2-22-65 (64-18761)

A NEW EUROPE?

A NEW EUROPE?

EDITED BY STEPHEN R. GRAUBARD

Illustrated with photographs

HOUGHTON MIFFLIN COMPANY BOSTON
THE RIVERSIDE PRESS CAMBRIDGE
1964

PREFACE

EUROPE was until very recently the part of the world which Americans knew most intimately outside their own continental limits. Since the end of the Second World War, national political and military requirements have necessitated the giving of attention to other foreign areas, with a consequent relative decline of scholarly interest in Western Europe. With limited resources and with great new needs for competence in the Soviet, Middle Eastern, Far Eastern, African and Latin American fields, contemporary West European studies have been scanted. This situation is made all the more serious by the fact that it comes at a time when Europe is in the process of large-scale change, so much so that knowledge acquired earlier is rendered quickly obsolescent. This book considers the character of this "new" European society, suggesting both what is traditional in its forms and what may be considered as genuinely innovative.

The work is a joint European-American venture in every sense. It could not have been produced without the active support of individuals and institutions on both sides of the Atlantic. These connections, maintained over several years, insured the maximum exchange of ideas and opinion. It made possible an acquaintance between European and Americans that is recollected with pleasure by all who benefited from it. Whatever merit the book has is largely owing to this continuing relationship.

The history of the preparation of the volume deserves telling. Early in 1961, conversations originated in the editorial offices of *Daedalus,* the Journal of the American Academy of Arts and Sciences, anticipating the publication of such a study. Although European economic change was then a principal subject of discussion, other equally important developments appeared to be receiving meager attention. The initial objective was to redress this imbalance, and thereby provide American and European readers with a report which would offer a more comprehensive view of what one of our number called the "silent European revolution." The expectation was that a volume conceived on such very broad lines would have great utility both in this country and abroad.

We recognized from the beginning that some sort of selectivity in the choice of topics would be necessary. This led to a decision to limit the study largely to the "Six" and Great Britain, and to give less attention to eastern Europe, Scandinavia, Spain and Portugal. This was not an arbitrary decision; considerations of space and organization suggested that such a concentration on specific areas was both necessary and legitimate. As a consequence, certain important questions, such as, for example, relations between Western Europe and the Soviet Union, have not been extensively treated. Had a volume twice the size of this present one been possible, such topics would certainly have been included. Under the circumstances, they have perforce been omitted.

Early in 1962 the Carnegie Corporation made a grant to the American Academy of Arts and Sciences to support this effort. It is impossible to exaggerate the debt we owe to the Carnegie Corporation for making the inquiry possible. Thanks are due especially to Mr. James A. Perkins, at that time vice-president of the Carnegie Corporation and now president of Cornell University, who encouraged the project from the start. A Planning Committee was established, which met in Cambridge to discuss the proposal and to develop a set of procedures for the study. Members of this committee, whose assistance proved invaluable, included Adolf A. Berle, Professor of Law, Columbia University, and formerly Assistant Secretary of State; Frederick Burkhardt, President, American Council of Learned Societies; Mario L. Einaudi, Professor of Government, Cornell University; Stanley Hoffmann, Professor of Government, Harvard University; Gerald Holton, Professor of Physics, Harvard University and at that time Editor of the Academy; Charles P. Kindleberger, Professor of Economics, Massachusetts Institute of Technology; Henry A. Kissinger, Professor of Government, Harvard University, and Director of the Harvard Defense Studies Program; Ben T. Moore, Associate Director of The Twentieth Century Fund; James A. Perkins and J. Robert Schaetzel, Deputy Assistant Secretary for Atlantic affairs, Department of State. The committee agreed to enlist the active cooperation of European scholars and to exchange views about various specific proposals. The plan was to emphasize political, social, educational and intellectual changes, with some attention being given also to European integration and to questions of foreign policy.

Members of the committee, in Europe that summer, consulted widely to determine whether the proposed outline coincided with what was felt there to be significant. These conversations encouraged the committee in its general approach while providing it with invaluable additional suggestions. It afforded the committee a unique opportunity to become better acquainted with persons already engaged in studies analogous to our own. Many Europeans commented on the extent to which purely national approaches predominated in contemporary studies; they urged that every effort be made to develop a comparative approach.

In the early autumn of 1962 invitations were issued to twenty-two persons, asking them to contribute articles to the issue. Since most of the authors were in Europe, a subcommittee of the Planning Committee traveled to Paris in January, 1963, to consult about the papers and to make final arrangements for a conference which would bring the whole group together. M. Jacques Vernant of the Centre d'Études de Politique Étrangère generously furnished conference facilities for these meetings.

Papers began to arrive in Cambridge during the spring. In June, 1963, at the Villa Serbelloni in Bellagio, Italy, the Planning Committee and the authors, joined by Professors Gordon Craig of Stanford University and Talcott Parsons of Harvard University, met for a six-day conference to discuss the papers and to consult about the larger issues raised by them. The Rockefeller Foundation provided us with an incomparable setting for our deliberations. We remember with great pleasure the hospitality of that week, and the many kindnesses of Mr. and Mrs. John Marshall, who did so much to make our stay agreeable.

This volume, in an earlier version, appeared as the Winter 1964 issue of *Daedalus*. Various revisions have been made in the articles since then, and three new ones have been added, to cover matters which seemed insufficiently treated in the original *Daedalus* volume. We are very pleased to have the contributions of Professor Hans Küng, who writes on "Theological Currents in Europe Today," of Professor Ernst Haas, whose essay "Technocracy, Pluralism and the New Europe" appears here for the first time, and that of Professor Klaus Epstein, who has written on "The Adenauer Era in German History."

Last year, the American Academy of Arts and Sciences and Houghton Mifflin Company arranged for hard-cover book publication of all issues of *Daedalus*. We are pleased that this volume should be the first of the new series. The book, we believe, is unique in its ambition and in its authorship. If it serves to stimulate study of contemporary Europe, and if it provides a pattern for further transatlantic intellectual cooperation, the effort to produce it will have been fully justified. We hope that it may raise new questions but that it will also provide at least a few answers to the many that already exist. The title of the book, *A New Europe?*, is conceived not as an expression of doubt or bewilderment about Europe but as evidence of our continuing curiosity about a society that is changing in unexpected and unparalleled ways, raising possibilities whose long-range effects are only beginning to be examined.

S. R. G.

CONTENTS

A NEW EUROPE?

ACHILLE ALBONETTI

The New Europe and the West

PEOPLE often talk about Europe, tending to forget that on the one hand it is only a geographical expression—to borrow the phrase of a distinguished Austrian statesman—and that on the other, the European nations, even divided, were for many centuries the center of the world. Until a few decades ago no region in the world could compare with Europe in wealth, productivity, military power or political influence. At the end of the nineteenth century, all the great powers were European states. Europe, with its virtual monopoly of political and economic power, was the pivot of world civilization.

The political situation in recent decades, especially since World War II, has been disastrous for European countries, and not only on the continent. The maintenance of order and the task of checking the expansion of Soviet Russia and its satellites in the Far East, in Southeast Asia, in the Near and Middle East and even in North Africa and certain parts of Europe itself often became the responsibility of the United States. Two great powers, the United States and Soviet Russia, confronted each other with two opposing ideologies and two opposing spheres of influence.

The French and especially the British, in accepting Hitler's challenge, destroyed the European equilibrium they wished to preserve, and Russia assumed Germany's position as the dominant power on the European continent. Stalin was able to obtain from Roosevelt and Churchill what Hitler had not been able to obtain. However, those peoples who are inspired by the liberal and democratic ideal and whose civilization is founded on Christianity can hardly fail to rise to certain challenges. Also, if wars have any purpose, it is certainly to test what nations really are and not what they would like to be, for reasons of tradition or for other reasons.

As a result, while it is no doubt correct to say that World War II contributed to the decline of Europe, to the destruction of the equilibrium within the continent and to the emergence of the un-

1

contested supremacy of only two great powers, Russia and the United States, it is even truer to note that the last world war only strikingly confirmed the forces already latent in the facts of the situation—a situation which involved a whole new way of thinking and acting even for the most farsighted Europeans.

This renewed approach was already underway at the beginning of the war. The idea of a united Europe was taken up in different countries during the most difficult years of the Resistance. The voluntary unification of European nations on a democratic basis is a theme found frequently in the clandestine press and manifestoes of the Resistance movements, whether French, Italian, Dutch or Belgian—in opposition to the Nazi attempt at unification by force.

The ideal of a united Europe certainly is not new and one can trace its origins through the course of past years and even centuries. It can be said that over the centuries, statesmen, philosophers, and great thinkers generally have dreamed of a united Europe. What is new since the war is the transposition of the ideal of a united Europe into a political program and a criterion of political action by leading parties and governments. Without taking cognizance of this new and rather revolutionary fact, it is without doubt hard to understand the profound evolution which has taken place in all aspects of life in the European nations. Perhaps for the first time in European history, parties with very different ideologies and successive governments have held this ideal as a political objective. This goal has motivated the action of men in public life, experts and diplomats in France, Germany, Italy, the Benelux nations and, more recently, in Great Britain. There have been ups and downs in the course of events, but the difficulties in all spheres, though often enormous, have not succeeded in eliminating the determination to unify Europe. Inevitably some men get lost on the way, but others take their place.

In a little more than two years, between 1947 and 1949, after the European Congress in The Hague and with the signing of the Treaty of Dunkerque and that of Brussels, with the creation of the Council of Europe, the Organization for European Economic Cooperation (OEEC) and the Atlantic Pact, a whole series of international institutions came to life through which European collaboration took form and developed in the political, military and economic spheres. These were the years of the greatest enthusiasm for the European cause. The New Europe as a political unit seemed within grasp. It was the period of Schuman, Monnet, Bidault, Adenauer, De Gasperi, Sforza, and Spaak. It was the period of the Marshall Plan and of the attempt to unify Europe economically in the OEEC and politically in the Council of Europe.

Nevertheless, the limitations of the intergovernmental organizations thus created were soon realized. Great Britain's resistance began to exercise a decisive influence at that time also. In 1950, a key year in the history of European unification, a new method was tried: that of vertical economic integration, applied for the first time to coal and steel. Despite Britain's refusal to participate in the negotiations, the Schuman-Monnet initiative led to the European Coal and Steel Community (ECSC), uniting France, Germany, Italy, Belgium, the Netherlands and Luxembourg.

It was about this time that the distinction between "little" Europe and "greater" Europe began to be made. It was also about the same time—after the first setbacks to the expectations of unity deriving from the OEEC (1948) and the Council of Europe (1949)—that the European policy began to lose its monolithic character to a considerable extent. Gradually the view began to prevail that the Europe of the Six (France, Germany, Italy, Belgium, the Netherlands and Luxembourg, that is, the nations disposed to accept the principle of economic integration based on the coal and steel pool of May, 1950) was the only possible "Europe" in the political sense. It seemed that only this "little" Europe—as the British somewhat scornfully called it—could pursue a basically European policy independent of the looser policy of "greater" Europe, that is, of the whole group belonging to the Council of Euorpe. This is what happened, especially after Great Britain's failure to join the ECSC, which implied the abandonment of the "functional" thesis. At one time this latter had seemed to provide a compromise between the federalism of the most advanced advocates of European unity and the form of Europe desired by the British and Scandinavians. Indeed in 1948–1949, the federalism of the foremost proponents of Europe was opposed not only by those—especially the British and Scandinavians—who thought it possible to achieve the unification of Europe by means of cooperation between governments, but also by the so-called "functional" school, whose method went beyond such cooperation to include the creation of common institutions for particular sectors.

The rejection of the Mackay Plan by the British and Scandinavian representatives on the Council of Europe, as well as Great Britain's intransigent attitude toward the OEEC and its refusal to participate in the ECSC and in the plan for the European Defense Community (EDC), precipitated a crisis within the Council of Europe toward the end of 1951. (The Mackay Plan envisioned the establishment of a European political authority under whose aegis the ECSC, the EDC and other such organizations would be coordinated.) The crisis, which almost brought about the collapse of

3

the council itself, reached its culminating point with the resignation of Paul Henri Spaak, chairman of the Consultative Assembly. His parting speech is perhaps worth citing again today:

There is a simple choice facing Europeans: either we must line up with Great Britain and renounce the attempt to create a united Europe, or we must endeavor to create Europe without Great Britain. For my part, I choose the second alternative, despite the risks and all the dangers involved, because, reckoning all the possibilities, I think the risks are less great and the dangers less serious than those which inaction and renunciation would inevitably imply.

In these years, the political objective of the New Europe—unity—began to be subjected to harsh trials. Governments, political parties and statesmen, whose actions were inspired by generous but also general ideals, had to mark time, faced with the necessity to commit themseves more resolutely. In 1950–1951, as mentioned above, the most ardent partisans of Europe realized that only the Europe of the Six was politically possible. Indeed, even as early as the Schuman Plan, they had thought that there were two possible ways to unite Europe. The first was to wait until all the European nations were ready to associate themselves with concrete moves toward unity. This method had been enthusiastically tried already in 1948 in the OEEC and the Council of Europe, and it produced important but not decisive results. The second method was to unite first the nations which, for political, economic and even geographical reasons, were ready to assume serious commitments toward unity, and then to bring the others in later. The history of the last ten or fifteen years seems to prove that each time an attempt has been made beyond the framework of the Six, the results have been meager—as far as effective political unity of the continent is concerned. The various horizontal plans of integration presented by Pella, Stikker and Petsche in the OEEC after 1950 and the several "pools by sector" negotiated in the framework of greater Europe met with only feeble success.

The negotiations to work out the treaty establishing the ECSC had hardly begun in June, 1950 when the international situation was disturbed by the war in Korea. The resulting deterioration gave rise to a new European initiative, the European Defense Community (EDC), analogous to the Schuman Plan. Again, the idea was Jean Monnet's, even though the necessity of a European army had been mentioned earlier in Strasbourg. It has been justly said that a complete history of the EDC, national and international, parliamentary and diplomatic, would end by merging with the history of French policy and of western policy in the four years between September, 1950—when President Pleven proposed the EDC—and August,

1954, when it was rejected by the French National Assembly. One might add that the history of postwar France is intertwined with the fate of European unity. It is, in fact, impossible to speak of Europe while excluding France. Geographic, political and cultural factors require the inclusion of France in any move for effective European unity. This explains why a second phase in the history of the unification of Europe and a new period of French postwar diplomacy both began on the day Schuman presented the Coal and Steel Plan—May 9, 1950. Between 1944 and 1947, France had tried to assume an intermediary or mediator's role between East and West; only between 1947 and 1950 did it reluctantly consent to belong to the western camp. With the initiatives of Schuman and Pleven, it tried, for the first time, to make an original contribution to the building of Europe and the West. Instead of delaying the inevitable rebirth of West Germany, France opened a new perspective by offering West Germany an honorable place in a united Europe. Through the policies of Schuman, through the ECSC and later the EDC, France combined guarantees against the revival of German power with Franco-German reconciliation. France no longer sought guarantees against Germany through reparations, demolitions, and the controls envisaged by the Ruhr Agency and the Disarmaments Agency, but rather through a European system in which Germany would be admitted with equal rights. The Europe vocation began to take precedence over the "vocation mondiale," which is always present in different sectors of French public opinion, left or right. Even the most recent attempt to mediate between Russia and the United States, through a policy of close cooperation with Great Britain, was put aside. The French realistically preferred a policy of narrower European union, even while remaining closely tied to three other western powers—the United States, Great Britain and Canada—through previously established pacts such as the Treaty of Dunkerque, the Western Union, and the Atlantic Pact.

The governments of the Six, including that of France, signed the treaty establishing the EDC on May 27, 1952. In spite of the government's adherence, months went by before it came up for ratification by the French parliament. Meanwhile one of the most serious ideological and political debates in recent French history broke out. This debate, while concerned with the rearmament of Germany, revolved essentially around the very existence of the French state and its sovereignty. It took shape between those who believed the concept of national sovereignty to be obsolete and who favored the unification of Europe and the absorption of the state into a community of states, and those who thought it still possible for France to play a political role in the world on the basis of national sov-

5

ereignty and within the narrow confines of a single state. There were also those who refused to consider a policy of merging the French state with five other nations among which were the chief enemies of yesterday. This group maintained that France should not tie itself more closely to its ex-enemies and abandon its traditional allies: hence the slogan, "no Europe without Great Britain." Still others saw in a Europe of the Six the outline of a clerical Europe dominated by the powerful Christian-Democratic parties of France, Italy and Germany. (One must bear in mind that indeed the leaders of the enterprise were Schuman, De Gasperi and Adenauer.)

An attempt was made to find a drastic remedy and to support the EDC by a new spurt of political activity. De Gasperi proposed and the Six decided to establish the European Political Community (EPC) during the summer of 1952. The plan was drawn up in record time and approved by the consultative European assemblies in the spring of 1953. This considerable effort to give new impetus to the process of European unification by constantly renewed initiatives was to flounder before increasingly powerful obstacles. In spite of American pressure and some optimism on the part of Dulles and certain European groups, and in spite of the fact that the United States government never seemed to have lost hope that France would ratify the EDC, the outlook for French parliamentary approval grew progressively worse. Innumerable attempts were made to meet French objections, but in vain. On August 30, 1954, the treaty establishing the EDC was rejected by the French parliament on a motion of procedure, by which a postponement of the debate without indicating a time for its resumption was requested.

The skillful re-entry of Great Britain on the European political scene brought about a solution to the problem of German rearmament, with the creation of the Western European Union in the autumn of 1954 and with Germany's membership in NATO, but within a few months opinion grew stronger that the moment had not arrived to take concrete steps toward the economic and political union of the continent beyond the framework of the Six. Great Britain was certainly not ready to assume a dynamic role in the process of European unification. There was therefore nothing to do but resume the attempt among the Six, because the desire to do so was not extinguished among them, even in France.

Out of the crisis of the EDC, and despite the creation of the Western European Union, there was born, at Messina in June 1955, the idea of a new European "relance" by the Six. The British were invited to participate in the negotiations and they sent an observer for some months, but then they recalled him. They preferred to put their trust first in the OEEC and then in the EFTA to offset the integration attempts of the Six, even though these attempts were initially limited to the economic sector. The "relance" of Messina and the Brussels Conference, with the unexpected additional aid of the Suez crisis of 1956 (which made clear the precarious position of the European nations) gave rise to the Treaty of Rome, that is, to the treaty establishing the European Economic Community (EEC), or Common Market, and the European Community for Atomic Energy (ECAE), or Euratom.

Faced with the limited success of the Council of Europe and the OEEC, on the one hand, and setbacks in the sphere of political integration (whether military or political in a narrow sense) on the other, the partisans of Europe fell back on vertical economic integration (Euratom) and later, encouraged by the Suez crisis, on horizontal economic integration (the Common Market). The political hopes on which the Common Market was based are relatively simple: the Customs Union could not be realized without economic integration. To this point the partisans of Europe would add: economic integration cannot be achieved without political union. This is the principal explanation of the unwillingness of the Six to accept Britain's proposal of 1957–1958 in the OEEC to create a European free trade area. Indeed, once economic integration was arrested and made difficult, not only would its economic advantages be lost but also political hopes would be compromised. But if the more or less automatic mechanism (which certainly inspired the action of the partisans of Europe who promoted, defended and drew up the Treaty of Rome) is sound in its general structure, on the other hand, no one overlooked the fact that difficulties would accumulate with time.

The results yielded by the European communities in general and the Common Market in particular have surpassed all expectations. The increase in national income and the growth of industrial production and of trade within the community since the beginning of the Common Market were greater than those of the United States, Great Britain and other major industrial nations. Is this the result of coincidence or luck? In any case, it is a fact and has had extraordinary consequences. Although these successes were not enough to resolve the key problem—that of Europe's political unity—still they made it seem that the moment political discussions could be resumed was drawing closer each day.

After the refusal of the French National Assembly to ratify the EDC and the postponement *sine die* of the examination of the European Political Community in August, 1954, the partisans of Europe did not dare to bring up the political implications of Europe's economic integration again for several years. For one thing they thought that the gradual integration of the economies of the Six would create a more propitious climate, and for another they believed that the very fusion of the six economies would bring about a European political authority, if not automatically, at least with a minimum of effort. So they applied themselves to the difficult task of carrying out the Treaty of Rome and of developing for the future some political possibilities, for example, the election of a parliamentary assembly by direct suffrage, deliberately leaving aside the problem of the political construction of Europe.

One could say that already in 1960 the advocates of Europe thought there were two possible ways to achieve the ultimate political goal implied by the economic initiative begun at Messina. One would be by way of the existing European communities. Indeed, the first years of the Common Market seemed to allow a glimpse of the time when it would be necessary to create political organs in order to surmount the technical difficulties arising from the mere application of the treaty itself. This would reinforce the existing institutions. Besides, the treaties themselves, and the Common Market in particular, anticipated that the Council of Ministers would evolve gradually toward a supranational function by taking decisions by majority vote, beginning in the second stage of development. One should thus expect its jurisdiction to extend from the purely economic sphere to that of foreign policy, defense, etc. Similarly, the commissions of the Common Market and Euratom and the high authority of the ECSC could be fused into a single executive body. The powers of the Parliamentary Assembly would be reinforced by the direct election of its members by universal suffrage, according to a plan proposed to the Council of Ministers of the three communities by the president of the European Parliamentary Assembly on June 20, 1960. In this way the mechanism established by the European treaties would have slowly given rise to a European political power with accompanying institutions—a future confederation or federation.

A second way of developing a political construction from the economic initiative was thought to be through action by the governments. The existing organizations would have preserved their full economic function, but the political impulse would have come from new moves by the six governments, integrationist or federalist in character.

Whatever the way followed, the advocates of Europe thought that the potential inherent in economic integration and in the Common Market's success should be used to the utmost. As early as the first half of 1960, however, it became clear that it was not possible to wait for the normal development of the process begun in 1950, brusquely interrupted by the failure of the EDC in 1954, given new impetus in 1958 and accelerated by the implementation of the Treaty of Rome. The advocates of Europe themselves brought out the fact that the Parliamentary Assembly—elected by universal suffrage as outlined in the Dehousse Plan—could be only one element in this process. The same applied to the eventual fusion of the executive bodies of the three communities. Their political potential would have been limited in any case. To take a new step forward, the partisans of Europe therefore thought that it was not only necessary but politically possible to present a new goal to public opinion, clearly and without ambiguity, by asking for parliamentary ratification, as had been done in the case of the three existing treaties.

No doubt the unexpected success of the Common Market and the rapidity of the strides taken toward economic integration as early as the first years of the EEC encouraged this line of thought. Furthermore, it now seemed that the policy of the Fifth Republic was not as insurmountable an obstacle to the construction of Europe as General de Gaulle's attitude when he first came to power had seemed to indicate. At first the de Gaulle regime was silent—in contrast to the professions of faith of the Fourth Republic—and this was disquieting to the partisans of Europe. Only after certain events were their fears quieted: first, the initial meetings between de Gaulle and Adenauer toward the end of 1958, and above all the French economic reforms in December of the same year established a basis enabling the French economy to cope with the opening of the Common Market. Later, early in 1960, France, surprising even the most skeptical, supported the recommendation of the commission of the EEC to accelerate its pace of implementation. All of this took place while the Fifth Republic was directed by men like de Gaulle—and even more by Debré—who had for years opposed all serious attempts to unify Europe politically or economically, especially in the framework of the Six. But if fears of French sabotage of the Common Market and the other two communities were fairly rapidly dissipated, one could not say as much for the political extensions that should have grown out of the European treaties. On the contrary, everything indicated that French official thinking was different from that of the partisans of Europe.

One sentence of the communiqué issued after the meeting of de Gaulle with Italian President Gronchi and Italian Premier Segni on June 25, 1959—a sentence almost unnoticed at the time—announced a new common action to develop political cooperation among the Six. This cooperation was supposed to take concrete form at first through the creation of a permanent political secretariat. De Gaulle's initiative received a rather lukewarm reception in the other interested capitals, more because of its author than because of the proposal itself. In spite of this, the initiative—which was taken up only about five months later during a meeting of the Council of Ministers of the Six in Strasbourg, November 23 and 24, 1959—was given substance when the foreign ministers of the Six undertook to meet every three months. The creation of a political secretariat was, nevertheless, ruled out. The television speech of General de Gaulle on May 31, 1960, confirmed the impression that something was again moving on the political plane.

But the first real initiative, which revealed not only the thought but also the objectives of the president of the Fifth Republic, came about at the end of July, 1960, about a year after de Gaulle's advances during his visit to Italy. Before retiring to the peace of Colombey-les-deux-Eglises, General de Gaulle met Chancellor Adenauer on July 29 and 30, 1960. He wished to give the German chancellor his first thoughts. During these conversations, General de Gaulle submitted to Adenauer a certain number of suggestions about the urgency of reinforcing Europe's political position. De Gaulle's new plan, which represented a sort of new political "relance" and a reaffirmation of the necessity for greater solidarity among the Six (already foreshadowed during his visit to Italy in June, 1959), far from creating enthusiasm, aroused anxiety in the capitals of Europe. After a whole series of meetings, evasions, interviews and speeches, there was finally a clarification which took place during the important visit of Debré and Couve de Murville to Bonn on October 7 and 8, 1960. This seemed definitive and opened the way to the first European summit meeting in February, 1961.

The first summit meeting between the government leaders and chiefs of state of the six European nations finally took place in Paris on February 10 and 11, 1961, under the chairmanship of General de Gaulle. The meeting decided to create an intergovernmental commission whose task would be to present a series of propositions on the main outlines of a European political union. The second European summit meeting took place in Bonn, July 18, 1961, under the chairmanship of Adenauer. On the basis of the previous work of the intergovernmental commission presided by Ambassador Fouchet, the conference approved an important document which was supposed to constitute a point of departure for the future work of that same commission. Following the outline of this document, the French government presented a formal draft of a treaty for the political union of Europe. The French draft aroused interest throughout Europe. Nevertheless, the fears formerly raised by the Gaullist propositions for a "Europe of States" reappeared. Certain nations, especially Belgium and the Netherlands, expressed reservations principally about the minimal degree of integration in the draft of the treaty and about the inclusion of problems of defense. The same nations also raised a question of principle about the non-participation of Great Britain in the negotiations of the Fouchet commission.

After a few months of negotiation in the Fouchet commission during the winter of 1961–1962, it seemed impossible to overcome the differences between the other five and France. De Gaulle then took the initiative by going to Bonn, and then to Turin, to try to resolve the controversial points personally with Adenauer and Fanfani. Following these meetings the situation seemed to have become unblocked, and people had the impression that the signing of the treaty was imminent. But at the conference of the foreign ministers of the Six in Paris, April 17, 1962, whose purpose was to prepare the third and final European summit meeting, agreement was not reached. Quite the contrary, the enterprise was brusquely interrupted. Even though France had shown that it could not renounce its project for a "Union of States," the final blow was delivered by the Benelux nations, encouraged by a speech by Edward Heath at a meeting of the Western European Union a week earlier. Spaak declared clearly, indeed, that negotiations could not be carried further before the entry of Great Britain into the EEC. This attitude reflected the determination of certain nations of the community to prevent the transformation of the embryonic political union into a kind of Franco-Italo-German directorate, without guarantees concerning integration properly speaking. Given the situation, if it was impossible to anticipate developments on the plane of political integration, it would be better—according to Spaak—to include Britain in the enterprise. Britain's weight would offset all attempts at leadership on the part of the France of General de Gaulle.

Since then, despite some vain attempts, nothing more has been done on the level of European unification. On the contrary, the atmosphere has become heavier, despite the liquidation of the Algerian problem and the solution of problems posed by the retirement of Adenauer. The failure of the negotiations for Great Britain's entry into the EEC in January, 1963 contributed to making this situation even more difficult.

I The Obstacles to European Unification

This rapid summary of the chief events and major difficulties characterizing the history of the European nations in the years since the war should permit us to draw conclusions of some importance. First of all, beyond the fluctuations of domestic and foreign policy of the European states, and of the Six in particular, it seems impossible not to discern one consistent main theme—a determination to achieve the political integration of Europe. I use the word "integration" deliberately to underline the existing will, especially on the continent, to go beyond a policy of unity based on the traditional instruments of relations between states, that is beyond treaties sealing alliances and intergovernmental conferences. These latter, indeed (and here we refer especially to the OEEC, the Council of Europe, NATO and the Western European Union), are differentiated in certain respects from traditional alliances in that the contracting parties decide to create permanent secretariats and diplomatic representations *ad hoc*. Nevertheless, joint institutions which would be the prelude to the real fusion of states, that is political federation, are lacking.

The awareness of the necessity to go beyond the nation-state and to achieve the gradual creation of a political federation through common institutions has been constantly present in the action of the six continental governments, or at least it constitutes the political objective of some of the principal parties of opposition. Despite difficulties and disillusions, it seems clear to me—as I shall try to prove—not only that the necessity for federation increases as time passes, but also that the results obtained by the progressive fusion of the policies of European states are increasing, especially in the economic sector. The aspiration toward unity is not only expressed by political groups of the idealistic type—like the European Federalist movements—but above all by men who have a prominent position in the parties, in diplomacy and in the national and international bureaucracies. Public opinion is familiar with the most eminent representatives, such as Adenauer, Beck, Colombo, De Gasperi, Maurice Faure, Mollet, Monnet, Pleven, Schuman, Segni, Sforza, Spaak, Taviani, von Brentano and others. No less important is the daily patient action over the years of men in public life, leading civil servants and experts such as, for example, in France, Armand, Aron, Clappier, Deniau, Hirsch, Marjolin, Pflimlin, Uri and Wormser; in Germany, Hallstein, Karstens, Ophuels and von der Groeben; in Italy, Cattani, Ducci, Malagodi, Petrilli and Saraceno; in Belgium, Forthomme, Kervyn de Lettenhove, Rothschild and Scheyven; in Holland, Luns, Spierenburg, Tinbergen and von Stiikel. This phalanx has matured in action and has certainly lost neither the will to go ahead nor the hope of arriving in the fairly near future at the political construction of Europe. Let us add that it is precisely in the most important nations and in France in particular—even though the leadership of de Gaulle seems to prove the contrary—that the influence of Europeanism has deepened and grown. Furthermore, this influence has extended to other nations, especially to Great Britain, where, until very recently, the movement for European integration had very few advocates.

A second characteristic that emerges from examination of the fifteen years of struggle for the political unity of Europe is that in each crisis the European movement has been faced by difficulties raised either by France or by Great Britain or by both at the same time. It is interesting to note, in my opinion, that the struggle for unity merges with the struggle to reduce the policy of the nations of Europe (and especially of the most important ones like Great Britain) to strictly European dimensions. This observation may seem banal, yet many errors could have been avoided and others still can be by bearing it in mind. France and Great Britain have had and have still the greatest difficulty in accepting the European dimension which would be imposed on them by the creation of a United States of Europe because their recent tradition still leads them to attempt to develop an independent policy on a world scale.

It was not by accident that the root of the first great crisis of the European movement (1950–1951) lay in Britain's unwillingness to commit herself deeply to the OEEC and the Council of Europe. In the second great crisis, that which brought about the failure of the EDC and the EPC, France provided even more striking evidence of this same feeling. French action, furthermore, seemed to be provoked if not justified by Britain's unwillingness to commit itself fully on the continent. In the two other serious crises, those of November, 1958, which marked the failure of the plan for a free trade area, and of January, 1963, which caused the interruption in the negotiations for Great Britain's entry into the European communities, we also find France and Great Britain in the foreground. It is perhaps opportune, therefore, to pause a moment to review the European policy of these two states—an effort which should permit us to grasp more easily the difficulties encountered and to evaluate better those which still remain to be overcome.

France, even before its liberation in December, 1944, wanted to resume its traditional policy in relation to Russia, characterized by direct alliances against Germany and by maintaining a half-way position between Russia and the United States, or perhaps even between Russia and the Anglo-Saxon nations. Indeed, it was not accidental that France did not decide to sign the Treaty of Dunkerque until after the hardening of the Russian attitude, about two years after having made a fifty-year alliance with Moscow. Germany surrendered unconditionally; it was destroyed, divided, or rather, dismembered. So was France. Russia, enormous and powerful, was at the gates. But de Gaulle and Bidault resumed the tradi-

13

tional policy as if nothing had happened and as if the world and Europe would be reconstructed as before. It took many disillusions and crushing humiliations, it took the great fears of the years 1947 and 1948, which saw crises in Iran and Czechoslovakia, the Berlin blockade, the Korean War, and, last but not least, United States pressure, to make France change its course and to adopt a more realistic policy toward Germany and toward the world. The Schuman Plan for the ECSC and then the EDC were the first signs of this change.

No sooner had the letup of Russian pressure and the economic revival allowed Frenchmen to forget their difficulties for a short time than the atavistic fear of Germany and especially the traditional French ambitions for great power—the so-called *vocation mondiale*—reawakened and paralized the French parliament. The great "no" of August, 1954 came only two years after the ECSC began operating fully and the treaty of the EDC was signed. This refusal was not very significant because Germany was rearmed anyway and entered NATO, but even so, national sovereignty and the right to fulfill a world mission had been solemnly affirmed.

The Suez adventure of November, 1956 was the logical end of a cycle. The two world powers, France and Great Britain, did not succeed in stopping Nasser, and a war of a few days isolated those two powers politically and seemed likely to provoke an economic crisis in Europe. This time, the lesson seemed to have been learned. A pro-European policy founded on Franco-German reconciliation was rapidly resumed and the negotiations of two treaties which had been dragging for months were wound up in record time. Within a few months of the setback at Suez, France signed the Treaty of Rome with Germany, Italy and the Benelux nations. This time the French parliament gave its approval by ratification. The line laid down for French policy by the Treaty of Rome was followed by de Gaulle himself, although his conversion was probably facilitated by the marked isolation of France at the time of the Algerian crisis.

As far as colonial policy is concerned, Great Britain seems to have learned better than France to adapt itself to the times and to the level of its actual power since the war. But in its European policy, it seemed to be following the traditional paths just as much as France. British policy toward Europe was consistent, at least until July, 1961, and it followed tradition regularly and monotonously in the postwar years. British opposition, although more polite and more subtle than that of the Soviets, was nonetheless often equally painful for Europe. Europe considers that it has received and continues to receive support from Great Britain, as well as an indispensable example for its own liberal and democratic development. Although the ideas for the Council of Europe and the European army were practically launched by Sir Winston Churchill in two memorable speeches, and although Franco-German reconciliation has always been a desirable thing in the mind of that great Briton, the policy of the British government, even when led by Churchill, did not depart from traditional lines. The Foreign Office, the Treasury, the Admiralty and the Board of Trade openly opposed the unification of Europe for years. Some liberal groups connected with certain journals of the intellectual *avant-garde,* such as *The Economist* and *The Manchester Guardian,* attempted to go in the opposite direction. However, their influence was not political but only ideological and the English have little sympathy for ideologies.

British opposition has been and will continue to be costly to Europe. Britain took many negative positions toward the Council of Europe, the OEEC, the ECSC, and later—with disastrous results —to the EDC. Its opposition to the Common Market and Euratom was for years subtle, tenacious and consistent. It is no exaggeration to state that events seem to prove that the British fear the Germans perhaps even more than the French do. All, or almost all, the British press in 1958, during the French opposition to the British plan for a free trade area, did nothing but repeat that the British presence in Europe was necessary to offset German influence and that when de Gaulle had had time to make up his mind, he would open his arms to the British ally. It is very possible that the British interrupted the negotiations of the intergovernmental committee on the free trade area in November, 1958 in order to solicit the advice of General de Gaulle. But at the peak of the Franco-British crisis, de Gaulle, instead of flying to London, took the train to Bad-Kreuznach, where, among other things, the foundations of the real entry of France into the Common Market were laid.

The fact is that in the course of the preceding years and with particular insistence at the time of the EDC, the British had been repeatedly invited by the French to participate in the European enterprise and to offset the expanding power of Germany, but they had refused. The British would like to influence European policy but not to be influenced themselves. After the launching of the Common Market they seemed almost to fear Franco-German rapprochement. Briefly, the British would want Franco-German relations to be close enough to avert any danger from Russia, but not so close as to challenge British leadership or London's direct relationship with Washington. But this policy is out of date. It is to be doubted whether Europe, including Great Britain, could survive very long without Franco-German reconciliation guaranteed by European integration. Much can be done in Europe, assuming a

15

stable agreement between France and Germany. Nothing can be done without such an agreement.

The crisis over the project for a free trade area, on the eve of the implementation of the Common Market, revealed significant states of mind. The British press and official spokesmen both stated in December, 1958 that the free trade area was more important to London than the problem of Berlin. They finally went so far as to threaten to withdraw from NATO, the OEEC, and the Western European Union and to remove their troops from the continent. Intervention by the United States was required to restore a sense of proportion in certain British circles. These opinions and threats are nevertheless significant.

Aside from traditional fears and the age-old British policy of opposition to the unity of the continent, it is understandable, even though frightening, that Great Britain, faced with the impossibility of leading and controlling a European coalition in 1959, should have followed two lines of action. First, it sought to obtain what it wanted, if not by a really pro-Soviet policy, at least by a more flexible policy toward Russia on Germany and Berlin. Second, it hastily organized a coalition of nations which were at least rivals of the Six if not their opponents. The resulting organization, the European Free Trade Association (EFTA) included the Scandinavian countries, Austria, Portugal and Switzerland. After all, from the point of view of traditional policy—such as France has followed up to 1950 and tried to resume in 1954 with the rejection of the EDC—it is understandable that Great Britain, perhaps unconsciously, should prefer a neutralized Germany to a Germany that is the pivot of a coalition of six nations. Great Britain remembers, on the other hand, that one of the reasons for European integration is Russian expansionism. If Russian pressure should let up, Franco-German understanding and the European integration which guarantees it and is founded upon it could become less necessary. Khrushchev, who fears all coalitions from NATO to the Baghdad Pact and SEATO, could be receptive to this line of thinking. Besides, what Russia fears most of all are coalitions which seem solid and likely to become more so. One must not forget the tenacious Communist opposition to all policies of collaboration or integration in Europe from the OEEC to the ECSC, and especially to the EDC, the Common Market and Euratom. It is therefore not necessary to agree with or to sympathize with certain Russian positions in order to obtain the desired effect; it suffices to oppose them without violence or to oppose them only with great patience.

This is why any unilateral initiative for disengagement, and still more any initiative capable of weakening and therefore of neutralizing Germany, is likely to be more harmful to western unity than to Russian propaganda. British policy in 1959—even if its purpose was to embarrass the Russians—should have been developed in full agreement with all the other allies, and especially with Germany and France. Its polemical character, anti-German and therefore anti-European, made it extremely dangerous. The visit of Adenauer to London which finally took place in November, 1959, that of Macmillan to Bonn in August, 1960, and especially the failure of the summit conference and the intransigence of Khrushchev, seemed to have re-established a better atmosphere between London and Bonn; but fears and suspicions have not been altogether dissipated.

Revision of British policy toward Europe did not really begin until July, 1961, with its request to join the Common Market. Yet, at the same moment, the success of the European communities and the failure of the East-West summit meeting seemed likely to detach that island from the course of history. If Great Britain's conversion to the European idea in the economic sphere seemed likely because of the pressure of events, it was not the same in the political and military spheres. Here Britain's policy continued to be centered on the Atlantic, scarcely concealing its desire to maintain special relations with the United States.

British lack of comprehension, as far as European policy goes, reveals itself particularly in the way Britain sees the problem of its security, that is, in its conception of East-West relations and specifically, in relation to solutions of the German problem. It is useful to consider the question of Germany before going any further. Berlin divides Europe and the world; Germany remains the key to coexistence and the principal obstacle to stability and peace. East Germany and West Germany symbolize and perpetuate the great majority of unresolved postwar problems: the Iron Curtain between these two zones is the only front along which Soviet and American troops face each other. The United States and the Soviet Union could always—with the partial test ban, with the "hot line" or other measures—re-establish an atmosphere of confidence and eventually reduce their armaments. But if they want to organize peace, they must really grapple with the German problem.

Personally, I do not believe in the possibility of the neutralization of Germany. On the contrary, I think that Germany belongs definitively to the West. If Russia could take over Germany by disengagement, neutralization or the ruin of the Atlantic Pact and of the movement for European integration, it would most probably hold the key to the domination of Europe and the world. In short, a solution of the German problem is one of the principal reasons in favor of a European federation capable of reinforcing the Atlantic

Alliance through bonds of association with the United States and of fostering a dialogue with the East for the organization of peace. The problem of Germany can be summed up in the necessity to tie it to the West by economic, political, psychological and military bonds stronger than those which could derive from simple participation in the Atlantic Alliance.

This is why the fundamental goal of the partisans of Europe has been to integrate Germany with the West in a European federation, because the more Germany feels itself tied to Europe and the West, the less it will tend to raise the painful problem of its reunification in dangerous terms. This is also why there has been such a consistent effort to prevent Germany from feeling isolated and therefore from basing its policy on political resentment. Such a policy would have led Germany to pursue dangerous mirages: at worst, a desire for revenge, at best, a new Rapallo and a policy of playing off the East against the West.

Monnet, Schuman and later, after Suez, Mollet and Maurice Faure understood this problem very well. In a certain sense, de Gaulle himself could do nothing but follow this new direction in Franco-German relations. Nevertheless, there is a discrepancy between the goal envisaged and the means adopted. Indeed, it is not by treaties, nor by consultations at all levels, still less by an exceptional and personal relationship between two chiefs of state soon to retire that two great nations unite in a common destiny. Here the conception of de Gaulle seems clearly inferior to that of Schuman and Monnet. A common destiny implies something much more organic than an agreement to consult each other; it implies the pooling of sovereignty on essential questions such as foreign policy, defense and direction of the economy. In the long run, a federal relationship is therefore necessary. However this may be, de Gaulle himself seems to have understood the German problem and the problem of European security better than the British and better than the Kennedy administration.

To sum up, Great Britain has had great difficulty in following the pitiless logic of the only line of reasoning that seems to me to fit the situation today: the reinforcement of the Atlantic Alliance through European integration is the only policy capable of guaranteeing both the independence and development of the European democracies, and international equilibrium and world peace. The United States has always been convinced of this thesis, at least until the election of Kennedy. Continental Europe seems to have learned the lesson better than Great Britain, even if the forces of nationalism, left or right, are far from completely eliminated and even if the temptation to follow the traditional paths is always at hand.

II *Is European Unification Progressing or Degenerating?*

The success of the Common Market in the years 1959 to 1962 almost made people forget the somber years between 1951 and 1954, and gave rise to hopes of even better times. But the crisis created by the rupture of negotiations for Great Britain's entry into the EEC in January, 1963 seems to have set back by about ten years progress toward the unification of Europe. As at the time of the failure of the EDC, relations among the Six are tense, full of suspicion and distrust. Among the results are harmful repercussions in the rate of progress of the Common Market and the suspension of all progress toward political unification. Relations between the Six and Great Britain are cold, despite the decision to resume negotiations every three months at the meetings of the Western European Union and despite the bilateral contacts begun between some members of the Six and London. The Atlantic Alliance is in a state of crisis. The presence of de Gaulle—in comparison to whom Mendès-France looks like a simple boy scout, although further to the left—seems to make all communications between the Allies more difficult, not to mention all relationships. The liquidation of the Algerian problem, the considerable stability of the regime and of the economy in France, as well as the conclusion of the Franco-German pact, instead of making the situation easier, have complicated it. Finally, it is precisely at this moment of crisis for Europe and the West that the United States is preparing to reopen the dialogue with Russia. The New Europe is not only absent, it is divided. The West is disoriented.

It is useful to note that this pessimistic view is not new. It has reappeared with each grave obstacle on the road to the unification of Europe. One should also add that despite the success of the Common Market, a whole sector of public opinion has never ceased to perceive growing elements of degeneration in the process of European unification ever since the failure of the EDC. This process of degeneration would have gained momentum with the disappearance of De Gasperi and Schuman, with the deaths of Stalin and Dulles, with the decline of Adenauer and above all with the accession to power of de Gaulle. The general has long been for the European movement the symbol of nationalism. It is perhaps among the least pessimistic views that all the present difficulties are imputed to de Gaulle. The Common Market was the offensive weapon of the New Europe, which, through its gradual but automatic and efficient mechanism, was supposed not only to destroy customs barriers— symbols of national sovereignty—but also to accomplish the fusion of economic policy, thus tacitly imposing the eventual fusion of policies of whatever kind. The Common Market—which has really produced abundant fruit—had finally forced Great Britain to request membership in the European community and was laying the basis for an Atlantic partnership which would make possible a constructive dialogue with the East for the organization of world peace. Then General de Gaulle dared not only to defy the European communities, but even to veto Great Britain's membership in the EEC and to dispose of the great design, dear to partisans of Europe on both sides of the ocean, at the very moment when its realization seemed to be taking place.

Everyone is not agreed about the beginning of the degeneration of the process of unification, nor about putting the entire responsibility on General de Gaulle in an oversimplified way, but many observers have no difficulty in admitting that, at least for some time, the forces working for the unity of Europe and the organization of the West have been weaker. To use a fanciful comparison, people have tried to apply a sort of litmus test to the situation and have concluded that the colors are not as bright as they used to be. "To degenerate" means to deviate, fall, decline or descend, which means that to have "degeneration" one must refer to something in the past. The process of European integration would today be understood as declining. I do not agree with this opinion. Indeed, I do not think that it is valid either from the economic point of view or from the political or diplomatic point of view. I think, on the contrary, that the forces existing today on all these levels, both within and outside the Six, are no weaker than those of past years and, in particular, than in the years of the OEEC, the Council of Europe and the EDC. If we had consulted the litmus paper in the course of the years 1949–1950, 1950–1951, or in the following years, I am sure that it would have shown some elements "less brilliant" and certainly not "more brilliant" than today.

Let us begin with the economic point of view. Up to the time of the signing of the Treaty of Rome in 1957, the history of the attempts to integrate Europe economically is a history full of setbacks and disillusions. If one compares the plans presented at the OEEC between the years 1948 and 1952 with their results, one obtains a realistic perspective on the discrepancy between hopes and realizations. This is why the partisans of Europe, as early as 1950, had to fall back on the system of vertical economic integration. Already in 1950–1951, the years when it is generally considered that the European movement was in full expansion, the partisans of Europe fell back from a horizontal conception of economic integration (that is, a conception embracing all economic sectors and the whole continent) to a conception of integration by sectors (coal and steel)

and limited to six nations. As proof, it is sufficient to remind ourselves of the failure of the Franco-Italian customs union, the proposition for Fritalux and especially of the expectation that the OEEC, as
such, could create a European Market or, at least, a European Customs Union.

Until the end of 1956, in spite of the "relance" of Messina, Spaak's
report and months of negotiations in Brussels, even the most sincere
friends of Europe recognized that it would be futile to present a
treaty for horizontal integration like the Common Market to the
French parliament (as modest as it was, in some eyes). One remembers, indeed, the strong opposition in France on the part of
management, of the agricultural interests and of various sectors of
public opinion. The most eminent partisans of Europe, both Monnet and Spaak themselves, advised proceeding at most to the establishment of a second community of the sector type (Euratom)
in order to enlarge the area of the community which at the time
was limited to ECSC alone.

What is the situation today? The Treaty of Rome has been signed
and ratified by France and by the other five nations of the ECSC.
Even more important, the Common Market began functioning punc-
tually, despite serious difficulties which arose in the very early years
of its effective existence; customs duties have been reduced by more
than half and the common external tariff is on the point of being
applied. The EEC had made France, the nation most opposed to
horizontal economic integration, undertake a radical revision of its
economic and financial policy and submit itself to a merger with
dynamic and highly competitive economies like those of Germany,
the Benelux nations and Italy. This would have been unthinkable a
few years ago. Nor did this change of attitude in France come about
only by the will of General de Gaulle. On the contrary, the Common
Market has imposed a certain economic policy on de Gaulle. A series
of events and men sincerely devoted to the European cause have
contributed this development. Well before de Gaulle came to power,
the Suez crisis and the gradual liquidation of the French empire
imposed this economic revision, whose necessity had already been
foreseen some years before by the most farsighted partisans of
Europe in Italy, Germany and even in France. A capillary action,
undertaken by men in public life and civil servants, had transformed
the situation when de Gaulle was not yet in power and the Gaullists
were reduced to a small scattered group. Nor is this all.

Even before de Gaulle reappeared on the political scene, the
governments of the Fourth Republic, together with other member
countries of the Common Market, were struggling to prevent it from
being diluted into a free trade area. Between 1958 and 1960, the

21

Common Market brilliantly overcame terrible crises, both internal and external. In 1960, after the conclusion of the difficult negotiations over the definition of duties on the G list, the schedule was accelerated, the common external tariff was announced, and the first step toward its adjustment to the tariffs of the six nations was taken. In 1962, the Common Market entered its second major stage and in 1963 a 60 per cent customs reduction among the six was achieved.

In short, I think we can state that whereas up to 1956 there was at least one obstacle to the economic integration of the Europe of the Six, namely the attitude of France, which was judged insurmountable even by the most optimistic, in these recent years this obstacle has diminished considerably. Incidentally I would underline the fact that de Gaulle did not appear on the political scene until May, 1958.

Important steps have been taken, even in Great Britain, toward the economic integration of that island with the continent. There is no doubt that even though the first British propositions in the autumn of 1961 were intended more to radically modify the system of the Common Market than to adapt British economy to it, Heath—after ten months of negotiations—accepted the original conception of the Treaty of Rome almost in its entirety. It is an uncontested fact that the Macmillan government had the political courage to declare itself ready to bring Great Britain into the European communities under conditions which would modify the British system. In practice, the special economic relations which the British Commonwealth (which together with the special political relations with the United States made the integration of Great Britain with the continent difficult) had been virtually abandoned and a good start had been made toward a common agricultural policy. The prospect opened for the relations of the New Europe with the United States (the Dillon negotiations, followed by the "Kennedy round" based on the Trade Expansion Act of autumn, 1962) confirmed the enormous progress made in the economic unity of the continent and provided a basis for a new dialogue within the Atlantic Alliance.

Now let us look at the litmus test from the political and diplomatic point of view. Here also, even though appearances may seem to contradict, I think that it is not difficult to ascertain that the situation, far from having deteriorated, has improved by comparison with earlier years. Until very recently, no one would have dared submit to the French parliament a project of any kind that would tie the six nations of continental Europe together politically in order to re-enforce the EEC, the ECSC and Euratom. Beginning in 1956, the situation has been gradually and radically modified. There is virtual unanimity not only among the M.R.P. and the "Independents" but also in the Socialist and Radical parties on the opportunity for a common political policy of the Six and on the necessity, consequently, to renounce the policy of traditional power. One even finds many partisans of Europeanism among the Gaullists.

The fact is that up to 1956 the pro-European forces were preponderant in only five of the six nations: in Italy, Germany and the Benelux countries. Let us examine the Europeanism of these countries in greater detail. It is undeniable, even if this truth is hard to admit, that for Germany, Italy and the Benelux nations the renunciation of national sovereignty—implicit in integration—represents a much less painful choice than for France. It is easier for a nation to renounce national sovereignty when its national sovereignty is threatened. Did not Churchill propose, for example, that Great Britain merge with France in the tragic hours of 1940? Also one should not forget that up to 1951 Germany did not even have the right to have a ministry of foreign affairs, and we would not for the world cast any doubt on the sincerity of Adenauer's "Europeanism."

It is a fact and an altogether natural one that Europeanism should become a political reality and not just a dream at the time when economic and political necessities became pressing. In Italy, Europeanism, among other things, is a reply to Communism and a source of hope for an overpopulated and underdeveloped country. In Germany it represents an anchor to windward against the attraction of Soviet plans for reunification and the temptations of power politics. As for the Benelux nations, it is natural that nations which have had twice endured invading armies should strongly feel the necessity to protect their sovereignty by renouncing it. For France, the problem has always been more complicated, and this must be recognized frankly, because for France to be "European" means detaching itself in some degree from Great Britain, the traditional ally, renouncing a policy of power, and merging with two ex-enemy nations and two other smaller nations—hence the constant fluctuations in French policy between 1944 and 1956.

Here economics and politics come together. This is why I affirmed above that the treaty establishing the Common Market has controlled not only economic policy but also the domestic and foreign policy of France by obliging de Gaulle himself to accept its consequences. The paradox is that de Gaulle, even while exalting the French nation and its independence, could not avoid helping to contribute to the integration of Europe. No other government could have taken France into the Common Market on January 1, 1959, without covering itself with safety clauses from the Treaty of Rome. From the economic point of view, financial disorder and chronic inflation had constituted insurmountable obstacles to European integration. The Fifth Republic has overcome them, and it has also consistently applied the European treaties favoring the acceleration and elaboration of agricultural policy and even the advance to the second stage of the Common Market. De Gaulle's political contribution is equally paradoxical. Even while speaking of *grandeur*, the general has granted independence to a dozen African peoples and has liquidated the previously insolvable problem of Algeria, which had for years blocked France's participation in a European policy. De Gaulle has swept up the last remains of the French empire and has dissipated the concomitant illusions. There is no other way for France, therefore, than that of greater and greater integration with Europe. De Gaulle's motives are perhaps quite different, but what counts is what he has done and not the reasons why he has done it.

No doubt, the Franco-German pact is difficult to reconcile with the construction of Europe, and it gives the unpleasant impression of attempting to impose an inadequate formula of European political unity on four other countries by force. Basically, however, this pact does nothing more than resume the policy of reconciliation with Germany begun by Schuman and Monnet, it facilitates the limitation of France and Germany to European dimensions. Firmness toward Britain's European policy—a firmness indispensable for the construction of Europe in view of the danger of dilution of economic integration—could come only from France. This is also true of the political construction of Europe, which nobody dared to resume after the failure of the EDC.

Furthermore, it is not only on the continent and particularly in France that substantial progress has been made in laying the foundations of political integration in Europe. Progress can also be seen in Great Britain. After the crisis of Suez in 1956, and especially after the crisis over the free trade area and after the success of the Common Market, the partisans of a bolder European policy for Great Britain increased, not only in the Liberal party, but above all in the two major British parties, Conservative and Labour. Even within the Conservative cabinet there is a "European party" which includes in its ranks men like Heath, Thorneycroft and Emery, all of whose influence has sometimes been decisive. British bureaucracy also has undergone an important change. In spite of the interruption of negotiations caused by de Gaulle's veto in January, 1963, these trends have not disappeared. The British have realized the error committed at Nassau, and they have understood that the economic commitments assumed in the course of the long months of negotiations in Brussels are insufficient and that it is necessary to take revolutionary decisions in the military and political sectors.

There is further proof of the development in the policy of European unity when one looks across the ocean. Was not President Kennedy's offer of an equal partnership to a united Europe made only a year ago? Did not the great debate on the respective nuclear responsibilities of a united Europe and the United States begin only a few months ago? Are these not signs that, in spite of obstacles and reverses, the European states, beginning with the most reluctant—France and Great Britain—are in the process of realizing that the essential condition of the attainment of their political destiny is unity, that is, the construction of a New Europe, associated with the United States?

In conclusion, I do not believe that the litmus test shows worse results today than it would have shown in 1948–1950, 1950–1951, or in the following years, whether from the economic point of view or from the political, diplomatic or military points of view. There were larger hopes then, a fact which perhaps explains the present disillusion, but there has always been a discrepancy between hopes and reality, and today's discrepancy is no greater in the sphere of European policy. On the contrary, it has been reduced. Does this examination of the facts lead to the conclusion that a European political federation, that is, a United States of Europe, is imminent? One would have to be a prophet to answer this question. I have only tried to show by a brief historical review that the European forces existing today on any level, economic, political or diplomatic, either within or outside the Six, are not in the process of dissolution. On the other hand, I think that it is difficult if not impossible to estimate whether or not these forces will be sufficient to unite Europe.

III The Formulas for Organizing the West and Europe

If the struggle for unity has been a dominant characteristic of the policy of European states in the last fifteen years; if this struggle merges with the struggle to reduce to European dimensions the European nations, particularly those of the most important ones such as Great Britain and France; if each European crisis has been precipitated by difficulties raised either by France of by Great Britain or by both at the same time; if one of the most important aspects of European policy concerns the differences of opinion between France and Great Britain on the subject of the German problem: if all this is true, it does not therefore mean that the unity of Europe has necessarily been conceived by its partisans as an end in itself, as the affirmation of a new will to power or as a subordination of obsolete nationalisms in each state to a new European supranationalism. There is no doubt that certain partisans of Europe conceive their goal in these terms. The Europeanism of certain movements of the extreme right in France, Italy and other continental countries also presents this debased characteristic. Incontestably, however, the great majority of "Europeans" have always visualized European unity within a framework of western and especially Atlantic solidarity; they have considered European unity as a step indispensable for the organization of the West and—through negotiations with the East—for the organization of world peace.

Until the last few years the most farsighted partisans of Europe, encouraged by responsible American circles, have expected that the organization of the West would evolve from British and American, especially American, hegemony toward a better balanced and more harmonious system. Such a system, which one might call tripolar organization, would be based on three pillars: the integration of the six continental nations; the United Kingdom and the British Commonwealth; and the United States.

In practice, the most important objective was to rapidly reinforce the Atlantic Alliance on the European continent, where East and West are in most direct contact, by the formation of a solid political and economic union among the six nations which had already begun the movement toward unity with the establishment of the ECSC in 1950. This objective also had the advantage of resolving, at least temporarily, the delicate problem of relations between Great Britain and the Six. At a later stage, the system would be perfected by the fusion of the continental nations and Great Britain in a single community. The result would be the foundation of a bipolar Atlantic Alliance which would strengthen the existing alliance because it would be better balanced and because its internal relations would be simpler by being reduced to a dialogue between two comparable powers, closely tied politically, militarily and economically.

The "grand design" set forth by President Kennedy in 1962 was actually the summation of all American postwar policy. American administrations, Democratic and Republican, supported all efforts toward greater unity of the continent of Europe openly and with conviction beginning with the first initiatives. The prime object of American policy in Europe has been to develop a community of free and strong nations, economically and politically integrated to the point where they could resist absorption, total or piecemeal, by the Soviet Union and capable, if necessary, of serving as the first line of defense against Soviet attack. After the Truman Doctrine came the Marshall Plan of economic aid and the encouragement given to the Europeans to form the OEEC, that is, to pursue economic unity. Then, later, came unconditional support for the establishment of the ECSC, the EDC, the Common Market and Euratom—even in spite of British opposition.

The United States rightly thought that only in this way—by establishing in Europe a tight and effective united nucleus—would Europe be in a position to cope with the double threat that the war left hanging over the continent: the closeness of a Soviet Russia not yet tired of expansion, and the trap set by Communist parties aiming to destroy the vacillating European governments from within. Only thus, by the creation of a solid European construction in which Germany would be admitted on an equal footing, could the organization of the defense of Europe and the Atlantic association be made effective. This defense would certainly depend on the United States at first, but later it would be capable of providing a sufficient rampart to protect western civilization by its own means.

The American hope of finding in Europe a viable and efficient ally, united in will and in resources, extended from the economic sphere to the political and military spheres. Instead of following the traditional policy of "divide and conquer," the United States has never hesitated to encourage the formation of a united Europe and has recognized the value of strong and united allies as opposed to feeble and divided allies. If the exact nature of the relations between a united Europe and the United States have never been carefully worked out, it is because the necessary condition of such elaboration—the unification of Europe—is still far off. And it was certainly not by accident that President Kennedy's speech of July 4, 1962, in which he expressed a desire that the partnership between the United States and a united Europe should be the partnership of equals, was delivered at the height of the success of the Common Market and on the eve of the European summit meeting in Rome where the treaty of political union among the Six was to be signed.

The American vision of the organization of the West has therefore always been evolutionary, and has gone beyond the unipolar and centralized conception of the Atlantic Alliance. The Kennedy administration took up this direction of American postwar policy and tried to speed it up. This is its original contribution and, perhaps, the cause of the difficulties it has encountered. The "grand design," which was to start with a tripolar arrangement, has been speeded up. According to the Kennedy conception, the success of the Common Market as well as the necessity to offset the authoritarian tendency of General de Gaulle and to reinforce to some extent the young democracy in West Germany, made necessary a rapid advance from the tripolar phase (United States, Great Britain and Commonwealth, and United Europe), to the construction of an

27

Atlantic Alliance based on the United States and united Europe including Great Britain, that is, to a bipolar situation.

This design for the organization of the West as well as the concept of the role which a united Europe should play within the Atlantic Alliance has always been shared by the partisans of Europe. They have consistently believed that the Atlantic Pact is an indispensable guarantee of the unity of the West and the survival of Europe. They have always thought, on the one hand, that the Atlantic Alliance was not incompatible with the unification of Europe and, on the other hand, that it could not be a substitute for it. On the contrary, Atlantic association and European unity complement and reinforce each other. European unity, to be viable, must indeed develop in the framework of the Atlantic Alliance, that is, Europe must be closely associated with the North American continent. Gaullist and neutralist conceptions of a Europe envisaged as an autonomous third force have always been rejected by the most representative partisans of Europe as abstract, nationalistic and dangerous conceptions which, moreover, would not stand up to a careful examination of the facts. The destiny of the West is indeed indivisible. How could Europe assure its own defense and, consequently, its own existence if separated from the United States? How could it cope with the dialogue with the East, the German problem, disarmament and assistance to underdeveloped nations if it was not closely associated with the United States economically, politically and militarily? There is no doubt that the construction of a united Europe would have a considerable influence on the course of world politics and, among other things, that it would assure Europe of a more important role in the decisions of the Atlantic Pact. It is no less evident, on the contrary, that divisions among the European states, a source of antagonism, would weaken NATO itself and diminish its importance.

The partisans of Europe therefore greeted President Kennedy's declaration of "interdependence" on July 4, 1962 with enormous satisfaction. As has been said, in this declaration the President of the United States expressed the desire for a partnership of equals between the United States and a united Europe. Furthermore, Kennedy declared himself ready to take the first step toward this partnership and to negotiate first new transatlantic commercial relations under the terms of the Trade Expansion Act. Kennedy also showed that he was willing to review the very foundations of the Atlantic Alliance, in order to transform it from an alliance centered on the Anglo-American monopoly of atomic weapons into a partnership where the responsibilities—financial, political and military—would be shared between the United States and a united Europe.

If the partisans of Europe have always opposed the conception of Europe as a third force and the construction of a detached Europe of the Gaullist type, however, they have also always rejected a static Atlantic conception of the British type. In such a conception, Europe would remain substantially and definitively subordinated to the leadership of the United States. To desire a politically, militarily and economically united Europe in close association with the United States means, indeed, to desire also an organic and balanced organization of the Atlantic Alliance.

IV *A Partnership of Equals for Dealing with the East*

The interruption of the negotiations for Great Britain's entry into the Common Market stimulated new discussion on all the problems of organizing the West and, perhaps, contributed to their solution. It is possible that, despite everything, the happenings in Brussels in January, 1963 indicated a crisis of strength in the West and not a crisis of decadence. If the European nations had really been weak, they could not have permitted themselves the luxury of such polemics; if the peril had been as grave as in past years, certain differences could not have been tolerated. Moreover, precedents for this interpretation are not lacking in the history of the European movement, for after the crisis of the Council of Europe and the OEEC in 1949, when everything seemed lost, the revolutionary enterprise of the ECSC was born. After the still more serious failure of the EDC in 1954, and the apparent burial of the political community project, hardly a year later came the "relance" of Messina which led to the Treaty of Rome establishing the Common Market and Euratom. After the serious break in negotiations for the free trade area between Great Britain and the other countries of the OEEC in November, 1958, and despite the increasing disunity of Europe caused by the EFTA, there was the courageous demand of Great Britain to join the EEC in July, 1961.

Today, we can glimpse the possibility that from the break of the Brussels negotiations might arise a political and military European community, including Great Britain, if it so desires, which would be closely associated with the United States in the framework of the Atlantic Alliance. It is not by accident that today as yesterday, France (Democratic or Gaullist) and Great Britain (Conservative or Labour) create the major difficulties. The struggle for European unification is still basically only an important battle in the struggle to reduce all the states of Europe to European dimensions, and it is therefore natural that the states which carry or have in the past carried greater responsibilities should offer the strongest resistance.

For a long time it was thought that the suspension in April, 1962 of the negotiations designed to develop political institutions out of economic integration would involve dangers both for the negotiations for Britain's entry into the European communities and for relations among the Six themselves. Failure to evolve political construction from economic integration has increased the temptation to substitute other policies for the policy of European unification. In the absence of a political construction, there occurred both a Franco-German reconciliation and increasing difficulties in the negotiations between Great Britain and the Six, a tension which led to the French demand to break off the negotiations. These political differences, if they are not rapidly resolved, might destroy the European communities, the Common Market in particular.

The major difficulties, as I said above, began, perhaps, when the attempt was made to organize the West too fast. The United States is responsible in that it pushed Great Britain to enter the European communities rapidly, reversing American policy of the past ten years; the United States even let it be understood that the nonadmission of Great Britain would be a grave disillusion and would without doubt modify its policy toward the Atlantic Alliance. Great Britain is responsible because, in spite of its revolutionary request for admission to the community in the summer of 1961, and despite the concessions made in Brussels, it has not yet showed itself ready to accept—especially in the nuclear sphere—the consequences of a bipolar conception of the Atlantic Alliance. The other five nations are also responsible because they did not propose a more integrationist plan of union to General de Gaulle, and they limited themselves mistakenly to focusing the battle for European political unity on the necessity to include Britain.

However this may be, it is now impossible to turn back and the only way open is that of an Atlantic Alliance based on a united Europe and the United States. Naturally, each country must take longer strides and commit itself more fundamentally as is true each time one wishes to force ahead. France should accept Britain's participation, political and economic, in the Europe of the Six. On its side, Great Britain should renounce all privileged relations with the British Commonwealth and the United States and become a part of Europe without reservations. The United States should accept—and not only in words—a united Europe bearing responsibility equal to its own in the common defense of the West; it should therefore admit, among other things, that the privileged nuclear arrangements with Great Britain should be extended to Europe as a whole. Italy and the Benelux nations should make the necessary political and financial effort to participate in the nuclear defense of Europe.

The organization of the West, based on a bipolar Atlantic Alliance, has consequences which inevitably affect defense. It should be frankly recognized that this problem has long been neglected by partisans of Europe and by Americans, for both economic and political reasons. Europeans took the easy way out by leaving their own defense, with all the responsibilities that it involves, to the trans-Atlantic ally and, in particular, to the American thermonuclear deterrent. But an effective partnership between a united Europe and the United States presupposes a real equality, even in the nuclear sector. It is only thus that Europe and the United States can be made to feel that they are defending a common civilization and not only their national territory. Between the two extremes of the American atomic monopoly—an atrophied, centralized and conservative Atlanticism—and the proliferation of national atomic forces in Europe, it seems to me that there is no other possible choice than that of a European deterrent closely coordinated with the American one. Naturally, this European deterrent would not only be associated with the American deterrent but would also be based on a democratic European political institution. The economic and financial resources of a united Europe would give such a nuclear force the necessary dimensions to make it credible. Finally, there are good reasons to suppose that the United States is ready to support such a European deterrent presented within the framework of a new burst of political and economic activity in Europe.

Naturally, the integration of foreign policy and defense policy brings out more than ever the political features of the New Europe and its relations with the United States. It should be clearly stated that the integration of both foreign and defense policies necessitates more than ever the eventual establishment of some sort of federal relationship. Only in the name of an integrated European structure could one bring about in the European states the sacrifices required on the plane of foreign policy and national defense. Only federal institutions would be sufficient to assure the abandonment of obsolete and nationalistic ideas by guaranteeing the formation of common political will in Europe and the acquisition of responsibilities in the domain of nuclear defense. Only a potentially federalist Europe could become a viable partner and meet the proposition of interdependence outlined by President Kennedy in Philadelphia on July 4, 1962. On that occasion, Kennedy gave the Europeans to understand that the United States was disposed to enlarge the privileged relationship with Great Britain to include a united Europe. But at Nassau, only a few months later, faced with a deadlock in the construction of Europe as a political unit and the dragged-out negotiations for Great Britain's entry into the European community,

Kennedy offered France the Polaris missile at the same time as Britain. The refusal of General de Gaulle to subscribe to the Nassau agreement, expressed in his press conference on January 14, 1963, should not lead one to believe that the game is over.

Great, therefore, is the temptation for the United States to give up the "grand design" and the great challenge to have a united Europe as a partner; great is the temptation for the United States to choose the easy way out, that of the atomic monopoly, camouflaged more or less by "directorates" including two or three other nations. But this does not seem to me to be the real solution if the West is to have the necessary and effective unity required for negotiations with the East.

In the course of the last fifteen years the alliance has achieved its principal and most immediate objective: that of avoiding war. The menace of direct Soviet attack is dissipated, at least for the time being. One should not forget this great gain when one speaks of the crisis in NATO. After the affirmation of the military power and the determination of the West, however, the Russian menace transformed itself from a military threat into a political threat. This is why the most important problem for the future is not only that of avoiding war, but even more that of organizing the alliance and reinforcing it to meet the political menace head on, and consequently to organize world peace.

The political cohesion of the alliance is therefore important and will become more so in the future. To achieve this cohesion, economic problems and above all political and military problems become mutually entangled. The proliferation of nuclear arms or nuclear discriminations within the alliance is not a solution: a unipolar alliance, comprehensible in time of imminent danger, seems to be excluded as a long-term solution, whereas a multipolar alliance is dangerous and, furthermore, impossible.

The Atlantic partnership based on the United States and a united Europe seems to be the only solution, even in the military sector. It will allow the West not only to resist but also to negotiate with the East on the long and difficult road to coexistence. The Atlantic partnership, although it has both political and military consequences, is primarily a political solution because if one achieves satisfactory political relations, military problems will be more easily solved. If, on the contrary, one does not succeed in assuring a political balance within the alliance, one must expect the resumption of nationalism and a policy of power politics or neutralism.

It is dangerous to contend that the existence and the cohesion of the Atlantic Alliance are established facts. This is why the nuclear multilateral force proposed by the United States allows room for many doubts. Such a force does not in fact represent a military necessity and it seems likely to make the present structure of the Atlantic Alliance, already out of date and unsuited to solving the problems of the future, all the more rigid. The multilateral force would probably hinder the creation of the European partner as a second pillar of the alliance and would arouse nuclear appetites that could not be satisfied. Finally, it seems likely to encourage neutralism in certain countries and to focus attention and efforts on the wrong track. Nevertheless, the problem is so complex that for a final judgment on the multilateral force—the so called MLF—one should wait a few years.

The partnership therefore presupposes European integration in political, economic and military terms. Only in this way will it be possible to strengthen the alliance and to give it the political cohesion needed to meet the political menace coming from the East and accordingly to undertake negotiations for the organization of peace. European integration therefore suggests a solution to the political problems both inside Europe and in the Atlantic Alliance. It also resolves the military problems because, through the establishment of a European deterrent, it avoids the proliferation of atomic arms and prevents the discrimination evident in the proposals of "directorates" including two, three or more countries. Finally, it is a means of control over arms because it permits the organization of a more elaborate and accurate European deterrent.

Though the responsibilities of the European nations are great and their nationalistic longings worthy of scorn, it is no less true that the responsibility of the United States as the leader of the alliance is equally heavy. The United States would be wrong to think that Europe, whether united or divided, would be satisfied in the long run with an American atomic monopoly. The United States will not be able to maintain its special atomic relations with Great Britain without creating resentment not only in France but in other European countries as well. There is a contradiction between the offer of partnership on the one hand and the special Anglo-American relations or an American atomic monopoly on the other.

If the European nations should decide to act rashly, a policy of monopoly on the part of the United States—evidently motivated by mistrust of Europe—would, far from stopping the effort, only push it toward a dead end. I would be surprised if the resources of Europe, freed from colonial responsibilities and directed toward reconstruction, were not now employed for the expansion of European influence in the alliance and ultimately in world affairs. The present anxiety about and criticisms of the United States are nothing more than signs of the success of American policy and are a proof of the birth of a dynamic, strong and self-confident new Europe.

I hope that the USA, in its negotiations on the subject of Berlin and Germany, will not yield to the temptation of the easy way by adopting certain dangerous attitudes of the British policy toward the German problem. Repeated bilateral initiatives, with emphasis on direct relations between Washington and London, Washington and Bonn, Washington and Rome—although they may flatter national ambitions—do not constitute a policy but merely a series of expedients. If this game is prolonged, it will be the prelude to disaster. The United States should above all avoid giving the impression that it is ready to renounce a policy of European unification and Atlantic partnership as a concession to Khrushchev—in payment for a *détente*. The dialogue with the East will yield bitter results if it is based on the fictitious unity of the West and its disorganization. Although the immediate results might be spectacular, the balkanization of Europe would probably result, followed by its neutralization and finally its annexation to the Soviet sphere of influence. The United States should avoid giving the impression to Germany, and even more to Europe, that it is seeking a collaboration with the enemy rather than with the allies. For a long time the Communists have maintained that there was a contradiction between the Atlantic Pact and a united Europe on the one hand and peace on the other. For a long time the partisans of Europe, supported by the Americans, have maintained, on the contrary, that peace could not be organized without a united Europe and the unity of the West. An irresponsible Atlanticism, even if it is covered with the high-sounding title of "Community," is no substitute for an equal partnership that requires the construction of the European partner—which is precisely what is lacking.

It will certainly not be the departure of de Gaulle or of Macmillan that will resolve these problems. On the contrary, if there is a reason why the former should leave the scene soon and the Conservative Party be defeated in the next election, it is precisely because, after these events, the problems of the organization of the alliance will be more clearly in evidence.

It is difficult to believe that the European nations and, even more, a united Europe, would be willing in the long run to share the risks of the modern nuclear era without sharing the political decisions whose purpose is to avoid or to reduce such risks. What must be gained is not so much the nuclear arms themselves as participation in the political decisions on their use. History teaches us, alas, that influence and the possibility of control are related to power. I do not believe that it will be possible to increase the real influence of Europe within the Atlantic Alliance while renouncing definitively the claim to nuclear power.

In conclusion, I do not believe—despite the extreme difficulty of the present situation—that either the European nations or the United States have a serious choice. Today, still, the only framework favorable for Europe, the West and world peace is a bipolar Atlantic Alliance. It is precisely at this time, when things seem at a deadlock, and when the European nations are preparing to open their ears again to the unsound appeals of nationalism and power politics, that it is necessary to affirm that, for Europe and the West, there is no other way than the construction of a European community, political and economic, associated with the United States in the Atlantic Alliance.

The situation does not seem to me serious enough to warrant renunciation of the attempts to construct Europe, nor are the European nations divided, weak and disoriented enough to have to take the consequences. Hasty moves could accomplish nothing but the ruin of the European communities which represent the point of departure for the political construction of Europe and for a more efficient organization of the Western world. The interruption of the negotiations for Great Britain's entry into the European community has brought into the open this series of important problems, whose solution will determine the future.

In 1955, with the relance of Messina, the partisans of Europe pushed aside the political problem of constructing Europe, when faced with the impossibility of establishing the EDC and the EPC. In July, 1961, after the success of the Common Market, Great Britain, by asking admission only to the *economic* European communities, avoided the problem again. The partisans of Europe also thought that it could be resolved by further delay and by the solution of economic problems alone. Today it is essentially the political aspects that are uppermost once again.

I hope that the United States will not make the same mistake of thinking that a largely political problem can be resolved by economic partnership alone, the so-called "Kennedy round." It is futile to harbor illusions: beyond the economic problems, an agreement among the nations of the Atlantic Alliance will be difficult and even impossible as long as the political problems are not resolved.

The possibility of the Common Market's complete success and of Great Britain's membership in it will remain slim as long as no overall solution is found for the various problems, economic, political and military. Today, more than ever, we must have the courage to resist resurgent nationalist myths. We need a clear vision of the ultimate goals and a strong dose of realism to choose the means best adapted to those goals. The sole solution which seems viable for the future is the construction of Europe with the objective of reinforcing the West. This would provide a true basis for a stable and efficient Atlantic Alliance and, as a result, for an understanding with the East which would guarantee a lasting peace. Negotiations with Russia will be fruitful only when Europe has proven that it wishes to renew itself and to unite once and for all.

BIBLIOGRAPHY

Albonetti, A. *Préhistoire des Etats-Unis d'Europe*. Paris: Sirey, 1963. Published also in German and in Italian.

Aron, R. *Introduction à la stratégie atomique*. Paris: Institut d'Etudes Politiques de l'Université de Paris, Amicale des Elèves, 1962–1963.

Aron, R. and D. Lerner. *La querelle de la C.E.D.* Paris: Librairie A. Colin, 1956.

Beloff, N. *The General Says No*. London: Penguin ed., 1963.

Comité d'action pour les Etats-Unis d'Europe. *Déclarations communes et documentation relative aux dix sessions tenues à Paris, de 1955 à 1962*. Paris: 83 avenue Foch.

Carmoy (De), G. *Fortune de l'Europe*. Paris: Domat, 1953.

Diebold, W., Jr. *The Schuman Plan (1950–1958)*. New York: Praeger, 1959.

Drouin, P. *L'Europe du Marché Commun*. Paris: René Juillard, 1963.

Grosser, A. *La IVe République et sa Politique Extérieure*. Paris: Librairie A. Colin, 1961.

———. "General de Gaulle and the Foreign Policy of the Fifth Republic." *International Affairs*, April, 1963, Vol. 39, no. 2.

Hallstein, W. *Several Speeches, Declarations and Interviews*.

Kissinger, H. A. "The Unsolved Problems of European Defence." *Foreign Affairs*, July, 1962.
———. "Strains on the Alliance." *Foreign Affairs*, January, 1963.
———. "Nato's Nuclear Dilemma." *The Reporter*, March 28, 1963.

Mayne, R. *The Community of Europe*. London: Victor Gollancz, 1962.

Monnet. J. *Interviews and Speeches*.

Nutting, A. *Europe Will Not Wait*. Hollis et Carter, 1960.

Perroux, F. *L'Europe sans rivages*. Paris: Presses Universitaires de France, 1954.

Pryce, R. *The Political Future of the European Community*. London: John Marshbank, 1962.

Uri, P. *Dialogue des Continents—un programme économique*. Paris: Plon, 1963.

Werth, A. *La France depuis la guerre (1944–1957)*. Paris: Gallimard, 1951.

Zurcher, A. J. *The Struggle to Unite Europe 1940–1958*. New York: New York University Press, 1958.

Daily newspapers: the New York *Times*, New York *Herald Tribune*, *The Times, The Financial Times, Le Monde*.

Weekly publications: *The Economist, The Observer*.

Collections of the *Agence Europe* and of the *Opera Mundi Europe*.

RAYMOND ARON

Old Nations, New Europe

THOUGH historians and sociologists rarely foresee events, they never have any trouble explaining them after they have happened. No economist could have foreseen in 1945, or even in 1949, that between 1950 and 1960 the nations of continental Europe would experience a rate of economic growth about double that of the United States or Great Britain. American sociologists were still listing the structural reasons why the economic growth of France had been and continued to be slow at a time when, if they had only observed attentively what was really going on, they would have seen the first signs of the "French miracle." As for the Italian miracle, if almost no one had demonstrated its impossibility, it was primarily because no one had conceived of its possibility. No visible social change came before it or announced it. Secondary and university education will be transformed by the Italian miracle, but the miracle is not a consequence of such a transformation. Men educated under the old system have created the new Italy.

At the risk of tiring the reader, let me cite some figures that bring out the exceptional nature of the period 1950–1959 in regard to economic progress. According to a study by D. C. Paige, F. T. Blackaby and J. Freund* the growth rate of the national product per worker per year between 1950 and 1959 was 4.7 per cent for Italy, 4.5 per cent for Germany, 3.6 per cent for France, 2.2 per cent for the United States and 1.2 per cent for the United Kingdom. But the same growth rate calculated over a long period† for these countries was only 1.2 per cent; 1.5 per cent; 1.5 per cent; 2.0 per cent, and 1.2 per cent respectively. In other words, the growth rate of the United States in the course of the past decade is slightly

* National Institute Economic Revue, No. 16, July, 1963 (French translation in *Sedeis,* supplement 804).

† For Italy since 1863, for Germany since 1853, for France since 1855, for the United States since 1871, and for the United Kingdom since 1857.

above its long-term rate (2.0 per cent.) It is the growth of the three principal nations of continental Europe—Italy, Germany, and France —that has strikingly increased.

Economists might well inquire into the causes of this accelerated growth and try to calculate the probability of its continuation. Some nations have already experienced eight if not ten years of accelerated growth. From 1922 to 1929 the gross national product and the product per worker per year in France increased annually by 5.8 per cent. The corresponding figures for Germany were 5.7 per cent and 6 per cent. In the same period, from 1922 to 1929, French industrial production grew 7.3 per cent annually, that is, faster than between 1950 and 1959 (6.3 per cent). In quantitative terms, what is new in Old Europe consists, therefore, in the fact that it has maintained for fifteen years a growth rate formerly attained only for short periods and which is considerably above the rate of the United States calculated over a much longer time. (This is true of the total product and of the production per worker per year, the last of which represents a measure of productivity.)

These results, which were not brought about by educational reform or by a revolution in the system of values or in family organization, seem to have been caused by a conjunction of three factors: a better economic understanding that fostered more efficient management and that was able to avoid crises; the transfer to Europe of techniques already known and practiced across the Atlantic; and a weakening of resistance to change which has facilitated modernization in all aspects of society.

Evidently, it has not been proved that tomorrow's circumstances will remain as favorable as yesterday's. The growth in productivity cannot continue indefinitely at the same rate, even if the maintenance of the present rate is not impossible for the next twenty or thirty years. In any case, western Europe has clearly entered the era of what W. W. Rostow calls "self-sustained growth and mass consumption." Throughout western Europe the type of society some call technical and others scientific has come into existence and it disrupts the system of human relations inherited from the *Ancien Régime* or even from the bourgeois property-oriented society of the last century.

It is worthy of note that in this issue of *Dædalus* the sociologists Alain Touraine, Ralf Dahrendorf and S. M. Lipset concentrate on the conceptual and theoretical elaboration of the changes that have occurred and on the analysis of their repercussions in social relationships. As for the changes themselves, everyone is familiar with them: industrial growth, increased mobility, enlargement of educational facilities, weakening of the "revolutionary" attitude of the proletariat, an increase in the number of persons with a bourgeois standard of living, diffusion of durable consumer goods, the search for individual success and prosperity, the swelling of the tertiary sector and of various parts of the middle class and many others. To describe these changes as the Americanization of Europe would be superficial and basically unjustifiable. Neither the automobile nor the airplane are, properly speaking, American inventions; in the early stages, Europeans played at least an equal part with Americans in creating the means of transportation that revolutionized the modern way of life. The truth is that mass production and consequently mass consumption of goods and gadgets developed in the United States one or two generations earlier than in Europe, and that by the same token a normal development, interrupted by the catastrophes of the great depression and the war, takes on the aspect of Americanization because it was brought about under the protection of American deterrent forces with the aid of American capital and in imitation of certain American techniques.

The prosperity of continental Europe, therefore, is new from two points of view: first, the Old Continent is for the first time achieving the stage of what is called mass consumption in which a sufficient proportion of the population feels the advantageous effect of economic growth so that the age-old obsession with the distribution of profits is weakened and the modern concern with development is reinforced.

In the second place, the growth rate is so far above the rate considered normal, according to past experience, that economists are wondering if we are witnessing a *qualitative mutation* of the modern economy. Le Commissariat au Plan en France, in its projections for 1985, expects as a hypothesis an annual increase of production per man per year (that is, reckoning with a shorter work week) of 4.7 per cent in agriculture and 4.2 per cent in industry. These projections attest to an extraordinary optimism. If they are realized, the European economies will not only be following the trail blazed by the American economy, but they will be following it at an accelerated speed.

This "economic novelty" can also be considered as the resumption of a movement interrupted by the catastrophe of the war and as a catching up with the lag for which the war was partially responsible. Of course it was fostered by the many organizations for European cooperation, but it began before the implementation of the Common Market. The extent to which the Common Market should be credited with the German, French and Italian "miracles" is very uncertain. As an experience common to all western Europe, it leaves open the question which is the subject of this article: To what extent have the separate nations remained the supreme political, historical and spiritual realities of the Old Continent?

People marvel that France and West Germany should have been able to sign a treaty of friendship and cooperation less than twenty years after the most horrible of wars. The political miracle is no less striking than the economic miracle. In 1945, western Europe was a mass of ruins; today it is one of the most prosperous regions of the world. In 1945, Europe was torn by hate and memories; today the historic enemies are united by the Treaty of Rome, and they are working together in the EEC. I will not push the paradox so far as to claim that the political miracle was more foreseeable than the economic miracle; but certainly it was no less so. By 1945, or more conservatively 1946, it was evident that the conflict between the Soviet bloc and the West would dominate the diplomatic scene for a long time. In these historically unprecedented circumstances the so-called traditional quarrels between European nations lost all meaning. Willy-nilly, the victors and the vanquished of the last war found themselves on the same side, and they had to work together. How could relations between the fragment of Germany called the Federal Republic and France be similar to the relations between the Reich of Bismarck or William II and the France of Napoleon III or Clemenceau? As long as the Soviet bloc exists, as long as the Red army is stationed two hundred kilometers from the Rhine, as long as the western fringe of the Eurasian land mass owes its liberty to the protection of the maritime powers, the former enemy nations are doomed to live together in an alliance imposed by events. The real question was to determine whether this alliance would be borne as a cruel fate or accepted as a challenge to be met by the will to construct. The second of these alternatives has been brought about not by a miracle, but thanks to a positive reaction on the part of the European peoples and the initiative of certain men.

By 1950 French public opinion in general had accepted the Schuman Plan, which implied some kind of reconciliation with Germany. It is true that between 1950 and 1954, the plan for a European army set off a great debate comparable to the great ideological debates so frequent in French history. There were two reasons for this conflict of opinion. On the one hand, the issue was not only that of working with Germany; it meant giving Germany arms when the Germans themselves did not seem to want them. On the other hand, the formula adopted—on the pretext of taking precautions against German rearmament—envisaged a kind of fusion between the armed forces of the Federal Republic and those of France. Hence the slogan tirelessly repeated by the opponents of the EDC: "The European Army destroys the French Army and rebuilds the German Army."* Since 1954, as if French opinion had been delivered at one stroke from its anti-German obsession, the following steps of European unification have been accepted with neither enthusiam nor visible indignation. Whereas from 1950 to 1955 French leaders were urging Great Britain's participation in European unity, and whereas even after the rejection of the EDC they were demanding British guarantees in the framework of the Western European Union as the condition of French agreement to German rearmament, in January, 1963 General de Gaulle vetoed Britain's entry into the Common Market. At that time Frenchmen were asked the following question: "When you think of France's future relations with England and Germany, with which of these two nations should we have the closest ties?" Of those asked, 40 per cent replied Germany; 25 per cent, England; 35 per cent did not declare themselves. In January, 1963, 61 per cent of Frenchmen polled judged the Franco-German treaty "desirable"; only 14 per cent judged it undesirable. In comparing these figures with those of ten years earlier, one can assert without hesitation that the percentage of those opposed to Franco-German reconciliation had diminished. There appear to be three causes of this diminution. Ten years ago the rearming of Germany, if not Franco-German reconciliation, seemed to be an aspect of the Atlantic alliance and even an expression of American will. However, when signed by General de Gaulle after the rejection of Great Britain, the Treaty of Association became an affirmation of French will. The Nationalist opposition to the EDC no longer existed to oppose the 1963 treaty. The Communist and *progressiste* opposition to the Atlantic policy continues, but both have lost in virulence. The opposition I call *progressiste* tended toward neutralism between 1947 and 1955; it refused to choose clearly between the two great powers, it hoped to stay neutral in case of war. This opposition no longer entertains toward the Franco-German Treaty the hostile motives it had toward the EDC. Finally, the percentage of Communist voters has diminished since the advent of the Fifth Republic, and there is reason to

* The rejection of the EDC was not merely a manifestation of anti-German sentiment. According to the polls, indeed, the Atlantic policy had resolute enemies on the extreme left, opponents with more qualified objections among the left-wing Socialists or *progressistes*, and finally intermittent opponents on the right among the traditional Nationalists. At the time of the EDC, these three types of opposition combined: the left-wing Socialists were hostile to the rearmament of Germany, the Nationalists to the dissolution of the French army, and the Communists to the entire Atlantic policy.

believe that even those who remain faithful to the party do not follow passively the party line of the Central Committee.

I have chosen the case of France because I know the situation at first hand and because France's action was decisive in this matter. The evolution of opinion could be summed up thus: Since 1947 majority opinion in France and in the other nations of the continent has been favorable to the unification of Europe, but war memories and hostility to Germany have subsisted in varying degrees in different nations and milieux. In the ten years that followed the war, the positions taken toward Germany, toward the rearmament of the Federal Republic and toward European unification were greatly influenced by domestic repercussions of the great diplomatic schism between the Soviet world and the free world.

In France after World War I, the left favored reconcilation with the Weimar Republic because of its pacifism, its internationalism. The right, on the contrary, was opposed to the policy of reconciliation because of its nationalism, because of its concern for security, and because of its defiance of the "eternal Germany." After World War II, the situation was reversed. The extreme left, Communist or *progressiste,* was hostile to the unification of Europe and to the membership of the Federal Republic in the Atlantic Alliance because it saw these institutions as manifestations of the cold war directed against the Soviet Union. Today European unification and reconciliation with Germany no longer seem exclusively to be instruments of the cold war, even in the eyes of the extreme left. By now, in spite of the continued strength of the Communist party in France and in Italy, public opinion in those two nations no longer reacts toward European unity in a manner perceptively different from opinion in nations where the Communist party has little influence.

Simultaneous polls of opinion in the six nations were taken for the first time during February and March of 1963. Some of the results are worthy of note. First and foremost, the minority which declared itself hostile to the European idea is extremely small: 4 per cent in Germany and Italy and the Netherlands, 5 per cent in Belgium and Luxembourg, and 8 per cent in France.* The combined total of those who declared themselves "very much for" or "more or less for" the unity of Europe reached 81 per cent in Germany, 87 per cent in the Netherlands, 72 per cent in France, 60 per cent in Italy and 65 per cent in Belgium. The idea of European unity is

---

* It is possible that the Communists, who are really opposed, were among those who did not reply. Yet if the Communists hesitate to declare themselves hostile to the European idea, this very fact is revealing of its virtually irresistible popularity.

today separated quite clearly from the cold war and from the conflict with the Soviet world. Asked what they expect from European unity, there are very few who see in it the safeguard of the West and a weapon against the East (15 per cent in Germany, 3 per cent in France, 6 per cent in the Netherlands.) Hardly more numerous are those who see it as a third force (3 per cent in Germany, 11 per cent in France.) Other reasons for favoring European unity are first to assure peace; second, to secure economic development and an increase in individual well-being. The third, more idealistic reason was expressed in various formulas: "to bring peoples closer," "unity," "to develop solidarity and equality," "to advance humanity." The percentages in this category are lower.* Some conclusions are self-evident from these unequal percentages: the economic motive overrules all others in the eyes of the Italians, the Belgians and the Dutch. The French and the Germans, on the contrary, more willingly justify European unity in political terms.

Favorable by a large majority to the *idea* of Europe, Europeans also declare themselves overwhelmingly in favor of measures which will require what is called integration or federation. For example, 71 per cent of the Germans, 60 per cent of the Belgians, 60 per cent of the French, 45 per cent of the Italians—but with only 7 per cent explicitly opposed—and 75 per cent of the Dutch recorded themselves in favor of a common foreign policy. Asked how they felt about the abolition of customs duties, free circulation of labor and business, equal social opportunity and a common agricultural policy, the majorities were as large or larger. Only on the subject of the use of national taxes to aid poorer European or African nations can important opposition, sometimes even opposing majorities, be discerned.†

Reduced to the essence, it seems to me a fact that the citizens of the six nations of the Common Market favor European unity by an immense majority, with the left and extreme left being carried

* The poll showed 23% in Germany, 8% in Belgium, 24% in France, 7% in Italy, 11% in the Netherlands. All these are the percentages of the total of those who declared themselves favorable to a united Europe, not of the number of people polled. Furthermore, some gave several reasons. The percentages of those who gave "survival, to be strong" as a reason were: Germany, 13%; Belgium, 10%; France, 11%; Italy, 6%; the Netherlands, 18%. The percentages for economic development and individual well-being combined as a reason were 20% in Germany; 39% in Belgium; 23% in France; 35% in Italy; 41% in the Netherlands. Percentages for the more idealistic reason were 6% for Germany; 9% for Belgium; 18% for France; 12% for Italy; and 14% for the Netherlands.

† Concerning the African nations, the figures are Germany, 38% for and 35% against; Belgium, 29% and 53%; France, 26% and 56%; Italy, 30% and 34%; the Netherlands, 65% and 24%.

along by the movement as a whole. They are all the more favorable as they are better informed, have traveled abroad more, and belong to the upper classes. However, while favoring European unity, public opinion is only faintly militant or impassioned about it. A majority of Germans, French, Italians and Dutch think that the Common Market will bring them more advantages than disadvantages; but, except in Italy, those who think that up to the present the Common Market has not made a great difference are nearly as numerous as those who consider that it has had good results.* Although many groups harbor various fears, either general or specific, there is no coherent opposition to the Common Market in any of the six nations, no theme around which anxieties and objections can crystallize. Finally, Europeans are only moderately confident that the unity they desire will be achieved. Taking the six nations combined, 19 per cent expect it in the next ten years, 14 per cent think it will take from ten to fifteen years, 12 per cent think it will take from twenty to thirty years, 6 per cent think it will take several generations, 13 per cent do not think it will ever be achieved.

Such a view, favorable but not ardent, leaves great freedom of action to the leaders. Public opinion will not oppose so-called measures of integration, but it will not suggest or impose them either. The public will be neither very much disappointed nor very much surprised if the Common Market continues without progressing. The average Frenchman does not perceive clearly the distinction between partisans of a "Europe of States" and those of an "integrated Europe." M. Pinay does not seem any more "European" to them than General de Gaulle (and 61 per cent refuse to declare themselves on this point). At the end of January, 1963, asked whether the entrance of Great Britain into the Common Market would foster or oppose France's interest, 43 per cent of those asked refused to reply. Of those who did reply, a plurality (35 per cent) thought it would be in France's interest and 22 per cent thought the contrary. At almost the same date, however, 40 per cent of the French approved General de Gaulle's policy toward England and only 21 per cent disapproved.

The future of European unification does not depend on public opinion, at least in the sense in which the pollsters use the term. On whom or on what does it depend? A possible reply would be

---

* In Germany, 36% thought something has been gained against 30% who did not see any great change. The respective figures of the other countries are Belgium, 35% and 24%; France, 29% and 32%; Italy, 23% and 4%; the Netherlands, 49% and 20%.

that it depends on the degree to which the six nations have already become a community comparable to a national community. In that case, the prospects would be poor because the Six are not—they are not even in the process of becoming—a national community. Relations among them are still very far from resembling those among the provinces of a single country. In many respects outside the economic field, relations among them are not basically different from those that existed in the past.

Let us consider intellectual matters. Throughout the centuries ideas and knowledge have crossed frontiers. Whether allies or enemies, the English, Germans, Italians, French and Spanish have exchanged inspirations without which none of the so-called national cultures would be as they all actually are. It would not be difficult to find in French literature and thought an English thread, a German thread, a Spanish thread. Major intellectual movements have been international and have affected several European nations almost simultaneously. At times one country has taken the lead. In this respect there is no change.

It would be interesting, for each sector and each nation, to find out with which partner cooperation has been closest and exchanges most fruitful since 1945. In philosophy, it is from Germany that France has received the most; that is, from prewar Germany. No postwar German thinker has come to the fore. It is with the heirs of Hegel, Marx and Husserl that French philosophers have carried on their exchanges. The Germans in turn have been influenced by existentialism in the literary form given it by Jean-Paul Sartre—an existentialism inconceivable without Husserl and Heidegger. French plays have been in fashion in Germany for the last ten years, but French thought, at least the school that has made the greatest stir at home and abroad, preserves the marks of its Germanic origins. At the same time, English and American philosophy have been following a very different path, toward logical positivism or analytical thought. To this extent there is no unity in European philosophy at the present time, because it would be senseless to exclude from Europe either phenomenology or linguistic analysis. As for the Italians, they justly complained that Croce is either unknown or misunderstood in France. Part of Ortega y Gasset's work has been translated, but his books are regarded as those of a literary writer.

In sociology, in anthropology, in social psychology it is to the United States that the majority of professors and students look for the completion of their training, borrowing American methods or seeking out American lecturers. Here again there is to some extent a return to European origins. The American social sciences have absorbed the European heritage that the émigrés of the 1930's brought them; Europeans are now finding it again, enriched by rigorous techniques of research.

As for literature, what strikes me is the slight acquaintance in France with English writers of the last fifteen years. Rarely has the intellectual climate been so different on the two sides of the channel. A special issue of the *Times Literary Supplement* in 1962 attested to this lack of communication across the channel. On the contrary, although no American novelist has today the influence that Faulkner, Hemingway or Dos Passos had a generation ago, American authors and books, of all kinds and on all levels, easily find a wide public. France hails Italian movies with enthusiasm; from Spain she receives almost nothing.

The universities do not seem to me to have changed perceptively. They have remained more nationalist than is desirable for the good of culture. Even though no scholar worthy of the name sticks only to works written in his native tongue, I do not have the impression from my own personal experience that the universities in France, Germany or Great Britain have become more or less European than they used to be. In France, it is with the United States that university exchanges have been most intense. Perhaps the Franco-German Treaty of Association will bring about a change in this respect, but I am not sure of it.

These remarks are banal and, it seems to me, almost self-evident, but they nonetheless have a paradoxical aspect because other phenomena, equally incontestable, strike the eye. Every summer, whole human migrations upset the Old Continent. For the tourist, Europe is a unit. Never in the past has such a number of Frenchmen, Germans, Belgians, Dutchmen and Englishmen found it so natural to cross their own frontiers and travel abroad. High quality movies are usually successful in various nations simultaneously. Television networks are increasingly exchanging programs and Eurovision is, of course, a European institution. Certain elements of so-called mass culture escape the national framework; but do they not also escape the European framework?

In certain respects, European culture since 1945 has had less unity than in the past because of the facts that it has been open to the rest of the world and that it has had a protector-partner of unprecedented size and importance. In many fields the dominating influence in every European country has been that of the United States rather than that of another European country or of Europe as a whole. One cannot doubt that this has been the case in the spheres of economics, organization and technique as well as in that of the social sciences. As a cultural unit, Europe, strictly or broadly defined, is less today than fifty years ago, not because internal frontiers stop men or ideas but because Europe as a whole no longer has external frontiers and because each nation has opened a dialogue with the whole world.

In what sense, then, is it possible to speak of Europe in the singular, as if it constituted a unit? First and foremost, it is the view of others that transforms a diversity into a whole. It is the non-Europeans or better yet the ex-Europeans—that is, the majority of Americans—who call Europe the Old Continent and who see in it specific traits that make it different from the New World. The initial impulse for the European unification movement came from Stalin, who threatened us all, and from Marshall, who made close cooperation between European nations the condition of his plan.

The nations of Europe also form a community in itself (*an sich*) in the sense that they have enough traditions and values in common to merit recognition as one and the same historical civilization (or culture in the sense of that word as used by Spengler and Toynbee); yet this sort of unity already existed yesterday and it has nothing in common with the political unity aspired to by those who are called "Europeans."

It could be said that European unity is revealed and illustrated by the same evolution experienced by the individual European nations already referred to. The same phenomena as analyzed by Ralf Dahrendorf, S. M. Lipset and Alain Touraine are visible throughout western Europe, although not without national differences. All of western Europe is arriving at the stage of mass consumption, urbanization, motorization and the dizzy diffusion of television at approximately the same time. A common economic destiny—in which, to be sure, Mediterranean Europe does not yet fully participate—is also an incontestable fact; but, on the other side of the world, Japan has experienced its "miracle" to an even greater degree. Once a certain level of economic development is reached, all nations seem destined to experience mass consumption and the revolution in organization, at least when the economic development does not come about under the rule of a totalitarian state.

Finally, in order to exist as such and not only as a common culture in the eyes of others, Europe must become either an economic unit or a political unit, or better still, both economically and politically unified at the same time. In short, there will not be a historical revolution properly speaking, except to the extent that nation-states, which seemed to nineteenth-century historians the supreme form of political organization, are in the process of melting into a larger whole, into a superior form.

The polls whose results I cited above suggest that the citizens of the Six will be ready to abandon sovereignty (since the majority of them accept the notion of a common foreign policy). But this consent signifies almost nothing. The man in the street has a very dim idea of what a common diplomacy could be. Such decisions are neither taken by the majority, nor do they carry out the preferences of the majority; they are taken by the ruling minorities. Furthermore, the same Dutch who subscribe to a common foreign policy would willingly substitute Great Britain for France in the Common Market. After General de Gaulle's famous press conference, the Dutch were asked, "If France continues to oppose Great Britain's entry into the European Common Market, would you prefer the Common Market without Great Britain or the Common Market with Great Britain but without France?" They replied 52 per cent in favor of British participation and French absence and only 10 per cent in favor of a Common Market without Great Britain but with France.

The meaning of such a question and answer extends far beyond the circumstances that provoked it. Some Common Market nations feel closer to certain nations outside of the European Community than they do to other members of it. The Six are only one part of Europe considered geographically and culturally. Can the Six form a confederation? Do they wish to? How does the rest of Europe stand in relation to the community?

Following the success of the Coal and Steel Pool and the defeat of the European army, the European party, which had followed the lead of Jean Monnet, decided to turn back to economics. The Treaty of Rome was signed and the first steps toward a customs union were successfully taken. If I had made this study a year ago, I would probably have been tempted to emphasize success, to stress the European Community as a going concern which had been assimilated into men's habits and which had become a reality to a point where the tide could not be turned back. Now I am writing six months after General de Gaulle's press conference, and even if the existence of the community does not seem to me in danger, I shall stress more than I would have the mortgages upon which the whole undertaking depends.

Enthusiasts for the Common Market used to think and willingly said that political unity—a single government—would result spontaneously and inevitably from economic unity. Others, like M. Monnet, were not aiming for the constitution of a European state, a great power comparable to the other superpowers. For them the Coal and Steel Pool and the Treaty of Rome were neither ends in themselves nor means to predetermined ends. They were the means for a *planned institutional transformation*. They were creating institutions which would transform reality and which were themselves destined to change as reality changes.

Both conceptions have recently received a severe blow. In M. Monnet's eyes, Great Britain's request to join the Common Market was the normal result of the latter's success. Experience had brilliantly proved the benefits of the Common Market; Great Britain, skeptical of ideas as usual, would pay attention to facts and learn the lesson. Up to the last moment M. Monnet refused to believe that the Brussels negotiations would fail. Probably even today the setback appears to him temporary, opposed to the inevitable nature of things.

As for those, more Marxist than they realize, who do not doubt that there is an inevitably smooth progression from economic unity to political unity, they are doubly mistaken. The Treaty of Rome, apart from the dismantling of customs barriers, is primarily a catalogue of tasks and intentions. Everything remains to be done in regard to harmonizing legislation and common agricultural policy; it can be done only if the various governments wish to reach agreement. In other words, the *text does not create an automatic unification.* It urges the governments to reach an agreement *to the extent that they refuse, on principle, to resign themselves to disagreement.* In the second place, even if they form a single economic unity, the six nations are not obliged to have one identical foreign policy. It is pure fantasy to imagine that the governments of Bonn and Paris will necessarily take the same attitude toward East Germany on the day that goods, capital and men circulate freely between France and West Germany.

The controversy between the partisans of a Europe of States and an integrated Europe has rarely reached the heart of the matter. To give—on paper—such and such so-called supranational powers to the High Authority or to the European Commission is not sufficient to place these agencies in a position to resolve differences or to impose decisions on the national governments. In this sense, the partisans of a Europe of States are not wrong in casting doubt on the importance of the particular structure of institutions; and it is even less true that regular meetings of government leaders or ministers should, in the long run, create the unity to which they claim to aspire. The real question is different and it is much more basic: Do the old nations wish to abdicate in favor of the young Europe—and can they? Do Frenchmen, Germans and Italians wish to be Europeans in the sense that citizens of Geneva, Zurich or Berne are Swiss citizens? I have never been convinced that the answer to this question is in the affirmative. And the advent of Gaullism in France makes such an answer still more uncertain.

General de Gaulle calls himself a "European," and in one sense he is. The majority of Frenchmen accept him as such. However, he is hostile to integrated institutions and wishes to reduce to a minimum the role of the High Authority or of the commission, that is, the very institutions that represent and embody the community will. The Treaty of Association with Germany, without being incompatible with the European undertaking, derives from quite a different concept and brings us back to the diplomacy of alliances. General de Gaulle's veto of Britain's entry into the Common Market was not contrary to the letter of the Treaty of Rome, but it certainly was out of tune with the spirit of the community. If one of the states acts alone in a decisive matter without even consulting its partners, the others will do the same, and the will to agree, without which the community would be paralyzed, will rapidly disintegrate.

In one sense General de Gaulle's responsibility for the present crisis cannot be questioned. He himself proclaims it aloud. But sooner or later Europeans would have come, in one way or another, to ask those questions of principle whose resolution they had been leaving to time and experience. What kind of Europe do they wish? Do they wish a federated Europe, capable of defending itself and limited to states willing to sacrifice their sovereignty? Do they wish a Europe which will be a great power dealing with the Soviet Union and the United States as an equal? Do they wish an enlarged Europe, including Great Britain, Denmark and Norway, which will leave the main responsibility for defense to the United States? In short, are the old nations, theoretically not opposed to a common diplomacy, capable of having one? In other words, do they have the same image of the world, of their goals and their interests? The present crisis obliges us to answer this question in the negative.

The German Federal Republic is dependent on the United States for its security, and it is therefore especially anxious to assure the maintenance of American troops in Europe and to do nothing that would provoke American leaders into a policy of disengagement. Incapable of achieving a national deterrent force, West Germany still hopes to participate in nuclear strategy, and for this reason it favors military integration in NATO. De Gaulle's France harbors a national ambition to possess its own deterrent force and is opposed to all forms of military integration. It does not, for the moment, reject the Atlantic Alliance, but it claims to see in it only a provisional organization, useful until the day when the Soviet Union, having reverted to the Old Russia, will favor the reconciliation of the two halves of the Old Continent. The supranational institutions recommended by M. Monnet's party can contribute to the realization of an integrated economy, but they cannot give to

51

the various nations the unity of vision and goals which a common diplomacy requires. Atomic weapons have added another dimension to the disputes over the solidarity of Europe, but even leaving atomic questions to one side, there are already schools of thought that would be difficult to reconcile.

To simplify the situation, it could be said that there are four pairs of alternatives: 1) Europe in the narrow sense (the Six) or a greater Europe (with Great Britain and the Scandinavian nations); 2) an integrated Europe or a Europe of States; 3) an autonomous (independent) Europe or an Atlantic Europe; 4) a Europe possessing a nuclear force or a Europe militarily integrated in an Atlantic alliance in which the United States retains a thermonuclear monopoly. General de Gaulle would choose the first in each of these pairs of alternatives except the second, a fact which gives rise to doubt about his real intentions. Probably he is following a basically French policy, without forgetting that on the day when the Americans leave Europe or when the Soviet Union has become a bourgeois state, France, with its own deterrent force, will play a decisive role in the reorganization of western Europe and in the reconciliation of the two halves of the Old Continent. France's partners would accept a small Europe if it were at least integrated, but they refuse the combination of the small Europe with a Europe of States. Their position is: If Europe is not to be integrated, then it should at least be a larger unit.*

With regard to the first pair of alternatives, France's partners in the Six would refuse an either-or choice and declare themselves for an autonomous Europe within the Atlantic Alliance. Finally, on the question of defense, up to now only the British and the Germans seem interested in it. The British hesitate between the Gaullist position of a strictly national force—until recently their own position—and acceptance of a unified Atlantic deterrent force. The Germans do not challenge the American strategic monopoly.

Is this confusion temporary? I am not sure. The creation of a superior political unity, embracing old nations weighed down by history like Great Britain, Germany or France, demands a real political will—unless it is to be a sort of abdication. But a political will is inseparable from a will to be independent, even if it is not equivalent to a will to power. Many of the Brussels Eurocrats are conscious of this fact and see the constitution of a European state, capable of taking a stand and thus of defending itself, as the in-

---

* An integrated Europe gives better safeguards to the small states than a Europe composed of sovereign states. Belgium and the Netherlands are slightly afraid of a Franco-German common policy whose weight would be decisive in the councils of the Six.

evitable final outcome of their efforts. Such a Europe would not consequently be a third force; it would remain tied to the United States, but as a single unit, whereas today, within the alliance, the United States can easily impose its will on the plurality of states, small or middle-sized, whose connections with each other are less close than their subservient relations with the Big Brother across the Atlantic. Such a will to create a politically and militarily united Europe seems to me to be almost nonexistent in the Scandinavian countries (which have always been more Atlantic than European), and feeble in Italy, Holland and Belgium. All of these nations could have been carried along eventually if France had openly played the card of integration. Barring an improbable reversal in French policy, the opportunity has passed, and for the coming years one can count only on the survival of the Common Market and hope for some slow progress toward the goals of the Treaty of Rome. It is most likely that France will pursue its own way in political and military policy without carrying any of its partners in the community along with it.

Events may invalidate such an analysis. I do not deceive myself on this point and I have tried to avoid categorical judgments and to make allowances for the unforeseen, but after all, nearly twenty years after the end of World War II and thirteen years after the start of the Schuman Plan, it is legitimate to draw up a balance sheet, however provisory.

1. The old nations, which were ruining themselves and imperiling a common civilization, have overcome their memories and their resentments. They have learned to live together and to live in peace. Economic development and its concomitant well-being have facilitated this reconciliation. This gain can be considered solid without undue optimism.

2. On the economic plane, cooperation within the Common Market and sometimes outside it has become the rule. Both French and English share in the production of the first commercial supersonic airplane. Great Britain is part of Europe in that it participates in the European Nuclear Center in Geneva and in the space program—to the general satisfaction, although the problem has never been explicitly raised. Besides, the freeing of trade has allowed Britain also to profit from the rapid growth of the continental nations. The question of whether or not Britain will finally join the Common Market has probably less economic importance than either its advocates or its adversaries are inclined to think at present. The common external tariff is not and will not be raised to a point which will constitute a serious obstacle to trade. The dichotomy, re-

peatedly emphasized in the British and American press, between an "inward-looking" and an "outward-looking" community, seems to me to belong to the sphere of polemic and propaganda.* In the short run, to be sure, some hundreds of millions of dollars' worth of American agricultural exports could be imperiled as a result of Common Market policy, but this is a diplomatic incident and not a historic event.

3. It must be admitted that the exclusion of Great Britain, and especially the way in which General de Gaulle did it, has shaken both the European Community and the Atlantic Alliance, but it is useful on this point not to lose a sense of proportion and to resist the pressures of the moment. If the Brussels negotiations had failed because of technical difficulties, nobody would have thought it a catastrophe for the Common Market to be limited to the Six and for the three groups (the European Community, the small free trade zone and the British Commonwealth, the United States) to continue within the Atlantic Alliance. These three groups would have been able to negotiate the lowering of tariffs, as they will now attempt to do. If the veto of General de Gaulle had such repercussions, it is due to the disappointed hopes of the Kennedy administration (aside from the aggressive style adopted by the president of the French Republic). Preceding administrations in Washington were rather more hostile than favorable to the free trade zone, vainly negotiated in 1957–1958. They never actively desired Great Britain's entry into the Common Market. It is President Kennedy

* Indeed there has been a development toward regionalization in European commerce in the course of recent years. In 1959 trade with the members of the OECD, leaving aside the United States and Canada, represented for West Germany 53.9% of the total imports, 58.4% of exports. In 1961 the German figures were 53.7% and 63.4% respectively; in the first half of 1962, they were 55.9% and 65.6%. Italy exported to OECD nations 53% of its total exports in 1959, 59.2% in the first half of 1962. France exported 42.7% to OECD nations in 1959, 55.8% in 1962. But the United Kingdom, although not a member of the Common Market, has experienced a similar phenomenon. Britain's imports from OECD nations in 1959 were 28.4% of its total; its exports to those nations accounted for 30.1%. In the first half of 1962, the percentages had risen to 31.6% and 37.8% respectively. In other words, the share of the European nations in Britain's total exports rose from 30.1% to 37.8% in spite of the "inward-looking" attitude of the community. There are many causes for this phenomenon, but declining import capacity of countries producing raw materials and the slowing down of the economic growth rate in the United States are two of which we can be sure. Common Market preferences and the small free trade zone are probably factors also. But this was an inevitable development for a Europe moving toward unification. We should add that during this period, 1959 to 1961, imports of the Six from the United States rose considerably while exports of the Six to the United States were either stagnant, as in the case of Germany, or declining, as in the case of France.

and his advisers who saw in the enlargement of the Common Market a necessary step toward the Atlantic partnership. I am not sure that they were not laboring under certain illusions. The enlarged European Community would not have been an easier partner than the narrow community, so far as commercial negotiations are concerned.

The destiny of Great Britain since 1945 has been curiously different from that of the continental nations. Eighteen years ago Britain was laden with glory, exhausted by her victory to be sure, but less so than Italy or Germany by their defeats or France by the disaster of 1940, which the participation of Fighting France and the Resistance could not wipe out. Today it is Great Britain that appears to be affected by a profound crisis while the continental nations, at least on the economic plane, have succeeded in adapting themselves to the new world and have attained a growth rate envied by British economists.

This is not the place to undertake a detailed analysis of the British crisis, which, it seems to me, is as much moral and social as economic. Great Britain, aside from the irrational and disastrous Suez expedition, resolved or resigned herself to the abandonment of its empire with a facility and a kind of good grace without parallel in history. (One cannot say the same of France after the long wars in Indochina and Algeria.) The accession to power of the Labour party in 1945, the return of the Conservatives and their long term in office were not accompanied by any serious trouble. The Labour reforms were taken over by the Conservatives, and neither the unions nor the Labourites offered a coherent opposition to the ministries of Sir Winston Churchill, Sir Anthony Eden or Mr. Macmillan. But all this wisdom has led to two striking setbacks, one in the economic sphere, marked by repeated monetary crises, and one in diplomacy. Having misjudged or misunderstood the scope and importance of the movement toward European unity, British diplomacy tried to correct this error when it was too late.

In a recent issue of *Encounter** the English performed—with surprising ferocity—an exercise in national self-criticism. This kind of performance goes in and out of style according to the vicissitudes of a nation. Virtually none of the most characteristic and original aspects of English society—the public schools, Oxford and Cambridge, classical education, the prestige of gentlemen, the orderly game of politics—escaped the critics, who violently denounced the distance between social classes and the undemocratic system of education. Probably all these criticisms contain some truth, as did

* July, 1963.

those the French did not spare themselves between 1930 and 1940, and between 1945 and 1960. Yet I cannot help being somewhat suspicious of too heavily sociological explanations for changes in the economic sphere. Yesterday the graduates of the Ecole Polytechnique and the *inspecteurs des finances* were held responsible for France's stagnation; today *Encounter* sees in them the builders of France's economic renewal. I do not doubt that there is much to be done in Great Britain to improve the training of businessmen, to raise the expert's prestige at the expense of the gentleman's, to increase the number of students and technical schools and to foster opportunities for lower class children. British society being what it is, however, Britain's relatively slow economic growth is directly attributable to difficulties in the balance of payments, which required restrictive measures on three separate occasions and which, as a result, brutally checked expansion. These difficulties in the balance of payments are caused simultaneously by the power of the trade unions, by the basically precarious position of the pound, which serves an international function disproportionate to the present dimensions of the English economy, and probably by a rather inefficient policy dictated by the Treasury. Bad economic policy in the course of the 1930's was likewise a direct and sufficient cause of the stagnation of the French economy at that time.

The diplomatic setback is to be imputed, if one may say so, to the force of tradition. Since the sixteenth century Britain has not belonged to Europe politically in the same sense as Spain, France or Germany. For four centuries England, under the pressure of events if not by deliberate design, has followed a basically negative policy toward Europe. It has intervened on the continent to prevent the hegemony of any continental power. It has preserved the freedom of European states whether threatened by Philip II, by Louis XIV, by Napoleon, by William II or by Hitler. As a protector of threatened states, it could be either acclaimed as a protector of liberty or accused of blocking the unity of the Old Continent and of profiting from the struggles in which the rival nations exhausted themselves while it, a small insular nation, became the center of an immense empire.

After World War II, British leaders understood that times had changed and that, confronted by the Soviet Empire, some sort of cohesion on the continent would serve Britain's interest and would even be a guarantee of security. This involved a reform but not a revolution. While Sir Winston invited France to extend a hand to beaten Germany and to lead the "hereditary enemy" back into the Community of Nations, he did not propose to take the initiative himself. From 1945 to 1950 the continent would have followed the leadership of Great Britain if the British had wished to play the part; but the Labour government wished to confine relations to those between governments and to international organizations; it merely encouraged the nations of the continent to cooperate peacefully. Afterwards, the Conservative government helped the Atlantic Alliance to overcome the crisis provoked by the rejection of the EDC.

Neither Mr. Attlee nor Sir Winston nor Sir Anthony hesitated to refuse to participate in the Coal and Steel Community, in the EDC or in the EEC. It has been the success of the latter that has shaken British conservatism for the first time. If continental Europe were becoming a real economic unity, could Great Britain remain outside? Should it? Those who lost World War II, by joining together, forced the only European nation who felt really victorious in 1945 to a self-examination of historic proportions. They forced it to a revolution which, because of its victory, it had considered useless. This was an illusion: the revolution was necessary.

In certain respects and by certain of its reactions, England since World War II resembles France after World War I. This time anti-German feeling has remained more lively and has lasted longer across the channel than on the continent, while after 1918 it was France who found it most difficult to overcome hatred for Germany. (It is as if nations found it more difficult to forgive the enemy when they felt themselves defeated in and by victory.) It is in Great Britain that the return to the pattern of past social relations has been most pronounced, despite the reforms of the Labour government. It is in Great Britain that one sees most clearly the maintenance of the old class structure and of the institutions that symbolize it, despite prosperity, mass consumption and television. France in 1918, likewise victorious but anguished, also attempted if not to restore at least to maintain the essential characteristics of the prewar era. If I dare to carry the comparison further, one could add that France seemed to have succeeded in the first postwar decade (the years 1919–1929 saw rapid economic progress), just as in 1955 Great Britain in turn accomplished the task history imposed by absorbing the Labour reforms and by consenting to retreat gracefully from its imperial position.

The French crisis broke out in the 1930's because the traditional France and the Third Republic, which had been capable of picking up the pieces after World War I and of restoring the old order, were incapable of responding to the double challenge of an unprecedented economic crisis and the threat of Hitler's Germany. Likewise, the present British crisis results from the inability to respond to two challenges: the accelerated growth of continental Europe and the formation of the Common Market.

According to tradition, England should have put its bonds with the United States and the British Commonwealth—with the English-speaking peoples—above its relations with nearby Europe, but after long deliberation the majority of British leaders decided that tradition was now a poor guide and they chose to join the Common Market. According to the polls, opinion was divided. To the question, "If the British government were to decide that it is in Great Britain's interest to join the European Common Market, would you approve or disapprove?" the percentages for and against varied in the course of the years 1961 and 1962; but the number of those ready to approve remained consistently greater than those who disapproved, with between one quarter and one third of those asked refusing to declare themselves. In October, 1961, 48 per cent would have approved and 18 per cent would have disapproved; in September, 1962, 46 per cent would have approved and 30 per cent would have disapproved. At the end of December, 1962, the respective figures were 37 per cent and 29 per cent. The majority of Labour voters were against Britain's joining. Of the conservative voters, one half favored it and one fourth definitely opposed it. A clear majority of persons asked would have refused to join if the price to be paid had been political union with France and Germany. At the end of December, 1962, 23 per cent of those asked thought that Britain would suffer a considerable loss if it did not join, 26 per cent thought there would be little harm done, 51 per cent thought there would be none at all. British opinion was therefore substantially different from the continental economies. We have only to remember that Britain, by importing one half of its food supply at very low prices, is in a position to subsidize English farmers instead of supporting the price of domestic agricultural products. Furthermore, it allows industrial products from the British Commonwealth to enter freely; it continues to benefit from certain imperial preferences; and it applies, on the average, very high duties to manufactured goods and low duties or none at all to raw or unfinished goods. Finally, Britain's trade with the rest of Europe represents a lesser percentage of its total trade than does their trade with Britain represent for the continental countries. (In 1959 the percentages of British trade with the Six and the Seven were 28.4 per cent of its imports and 30.1 per cent of its exports. These figures rose to 31.5 per cent and 34.1 per cent in 1961; but in this same year the corresponding figures for trade with Britain for France were 43.7 per cent and 51.5 per cent; for Italy, 47.3 per cent and 56.4 per cent;

for Germany, 53.7 per cent and 63.4 per cent.) It is therefore true that on the economic plane as well, Great Britain is not European to the same degree or in the same sense as the continental nations.

These facts do not at all mean that Great Britain could not or should not join the Common Market. The economic problems are difficult, but they were not really insolvable if the will to do so had been shared by all members of the community. The final setback had political causes: General de Gaulle, supported on this point by a large section of French opinion, probably estimated that the enlargement of the Common Market would lessen the chance of integrating the economies and would reduce the Common Market to a mere common external tariff and free circulation of industrial goods, without a common agricultural policy and without coordinate legislation.*

Furthermore, and most important in the eyes of General de Gaulle, Europe could not achieve an independent existence and any real sense of itself if it accepted American protection passively. Great Britain, as the leader of Fighting France had known it between 1940 and 1945, would subordinate all other considerations to its alliance with the United States. In this sense Britain was not yet "European," at least in the context of the general's image of the world, in which the American presence in Europe is temporary; the evolution of the Soviet Union into a bourgeois state inevitable; and the schism between Russia and China, as well as the liquidation of Russia's Asian empire and its return to the family of European nations, are all written in the book of history.

Even if one were to admit that such a reversal of the world situation might come about in the indefinite future, it would remain an open question which policy would encourage Russia's return to the European family—the maintenance or the loosening of the bonds between western Europe and the United States. At present, contrary to what his followers think, if not the general himself, the Soviet Union prefers to deal with the United States alone rather than with several western groups. A European nuclear deterrent force, in which Germany would play an important part, would hinder rather than facilitate the reconciliation between the two Europes, a reconciliation which is conceivable only after the unification of Germany and therefore after the Soviets have renounced

---

* As reflected in polls at the end of January, 1963, 40% approved General de Gaulle's stand toward England against 21% who disapproved; 39% did not declare themselves. At the same time, 35% thought England's entry to be in France's interest against 22% who thought the contrary, with 43% not declaring themselves. French industrial circles were, as a whole, hostile to England's entry.

their zone of military security in Europe and their policy of expansion. This situation is unforeseeable today. There seems to me to be a contradiction between the desire for a Europe with atomic weapons and the desire to achieve an agreement or even a balance between the two Europes. The present leaders of France refuse to recognize this contradiction.

Our concern is not to choose between the conflicting theses of President Kennedy, Prime Minister Macmillan and General de Gaulle. Our concern is to show that beyond unanimous agreement in the West on a certain degree of cooperation between European nations and some form of Atlantic alliance, differences are multiplying. The outlet for Europe, narrow or enlarged, federated or not, depends on the images world leaders hold and the degree of probability that these will be realized. President Kennedy would like a Europe enlarged and organized but without the capacity to defend itself. Great Britain would like to join the Common Market but without giving up its national deterrent force or its special relations with the United States. Above all, General de Gaulle would like France, and then Europe, to escape the kind of protectorate status implied—in his eyes—by the American monoply of nuclear arms. Germany would like simultaneously to keep the benefit of American protection and to continue the work of European integration. The other European nations are divided between the vague desire to depend less on the transatlantic Big Brother, the fear of compromising their security and the refusal to accept as leader a European state which, unlike the United States, cannot justify its domination by the immensity of its resources.

Will the old nations, with their centuries-old concern for national sovereignty, survive? Is the passion with which the public supports national athletic teams a symbol of a nationalism which raises still another insurmountable obstacle to block federation? Yes and no. I believe that consciousness of the nation remains infinitely stronger than a sense of Europe. I do not perceive any European nationalism beyond an aspiration to a degree of autonomy in relation to the United States and, especially, to the rejection of the bloody quarrels of the past. Will this reasonable desire be enough to give birth to a European federation? In terms of the next twenty years, I do not think so, and I am not even sure it would be desirable,* because on this point General de Gaulle seems to me absolutely right: to exist as a political unit, Europe would have to acquire the capacity to defend itself, or at least to acquire a relative autonomy in the

* I desire it sincerely, but I am not sure that I am right.

Atlantic Alliance. Without this political will, Europe will have to settle for continued economic growth, with the Common Market tightening bonds with Great Britain and the other European nations in one way or another. Will the situation arouse the European nations to a massive effort to acquire a deterrent force in the next twenty years? What will be the relations among China, Russia and the United States?

Nobody seems to me to be in a position to answer these questions, yet it is these answers that will determine the ultimate significance of the European undertaking. The old nations still live in the hearts of men, and love of the European nation is not yet born—assuming that it ever will be. But the federation of the Old Continent is held in check less by the survival of nationalism, large or small, than by another cause, simpler and often unrecognized: the present mixture of cooperation and integration in Europe and within the Atlantic Alliance is sufficient to assure the achievement of prosperity and security. It is not sufficient to create a European state. Rather, one must ask: What would be the object of a European state? To have a sense of vocation, Europe would have to discover a goal. What could this common goal be? A will to push Soviet Communism out of eastern Europe? But if this Soviet retreat is to be peaceful, is a European bloc something to be hoped for or something to be feared? A will to become a great power? But, in the nuclear world, do we want one more superpower?

ERNST B. HAAS

Technocracy, Pluralism and the New Europe

THE PRACTICES associated with regional integration in contemporary western Europe correspond to a type of society and economy variously labeled "post-industrial," "post-bourgeois" or merely "the New Europe." [1] This New Europe evolved historically from the interconnected strands of capitalism, industrialism and pluralistic democracy. It resembles in many respects the type of economy and society familiar to us in North America. Regional government in such a society is thus merely an adaptation on the scale of half a continent of forms of social and economic organization which evolved historically at the national level. Regional government in the New Europe is the institutional and political recognition that societies have changed dramatically since 1945, so dramatically that they cannot be adequately described in the doctrines and ideologies made familiar by nineteenth- and early twentieth-century political thought. Hence the New Europe and its regional government is the future of that part of history which has also been aptly described as "the end of ideology." It owes so little to the visions of the Abbé de Saint-Pierre, of William Penn, of Immanuel Kant and of Victor Hugo that these oft-invoked precursors of the contemporary movement could scarcely be expected to recognize their brainchild.

Yet the news of the last few months seems at variance with this extreme view of things. Disintegration and nationalist *immobilisme* appear to dominate, rather than the advance of regional government. France's veto of January, 1963, stopped not only the entry of Britain into the European Community of the Six, but in effect postponed the merger of the Europe of Seven with the Community. EFTA, after appearing to be on the threshold of dissolution, ac-

This paper is a revised version of an address originally presented at the McGill Conference on World Affairs, McGill University, Montreal, P.Q., October 31, 1963.

quired a new lease on life as a result. In agriculture, the Community has succeeded in translating the general policy adopted a year ago only to some commodities; but disagreement on target prices and levies continues with respect to others, while interest group representatives, parliamentarians and government experts continue to squabble about the proper compromise. In the field of energy, the Council of Ministers is now considering the fourth "interim memorandum" of the Community executives regarding the proper role and pricing of oil, coal, natural gas and hydroelectric power. Again, the interest groups press their claims and governments support or reject them in line with national perceptions of interest, thus far to the detriment of a coherent regional policy. During the summer of 1963, the special political agreement between Bonn and Paris went into effect, thus symbolizing to some Europeans that special Franco-German relationship which might institutionalize the hegemony of de Gaulle over the Community of the Six. The General's offer of a lilliputian French nuclear umbrella to his five partners has done nothing to dispel this impression. If the Fouchet Plan for a political confederation, a *Europe des patries,* superimposed on the existing regional government was turned down by four of the Six, its institutionalization among two of them is still perceived as disturbing.

Nor are things any better outside the framework of the Six. Long-standing efforts to refurbish NATO as a dynamic agency for working out common Atlantic defense and foreign policies have achieved little. The American proposal to share control of the safety catch on the nuclear deterrent by means of the NATO Multilateral Nuclear Force has been cold-shouldered by France and greeted with reserve by Britain. Only Germany seems fully committed to the idea. The Organization for Economic Cooperation and Development, for all its promising work on the sharing of aid to the non-western world, has done little to smooth the incipient United States-Common Market tariff war, of which the chicken rather than the rooster or the bald eagle is the symbol.

The unfortunate image of the dumbbell has been invoked to describe the desirable relationship between North America on the one hand and a united western Europe on the other, an image more respectfully labeled "partnership" by President Kennedy as well as by President Hallstein of the EEC Commission. Partnership connotes close cooperation tied to mutually respectful distance; hence people affiliated with the Atlantic Council of the United States prefer to speak of "community," or of close institutional and quasi-federative ties, to take the place of the current Atlantic structure, which merely perpetuates disarray. Yet the notions of partnership or community among two equal and allied blocs have begun to compete with rival images invoking a vision of concentric circles with the European Community at the core, or of an even looser system of polycentrism in which both Britain and France would retain independent relations inside as well as outside the Atlantic world.

These events and the prescriptions for reform bespeak disintegration rather than a shiny New Europe or New Atlantis. Have they undermined the system of regional government which has developed in the Community of the Six, the system which goes under the label of "supranationality"? To answer this question the nature of supranationality must first be well understood.

General de Gaulle equates supranationality with a federalism which he detests; Jean Monnet identifies it with a federalism of which he is a leading partisan. Both gentlemen mistake the essence of the phenomenon, even though Monnet is rightfully considered its founding father. British statesmen were repelled by the European Community for a long time because they could conceive only of federal or traditional intergovernmental international institutions, and they held the Community to be almost federal. Supranationality, however, is neither federalism nor intimate intergovernmental co-operation, even though the institutions it employs resemble those of a federation more than the United Nations or NATO. Supranationality is a unique style of making international decisions, unique because of the nature of the participants, the context in which decisions are made, and the quality of the decisions produced.

The participants in the supranational decision-making process include of course "governments"; indeed, governments theoretically dominate it because their representatives constitute the Councils of Ministers which rule the three communities. But these representatives are for the most part high civil servants meeting in almost continuous confrontation with their opposite numbers and working out common policies on the basis of their perception of the technical possibilities inherent in whatever is being discussed. Only exceptionally are decisions wholly made by the ministers themselves, and then only on the basis of suggestions and proposals prepared by the European Commission or the High Authority; that is, by experts whose job it is to find common ground among the six nations. Other participants include spokesmen for all major national and European interest groups, who confer almost all the time with the specialists in the Community executives. Proposals by the executives to the ministers always take into account the demands of the major interest groups. Finally, the legislatures of the six countries participate in the form of the European Parliament, which makes its wishes known and which demands to be consulted by the commissions and the High Authority. If it is still true that the representatives of the six governments dispose, this is so only because the European executives, in consultation with private and parliamentary groups, propose. The alternative dispositions in areas subject to regional jurisdiction are defined and limited by the range of proposals stemming from extragovernmental sources.

The context of supranational decisions is economic, social and technical. But this should not lead us to conclude that just because expressly "political" and military issues are excluded, supranational decisions are somehow secondary. The essence of supranationality lies in the tendency for economic and social decisions to "spill over" into the realm of the political, to arise from and further influence the political aspirations of the major groupings and parties in democratic societies. The supranational style stresses the indirect penetration of the political by way of the economic because the "purely" economic decisions always acquire political significance in the minds of the participants. In short, the kind of economics and social questions here dealt with are those at the very core of the modern welfare state.

The quality of supranational decisions differs sharply from the federal and the intergovernmental norms. In intergovernmental negotiations differing initial positions are usually compromised on the level of the lowest common denominator. That is, the least cooperative participant defines the limits of the compromise. In federal systems simple majoritarianism decides in ultimate situations of conflict, even if this be the majority of one vote on a federal Supreme Court. In supranational systems, on the other hand, the compromise pattern often involves "splitting the difference" between the final bargaining positions of the participants. More significantly still, supranational systems feature a bargaining process which I call "upgrading common interests." It occurs when the participants have great difficulty in arriving at a common policy; yet they do agree that they should have some common stand in order to safeguard other aspects of interdependence among them. Hence they tend to swap concessions in related fields, but outside the specific contexts in which disagreement prevails. Further the swapping takes place on the basis of services rendered by an institutionalized conciliator with powers of its own, the European executives; that body is able to construct patterns of mutual concessions from various policy contexts and in so doing usually manages to upgrade its own powers at the expense of the member governments. Yet those governments do not feel as if they had been bullied: common interests are upgraded also in the sense that each feels that by conceding something it gained something else. The final compromise, far from somehow debasing the bargaining process, induces a feeling of commitment, of creativity and of gain in the participants.

Hence it is a mistake to argue, as spokesmen for the communities usually do, that "the criteria by which policy decisions are made are no longer purely national criteria: there is also recognized to be a 'Community' point of view which arises out of a consideration, from an objective standpoint, of the interest of the economic unit as a whole." [2] In an objective sense there is no demonstrable "Community viewpoint," if by that we mean a voluntary national subordination to the general interest as defined by the executives. But there is a cumulative pattern of accommodation in which the participants refrain from unconditionally vetoing proposals and instead seek to attain agreement by means of compromises upgrading common interests.

Having defined the supranational style, we can now answer the question of the disintegrative effects of recent events. Clearly, General de Gaulle does *not* play the game according to these rules. Supranationality evolved gradually since the inception of the Coal and Steel Community in 1952 in a manner falling short of Monnet's federalism but exceeding British ideas of intergovernmental cooperation. De Gaulle is coming close to stopping that evolution. This is true despite the admitted fact that the Fifth Republic has honored its obligations under the treaties establishing the three communities even though it deplores the surrender of sovereignty implicit in this. It is true even though the Fifth Republic has taken the initiative in proposing and executing several measures which involved the upgrading of common interests, as for example in the case of agriculture and the acceleration of tariff dismantling. The point is that such steps were taken only when the government felt these steps to be in the national—rather than the European—interest, and that it has adamantly resisted other attempts to upgrade common interests when de Gaulle considered the surrender of further sovereignty undesirable.

The Gaullist vision of the New Europe is neither supranational nor federal. It is confederal; it limits the participants to ministers, the contexts to the political in the grand sense and the quality of the decisions to unanimous agreement defined by the leading nations. In the words of former Prime Minister Debré:

In Europe, legitimate power is the power which comes from national sovereignty and against this power arbitrary outside tyrannies like the so-called "supranational" institutions can do nothing. European unity is becoming, and will continue to become, a reality through the will of those who legitimately wield power in each of the countries which together make up Europe.[3]

The appeal is to a pre-modern notion of national sovereignty which exalts the political at the expense of the economic and social. The Fouchet Plan and the bilateral treaty with Bonn exemplify the Gaullist conception of a European confederation. Will it successfully impede supranational integration which reverses the emphasis and thereby avoids the notion of sovereignty altogether?

This formulation contains the larger question of the ultimate future of Europe, the shape of European society and the manner of governing it. De Gaulle agrees with the European Federalists in believing that the present structure is an impossible halfway house. The Federalist position disdains "mere" economics; or at best it considers it a necessary area of joint action among nations before the ultimate political stage of constitutional federation is reached, with its panoply of directly elected European legislature, federal executive enjoying general powers and federal judiciary. Emphasis is on commitment, faith, vision and a certain method of politics. Little is said about the content of politics except to stress the mystical superiority of a "political" quality over the humdrum collection of social welfare measures. For de Gaulle the supreme element is belief in the immutable nature of "high politics," of *Grosspolitik* in the expressive Bismarckian phrase. Economics, military strategy, social welfare, agricultural prices, relations with underdeveloped countries—all these are so many substantive sub-items in the pursuit of the supreme substance, the defense of the national interest. It so happens that this interest is held by de Gaulle to be closely tied to that of the other continental European nations. But a confederacy is all that is required to realize and assert it against others. In short, this argument asserts that the Europe of the three supranational communities cannot last: it must become either a full-fledged federation or a confederacy under the hegemony of the most important constituent nations.[4]

Few people believe that the existing system of regional government, that supranational method now under French attack, has a claim to longevity. I believe that it does. Because it corresponds to the nature of the New Europe, the Europe of adaptative interest groups, bureaucracies, technocrats and other units with modest but pragmatic interests resembling the traditional nationalisms of *Grosspolitik* only very remotely, it may well be a real system of government rather than a mere temporary style. "There are more things in Heaven and Earth, General de Gaulle, than are dreamt of in your philosophy."

What are these characteristics of the New Europe? Its main economic component is neither capitalism nor socialism: it is industrialism. Industry, under whatever management, easily produces enough to make everybody comfortable. Minimum standards of consumption are assumed as given for the entire citizenry. If the market mechanism and freely negotiated wage levels fail to attain the minima the state intervenes with subsidies, family allowances, social security payments, educational scholarships and retraining funds. Rising production and rising consumption are brought into gear by more or less systematically pursued policies of full employment or income guarantees. The flow of investment necessary for this is assured by policies of central steering through tax laws, credit policy and direct consultation among government, industry and organized labor. Foreign trade policy becomes particularly important in such a context because it tends to be manipulated to serve the ends of domestic production and consumption; this is as true at the regional as at the national level.

The New Europe has worked out a pragmatic synthesis of capitalism and socialism in the form of democratic planning. Nationalization of industries is sometimes, but not consistently, employed; the price system and the market remain the central regulatory agents. Planning takes place in the form of forecasts of demand for specific products in specific industrial sectors, which are then presented in the form of aggregate forecasts. Planning, unlike the communist variant, avoids fixed production targets. It "programs" desirable investment and production levels in line with predicted demand and interferes with the self-adjusting market only to that extent. For our purposes, the mechanism of this programming process is of central importance. It features the continuous participation of all major voluntary groups in European society through elaborate systems of committees and councils. The technical bureaucracies of trade unions, industrial associations, bankers and farmers sit down with the technocrats from the ministries of finance, labor and economics—or with central government planning offices—to shape the future. Statistics tend to replace ideology and dogma. Permanent negotiation and occasional conciliation tend to replace active confrontation, doctrinaire discussion and class warfare. The symbol is compulsory arbitration rather than the general strike. Even in countries in which "planning" is taboo, such as West Germany, key government officials consistently use techniques of consultation and of fiscal policy to attain results similar to those sought by the planners.

These economic features clearly rest on a social substratum very different from that portrayed in the inherited western ideologies.

Relative upward mobility now obtains. Relative social equality, at least as compared to the situation fifty years ago, is in the ascendency. The formerly alienated working class seems to have made its peace with the industrial system, perhaps because stronger unions in large-scale enterprises give it more scope for participation than was true in the earlier period of small family owned and managed plants. Ideology has lost its former relevance in the relations among workers, industrial managers and middle-class professionals. The groups which find it difficult to adjust to industrialism are the ones for whom ideologies remain important. The lower middle-class shopkeepers, artisans and inefficient farmers who are hard pressed by the advent of massive industrialism and large-scale bureaucratized enterprises of all kinds are the main consumers of doctrinaire ideology today, whether this be communism or some form of organic, status-oriented fascism. But even here the advent of the regional logic is manifest: contemporary neo-fascist groups in Europe profess a species of pan-European nationalism directed against Russia, the United States and the Afro-Asian world rather than the more familiar Germanic, Gallic or Roman varieties; it is a "white man's" nationalism directed against "inferior" extra-European races. The communists, for their part, are beginning to make their peace with the erstwhile "clerical-fascist conspiracy" by encouraging their trade unions to participate as just another interest group in the decision-making process of the communities.

Ideology, then, is still with us. But it manifests itself in religious, ethnic and educational policy confrontations rather than in the realm of the economy or the large issues of defense and foreign policy. Thus we find its continued role primarily in Belgium, Italy and France rather than in Scandinavia, Britain, Germany or Austria. Ideology is muted to the extent that cleavages in the national populations cut across contexts rather than clustering in firm groups united on a variety of issues. If a citizen can bestow his support— or his indifference—to differing groups for purposes of education, welfare measures, religion, defense, recreation and ethnic identity the logic of a pluralism based on cross-cutting cleavages will continue to mute ideology. Only if a citizen relies on his party or association for *all* of these aims will the logic of pluralism be defeated. The Communist poet Louis Aragon might have spoken for some Socialists and some Christian Democrats when he said:

> mon parti m'a rendu mes yeux et ma mémoire
> mon parti m'a donné le sens de l'époque
> mon parti, mon parti, merci pour tes leçons . . .

In the New Europe, however, this clustering of affections and expectations seems to be a thing of the past.

Indeed, when we turn to the political style of the New Europe, perhaps indifference is the key term. Political parties remain intact; but they are no longer divided by glaring controversy because all the major social and economic issues of fifty years ago no longer plague the body politic. Campaigns tend to avoid the great principles and to stress efficiency in administration. As a Swedish commentator put it, "as the general standard of values is so commonly accepted, the functions of the state become so technical as to make politics appear as a kind of applied statistics. . . . Voting in our day is much less than in earlier times a proof of political interest; elections should rather be considered as a general census."[5] In many European countries cabinets are now formed on the basis of more or less permanent coalitions among powerful parties united in a general consensus on the desirability to preserve and develop industrial society. Moreover, they agree on subordinating most other public questions to this desire. Industrial society is run by technocrats, inevitably. And so the technocrat has become the *éminence grise* of all government, public and private, local, national and regional. As the function of a parliamentary opposition has lost its sharpness the average citizen has lost much of his interest in politics. Politics in such a setting has been aptly described as the politics of collective bargaining among groups, all of whom accept the legitimacy of representation of each participant. The argument among the groups, then, is merely over the slice of the pie to be given to each. At the European regional level this image need not undergo any qualitative restatement: the argument is no longer over the slice of the pie to go to each; it is increasingly over the means for increasing the overall size of the pastry. But otherwise the style of moderate accommodation, universal representation and mediation by technocrats remains as central at the regional as at the national level. Holland, Belgium, Austria and Sweden epitomize this trend. In Germany the reunification issue somewhat blurs the same phenomenon, while in Italy the relative immaturity of industrialism contributes to the continued presence of the older pattern of politics. In Britain the modal pattern prevails even though it is obscured by the dominance of the two-party system, which normally makes coalition politics unnecessary. The major exception to the trend is France, where the towering figure of General de Gaulle imposes an unnatural style on politics which would otherwise conform to the depoliticized trend, as indeed it did under the Fourth Republic.

In such a setting there is but little trace of a purely political dimension. *Grosspolitik* is merely a phrase left over from a pre-industrial setting, national grandeur and national destiny conceptions which the upward mobile citizen weighs distrustfully against the new "telly," Renault, or that trip to the blue Adriatic. In a sense, everything is political simply because the modern industrial system engenders public concern—if not control—over so many aspects of economic and social life. But by the same token there is no longer a distinctly political function, separate from economics, welfare or education, a function which finds its reason for being in the sublime heights of foreign policy, defense and constitution-making.

It will have become clear by now that the supranational scheme of government at the regional level bears a very striking resemblance to the prevailing nature of government at the level of the industrial nation in everything but constitutional terminology. Supranationality, not federation, confederation or intergovernmental organization, seems to be the appropriate regional counterpart to the national state which no longer feels capable of realizing welfare aims within its own narrow borders, which has made its peace with the fact of interdependence in an industrial and egalitarian age. It represents the method adopted to secure maximum welfare, including military security, for a post-capitalist state which no longer conceives of its interests in starkly political and nationalistic terms. The advent of supranationality symbolizes the victory of economics over politics, over that familiar ethnocentric nationalism which used to subordinate butter to guns, reason to passion, statistical bargaining to excited demands.

Recent history offers a number of instances in support of this conclusion. Britain's decision to make its independent nuclear deterrent dependent on American Polaris technology was motivated by considerations of cost; that is, by the decision not to sacrifice welfare. Its ill-fated decision to join the Community of the Six implied very serious soul-searching and ended with the serious weakening of a nationalist mood and calculus which had long been taken for granted. Norway and Sweden have been known for their moderation in international affairs, but also for their fierce independence from entanglements and passionate belief in the value of their national ways of life. Notwithstanding these facts Norway applied for full admission to the inner circle of the Six, with all its supranationality, and Sweden sought the less binding tie of economic association with the Community. Upon being rebuffed in the crisis of January, 1963, neutral Sweden was in the forefront of those seeking to give EFTA a much more supranational scope than it had hitherto been permitted to acquire. Even Switzerland, to which neutrality and aloofness *is* the national way of life, anxiously discusses the alternatives open to it. Like many others, the Swiss would prefer a clear-cut distinction between the constitutional and political dimension on the one hand, and the politics of economics on the other. If Europe opted for political unification they would stay aloof; but if a "mere" economic union were the final plan they could make their peace with it. "Only when that decision is made can we distinguish once more between the two plans whose confusion obstructs all discussion," complains Herbert Lüthy. "Customs officials will cease making policy and statesmen will cease building Europe by organizing a market for beasts." [6] But it is the essence of the New Europe that the market for beasts and the discussion of ultimate political destinies can no longer be separated. In a welfare-oriented, industrial and technocratic order ultimate political concerns are ever more closely intertwined with these more mundane considerations.

Our argument, however, runs into the very obvious obstacle of active dislike for the supranational method on the part of some Europeans and of their practical resistance to continued integration, both among the Six and between the Six and the rest of Europe as well as North America. This resistance is explained by some scholars as a manifestation of the reassertion of the poltical function. Supranational integration may well take place on the basis of economic policies spilling over into more and more neighboring fields of activity, they suggest, until the *economic* potentialities of the process are exhausted. As long as we are merely dismantling tariffs, establishing fair pricing rules for steel, harmonizing social security rates and facilitating the free movement of manpower we remain within the logic of the economic spill-over. But once the limits of these tasks are reached, once these objectives are attained, we are up against the hard core of politics: foreign policy coordination, defense arrangements and the ultimate relationship between *national* political planning and *national* economic welfare. When statesmen feel that this point has been reached—as de Gaulle clearly does—the spill-over will trickle away and integration will either stop or take on a purely political-constitutional hue. Supranationality will then be condemned to linger listlessly in the economic institutions already created but foreclosed from further development.[7] The Europe of the Six may be at this point now.

This formulation mistakes the nature of the New Europe. It is not only the outer military shell of nations which has become very penetrable. Self-reliance equals the flirtation with suicide not only in the realm of defense. The outer shell of nations has become pene-trable even more in terms of trade, travel, investment, values and welfare in proportion to the degree of industrial pluralism which prevails domestically. The image which characterizes the nation-state as a warm and self-contained community and juxtaposes it to the colder and more calculating world of nation-states labeled "international society" is oversimplified and misleading, at least in the North Atlantic area. The internal *as well* as the external network of relations of nations constitute a species of society; both increas-ingly function on the basis of calculated interest and adjustment among interests, on the part of voluntary groups as well as of govern-ments. And the extent of the adjustment is deeply influenced by the degree of penetrability which the outer shell of the total national corpus permits.

Armed with this perspective, let us have another look at the spill-over process. While it assumes the continued commitment of major participants to the process of integration, it does not presume passionate enthusiasm and takes for granted opposition to specific items in the catalogue of integrative ventures. The support for given steps rests on the convergence of expectations of the participants; competing expectations and goals can be compromised on the basis of swapping concessions from a variety of sectors, all under the generalized purview of supranational insti-tutions and processes. Lack of agreement among governments can thus give rise to increased delegated powers on the part of these institutions. Dissatisfaction with the results of partial eco-nomic steps may lead labor and industry to demand new central action. Supranational institutions and national groups may create situations which can be dealt with only through central action, unless the nations are willing to suffer deprivations in welfare. The very penetrability of the national shell leaves the nation open to the lure of intersectorial bargains whereby one government is willing to take a loss in exchange for a gain in another sector. Nations outside the economic grouping but deeply intertwined with it through the activities of their citizens may experience prob-lems which can be solved—if welfare is not to be sacrificed—only by joining the grouping and upgrading its central powers.[8] No statesman, even if he deeply dislikes the process, can permanently isolate his nation from a commitment to unity which is already partially implemented, unless he is willing to pay the price in diminished welfare. De Gaulle may be willing to pay that price; but I doubt that French society is. Moreover, if de Gaulle expects Holland, Belgium, Italy and post-Adenauer Germany to endorse certain French goals he will be obliged to pay for this support by acquiescing to the goal expectations of his allies. And this involves him willy-nilly in more supranational integration.

What, then, is spilling over in the Europe of the Six despite current French policy? Where does the generalized post-national statistical mood manifest itself even though it does not fit the nineteenth-century national sentiments of the General? Despite a snail's pace, but because of French insistence, the integrated agricultural marketing system is beginning to operate for certain commodities, even though no single interest group or government seems to be completely happy with it. The harmonization of turn-over taxes is making slow progress under the active mediation of the EEC Commission. The first regulations concerning a harmonized social security system have come into operation. Europe has its first modest common regulation governing competition, even though the appreciably different approaches of the Common Market and the Coal and Steel treaties are creating confusion in this realm. The relative inflexibility of the Coal and Steel treaty, even though this was supposed to conduce to stronger suprana-tional powers, also clashes with the more permissive approach of the Common Market treaty in the fields of transport policy, aid to redundant industries and national subsidies, with the result that very little has been done in these areas. Lack of success in agreeing to a common energy policy is partially attributable to the same cause, even though the governments of France and Italy also have here shown that so far they are quite unwilling to sub-ordinate the national to the European interest. Another reason for lack of success lies in the adamant opposition between private and public interests identified with coal and oil, respec-tively, in each nation. In these fields, then, the spill-over has turned into a trickle.

But this does not exhaust the picture. The Court of the Com-munities has recently pronounced its equivalent of Marbury v. Madison in the *Van Gend* Case, laying down clearly the supremacy of Community law and holding that it applies directly to the individual citizen. Several European governments were found guilty of violating portions of the Treaty of Rome; in all cases they faithfully carried out the court's rulings. The Netherlands, in ex-change for accepting the Community's association agreement with eighteen African states (an agreement which conduces primarily to the benefit of France), extracted a promise that in the future single vetoes could not validly hold up the association of additional outside countries. Despite the exclusion of Britain numerous coun-tries still feel sufficiently attracted to or threatened by the Com-munity to demand the opening of negotiations for some form of economic association with it.* All these manifestations imply a continuation of the spill-over process despite the preferences of the most active opponents of supranational integration. There are further such examples. It is the Community which decides the criteria of political respectability applied to candidates for association: Turkey proved respectable, Spain did not. Similarly, it tacitly decided that permanent neutrality was incompatible with the political goals of union. Because of the logic of intersectorial bargaining the Six were forced to accelerate their own schedule of tariff dismantling. In addition they were obliged to work out a common economic and commercial position toward the United States, Latin America and Africa earlier than planned in order to be able to present a common front in GATT. The association agreement with the African nations compelled the preparation of a common policy on aid to underdeveloped countries, even though France had been far more interested in development funds from its partners than in advice and consent on policy.

Still, the events of the year 1963 gave some justification to those who dispute the longevity of economic-supranational approaches to regional government. It is therefore natural that the Commission of EEC and the High Authority of ECSC should have fallen back on the very dynamic of the New Europe to advance their cause. And this they did do. The Coal and Steel Community was checked in its endeavor to work out a common energy policy. But, conscious of the implications of this problem with respect to upgrading common interests among governments, consumers, producers and workers, the High Authority proposed the amendment of its treaty: "retrenchment" cartels for collieries should be authorized,

* In January, 1963, all members of EFTA had applied either for full or associate membership. As of October, 1963, only Austria was conducting active negotiations for some kind of association, while France was obliged to accede to its partners' demand for continued contact with Britain by way of the Western European Union. Other nations with whom various types of association were being negotiated at the time of writing are: Turkey, Israel, Cyprus, Ireland, Algeria and Iran. Greece has become an associate member with the intention of becoming a full member in 1984; its economic ties and obligations to the Community were so defined as to amount to complete union by that date. The agreement of association with the eighteen African nations (all former French, Italian and Belgian possessions, except Guinea) provides for a preferential EEC tariff on some African exports and for a nil tariff on some others, but opens Africa to EEC exports on a preferential basis and confirms the right of establishment. It steps up and diversifies EEC financial aid to African development, creates a standing institutional mechanism and a system of compulsory arbitration for the settlement of trade and financial disputes. For an official summary of the Convention see *Bulletin of the EEC*, Vol. VI, no. 2 (Brussels, February, 1963), pp. 21–25.

subsidies to permit the conversion of mines should be permitted, and the Community should be able to conduct its own commercial policy toward third countries. The administration of these plan-like activities, of course, would rest in the hands of the High Authority.[9] The proposal was endorsed by all parties in the European Parliament and all socialist trade unions, except the miners' unions. It was rejected as not sufficiently protective of coal by the European Committee of Coal Producers and opposed by some Dutch interests as too protective. French government and producer spokesmen rejected it because it would limit the ability of national governments to adjust the importation of oil in response to coal production needs. While nothing has been finally decided, the High Authority has opened the door to a sweeping compromise conciliating a variety of attitudes.

Even the politics of national grandeur, even when equipped with Mirage IV nuclear-armed bombers, seems to find the expansion of supranational authority palatable in the New Europe when welfare planning is at stake. Such, at least, is the conclusion to be drawn from the favorable reception the French government gave to the EEC Commission's audacious program for "medium-term economic coordination." In October, 1962, the commission presented a scheme for centralized monetary policy and intensified business-cycle research with a view toward the evolution of a central antirecession and income policy. Free enterprise-oriented interests responded by denouncing central economic direction and deliberate economic "programming" of the type already practiced in France, Holland and Italy. But the governments cooperated in the first systematic comparison of their national budgets in terms of expected future economic performance; however, they were slow to initiate the advance planning of desirable antirecession measures. The commission thereupon scrapped the term "programming" and began to refer to "medium-term economic coordination," which is to involve aggregate demand and supply forecasts for a four-to-five-year period. Since governments were already responsible for spending one third of the national income under medium-term conditions, efforts to coordinate government spending for cyclical and developmental purposes would in fact usher in Community-wide planning under a label found acceptable even by Mr. Erhard. The almost uniformly favorable response of nearly all interest groups and of the major governments presages the early implementation of this reaffirmation of the supranational style.*

* The formulation and negotiation of the Commission's approach is under the direction of Robert Marjolin, who did much the same kind of job in France under the authority of the Commisariat au Plan between 1946 and 1948. The

The spill-over process, though rooted in the structures and motives of the post-capitalist welfare state, is far from automatic. Our survey of specific areas of decision-making indicated where the slowing down has occurred. Once the initial *élan* of the supra-national style was dissipated (a development also connected with the advent of de Gaulle and the retirement of Adenauer) the quality of supranational bargaining subtly altered. If one important member unit started to evince reservations it followed that the remaining governments felt that a proportional amount of caution was required of them. As William Diebold diagnosed matters:

> The change will surely be in the direction of giving less weight—though perhaps not very much less—to agreement for the sake of agreement and of calculating national interests in a more conventional way than that which had been developing in "the Community method." This is not a matter of black and white, of separate national action versus common action, or supranational versus intergovernmental power. . . . It is enough to say that the French action and the inevitable reaction to it on the part of the other five governments move the Community along the spectrum away from common action and towards national action.[10]

Yet the spill-over process does not presume the continuation of enthusiasm so as to produce agreement for the sake of agreement. Its continued sway is manifest precisely in this hardening of the bargaining attitude among the Six. On behalf of a Germany far from eager to implement the agricultural agreement of 1962, Gerhard Schroeder advanced the new concept of "synchronization" of joint policies: "we should equalize as far as possible the advantages and disadvantages of the measures of the Community as applied to the separate member states. We cannot embark on a system of advance concessions to be made notably by those countries which have already made considerable concessions up to now." [11] Immediate and proportional counter concessions seemed implied rather than deferred benefits. The upshot of this doctrine was the very supranational manner in which the agricultural crisis of December, 1963, was resolved: in exchange for implementing the common agricultural policy (a German concession to France), the foreign trade policy of the Community was to be so carried out as to offer broad and real tariff concessions to third countries (a French concession to Germany and the Benelux countries).

bundle of proposals was endorsed by a variety of French officials, including M. Bokanowski, Minister of Industries, several German industrial and CDU spokesmen, all socialist parties and socialist trade unions, and the Dutch employers. It was opposed by the German FDP and cautiously endorsed by Erhard. See *European Community*, No. 65 (September, 1963), p. 3; *Bulletin of the EEC*, vol. VI, no. 3 (March, 1963), pp. 23–26.

The loss of *élan* is far from fatal with respect to the operation of the integrative logic, though it produces a clearly visible decelerating effect. There remains one admittedly "political" factor which could bring the whole process and its underlying logic to a dead stop: the reunification of Germany. The end of ideology in West Germany is itself partly a function of a recognition of the loss of the older national power. The interest of Germany's neighbors in complete integration is in large measure the result of their fear of a strong Germany and their continued desire to enmesh the Federal Republic in a web of interdependencies. A Germany of over seventy million people and Europe's greatest concentration of industrial might on the soil of one nation would quickly rekindle the older fears and trigger once more the old stereotypes, whether warranted by the nature of the new German society or not. The continued sway of the spill-over process, therefore, does rest on the indefinite division of Germany and on the tacit recognition of that status in the minds of West German leaders.

To what extent is the future of Europe determined by this version of the past? It seems to me incontestable that the future is determined in the sense that the supremacy of welfare-dominated policies is assured. If supranational institutions already charged with further penetrating this field are firmly anchored in this supremacy, they will survive and flourish. Determined is the role of the technocrat, the technical expert whose statistics and negotiations fashion welfare policies, whether this technocrat is on the payroll of a powerful interest group, a national government or a supranational executive. Determined is the citizen's distrust of simplistic nationalist slogans, the realization of which would involve him in sacrificing his peace or his standard of living. Determined, therefore, is indifference to militarism, adventurism and heroics. If by the term "americanization" we merely mean the progressive *embourgeoisement* of tastes and behavior patterns which goes along with industrial society in the West as well as in the East, then the americanization of the New Europe is equally determined.

What is far from determined by history, however, is the extent of the region so ruled, the degree of supranationality the rule will imply, and the region's relationship with the rest of the western industrialized world. Let us consider each of these indeterminate points.

The Europe of the Outer Seven, of EFTA, corresponds to the profile of the New European society even more closely than does the European Community. In principle, and neglecting the current foreign policies of the Community, it would "fit in" perfectly.

Indeed, the history of EFTA until February, 1963 was mainly one of waiting and watching for the best time and terms for disbanding and entering the EEC. With the French veto on this step it should not really come as a surprise that the supranational-integrative logic began to assert itself rapidly within EFTA. Even though the Outer Seven had foresworn any political plans, had shied away from a customs union and had kept the politically sensitive issue of agricultural trade out of their constituent agreement, all this began to change. Even though the very word "supranational" was taboo in their circle, the style of upgrading common interests by means of intersectorial bargains made its advent in 1963. EFTA became a success by default; it embraced supranationality as an unintended but inescapable consequence of exclusion from the Community, despite all earlier British, Swedish and Swiss disclaimers to the contrary.

In 1963 EFTA began the discussion of a common commercial policy against outsiders; it initiated studies and discussions of agricultural trade and concluded several agricultural and fisheries agreements; like EEC, it undertook a dramatic acceleration in the schedule of removing trade barriers among the members, keeping the schedule closely geared to its rival's. The developed EFTA nations began to study concerted policies of development aid to the underdeveloped members. On the institutional side this, of course, involved an increase in the powers of the expert; it also called into being the need for consulting private interest groups who are now represented in a consultative committee. And it gave rise to a nuclear parliamentary gathering in the form of meetings of delegates of EFTA parliaments to the Council of Europe. As the spokesman for this group, Per Federspiel, remarked:

> . . . whereas EFTA has always been considered an economic association, and the EEC a political union, we found that the political approach by the EFTA countries to the problems concerning us was generally coherent and that EFTA in itself was capable of developing a political policy.[12]

But how long will this last? Every protestation that EFTA now is here to stay is balanced with the assurance that no fight with EEC is intended and that all bridges to it must remain intact. While intra-EFTA trade took a marked swing upward in 1963, this had not been true previously and may not remain true indefinitely. And in the meantime the actual joint policies pursued in EFTA would facilitate an eventual merger with EEC by eliminating many national rules and practices and substituting therefore unified regional rules which resemble those adopted within EEC. Hence we cannot assume the inevitable, continuous and autonomous evolution of the Outer Seven, since only Sweden seems to be certain that this would be desirable.

The continued uncertainty regarding the extent of the New European policy increases the doubts regarding the future of supranationality as a form of government. Simple federation remains excluded simply because there is no generalized enthusiasm for it; the constitutive federal act in the New Europe of mass politics would have to rest on a substratum of passion and devotion which would differ from the older nationalism in name only. If a genuine "European sentiment," a sense of vocation and spiritual uniqueness, were actually in existence on a mass scale rather than being confined to the minds of a few intellectuals, such a feeling would be identical with a new nationalism writ large. But there is little trace of this sentiment. Without it, formal federation is inconceivable. But de Gaulle's confederal approach is equally irrelevant because it rests on false premises and enjoys few supporters apart from the aged Konrad Adenauer. Both federation and confederation remain tied to the concept of sovereignty and the pre-eminence of the political. As long as political figures are more interested in concrete problems and specific administrative tasks, these concepts are anachronisms of an earlier legal vocabulary. They remain irrelevant to the future of the New Europe.

A more relevant controversy, however, exists with respect to the degree to which existing supranational institutions perform satisfactorily. Many Europeans complain that they do not because they are not sufficiently powerful to carry out all the economic tasks wished on them, because they cannot formulate a strong policy vis-à-vis the outside world, and because they do not permit continuous democratic control over technocrats and ministers. All these charges are true enough, but whether there is any sense in devising institutional devices for overcoming them is another question. The common formula proposed for perfecting supranationality among the Six involves a modest and pragmatic federalization.

First, the three executive bodies are to be merged into one European High Commission which would enjoy all the powers now wielded separately by the three organs. Second, the three Councils of Ministers would be fused into one Council of the European Communities, but otherwise undergo no change in competence.* Third, the economic competences of the communities

---

* This is the essence of a Dutch proposal for the fusion of the executives, presented to the Councils of Ministers on June 27, 1961, the text of which may be found in Roy Pryce, *The Political Future of the European Community* (London: Marshbank, 1962), pp. 100–102. For the text of the Draft Convention for direct elections to the European Parliament, see *ibid.*, p. 98. The

would be extended further, following the proposals of the commissions and High Authority, and approaching gradually a competence over defense and foreign policy. Fourth, democratic control
would be provided over the ever more powerful technocrats by
strengthening the powers of the present European Parliament,
whose competence now is confined to *a posteriori* review of executive action and dismissal of the executives. Under the new dispen-
sation the Parliament would be elected directly by the European
citizenry, thus for the first time enabling it to participate in regional
government; further the competence of the Parliament would be
expanded by giving it the power of *a priori* review over all executive
policy, but not the ability of legislating.

It may be doubted that the direct election of the Parliament,
apart from giving the Communists representation for the first time,
will result in a dramatic change in the personalities now inhabiting
the assembly, or in a change of the party balance. *A priori* review,
in a setting of inevitable technocratic dominance, may delay the
preparation of policy but not change its content. Public participation may confuse rather than accelerate integration by giving the
victims of industrialism a European platform. The point is, rather,
as the EEC Commission's Action Program said, "what we call the
economic integration of Europe is in essence a political phenomenon." [13] In other words, even without formal constitutional
change the present supranational institutions are likely to acquire
the powers necessary to advance welfare.

In the meantime, the implementation of the reform program is
apt to hinder the integration of the EFTA bloc into the New
Europe. The outsiders are unlikely to advance as enthusiastically
to all-European integration—once this becomes politically conceivable—if they are confronted with an already highly developed
set of quasi-federal institutions. This, of course, is a reason for
advocates of an "Inner Europe" to proceed with institutionalization
as rapidly as possible. The supranational-integrative logic suggests
the tightening of relations *among* the Six and *among* the Seven.
It can teach us little about the tie *between* the two blocs, except
to suggest that rapid federalization in one is likely to repel the other.

Even more indeterminate is the future relationship between
the New Europe and the North American world. Neither the
military ties of NATO nor the economic links of OECD have
engendered the kinds of relationships on which a self-sustaining
spill-over process could thrive. Short of inaugurating a single At-

fusion of the executives was accepted in principle by the six governments in
1963, even though neither the composition nor the administrative structure of
the new European High Commission has been decided.

lantic defense and arms production policy and an Atlantic customs union, it is doubtful that the basis for such a process could be created. In the absence of any such trend the competing formulas of federation, partnership, concentrism and polycentrism all remain equally plausible in terms of logic, though not in probability of implementation.

The sweeping and audacious institutional formula pressed in the famous Declaration of Atlantic Unity is the least probable. [14] It places the need for an active federalizing impulse in the Atlantic world on the Communist threat; but the example of the Community of Six suggests that an external threat is of secondary usefulness among the many stimuli pushing toward permanent unity. It indiscriminately lauds all strictly European efforts toward unity on the mistaken assumption that this must necessarily conduce to the greater benefit of North America as well. And it stresses the need for the immediate creation of new federal Atlantic institutions while saying next to nothing about the concrete tasks facing the Atlantic nations or the duties these institutions might be expected to perform. Atlantic federation substitutes institutional gimmickry for efforts at upgrading common interests in substantive and pivotal policy conflicts.

In the military field the substantive task revolves around the active hegemonial role of the United States, especially in the field of nuclear strategy. The Nassau Agreement and its possible extension to France, as well as the scheme for a multilateral nuclear fleet for NATO, disguise but do not obliterate this hegemony. While these schemes multilateralize control over the safety catch they merely perpetuate the American preponderance as concerns technology, arms procurement and strategic doctrine; the choice left to the European participants is so limited as to affront their own sense of purpose and competence. In the economic field, the task hinges around the fact that the interests of the Atlantic nations are neither homogeneous nor equally intense with respect to intra-Atlantic and world-wide trade and investment. Japan, Latin America and parts of South Asia are more important to the United States; Africa, the Middle East and the temperate-zone Commonwealth countries tend to preoccupy Europe. No amount of federalizing and invocation of Communist dangers can gloss over the differences in interests regarding international monetary liquidity, price stability for agricultural commodities and economic development needs.

Those most impressed by these conflicts consider and sometimes accept the opposite of the federal formula: the path of western polycentrism, a sort of *sauve-qui-peut* policy under which each major country or bloc would seek its own salvation as best it can in terms of heterogeneous and asymmetrical ties within and outside the Atlantic world. NATO might well survive here, but its tasks would remain confined to the narrow aspects of military policy on which interests converge.[15] Both EFTA and EEC would prosper, the Commonwealth would remain identified with Britain, but Canada and the United States would have to make the best deal they can.

The concentric approach was devised to head off such tendencies but it despairs of a real meshing and upgrading of Atlantic interests. This approach grants that the West has a great deal to gain by maximizing its contribution to economic development in the non-western world, through tighter planning and coordination in OECD. It grants further that the confusion in agriculture could logically be solved only in terms of some joint Atlantic policy geared to that of the major one-crop exporting nations. Monetary matters also would have to be jointly discussed. But the approach takes for granted that asymmetries between the United States, Britain and the EEC would continue just the same. Therefore it conceives of a series of concentric circles, with the Community at the center and radiating outward in ever weaker ripples to take in the Atlantic world as well as Japan. Coordination could not be expected to proceed beyond the pattern of discussion and confrontation concerning monetary, trade and aid policies now being carried on leisurely in OECD.[16]

That leaves us with the "partnership" formula. It should be noted from the outset that the soul-searching and planning associated with this approach is to be taken very seriously, because for the first time in the Atlantic setting it proceeds from a concern with internal conflict rather than merely from a response to a temporary and intermittent external threat, such as NATO. If partnership is to unite the West "there must be a genuine division of labor between the two halves of the alliance. The concept of 'interdependence' will not be satisfied by any formula that assumes that advanced technology is an American prerogative, and which attempts to apply a division of effort which is at variance with economic realities and capabilities."[17] In short, it must involve a military policy of sharing not only weapons as end products and joint control over launching them, but also a common policy of research, production, targeting and command. Unless complete rather than fragmentary multilateralization takes place, the Gaullist claim of a "special relationship" between the United States and Britain retains its plausibility. And de Gaulle's offers of a separate continental deterrent, perhaps linked to Britain's by way of the

Western European Union, will become increasingly attractive to Europe. It has already been partially endorsed by the Western European Union. A mere coordination of national efforts, as now in NATO, will not advance Atlantic integration. A true integration under United States leadership will be resented and cause fragmentation. Only complete sharing can set the scene for the upgrading of common interests from which further integrative steps can spill over into other policy contexts. Such an approach is facilitated by the fact that we seem to have reached the political limits in Europe with respect to the size of conventional forces which are to be deployed. Emphasis can therefore be placed on an effective division of labor between these forces, including the equipment they will carry and the auspices under which it will be manufactured and procured. By capitalizing on this point an economic spill-over can be built into military planning. But by the same token the United States would have to agree to a nuclear division of labor not yet officially accepted in Washington.

And so it is in the economic realm. Short-run discussion concerning small steps for easing the United States gold outflow will not create a spill-over. Neither will practices in OECD under which growth rates and economic aid measures are frankly discussed and criticized. Joint policies in the fields of commercial policy, agricultural marketing, fair competition and monetary stability are called for. The nature of the task must define the creation of appropriate institutions. These, since the task bears so much similarity to what has been done by the European Community, will approximate the supranational style no matter by what name they are called.

The Atlantic Institute in Paris took the initiative in exploring these tasks under the general aegis of the partnership doctrine. Further, it devised institutions capable of carrying out the tasks *after* exploring what ought to be done.[18] The substantive proposals stress the interconnected aspects of tariff policy, trade in agricultural commodities, aid to economic development in non-western countries, and the stability versus liquidity issue in the international payments system. In the field of tariff reduction in the transatlantic trade in manufactured goods, the Atlantic Institute proposed a fixed method of negotiation tied to a new set of criteria for judging the protective character of existing duties and the reciprocity of concessions. Rules governing dumping and discrimination in the home market would be worked out for the Atlantic nations. In the realm of agriculture, the Atlantic Institute proposes an ambitious formula for multilateralizing the sale of agricultural surpluses to underdeveloped countries, stabilizing the terms of trade so as to end the victimization of exporters of primary products and computing development aid in connection with this stabilization. At the same time the manufactures of underdeveloped countries are to be given a slowly expanding market in the Atlantic nations. In short, the Atlantic Institute proposes to end competition among the members of the Atlantic partnership in their relations with third countries, a formula which requires a great deal more coordinated and joint action than in the past. The payments problem is to be solved by short-term measures of balance-of-payments aid at the Atlantic level tied to the creation of a Common Market foreign reserves fund in Europe.

That these measures would require a high degree of technocratic autonomy for the officials called upon to carry them out is clear beyond argument. But following the integrative logic of the EEC, the Atlantic Institute proposed a modest body of institutions with vaguely articulated powers, yet flexible enough to develop additional competences by following the functional lines of task-oriented policy-making. It is a suggestion which looks forward to an eventual *bipartite* Atlantic partnership, transcending the present division of Europe.

For the immediate future, a tripartite committee is to be set up with the task of exploring and defining the policy areas requiring attention and preparing the necessary negotiations, notably in the "Kennedy round" of tariff cutting. This committee would be composed of the EEC, the United States and Britain, each representing the nations associated with it in terms of world trade blocs. The most important task of this committee would be the easing of tensions between EEC and EFTA and the eventual merger of the two. Following this development, the bipartite machinery would begin to work. At the top there would be a Council of Partnership, made up of European and American economic administrators *and* ministers. They would enjoy supreme authority to dispose. Power to propose, however, would be lodged in a Committee of Wise Men responsible to no government and inspired by the example of the executives of the European communities. The prestige of the Wise Men would be such as to make the adoption of their proposals by the Council a fairly certain outcome. The power to review and criticize—but not to alter—these decisions would be lodged in an Atlantic Parliamentary Assembly, following the model of the current European Parliament.

The essence of this proposal remains true to the technocratic nature of pluralistic, welfare-oriented modern states. Democratic accountability, majority voting, and public discussion are balanced at all levels by permanent bodies of experts negotiating away from the glare of public confrontation. OECD is to provide the expert committees and the secretariat for the entire operation and thereby gain a new lease on life as the technical body charged with unifying western economic policy, representing both the enlarged European Common Market and North America. As the Atlantic Institute put it:

We shall thus have an organization systematically conceived as a *network* of committees, organized on a functional basis and served by a single secretariat. Such a body would prove an invaluable forum for the submission and wider discussion of the ideas of the two main partners before they are finally dealt with in the appropriate international bodies.[19]

We can now restate, at the Atlantic level, the formula of cross-cutting cleavages in popular expectations and loyalties which we adduced in the characterization of post-capitalist and post-ideological western society. It is the supreme merit of the Atlantic Institute's proposals to have grasped this point and to have married the continuation of the supranational process of integration in Europe to the splitting of the task so as to prevent Europe's pre-empting the future. Integration in any network of autonomous units is advanced if no single unit is the supreme repository of hopes, hates and tasks. If a united Europe were to become the vessel for the simultaneous execution of a nuclear military policy and a comprehensive economic approach to its internal trade *as well as* to the underdeveloped world, we would have to bury both NATO and OECD and forget about partnership. There would no longer be an opportunity, in terms of tasks and institutions, for technocrats to prepare policy and for voluntary groups to coalesce across national boundaries. Hence military matters must be kept out of the hands of purely European and North American agencies, and economic issues must be divided among those which can be dealt with by an enlarged EEC and others which properly belong to an Atlantic structure. A future confrontation of the autonomous units on both sides of the Atlantic—one an old nation and the other in the process of making a new one out of established nationalisms—might well lead to the revival of that very *Grosspolitik* which we dismissed earlier. The preservation and cultivation of cross-cutting cleavages at the Atlantic level can prevent this; indeed it is a necessary condition for partnership.

REFERENCES

1. The term "the New Europe" was made familiar by George Lichtheim, *The New Europe—Today and Tomorrow* (New York: Praeger, 1963),

whose general view of things I share almost completely. The economic and sociological reasoning and analysis which underlies the concept is developed in the following publications: Ralf Dahrendorf, *Class and Class Conflict in Industrial Society* (Stanford: Stanford University Press, 1959); Raymond Aron, "Fin de l'age idéologique?" in Adorno and Dirks (eds.), *Sociologica* (Frankfurt: Europäische Verlagsanstalt, 1955); Daniel Bell, *The End of Ideology* (Glencoe: The Free Press, 1960); Gunnar Myrdal, *Beyond the Welfare State* (New Haven: Yale University Press, 1960); S. M. Lipset, "The Changing Class Structure and Contemporary European Politics," *Daedalus* (Winter, 1964).

2. Roy Pryce, *The Political Future of the European Community* (London: Marshbank, 1962), p. 19.

3. Press Conference, Paris, September 5, 1960. PEP, *Occasional Papers*, No. 11, p. 12. Nothing which has been said by de Gaulle since changes this view of things.

4. These alternatives are convincingly and perceptively explored by Stanley Hoffmann, "Discord in Community: The North Atlantic Area as a Partial International System," *International Organization*, vol. XVII, no. 3 (Summer, 1963), pp. 537–538. My understanding and rejection of the newly rehabilitated concept of "confederation" owes much to Max Beloff, "International Integration and the Modern State," *Journal of Common Market Studies*, vol. II, no. 1 (1963).

5. Herbert Tingsten, "Stability and Vitality in Swedish Democracy," *Political Quarterly*, vol. 26 (1955), pp. 140–151.

6. Herbert Lüthy, "La Suisse à contre-courant," *Preuves* (October, 1963), p. 27.

7. This argument is fully developed in Hoffmann, *op. cit.*, pp. 526–531.

8. These formulations are developed by Leon N. Lindberg, *The Political Dynamics of European Economic Integration* (Stanford: Stanford University Press, 1963), pp. 10–11.

9. European Coal and Steel Community, High Authority, *Résumé du Douzième Rapport Général* (April, 1963), pp. 29–31.

10. William Diebold, Jr., "European Economic Integration in a New Phase," paper given at Ohio State University, October 24, 1963, mimeographed, p. 15.

11. "What is 'Synchronization'?" *European Community* (June, 1963). Quoted in Diebold, *op. cit.*, p. 18.

12. *EFTA Reporter*, (No. 82, Sept. 17, 1963), p. 2.

13. For a full exposition of this line of thought in the mind of the EEC Commission see Walter Hallstein, *United Europe* (Cambridge: Harvard University Press, 1962), pp. 62–66.

14. For a summary of the Declaration of Atlantic Unity and a variety of endorsements see *The Atlantic Community Quarterly*, vol. 1, no. 2 (Summer, 1963), pp. 275–276, and the bulk of the articles which appeared in the Spring, 1963 issue of the same publication.

15. See Max Beloff, "Britain, Europe and the Atlantic Community," *International Organization,* vol. XVII, no. 3 (Summer 1963), pp. 587, 589–591.

16. The concentric formula is suggested by Livingston T. Merchant, "Evolving United States Relations with the Atlantic Community," *ibid.,* pp. 626–627. The economic issues at stake are discussed by William Diebold, Jr., "Economic Aspects of an Atlantic Community," *ibid.,* especially pp. 671 ff.

17. Alastair Buchan, "Europe and the Atlantic Alliance: Two Strategies or One?" *Journal of Common Market Studies,* vol. I, no. 3 (1962), p. 250.

18. Pierre Uri *et al., Partnership for Progress: A Program for Transatlantic Action* (New York, Harper & Row, 1963), especially pp. 96–107.

19. *Ibid.,* p. 106. Italics in original.

OLIVER FRANKS

Britain and Europe

THE PRESS conference of General de Gaulle on January 14, 1963, was a major political event. It put an abrupt end to the long negotiations between Britain and the European Economic Community and, since one black ball excludes, made it certain that Britain for the foreseeable future would not be a member of the Community. By a stroke of policy as sudden as the peripeteia of a Greek tragedy, General de Gaulle ensured that the negotiations, at long last near success, must fail. His action has important consequences, not only for Britain but also for the Six of the Common Market, and indeed for the United States and the whole Atlantic Community of nations.

The first point of interest is that the considerations which led General de Gaulle to act as he did were different from those which had induced many observers to fear the breakdown of the negotiations. To them it had appeared that there were three difficulties standing out from the mass of detail, any one of which might have proved insuperable: one political, two economic in character.

The political difficulty had two aspects: whether Britain was really prepared to accept the political aims and institutions of the Six, and whether the Six would believe the British. There were grounds for thinking there might be problems here. At earlier stages of the realization of the European Idea, the foundation of the Coal and Steel Authority and then the elaboration of the Treaty of Rome, Britain had made it clear that to her the political aims embodied were unacceptable. Thereafter the British Government had insisted on treating relations with the Community as purely economic in nature and had sent Mr. Maudling, then President of the Board of Trade, to a foredoomed negotiation on this basis. Britain had seemed to have a deep emotional commitment to the notion of independent national sovereignty and an equally strong sentiment for the unique relationships of the Commonwealth. It is true that acceptance of the provisions of the Treaty of Rome did not include acceptance of a United States of Europe. One of the surprising things about the treaty is the cautious empiricism of its approach to the political goal: "an ever closer unity" is the description offered. Nevertheless the application of Britain to join the European Economic Community did involve the acceptance of a real limitation on national sovereignty. But the British Government accepted the political aim and, what was far more important, the political institutions designed to keep the member nations moving toward the end desired. Early on in the negotiations the minister in charge of the British negotiating team made the British position clear. His exposition was accepted and from then on it ceased to be a primary issue in the long discussions.

The second expected difficulty was economic and arose from monetary questions about the pound sterling. Sterling plays a different role in the world from the currencies of the Six. They are all national currencies. Sterling, like the dollar, is that and more, for it is also a reserve currency; that is to say, a number of nations keep sterling as well as gold in their central banks as an acceptable means of settling their international debts. They also use sterling as a currency in which they carry out international transactions. In consequence sterling, like the dollar, is vulnerable in ways in which the western European currencies are not. If a country which keeps its reserves in sterling and so belongs to the sterling area runs a deficit on its balance of payments with the world outside the sterling area, then it cannot use the sterling in its reserves to settle this deficit. It has to turn to Britain, to the central reserves of gold and foreign currency in the Bank of England, and exchange its sterling for gold or, perhaps, dollars to extinguish the debt. But this can be a large additional strain on the British reserves.

What would be the attitude of the European Economic Community to the pound sterling? Would the Six agree to underwrite sterling, in which case this reserve currency would be fortified by the great strength of the reserves of western Europe, or would they refuse? In the latter event the British, in assuming the obligations of the Community, would have to do one of two things, either ask for sanction for escape clauses so as to be able to protect sterling when necessary, or accept the inevitability at times of subjecting their own economy to severe deflation. Here were real problems adding up potentially to a major difficulty. But the remarkable thing about the course of the protracted negotiations in Brussels was that these monetary issues never appeared on the official agenda and, since they were never discussed, did not prove a cause of stumbling.

The third difficulty, the economic problem of the temperate zone agricultural products, came under discussion in the negotiations and proved troublesome. It can best be illustrated by taking the most awkward case, wheat. This commodity is in burdensome surplus: much more of it is grown than people can buy and consume, though much less than would be consumed if all the people who need wheat became possessed of the foreign currency to buy it. Now of the countries which import wheat and can pay for it, Britain provides the largest single market. It has traditionally been supplied from Canada, Australia or Argentina. But during the last few years France has reached the point of breakthrough in agriculture. In wheat, for example, France has a surplus over and above domestic requirements and needs export markets. One was found at the time of negotiation of the Treaty of Rome: in effect West Germany guaranteed a market for wheat in return for access to the large market of the Community for German industrial goods. By the time the British application for membership of the Community was being discussed, France needed another outlet and demanded a large share of the British market. This meant of course the displacement of traditional suppliers. But, because wheat that could be paid for was in world surplus, any share of the British market lost by Commonwealth countries left them with wheat which could not be sold. Hence the acuteness of the difficulty. In the case of wheat and other agricultural products problems of surplus on a world scale were looked at from the narrow perspective of the British market and the new need of France to export. In such a context there were no reasonable solutions. Yet at the same time it is hard to suppose that the difficulty would not have been overcome, if it had been the only major obstacle to agreement.

None of these substantial and relevant considerations played any real part in the decision of General de Gaulle. The arguments he put forward were two in number and were derived from political convictions of a more general kind. The first was that Britain, the offshore island, was not really part of western Europe and that therefore to include her in the Community was so difficult as not to be practicable. General de Gaulle was not just stating a geographical truism: he was claiming that the six nations of the European Economic Community have a basic affinity whereas Britain is quite different in outlook and in economic habits of life. He said:

The Treaty of Rome was concluded between six continental states, states which are, economically speaking, one may say, of the same nature. Indeed, whether it be a matter of their industrial or their agricultural production, their external exchanges, their habits or their commercial clientele, their living or working conditions, there is between them more resemblance than difference. Moreover, they are adjacent, they interpenetrate, they prolong each other through their communications.

It is therefore a fact to group them and to link them in such a way that what they have to produce, to buy, to sell, to consume—well, they do produce, buy, sell, consume, in preference in their own ensemble. Doing that is conforming to realities. Moreover, it must be added that from the point of view of their economic development, their social progress, their technical capacity, they are, in short, keeping pace. They are marching in similar fashion.

But Britain is fundamentally different. England, in effect, is insular, she is maritime, she is linked through her exchanges, her markets, her supply lines to the most diverse and often the most distant countries; she pursues essentially industrial and commercial activities, and only slight agricultural ones. She has in all her doings very marked and very original habits and traditions.

In short, the nature, the structure, the very situation that are England's differ profoundly from those of the continentals.

First of all it must be admitted that the general characterization of Britain is just. It is true in detail as well as in the large. Consider my breakfast table: coffee is from Brazil or Africa, tea from India or Ceylon; sugar from the West Indies or Mauritius; the oranges in the marmalade from Spain; butter from New Zealand or Denmark; the grain that went into the bread from Canada and, perhaps, Australia. The supply lines to my breakfast table come from five continents, from "the most diverse and often the most distant countries." But what weight has the argument? Do the Dutch, the Belgians or the Germans think the British situation so different in kind from their own? Further, it is probable that so far as they thought these were real differences, they would think the introduction of these differing habits of mind and practices good rather than bad for the Community. But surely on any view these considerations can have played only a quite minor part in the decision. What is said about Britain has been true and known to be true for the best part of a hundred years. The negotiations had been going on for eighteen months. It does not make sense to suppose that these well known characteristics of British life suddenly assumed decisive weight in the mind of General de Gaulle during January, 1963. For him the conclusive argument is the second.

General de Gaulle believes that France and the European Economic Community must develop in their own style, in their natural European way. He therefore does not desire close links with the United States, dependence, interdependence, partnership, call it what you will. He thinks that the influence of the United States in European affairs is too great rather than too small. But he is certain that in crisis Britain will always choose the United States rather than Europe. This is what Churchill said to him on a number of occasions during the war. General de Gaulle believes this to be a fundamental position of British foreign policy. It follows therefore that to admit Britain to the Community would be to readmit interdependence with the United States, and this is inadmissible. The conclusion is that Britain must go her way outside the Six. This is why negotiations between Britain and the Community collapsed in January, 1963.

It is ridiculous to suppose that this decision was dictated by personal prejudice against the Americans or the British, against Roosevelt or Churchill. General de Gaulle may not like the Anglo-Saxons but the decision was a matter of high policy. It was the consequence of a theme, a positive vision of the role that France and her neighbors in western Europe should play in the world. He is utterly convinced of the historic civilizing mission of France. He is sure that under French leadership, but not under that of the United States, western Europe can regain its soul and make a future. There is no aspiration here to dominate Germany or Italy or the Low Countries. General de Gaulle is not a Louis XIV or a Napoleon reincarnate. For him the French are French and the Germans are Germans; just as there are also the Italians and others. His desire is that France should take her natural position of leadership, in policy as in the arts of civilized life, so that Europe once again becomes the place where much of the history of the world is made.

He is convinced that the Soviet Union no longer represents an instant danger to western Europe. Once sixteen years ago things were different, but the menace was overcome with the help of the United States in the Berlin Airlift, the Marshall Plan, the forging of the North Atlantic Alliance and the establishment of NATO. Now and for the future the Russians are not in that sense a menace to western Europe. In fact the time will come, though not necessarily soon, when Russia will rejoin the society of European nations. No date can be set but the trend is there. In the interval one must wait, patient but firm. This is a different view of the posture of the Soviet Union from that commonly accepted in the United States at the present time. It makes a considerable difference to the way one looks at the world and its problems.

Again General de Gaulle believes that France through the length of her experience as a nation has come to possess a certain style of thought and action. She has developed a sense of measure, a sense of proportion which give order and regularity to the national temperament. He would accord the same qualities in an individual version to the British nation, which also has a long history and has therefore developed a characteristic outlook. He does not accord the same qualities to the United States, which he regards as a nation still in the process of formation, not yet possessing a sense of measure. It is therefore important that France should not be too closely linked with the immoderation of the United States.

Lastly he does not think that the United States alone should have a finger on the nuclear trigger. In the last resort the United States will act as it sees its own self-interest and not because of the interests of France and western Europe. General de Gaulle approved of the action of President Kennedy in the Cuban crisis: in the circumstances it was the right action for the United States to take. But equally the point had been proved: the United States, consulting its own interests, would take such action as might be required, action as in this case involving a risk of thermonuclear war on the world scale, without consulting her allies. In similar circumstances the United States would do it again. The reasonable line for France to take is to stay away from this finger on the trigger, not becoming involved in unrealities like partnership or interdependence, and in the meantime to build up her own nuclear capability. Such then is the nature of the decision taken by General de Gaulle and such the high policy from which it derives. What consequences follow from it?

It is obvious that the decision entails major consequences for Britain. The British Government made a historic change in policy when it applied in July, 1961, for membership of the Community, and the bid failed. What are the prospects for Britain now and what has she lost by the failure?

Any appraisal must start from the simplest facts. The power of Britain, her standards of life, her ability to make views and policies count in the councils of the world, these are all directly conditioned by the nature of the economy. We are an industrial nation of over 50 million people on a small island, grow half our food, have few raw materials and virtually no sources of power except coal. Our life depends on the amount earned from exports being large enough to pay for the other half of our food and for the raw materials and oil without which industrial plant stands idle. This is why the reserves in the Bank of England are continuously watched: if imports surge, if exports sag, if the terms of trade turn against us, we depend on these reserves of gold and foreign currency as a first line of defense to buy time to adjust to the changed circumstances.

At the present time there is a widespread inclination abroad to discount the future of Britain and write us off as a power in the world. Membership of the Common Market was our chance and it has been lost. These melancholy opinions have been held abroad before: they were prevalent in 1947 and 1948; they were almost universal in 1940. Is it true that our prospects are dim? What are the facts? Over the last fifteen years we have earned our living in the world. Britain has enjoyed a high standard of living and, almost continuously, a high level of employment and industrial activity.

There have been crises, immediately reflected in a drain on the reserves, but they have been surmounted. We have had the capacity to regulate the situation and the reserves have fluctuated around the figure of 1000 million sterling. Judged by the outlook in the immediate postwar years we have done well. Why then the present doubts?

They arise for two reasons. First, in a world addicted to economic growth and tending to judge economic well-being by this criterion, the British economy has grown more slowly than many. And it has suffered from an abrupt cycle of expansion and stagnation again and again. This has been the price of our capacity to regulate the situation when the balance of payments suddenly went into deficit. It has seemed impossible to break out of this rhythm and secure that continuous growth which others enjoy. The forecast has therefore been made that the British economy will dwindle in strength relatively to those of more vigorous nations. Second, in the last few years a malaise has come over the British people, a sense of discomfort, of generalized dissatisfaction with the way things were going. This too has been noticed abroad, and it has reinforced a pessimistic view of Britain: if the British are dissatisfied and uncertain about themselves and their future, the prospect cannot be good. Furthermore, in commending to the electorate the decision to ask to join the Community, the Government had raised high hopes that membership of this large and prosperous market would of itself cure these ills. The death of these hopes increased the malaise.

How much in fact has exclusion from the Common Market weakened the prospects for Britain? The first test must be on our capacity to export and earn a living. It would be foolish to deny that direct access to a market as big as the United States would have been advantageous to British industry. But it is not clear that it would have made a vast difference to our exports. The Community has been in existence for six years but British exports have successfully jumped over the common tariff. In fact exports to the Common Market have increased faster than any others. The disappointing sector has been the sterling area, the Commonwealth countries old and new, to which exports in total have been declining. There is little reason to think that in future years British exports to the Community will fail to grow satisfactorily. The problems of Britain in increasing exports lie elsewhere. Membership of the Community would have had another advantage. Britain would have exchanged a domestic market of 50 million for one of 220 million. There would have been the gains of specialization and division of labor. These would have counted for something, but Professor James Meade of

Cambridge University has shown that it would be mistaken to attach great importance to this point. The difference would have been real but quite small.

But the cost of exclusion is not to be measured by these economic considerations. The loss is essentially political, not economic. Britain lost the opportunity of a new start, a fresh inspiration, new horizons and purposes, an end to malaise and dissatisfaction. For what is so boring, so irritating and frustrating, what feels so unprofitable as prolonged retreat? For more than forty years Britain has been making a strategic retreat. We have had a great deal to retreat from: a position of eminence unchallenged in the nineteenth-century world. Even in the early years of this century the Navy, symbol of Britain's power, was designed and built to be strong enough, and was strong enough, to take on any combination of hostile fleets which could be envisaged. After the 1914–1918 war this ceased to be true. The facts were overtly recognized in the Washington Naval Agreement, which assigned ratios of 5, 5 and 3 in capital ships to the British, American and Japanese fleets. Britain agreed to equality on the sea with the United States and to inferiority in face of a theoretical combination of naval powers. Perhaps the next great milestone was passed when during the 1939–1945 war Singapore fell: it was proof that the British no longer had the power to wage full-scale war on two fronts on opposite sides of the world. Then came the birth of India and Pakistan, the peaceful emergence of new nations from the dissolution of the Indian Empire, one of the most successful acts of statesmanship seen during the troubled history of the postwar world. But like all great successes it had its reverse side. Britain lost the services of the British-Indian Army, the complement on land to the Navy, a great force of trained manpower which Britain herself could neither provide nor maintain and which had for many decades kept order in the Indian Ocean from Suez and Aden to Malaya and Hong Kong. The process went on inexorably: the next stage was the evacuation of Suez and loss of control over the Canal. This brought home to the British people as no earlier change had done the nature of the strategic retreat that was occurring. And still the retreat is going on, though it is nearly ended.

On the whole this long movement of disengagement has been amazingly well conducted. It has been slow, steady and economical. Its pressures have never been allowed to undermine the unity of the British nation. But as the years have become decades the process has increasingly been felt as a weariness of the flesh, with no adventure, no inspiration in it, nothing positive, only an endless negative. It is the ultimate source of the British malaise and our present discontents. How pleasant it would have been, how encouraging if, instead of concentrating on making the retreat as slow, orderly and inexpensive as possible, Britain had been able to look forward, go forward, helping in the creation of something new, a new framework of life in Europe, political, economic and social, with so many of our neighbors. It would have given a different savor to life, a relish we should have enjoyed. This is the great loss of our exclusion. For a little longer we have to go on living with this phase of our history before we can know and build the future.

In this context the absoluteness of national sovereignty is not a vital issue. We are all interdependent nowadays, whether we like it or not: all national sovereignties are in degree in commission to others. This is most obviously true in matters of strategy and war: the old dictum that peace is indivisible has gained in validity. But it also holds of two other great branches of human activity. In the Middle Ages learning and trade knew no frontiers. Today the discoveries of science overleap all boundaries offering in their application good or ill to men; while prices for large ranges of manufactured and primary products are increasingly set in the international market, thereby limiting the freedom of governments to determine their internal policies as they wish. This is as well understood in Britain as elsewhere. The questioning and debate which arose particularly in the six months before General de Gaulle made his decision was not essentially about whether sovereignty would be compromised by entering the Community. It was due partly to the silence of the Government maintained in the belief that this was necessary if Mr. Heath was to have a free hand in negotiation in Brussels. It was due also to confusion and uncertainty in the minds of the British people because of the historical conjuncture that has been described: the past, present and future of Britain clashed together in thought, feeling and imagination.

There remains one further consequence to note, a consequence of long-range importance to the economy. Membership of the Common Market would have acted swiftly as a stimulant to enterprise. It would have increased competition and shown up restrictive practices in both management and labor. The British Government has known for some time that this is desirable, indeed necessary. So have most people. But this is a matter on which it is unpopular to take a strong initiative. It was the hope of the British Government that beyond the measures it had already taken matters could be left to the stimulating disciplines of the Common Market. High expectations were based on this external leverage: it was an added recommendation in the judgment of many for joining the Community. Old habits, bad habits would be swept away. There would be more room for youth, ideas and enterprise. Now this will not happen

97

in the easy way. But the problems remain and have still to be dealt with. We shall have to pull ourselves up by our own bootstraps, to buy ourselves a do-it-yourself kit. This can be done, and without extreme difficulties, if it is seen to be a necessary part of a larger future. But this requires a new vision of British society, new themes of policy, internal and external, and for the reasons given the immediate conjuncture is unfavorable to this act of statesmanship. A beginning has been made with the National Economic Development Council, on which sit three Ministers of the Crown, six industrialists, six trade unionists, two chairmen of nationalized industries and two independents. The Council has begun to make progress in this area of difficulty, but how far and how fast it can go cannot yet be foreseen. Exclusion from the Common Market has imposed a delay.

The British in self-depreciation often speak of themselves as muddling through. It looks as though the decision of General de Gaulle means that Britain must engage in one further round of this unexciting form of activity while the final adjustments of our position in the world take place. This is a pity but not a disaster. It is a waste of time. But there is ample stubbornness in the British people to bring them through, and they have the capacity under pressure, at times when their friends are despondent about the future of Britain, of responding with bold and constructive enterprise. The only question is how quickly the response will be elicited.

There will be consequences too for the European Economic Community as a result of the decision to exclude Britain, though not the consequences which many feared and some hoped for immediately after the breakdown of the negotiations. At that time people wondered whether the five members other than France might feel compelled to go it alone, whether conceivably they might make an agreement with Britain or, if not that, oppose all advance in the directions wished by France, even to the extent of forcing a breakdown in the Community itself. All this is fantasy and out of relation with the realities. And what is more, such courses would be in the interest of no one. The interest of each member of the Six must be that their great experiment should go forward. It is equally in the long-term interest of Britain and the United States that it should continue and prosper.

Clearly the basic conditions which led the six nations to agree upon the Treaty of Rome still apply. They are both political and economic. The political conditions spring from the history of the present century and the realization of what the nations of western Europe had done to themselves and had suffered. Twice there had been in effect civil war and the peoples had torn each other to pieces with terrible loss of human life. There had been too the experience of defeat and occupation in the 1939–1945 war. It was no accident that many felt constrained to look beyond the nation-state as the sole embodiment of their hopes for civilization and the sufficient guarantee of protection against external force. They acknowledged the compulsion of fact and saw there was no point in a loyalty which could not look beyond the confines of the nation-state.

Beyond this there was a sense that, despite all the quarrels and the wars, the differences of language and of custom, the peoples of western Europe sprang from a common root, shared one civilization, partook of one great inheritance. There was a unity underlying all the differences. Just as western Europe had counted for much in history, so it could again if civil war could be ostracized and Europe united could make its policy and action of account in the world. All these elements, revulsion from the past, the inadequacy of the present and hope for the future came together in the minds of the drafters of the Treaty of Rome.

The builders of the Community did not attempt to embody their political aims in a formal constitution. That they were prepared to leave to be worked out over the years provided that the institutions they devised pointed the member nations steadily toward unity. They further believed that immediate objectives should be practical and therefore limited. They laid primary emphasis on economic affairs because through them they saw the best way of realizing their aims while at the same time progressively linking and integrating the economic life of the nations so that in the future separation would become harder and less inviting. Hence the concentration on the well-known economic outlines of the Community, the reduction of the individual national tariffs to one tariff of the whole Community and the promotion by successive stages of the free movement of men, goods and capital within it.

But the new creative element in the treaty lay in the relationship established between two principal organs or institutions of the Community, the European Economic Commission and the Council of Ministers. They set up the Commission as a body of experts drawn from the six countries charged to think and work internationally for the common good of the whole Community. They gave it the sole power of initiative but only such powers of execution as might expressly be delegated to it by the Council of Ministers. The business of the Commission was to plan and propose in the common interest within the articles of the treaty. The Council was composed of ministers, each holding political office in his own nation, and to it was given the power of decision. The Commission proposed, the Council disposed. But in the debate or, as the French term it, the dialogue between these two bodies lay the secret of success. It was

the new way of doing things which got over and around the difficult and delicate issues of national sovereignty without tackling them
head on. For when the ministers met in council to argue out what
should be done and seek the normal compromise between national
interests, they were checked in two ways from bargaining solely in
the traditional manner. Their agenda was not chosen by themselves
or by their own officials but by an international commission thinking
in terms of the common interest. The ministers could decide only
whether to accept or reject the proposals of the Commission. Again
it followed that in their discussions the ministers were not simply
arguing with each other in the effort to compromise out national
interests: they argued in the presence of and with a solution proposed for the good of the Community as a whole. This they could
not escape: throughout they were up against this new party to the
debate. Much of the progress made has been due to the dialectical
process so set up. It has proved the dynamic element.

In the last six years the Common Market has enjoyed great prosperity: the industries of the Six have flourished, trade has expanded,
the balance of payments has been very favorable. So far it has all
been a considerable success. No doubt all the growth and prosperity
is not due to the Treaty of Rome and the experiment of the Community: much of it would have occurred in any case. But equally
and unquestionably so much would not have happened so fast but
for the dynamic forces engendered and released by the Community
working through its institutions.

Given the political aims, these economic activities and successes,
it is surely nonsense to suppose that the Community will fall apart
and be destroyed because of the decision to exclude Britain. Yet the
absence of Britain has relevance to the future development of the
Community. In September, 1961 I was invited to attend a conference at Bari in southern Italy. To it there had been invited, apart
from one or two outsiders like myself, some two hundred ministers,
civil and foreign servants, businessmen, bankers and trade unionists
from the Six. The business was to discuss the relationship of the
Community to the underdeveloped nations and to make recommendations. Early on it became evident that two widely differing
views were held. On the one hand, some of the French and Italian
representatives argued that the Community was essentially a European affair which should be concerned with those developing peoples who lived in Africa on the other side of Europe's central sea,
the Mediterranean. This Roman view entailed that the conference
should concern itself with those new states which had been African
colonies of France and Italy. They formed a natural complement
to European economies and their development should be pursued

through a special association with the Community. The German and Dutch participants were strongly opposed: they argued that the Six must be concerned with all the developing peoples; in Africa certainly but equally with those in Latin America, the Middle East or South Asia. All the world, so far as it was not fenced off by the Communist bloc, lay in the perspective of the Community, which in aid as in trade must look outward with expansionist policies.

That discussion at Bari continues today in the Community, not only in the context of the developing peoples but generally. Is the European Economic Community essentially a European affair, building itself up behind a tariff wall and acknowledging a special association with the new African states, or does it take the world as its province, seeking through successive reductions of the common tariff to encourage commerce with all the world, industrialized nations and developing peoples alike?

If Britain had entered the Common Market, our nature, history and trading needs would have compelled us to throw our whole weight on the side of the world-wide perspective and reject any view of the Community as essentially European and Mediterranean. And the added weight of Britain would have been decisive. As it is, the debate continues. There is no question that the outward-looking view has always been held by creative minds like that of Jean Monnet. It has also, by and large, characterized the outlook of the European Commission. But it is not so clear that the western Europe which General de Gaulle envisages would hold these opinions. It seems more probable that, so far as his vision prevails, the Community will look within and shy away from too close ties with the world outside.

There is a further consequence for the Community and western Europe which flows from the broad policy of General de Gaulle revealed in his decision. He believes in *L'Europe des patries*. For him the day of the independent and sovereign nation-states of Europe is not yet done: in particular the star of France will shine again in the company of her neighbors as brightly as in former centuries. French ideas, French inspiration, French leadership, close alliance with West Germany: these are the foundation of the new Europe. Such were not the beliefs of the men who made the European movement after the war and later framed the Treaty of Rome. They were convinced that they had verified in their personal experience that the future of Europe could not lie in a return to the nation-states of the nineteenth century. Alcide de Gasperi was Prime Minister of Italy but before that he had been a member of the Austrian Diet; Robert Schumann, Prime Minister and Foreign Secretary of France, had earlier been a German official; Konrad Adenauer, Chancellor of the German Federal Republic, once as mayor of Cologne contemplated the detachment of the Rhinelands from Prussia. The evidence of their own lives made them Europeans. There will therefore be argument in the Community about its future development. Progress toward that ever closer unity will be slowed down. Insofar as General de Gaulle can make his views prevail there will emerge a grouping of nation-states in close alliance under French leadership, not that unified Community which inspired the efforts of those whose aim was *faire l'Europe.*

How far does this policy of General de Gaulle affect the Atlantic Community and the purposes the United States has been pursuing? Here too there are consequences of importance. Take the statement made by President Kennedy in his speech at Philadelphia on the Fourth of July, 1962:

I will say, here and now, on this Day of Independence, that the United States will be ready for a Declaration of Interdependence—that we are prepared to discuss with a United Europe the ways and means of forming a concrete partnership—a mutually beneficial partnership between the new union now emerging in Europe and the old American Union founded here a century and three-quarters ago.

Bring into consideration the large vote which in the same year carried the new Trade Expansion Act through both branches of the Congress. Whether one takes the speech of the President or the act of the Congress, there is a clear policy expressed of closer relations between the United States and western Europe within the Atlantic Community.

Then contrast with these expressions of policy two statements of General de Gaulle, the first from his press conference of January 14, 1963, and the second from his message to the National Assembly on December 11, 1962. In the press conference he considers the hypothetical case of the British entering the Common Market and then the other states of the European Free Trade Area. He says:

Then it will be another Common Market whose construction ought to be envisaged: but one which would be taken to 11 and then to 13 and then perhaps 18 would without any doubt no longer resemble the one which the Six built. Further this Community, increasing in such a fashion, would see itself faced with problems of economic relations with all kinds of other states, and first with the United States. It is to be foreseen that the cohesion of its members, who would be very numerous and diverse, would not endure for long, and that ultimately there would appear a colossal Atlantic Community with American dependence and direction which would quickly have absorbed the Community of Europe. It is a hypothesis, which in the eyes of some can be perfectly justified, but it is not at all what France is doing or wanted to do—which is a properly European construction.

Next from the message to the National Assembly:

In order gradually to resolve the greatest problem of the world, in other words, the attainment of modern civilization by all peoples, how heavily can and should France count, given that she knows how to develop her economic, technical and cultural capacities, and provided that her authorities are in a position to apply to this end ordered and sustained effort. How true this is above all for the African states, including Algeria, with which our historic mission is realized from now on through cooperation.

Here is a confrontation of policies: on the American part an effort to bring together the two sides of the Atlantic in real partnership which would through growing interdependence give substance and form to the Atlantic Community; on the French part the need to avoid partnership or interdependence with the United States lest dependence result and prevent the development of the Community of the Six as an essentially European construction. The historic mission of France could not be realized in a great Atlantic Community: she must think first of Europe and then of the Mediterranean world.

No one can foresee the outcome of this conflict. At the moment General de Gaulle bestrides the European stage. But the voice of France is not the voice of Europe, and it does not express the united opinion of the European Economic Community. It cannot be assumed that these policies will go unchallenged or prevail unchanged. The argument is only now beginning, and General de Gaulle, on other matters of great importance to France, such as Algeria, has admitted the constraint of events and modified his views.

Perhaps one or two comments can usefully be made. There is a large body of opinion which favors British entry to the European Community. These opinions are not based upon sentiment but upon a rational judgment of enlightened self-interest. There are problems of the first magnitude for the Six which cannot be effectively dealt with in European or Mediterranean context. There is the problem of defense. There is the whole question of the free world, the assurance of its freedom and development, the issues of trade and aid, so vital for the prosperity of the European industrialized nations. There are difficulties about agricultural policy, commercial policy, monetary policy. None of these can be tackled satisfactorily without the United States and Britain. There is a logic of fact which compels attention.

Second, because Britain is now excluded from the Common Market it must not be assumed that this will always be so. Britain is part of Europe, and an important part. It is true that she is a member of a Commonwealth of Nations but this is to the advantage of an outward-looking and expansionist Europe. And in the longer

103

run the pressures on the highly industrialized states of the Community will reinforce this attitude. The Six, like Britain or for that matter the United States, need a large environment in which to move and trade and live.

Last, the fact must be faced that the policy of partnership and interdependence between the two sides of the Atlantic has received a serious setback for the time being. The pace President Kennedy hoped to set has been slowed. But this does not mean that nothing can be done to strengthen the relations between the Atlantic group of countries. There already exist two great multilateral institutions, NATO and the OECD, through both of which progress can be made. There is no reason to believe that General de Gaulle rejects the North Atlantic Treaty or concerted measures for the common defense. There is evidence for this in the recent agreement to set up an interallied nuclear force. His objection is to an American monopoly of nuclear capability, to dependence on the United States: hence the insistence on France developing her own nuclear weapons. Again there is no reason to think that he will object to cooperation, when it is expedient, in economic matters. Partnership or interdependence he will not have: these imply agreed common objectives of policy and a commitment to continuous joint action to bring them into being. He is convinced that this would lead to dependence on the United States. The risk is that there will be substituted for joint working based on mutual trust a retrogression to suspicious, traditional diplomacy between sovereign states, which will limit and retard their cooperation.

There are those who, impatient with this ebullition of nationalism, would wish to press on through NATO and the OECD to the multilateral solution of problems. If France will not join in, they say, let her be excluded. Surely this is a short-sighted point of view. Like Britain, France is an essential part of western Europe. It is a time for firmness of purpose and patience in action, both exercised in the belief that the policies of General de Gaulle in the end look to a past which is gone beyond recall, and that the nations of western Europe will remain true to their inspiration and will go on building a united Community, in due time including Britain.

KLAUS EPSTEIN

The Adenauer Era in German History

THE POSTWAR POLITICS of West Germany have been dominated, to a far greater extent than is the case in any other European country, by a single man, the monumental figure of Konrad Adenauer. His retirement from office on October 15, 1963, after holding the chancellorship for fourteen years, affords a good occasion for assessing the development of the Bonn Republic since its founding in 1949.

Where does the Federal Republic stand today in its international position and domestic structure? What have been the major achievements, what the significant failings of the fourteen years of the Adenauer era? To what extent has its history been shaped by objective factors beyond the influence of any man; to what extent has Adenauer personally influenced events which another chancellor would have determined otherwise? The following essay can be only a preliminary attempt to answer these questions, since it is obviously too early for a truly historical perspective; yet the present moment appears as a suitable time for taking stock, measuring achievements, and pointing out problems still unsolved.

I Foreign Policy

The most notable achievements of the Bonn Republic have without question been in the field of foreign policy. The Germany of 1949 was ruined by the Second World War, degraded by Nazism, and filled with resentment and disappointed hopes after four years of military occupation. It was morally isolated in the world by the continued hatred of the numerous victims of Nazi policy. There was general agreement that Germany must never again possess an army which might repeat the aggressions of the past. The partition of Germany between an East Zone, occupied and communized by Russia, and three western zones (only recently

105

merged into a single political and economic unit) was an accomplished fact. The federal government was formed under a constitution substantially influenced by the wishes of the occupying powers, which incidentally retained control of many important matters—including foreign policy, foreign trade, and military security—under a far-reaching Occupation Statute. It was a crippled government with territorial jurisdiction over only 60 per cent of prewar Germany which was launched in 1949. The sole consolation could be found in the fact that there was no direction to go except *upwards*—and that the new government was therefore likely to achieve some aura of success as it led Germans out of the nadir of their history.

How different was the position of West Germany in 1963! The residues of the occupation regime had been dismantled in rapid stages, with "sovereignty" being achieved after only six years in 1955. The moral isolation had been pierced by means of a far-reaching reconciliation with its western former enemies—a reconciliation which took on special intensity in the case of France. Germany had been welcomed into NATO and had become an influential and valued member of the western community of nations. It was a strong champion of western European unity and held original memberships in such important institutions as the Schuman Plan Community for Coal and Steel and the European Common Market. Rearmament, which had seemed quite inconceivable in 1949, was an accomplished fact, and West Germany possessed the strongest conventional military power in Europe west of the Iron Curtain. Its return to a position of power and influence had been widely accepted as a "normal" and even desirable development. The sole drawback in the record of magnificent achievement was the failure to make the slightest progress in the direction of reunification.

THE OPTION FOR THE WEST AND
THE PERSONAL ROLE OF ADENAUER

How were these great successes achieved? Partly it was through the operation of objective factors of which Germany was the beneficiary. Public opinion in the West—and more especially in the United States—inevitably abandoned the vindictive follies which had marked the first years after 1945; it became anxious to receive a Germany purged of Nazism as an alliance partner. The European movement, which transcended the suicidal nationalism of the past, was eager to accept Germany as an equal partner. Most important of all, however, was the intensification of the cold war between the Soviet Union and the free world, with the latter desiring to build "positions of strength" everywhere along the Soviet periphery as part of a policy of "containment." The West simply could not afford to leave Germany's potential strength—economic, political, and soon military—idle in the face of the Soviet challenge.

It is to the credit of Konrad Adenauer, who personally dominated German foreign policy throughout his chancellorship, that he understood these facts better than anybody else, and that he pursued with singular tenacity a policy which took maximum advantage of them. His policy was in essence one of clear-cut option for the West in the belief that Germany's interests were essentially identical with those of the western powers, and that the latter were willing to give Germany genuine partnership by progressively dismantling the discriminatory status of the occupation regime. Adenauer saw, moveover, that the crucial first step was to establish an atmosphere of trust and cordiality which would gradually remove the suspicions of the past: given such an improvement in the overall climate there would be little difficulty about achieving close institutional ties between Germany and the West. This improvement in overall climate presupposed an unmistakable and irreversible German option for the West since the West had unfortunate memories of Germany's seesaw policy between East and West during the Weimar Republic. This option was made easy for Adenauer because he hated Communism with a missionary fervor; because he had never been a German nationalist, with all that this implied in terms of suspicion of and contempt for the "philistine, hedonist, materialistic West"; and because he was a sober realist who understood the fact that Germany was no longer in a position to conduct an independent foreign policy of its own. Adenauer saw that West Germany was too big to become a neutral buffer state between East and West, like Austria or Sweden, and too small to conduct a genuinely independent foreign policy. Alliance with Communism was unthinkable; hence alliance with the West was the correct policy for Germany. This result of sober analysis was backed in Adenauer's case by a strong attachment to the European idea, an emotional sympathy for France, and a deep appreciation of the commanding role played by the United States as the leader of the free world since 1945.

Could another chancellor have acted differently in Adenauer's place? His Socialist opponents were until recently opposed to the policy of exclusive reliance upon the western alliance. They favored some kind of arrangement with Russia, in order to secure the reunification of Germany, which they correctly predicted

Adenauer's pro-western orientation could not bring—hence their opposition to such crucial Adenauer policies as the Schuman Plan, NATO membership, and rearmament. It should be stressed that their opposition was in no sense indicative of any "softness toward Communism"; it was exclusively the result of a passionate preoccupation with Germany's reunification. It will be argued below that the alternative policy—reunification through neutralization, that is, the nonacceptance or repudiation of Western ties—was unrealistic and offered little prospect of success; but this is irrelevant in considering the question of whether a Socialist chancellor would have conducted a foreign policy different from Adenauer's. It would be insulting to the Socialist leaders to suggest that they opposed Adenauer's pro-western orientation *only* because they were in opposition; hence it is the view of this author that Adenauer's personal role was very important in shaping the course of German foreign policy.

The point may be summarized as follows: If it is true that the great foreign policy achievements could be won only through Adenauer's clear-cut option for the West; if it is true that the Socialists opposed that option on principle and would have refused to make it if they had formed the government in 1949; then it follows that Adenauer's formation of an anti-Socialist coalition in 1949 (in opposition to the widespread clamor even within his own Christian Democratic party for a "great coalition" with the Socialists) was the necessary prerequisite for the great achievements won by Germany on the international stage since 1949. This is certainly the view of Konrad Adenauer himself.

Adenauer's personal contribution is by no means limited to making the not-inevitable western option; he was also in many ways the ideal man to preside over Germany's reconciliation with its western former enemies. Adenauer showed great persistence of aim. He established especially cordial relations with western leaders; and he clearly understood the role of moral factors in drawing Germany out of the isolation wrought by Nazi crimes.

The Chancellor showed exemplary tenacity of purpose in the face of temporary reverses, painfully slow progress, and the opposition of large strata of German public opinion to his policy. All of these qualities were necessary in the course of the long struggle over German rearmament. The settlement of the issue was dragged out over five years, from the initial decision for rearmament produced by the "Korean panic" of 1950 to Germany's admission to NATO in 1955. Rearmament received a serious setback when the French killed the plan for a European Defense Community in 1954 after more than two years of protracted debate—yet Adenauer refused to despair and in fact quickly joined British Foreign Secretary Sir Anthony Eden in working out an alternative arrangement. Adenauer ignored the formidable German sentiment against rearmament revealed by public opinion polls and the various *Länder* elections of the summer of 1951. The Chancellor rightly foresaw that conditions would change; he was resolved, in any case, to be right rather than popular, and he had the eventual satisfaction of being both. His conduct added very much to his public stature in the long run by impressing both his fellow countrymen and foreigners with his steadiness of purpose.

Adenauer's willingness to make concrete concessions to France in return for the mere *intangible* of French good will has been one of the most controversial aspects of his foreign policy. Germany agreed to join the International Ruhr Authority demanded by France in 1949, although it meant a discriminatory internationalization of its key industrial area; the concession became harmless when the multilateral Schuman Plan supplanted the International Authority in 1952. Adenauer publicly gave his support in 1955 to a French plan to internationalize the Saar territory (which France had administered through a puppet government since 1945), although this implied the permanent loss of undisputably German territory and the continuation of thinly veiled French control. He placed friendship with France above Germany's legitimate claims, and he was rewarded by the good fortune that an unforseen development, the rejection of the International Statute by the Saar population, killed that statute and left no alternative but the return of the disputed territory to Germany. Adenauer achieved the almost impossible feat of securing the return of the Saar and cementing Franco-German friendship at one and the same time. (It may be added that the claim of his more fervent admirers that he had foreseen this entire course of events from the very beginning is historically untenable.) The German government unhesitantly supported many steps of western European integration under which Germany paid most of the bill and France received most of the benefits, for example the so-called "development fund" for promoting economic progress in France's former African colonies, now members of the French Union. This policy of unilateral concession to win the friendship of France—a policy incessantly criticized by the German opposition—must be considered fully justified by the course of Franco-German conciliation.

Adenauer's excellent personal relations with leading American and French—less so with British—statesmen contributed to Germany's cordial acceptance by the western alliance. The confidence which was at first bestowed upon him personally was gradually extended to his fellow countrymen as well. Adenauer worked especially closely with John J. McCloy, the first American High Commissioner who played the central role in America's German policy in the crucial years 1949–1952. The German Chancellor became America's favorite ally in the six years that John Foster Dulles was Secretary of State (1953–1959). His relationship to the leading figures of the Kennedy Administration was considerably less happy, but this proved of comparatively little importance since the Federal Republic had by 1961 less to hope from American favor and less to fear from American resentment. The Chancellor's cordial relationship with leading French statesmen proved even more important. He worked well with Foreign Minister Robert Schuman, who courageously defied much French opinion to secure a reconciliation with Germany. The ideological principles of Schuman's Mouvement Républicain Populaire were very close to those of Adenauer's CDU. The German Chancellor proved equally fortunate—and skillful—in establishing excellent relations with President Charles de Gaulle, whose authoritarian and antiparliamentary views (not to speak of his anglophobia) were not unlike Adenauer's. The rapprochement with France—even de Gaulle's anti-American France—became indeed something of an obsession with the aging Chancellor, as will be discussed in detail below.

Adenauer showed superb skill in influencing the public opinion of western countries in a manner favorable to Germany. His virtuosity in using interviews with the foreign press to promote understanding for German problems—and to apply pressure on the Allied High Commissioners while Bonn was not yet permitted to have a foreign office during the years 1949 to 1952—is generally acknowledged. He has understood the role played by moral factors in molding western public opinion, and this has certainly influenced his decision to press hard for a restitution agreement with Israel. Adenauer not only—it goes without saying—personally abhorred the criminal genocide practiced by the Nazi government against European Jewry; he also clearly saw that Germany could never regain normal relations with other countries unless it made whatever token reparation that could still be made for this unparalleled crime. When the Israeli government—for understandable reasons—refused to open negotiations with West Germany, he used the mediation of American Jewish leadership to secure agreement to a treaty whereby Germany made an important contribution to Israel's economic development for a ten-year period. It is to Adenauer's credit that he saw this question as one of morality and public policy, and swept aside all the legalistic obstacles which some of his advisers urged upon him, for instance, whether Israel was entitled to claim reparations for the murdered European Jews who had never had any connection with the then nonexistent state.

It is clear that Adenauer's option for the West has resulted in a *fait accompli* for the Federal Republic—a fact signalized by the Socialist abandonment of opposition to this policy in 1960, to be discussed below. Germany is today economically, militarily, and politically so interrelated with the West as to make withdrawal into neutralization or rapprochement with Russia quite unthinkable. Its economy is geared to the Common Market, its coal and steel industries to the Schuman Plan, its atomic program to Euratom— to withdraw from these bodies would obviously have catastrophic consequences for the German economy. Its army is wholly committed to NATO and stands under NATO command, while the voluntary German renunciation of the manufacture of atomic, bacteriological, and chemical weapons makes it incapable of fighting an independent war. Its security—and more especially that of Berlin—is completely dependent upon the support of its western partners, and more especially that of the United States. Its capitalist system and democratic form of government, and allegiance to the principles of liberty and self-determination for East Germans, make it an object of suspicion to the Russians quite apart from its Nazi past. Even if it were able to break loose from the West— which it is not—it would be quite incapable of establishing a cordial relationship with Russia through neutralization or any other relationship other than the status of a total satellite (a point which will be discussed in detail below). It may be safely asserted, then, that the Federal Republic has under Adenauer become a reliable member of the western alliance—and that this fact constitutes a major turning point in German history.

THE FAILURE TO ACHIEVE UNIFICATION

All of Adenauer's great achievements in foreign policy—German sovereignty, western European integration, participation in NATO, reconciliation with France, and close friendship with the United States—have been purchased at a great, and for many Germans an intolerable, price: there has been no progress whatsoever towards German reunification. The German people find themselves divided, in 1963 as in 1949, into two hostile states marked by antagonistic social structures, antagonistic principles, and participation in the antagonistic alliances of the two sides which divide the world in the cold war. It is most improbable that this situation could have been avoided if Germany had pursued a policy other

111

than Adenauer's option for the West and refusal to parley with the Russians. The policy advocated with vacillating persistence by his Socialist opponents until 1959—loosening of western ties through demilitarization and neutralization as an inducement to achieve Russian consent to reunification—never stood much chance of Russian acceptance at any time, and it was formally rejected by Khrushchev in 1959. It must always be remembered that the Russian military administration had gone far towards socializing the East Zone by 1949; that it had united the Communist and Socialist parties through a shotgun marriage as early as 1946; and that it stood committed to maintaining its own adherents—Pieck, Grotewohl, and above all Ulbricht—in power. It has been clear since 1949 that meaningful unification through free elections must lead to the elimination of Moscow's supporters, the re-establishment of a free Socialist party, and the dismantling of at least some of the collectivist institutions established in the Russian zone of occupation. Is it conceivable that Russia would have allowed all this? Would such a settlement not have had vast repercussions throughout the Russian satellite empire? And would the neutralization of West Germany have in fact constituted an adequate purchase price for the Russian surrender of East Germany, especially as there could be little question that a neutralized, reunited Germany of the future would be economically and culturally tied to the West, even if prohibited specific military and political ties.

It appears probable, at least in the opinion of this writer, that Adenauer's policy of opting clearly for the West did *not* prevent the unification of Germany, as charged by his opponents; it appears that there never was a realistic chance to achieve unification. It will be long debated, however, by future historians whether Adenauer actually saw the situation in this light and deliberately based his policy of western integration upon the premise that reunification was objectively *unattainable,* and that its pursuit through a policy of neutralization could only compromise the attainable goal of close ties with the Atlantic Community without bringing the least benefit to the East Germans. The problem of unfathoming Adenauer's real views is created by the fact that it would have been political suicide for any German chancellor to base his policy upon the open avowal that reunification was unattainable. Adenauer in fact always insisted—was by political necessity compelled to insist—that western integration was in no sense an alternative to reunification, did not imply any renunciation of unification, but was rather a step towards unification.

This was the famous policy of building western "positions of strength" which could subsequently be exploited to compel—by means which were never specifically elaborated—the Russians to concede reunification. It is abundantly clear today that this policy was totally mistaken in its premises so far as the attainment of its avowed goal of reunification was concerned. How could even a very strong West extort freedom for East Germany through merely diplomatic pressure? That no one would be willing to apply military pressure in an age of atomic weapons—and Russia possessed the A-bomb after September, 1949—was abundantly demonstrated by western passivity at the time of the 1953 East German uprising. There was an additional obstacle to the implementing of Adenauer's "policy of strength," namely the notorious reluctance of some western powers—and more especially France—to engage in any exertion to achieve German unification; it was an open secret that they were far from displeased by the partition of Germany and feared the hegemonial position which a reunited Germany would inevitably claim within western Europe.

It is clear, in the light of these considerations, that Adenauer's "policy of strength" never had the slightest chance of achieving German unification. This does not, of course, mean that this policy was intrinsically mistaken; on the contrary, it achieved what was attainable—a viable West Germany closely linked with the Atlantic Community—and failed to achieve only what the alternative policy of neutralization was also unlikely to achieve, because it was objectively unattainable—German unification. What is certain is that Adenauer's "policy of strength" served the essential function of winning German public opinion for western integration while concealing from the nation the terrible fact that all reunification hopes must be abandoned for the foreseeable future. It is an interesting but insolvable problem whether Adenauer ever subjectively believed that the "policy of strength" would in fact lead to unification, or whether he employed it consciously as a "royal lie" on the maxim that a German statesman after 1949 could not pursue the sensible thing—western integration—merely because it was sensible, but had to sell it to German public opinion with the false claim that it also led to unification. There is much evidence for the view that the Chancellor genuinely believed, at least until the late 1950's, that Russia would concede unification to the "policy of strength." Some of his speeches showed an amazing primitivity in assessing the strength of the Communist world: there were occasional predictions of the imminent general collapse of Communism, or at least the depiction of a Russia standing under such severe overall strain —from internal problems, Chinese rivalry and western pressures— that it must seek an accommodation with the West even if this meant the abandonment of Ulbricht and Co. (It is well known that John Foster Dulles occasionally suffered from similar illusions.) It is, in short, possible to vindicate the honesty of Adenauer's "policy of strength" at the price of his intelligence. There can, on the other hand, be no question—nor is this necessarily discreditable to him—that Adenauer was perfectly capable of foisting a "royal lie" upon his people if he considered this necessary to achieve a laudable end—Western integration—which otherwise might remain unachieved.

The problem of defining what were Adenauer's real intentions is further complicated by the widespread impression that it cost Adenauer little internal sacrifice to renounce the prospect of early unification. His outspoken critics have often asserted that at heart he did not really desire reunification, or at least did not desire it with the proper emotional intensity. They ascribe this "defect" either to a Rhenish provincialism which believes that "Asia starts at the Elbe," or a partisan view that a reunified Germany—with a big Protestant majority—might be less solidly CDU than what his opponents call the "Rhenish Republic." It is certain that there is much exaggeration in these insulting charges; but it is probably true—and in fact in no way to Adenauer's discredit—that he has not made German reunification the highest priority aim of his foreign policy, and he has certainly not wanted reunification at any price. He has never been a nationalist in his long public career, even when it was politically expedient to act like one (as was true during the Weimar Republic); he has always been a good European in the sense that he wanted his native Germany to emphasize the European heritage that it shared with its western neighbors and more especially with France. It is, therefore, probable that he wanted western integration after 1949 at *almost* any price, including a delay in achieving (or even the abandonment of) the goal of national unification. There is, however, let me repeat, no conclusive evidence that he believed that Germany would have to make a choice between unification and western integration. His unhesitant and inflexible support of an unambiguously pro-western policy can best be explained by his belief that there was no necessity to make a choice between two desirable goals—Western integration and German unification—which his opponents believed to be incompatible.

Adenauer's belief in the "policy of strength" as the road to unification was no doubt confirmed by his clear understanding of the above outlined reasons why Russia was most unlikely to concede unification, if the alternative policy of separation from the West through an offer of neutralization were tried. It is certain, moreover, that Adenauer saw great disadvantages in a reunification achieved through neutralization (if by a miracle the Russians should have conceded it). He obviously feared a Germany which was thrown upon itself and deprived of the stabilizing force of full integration into the West. There would be danger of a resurgence of a self-centered nationalism and an abandonment of allegiance to the common European traditions which had won a perhaps precarious ascendancy after 1945. There would be a significant Communist "fifth column" in a reunited Germany, since the Russians would presumably insist upon some kind of guarantees for their supporters as part of any reunification settlement. There would be the probable loss of a CDU majority, if not in the first then in the second national election following reunification, in view of the traditional Protestant and Socialist outlook of the East German population. There would, last but not least, be the danger of a total collapse of NATO if West Germany ceased to be a member of the anti-Communist alliance. It was doubtful whether western Europe minus West Germany was, geographically and strategically, large enough as a staging area for the deployment of modern armies; it was certain that American troops would be withdrawn across the Atlantic whereas Russian troops would presumably continue to be stationed in Poland. How secure would a neutralized Germany be under these circumstances, and how likely to resist future Communist threats and subversion? The force of these arguments suggests that Adenauer had good reasons (in his own mind at least) to prefer a democratic West Germany tied securely to the West to a neutralized reunited Germany with precarious external and internal prospects. It should be repeated, however, that there is no reason to believe that Adenauer ever thought in terms of such alternatives. There is much evidence that he believed that a successful "policy of strength" could result in a Germany reunited upon his own terms and remaining a part of the Western alliance.

If one concedes that unification through western strength was unattainable—the thesis of Adenauer's Socialist critics—and that unification through a neutralization was probably unattainable and certainly undesirable—the thesis of Adenauer—one cannot criticize Adenauer for his failure to achieve unification. It remains to be said, however, that Adenauer did not do enough to counteract the legend—if it is a legend—that his government never really desired unification of any type. The widely believed charge is given apparent substance by Adenauer's curt rejection of various Russian offers, more especially in 1952, to reunify Germany upon terms of neutralization. We have seen above that it is most unlikely that these proposals were seriously meant; they were most likely pure propaganda measures calculated to sow dissension between Germany and its new western friends at the critical moment when the fate of the European Defense Community hung in the balance. If Adenauer had entered into negotiations, he certainly would have helped to kill the EDC and to provoke grave western suspicions that Germany was reviving the old "seesaw" policy between East and West. The result of negotiations, ending in inevitable failure, would have been to place Germany between two stools, with its western friendships compromised, reunification unachieved, and relations with Russia embittered by frustrated hopes and recrimination about who was responsible for failure. I believe that the federal government cannot, in the light of these circumstances, be blamed for its refusal to negotiate in 1952; the alternative policy of unmasking the insincerity of Russian proposals through detailed negotiations simply entailed too great risks. The domestic result of the former policy must, however, be described as deplorable: millions of West Germans have today the fixed belief that Adenauer is *as* responsible as Ulbricht for Germany's continued partition. This suspicion has contributed enormously to poisoning the entire political climate of the Federal Republic; and Adenauer has—irrespective of the defensibility of his curt reply to the Russians in 1952—done too little to prevent it from arising in the first place and assuming a good deal of plausibility from his overall conduct.

WEST GERMAN POLICY TOWARDS THE D.D.R. AND THE EASTERN FRONTIERS

While failing to achieve unification, the Federal Republic has insisted—with broad success so far as the non-Communist world is concerned—that it is the only legitimate German government. It has refused to extend formal recognition to the Russian satellite government ruling in East Berlin, and it expects its friends and allies to take the same attitude. Under the so-called "Hallstein doctrine," named after the former Foreign Office Staatssekretaer who is now president of the European Common Market, the Federal Republic breaks off, or refuses to take up, diplomatic relations with any country other than Russia which has, or enters upon, diplomatic relations with the so-called German Democratic Republic (D.D.R.). The mere threat to break off relations has generally sufficed to keep the D.D.R. isolated diplomatically; its implementation has so far proved necessary only in the single case of Yugoslavia when Marshal Tito recognized Ulbricht's government in 1957.

The Hallstein doctrine is not based—as ignorant critics some-times charge—upon the premise that the East German regime does not exist; it is based rather upon the correct premise that there is no moral equivalency between the Bonn and East Berlin govern-ments. The former is based upon the free mandate of a free people given in free elections; the latter is feared and hated by its people and is propped up exclusively by Russian bayonets. To expect the West German government to treat its East German rival as an equal (for example, by entering upon bilateral negotiations to achieve German unification) is to ignore this obvious fact. The Hallstein doctrine symbolizes the West German claim to speak for the entire German people, and the hope that Germany will some day be reunited under a single, democratically elected govern-ment, which would in fact be an extension of the present West German political system to all of Germany. The East German de-sire for diplomatic recognition symbolizes, on the other hand, the desire to perpetuate the present partition of Germany into two states with antagonistic political and social systems. The leaders of East Germany know that they cannot extend their system to all of Germany through free elections; they know, indeed, that they cannot survive in their present territory if free elections were held there. They desperately seek, therefore, to buttress their position—equally precarious at home and abroad—by securing diplomatic recognition. The function of the Hallstein doctrine is to prevent the upgrading and consolidation of the East German regime which this would signify.

The sentiments behind the Hallstein doctrine are impeccable, but it is unfortunate that they have been crystallized into doctrinal rigidity. The doctrine was—and still is—understandable as the theoretical affirmation of West Germany's claims and hopes; but it made sense as a practical policy only as a temporary measure isolating an already toppling D.D.R. It has become something of a liability to the Federal Republic in a world situation where the D.D.R. is likely to stay with us for a long time to come. The doctrine offers the "uncommitted nations" extensive blackmailing opportuni-ties against Bonn, for example in the matter of foreign aid; it is generally believed that the threat of opening diplomatic relations with East Berlin is sometimes used to extort aid allocations from Bonn. The Hallstein doctrine has also prevented the normalization of relations with the various East European peoples which as Russian satellites have no choice but to recognize the D.D.R.

Normal relations with Poland, Russia's most important satellite, have also been prevented by the troubled issue of the Oder-Neisse territories occupied by Poland "provisionally" since 1945. No one can reasonably expect any independent German government to formally renounce all claims to these territories prior to a general peace settlement; but this consideration cannot excuse the sometimes disgraceful activities of the German refugee groups (the so-called *Landsmannschaften*) whose annual monster gatherings, financed in part by the Ministry for All German Affairs, are an embarrassment to all foreign friends of Germany. Their constant verbal reiteration of a policy of "no vindictiveness" towards the Eastern peoples is belied by their spirit of crude nationalism and irresponsible defamation of all *Verzichtpolitiker,* a wide term covering all Germans who talk sense about the Eastern boundaries. Adenauer has taken, on several occasions, cautious preliminary steps for improving relations with the Eastern peoples; this has regularly provoked a howl of indignation from refugee groups to which the Chancellor has usually surrendered. His government cannot be absolved from the charge of having at times given encouragement to the unrealistic hope that these Eastern territories will return to Germany at some time in the future. This encouragement has certainly contributed to the enormous amount of wishful thinking and calculated hypocrisy which befogs the entire Oder-Neisse issue in German public opinion. The explanation for Adenauer's irresponsibility is easy to find; he needed the organized refugee vote in order to maintain himself in power. It was a clear case of the primacy of domestic over foreign policy. There is no evidence that Adenauer ever strove to undercut the refugee leaders by making an agreement with the Socialist leadership to avoid an irresponsible competition for the refugee vote.

GERMANY BETWEEN THE UNITED STATES AND FRANCE

The magnificent clarity which characterized German foreign policy during the entire 1950s was unhappily shattered during the last three years of Adenauer's chancellorship by three interrelated factors: the obvious failure of the "policy of strength" to achieve anything more than the containment of Russia, instead of the hoped-for rollback including unification; the atmosphere of suspicion and recrimination which entered into the relations between Washington and Bonn; and the increasing intimacy between Bonn and Paris despite the fact that de Gaulle's foreign policy could be described only as anti-American. The result was that German foreign policy began to flounder and that Germany was placed in the embarrassing (albeit flattering) position of being wooed (but also implicitly threatened) by President John F. Kennedy and General Charles de Gaulle at one and the same time.

The limitations of the "policy of strength" became dramatically apparent when the Allied powers proved unable to prevent the building of the Berlin Wall on August 13, 1961. It was clear that a policy which could not even prevent the deterioration of the precarious Berlin position was little likely to achieve the forward step of unifying all of Germany. This "moment of truth" certainly cost Adenauer a great many votes in the ensuing September elections—enough to make his CDU party lose its absolute majority and thereby impair Adenauer's political standing during the last two years of his chancellorship. There can be no question that Adenauer felt betrayed by the American government, which had contributed to his poor pre-election "image" by vetoing his plan to go with Vice President Lyndon B. Johnson on the morale-boosting trip to West Berlin. (The American government feared that Adenauer's presence might trigger off an explosive uprising in East Germany with which it was not prepared to cope.)

The American passivity in the face of the Berlin Wall was only one of several factors which convinced the Chancellor that President Kennedy was basically "soft on Communism." The German government disliked the plans of the Kennedy Administration for a new Berlin settlement which would include an International Access Authority. Such an authority must involve an upgrading of the D.D.R. (whose participation was contemplated) and a downgrading of Allied responsibility for the security of Berlin (in view of the international features of the plan). The plan was killed at least temporarily through premature publicity resulting from what was generally believed to be a German journalistic indiscretion; its demise gave the Bonn leadership a bad reputation in Washington as incorrigible cold warriors.

The real damage to German-American relations was, however, produced by the close intimacy between Germany and France symbolized by the Pact of Friendship and Consultation signed at Paris on January 22, 1963. The United States had, of course, long favored Franco-German reconciliation as the cornerstone of a strong and unified western Europe: but it wanted a Europe eager to cooperate with the United States within the overall framework of the Atlantic Community. This was not De Gaulle's conception of the new Europe, as was shown by his veto of Britain's membership in the European Common Market and by his insulting suggestion that America would not honor its strategic commitments in the face of Russia's threat of atomic retaliation. These Gaullist positions were announced eight days before the Franco-German pact was signed, and the American government obviously resented the fact that Germany signed the treaty nonetheless. For some time thereafter nothing done by the German government could erase the impression that Bonn had become a satellite of De Gaulle's anti-American policy, though Germany accepted the American-proposed multilateral atomic fleet despised by De Gaulle, who was bent upon his own *force de frappe,* and vigorously supported Britain's application to the Common Market, though Bonn could not override the French veto. The cloud upon German-American relations was lifted briefly by President Kennedy's successful visit to Germany in June, 1963, which stood in clear competition to De Gaulle's triumphant tour nine months earlier. The recrimination was resumed, however, when the Germans believed themselves inadequately consulted before the signing of the Moscow Test Ban Treaty, whose "accession clause" inevitably gave some upgrading to the D.D.R. It continued when Adenauer denounced the American plan to sell wheat to Russia as an example of Kennedy's "softness towards Communism." These cumulative frictions led to the development of what one might call a "Gaullist" party within Germany's ruling CDU, that is, a group which was deeply suspicious of America and was therefore willing to cooperate with most of De Gaulle's policies. The real chief of this party was Konrad Adenauer himself—a sad anticlimax of a career whose great foreign policy achievements were primarily the result of his intimate alliance with the United States.

It is unlikely, however, that the aberrations of Adenauer's last phase have done any permanent damage to Germany's international position. The new chancellor, Ludwig Erhard, and his foreign minister, Gerhard Schröder, who was far from happy about Adenauer's Parisian flirtation, are both determined champions of the American alliance. They are willing to cooperate with the American policy of negotiating with the Russians on Berlin and other questions, and they are quite free of Adenauer's suspiciousness towards America, born of thwarted love. They know the importance of the reconciliation with France, but they have told De Gaulle in unmistakable terms that Germany will not accept his lead in foreign affairs. They are eager to work with Great Britain and hope that its admission to Europe has been postponed rather than prevented. Their views on all these questions are supported by a majority within the Christian Democratic and with virtual unanimity by the Social Democratic and Free Democratic parties. The only chance for the competing "Gaullist" sentiment, headed by the retired but still active Adenauer, lies in the remote possibility that America might disregard vital German interests (for example, by recognizing the D.D.R.) or live up to De Gaulle's prediction that it is an unreliable ally (for example, by electing an isolationist President).

It may be said in conclusion that Adenauer's legacy is better than his conduct of foreign policy after 1961 would suggest. Germany's commitment to the West is an irreversible fact, and it is determined to play a loyal role within the NATO alliance, of which it is the second strongest conventional military power. Reconciliation with France is a permanent achievement which does not require servility towards De Gaulle to be maintained. Involvement in the Common Market economy is an incontrovertible fact, since withdrawing from it would have catastrophic consequences for the German economy. Germany has won the respect and in some cases the friendship of its numerous former enemies, and the moral isolation of 1949 has become nothing but an unhappy memory. Most important of all is the alliance with America, which is so much based upon mutual self-interest that it can only be impaired, not destroyed, by suspicions and recriminations like those of recent years. It may be said, then, that the foreign policy legacy of the Adenauer era is a magnificent success—though rejoicing must be tempered by the bitter fact that progress towards reunification has been nonexistent.

THE USE OF FOREIGN POLICY FOR PARTISAN PURPOSES

One further point must be made in connection with Adenauer's foreign policy since 1949. The Chancellor has brilliantly succeeded in converting foreign policy into an electoral ace to maintain himself domestically in power. He has never hesitated to defame the Social Democratic party's opposition for its alleged insufficient firmness against Communism—a completely unjustified charge reminiscent of American McCarthyism at its worst. Adenauer for years poisoned German public discussion of the unification question by denouncing various SPD plans—which were born of patriotic concern and an emotional solidarity with the people of the East Zone which Adenauer did not happen to feel with the same intensity—as arising from a "soft on Communism" mentality. Yet there can be no question that the SPD has been a consistent and intransigent foe of Communism ever since the Russian Revolution of 1917. It is probable, but not absolutely certain, that Adenauer acted contrary to his better knowledge in this campaign of defamation against the SPD; though it is just barely possible that he has really never overcome the anti-Socialist complexes which bedevilled the German bourgeoisie at the time of his early manhood during the Wilhelmine period of the 1890s. It is certain, in any case, that he made no genuine attempt to achieve a common foreign policy with the SPD in the early years of the Bonn Republic; though it must be said in extenuation that the passionately nationalist opposition leader Kurt Schumacher was about as difficult a negotiating partner in this field as one can imagine. What is regrettable is the fact that Adenauer was quite satisfied with the opposition of the SPD to his foreign policy; it led the Socialists into a *cul de sac* and allowed Adenauer to monopolize the winning policies of western integration and the American alliance for his Christian Democratic party. When the SPD "came over" to his foreign policy in 1960, Adenauer feared to lose his best election ace; he consequently took the lead in questioning the sincerity of the Socialist "conversion" to NATO and the Atlantic Community. It was a case of the Chancellor placing the interests of his party before those of the country as a whole, which obviously would gain from a common foreign policy to meet the difficult challenge of the 1960s. Adenauer's conduct was symptomatic of the fact that the party politician was never far from the statesman's heart. Perhaps this should not be criticized too harshly; the virtues of statesmen out of office have little interest for the later historian. Adenauer needed fourteen years of firmly entrenched power—confirmed by three successive national elections—in order to place his imprint upon an entire era, and his election victories would propably have been impossible but for his habitual employment of unfair electioneering techniques.

Adenauer's continued libels against the SPD have tended to obscure what is in many ways the greatest of all of his triumphs in the foreign policy field—the above mentioned conversion of the opposition Socialist party to the basic position it had bitterly opposed for a decade. When Herbert Wehner, the leader of the SPD, emphasized his party's loyalty to NATO in his famous speech of June 30, 1960, West Germany at last secured that "agreement on fundamentals" in foreign policy which is characteristic of mature democracies. When the SPD began in 1961 to criticize Adenauer's alleged inflexibility in the cold war on the ground that it threatened the American alliance (as the Kennedy Administration strove for a new Berlin settlement), the Chancellor could tell himself that *that* kind of criticism from *that* source was the finest vindication of the way he had conducted foreign policy during the previous twelve years. He had always insisted that it was more important to have the right than a common foreign policy; he left a Germany where his successor could have both without encountering partisan difficulties.

II Domestic Policy

The domestic record of the Adenauer era is also marked by very solid achievements. The major accomplishments may be listed as follows: the development of a prosperous economy out of the greatest rubble heap in history; the achievement of a well-functioning democracy based upon virtually-unanimous consent; the reduction of the pre-Nazi party chaos to three parties, of which each combines heterogeneous elements and is predisposed to the art of political compromise; the prevention of any significant neo-Nazism or other radicalism; and the building of a new army under firm civilian control (instead of restoring the deplorable Weimar situation where the army was a "state within the state"). It will be shown that each of these accomplishments is by no means free of blemishes, but it must be stressed that the overall record is very impressive indeed. Who would have been willing to predict confidently in 1949 that democratic government would flourish, the German party system gain simplicity, neo-Nazism vanish, a German army be recreated, and prosperity create a completely new pattern of life?

The success of West Germany in all these matters is primarily due to the Germans themselves under the great leadership of Konrad Adenauer, but some credit must also be given to the much-maligned work of the military government in the years 1945–1949. It did much of the "dirty work" which had internally discredited the Weimar Republic a quarter century earlier. The Bonn Republic did not have to accept a humiliating peace treaty, as Weimar accepted Versailles after fratricidal debates; the terms of peace were dictated *de facto* before the Bonn government was inaugurated in 1949. That government did not have to liquidate a revolution, as Ebert and Scheidemann were forced to do in 1919; it did not confront anti-republican leagues capable of criminal adventures like the Kapp putsch of 1920. It took over a tranquil and orderly country where the few political extremists knew that disorder would never be tolerated by the Allied garrison as it had been tolerated by the too tolerant democrats of the Weimar period. The military government had reformed the German currency in June, 1948, by one stroke with an operation more drastic than the Weimar currency reform which ended the famous inflation of 1923. The stage for the numerous accomplishments of the Bonn Republic was in fact prepared by the military government to a far greater extent than Germans are generally willing to admit today.

THE "ECONOMIC MIRACLE"

The most indubitable achievement of the Federal Republic has been the remarkable economic progress which has led Germany from utter ruin to unprecedented prosperity. West Germany's gross output nearly quadrupled, from $22 billion to $84.3 billion, in the fifteen years from 1948 to 1963. Foreign trade rose from something close to zero to nearly $25 billion, the second highest of any country in the world. The currency remained comparatively stable and was in fact revalued upwards by 5 per cent in the spring of 1961. Gold and convertible currency reserves (mostly dollars) stood at $6.4 billion in 1962, while Germany continued to have a favorable balance of trade. Wages recovered their prewar real value by 1950 and nearly doubled in the next decade. All these figures demonstrate the existence of a booming economy where a well-distributed prosperity was rapidly altering traditional patterns of living. The automobile, to give only one example, was once the status symbol of the German rich; it has now become the possession of many German families and the aspiration of all.

The architect of this "economic miracle" has been Economics Minister Ludwig Erhard, who succeeded Adenauer in the chancellorship in October, 1963. He has been a fervent apostle of the creed of neoliberalism, which relies upon initiative, competition, and the profit motive in order to achieve maximum economic results. These principles have been remarkably successful since Erhard introduced them by discarding the entire mechanism of rationing and price control set up by the military government. It will long be argued whether his laissez-faire principles possess general validity or only happened to be suitable to the specific German conditions of 1948; there can be no argument, however, about their magnificent success in Germany during the last fifteen years. They made the name of Ludwig Erhard a household word and symbol for prosperity, helped win election victories for his party, and made him Adenauer's inevitable successor.

The extraordinary prosperity produced by the "economic miracle" has had two important political consequences. It has, in the first place, given much needed prestige to Germany's fledgling democracy under which it was achieved—in welcome contrast to the economic record of Weimar, marked by inflation and depression. It has, in the second place, done irretrievable damage to the cause of German socialism as an economic program. When Erhard began his laissez-faire economic policy in 1948 it still seemed as if socialism—defined as government ownership of industry and a comprehensive apparatus of economic controls—were the way of the future in Europe. The results achieved by Germany through the application of Erhard's principles gave a completely unexpected impetus to the economic neoliberalism which Socialists too easily despised as a sectarian anachronism. Erhard enjoyed in 1959 one of the greatest triumphs of his career when the SPD, at its special Bad Godesberg congress, practically abandoned its Marxist heritage and substantially embraced the neoliberal economics it had bitterly opposed for nearly a dozen years. This triumph is comparable to Adenauer's when the SPD embraced his foreign policy principles in 1960.

It is important not to confuse Erhard's neoliberalism—which he calls *soziale Marktwirtschaft,* that is, a market economy with a social purpose—with what some American reactionaries call the "golden days of William McKinley." Erhard's neoliberalism is propped on top of a cradle-to-grave welfare state which goes back eighty years to Bismarck's time, and which is completely noncontroversial in its major principles (including, for example, national health insurance). It subsidizes agriculture exactly as other states do, for political as much as economic reasons. It intervenes in all major strikes, though these are happily infrequent in Germany's excellent industrial climate. It has intervened successfully to remedy a housing shortage endemic since the Second World War. Approximately seven million housing units have been built since 1949 with various types of governmental subsidies. It has shown an admirable openmindedness towards new forms of industrial organization by accepting the principle of codetermination (*Mitbestimmung*) for major industries in 1951. Under this principle labor elects some members to the directing board of every industrial firm, and these "labor directors" have exactly the same rights as all other directors, including access to company books. The principle aroused grave fears and enthusiastic hopes when it was originally established: neither have been justified, for labor directors have in fact made little practical difference in actual economic operations. They quickly shed any distinctive working class outlook and have as frequently explained management's case to labor as labor's case to management. It remains true, nonetheless, that codetermination has proven a valuable institution, part symbol and part cause of the harmonious industrial climate of the Bonn Republic.

The greatest failure of the Erhard brand of neoliberalism has been the neglect of the "public sector" of the German economy. The governmental antipathy to every kind of planning has made Germany a land with inadequate roads (despite the legacy of Hitler's *Autobahnen*), inadequate schools, and inadequate hospitals. City planning is woefully backward, and such prosaic but important problems as water supply and smoke control have been completely neglected. Worst of all has been the inadequate encouragement of science and the failure to pursue realistic plans of university expansion and reform. Germany stands today in serious danger of becoming a second-rate scientific and industrial nation. Its young scientists are emigrating to America in flocks, the application of atomic power to industrial purposes remains embryonic, and Germany's electronics industry is a generation behind America's. It must be said in extenuation that the absence of military contracts have complicated the development of atomic and electronic industry, but it cannot be said that the government has sought any alternatives for military incentives for industrial modernity. It is a neglect which raises gloomy perspectives for Germany's economic future.

There are few votes to be had by the expensive encouragement of scientific progress. Instead of making it a top priority, the government has attached far more importance to showering "election gifts" upon the country every four years just prior to federal elections. It has not scrupled to unleash economic appetites in a manner unparalleled in previous German history, and pressure group politics have become the order of the day. These government handouts have been bestowed for political purposes with little regard to economic rationality; thus the vast sums handed to farmers have been used as much to temporarily save small, unviable plots of land as to modernize plots of a rational size. Erhard, who is verbally a stern puritan in his fiscal principles, has repeatedly protested against this policy of handouts and found strong words against egotism, materialism, and the degradation of the "handout state." He has, however, been repeatedly undercut by the Chancellor, who has often made promises to lobby leaders after they had been previously turned down by the Minister of Economics. It has been a demoralizing practice, and it has established a pattern which will be difficult to break in the future.

THE ACHIEVEMENT OF DEMOCRATIC GOVERNMENT

The unleashing of pressure group egotism is certainly one of the most unattractive aspects of the Bonn political scene; to keep matters in perspective, however, it must be said that such egotism is far from new in German history and far from untypical of modern democracies in general. Its political significance in the new German democracy will be explored further below. First it is necessary, however, to say a few words about the spectacular fact that Germany has become a well-functioning democracy at last. There can be no question that the façade of the democracy of the Bonn Republic is *prima facie* extremely impressive. Parliamentary government flourishes on both the national and the *Länder* level; free elections are vigorously contested, and a voting participation of upwards of 80 per cent puts the record of an old-established democracy like the United States to shame; the press is free despite the unfortunate aspects of the *Spiegel* affair, to be discussed below; courts are independent and the Karlsruhe Supreme Court has not hesitated on occasion to thwart the actions of the Adenauer government. The electoral law combines equity with utility by being based upon a perfect mixture of the proportional and the majority system; the clause which denies parliamentary representation to parties with less than 5 per cent of the national vote has successfully curbed all splinter parties and limited the Bundestag (national parliament) to three parties, where the Weimar *Reichstag* had as many as a dozen. Each of the three national parties—the Christian Democratic, the Social Democratic, and the Free Democratic—is composed of very heterogeneous elements, and the necessity for internal compromise develops the mentality which favors external compromise as well.

None of these three parties is attached to any overall ideology encouraging extremism or tactical rigidity. The self-proclaimed attachment to Christian principles of the CDU should not be taken too seriously; the party is in fact a congeries of pressure groups—including peasants, heavy industry, many professionals, Roman Catholic workers, and most of the lower middle class— bent upon winning elections where access to the public trough is the main prize (although this fact has long been concealed by Adenauer's stress upon the "correct"—but long controverted—pro-Western foreign policy at election time). The SPD practically abandoned its Marxist ideology at the Bad Godesberg Congress of 1959; it is trying frantically to enlarge its social basis by repudiating its traditional anticlericalism, which long immunized much of the peasantry and Roman Catholic working class to its propaganda, and by seeking to assure professionals and progressive businessmen that it is not the red bogey which CDU orators still claim it is. The FDP has never had a specific ideology; its main problem is to keep its "progressive" liberal and its "conservative" nationalist wings from breaking apart and to maintain its balance of power role between the two big parties.

The best index of the health of German democracy is to be found in the attainment of that "agreement on fundamentals" so essential for the good functioning of constitutionalism. Germany's three parties are all dedicated to parliamentary democracy and the maintenance of the existing Bonn constitution. This fact constitutes an important and welcome change in the entire German political situation. A brief backward glance over the last one hundred and fifty years of German history shows that the prevalent monarchical absolutism of the pre-1848 period was confronted by the champions of democratic sovereignty; the Bismarckian Empire by the challenge of radical Social Democracy; and the Weimar Republic by intransigent Nazi, Nationalist and Communist opposition parties. In every case mentioned the opposition struck at the very *fundamentals* of the existing state structure in a manner which precluded compromise and made political controversy either a radical attack upon or an intransigent defense of its established order—instead of being a contest for office in which each side freely submitted to mutually accepted "rules of the game." It is one of the few advantages of Germany's tragic recent history that it has eliminated so many alternatives that Germans now have no choice but to be good democrats.

This agreement on constitutional fundamentals is the main reason for the quiet and even dull character of German domestic politics today. The second reason is that the political consensus has been recently extended from constitutional to other issues as well. The economic policies of Erhard were largely accepted by the SPD in 1959, the foreign policies of Adenauer only a year later. There is danger in today's Germany that the range of political controversy is becoming too narrow—a welcome change from the traditional evil of controversy being far too broad, but a danger nonetheless in the apathy which can easily be produced if there are too few differences between the "ins" and the "outs."

The reduction of the number of parties to three is partly due to the amalgamation of the followers of various Weimar parties into a few parties characterized by comprehension (even though it means much internal friction), partly due to the elimination of all extremes from German political life. Thus the CDU—to mention the main beneficiary of the former tendency—combines followers of the exclusively Roman Catholic Zentrum party of the Weimar period, the primarily Protestant Nationalist party, the bulk of the pre-1933 Nazis, and a good many followers of the right-wing Liberal People's party. The achievement of this kind of comprehension—and its cementing into a governing coalition which could three times renew its mandate in sharply contested elections—makes Adenauer one of the greatest party leaders in history. He has combined Protestants and Roman Catholics, centralizers and particularists, capitalists and workers (primarily of Roman Catho-

lic religion), farmers and urban professionals. The loose, heterogeneous, indefinable party which embraces all these elements
has the same character as the diverse and unideological parties of
such outstandingly successful democracies as Britain and the
United States. The SPD has recently paid the CDU—in this field
also—the sincere compliment of imitation by aiming to embrace
a similarly broad gamut of social forces.

THE PREVENTION OF POLITICAL EXTREMISM

The elimination of extremism is partly the result of general
factors, partly the result of the intelligent actions of the federal
government. Communism was hopelessly discredited by the brutal
tyranny which Ulbricht established in the East Zone—quite apart
from the atrocious misconduct of the Russian troops in 1945. It
was given its *coup de grâce* when the West German Communist
party was formally outlawed, after long judicial proceedings, in
1956 under a constitutional provision prohibiting antidemocratic
parties. (This regrettable action, whch has tarnished West Germany's liberal image as opposed to the D.D.R., was necessitated by
considerations of "parity," since neo-Nazi organizations have been
regularly outlawed.) The prevention of the development of any
significant Nazi or other right-wing extremism is without question
one of the major achievements of the Adenauer government, and
one which constitutes one of the major differences between the
Bonn and Weimar republics. The problem was simplified by
Nazism standing condemned of the worst crime possible in the
eyes of its followers—namely, failure. Hitler left Germany a heap
of rubble, while the dreams of world conquest yielded to the
nightmare of national partition. A problem nonetheless existed
in view of the fact that some 80 per cent of the German people
had, at one time or another, and with various degress of enthusiasm,
supported the criminal Nazi regime. How would postwar Germans
come to grips with this ugly skeleton in the national closet? How
would they digest Germany's—meaning their own—past? There
was much chest-beating, talk of collective guilt, and so forth, in
the first years after 1945—and there was an initial resolve, which
was not decreed only by the Allied occupation, that former Nazis
should never again play a prominent role in German political,
economic, and cultural life. The impracticability of this resolve
became quickly evident as it proved impossible to run Germany
with a minuscule band of returned émigrés and concentration
camp survivors. It was inevitable that men compromised by mere
error, that is, support of Nazism without full recognition of its

criminal program, should return to positions of leadership in all walks of life. Adenauer, himself admirably uncompromised by complicity in Nazism, accepted this fact with the prosaic realism which is one of his most conspicuous qualities; he made it a general policy not to look too closely into men's pasts. His party, the CDU, has regularly won the major share of the ex-Nazi and right-wing nationalist vote. It has done so without significant concessions to Nazism by applying the Christian doctrine of hating sin but loving the sinner (or ex-sinner), or at least his vote. One can go further and say that CDU election propaganda has on occasion appealed to some of the instincts and sentiments of former Nazis. The noisy appeal to the Allied powers to amnesty men convicted of Nazi crimes falls in this category; so does the virulent antisocialism and constant invocation of the Red scarecrow. It is probable that Adenauer's systematic and unfair defamation of the Socialists has served the "conservative" function (and was presumably so intended) of incorporating old Nazis within the new political framework by giving due ventilation to some of their less estimable, but evidently incorrigible, instincts.

The employment of men with a compromised past was symbolized by Adenauer's appointment of Hans Globke, who had written a commentary on the infamous Nuremberg racial laws, to head his Federal Chancellery (Staatssekretär im Bundeskanzleramt). Globke is without question a man of enormous ability and subjective integrity, and his commentary was relatively favorable to the Jews; it was nonetheless a highly questionable appointment because it made the emergence of men tainted by the Nazi brush into positions far less important than the Federal Chancellery appear a relatively innocuous matter. The result of this policy has been a situation where men whose own pasts prevent an unconditional repudiation of Nazism hold positions of power in German industry, the bureaucracy, and the judiciary, thereby creating a problem which only time will be able to solve.

It should be stressed, however, that to deplore the presence of ex-Nazis in high positions is something very different from asserting the existence of a *present* Nazi danger in the Federal Republic. On the contrary: to give ex-Nazis (compromised in various degrees) power and responsibility was the one certain method of preventing the rise of an overt neo-Nazi radicalism. No significant group was driven into a ghetto where personal despair would create a fruitful soil for radicalism. Adenauer—and with him the overwhelming majority of German public opinion—was only too eager to accept the sincerity of latter-day conversions to democracy. The small remnant of genuine Nazism has, on the other hand, been relentlessly crushed by police and judicial methods whenever it took on an institutional form. The remnants of anti-Semitism have been similarly crushed; Adenauer indeed went a bit too far in this direction when he publicly advocated lynch justice (*Verprügeln*) against anti-Semitic hooligans at the time of the over-publicized Cologne swastika daubings in 1959.

The Adenauer government clearly saw the danger of radicalization presented by the presence of some ten million impoverished refugees from Germany's lost eastern provinces. The program it developed for incorporating them into the economic and political life of the Federal Republic has proved a brilliant success; it included a far-reaching "equalization of burdens tax" (*Lastenausgleich*), under which the refugees received approximately $11 billion in compensation, and a systematic resettlement program under which millions of refugees were taken out of the economically backward border areas and distributed throughout the Federal Republic. When a distinctive Refugee party (the BHE) appeared in the early 1950s, Adenauer clipped its wings by taking it into his governing coalition. Its most active leaders, including some with an unusually tainted (though of course not criminal) Nazi past, were practically bribed into conducting themselves responsibly by the offer of cabinet seats. The degree of refugee assimilation was soon shown by the decline of the BHE, which fell a victim to the 5 per cent clause of the electoral law in 1957; most of its leaders found a not uncongenial new political home in the broad bosom of the CDU.

The result of all these policies towards neo-Nazism, real and potential, has been a paradoxical situation where Germany is at one and the same time without a Nazi danger yet has not come adequately to grips with its Nazi past. I believe that this situation is the best that could reasonably be expected in the face of very difficult circumstances. Repentance is of necessity an individual rather than a mass phenomenon; a whole nation cannot walk for an entire generation in sackcloth and ashes. The German nation refused to tear itself apart about its recent past, and oriented itself instead towards the present and the fuure. Moral purists will regret this attitude of evasion; men of the world will be gratified, and indeed surprised, that there is so little overt Nazi sentiment in Germany today.

BUILDING A DEMOCRATIC ARMY

One of the greatest achievements of the Adenauer era has been the rebuilding of the German army, this time—in sharp contrast to the Weimar Republic—under firm civilian control. Rearmament took place in a very difficult psychological situation characterized by a too precipitate reverse of the antimilitarist campaign conducted by the military government, which had sometimes gone to the ludicrous extent of removing monuments to the dead of former wars; the collapse of elementary patriotic feelings, leading to young men resenting military service as an improper intrusion upon private life; and a well-justified conviction that the army had exercised a disastrous influence upon Germany's political development in the past. Adenauer showed great courage in nonetheless embarking upon the initially very unpopular rearmament course, because he saw its necessity if Germany were to play its proper role in the NATO alliance. He was in full accord with German public opinion, however, in his insistence that the new army must be purged of some of the undesirable features of the old, including most notably the absence of civilian supremacy. The right man for heading the Defense Ministry was found in the person of Franz Josef Strauss (if *found* is the right word in view of Strauss' incessant intriguing for the job). Strauss' dishonorable role in the *Spiegel* affair, and his deserved fall from power in November, 1962, should not detract attention from his monumental achievement in building up Germany's new army. He is the first defense minister in German history (if one excludes Hitler) who made civilian supremacy a fact rather than a theory; his ruthless personnel policies—however unfair in individual cases —succeeded in making even stiff-necked generals realize who was boss. He gave some support to the idealistic attempt to make the German army a body of "citizens in uniform" rather than a group of conscripts owing unintelligent and mechanical obedience (the so-called *Kadavergehorsam*). He probably went as far in this direction as was compatible with military efficiency, and the angry frustration of idealistic ultrareformers should not be taken too seriously. Strauss' technical achievement of building up the Bundeswehr is generally recognized, while his obvious desire for direct German control of atomic weapons (an understandable demand from a military point of view) was happily vetoed by Chancellor Adenauer for political reasons. There is no gainsaying the great achievement of building up, in the short period of seven years, an army of 420,000 men which has become the backbone of the conventional forces of NATO. Apart from its military importance it has given the Federal Republic a strong voice in western councils and contributed to West Germany's firm alliance with the western world.

SOME REMAINING POLITICAL WEAKNESSES

It is important to recognize the solid achievements of the "democracy of Bonn"; but one must also remember that there are important shadows in this remarkably bright overall picture. Many democratic habits are as yet underdeveloped in the Federal Republic, and there is a disturbing persistence (in some cases even a restoration) of predemocratic attitudes. There is a deplorable political apathy in broad sections of the population. Millions of Germans have accepted the course of developments since 1949 more as a fate imposed from above—for once a benevolent fate!—than something achieved by *their* government for whose actions *they* share responsibility. Volunteer activities—the hallmark of a sense of civic responsibility, whether in the fields of religion, charity, education, or "clean government"—remain virtually unknown in Germany. The mentality of the authoritarian *Obrigkeitsstaat* (that is, one where rulers rule "from above" rather than as agents of popular sovereignty) is far from dead; many bureaucrats consider themselves rulers, possessing the *arcana imperii,* rather than servants of the people. Highly placed ministerial bureaucrats frequently do not take their parliamentary chiefs seriously. Adenauer has administered the chancellor's office in a highly autocratic manner which has frequently degraded cabinet colleagues to lackeys and reduced parliament to a rubber-stamp role. He has viewed the opposition SPD not as a legitimate rival for power but rather as an enemy of the state, which he has—in this following his great predecessor Bismarck—too much identified with his own person.

It would be incorrect to say that Adenauer has broken the letter of the constitution, but his fidelity to its spirit has left something to be desired. It must be remembered, however, that the constitution framers of 1949 intended the chancellorship to be the centerpiece of the political system (the SPD expected that their leader Kurt Schumacher would become the first incumbent.) No one could of course foresee just *how* strong it would become when its powers were wielded by a skilled and determined autocrat like the first Chancellor.

It is improbable that Adenauer possessed any long-range aims in domestic policy similar to those he designed and executed in the field of foreign policy. He was interested above all in maintaining himself in power, and he was willing to employ all means—fair or foul—to achieve this end. We have seen above that he shamelessly tarred the SPD with the Red brush throughout the fourteen years of his chancellorship. He did not hesitate to refer to the illegitimate birth of his SPD rival Willy Brandt during the 1961 elections. His demagogy was often unbelievably crude, and his political methods did not exclude intimidation and character assassination. Worst of all was his utter unscrupulousness in manipulating men, confessions, parties, and pressure groups. He positively encouraged the latter to register their claims upon the public, and accustomed Germans to the practice of extensive governmental handouts every four years just prior to federal elections. This has made for a cynicism and materialism that goes far beyond what is normal under democratic government.

The worst of it is that Adenauer has set the tone of federal politics during the crucial beginning phase of the Bonn Republic. He has surrounded his malpractices with the aura of success and has thereby given his fellow countrymen a very unfortunate image of what to expect from a great democratic statesman. He has clearly subordinated the reverence owed to institutions to the paramount consideration of perpetuating his own power: the worst example of this was his on-and-off candidacy for the presidential office in 1959, which did considerable damage to that essentially ceremonial but by no means unimportant office.

Another unfortunate legacy of Adenauer is that he associated the chancellor's office with a regrettable want of intellectual distinction. It would be hard to think of a statesman in European history who combined Adenauer's great political achievements with a similar cultural mediocrity. His speeches have been pedestrian in character and *ad hoc* in purpose, and they are unreadable outside of their specific context; there are no literary allusions, no historical parallels (except an occasional reference to the Weimar Republic), no general maxims of statecraft, and preciously few calls to service and sacrifice. Perhaps one should not be too harsh concerning this aspect of the Chancellor's record: the oratorical greatness of Adlai Stevenson—who is in almost every way a type antipodal to Adenauer—did not pave his way to the White House. It remains true, nonetheless, that Adenauer established a political style devoid of elevation, fair play, and even the ordinary decencies which are, if not the essence, at least a valuable accessory of public life in a well-functioning democracy. The most urgent task confronting his successor, Ludwig Erhard, is to elevate the overall tone of German public life.

Most of the unfortunate aspects of the Adenauer era were reflected in the revealing prism of the *Spiegel* affair of November, 1962. A government aware of the central importance of the freedom of the press never would have sought to destroy an important opposition journal through a bogus accusation of treason. The incriminating article was in fact little more than a summary of previously published facts about Germany's unsatisfactory defense posture. The temporary confiscation of the entire *Spiegel* archive was a barefaced attempt to intimidate future informants and to find material warranting prosecution *ex post facto*. The employment of a man with a tainted Nazi past (Police Commissioner Saevecke) to direct the arrests was more than an unfortunate accident—it was symptomatic for the degree to which former Nazis had penetrated into sensitive positions in Adenauer's government. The failure to inform the responsible minister of justice (Stammberger of the FDP) before launching the entire action showed a blatant defiance of the principles of parliamentary responsibility. The arrest of Conrad Ahlers, the author of the controversial article, in his Spanish vacationing retreat took place without the slightest respect for international extradition practices. The lies told to the Bundestag by Defense Minister Strauss about his role in this arrest showed an indifference to truth and a contempt for parliamentary dignity singular in a parliamentary minister. In many ways worst of all was the conduct of Chancellor Adenauer himself: he exposed his underdeveloped sense of justice by using the forum of the Bundestag to denounce Rudolf Augstein, the editor of the *Spiegel*, as a man dominated by low (*gemeine*) motives as he made money out of treason: surely a singular *obiter dicta* delivered by the head of the executive while commenting about a pending judicial case. Adenauer compounded his outrageous conduct by publicly calling upon all advertisers to boycott the *Spiegel*, a really remarkable attempt to supplement judicial harassment of an opposition journal by economic strangulation.

The *Spiegel* affair was, however, not all loss for Germany. The outcry of public opinion against the government's arbitrary actions showed that Germans had learned that eternal vigilance is the price of liberty. (There had been far less protest against the far more arbitrary actions of the Nazis in 1933.) The press attacked the government with a high degree of unanimity; university professors actually signed petitions against the government—a remarkable action for those acquainted with the mores of German university life. The Chancellor's own position seemed in danger for several days, but he soon recovered from his fumbling and skillfully ejected the especially incriminated Strauss from the cabinet. He saved his own position temporarily by great tactical skill in negotiating a new coalition with the FDP, whose leadership had possessed close ties to the *Spiegel* and which was especially enraged by the entire affair. The FDP leaders were intimidated by the possibility of a "Great Coalition" between the CDU and SPD, which SPD leader Herbert Wehner desired because he despaired of his party winning an independent electoral majority in the foreseeable future. Wehner probably had few illusions about achieving the "Great Coalition" in 1962; but he valued the "certificate of respectability" implicit in the mere fact that Adenauer had publicly contemplated taking the SPD into his own government. This gain more than outweighed, at least in Wehner's eyes, the indignation felt by many SPD militants at the fact that Wehner had come to the Chancellor's rescue at the very moment when the latter's prestige stood at a nadir point. The entire *Spiegel* affair did much, nonetheless, to destroy Adenauer's public image and was partially responsible for the decision of the CDU party leaders to force his retirement in the autumn of 1963. Its historic importance lies in the fact that it brought to the surface much that is still predemocratic in the public life of the Bonn Republic, but it also showed the vigilance of German public opinion to any overt threat to the democratic liberties enshrined in the 1949 constitution. The Republic passed its first real internal crisis not exactly with flying colors, for Adenauer remained in power for another year despite his really impossible conduct; fallen Defense Minister Strauss was hailed by his Bavarian fellow provincials as the martyr of an alleged Communist (or Protestant, or American) intrigue; and the Karlsruhe Supreme Court has not as yet condemned the arbitrary conduct of the government. Yet it must also be stressed that the *Spiegel* still exists, neither Augstein nor Ahlers has been convicted, Adenauer was discredited, and Strauss ceased to be an active contender for the chancellorship in the foreseeable future.

A SUMMARY OF THE DOMESTIC RECORD

The domestic record of the Adenauer era is less clear cut than its record in the international field. There has been no success comparable to Germany's acceptance in the western alliance, no failure as unmistakable as the nonachievement of unification. There has been, rather, a pattern of respectable achievement accompanied by blemishes which only time can ultimately remove. There is no denying the spectacular success of the "economic miracle"; yet it has been accompanied by neglect of the public sector and an unleashing of the type of materialism which ignores the ancient truth that man does not live by bread—or status seeking—alone. A viable democratic system has been achieved which far exceeds the most optimistic expectations of fifteen years ago; yet authoritarian patterns persist and grassroots democracy is still in its infancy. NeoNazism has remained a completely marginal phenomenon, yet a forthright confrontation with the ugly Nazi past remains limited to a minority elite (though fortunately one which dominates public opinion). A remarkable "agreement on fundamentals," the prerequisite for a civilized political life where rivals compete for power under mutually accepted rules, has been attained; yet political struggles retain a ferocious—and even indecent—character; and a permanent government party, the CDU, has confronted a permanent opposition, the SPD, without interruption since 1949. Complete confidence in German democracy must be postponed until there has been at least one electoral transfer of power from the government to the opposition; until predemocratic attitudes have so far disappeared that a *Spiegel* affair becomes inconceivable; and until all men who were tainted by Nazism—and therefore cannot repudiate it unconditionally—are removed from influential positions through retirement or death. The establishment of a collegial nonauthoritarian pattern of government by Ludwig Erhard is to be welcomed, provided that it proves effective in governing Germany. There was something to be said for Adenauer's authoritarian methods in the nonage of German democracy: they convinced millions of latently antidemocratic Germans that Germany could have order and strong government despite the fact that the polity was democratic in formal structure. This was a very indirect method of making converts for democracy, but it has proved highly effective in the critical early stage. It became a misfortune, however, long before the end of the Adenauer era—one of the many examples of the fact that the old Chancellor had the misfortune politically to outlive his usefulness.

There is one other desideratum which only time can fulfill: an enthusiastic general acceptance of democratic government by the broad mass of Germany's population. The democracy of Bonn has won universal acquiescence and much grudging respect; of enthusiasm or devotion there is, however, very little trace despite the tremendous achievements attained by Germany under the democratic form of government. Why is this so? One suspects that the German capacity for enthusiasm and devotion—once both the envy and the terror of the world—was drained to the limits by Nazism, which exploited so many noble qualities for such utterly criminal ends. The post-Nazi German has lost much of the idealism, devotion, and capacity for self-sacrifice which used to characterize the nation; he has become skeptical, materialistic, and pragmatic in his outlook and tends to be absorbed in his private affairs, becoming indifferent to the problems of public life where his fathers burned their fingers. This kind of mentality is not without some value in running a democratic polity, which suffers when too much idealism and romanticism (especially when accompanied by German metaphysical absolutes) enters public life and inhibits tolerance and the art of compromise. The rise of skepticism, pragmatism, and materialism has in fact bridged the spiritual gap which too long separated Germany from the western democracies (non-Socialist Germans were almost unanimous until 1945 in feeling contempt for the decadent, philistine "bourgeois" West with its skepticism, pragmatism, and materialism). These qualities, while valuable in running an old established democracy, however, are handicaps in *initially* establishing enthusiasm on behalf of a newly established form of government.

The German attitude of 1949 was one of "wait and see" concerning the results of the seventh type of government consciously experienced by all Germans of fifty years and older: authoritarian monarchy (until 1918) all-Socialist provisional government (winter 1918–1919), parliamentary democracy (1919–1930), presidential dictatorship (1930–1933), Nazi dictatorship (1933–1945), military government (1945–1949) and finally the parliamentary democracy of Bonn. The new political system had the initial advantage of being untroubled by any serious opposition, because the prevalent wait and see attitude encouraged universal *acquiescence.* Strong grievances and some capacity for sacrifice are necessary to start a movement to overthrow an established government. The Germans of the Federal Republic have had neither, and it is true—though paradoxical—that the democratic government of Bonn was from the beginning buttressed by the formidable indifference and political apathy of its population.

This mere acquiescence has, however, gradually changed to a more positive attitude by the respect earned by the achievements of the Adenauer era. These have succeeded in attaching favorable connotations to democracy for the first time in German history. The prestige of any form of government in any country is largely dependent upon the successes and failures with which it is associated in the public mind. We Americans value our libertarian democracy not only because we love liberty; we also associate it with a glorious national history which has seen a string of seaboard colonies turn first into a continental giant and later into the leading world power. Libertarian democracy was, prior to Adenauer, associated in German minds with impractical professors debating in the Paulskirche in 1848, doctrinaire liberals opposing the great Bismarck in 1862, and feeble Weimar politicians surrendering to Nazism with only token resistance in the early 1930s. This "negative image" has begun to be replaced by a more "positive image" based upon the solid successes—especially in foreign and economic policy—which have marked the fourteen years of the Adenauer era. It is but a question of time—and future accomplishment—until respect will turn into at least moderate enthusiasm, insofar as the German people will again be capable of feeling political enthusiasm. More important still will be the sheer force of habit— the habit which makes government noncontroversial by precluding the very idea of any fundamental political change. The crowning stone of national pride in a long tradition of constitutional democracy, which explains so much in the stability of countries like Britain and the United States, is, of course, still decades away; but the Adenauer era has made a good start in the right direction. In terms of domestic development—and always excluding the tragic, and insolvable, problem of national partition—the German scene has never previously looked as promising as it does at the present moment.

MAX KOHNSTAMM

The European Tide

I There is a tide in the affairs of men . . .

NEITHER the position of the Netherlands in world affairs, nor its attitude toward them, was changed drastically by World War I.

Neutrality, which had served the country well for nearly a century, continued to be accepted by all Dutch citizens as the basis of the country's foreign policy. At the Hague peace conferences earlier in the century, the Dutch had shown the deep interest in international law and the organization of peace that was traditional to the country. The horrors of World War I, witnessed from afar, strengthened the Dutch desire for international organization and peace in Europe. The birth of the League of Nations stirred great hopes: here, it seemed, was the beginning of a new order in which the rule of law would at long last replace brute force as the governor of international relations. Locarno, in the second half of the twenties, followed by Germany's entry into the League, that Indian summer of Europe's old order, looked like spring, a fore-taste of great things to come.

The Netherlands, of course, did not escape the economic consequences of the peace: the twenties were lean years; how could it be otherwise, as they were lean for Holland's neighbors? Nevertheless, free trade and the gold standard remained two unquestioned articles of the national credo.

But if the twenties were lean, the thirties were disastrous—as nearly everywhere in Europe. The rise of Nazism, from its first beginnings, caused deep dismay, and so did the sudden, unexpected agony of the League: Manchuria, Germany's departure from Geneva, then Abyssinia. Only a few years after the high hopes of Locarno, international law had been reduced to meaningless

This article is an account by an eye-witness. As is the case with many of his contemporaries, he first watched events from inside his nation; gradually his point of view became European.

words. Brute force had become more decisive than ever. Free trade, indispensable to a small trading nation such as the Netherlands, was swept away in England, Germany, and everywhere; a new economic nationalism took its place, regulating in minute details the flow of goods and money across borders. Deeply reluctant, the Netherlands felt itself compelled to follow suit. The name of Schacht—the economic overlord of Germany during those years—became the trademark of these hated policies. There was one short-lived glimmer of hope when, at Ouchy, the three low countries (Netherlands, Belgium, Luxembourg) decided to study the setting up of a customs union. A warning from Britain that it would not tolerate any discrimination against it (of course, it did not for a moment think of joining the union) brought the enterprise to an abrupt end.

Yet, notwithstanding heavy unemployment and economic misery, the Netherlands, in the last few years before World War II, seemed more united than before. In 1938, for the first time in twenty-five years, Queen Wilhelmina was allowed by her advisers to visit one of Amsterdam's few radically leftist districts, where, only a few years before, bitter street fighting had taken place between police and rioting unemployed. Now the narrow streets were covered with banners saying, "We don't want Hitler, we don't want Stalin, we want Wilhelmina."

The Socialist opposition abandoned unilateral disarmament, popular in the idealist twenties. United, the Netherlands was passionately resolved to keep out of the coming conflict if it could, but also, if necessary, to defend itself against anyone who would try to violate its neutrality. On May 10, 1940, Germany invaded. Four days later, all was over. Queen and government had fled the country. Rotterdam had been turned into a smoking heap of rubbish. With lightning speed, the old, trusted, and beloved order ceased to exist. In the harsh light of disaster things which only yesterday were absolute certainties ceased to be so. What about neutrality? Had it made sense that when Germany's attack came, a part of the army, albeit a small part, lined the Dutch coast, with weapons pointing out at sea, in case England should violate its neutrality? Wasn't it shaming that, in the name of that same neutrality, Dutch and Belgian defenses, where their eastern borders met, had not been coordinated, leaving an opening between them, which of course the Germans had known about and used to their advantage? Was it honorable to have tried to remain neutral in a war between Nazism and those who were defending their own countries, certainly, but defending also a political order in which freedom and human dignity were permitted to exist? Looking back at the lean twenties and hungry thirties, on unemployment and class bitterness, on the results of neutrality, could it really be said that the Netherlands' democratic institutions had been able to cope with the problems of the times? That question remained even when the results, first in Belgium, then in France, of a royal family, of a government, remaining under German occupation, showed how wise it had been for Queen and government to leave the country. These were not the only questions which troubled people's minds during the following five long, dark years of Nazi occupation. When the workers of Amsterdam, without weapons, without the remotest chance of success, rose in revolt to defend their Jewish co-citizens, were they defending national independence, or something even more fundamental? In concentration camps and prisons words once thought stirring, like "for God, Fatherland, and the House of Orange," seemed to sound hollow, while others, like justice and human dignity, not bound to any nation, seemed to grow in force and meaning.

Neither darkness nor oppression keeps men from dreaming about a better world. Wherever men could still meet and talk, they dreamed about peace and the renewal to come. But their dreams about renewal did not remain confined to internal affairs. The international order, the structure of Europe itself had to be changed, so changed that history could not repeat itself, that force would be lastingly bridled by justice in international as well as it had been in internal affairs. What was the use of reconstructing internal democracy, if the country could once again become a prey to neighbors, if internal democracy could not be safeguarded by international democracy?

Then, at last, peace came. At first, all available energy had to be directed at carrying out the most essential tasks of the moment, such as providing people with food and clothing. Everything had to be rebuilt, parliamentary institutions as well as railroads, the machinery of government as well as harbors and factories. When at last there was time to look at the world outside, the Dutch East Indies were in turmoil and on the road to becoming independent Indonesia. For three years the country resisted the inevitable—then the proudest chapter of its history came to an end. Few were fooled by the Dutch-Indonesian Union, a shortlived attempt to save appearances. The colonies, "the East," had built Dutch cities, had been the mainstay of trade and even of certain industries. Could the country survive without its colonies?

In Europe Schacht had gone, but the seeds he had sown flourished profusely. The rich arsenal of commercial and monetary beggar-your-neighbor policies of economic nationalism had been invented before the war, when the European nations were still relatively well off. Now that all had really become beggars, they seemed to have no choice but to apply the same techniques again. International trade was reduced to barter arrangements, international payments had to be settled in cash, currency reserves had disappeared, credit did not exist. How did one fix the exchange ratio of tulip bulbs or cheese to be traded against coal or pig iron?

Germany posed an insolvable dilemma. For decades it had been the Netherlands' trading partner. Holland's biggest harbor, Rotterdam, owed its prosperity to a large extent to the Ruhr, which had also produced the bombs that destroyed it. After the years of occupation Germany was hated, despised, feared—and needed, at the same time. Poverty in Germany meant poverty in the Netherlands. But a prosperous Germany meant a powerful, therefore a dangerous, Germany. How right the French were to want to keep Ruhr production low and under control, but how much one needed Ruhr coal and steel, and the trade and transport that went with them! If only the circle could be squared! Germany was disquieting in still another way. The occupying powers, just as Schacht before them, did not want to spend their foreign currency, and they wanted German workers to find work. They shipped food into Germany via Hamburg and Bremen and not through the natural—and allied—port of Rotterdam. They refused to buy Dutch vegetables or to exchange them against bitterly needed coal, for which they demanded gold or dollars the Dutch did not possess. Did something inherent in the situation lead to these tricks, previously thought of as just wicked Nazi methods? Could it be that in a system where everyone was responsible for the solution only of *his* part of the problem, the problem itself simply could not be solved? Was everyone, either German or allied, whose responsibility was limited to Hamburg and did not extend to Rotterdam obliged to act in this way? If so, then only a common responsibility could change these policies.

Since those terrible days of May, 1940, all experience seemed to point to the failure of the old order, to the need of a drastic change in the relations between European nations. No one in the Netherlands, therefore, was astonished that Europe could not find its way back to recovery and solvency on its own and within the old context. The Marshall Plan was welcomed by everyone as a source of help and hope. What did astonish and disappoint in the years that followed was that so little headway could be made in the direction of freeing intra-European trade from the strangling influences of economic nationalism. Benelux, the economic union between the Netherlands, Belgium, and Luxembourg, was extremely useful, but it could not solve Dutch problems, because it was too limited in scope. In the OEEC the British, more even than the French, opposed every attempt to go beyond the elimination of quota restrictions and to tackle the tariff problem itself. In view of British unwillingness to cooperate, a French proposal to form a customs union among only the Benelux countries, Italy, and France (Fritalux) came to nothing because no one really believed that such a union—with neither England nor Germany—could be viable. The Dutch could not but heartily agree with the Americans, who never tired of stressing the need for the OEEC to go beyond simple *cooperation* to *integration* in order to create the big single market which alone could provide the desperately needed increase in European productivity, now lagging far behind American.

In the autumn of 1949 Dr. Hoffman, the American administrator of Marshall aid, defined what was needed: "the substance of such integration, would be the formation of a large single market within which quantitative restrictions on the movements of goods, monetary barriers to the flow of payments, and, eventually, all tariffs are permanently swept away." A group of Dutch officials, studying during those same months how such a European market could be created, reached the conclusion that it could not be done if governments did not give up their veto power and accept majority decisions in the OEEC ministerial council. Mr. Stikker, then Dutch foreign minister, proposed, in the spring of 1950, a plan with provision for majority voting, to the OEEC. Nothing came of it, mainly as a result of British unwillingness seriously to discuss anything going beyond the elimination of quantitative restrictions.

In political and military matters the Netherlands readily accepted proposals for closer cooperation. It became a member of the Western European Union (founded in 1948 and grouping England, France, Italy, and the Benelux countries) and of NATO, welcoming this organization warmly as a guarantee of continued American presence in Europe. Also, in 1948, the European movement organized an impressive congress in The Hague. Churchill became its leader and hero. Here, it seemed, was real hope. Would the dreams of occupation days, the hope of a new European order, be fulfilled at last?

The Council of Europe, resulting in 1949 from this congress, was greeted with real enthusiasm. The restrictive attitude of Britain's Labour government during the negotiations leading to its foundation disappointed but did not destroy these high hopes. But the council's functioning quickly became a very sobering experience. Impressive speeches, above all from British conservatives, then in opposition, yes—but action, no. One could not help remembering the League of Nations and the Indian summer of Locarno. Words—but no reality; noble sentiments—but no lasting change. Again, what seemed to stand between the initial hopes and the disappointing results was the unanimity rule, the veto power. By 1950 it had become clear that solution of the problems facing the Netherlands could be found neither in the Council of Europe nor in the OEEC unless they were drastically transformed. And in the meantime, although the Federal Republic of Germany had began to function in 1949, the German circle remained unsquared, threatening to become a vicious circle.

II . . . which, taken at the flood . . .

Such was the rising tide in the Netherlands. Though circumstances were exactly similar in no two countries, comparable experiences created a comparable tide in every continental nation that had been involved in the war. The tide was strongest in defeated Germany. Seen from there, Europe seemed the only remaining hope. It was weakest in the Scandinavian countries, their tie being with Britain rather than with the continent. East of the Iron Curtain, of course, nothing but the Communist tide was allowed to flow, as the Russian prohibition of Czechoslovakia's acceptance of Marshall aid made abundantly clear. But west of it one cannot think of a single country that would not, in those first years after the war, have enthusiastically followed any proposal for economic or political unity put forward by the United Kingdom. Why was no such lead forthcoming?

During the war years, in which the tide had gathered strength on the continent, Britain's history had been more different from the continent's than at any time since Napoleon. Alone of all European nations, Britain came out of the war undefeated: its institutions had not crumbled, its government not been forced to flee before the enemy. While other European nations went through the humiliation of defeat and occupation, Britain had known its proudest hour. No political leader in Britain doubted that its role was as Churchill described it—the point of intersection of three circles: first that of the English-speaking nations, the Atlantic circle; second that of the British Commonwealth; and third that of Europe. Britain still felt itself to be, just as in past centuries, in but not of Europe. No lead was forthcoming because Britain simply did not see itself as part of a United Europe.

Of course, the Soviet Union was willing to lead, but only toward a Europe united under Communist rule. West of the Iron Curtain, neither defeated Italy nor Germany could, for obvious reasons, take an initiative. The Benelux countries lacked the weight and authority needed for leadership in such a difficult enterprise; they had therefore to confine themselves to working their own economic union, which they did very well, and to pushing forward the existing organizations, especially the OEEC. Once Britain had to be counted out, the only country which could possibly take the initiative and lead the way was France. But no one, certainly in the Netherlands, expected French leadership. France's record between the two wars had been far from brilliant. Its economy seemed backward, and only a very few were aware of something remarkable happening through "the Plan": Monnet's Plan de Modernisation et d'Equipement. France seemed, as usual, absorbed in its internal problems. Insofar as it thought of broader issues, it was much too obsessed by fear of Germany's recovery to think seriously about squaring that circle. All it did was drag its feet at every proposal to give more elbow room to West Germany, clinging to controls which became daily less effective as a result of diminishing American backing, although they remained irritating to Germany and to those allies who found it easier to forget the past. And then on May 9, 1950, the unexpected happened. Schuman, in the name of the French government, made his famous proposal.

How could it have happened, and why did it happen? It could happen, first and foremost, because the tide existed in France as elsewhere. But it actually did happen because of a special constellation of circumstances. Foremost among them were developments in Germany. By the spring of 1950 the Federal Republic had been functioning for about a year, and events were taking their natural course. The dismantling of plant, and even production controls could no longer be maintained; no one took very seriously the International Ruhr Authority, a control institution set up largely as a sop to France. Far-reaching decisions about Germany could no longer be postponed; the big three of the West were going to meet in London in mid-May to discuss them. Nevertheless, if the French governmental machine had been as highly organized as, for example the British, Schuman's declaration might not have happened. On the Sunday in June, 1940, when the British cabinet had to decide on the proposal for a Franco-British Union, time was taken to look for the red tape which must be attached to papers presented to the cabinet. In Paris, in 1950, the procedural requirements were less exacting. It is well known how summarily Robert Schuman presented his declaration to the French Cabinet before reading it to the press.

In such circumstances the influence of a few men can be decisive; it was in this case. Robert Schuman and Jean Monnet felt the tide as few others did. Schuman, a Lorrainer born in Luxembourg, to which his parents had emigrated when their homeland became German after the Franco-Prussian war of 1870, returned to Lorraine shortly before World War I and saw his province change from German to French, from French to German and back again to French control within a span of thirty years. To him the world wars had been a thirty years' civil war. He knew that France's policy of control over Germany was doomed, and he needed a substitute. He was willing to bank his political career on a good one. Jean Monnet provided him with it.

While creating and directing the Anglo-French shipping pool in World War I, Jean Monnet had become deeply convinced of the absurdities of purely national solutions and of the vital need to change the structure of Europe. In the early twenties, seeing before his own eyes that national sovereignty and the right of veto made such a change impossible, he had relinquished his deputy secretary-generalship of the League of Nations.

He had a few simple ideas on what to do about Germany and Europe. As he often says, he learned from one of his female ancestors, nicknamed "La Rabacheuse," * to have only a few ideas, and to repeat them constantly. He was convinced that in the interest of peace Germany had to be tied to the West, and that this could be done only by integrating it on a basis of complete equality into a European Community. In such a European Union there should be no veto power; governments would have to accept delegating some of their powers to a common executive. Only common institutions could solve the economic and political problems which Europe had to face; only they could give permanency to a new European structure. To get these changes accepted and rooted in popular support a common material interest between the peoples of Europe should be created first. Only on the realities of such a common interest, which would change man's outlook on his neighbor, could political unity be built, and political unity was necessary in order to change Europe from a deadly fire-trap into an element of peace and stability in the world. Coal and steel, the symbols of national power, the objects of French and German territorial conquests in the past and now at the center of the interallied discussion about the control of Germany, formed an obvious starting point. It did not matter that the field of action at the outset was limited; it was essential to begin.

Real change cannot be achieved wholesale; it must come gradually, step by step. To be effective action should be gradual,

---

* rabacher—to harp continually on a point.

based on necessity, rooted in reality and providing an answer to the burning questions of the day, while at the same time changing the existing context in which the great long-term issues seem unsolvable. Therefore, although indicating the final objective to be achieved—European federation—the concrete proposal Monnet submitted to Schuman was limited in scope—a European organization federal in structure but confined to the organization of production and distribution of coal and steel. Monnet was well aware of the fact that there was no logic in pooling only two sectors of the economy. But the limitation made it possible to start what one of his opponents later disparagingly called "l'engrenage" * and Monnet himself, the process of change.

How would the countries of Europe react to the French proposal? The need for a fundamental change had been brought home to Germany as to no other country. None was so exposed to the Soviet threat, none longed so deeply to be accepted as an equal, attempting to be freed from restrictive economic controls over its heavy industry while at the same time fearful of being sold down the river by its controllers, the three Western occupying powers, especially France.

Nevertheless, 17 million Germans were living in the Soviet zone of occupation. Was not this division Germany's primary problem? Could reunification be obtained, otherwise than through agreement with both East and West? Should Germany therefore not strive for a situation between the two blocks, refusing to become an integral part of the West? But to Chancellor Adenauer, Germany's primary problem was not simply reunification, but reunification *in freedom*. Liberty could not be sacrificed for unity. Germany should opt for freedom and for the West; it should work for reunification in freedom with and from within the West. Adenauer deemed European union not only possible but an absolute necessity for the success of the policy he had decided to pursue. His answer to Schuman's proposal was immediate and positive. He made his choice and upheld it, wavering neither then nor later. Had he made another choice, there would not now be a European Community.

Neutrality obviously precluded Sweden's or Switzerland's joining the proposed political enterprise, unambiguously announced as such. Austria was still jointly occupied by Russia and the West, who were negotiating endlessly about a peace treaty. Noncommitted Titoist Yugoslavia and Franco's Spain were not invited, though this was not overtly stated; certainly they did not them-

---

* Literally, a mechanism that swallows up.

selves consider participation. Countries like Portugal and Greece, though members of the OEEC and NATO, could not think of taking part in a market based on competition without tariff protection.

For the others, destined to become the Six, the answer was hardly in greater doubt than for Germany. Italy's largely Christian-Democratic government was fighting against the Communists at home and against isolation from its western friends abroad. The life of Italy's Prime Minister de Gaspari showed striking similarities with that of Robert Schuman. Born in that part of the Tyrol that had become Italian after World War I, under the Habsburgs he had sat in Austria's parliament. He too felt the tide. Neither did the Benelux countries have any serious hesitations. A few days after Schuman gave his press conference, the Dutch government, including both Christian-Democrats and Socialists, welcomed his declaration. The Netherlands might regret that the proposal was limited to coal and steel; but it might be wise to gain experience in a limited field first. Integration, not simply coordination, was proposed. Hoffman's elements, freedom of movement for goods and capital, were present. In any case coal and steel were important bottlenecks in the reconstruction of a country with insufficient steel and sources of energy. Above all, the proposal did promise to square the German circle! Not only would the proposed pool open an escape hatch to get away from the hopeless wrangles over the control of the Ruhr and the limitation and distribution of German production, but the proposed supervision of a common High Authority offered the hope of equal treatment while preventing domination by the Germans. Would it be possible after all to see Germany become prosperous again without becoming domineering? For Belgium the situation was not very different. A part of its coal mining industry, in bad shape and with extremely high production costs, had genuine fears; in the steel sector some were far from enthusiastic about free competition; some Socialists, when Britain refused to take part, feared what the German Socialist party (SPD) later called the three K's—Conservatism, Capitalism, and Catholicism.* But here too the tide easily swept over these reluctant elements.

But Britain's Labour government, after visits by Schuman and Monnet which were followed by an exchange of notes and letters, gave a negative answer. The discussion between Schuman and Monnet and the British government centered around the acceptance, demanded by France, of the principle of delegation

---

* All three words begin with K in German.

of powers to a High Authority, considered by Schuman and Monnet as the heart of their proposal. Monnet cannot have had many illusions about the British answer. A year previously, he and his closest collaborators had for several days discussed with a small group of high treasury officials sent by the British govern- ment the chances of setting up an economic union between Britain and France. Britain had refused, believing Monnet's aims to be completely unrealistic and willing to accept at most a bilateral commercial deal. But Schuman and Monnet were firmly decided to go ahead without Britain if need be. They believed that Britain would join later if European union proceeded from the hypothesis it was then to become a fact one day. To Monnet, Hitler's occupation of the Rhineland by the German army had contained an unforgettable lesson. France then had made its decision depend on Britain's—nothing had happened and war had become inevitable. Now, if necessary, France should take the lead alone, acting together with Germany, even if at the beginning Britain decided to stand aside.

Britain's refusal to participate, regretted in all the countries which had accepted the French invitation to negotiate, was felt as a greater shock in the Netherlands than anywhere else. Britain's absence, of necessity, meant the absence of Denmark and Norway, which would never dissociate themselves from Britain. Could the Netherlands enter into an important economic and political arrangement to which France and Germany were parties and Britain was not? Only a few years before, this would have been unthinkable. But through the loss of its colonies the Netherlands, deeply against its wishes, had become a continental country. The economic and political necessities of the situation were pressing. For five years the Netherlands had fervently hoped for a British lead, but none had come. Venerated men like Churchill had often urged the continent to unite, but never proposed that Britain itself should be a founding member of such a union. And now Britain refused to accept the principle of delegation of sovereignty as embodied in the proposed creation of a common High Authority. Although the Netherlands agreed that this proposal might perhaps be too radical, the political forces in the country nevertheless were convinced of the need to go in a federal direc- tion. Therefore, without much doubt and notwithstanding Britain's staying out, the Netherlands—more closely linked with Britain than any other of the Six—decided to go in.

Thus in June, 1950, in Paris, delegations of France, Germany, Italy, Belgium, the Netherlands, and Luxembourg, meeting for the first time as Six, began negotiations on what was to become the first of the European communities: the European Coal and Steel Community.

III . . . leads on to fortune . . .

For the next few years, the future of European integration depended on the success of the Schuman Plan.* First in Paris as president of the conference and of the French delegation, then in Luxembourg as president of the High Authority, Monnet concentrated all his energy, all his inventive capacity and all his contagious optimism on achieving this success. During the nine months that it took to turn the Schuman declaration into a treaty of one hundred articles and a number of annexes, he saw to it that neither the central objective, a European community, nor the proposed method, delegation of powers to common institutions, got lost in the mass of details about coal, steel, scrap, transport, wages, cartels, distortions, and discriminations. More than that, he never allowed the negotiations to become negotiations in the traditional sense. Apart from the basic objective and the method laid down in the Schuman declaration and accepted by each of the Six before negotiations began he showed great flexibility. The delegations were not confronted with French positions, as would have been normal and indeed as they expected, but were invited to discuss, to contribute, to help find common answers to common problems. Monnet never defended a merely national and therefore of necessity a partial view, but tried to define the general interest of the community the negotiations were establishing together. Some of the delegates, formed in the tug-of-war of economic negotiations of the "Schachtian" decade, at first believed that they were simply being tricked when, during meetings, they saw the little group of Frenchmen around Monnet disagreeing among themselves just as much as with other delegations. How could one negotiate one nation's special interest in orderly fashion against another's, if the inviting delegation seemed to have no clear view of the national interests it wanted to defend? But Monnet's method was so contagious, the attempt to find solutions for common problems instead of defending simply one's own national interests was so liberating and exhilarating, that none of the chief delegates resisted this new approach for very long. Monnet thus succeeded in creating

* About this moment the point of observation of the author moved from the Netherlands to the European Community. This was both the result of the influence of the Schuman Plan on Europe's post-1950 history, and of the author's participation, from June 1950 on, in the negotiations first, and the setting up of the Coal and Steel Community afterwards.

out of these hard-boiled negotiators a group of ardent Europeans, many of whom later came to Luxembourg to make the community work.*

Another development of outstanding importance took place during the negotiations. Even more than to the other political parties, the absence of Britain and its Labour government had been a serious disappointment to Socialists everywhere on the continent. Guy Mollet and his SFIO, the French Socialist party, now felt hesitant about it all. Were the French government (in which, at the time, they did not participate) and Monnet right in making British membership conditional on Britain's prior acceptance of the concept of a common High Authority and delegation of powers? Or was it a Catholic plot to keep Protestants out of the community?

In Germany, worse seemed to be happening. The SPD, recreated after twelve years of Nazi persecution by its leader, Kurt Schumacher, was turning against the plan. The causes of this were manifold and complex. Schumacher was bitterly opposed to Adenauer and his government. Nearly everywhere on the continent power was in the hands of center and right-of-center parties, mostly the Christian-Democratic parties. In France, Belgium and Italy, although not in Germany, they were exclusively Catholic. The SPD was a party not of the Catholic but of the Protestant parts of the country. Was there not some deep plot of Conservatism, Catholicism and Capitalism behind this apparently idealistic and internationalistic plan? Something else weighed even more with Schumacher. After World War I he had seen the upsurge of nationalism in Germany. With unflagging courage he had fought against it; he had spent ten years—an eternity—in concentration camps. Might not nationalism in his now tragically divided country raise its ugly head yet once again? And would it not be the mission and task of his SPD to canalize those feelings and bridle them?

---

* A typical example of this procedure was the introduction into the treaty of the Council of Ministers. The Schuman declaration had only proposed a common High Authority. The Dutch delegation suggested the introduction of a Council of Ministers. At first Monnet and Hallstein, the leader of the German delegation, were opposed to the idea. But in discussing the matter Monnet came to agree that the Dutch had a good argument—the national ministers *should* participate in the work of the community, both in the interest of its functioning and in that of getting them involved in the work of building a united Europe. But there never was any negotiation on the subject. The point was not granted to the Dutch in exchange for something else. It was simply accepted once the discussion had produced a general belief that the amendment was a good and even a necessary one. It was during one of these talks that Schuman, sitting in on a discussion, said: "Very good, I see that you are not negotiating, but looking for solutions together."

Never again should the SPD allow itself to be outflanked by nationalism; never again should it be possible to ostracize the Socialist leaders as "Vaterlandslose Gesellen." * Therefore the SPD could not allow itself to be in favor of a plan which integrated Germany into the West without at the same time offering a precise, clear road toward German reunification, Germany's number one national problem. Maybe something in Schumacher's inner self was equally fundamental. Ten years of the inconceivable hell of concentration camps, leaving him with a mutilated body, could not but have deeply marked his spirit. He may have seen and felt the tide—but somehow excess of suffering had dried up the inner well-spring which makes a man look toward the future, and believe in it. The political climate in the young Federal Republic was not propitious to the healing of such wounds. So Schumacher lined up his party against the coal and steel plan. This was a serious matter indeed. The Coal and Steel Pool, so Monnet thought, could fulfill its role as initiator of the process of change only if the new community was regarded as irreversible. But this would not be so if a change in majority and government in Germany could reverse everything.

From the very beginning, the powerful leaders of the German trade unions did not seem to agree with Schumacher's attitude. Men like Hans Bockler, then president of DGB (German Federation of Trade Unions), Hans vom Hoff, in charge of the economic department at DGB's headquarters, and many young leaders in their daily work were faced with the economic necessities which played such a part in creating the current. Not directly involved in party politics, they and their colleagues in the noncommunist trade unions of the Six discerned the political necessities unhampered by party-tactical considerations. During the negotiations, Monnet, who as head of the "Plan" had formed excellent relations with the French trade union leaders, now established close and regular contacts with all of them, urged trade union representation on the national delegations, and kept their leaders fully informed, convinced that the fear of Conservatism, Catholicism, and Capitalism would dissolve when the cards were laid on the table. Without the SPD later rallying to the policy of European integration, the "relance" after the defeat of the Defense Community would hardly have been possible; Europe's history might well have been different. During the negotiations Monnet laid the seeds for this development by the relations he created with the trade unions.

In August, 1952, after ratification in each of the parliaments

* "Fellows without Fatherland."

of the Six, the Coal and Steel Community began to function, with its headquarters at Luxembourg. Half a year later, as provided by the treaty, Europe's first common market came into operation. An impressive harvest was now quickly gathered in. After a few years it became difficult to deny that structural changes were taking place in the European economy. More rational patterns of trade in coal and steel were established, greater stability in the economies of the Six was brought about; modernization was spurred; gradual upward harmonization of conditions of work in the community countries was under way. Opposition among industrialists, at first strong especially in France but present in Belgium and even in the Ruhr, abated. Exaggerated fears about the deadly competitive qualities of the other producers evaporated —there proved to be room not only for everyone's existing business, but even for everyone's expansion. Industry, once the community had become established, accepted the new context and rapidly shifted its vested interest from the old to the new order, thus prefiguring the remarkable effect which the beginning of the general Common Market was to have in the years after its inception in 1958.

But for future developments the political results were even more important. First of all, the institutions, the High Authority, the Council of Ministers, the European Parliament, the Court of Justice, the Advisory Council (representing employers, employees, and consumers) all functioned and functioned well. Europeans from countries which had been at war with each other during the greatest part of history discovered their common interest and proved capable of working common institutions, finding solutions to common problems, obeying common rules, and even of paying a common tax! For the moment all this activity did not touch the masses, but it did touch a highly influential group of ministers, politicians, civil servants, industrialists, trade union leaders, and journalists. In their regular often weekly or even daily dealings with each other, mutual distrust and fear rapidly disappeared. New group interests, cutting across national borders, developed. Perhaps it was not so impossible after all to break away from the vicious circles of the past.

Other less visible, less spectacular, but no less important things happened. Monnet united the men who had come with him to Luxembourg into an able and devoted team, transmitting their enthusiasm for Europe to all of those with whom they dealt. The European Parliament became a graduate school in European integration for many of the leading politicians of the Six. Erich Ollenhauer, who upon Schumacher's death in 1952 succeeded him as leader of the SPD, and Herbert Wehner regularly came to Strasbourg and to Parliamentary Committee meetings in Luxembourg. Though they had voted against the community, they had not closed their minds to it but were willing to find out in what direction the enterprise was really going. Their trade union friends told them that they got more information in Luxembourg about what was going on in German heavy industry than they ever had obtained at home. Monnet never tired of explaining the need for and the way toward European unity. On closer acquaintance there seemed to be nothing sinister about either the man or his concept. Very few of the leading politicians and trade unionists failed during those years in Luxembourg to discuss privately and at length the problems of the day and of Europe with Monnet. They never found him seeking power, or keeping secret from one the thoughts which he had exposed to another. They also found him open to their own questions and problems, not brushing these aside but trying to relate them to the common task and problem uniting Europe. The grapevine, the secret telegraph which later seemed to link "good Europeans" in every one of the six countries and which contributed so much to the success of European integration, owed its origin to these conversations, as did the Action Committee for the United States of Europe, which Monnet formed at the end of 1955, after resigning as president of the High Authority.

In the meantime, outside Coal and Steel, things were not going well. In the autumn of 1950, during the Korean crisis, the United States had come to the conclusion that German rearmament was necessary. France, unwilling to accept the idea of a national German army but unable to hold out alone against the United States and its other NATO partners, proposed to apply the concept of the Coal and Steel Community to the problem of German rearmament. Thus the idea of a European army, the European Defense Community, was born. But the difficulties proved to be insuperable. From the beginning, France was torn between its wish to integrate Germany's military potential and its hesitations about integrating its own army. Even more than in the Schuman Plan, Britain's absence in this military affair formed a serious drawback. Why should France alone fulfill the task of providing a solution for German rearmament—something it did not desire and had not asked to accomplish?

Britain, now under a Conservative government, refused anything but vague promises of eventual association right until the defeat in 1954 of the European army in the French parliament. On the home front in France, the Communists and the Gaullists stood together in unholy alliance. Succeeding French governments, always in need of a few marginal votes, then mostly to be obtained from the right, temporized, adding a protocol here or a condition there and postponed ratification. In these circumstances, it was relatively unimportant that in the other countries of the Six all went well, ratification being never in doubt, although the SPD strongly opposed the European army plan and German rearmament in any form.

The unsolved problem of political command over the army led to plans for a political community elaborated by a group from the European Parliament presided over by Heinrich von Brentano. But although Monnet and his men in Luxembourg backed the results of their work wholeheartedly, these plans did not really coincide with the gradual approach of the Coal and Steel Community. The common interest, only just beginning to become manifest, did not yet form a foundation solid enough to withstand the divisive forces created by the prospect of German rearmament. Finally after nearly four years the end came in August, 1954. Mendès-France, the ministers of his government themselves abstaining, brought the treaty finally to a vote and to defeat. The Coal and Steel Community carried on; but the setback was serious. Any conceivable French government would need the votes of Guy Mollet's Socialist party in order to be in a position to cooperate with, let alone to be able to initiate a new European proposal. But though Guy Mollet himself favored it, the European army issue had deeply and bitterly split the SFIO. It was to be expected that the French Socialists and their leaders would be very loath to take up a European issue again. After the defeat of the European Defense Community, Monnet decided to retake his liberty of action in order to campaign for a European "relance" from outside the Coal and Steel Community, which was now on the rails and could manage without him. His plan was to set up an Action Committee of all the non-Communist political parties and trade unions of the Six, to act together as a guarantor to their respective governments that parliamentary majorities for new European proposals would be forthcoming; also, if need be, as a pressure group to push things forward; and finally as a kind of "Committee of Correspondence" of the Six, in which political and trade union leaders would together chart the course of action to be undertaken. In June, 1955, the foreign ministers of the Six met in Messina to appoint René Mayer as Monnet's successor. But things had happened in the meantime. Monnet, casting about for new opportunities, had been struck both by the prospects of the peaceful uses of atomic energy and by the impossibility of developing these prospects on the basis of action by separate European nations. In discussions with Spaak and between Spaak and Beyen* this idea, and a plan to set up a general Common Market in the wave of the common market for coal and steel, were both developed. Finally, the Benelux countries decided to take the initiative and launch a proposal to this effect, which was put on the agenda of the Messina conference. The British, finding Messina an outlandish place for foreign ministers to meet, declined the invitation to attend.

The Messina conference, birthplace of the Common Market, became a starting point for the "relance." Yet at the time this was difficult to believe, and the British impression that the whole conference did not seem worth a minister's trip was much more understandable than it seems with today's hindsight. France certainly did not seem intent to start the European business all over again. Still convalescing from the fevers of the European army debate, it wanted a period of calm. The new government† needed Gaullist votes; the name of Monnet and his trademark—integration and delegation of powers—were therefore unpopular in government quarters. Even the German government seemed hesitant, not about European unity as such but about the community method. The failure of the Defense Community with all the ensuing bitterness had been a profound disappointment to Chancellor Adenauer. He had wholeheartedly agreed with those who had been against the recreation of an independent, national German army. But events had taken their course—Germany had become a member of NATO, good relations with France had continued. Coal and steel, atomic energy, economic integration—all this seemed technical and the whole process too slow to help Adenauer solve his political problems. Ludwig Erhard, in whose domain as minister of economic affairs these matters lay, wanted a united Europe fervently but at the same time felt doubtful about the community approach, about institutions which contained the seed of "dirigisme" and in which only six of all the free European countries took part. Were there no simpler roads leading toward the liberalization of trade?

Nevertheless the current was there, everywhere present, even in France. Both the people and the press wanted the "relance" to begin. In France, where the great debate over national sovereignty versus the community approach had led to the defeat of the European army, public opinion noticed that the Western European Union, finally used to settle the problem of German rearmament, had not really solved anything; that the price of keeping things

* Then foreign ministers of Belgium and the Netherlands respectively.
† Led by Edgar Faure, who succeeded Mendès-France early in 1955.

as they were in France was to reconstruct them as they had been in Germany. In any case German rearmament, now decided upon, had ceased to be an issue; European integration and German rearmament ceased to be synonyms.

Under these circumstances ministers simply could not gather in Messina only to discard Monnet.* Spaak and Beyen brought along a paper—and a good one at that—which turned out to be invaluable when on the last day in the small hours of the morning, after an open air ballet and a supper, a communiqué had to be drafted. When the sun rose, the Benelux paper, watered down but not beyond recognition, had become the conference communiqué. In the following thirty months, things happened which turned the results of Messina from something seemingly accidental into the beginning of an important new chapter. Without the current and its lasting strength this would certainly not have been possible. With it, a series of actions and happenings led on to fortune. The procedure which the conference adopted, partly in order to avoid serious negotiations for the moment, proved to be immensely valuable. Without binding their governments, Spaak and experts from each of the six countries began to study how the Messina objectives could be realized. For more than six months they discussed together the outline of an integrated Common Market and a common organization for the peaceful uses of atomic energy. A few people from the Luxembourg team—in particular Pierre Uri—acting as technical counselors to Spaak and drawing upon their coal and steel experience, did a persuasive and excellent job. When negotiations began in earnest a year after Messina, the Spaak report, accepted as a guide line by the six governments, became the compass of the conference, keeping it on a straight course. It is doubtful whether anything would have been achieved if negotiations had started out simply from each nation's point of view, each nation's own particular interest. But now, with Spaak as president, his able advisers at his side and his report accepted as guide line by all the delegations, the common interest was present from the beginning, fulfilling much the same function as the European Commission was to fulfill when the Common Market actually got under way.

Liberated from his functions in Luxembourg, Jean Monnet

---

* After the fall of the Mendès-France government, Monnet had indicated that he was willing to serve another term as president of the High Authority if the governments of the Six decided to continue the European integration policy. Although the other governments would gladly have accepted Monnet, the new French government, for reasons indicated above, wanted a less controversial successor.

wasted no time in carrying out his plan. He began to make the first of his innumerable rounds of the capitals of the Six. Everywhere he met men who, through their work in the institutions of the Coal and Steel Community, had become his friends. If he needed someone he did not yet know, there was always someone who had known Monnet in Luxembourg and was willing to break the ice and undertake the introductions. Everywhere he found men, influenced by the tide, willing, even eager, to act if only they could see how. Monnet's plan was simple. An Action Committee should be formed—not of men, but of organizations. If the major political parties and trade unions would unite, meet, and make their common point of view known and felt, no government would resist. And the program was there ready to be taken: the Messina resolution. Why not, now that all the governments had agreed in principle, act together to see to it that the Messina resolution would be translated into a treaty, not in a watered-down form, but with real institutions, capable of acting in the same way as the institutions of the Coal and Steel Community?

There were no refusals and one acceptance was of fundamental importance: the acceptance by Ollenhauer on behalf of the SPD. From the beginning Monnet had little doubt that the German trade unions would accept. But the SPD had voted against Coal and Steel and against the European army. After three years of Luxembourg, however, little remained of the SPD's old hostility and fears about the three K's. The acceptance of the SPD not only meant that the committee would represent the vast majority of German political opinion, but also that it would become much easier for the SFIO to forget the bitterness of the past and unite again behind a European policy, now backed by the other major Socialist party of the Six.

The Action Committee met for the first time early in 1956, publishing the first of a series of resolutions intended to trace the road that the parties and trade unions of the Six were ready to travel together. By this time Guy Mollet had become prime minister of France, remaining in office during the vital period of the negotiation, obtaining from parliament a formal mandate to go ahead with the Euratom project in the summer of 1956 and with the Common Market early in 1957. Between those two dates lay the Suez episode. In France it strengthened the European current. It brought home beyond all possible doubt the changed position of Europe and its former great powers and so demonstrated forcefully the necessity of union. It also highlighted the danger of Europe's dependence on Middle Eastern oil. As in England, the shock of being cut from these sources placed the peaceful uses of atomic energy in the center of public preoccupation, turning it into a political matter of major importance. Especially in France the idea of pooling atomic energy became a source of strength to the integration concept.

For quite a while it seemed as if France would accept Euratom, but not the Common Market until a later date. Although the Coal and Steel Community had proved that French industry's fears of being inferior and of having too heavy a wage and social security bill to be able to compete, especially with Germany, were unfounded, this experience had not yet sunk in. But some of France's biggest and most modern enterprises were becoming increasingly export-minded. Exports had become more and more vital to growth and expansion and to earning necessary foreign currency. Those involved in export knew that they had to live in a competitive world even if competing with Volkswagen meant competing not in the home market but in North and South America. They were carrying the load of internal measures destined to help that part of French industry which was still "artisanal" and old fashioned. In this way they were having the worst of both worlds: competition in the export markets but not at home, where it would at least have forced the antiquated part of industry into making an effort too. Just as later industrial opinion convinced many a civil servant in Whitehall of the necessity of Britain's going into Europe, so the thinking of the leaders of the most modern, competitive, and export-minded part of French industry now influenced the French civil service.

One conversion proved just as decisive as the conversion of German socialism: that of French agriculture. The ablest French agricultural leaders knew that agriculture in their country was on the verge of a productivity explosion. Already the national market was ceasing to offer a sufficient outlet. Through the Plan de Modernisation they all knew Monnet, and they also felt that he was right in saying that the economic problems of France could not be solved within a limited national context. Germany was then importing about a third of its foodstuffs. What if the German market could become part of the home market? Maurice Faure, then dealing with European matters at the Quai d'Orsay, himself elected by a rural district, kept in close contact with agricultural leaders during the negotiations. With their backing a Common Market treaty could be ratified; without it, not. Gradually the farmers' leaders became convinced of the community concept, and their unspectacular conversion was decisive for the adoption of the treaty by the French parliament. In July, 1957, first the German Bundestag, CDU and SPD voting nearly unanimously in favor, then the French Assemblée Nationale, with a comfortable majority including all the Socialist and most of the farm vote, ratified what were now called the treaties of Rome, where they had been signed in March of the same year.

Industrial reaction was as it had been in the Coal and Steel Community. Even those who had opposed the Common Market as a new and unknown element in an already sufficiently uncertain world accepted it as the new context in which to work, now that it appeared irrevocable. From 1958 onwards trade within the community increased by leaps and bounds, probably more as a result of psychological than of pure tariff reasons. Interest groups, literally by the dozens, began to organize themselves within the new pattern even as industries began to plan their investments and build up their sales services in the new context, thus rapidly creating a new vested interest in its maintenance. Trade union leaders of the Six concluded that they had to defend their interests in common and should therefore define common attitudes. Across national borders political parties began to do the same. Monnet's Action Committee continued to act as a clearing house for ideas concerning further progress, contributing to keeping political and trade union leaders of the Six thinking along the same lines. Gradually the horizons widened from economic integration to political union, from organizing Europe to Europe's role in the world, from ending Europe's divisions of the past to Europe's becoming the equal of the United States in an Atlantic partnership.

Indeed, all this was bound to happen unless formidable obstacles were put on the tracks, unless something or someone managed to stop the tide.

President de Gaulle's European concept was very different from the community concept. But until he vetoed England's entry into the European Community his policies strengthened rather than weakened the community. By devaluating the French franc and accepting economic policies which prevented the price benefits of devaluation in export markets from being nibbled away too quickly, he gave French industry exactly that fillip it needed to get rid of the last shreds of its inferiority complex and make it rush into the new market with unexpected gusto. Seen from inside the community, only one event seemed like an attempt to stop the movement; and it came not from the inside but from the outside. This was Britain's proposal to include the European Economic Community in a large European Free Trade Area. The cause of Britain's abstention from the community has been discussed before, and a description of Britain's relation to the New Europe and the way it developed is dealt with in another article of this issue. Therefore only the impact of the free trade area episode on thinking inside the community is to be discussed here.

At first the British proposal, made even before the ratification procedure of the Treaty of Rome had been completed, seemed positively a real step forward, a British move toward the continent. But when the Common Market had begun to function and the consequences of the British proposal were more amply discussed and better understood, objections began to arise. Did the proposal take account of the political objectives of the community, as they had been discussed on the continent for nearly a decade? Did it not leave Britain, as so often before in European history, in and out of Europe at the same time? But if this was allowed to one nation, why not to every nation? And what then about integrating Germany irrevocably with Europe? Common rules, applicable to all without discrimination, were part of the basis of the community. Did Britain not ask all the privileges of membership, keeping at the same time all the privileges of being the center of the commonwealth? Above all, what would remain of the inner dynamics of the community? Certainly in theory the British proposal did not infringe the unity of the community. But shorn of its character as a custom union, would the community be capable of pushing on toward economic union, which was in any case more difficult to accomplish? And without economic union the final objective—political union—would never be attained.

Even in purely economic terms the proposal did not seem to make much sense or to be equitable. The economic debate on the continent had centered around the necessity of common economic policies to make free trade work. Now, as if nothing on this subject had ever been said, Britain proposed a return to a nineteenth-century free trade conception. And was it fair to leave agriculture out? Even to the Netherlands, ardently in favor of links between the community and the United Kingdom, this was unacceptable because it obviously jeopardized the community's common agricultural policy, still to be established. Furthermore, did it really make any sense to create a purely commercial European zone, to set up a sort of new imperial preference area, discriminating against the United States?

Slowly many of those who played leading roles in the community turned against the project. So did France, its political position strengthened by de Gaulle, its economic position by devaluation. But those who for different reasons had always been more attracted by the commercial than by the political side of the community hoped and fought for the success of the free trade area —Erhard on the basis of his deep attachment to economic liberalism; Dutch civil servants, looking traditionally toward England; trading circles in Hamburg, Bremen and Rotterdam, interested in trade, not in politics; industrialists with important markets in the United Kingdom and Scandinavia. But even in Germany and the Netherlands many industrialists, disliking the prospects of competing on unequal terms with British industries which would keep their tariff preferences in the commonwealth and which would profit from wages helped by cheap food, together with all those who looked at the community as primarily a political enterprise, became more and more convinced that the free trade proposal could not satisfactorily settle the relations between Britain and the community. Yes, the community should be open: but to those countries who wished to become members, accepting the same obligations in order to obtain the same privileges as the other members. And again, as at every important turn in the road toward a united Europe, the community view was backed by the United States. America's policy toward Europe, from 1945 on, has been remarkably steadfast. The United States has always favored an integrated European Community, hoping that it would develop into a political union, a United States of Europe. The only change in that policy was that the United States looked upon such a development at first mainly as an instrument for creating strength and stability in Europe, only then gradually beginning to see the unity of Europe as a necessary condition of establishing between itself and Europe the equal partnership which is urgently needed to carry out successfully the constantly growing tasks of leading the free world. The United States always wanted Britain to be part of the European Community, doing what it could to favor such a development. What it did not and could never want, because it was directly against its own economic interests, was a commercial zone, shorn of political promise and discriminating against it and the rest of the world. The common tariff of the European Community would be applied to outsiders only, not to insiders, and would therefore technically discriminate. But such discrimination, inherent in regional integration, could and should be accepted as a means to the objective of economic and political unity.

For many and complex reasons the slow and gradual change from first and generally favorable reactions to final opposition to the European free trade area was insufficiently explained to the United Kingdom. This contributed to making the "debate" between the community and Britain confused, and misunderstanding increased bitterness in England. Finally, at the end of 1958, seeing that the community—not just France—would not give in, Britain declared the long-drawn-out negotiation terminated. Inside the community the shock was not such that further internal progress was hampered or even delayed. Indeed, in the spring of 1960, though not without an internal tussle between the forces which had favored and those who had opposed the free trade area, the community decided to accelerate its pace by reducing tariffs between member countries more quickly than stipulated in the treaty. Ten years after the Schuman declaration it had become clear for everyone to see that the tide, taken at the flood, was leading on to fortune.

IV On such a full sea are we now afloat . . .

President de Gaulle's veto of Britain's entry into the Common Market, announced in his press conference of January 14, 1963, has created serious tensions in the European Community, putting to the test for the first time since the defeat of the European army the strength of the European tide. The decision of the British government, taken in the summer of 1961, to ask for negotiations in order to find out whether satisfactory conditions could be agreed upon for British membership had strengthened and broadened that current. More than anything thus far, Britain's decision brought the European Community from the economic page to the front page of Europe's and the world's newspapers, moving it into the center of political discussion everywhere, and helping public opinion to understand that the business of the community is politics, not business, as President Hallstein once remarked. Some of those who from the beginning had backed the community approach to European unity looked on Britain's application with doubt. They could not forget that for ten years Britain had been cool and aloof, on several occasions putting obstacles on the road ahead. Did this attitude now really belong to the past? Certainly, the customs-union part of the Common Market was functioning all right, being even ahead of schedule. But would not Britain's entry, bringing into the community new interests to be taken into account, endanger even among the Six future decisions on common economic policies, which are so much more difficult to arrive at than tariff reductions? And how did Britain feel about political unity, the most important objective of the community? Would Britain, once in, not stop all further movement in that direction, at least for years to come? Until the commonwealth conference in September, 1962, the British government, in explaining to Parliament and public opinion why it was taking the course it took, stressed the economic aspects of the community much more than its political character and objective.

And when after September, 1962, this political side was given more emphasis, the attitude of the Labour party and its leader, Hugh Gaitskell, became more and more openly hostile. Nevertheless, thinking in the parties and trade unions of the Six was largely and strongly in favor of Britain's entry. The British demand proved not only that their common enterprise was a success but also that the decision had been right to go ahead without waiting for Britain. Nothing succeeds like success; for this reason alone Britain's demand strengthened the community, and was therefore welcomed. Certainly, Britain's entry also contained risks for the community and its development. But how could the community without constantly accepting such risk remain dynamic; continue to generate the process of change, creating in an ever widening circle relations between states, based on common rules and common institutions, instead of on the law of the jungle? And how could Britain really ever become community-minded, except by becoming a member? In any case, once Britain had asked for them, the risks for the community of a failure of the negotiations were much more serious than those of Britain's entry.

More and more, over the years since its formation in 1955, the Action Committee for the United States of Europe had also stressed the importance of European political unity as an indispensable element in creating the necessary conditions for peace between East and West. At the same time, the idea that a United Europe, including England, should become an equal partner of the United States had gathered way. For Europe to have the strength and authority necessary to become such a partner, the contribution Britain could make to the community was felt to be important, even essential. In June, 1962, shortly before President Kennedy in his Philadelphia address on Independence Day declared himself clearly and eloquently a champion of an Atlantic partnership, the Action Committee adopted a resolution indicating as its next objective "the economic and political unification of Europe, including the United Kingdom, and the establishment of a partnership between equals of Europe and the United States." *

Of course, especially in countries like France and Italy, where protection had deep roots, certain industries were far from delighted by the prospect of increased competition inside the Common Market. Furthermore it was clear from the beginning that the French government was not enthusiastic about Britain's entry. But this seemed mainly a negotiating position, used to urge the community to dally no longer in creating the instruments for a common

* Resolution of the Action Committee for the United States of Europe, June 26, 1962.

agricultural policy and also in order better to defend French interest against British demands. Authoritative French voices repeated, right to the very end, that if only the technical problems could be solved France would not put any political obstacles in the way of Britain's entry into the community. On one point everyone inside the community agreed: Britain should enter on the same basis as the other members, accepting the same obligations and acquiring the same rights. Therefore there could be little or no changes in the treaty itself; subject for discussion could only be Britain's adjustment to the community and the way in which, once enlarged by British membership, the community should tackle its common problems, including those which before had been purely British. Without giving up the fundamental principle of equal treatment for all the members and thereby endangering the existence of the community itself, Britain could not be allowed after the adaptation period to maintain a special position within the community, nor could the British Commonwealth be given special conditions of access to the Common Market. On this point the American government, although warmly welcoming Britain's decision, entirely agreed with the Six: the negotiations should not lead to a new preferential arrangement between Europe and the commonwealth.

It is impossible within the context of this article to give even a short outline of the long and detailed negotiations which took place between the United Kingdom and the Common Market countries.* But when President de Gaulle forced the negotiations to be broken off, the most difficult commonwealth problems were already settled, with the exception of New Zealand's nearly complete dependence on the British market, and of some items like the future common external tariff on aluminum. As far as Britain's own farmers were concerned, Britain had accepted both the treaty and the regulations adopted since the community had began to function; discussion continued only on how Britain should adopt its agriculture to them in the years after entry. The institutional aspects of the treaty created no problems. One important question had not yet been discussed: the relations to be established between the community, once enlarged by Britain's entry, and the other members of EFTA.

Undoubtedly, during negotiations, the British government gave hostages to fortune by wasting precious time on details which should have been settled after, but not before, entry. Undoubtedly Britain weakened its case in presenting its decision to ask for

* Nora Beloff, who followed the negotiations for *The Observer*, has described them ably in "The General Says No."

membership for home consumption too much as based on economic, not on political grounds. But just as unquestionably, President de Gaulle did not break off negotiations because he believed technical solutions impossible, but because he believed them imminent. If he had insisted on bringing the negotiations to a speedy end, for example on the basis of a community proposal for the solution of problems still outstanding, he would have found little opposition among the Six. What caused the crisis, and is now putting the strength of the European tide to the test, is the fundamental difference which his action revealed beyond all doubt between his conception of Europe and Europe's place in the world and the conception concerning those matters held by the overwhelming majority of political opinion within the community.

First of all this difference concerns the method of uniting Europe. Although during the years de Gaulle had been out of office, he and his followers had fought against the Coal and Steel proposal as well as against the European army, rejecting their central element—common institutions based on delegation of powers —after taking office President de Gaulle did not act against the European communities. On the contrary, his actions strengthened them.

After the summer of 1960, when he discussed his proposals for political unity for the first time with Chancellor Adenauer, it became increasingly clear that his aversion of the community method had not abated. Nevertheless, for a time it seemed as if enough common ground between the Six did exist to make a start with political union. A large majority of those who were in favor of the community concept were ready to accept his proposal as a useful and even necessary preliminary to further progress in the field of foreign and defense policy, where delegation of powers is much more difficult to circumscribe than in the economic field and therefore can only be obtained through careful preparation.

At a meeting in Bonn, in the summer of 1961, very shortly before Harold Macmillan announced Britain's decision to seek entry into the community, an agreement about the principles of such a union was reached. However, it proved impossible to translate this agreement into a treaty text, largely because the French government demanded that the new organization should be entirely and exclusively intergovernmental in character and also seemed to intend to use the new union to weaken the existing community institutions, especially the European Commission, whose task it is to be spokesman and guardian of the common interest.

In the daily functioning of the communities and in the negotiations with the United Kingdom, however, France stuck to the rules of the community, written and unwritten.* But with his press conference of Januray 14, 1963, and the instructions he gave to the French delegation in Brussels to break off the negotiations President de Gaulle flew in the face of what is the essence of any freely formed community: that action must be preceded by collective decisions. President de Gaulle took his decision alone, acting against the strongly expressed views of all the other member governments and the European Commission. As according to the Treaty of Rome decisions concerning the entry of new members have to be taken unanimously by the member states and not by the community institutions, the French government did not violate the letter of the treaty. But its action did violate the spirit of the community, imposing on it, in a very important matter, a purely unilateral decision. Since 1958 the difference about the method of European unification had been a theoretical one: the community approach versus l'Europe-des-Etats; now it became a practical matter of the greatest importance.†

The first and inevitable consequence of de Gaulle's action has been that it is now much more difficult for member governments, when decisions have to be taken in the Council of Ministers, to give way to the community interest. The so-called "community spirit" is not something mystical. It is the institutionalized habit of seeking together the common interest and allowing it, with due regard to national interests, the ultimate right of way. The second difference that became manifest concerns the relations between the continent and Britain. Political opinion on the continent had accepted the need to go ahead without waiting for the United Kingdom, not because it doubted that Britain belongs to Europe, but because it believed that action could not wait and that only action would convince Britain to join. The Community of Six was accepted not as an ideal but as a temporary necessity in the knowledge, as Monnet once said before the European Parliament, that the boundaries of the Six were not drawn up by the Six themselves but by those who were not yet willing to join them. Now, according to the French president, the community should become a closed shop, open to

---

* With one serious and regrettable exception: in January, 1962, it ditched the able and European-minded French president of Euratom: Etienne Hirsch. This was not against the written, but certainly against the unwritten rules of the community.

† "C'est l'application à un cas concret des vues du Général de Gaulle. Préférant l'Europe des Etats à l'Europe Communautaire le président de la République a agi à l'égard de celle-ci comme si elle n'existait pas et comme si l'organisation des Six était fondée sur le principe de la simple association." Roger Massip: *de Gaulle et l'Europe*, page 124.

Britain only at some time in a nebulous future. His action conjured up old and recent memories of continental geopolitics and re-awakened fears of domination and of hegemony which the European Community was just beginning to relegate to the past.

The third difference which the action of the French government in January, 1963, revealed more clearly than ever before concerns the relations between Europe and the United States. No political voice of any importance within the community denies the necessity of adapting these relations to changing conditions. The Action Committee for the United States of Europe as well as President Kennedy himself declared to be in favor of a partnership of equals, of interdependence. "Europe for the Europeans," on the contrary, sounds like a strangely belated echo of an American doctrine formed more than a century ago, appears to be completely out of touch with reality, and at the very best promises a world of states, or coalitions of states, bigger, but in no other way different from those of the past. In a rapidly changing world, the European Community has appealed to people not as an end in itself but as a beginning of a process, as a ferment of change. The community has been built, as Monnet said in an address in London in May, 1962, "in order to find a way out of the conflicts to which the nineteenth century power philosophy gave rise."

Europe, as an independent third force, as opposed to Europe, equal but interdependent with the United States, appears not only as a dangerous anachronism but also as based on a static, antiquated conception of international relations devoid of even a shimmer of hope for the solution of the problems of our nuclear age.

It is relatively easy to establish the influence of President de Gaulle's veto on the functioning of the community. The tensions have not destroyed what has been constructed. The common interest has become a reality, the common institutions provide a crisis-resisting element of permanence. Europe is no longer dependent on the good will of a few mortal men, as in the days of Locarno. But at the same time further progress has become much more difficult, dependent of a quid pro quo at every step. This is what "synchronization" means, a formula accepted after de Gaulle's veto in order to set the community machine in motion again. More important than the impact on the daily functioning of the community, but more difficult to evaluate, is the influence of this veto on the European tide. More important, because the current remains the essential precondition to all future action. More difficult to establish, because less visible, therefore more difficult to measure. Almost no one in Britain and not so very many on the continent recognized after the defeat of the European Defense Community the unabated force of the tide. Furthermore, the strength of the current in its turn will be influenced by future political events inside and outside the community. Nevertheless an attempt must be made to evaluate what now is happening to the tide, how political opinion is affected by President de Gaulle's position on the three points mentioned: firstly the method of uniting Europe, secondly Europe's relation with the United Kingdom, and thirdly Europe's relation to the United States. As far as the method of European unity is concerned a return to the fundamentals of the community approach seems to be developing. During the years after 1958, with President de Gaulle and the community marching in practice in step, action appeared more important than theory and a "war of religion" seemed dangerous and unnecessary. Now that the conflict between the two approaches has become a practical matter, it is no longer possible to bypass the fundamental differences existing between them. Confronted by the consequences of President de Gaulle's "l'Europe des Etats," the necessity of delegation of sovereignty is appearing more clearly than ever. Difficult tasks are confronting the community, both internally and externally. Internally, common policies on agriculture, transport, energy, and economic expansion must be developed; externally, a success must be made of the Kennedy round and practical applications of partnership with the United States in defense, in monetary and economic policy, and in policies for the underdeveloped nations must be found. The community, in applying itself to these tasks, is beginning to find by painful experience that they cannot be achieved unless more powers are given to the community's institutions.

There are no indications that the dangers of nationalism and the absurdity of it in the modern world are being forgotten in European opinion. The Franco-German treaty, even allowing full credit for its psychological importance, is providing and will continue to provide practical evidence that bilateralism on the basis of intergovernmental cooperation only, has no force, no future, no reality. The negotiations with the United Kingdom have made it abundantly clear that "Brussels," with or without a Fouchet plan for political consultations, already, here and now, deals with political matters of the greatest importance. To deal with them successfully, greater powers are necessary.

But it is also appearing more clearly than before that the indispensable strengthening of the community institutions through delegation of powers is not possible without giving these institutions at the same time stronger democratic roots. The European Commission has been reproached with being technocratic. It is dealing with highly political matters, but receives its mandate only from the governments, not directly from the people. Also under present conditions it is often impossible clearly to define its responsibility before the European Parliament. During the first decade all this could not be otherwise; only gradual progress promised success. But events are now pushing forward—and are recognized to be doing so. Therefore the demand for "democratization" of the community institutions is heard with greater force, imposing itself on practical grounds, not as until recently mainly on theoretical ones.

Therefore, concerning the method of uniting Europe, President de Gaulle's action does not seem to weaken the tide. Neither does it appear to influence the current very much as regards Europe's relation with the United Kingdom. A "closed-shop" Europe looks like a new device for a highly unpopular and very old-fashioned product: the hegemony of one continental nation over the others, that is, the very opposite of the European Community the Six have begun to build. Nevertheless, there is one question that seriously worries even those who most warmly welcomed Britain's decision to seek entry into the community: that is, its position concerning nuclear defense. How can a country be convinced of the necessity of European unity and at the same time stay out of the only presently available plan for an integrated European-American nuclear defense organization (the Multilateral Nuclear Force), even stressing the importance of independent national nuclear defense? The attitude of the British government in these matters, incomprehensible to those inside the community, may result in convincing Europeans that next steps may be necessary, even if Britain once again, as in the past, is initially unwilling to go along.

What about the third point, Atlantic partnership? Here too what influences the tide in Europe is not the concept of a "Europe for the Europeans." There is a profound awareness in Europe that no important problem today can be settled by one country, even if this country happens to be the North American continent, or that part of Europe lying west of the Elbe, or even an imaginary Europe from the Atlantic to the Urals. Peace has become, for everyone to see, indivisible, and the organization of peace the central problem of politics in a way it never has been before. Only if the West remains united and at the same time proves capable of transforming the relations between free nations can progress toward the organization of peace be made. The policies of President de Gaulle threaten to divide the West; they do not contain elements for the transformation of relations among states. The European Community does transform them, basing the new relations on common rules and common institutions instead of on hegemony and domination as in the past. But in order to continue to do so, the community must remain an open community, a process of change, and not become simply a new superpower. The idea of such a community, open to others and progressing beyond itself, establishing the unity of the West through an equal partnership with the United States, remains immensely powerful and attractive. For the first time, during the summer of 1963, the trade unions of the Six organized a mass meeting to demonstrate in favor of the United States of Europe, "partner of the free world."

It is not lack of popular support which makes it difficult to translate the partnership concept into reality. Progress makes it necessary to gradually solve difficult problems. The principles of partnership are clear: it must be based on equality, and it must serve the organization of peace in the world as a whole; based not on domination but on common rules and common institutions. But what exactly does this mean in concrete terms? Does it mean in defense that Europe must have its own nuclear deterrent, integrated with the defense of the United States? Are there other ways of establishing equality? How can Europe voice its views in, and contribute to, the discussion about disarmament and "detente" between East and West? How should trade in such a partnership be organized so as to contribute the most to economic expansion and to the progress of the developing world? Trade should be freer, but is that enough? If not, how should the Kennedy round be used to obtain not only lower tariffs, but the beginning of a partnership in economic policy? What about agriculture in such a partnership? Should structural change in European agriculture be given greater emphasis than it gets at present? How, in this field, can the demands of economic common sense and those of social justice be harmonized?

Europe, hampered for the moment in its progress toward political unity as a result of the profound difference of view between President de Gaulle and political opinion elsewhere in Europe—including the French opposition parties—may prove to be a difficult partner during the next few years. The United States may become so absorbed by its internal problems or the problems of "detente" between East and West that it may lose interest in the partnership concept, which it will need a great deal of ingenuity and patience to realize. But it is not weakness of the current which will make it difficult to act on the Atlantic partnership, on Britain's entry into Europe, or on strengthening the community's institutions. Certainly the strength of the European tide, as it has manifested itself in the community approach, is put to a test today. Once before, in the years after 1954, this was the case; then the result was to strengthen it. Now, as then, the current, the essential prerequisite to successful action, continues to be strong. "And we must take the current when it serves, or lose our ventures."

RICHARD MAYNE

Economic Integration in the New Europe:
A Statistical Approach

I Introduction

TRADE traditionally follows the flag: but in the new Europe the order
is reversed. Since 1950, the six nations of what has come to be called
"the European Community"—Belgium, France, Germany, Italy,
Luxembourg and the Netherlands—have painfully sought to achieve
political unity under common rules and institutions; but the path
which they have so far followed to this long-heralded goal has been
the path of economic integration.

In 1950, the then French foreign minister, Robert Schuman,
proposed that France and Germany pool in a single market, un-
divided by trade barriers of whatever kind, their joint resources of
coal and steel. From this proposal, addressed equally to other European coal and steel producers, sprang the European Coal and
Steel Community, with its panoply of quasifederal "supranational"
institutions—the executive High Authority, the intergovernmental
Council of Ministers, the consultative "Common Assembly" of parliamentarians, and the supreme Court of Justice. Over a transition
period of five years beginning in 1953, the ECSC established a "common market" for coal, steel, coke, iron ore and scrap.

Meanwhile, a second attempt to pool resources came to grief.
This was the plan for a European Defense Community, or European
Army, which the French parliament failed to ratify in 1954. But one
year later, in June, 1955, ministers of the same six countries met in
Messina to propose further economic steps toward the goal of unity
which their countries had set themselves. From their deliberations
arose the European Economic Community and the European Atomic
Energy Community—better if less accurately known as the Common
Market and Euratom.

In these three organizations, an attempt is being made to combine the formerly national markets of the six community countries

in one single home market of continental size. From this progressive fusion of economic resources, it is hoped, full political unity will emerge.

Some commentators, indeed, would claim that within the limited field charted by the three community treaties, political unity is already a fact. The common institutions established by the treaties follow the broad pattern set by the ECSC: indeed, all three organizations share the same assembly, now renamed the "European Parliament," and the same Court of Justice. There is now a growing possibility that the other organs—the executives and the Councils of Ministers—will also be merged into a single Executive and a single Council. Likewise, the common rules governing the workings of the community organizations include a number of supranational aspects and call for common policies in a number of fields. In the official languages of the community—French, German, Dutch and Italian— the words for "policy" are identical with the words for "politics." It is therefore natural for community spokesmen to claim that what is being achieved is "political integration so far limited to the economic and social field." And there is at least some justice in their claim: for what the community seeks to integrate is indeed the part hitherto played by national governments in setting the conditions—holding the ring, or even weighting the odds—which determine the economic activities of private citizens, labor, capital, business and industry.

Nevertheless, the economist is likely to be interested less in semantic discussion of what the words "political unity" mean than in practical examination of whether "economic unity" is being achieved. That *something* is happening in the European Community is plain to the most superficial observer. But as Nicholas of Cusa once remarked, "knowledge is always measurement." Unfortunately, measurement in the present case is particularly difficult. Before attempting it, there may therefore be some value in surveying the much abused term "economic integration."

II The Theoretical Background

The simplest, as well as one of the earliest, of all the arguments in favor of economic integration was that advanced by Adam Smith. "The division of labor," he pointed out, "is limited by the extent of the market." [1] But while some advocates of larger markets may seem at times unduly trusting in their acceptance of classical economic theory, later work on the subject has shown it to be more complex. In 1947, a League of Nations study declared that "customs unions are to be advocated to the extent that they bring about greater freedom of trade, that is, to the extent to which greater opportunities are afforded for specialization in production, costs are reduced, and the exchange of goods is intensified." [2] In 1953, Professor James Meade drew attention to the fact that the mere "intensification" of trade was not enough; and he made a useful distinction between what he called "the optimization of trade" and "the maximization of resources." [3]

Both of these aims are traditionally associated as much with free trade as with customs and economic unions. Indeed, as Professor Jacob Viner remarked, "the customs union problem is entangled in the whole free trade-protection issue, and it has never yet been properly disentangled." [4] But Meade himself was careful to stipulate that arguments based on both the optimization of trade and the maximization of resources "rely throughout upon the assumption that prices correspond to marginal utilities to consumers and marginal costs to society"; and a large part of his own work was devoted to demonstrating that the full advantages of "a single free-trade market" could not be assured without some degree of economic integration:

> We may conclude that the free movement of labor and capital within our economic union is in general to be desired in the interests of economic efficiency and of raising standards of living to the highest possible level. But in order that such an integration of the market for the factors of production, as well as for their products, should have this desirable effect, three conditions must be fulfilled. First, the individual member-states must not be too out of line with each other in their domestic policies concerning the distribution of income and property. Second, the individual member-states must not be too out of line with each other in their choice among direct controls, fiscal policy, and monetary policy for the stabilization of their domestic economies. Third, the individual member-states must not be too out of line with each other in those social and economic policies which determine their domestic demographic trends.[5]

Or, as the League of Nations study put it, still more sharply:

> For a customs union to exist, it is necessary to allow free movement of goods within the union. For a customs union to be a reality it is necessary to allow free movement of persons. For a customs union to be stable it is necessary to maintain free exchangeability of currency and stable exchange rates within the union. This implies, *inter alia,* free movement of capital within the union. When there is free movement of goods, persons, and capital in any area, diverse economic policies concerned with maintaining economic activity cannot be pursued. To assure uniformity of policy, some political mechanism is required. The greater the interference of the state in economic life, the greater must be the political integration within a customs union.[6]

Comprehensiveness was thus now seen to be one requirement in any attempt to secure the benefits traditionally associated with the mere freeing of trade. A second was growth. Pierre Uri, in particular, has pointed out that "the classical argument for the redistribution of productive resources has only a limited scope. The gain derived from making better use of resources is out of proportion to that derived from a faster rate of growth. More precisely, the two factors must be combined, and the distribution of resources must be reconsidered from the growth angle. The gradual shift of activity from low productivity sectors to high productivity sectors, from declining industries to expanding industries, from one branch of an industry to another or from one firm to another in the same branch is the essential element for increased productivity in the economy as a whole, in other words of growth. Similarly, the classical argument of the size of markets is not conclusive in its elementary form: there are few industries for which the market of a large country is not sufficient to ensure the optimum size of the firm. But a larger market enables several firms to take advantage of optimum size, or, in other words, reconciles optimum size with the maintenance of competition."[7]

A good, if slightly overoptimistic, picture of how a larger market may thus be viewed in dynamic rather than static terms is provided by another French expert:

Only a larger market appears to be able to give full scope for research, productivity, lower production costs and increased consumption. . . .

A large market opens the way to mass production. . . . It is thus possible to ensure that machinery and equipment are fully employed. . . . It enables manufacturers to cut down those overhead charges which do not increase in proportion to output. . . .

The advantages which accrue to industry internally are matched by benefits arising from the degree of specialization which only a huge market permits. Moreover, a firm which is assured of a large number of consumers can enjoy the advantages of specialization without necessarily increasing its size. . . . The specialization of workers and staff, of equipment and tools, and of marketing channels, contribute both to the full employment of men and machines, as in mass production, and to their more rational use from the point of view of efficiency and lower production costs. In particular, a large and steady market for a specialized firm is an essential prerequisite for any serious attempt at staff training and industrial or scientific research. . . .

But . . . it is only competition which will ensure that all the benefits . . . will be passed on to the consumer. . . . By reviving and intensifying competition a large market is therefore a factor in economic progress and the raising of living standards. . . .

By guaranteeing the free movement of raw materials, manpower and capital, as well as of goods, it tends to bring the distribution of economic activity into line with the requirements of productivity. The borrowing of money becomes easier. There is less fluctuating in marketing, and hence less uncertainty attaches to expansion. . . . Industries such as atomic power and civil aviation, which it would be prohibitive, or at least very expensive, to operate in a limited market, become viable. . . .

All these factors tend to reduce production costs and selling prices.

In addition, there is the possibility of a net reduction of one element of the price through the abolition of customs duties. The result should be an increase of purchasing power and a rise in the real standard of living. The increased number of consumers of a particular product should thus permit an increase in consumption and hence a greater increase in investment.

Economic expansion then begins to snowball. . . .[8]

Many of these ideas, in slightly different form and with somewhat different emphasis, recur in the "Spaak Report," which was the first blueprint for the European Economic Community. This declared:

The aim of a European Common Market must be to establish a vast area of common economic policy, constituting a powerful productive unit and making possible continuous expansion, increased stability, an accelerated raising of living standards, and the development of harmonious relations between the States which it joins.

To attain these objectives, a fusion of the separate markets is an absolute necessity. It is that which makes it possible, by an increased division of labor, to eliminate the wastage of resources and, by a greater security in supplies, to abandon lines of production which are carried on irrespective of cost considerations. In an expanding economy, this division of labor finds expression less in the displacement of existing lines of production than in the more rapid development, in the common interest, of those which are the most economic. Competitive advantage will moreover be determined less and less by natural conditions. Just as atomic energy gives greater liberty to the settlement of industries, the common market will give full scope to the management of firms and to the quality of human beings: the pooling of resources ensures equality of opportunity.

This fusion of markets opens large outlets for the use of the most modern techniques. There are already productive activities which demand such vast resources, or machine-tools of so great an output that they are no longer appropriate to the scale of an isolated national market. But above all, in many branches of industry, national markets offer the opportunity of attaining optimum dimensions only to firms which enjoy a *de facto* monopoly. The strength of a large market is its ability to reconcile mass production with the absence of monopoly.

Protective measures which eliminate external competition, moveover, have a particularly bad effect upon the progress of production and the raising of living standards: that is, the means and the incentive which they provide for the elimination of internal competition. In a larger market, it is no longer possible to organize the maintenance of outdated methods which result at one and the same time in high prices and in low wages; and firms, instead of preserving the *status quo* unchanged, are subjected to continual presure to invest in order to increase production, to improve quality, and to modernize their methods: they have to progress in order to survive.

These advantages of a common market cannot be obtained, however, unless time is given and unless resources are made collectively available, to make possible the necessary process of adaptation; unless measures are taken to put and end to practices whereby competition between producers is distorted; and unless coöperation is established between the States to ensure monetary stability, economic expansion, and social progress.[9]

Such was the theoretical background of the Rome Treaty establishing the European Economic Community, signed on March 25, 1957. How faithfully this reflected the theories that lay behind it can be seen from its text:

It shall be the aim of the Community, by establishing a Common Market and progressively approximating the economic policies of Member States, to promote throughout the Community a harmonious development of economic activities, a continuous and balanced expansion, an increased stability, an accelerated raising of the standard of living and closer relations between its Member States.[10]

To this end it proposed:

—the elimination, as between Member States, of customs duties and of quantitative restrictions in regard to the importation and exportation of goods, as well as of all other measures with equivalent effect;
—the establishment of a common customs tariff and a common commercial policy towards third countries;
—the abolition, as between Member States, of the obstacles to the free movement of persons, services, and capital;
—the inauguration of a common agricultural policy;
—the inauguration of a common transport policy;
—the establishment of a system ensuring that competition shall not be distorted in the Common Market;
—the application of procedures which shall make it possible to coördinate the economic policies of Member States and to remedy disequilibria in their balances of payments;
—the approximation of their respective municipal law to the extent necessary for the functioning of the Common Market;
—the creation of a European Social Fund in order to improve the possibilities of employment for workers and to contribute to the raising of their standard of living;
—the establishment of a European Investment Bank intended to facilitate the economic expansion of the Community through the creation of new resources; and
—the association of overseas countries and territories with the Community with a view to increasing trade and to pursuing jointly their effort towards economic and social development.[11]

The treaty quoted above came into force on January 1, 1958; and it is due to have accomplished the whole process of establishing a Common Market among its signatories by December 31, 1969. How far can its effects already be traced in practice?

III The Community Context

The foregoing theoretical analysis, however summary and inadequate, makes it clear that the quest for the "results" of economic integration in Europe is beset by a number of difficulties. The first is the general problem summed up in the logical fallacy *post hoc, ergo propter hoc*. Statistics have been and will be quoted in an attempt to "prove" that integration has "succeeded"—or "failed"—in various ways: but any reader of Hume must be aware that conclusions drawn from them can at best be only tentative. In the present instance, this general caveat applies with even greater force, chiefly for two reasons. In the first place, some degree of economic interdependence already existed among the EEC countries before the Rome Treaty began to be applied; and by the same token their economies were already rapidly expanding. In the second place, these countries are still only midway along the course which the Rome Treaty charts; and academic theory would suggest that the full effects of integration can be detected only when the process is complete. In some degree, this argument is qualified by the phenomenon of "anticipation," whereby the business community in particular bases its plans and actions upon the future situation which it expects: but this merely adds to the difficulty of analysis a psychological factor which is even harder to assess. Finally, just as the dynamics of integration thus complicate the problem of isolating its "results," so its comprehensiveness increases the difficulty of disentangling one such "result" from another. Even elaborate theoretical discussion, in other words, may ultimately founder against both the continuity and the complexity of economic change.[12]

To forestall all the difficulties, it would no doubt be necessary to analyze in detail the long-term secular changes in Europe's economies which are clearly independent of measures or policies applied under the Rome Treaty. These would certainly include such things as the development of synthetics and the fertilizer revolution in world agriculture, as well as changing attitudes and priorities which now, for instance, place greater emphasis upon redistributive measures and general development policy. Likewise, it might ideally be desirable to attempt a detailed preliminary study of the situation and tendencies prevailing in the EEC's member states when the Rome Treaty came into force. This would require, in particular, a description of the measures and policies applied both within the Belgo-Luxembourg and Benelux economic unions and under the treaty establishing the European Coal and Steel Community. Some discussion of the latter, indeed, is inevitable in this context: but for the present it is perhaps sufficient to recall its existence. More to the point, however, is a brief summary of the setting for economic integration that has so far been achieved under the Treaty of Rome.[13]

By July 1, 1963, the customs duties between the member states of the European Economic Community had been cut across the board to 60 per cent of their original level as on January 1, 1957. Quantitative restrictions on trade in industrial products had likewise almost entirely disappeared, both within the EEC and *vis-à-vis* the rest of the world. Recourse to safeguard clauses had been comparatively limited. By the same date, the second of three moves had been made toward the establishment of the EEC's single external customs tariff. In the first move, made on December 31, 1960, those duties which were only 15 per cent higher or lower than the common tariff level were replaced by the common tariff, and in other cases the difference was reduced by 30 per cent; in the second move, made on July 1, 1963, this difference was again reduced by 30 per cent. On both these occasions, the calculation took as its basis the common tariff lowered by 20 per cent; and part of this reduction was confirmed in the so-called "Dillon round" of negotiations under the General Agreement on Tariffs and Trade (GATT), completed on July 16, 1962. In addition, a number of tariff quotas were conceded to member states in respect of particular products. At the time of writing, therefore, the customs union provisions of the Rome Treaty were some two thirds of the way to full implementation, and the EEC in this respect remained something of a hybrid between a partial customs union and a partial free trade area.[14]

Similar but less striking progress had been achieved in the liberalization of the factors of production. On June 12, 1961, a first Regulation was issued to facilitate the free movement of labor; and already in 1958 the EEC had adopted a system, first worked out under the ECSC, to reduce to the minimum any loss of social security benefits suffered by migrant workers. A number of restrictions and difficulties still remained at the time of writing, however, and the national labor market still enjoyed prior claim on vacant jobs.[15] For the liberalization of services and of the right of establishment, two broad timetables were agreed on December 18, 1961, but by July 1, 1963 only two specific directives on this subject had been issued, and the first major measures in this field were taken only at the end of the year.[16] The liberalization of capital, on the other hand, had gone somewhat further. A first directive on the subject, issued on May 11, 1960, granted unconditional freedom to a broad category of capital movements, including direct investments, and conditional freedom to a number of others; this directive was supplemented by a second on December 18, 1962. By mid-1963, the chief remaining official obstacles affected only noncommercial medium- or long-term loans, shares in national industries and a few other items.[17]

In agriculture, a first series of EEC regulations, covering grains, pigmeat, eggs, poultry, fruit and vegetables, and wine, was agreed to on January 14, 1962, and began to operate on August 1 of that year. Prior to that date, a number of minimum price systems had been maintained or introduced, and one long-term agreement—on grains—had been concluded by France and Germany in 1959.[18]

In transport, a proposed action program for a common policy had aroused much detailed discussion, and member states had agreed to begin on January 1, 1964, the abolition of differential freight rates favoring domestic over interstate traffic. But the chief practical measures affecting the present study were the ban on discriminatory pricing or conditions of transport based on the origin or destination of the goods in question, and the undertaking of a number of measures to improve road, rail and waterway communications. The former came into force on September 5, 1960; the latter, which included such projects as a Brussels-Paris motorway, a new Alpine road tunnel, and the electrification of a large number of railroads, were proposed in June, 1960, and for the most part were rapidly taken in hand.[19]

On competition policy, some degree of alignment of national laws had been achieved during the early years of the EEC's existence; and in December, 1961 and February, 1962 a first regulation on "anti-trust" policy was adopted. A fair start had been made on processing some 35,000 applications under this regulation by mid-1963, but its implementation was still too recent to have had verifiable results which would be relevant to the present study; and in this broad field the changes brought about in state monopolies, among other things, had so far been more measurably significant.[20]

If progress was thus difficult to measure here, the same was true of the EEC's attempts to coordinate economic policies and approximate national laws. The work of the European Social Fund was more easily quantified: by December, 1963 decisions had been taken for the payment of $14,135,900, affecting some 200,000 re-employed workers. At the same date, the European Investment Bank had approved loans totaling $335,300,000 and thereby facilitating a global investment of more than $1,535,300,000. Nevertheless, the integrating effect of these operations remained more difficult to assess. Finally, mention should be made of association with the EEC of African and other states, since the EEC had extended to them the same tariff reductions as had been effected between its own member states.[21]

This brief survey of the economic measures so far taken by the EEC suggests two main conclusions. The first is that although the Rome Treaty has been applied more rapidly than had originally been planned, it has still not had its full direct impact upon the economies of the six countries. Much remains to be done, particularly in the liberalization of the factors of production and in the gradual fusion of national economic and commercial policies. The full customs union and the full economic union thus lie in the future. Second, moreover, a number of factors may still stand in the way of full economic integration even when the implementation of the Rome Treaty can be considered to have been completed. Differences of language, tradition and even dietary habit are likely to continue; and even if these are discounted as permanently unalterable, it will still take time for even less deeply rooted characteristics to change. In some existing customs unions, indeed, there still persist many of the disparities that theoretically impede economic integration: in Switzerland and in the United States respectively, tax laws differ, for instance, from canton to canton and from state to state. Similar differences seem likely to persist within the EEC.[22]

It would be a mistake, therefore, to expect the economies of the six EEC countries to display the same degree of integration as that which might normally be achieved within a single nation-state. Nevertheless, the tendency is likely to be in that direction; and a study of the practical changes which have taken place within the complex of those economies suggests that, provided there be reasonable certainty that the customs and economic union will ultimately be achieved, the phenomenon of "anticipation" already mentioned may well be more influential than the specific measures so far taken on the way to such a union.

IV Integration in Practice

All that has been said hitherto serves to emphasize the interdependence of the various aspects of economic change. Production, productivity, trade, the flow of manpower, capital investment, industrial organization, the general pattern of economic life—all influence each other, and none can be discussed in isolation. For the sake of clarity, however, it may be permissible here to consider each in turn.

1. PRODUCTION

Strictly speaking, the growth of production is at best only a very indirect index of the "effects" of economic integration: but it is one which has been frequently cited as "proof" of the "success" of the European communities. *Per se*, the figures are certainly impressive. In the European Coal and Steel Community, steel production rose from 41.9 million metric tons in 1952 to an estimated 72.7 in 1962: this compared with increases in the United Kingdom from 16.7 to 20.8 and in the United States from 87.8 to 91.1. Iron ore production in the community rose from 65.3 million metric tons to 92.3 over the same period;[23] and if the figures for coal showed a decrease, this was due chiefly to changes in the overall pattern of energy consumption which were independent of the community's existence.[24] In the broader framework of the European Economic Community, the gross national product of the six countries, expressed in real terms, stood in 1962 some 27 per cent higher than the 1957 figure. This increase compared with figures of 14 per cent for the United Kingdom and 18 per cent for the United States. Community industrial production, meanwhile, had risen by nearly 40 per cent. During 1963, this expansion continued, with a further 4 per cent rise in gross national product, and 5 per cent in industrial production, while forecasts for 1964 predicted increases of 4.5 per cent and 6 per cent respectively.[25]   Italy's GNP has grown by 59 per cent since 1958, Luxembourg's by only 15 per cent. The Belgian record is similar to that of Luxembourg; while Germany with 35 per cent, the Netherlands with 34 per cent, and France with 29 per cent, take intermediate places in the scale.[27] In some degree, these differences may be explained by the differing levels of these countries' economic development: they reveal, indeed, a process of leveling upwards. But they also show that membership of the EEC has not so far ensured an automatically rapid growth rate. Second, the intermediate annual and monthly figures show continued cyclical fluctuations— a reminder that more general factors complete for influence with the specific effects of progressive integration. Third, the case of Austria, which between 1953 and 1960 achieved an increase in industrial production of nearly 70 per cent, demonstrates, if proof were needed, that a high growth rate was possible outside a community framework. Finally, the EEC countries themselves were already enjoying extremely rapid growth in the early 1950's. To this last objection it may justly be replied that their continued growth at a similar rate thereafter, when postwar recovery and the flood of refugees were both coming to an end, may itself be ascribed to the advent of the Common Market;[28] but in the welter of rival conjectures, the safest conclusion may be that of Professor Walter Hallstein, who expressed it thus: "It may be objected that these growth figures are no index of the success of the Common Market; but my reply would be that they certainly show that it has not failed." [29]

2. PRODUCTIVITY

At first sight, productivity may seem a more reliable indicator of the effects of economic integration. Progressive integration, that is, should theoretically lead to two main results. First, there should be a shift of activity to higher productivity sectors, industries and firms, leading to greater specialization internationally and even within national borders. Second, the same phenomenon should enable fuller advantage to be taken of latent capacity and of optimum size. In practice, of course, all of these advantages are likely to be interrelated, and no purely statistical approach to them is likely to disentangle cause and effect. This difficulty is increased, moreover, in a period of expansion, when such shifts as may occur do not necessarily result in greater mortality among less efficient firms, since these merely enjoy a declining proportion of the generally increasing prosperity. In such a period, finally, productivity may rise largely as a result of increased capital investment and modernization, much of which could be expected to take place irrespective of specific community measures or policies.

Nevertheless, the evidence in this field is not unimpressive. In the Coal and Steel Community, which undertook special programs designed to modernize backward pits,* coal output per man-shift underground has climbed steadily, despite the comparatively modest and unsustained rise in coal production. While coal production rose from 238,900,000 metric tons in 1952 to a peak of 249,100,000 in 1956, and then fell away again to 226,988,000 by 1962, output per man-shift underground increased progressively from 1389 kilograms in 1952 to some 2174 ten years later.[30] Over the same period, with an increase in steel production from 41.9 million metric tons to 72.7, the number of man-hours worked in the ECSC's steel industry remained fairly constant at around 1000 million per year.[31] In the broader field of the European Economic Community, productivity since 1957 has risen by some 20 per cent—faster than in either the United Kingdom or the United States.[32] Here too, while the figures by no means prove the success of EEC policies, they may more modestly suggest that at least those policies have not been counterproductive.

3. TRADE

The same general caveat applies, of course, to conclusions based upon the evolution of European trade; but in this field statistics are perhaps more directly indicative of the growing interpenetration of markets. This is evident, in particular, in three main ways. First, one may compare the figures for trade with those for production. Second, one may compare the early trade figures for ECSC products with those for products which did not then enjoy even the beginnings of a "common market." Finally, one may consider regional shifts in trade, and compare the development of trade among the

---

* Notably the Sulcis coal mines in Sardinia, and the Belgian coal-mining district of the Borinage.

EEC countries with that of their overall trade with the rest of the world. In all these respects, it would seem that integrationist policies have at least been accompanied by the kind of changes that one might expect to result from them.

Trade and production: The first comparison of trade and production figures is afforded by the early experience of the ECSC. Between 1952 and 1960, the output of products subject to the European Coal and Steel Community—coal, iron ore, coke, steel and scrap—increased by some 35 per cent: but intracommunity trade in the same products rose by some 200 per cent. In 1952, about 16 per cent of the community's output in these products was traded among the community countries: by 1960, the proportion was about 33 per cent.[33] A similar tendency can likewise be detected in the so far partial experience of the European Economic Community as a whole. Here, while gross national product and industrial production have risen by 27 per cent and 40 per cent respectively between 1957 and 1962, the figures for intracommunity trade have almost doubled.[34] While about one quarter of the EEC's internal trade was made up of trade in ECSC products, it nevertheless remained clear that even in other products intracommunity trade was increasing more rapidly than production. This at least showed that the interpenetration of markets was rapidly taking place.

Trade in "integrated" products: That such increased interpenetration was at least partly the result of integrationist policies is suggested by a second set of figures. As has been pointed out, the "common market" was established by the ECSC for coal, steel and other products long before intracommunity trade barriers began to be reduced by the EEC; and at first, trade in ECSC products reflected this discrepancy. Between 1952 and 1955, indeed, it increased by 89 per cent, as compared with 61 per cent for all other goods. The differential, however, was not completely maintained. By 1958, indeed, other goods had overtaken the global increase in ECSC trade. In part, this was no doubt due to a double phenomenon of "anticipation," which in the early days of the ECSC gave a spurt to intracommunity trade in its products, and later, as the EEC began to loom on the horizon, caused a similar spurt to affect other goods. At least equally important, however, was the change in the position of coal already mentioned: for while the lead of ECSC products in general was soon overhauled, trade in scrap and steel still continued to grow far more rapidly. By 1958, the intracommunity trade figures for these two products were respectively 300 per cent and more than 150 per cent higher than in 1952, while the corresponding figure for other goods was just over 100 per cent. In the following two years, the scrap and steel figures grew even more rapidly.[35]

Regional trade patterns: A little more body and color is lent to these general statistics by a consideration of the geographical distribution of the trade to which they refer. Here, once more, the first evidence is that of the European Coal and Steel Community. In 1952, before the opening of the "common market" for coal and steel, there was a tendency for supplies to be channeled, often over long distances, to outlets within the same country. With the advent of the ECSC, markets in other community countries began to assume greater importance.

In the case of coal, these regional shifts were particularly evident in the trade of the Aachen and Limbourg mining areas. In 1952, the Aachen area sent 56.7 per cent of its total sales to other regions of Germany, and only 15 per cent across the nearby frontiers to Belgium, the Netherlands and Luxembourg. By 1959, its sales to the rest of Germany represented only 35.5 per cent of the total, and its sales to the Benelux countries had risen to 34.9 per cent. Similarly, the Dutch Limbourg area, which in 1952 had sent 88.6 per cent of its sales to the Netherlands and very little to Belgium and Germany, was by 1959 sending only 61.5 per cent to the Netherlands, while its outlets in Belgium represented 10.1 per cent and those in Germany 4.9 per cent of the total, with a similar increase, from 3.1 per cent to 11.9 per cent, in the proportion of its sales to France.[36]

Corresponding changes meanwhile affected other ECSC products. Between 1952 and 1959, southern Germany's deliveries of rolled steel from the rest of the Federal Republic increased by 18 per cent: but its imports from other community countries across the nearby borders rose by 450 per cent. A similar phenomenon is observable in the movement of scrap supplies for northwestern Italy; and in general it seems true to say that the opening of the common market for coal and steel has been followed by a rationalization of trading patterns as well as a greater interpenetration of markets.

Whether this is also true of the much broader field covered by the European Economic Community remains more difficult to judge. One reason for this, as has been suggested already, is the degree of interpenetration which the markets of the community countries enjoyed when the EEC came into being.

The European Economic Community has been described, somewhat colorfully, as "a bargain between French agriculture and German industry." [37] Whatever the merits of this remark as an indication of future hopes on both sides, it does little justice to the trade patterns already in being at the time when the EEC treaty was signed. In 1957, it is true, Germany was the biggest importer of agricultural produce from other community countries; but her biggest supplier—and the community's biggest exporter to other community countries—was not France but the Netherlands. France, on the other hand, was the main exporter of raw materials to her community partners, and Germany the biggest importer; but slightly more of France's exports of these commodities went to Belgium and Luxembourg than to Germany. At the same time, Germany was France's biggest community supplier of fuels and oil: at $188 million, this was the biggest single trade item in the community. For animal and vegetable oils and fats, a comparatively small item, the Netherlands were the biggest exporter to other community countries, while Germany accounted for two fifths of intracommunity imports. For chemicals, Germany was the biggest supplier and Belgium and Luxembourg the biggest importers, although the trade was very diverse, with its biggest single current running from Germany to the Netherlands. Of machinery and vehicles, Germany was by far the biggest exporter; but here again the pattern of trade was fairly evenly divided between her partners, and the main single importer, by a short head, was not France but the Netherlands. For the final category of "other manufactures," Belgium and Luxembourg and Germany were the main exporters, and the Netherlands and Germany the main importers.[38]

The total picture was therefore more complex than might have been supposed. Moreover, it only partially bore out the supposition that the EEC countries were each others' chief customers.* On an average, one third of the community countries' foreign trade was done with other member states: the highest percentages—around 40 per cent—were those of the Benelux countries; next came Germany; and the lowest were France and Italy, with about 25 per cent. each. A similar disparity marked the proportion of each country's gross national product accounted for by foreign trade. Here, the highest figures—around 90 per cent—were for Luxembourg; the Netherlands followed, with some 60 per cent; next came Belgium, with some 35 per cent; then Germany, with 25 to 30 per cent; then Italy and France, with less than 20 per cent. Both as regards the proportion of its foreign trade that was intracommunity trade, and as regards the importance of foreign trade as a whole in the global economy, the EEC resembled Germany rather than Benelux at one extreme or France at the other.[39]

How far have these general patterns been modified since the EEC treaty began to be applied? The most striking fact is that trade between the community countries has shown a far greater percent-

* See the press conference given by President de Gaulle on January 14, 1963.

age increase than those countries' trade with the rest of the world. Between 1958 and 1962, intracommunity trade increased by 97 per cent, from $6790 million worth to $13,404 million worth. At the same time, the community's global imports from the rest of the world rose by 38 per cent, from $16,156 million worth to $22,327 million worth, and its total exports to the rest of the world by 29 per cent, from $15,911 million worth to $20,638 million worth. The absolute value of the increase in the community's imports from the rest of the world was thus slightly greater than that of the increase in intracommunity trade; but in the case of exports the discrepancy was reversed, and much greater, in absolute terms; while for both exports and imports the percentage difference was immense. This suggested, therefore, that something of the same interpenetration of markets was taking place within the EEC as had already occurred in the ECSC. It was true that in the five years 1953–1958 the increase in trade among the members of the then future EEC had been of the order of 80 per cent: but the fact that this rate of growth had now been increased, and in a period of slower economic expansion, seemed to justify the claim that integrationist policies were taking effect.[40]

Almost as striking as the difference in the rate of growth of internal and external community trade are the differences between various community countries. Here Italy leads the field, both as regards her trade with other community countries and as regards her total foreign trade. From 1958 to 1962, her total imports have increased by some 110 per cent, and her exports by some 99 per cent. Within the community, her imports have increased from $687 million worth in 1958 to $1887 million worth in 1962, and her exports from $608 million worth to $1625 million worth. The next biggest trade increase is that of Germany's total exports, which have gone up by 76 per cent since 1958: after that come the Netherlands with 50 per cent. On the import side of the balance sheet, France has registered the biggest increase, of 49 per cent, closely followed by Belgium and Luxembourg and by Germany. In intracommunity trade, Germany remains the biggest importer and the biggest exporter: but in the former respect her rate of increase, outstripped by Italy, is rivaled by France; while in terms of the rate of growth of her export trade, France actually joins Italy in outstripping her.[41] These figures may suggest that higher tariff countries, once inside a customs union, are likely to increase their exports to their partner countries at least as fast as the latter are able to invade the formers' hitherto protected markets. They may also, perhaps, show that the balance in trade within the whole area is likely to level up as the process goes on.

189

4. MANPOWER

Even the barriers to the movement of goods include human factors of taste and habit which are unlikely to disappear rapidly or as a result of administrative acts. *A fortiori*, the same applies to the movement of manpower. Here too the experience of the ECSC was indicative: in one early experiment, for instance, it sought to induce 5000 miners to move from the declining Centre-Midi area to new jobs in Lorraine, but in the event only some 650 felt it worth their while to move to a new environment, with poorer weather, fewer old friends, and the fear of uncertain prospects.[42] In a Europe still divided by language and custom, old habits die hard, and the mobility of labor remains small. Strictly comparable figures are not easy to obtain, partly because while all the Community countries maintain statistics of newly-arrived foreign workpeople, there are often no data about those who leave. One report, published in 1961, estimated at some 520,000 the total number of community nationals exercising a wage-earning activity in a country of the community other than their own—this out of a total force of some 74 million. To this figure should be added upwards of 25,000 seasonal workers and workers merely crossing the frontier to go to their daily work. A year later, the corresponding report evaluated the total at some 564,000, with some 87,000 frontier and an unknown number of seasonal workers: but the apparent increase should be treated with caution, since many of the component figures come from different years and may appear more imposing only because in the second report the statistical net was a little more finely woven.[43] A more reliable, if still only partial, picture is provided by the number of new work permits annually issued in each of the six Community countries to nationals of the remaining five. In the years immediately preceding the setting-up of the Common Market institutions, this number was 156,414 for 1956 and 186,400 for 1957. In 1958 it dropped to 156,476, falling in 1959 to 137,707. Then it rose very rapidly to 249,107 in 1960 and 292,192 in 1961, falling only slightly to 275,907 in 1962.

It would be tempting to regard these last figures as an indication of greater mobility of labor in the emerging Common Market; and in some degree this may be true. What is at least equally significant, however, is that recent increases are almost wholly confined to Germany, where the dwindling of the number of refugees has helped to create a severe labor shortage. New work permits issued in Germany to applicants from other Community countries rose from 53,502 in 1959 to 208,030 in 1962—nearly four times the previous figure. Common Market measures may well have facilitated this movement of labor; but they can hardly be held to have caused it, since over the same period the number of new work permits issued to non-Germans from outside the Community rose even faster, from 31,131 in 1959 to 186,958 in 1962—just over six times as many.[44]

Of all the Community workers employed in Community countries other than their own, the largest total number were in France, followed by Germany; an overwhelming proportion of the workers involved (68 per cent) were Italians, with Belgians, Germans and Dutch heading the very much smaller figures for the rest. The figures, such as they are, thus corroborate the familiar stereotype of Italian migrant labor; but owing to their disparate origins and often remote date they do little to suggest that economic integration has so far led to widespread migration of labor.

One reason for this comparative immobility is the high level of employment that the community countries at present enjoy. At the end of 1957, there were 2.6 million unemployed in the community, or 3.7 per cent as compared with 1.1 per cent in the United Kingdom and 4.3 per cent in the United States. By 1962, the figure had fallen to 1.8 million (2.4 per cent), and by mid-1962 there was an acute shortage of skilled labor in most areas of the community, including northern Italy.[45] Partly in consequence, wages were rising steadily: from 1958 to mid-1962, the increase was 33 per cent in Germany, 27 per cent in France, 17 per cent in Italy, and 20 per cent in the Netherlands; while for 1962 as a whole, the overall increase of gross income from paid employment in the EEC was 10 per cent. Surveys conducted by the ECSC indicated that real wages of coal and steel workers had not only increased but had moved closer together in doing so. As a result, there were sometimes greater disparities between the incomes of comparable workers in different regions of the same country than between the different national averages.[46] A similar trend seemed likely within the EEC, particularly since both the Christian (CISC) and free (ICFTU or CISL) trade union federations had organized themselves on a community basis, with special secretariats in Brussels and Luxembourg to try to coordinate their activities in the various community countries.[47]

5. CAPITAL

Given the imperfections of the "European money market" (if such it can be called, since stock exchanges in the Six still remain primarily national), as well as the tradition of secrecy that still shrouds many European business operations, it is even less easy to marshal evidence on capital movements than it is to assemble valid statistics for the movement of labor. A little simpler to evaluate is the volume of capital investment in general. During the 1950's, the European Economic Community was investing somewhat less than 20 per cent of its gross national product—more than in either the United Kingdom or the United States. The curve representing gross capital formation per year, after rising steeply during the early 1950's, flattened out somewhat, though still moving rapidly upwards, during 1956 and 1957. If this perhaps reflected uncertainties about the fate of the EEC and Free Trade Area negotiations, a marked change took place in mid-1958, when the investment curve moved suddenly upwards once again. By 1961, the annual rate of increase in capital investments stood at 9 per cent; and although in the following year this figure had dropped to 5.5 per cent, public expenditure had somewhat compensated for the slower rate of growth. In 1962, new public and private issues in the EEC totaled some $8.3 billion.[48]

Particularly striking, and particularly well documented in view of New York's dominant role, was the part played in this general development by the increase of United States investments in the European Economic Community. From 1956 onwards, while the total annual increase of all United States investments overseas fluctuated between roughly $2 and $3 billion, the annual increase in the community rose from $238 million to some $400 million in 1961, bringing the total to $3041 million by the end of that year—a rise of 81 per cent since the EEC began. The growth was fastest in Germany and Italy, and slowest in Belgium and Luxembourg. How far such investment was a direct result of the existence of the EEC remained impossible to judge; but subjective impressions, based on many conversations with businessmen of several nationalities, suggest that the link, if only psychological, was strong. During the four years 1958–1961, moreover, 608 American firms established themselves in community countries, as against 235 in all the rest of Europe.[49]

6. INDUSTRIAL ORGANIZATION

In addition to the increase of investment, one of the most evident features of European industry in the last few years has been the formation of new links, associations and agreements among firms. While capital formation is not always clearly traceable to the European Economic Community's existence, many of these other manifestations undoubtedly are. In the first place there may be mentioned the proliferation of industrial and commercial federations, associations and study groups, all organized on a six-nation basis and explicitly inspired by the existence of the EEC. By 1960, already, there were more than 200 such groupings, a full list of whose names and affiliates fills a volume more than an inch thick.[50] A similar if slimmer volume lists 81 similar organizations in the agricultural field.[51]

Such associations represent a reflection, on the business level, of the EEC organizations in the governmental and administrative field. More to the point, however, as indicators of economic integration in practice may be the various mergers, agreements, and other material links which have been formed by firms since the EEC came into existence. Obviously enough, a qualitative judgment about their effects is quite out of the question. Some may indeed be arrangements which will in due course be subject to the "anti-trust" provisions of the EEC treaty; some, while not necessarily falling under such a ban, may make little or no contribution to the rationalization which is one of the supposed benefits of economic integration. Many, nevertheless, may indeed serve that end. To list them all would be impossible, as well as tedious, for not all such links can be traced. Attentive reading of trade and financial newspapers and other sources, however, has resulted in the following figures, spread over the first few years of the EEC's existence.

Agreements between firms in different EEC countries: By June 1959: 50. By August 1961: 167. By February 1962: 189.

Mergers between firms within an EEC country: by June, 1959: Germany: 6, Belgium: 5, France: 50, Italy: 4, Netherlands: 13. By December, 1959: Germany: 12, Belgium: 14, France: 85, Italy: 3, Netherlands: 10. By August, 1961: Germany: 19, Belgium: 23, France: 85, Italy: 22, Luxembourg: 12, Netherlands: 20. By February, 1962: Germany: 26, Belgium: 49, France: 88, Italy: 34, Luxembourg: 22, Netherlands: 33.

Such crude figures as these can only be of impressionistic value; but—apart from the Luxembourg totals, swollen by the formation of holding companies partly as a result of governmental encouragement—they seem to indicate two main tendencies. The first is that, so far as one can judge, new mergers between firms in any one country still outnumber new international agreements; even in countries that were somewhat slow off the mark, this trend now seems to be well developed. This might suggest, if no more, that as trade barriers fall or threaten to fall competitive pressure is leading to larger scale organization. The hint seems to be borne out, secondly, by the fact that for the periods in question France shows by far the largest number of regroupings—an index, perhaps, of the stimulus exerted by the beginnings of economic integration upon an economy previously characterized by a fairly high level of protection from outside competition and by the survival of large numbers of small, sometimes family concerns. This general theme is supported, moreover, by sector studies made in various industries, as well as by personal observation; and it may be significant that French fears of the EEC quite quickly gave way to eagerness to exploit its benefits, at least on the part of such powerful organizations as the Patronat. The experience of the Coal and Steel Community, which had already pointed in this direction, may thus be borne out in the wider field.[52]

V The Pattern of Economic Life—Conclusion

It is comparatively simple both to predict the future impact of such changes as have been sketched out so far, and to show that the existing tendency is already set in that direction. What is well-nigh impossible, however, is to prove satisfactorily any connection between the two. One can foretell, for instance, a gradual decline in the share of agriculture in total European Economic Community production and a further drift from the land; one can foresee a further growth in the relative importance of services. In the marketing field, one can expect the growth of chain stores and self-service, of further vertical integration, of more installment selling, and other developments which at present especially characterize the United States. In the field of consumption patterns, one can foresee a continued rise in apparent steel and energy consumption, an increase in the number of consumer durables, and greater relative expenditure on rents and clothing, but less on food. All this it is convenient, if misleading, to call "an increase in the standard of living."

Such an increase, undoubtedly, is already taking place within the EEC. The proportion of national production represented by agriculture has fallen over the ten years 1950–1960 from 11 per cent to 7 per cent in Germany; from 14 per cent to 10 per cent in France; from 28 per cent to 17 per cent in Italy; from 14 per cent to 11 per cent in the Netherlands; and from 9 per cent to 7 per cent in Belgium. The drift from the land has continued, although too slowly to compensate fully for the rise in productivity. The importance of services in the total economy has increased, especially in Italy and France. The number of retail shops per head of population is decreasing, and the size of them is growing; while there are now some 37,000 self-service stores throughout the EEC as against a tenth that number in 1957. More generally, steel and energy consumption are increasing rapidly, and within family budgets the proportion represented by food is declining in France and Italy, while that for rent is growing in these countries as well as in the Netherlands. The face of

Europe is thus changing in a very real and measurable sense: in certain ways, it is becoming what some would call "Americanized," others "affluent," and others "less underdeveloped." [53] What is equally clear, however, is that these changes, for good or less good, are not developments that the creation of the European Economic Community has called into existence. They had begun before the drive for European integration was initiated: if it were to fail, they would continue after it was spent.

The European Community, however, is still young. Economists will probably always differ as to how much the integration of Europe's economies can be proved to have accelerated these processes. For my own part, I believe that its true impact is likely to increase. Ultimately, however, it must always remain unmeasurable, because it is psychological and political, not statistical. But for "unmeasurable" I personally prefer to read "immeasurable." Nicholas of Cusa was not always right.

REFERENCES

1. Adam Smith, *The Wealth of Nations*, Book I, title of chapter iii (Everyman's Library edition, London: 1910), Vol. I, p. 15.

2. *Customs Unions: A League of Nations Contribution to the Study of Customs Union Problems* (New York: 1947), p. 75.

3. J. E. Meade, *Problems of Economic Union* (London: 1953), pp. 9 ff.

4. Jacob Viner, *The Customs Union Issue* (New York-London: 1950), p. 41.

5. Meade, *op. cit.*, p. 12; p. 82.

6. *Customs Unions*, p. 47.

7. Pierre Uri, "The meaning of economic integration," in *Aspects of European Integration* (London-Paris: 1962), pp. 1–2.

8. J.-F. Deniau, *The Common Market* (London: 1960), pp. 13–16. Cf. also Tibor Scitovsky, *Economic Theory and Western European Integration* (London: 1958); R. Sannwald and J. Stohler, *Wirtschaftliche Integration* (Basel-Tübingen: 1958); Walter Hallstein, *United Europe: Challenge and Opportunity* (Cambridge, Mass. and Oxford: 1962), pp. 30–57; R. Mayne, *The Community of Europe* (London: 1962 and New York: 1963), pp. 63–67; 117–128.

9. *Comité intergouvernemental créé par la Conférence de Messine, Rapport des Chefs de Délégation aux Ministres des Affaires Etrangères* (Brussels: 1956), pp. 13–14. (Author's translation.)

10. *Treaty establishing the European Economic Community*, Article 2, (unofficial) English edition, p. 17.

11. *Ibid.*, Article 3.

12. For some instances of this general difficulty, cf. Alexander Lamfalussy, "Europe's Progress: Due to Common Market?" *Lloyds Bank Review* (October, 1961), New Series, No. 62, pp. 1–16; Mayne, *op. cit.*, pp. 16–19; L. L. Sermon, "Dynamics of Economic Integration," in J. Frederic Dewhurst and others, *Europe's Needs and Resources* (New York: 1961), pp. 818–861; J. E. Meade, *UK, Commonwealth and Common Market* (London, 1962), Hobart Papers, No. 17.

13. On the Belgo-Luxembourg Economic Union (BLEU), cf. J. E. Meade and others, *Case Studies on European Economic Union* (Oxford: 1962); on the European Coal and Steel Community (ECSC), cf. in particular L. Lister, *Europe's Coal and Steel Community* (New York: 1960) and W. Diebold, Jr., *The Schuman Plan* (New York: 1959). See also Sermon, *op. cit.*, pp. 821–830, and studies cited in Mayne, *op. cit.*, pp. 176–179.

14. For details, cf. the annual *General Reports* of the EEC Commission, and EEC Commission, *The First Stage of the Common Market: Report on the Execution of the Treaty (January 1958–January 1962)* (Brussels: July 1962), pp. 17–24. Tariffs on non-liberalized agricultural products had been cut by 45 per cent—i.e., less than those on industrial goods—but here tariffs had less effect.

15. EEC Commission, *Fourth General Report* (Brussels: 1961), pp. 52–56; *Fifth General Report* (Brussels: 1962), pp. 57–60.

16. EEC Commission, *Fifth General Report,* pp. 66–71; *Sixth General Report,* provisional edition, mimeographed (Brussels: 1963), pp. 27–31.

17. EEC Commission, *Fourth General Report,* pp. 60–66; *Sixth General Report,* provisional edition, pp. 32–33. It should be noted that even the first EEC directive on this subject represented an advance on the Code of Liberalization of the Organization for European Economic Cooperation (OEEC): cf. Å. O. Liljefors and J. A. Johnson, "International Capital Movements in Recent Years," in *Ekonomisk Revy,* Häfte 4, (Stockholm: April, 1961).

18. Cf. EEC Commission, *Fifth General Report,* pp. 140–166; *Sixth General Report,* provisional edition, pp. 126–162. On minimum prices and Franco-German grain agreement, cf. *Fifth General Report,* pp. 48–49, and *Third General Report* (Brussels: 1960), p. 92. Further regulations, on beef and veal, rice, and dairy products, as well as on the EEC agricultural fund, were approved on December 23, 1963.

19. EEC Commission, *Fourth General Report,* p. 149; and *Recommendations for the Development of the Infrastructure of Transport within the Community,* mimeographed document VII/COM(60)76 Final-E (Brussels: June 21, 1960).

20. Cf. EEC Commission, *Fifth General Report,* pp. 72–92; *Sixth General Report,* provisional edition, pp. 34–61. On state monopolies, *ibid.*, pp. 14–17.

21. On the Social Fund, cf. EEC Commission, *Sixth General Report,* provisional edition, p. 181; on the bank, *ibid.*, p. 124; on the associates, *ibid.*, pp. 210–213. Most of the associates' products remained subject to quotas, chiefly under national marketing organizations. In addition to its loans within the EEC, the bank had by December, 1963, approved loans of $23,000,000 in

Greece, facilitating a total investment of $54,700,000. Otherwise, however, the association of Greece with the EEC, which came into force on November 1, 1962, was too recent to have had any appreciable economic effects at the time of writing. The same was true of the Agreement of Association with Turkey, signed on September 12, 1963, and of the trade agreement with Iran, which came into force on December 1, 1963.

22. Cf. EEC Commission, *Rapport du comité fiscal et financier* (Brussels: 1962) —the "Neumark Report," so called after the president of the committee which produced it, Professor Fritz Neumark.

23. Statistical Office of the European Communities, *Eisen und Stahl* (Brussels-Luxembourg: 1963), No. 1, p. XXVIII; p. 2.

24. Cf. Mayne, *op. cit.*, p. 95.

25. EEC Commission, *Sixth General Report*, provisional edition, p. 107. 1963 and 1964 figures in Robert Marjohn, *Les Problèmes Economiques du Marché Common en 1964* (Documents de Commenanté Européenne No. 20, Paris: 1964), pp. 3–4.

26. Lamfalussy, *op. cit.*, pp. 5–8.

27. Statistical Office of the European Communities, *General Statistical Bulletin* (Brussels-Luxembourg: 1963), No. 2, p. 17.

28. Cf. Uri, *op. cit.*, p. 2.

29. W. Hallstein, "The European Community: A New Path to Peaceful Union" (Azad Memorial Lectures, New Delhi, 1963), EEC Commission, mimeographed document No. 3591/PP/63-E (Brussels: 1963), p. 17.

30. Rolf Wagenführ, "Sur le Chemin de l'intégration européenne," in *Informations Statistiques*, Office Statistique des Communautés Européennes (Brussels-Luxembourg, 1961), No. 1, pp. 5–41 (p. 8); Office Statistique des Communautés Européennes, *Charbon et autres sources d'énergie* (Brussels-Luxembourg: 1963), No. 1, p. 25; High Authority of the ECSC, *Third General Report* (Luxembourg: 1955), p. 46; Statistical Office of the European Communities, *General Statistical Bulletin* (1963), No. 2, p. 22.

31. Cf. note 23 *supra*, and *op. cit.*, p. 61.

32. European Community Information Service, *A New World Power* (Brussels-Luxembourg: 1961), p. 2. The precise figures in 1961 showed an increase over 1957 of 19% in the EEC, 12% in the U.K., and 13% in the U.S. The community's total labor force meanwhile increased from 71.9 million to 72.8 million.

33. Wagenführ, *op. cit.*, p. 11.

34. Cf. note 27, *supra*, and Statistical office of the European Communities, *Foreign Trade Monthly Statistics* (Brussels-Luxembourg) *passim*. In 1958, intracommunity trade totaled some $6790 million: by 1962, this figure had reached $13,404 million.

35. Wagenführ, *op. cit.*, pp. 9–12.

36. Wagenführ, *op. cit.*, p. 18.

37. Walter Lippmann, *Western Unity and the Common Market* (Boston-Toronto: 1962), p. 14.

38. EEC Commission, Direction Générale du Marché Intérieur, Direction "Industrie, Artisanat, Commerce," Division "Commerce," *Note sur les échanges intérieurs de la Communauté Economique Européenne en 1957* (mimeographed document no. 221/59).

39. EEC Commission, *Report on the Economic Situation in the Countries of the Community* (Brussels: September, 1958), pp. 111–112.

40. Statistical Office of the European Communities, *Foreign Trade Monthly Statistics, passim;* on 1953–1958, cf. Lamfalussy, *op. cit.*, p. 10. During the first nine months of 1963, trade between member countries increased by a further 16% over the corresponding period of 1962, while the Community's exports to the rest of the world rose by 4% and its imports by 11%.

41. Statistical Office of the European Communities, *Foreign Trade Monthly Statistics* (1963), No. 4, pp. 18, 24.

42. *Bulletin from the European Community for Coal and Steel* (London: 1956), Vol. III, No. 5, pp. 3–6.

43. EEC, Commission administrative pour la sécurité sociale des travailleurs migrants, *Premier rapport annuel* (Brussels: 1961), pp. 80–83; *ibid., Deuxième rapport annuel* (Brussels: 1963), pp. 88–90.

44. Statistical Office of the European Communities, *Statistiques Sociales* (1963), No. 4, *Statistique de l'Emploi 1958–1962*, pp. 247–261. The present figures are derived from a collation of those on pp. 256–260.

45. Cf. note 32, *supra;* and Chase Manhattan Bank, Economic Research Department, *Report on Western Europe* (New York, April–May, 1963) No. 23, p. 2.

46. ECSC High Authority, *Real Incomes of Workers in the Community* (Luxembourg, 1957), pp. 23–24.

47. Cf. R. Colin Beever, *European Unity and the Trade Union Movements* (Leyden: 1961), *passim.*

48. Cf. note 32, *supra;* EEC Commission, *Sixth general report*, provisional edition, p. 95.

49. Cf. note 32, *supra; Journal Officiel des Communautés Européennes*, 6e Année, No. 48 (March 26, 1953), pp. 974–978.

50. EEC Commission, *Répertoire des organismes communs créés dans le cadre de la Communauté économique européenne par les associations industrielles, artisanales et commerciales des six pays* (Brussels: 1960); Mayne, *op. cit.*, pp. 18–19.

51. EEC Commission, *Répertoire des organisations agricoles non gouvernementales groupées dans le cadre de la Communauté économique européenne* (Brussels: 1959).

52. EEC internal information; P. Fabra, G. Mathieu, A. Murcier and Pierre Drouin, *French Industry and the Common Market* (Information Service

of the European Communities, Community Topics No. 5, London: 1962);
on ECSC experience, cf. Diebold, *op. cit.,* pp. 412–415.

53. Chase Manhattan Bank, Economic Research Department, *Report on Western
Europe,* (New York: June–July, 1962), No. 18, p. 4; EEC Commission,
D. G. Marché Intérieur, *Les Appareils Commerciaux des pays de la CEE*
Document de travail (Brussels: December 1961); note 32, *supra;* Neumark
Report (cf. note 22, *supra*), p. 108. Cf. also Readers Digest Association,
Products and People, report of a survey carried out in January and February,
1963 (London, 1963), *passim.*

Note: The opinions and other statements contained in the foregoing article are
those of the author only, and cannot be considered as committing any
institution or other body, including those cited in the notes.

WILLIAM CLARK

New Europe and the New Nations

I The Imperial Past

THE most historically significant fact for Europe since the wars has
been that it has lost its empires. In a few years now the process
which began so recently will be complete and Europe will hold
dominion over no colonial territories beyond a few bases and
islands of which for historic or economic reasons it has been impossible to disembarrass itself. But the end of colonialism does not
denote the end of the colonies; these countries which we fathered
continue to exist as nations even though we no longer have full responsibility for them. The change is a change only of relationship;
Europe has to live with Indochina and the Gold Coast in the modern
world even though they have altered their names and become independent.

The question before Europe is what its new relationship with
these new countries is to be. How differently will its motives be
mixed in the postimperial era from the mixture that constituted
imperialism? For it is a profound, though common, historical error
to imagine that these motives of the imperialists, and their consequent relations with the colonies, were unmixed and unchanging.
In fact Europe acted for economic, strategic and philanthropic
motives; pride, fear, charity, greed, religion and adventure all
played their part in the relationship. So they will in the future,
though in a different mixture, for history is a continuum without
sudden breaks; the end of colonial power removes only one strand
in a complex relationship. To estimate the future it is necessary to
understand the past.

The saying that Britain acquired her empire in a fit of absence
of mind conceals the truth that neither Britain nor the other European powers had a conscious policy for building their empires. But
it was not a motiveless policy; rather it had many unexpressed
motives.

The most obvious motive was *economic*. The early Elizabethans were merchant venturers who sailed the seas partly for the reason that men today climb Everest, but partly because they hoped to find Eldorado. (What they in fact found on the Eldorado venture was British Guiana!) In the eighteenth century Europe was seeking cheap labor through the ghastly traffic of the slave trade. By the nineteenth century Britain was anxious to preserve and extend her empire economically as a market for the goods which she produced as the result of her early industrial revolution, and which were increasingly being produced more cheaply by newcomers to industrialization. The tropical colonies were also regarded (for instance by the Dutch in the East Indies) as a political method of pre-empting raw materials. Britain even became dependent on obtaining food supplies from her empire—wheat from Canada, meat from Australia, tea from India and coffee or chocolate from Africa. The idea behind empire free trade, or imperial preference (an idea which was never fully implemented) was to close this mutually beneficial system and consciously develop its resources and commerce at a time when world trade was in general stagnating. With less fanfare the French have gone further in this direction of making their empire an economically managed trading area, through the institution of the franc zone.

But powerful though this economic motive was, and profitable as it proved in the century 1815–1914, it was by no means always dominant even in that period. There was also a *strategic* corollary; if empire needed to bring food and raw materials from overseas, then the sea lanes must be protected and so must overseas territories. A great deal of the world was brought under imperial control for these strategic reasons. The British Navy put the Union Jack on coaling stations around the world's oceans; bases and protectorates were established around the Middle East to ensure the safety of the Suez Canal; the McMahon Line was drawn through the Himalayas; and the North West Frontier was adjusted to protect India against the threat from the north. Even as recently as 1945 the United States took over the Japanese-mandated islands in the Pacific on the grounds of strategic necessity.

A sort of mixture of commercial and strategic motives was the simple desire for *prestige*, which played a large part in the imperial story, just as it does in the "West Side stories" of today. Imperial nations wished to assert their right to exclude others from their turf, and to color such areas appropriately on the map:

> For most of it's Red
> And the rest's all Grey
> And that's the meaning of Empire Day.

The sense of Empire, the feeling that most of the world was "ours," was a very important psychological part of the imperial era, and has considerable implication for attitudes today, when this prop for the national ego has been removed. The earlier attitude of well-padded content was well expressed in a *Punch* joke of June, 1940: "Well now we are alone; all 600 million of us."

The rivalry among the European nations resulted in a great deal of land being placed under European rule for no very good strategic or commercial reason but to keep it away from the other side. Many of the colonial powers, and particularly Britain, were very reluctant to take over new territories but found themselves under pressure from military experts or jingoist public opinion. A British prime minister in the late nineteenth century complained that he would soon be asked by the armed services to garrison the moon to stop others from getting there first. At the time that was a joke.

Another semi-economic motive was the desire to *settle* surplus population, whether younger sons who wanted land or black sheep who were sent to penal settlements or merely to remote spots as remittance men. The rapid population growth of the nineteenth century in Europe might have fulfilled Malthus' fears more nearly if it had not been for this overseas safety valve, which also had the result of rapidly increasing the world's food supply. The settlements in North America and Australasia, where the white settlers took root and decimated the indigenous population, before protecting them as curiosities, have provided the most solidly based structures of imperialism—so solid that it is no longer customary to refer thus to their origins.

In contrast to all these political and economic motives, but not in opposition to them, was a strong *philanthropic* urge. As early as the sixteenth century the Cross followed the flag and sometimes led it. For St. Francis Xavier, saving souls was the main motive of Spanish imperialism, and Sir Francis Drake, propagandizing for American settlement, wrote:

> Their gain shall be the knowledge of our Faith
> and ours such riches as the country hath.

From then till today the Christian missionaries have remained a powerful instrument of European culture throughout the colonial world, and an important link between the colonial powers and their subjects.

In the nineteenth century the philanthropists actually reversed plain economic motives, got slavery abolished and turned the British Empire into a bridgehead against the slave trade. For instance it was largely as an assault on the slave trade that Uganda was reluctantly brought into the empire, and the railway was built for this "strategic" purpose. Then, in order to recoup the losses on that railway, Kenya was thrown open to white settlers—so confused and intermingled were the intentions and results of imperialism.

To the mid-twentieth-century student of the Age of Empire, the most surprising feature of our great-grandparents' outlook was their certainty that they knew what was right not only for themselves but for others. Looking back today we are perhaps too inclined to believe they were always wrong, just because they were so sure they were right. In India, from the time of Macaulay onward, the British were sure that their mission was to bring India forward into the mainstream of western political thought, and by education to prepare it for self-government. It was a large assumption, but there is as yet no reason to think it was wrong; most of the errors in the subsequent century were due to failure to remember the ideal. In Africa Britain was far less certain of what its mission was, or, at best she regarded the prospects of self-government to be so remote as to be hardly worth bothering about till the next decade. Nonetheless, British colonial rule there did aim at improving the lot of the African by giving him law and order, a slowly rising economic standard, and education toward western culture. The French, who concentrated more on education and on making an African-French elite class of society, have retained more of their self-confidence that what they were doing was right. The Belgians, who concentrated on social and economic improvement but denied political advancement "until the next stage," have seen their whole paternalistic system in the Congo destroyed by the Congolese and denounced by world opinion.

Yet with all their failures and mistakes, in the period of the Long Armistice in Europe this philanthropic-educational-religious motive was as powerful as any in the European imperial outlook. At this time Lord Curzon could say with conviction: "The British Empire is, under Providence, the greatest instrument for good that the world has seen."

II The Postwar Scene

It is tempting to see World War II as marking the end of this whole myth of Empire, but that is not how it appeared to the colonial powers as the war drew to its end in 1945. The skeptical self-questioning of the 1930's, the British jokes about the empire and Poona Colonials had, superficially at least, disappeared during the war. On the whole many of the motives which had led to colonialism were strengthened by the conflict. The European colonial powers saw ahead of them a long period of economic hardship in which the commercial advantages of the colonies might be crucial; the strategic value of colonial bases had not been disproved—India had proved a vital base and with Africa a source of good military manpower; rather negatively Japan had shown the military value of its mandated islands. The very losses of certain colonies to the enemy provided the strongest reasons of prestige and pride for reasserting sovereignty after victory.

It was true that the emergent United Nations, with three out of five great powers anticolonialist, showed signs of being an influence against Colonialism, but the colonial powers attempted to meet this by emphasizing the philanthropic aspect of their empires. Churchill, who signed the Atlantic Charter promising "to respect the right of all peoples to choose the form of Government under which they will live," also asserted, "I did not become the King's First Minister to preside over the liquidation of the British Empire." Neither the Dutch nor the French had any intention of yielding their sovereignty over former possessions and as the war ended the colonial system was reimposed *de jure* on much the same one third of the world's area and population which had known it in 1939—with the exception of those colonies belonging to Japan and Italy. At the San Francisco Conference, which established the United Nations, the colonial powers, led by Lord Salisbury for the United Kingdom, fought successfully to prevent any mention in the charter of "independence" as an objective for dependent territories.

Yet within two decades independence was to be granted to virtually all the dependent territories. Why so sudden and unpremeditated a revolution, and what did it portend for the future? Again it is tempting to write of the decline and fall of the European empires as if some single factor had brought about the collapse of the whole structure. But the whole structure of relationships between metropolitan and colonial powers has not collapsed; it has only changed.

III The British Commonwealth

The end of the empires was a result, and a signal illustration, of the passing of power from Europe to two superpowers, both anticolonial. That nationalism which wrung concessions from Europe was a powerful and determined antagonist, but the Dutch could have beaten it in Indonesia, the British in Cyprus, and the French (probably) in Indochina and Algeria, if they had not been opposed by their principal ally—the United States—and by world opinion expressed through the United Nations and reflected in their own domestic opinion. To some extent, too, the people of the imperial powers laid down their empires surprisingly quietly because they were war-weary and realized that the odds against them were too great. But it is a mistake to suppose that, at least for the older generation, the parting was not a bitter blow, leaving behind a feeling of deprivation and an antagonism to the deprivers, whether they were the nationalists, the U.S. or the U.N.

In almost every case an attempt was made to soften this blow of losing control by some more or less meaningful form which stressed the continuing relationship. Thus the Dutch originally offered their East Indies full self-government in a union under the crown; the French in 1956 declared their remaining possessions parts of the French Union of states, which shortly became the French Community of sovereign self-governing states, which finally became simply independent states speaking the French language; Britain made the historically crucial move in 1947 of granting India independence under the crown and in the British Commonwealth; two years later India became a republic in the Commonwealth (no longer British) of Nations.

Insofar as they have lasted, these special relationships have helped to salvage the prestige which was always one motive for empire—the British Commonwealth can still be colored red on the map. To some extent they have served to conceal the reality of change, and the new Europe of today still has the problem of finding its proper position in the new postcolonial world. How does it fit into this new world in terms of politics and strategy, of commerce and settlement, of culture and philanthropy—which can now be called "development"?

Britain set the pattern of converting "an Empire into a Commonwealth" in 1947, when the Indian empire was granted independence within the commonwealth. The fact that both India and Pakistan agreed to remain within the commonwealth was regarded as so important, and such a triumph, that the very real change in power and political arrangements was almost overlooked. In popular thinking, except on the far right, the new dominions were regarded as being just like the old (white) dominions of Canada or Australia—part of a happy family. After all, Mr. Nehru was, like Mr. Churchill, an Old Harrovian. This euphoric vision was not shattered when India decided two years later to become a republic and so sever the link with the crown that had been at the root of the commonwealth idea.

The official line about the commonwealth that was built up at this time, and which has persisted since with few modifications, was this: Britain was exchanging a position of power for one of influence; the old relationship of dominance was being exchanged for a special relationship of partnership. The Commonwealth Relations Office would ensure that this relationship was based on mutual understanding by maintaining a constant flow of secret telegrams explaining Britain's position and policy (there were 23,000 such telegrams in 1962) and acting as a sort of intelligence service (diplomatic and military) for the dominions. Commonwealth solidarity would be strengthened by fairly frequent meetings of the prime ministers, of finance ministers (before the World Bank annual meeting) and foreign ministers (before the U.N. General Assembly). At international conferences (e.g. the General Assembly) it would be usual for the commonwealth delegations to hold special private meetings to agree on a line (or often to disagree). Britain would continue to act as banker for the sterling area, and so for the commonwealth as a whole, with the exception of Canada. At the legislative level the Commonwealth Parliamentary Association would continue to maintain relations between the Mother of Parliaments and her numerous progeny, who could expect to receive a mace of a speaker's chair as a christening present.

All this paraphernalia has served to maintain in Britain a special interest in her world-wide commonwealth. In thought at least it does provide a certain bridge between the richest and the poorest parts of the world. There is, as a rule, a certain courtesy among commonwealth governments and an attempt to understand one another's views. In general, to use the favorite British analogy, there is something of the atmosphere of a club in which the members are completely independent of each other, but maintain certain civilities—this in strong contrast with the Hobbesian state of nature which characterizes the relations of most nations in the world.

Yet if we are looking to the future we must ask whether this is a living relationship capable of growth and adaptation, or whether it is a wax effigy of the past set up to conceal the death of empire. In particular, do the British people see advantages in their special relationships with their ex-empire as a mold for a new relationship with large sections of the developing world? If it is a club, whose club is it? A white club experimenting with new colored members, or a predominantly colored club founded, however, by whites?

Again, as in the time of empire building, we must recognize that there are varied motives for trying to preserve the special relationship. The first, in the postwar era, was certainly *political* in terms of international influence and security. Here it is hard to see how Britain's narrow national interests have been served by the commonwealth connection. A few bases have been saved, in particular those in Singapore and Cyprus, but on suffrance; the naval base at Trincomalee had to be surrendered when a neutralist government came to power in Ceylon, and the defense agreement made with Nigeria at the time of independence was a dead letter within a couple of years.

Many people feel that the influence of the commonwealth on British policy has been to broaden and modernize its outlook; but it should not be overlooked that a certain section of British opinion feels that the price paid in terms of British national interests for holding the commonwealth together has been very high, and they wonder what in fact the commonwealth has politically in common. No very satisfactory answer to that question has yet been given. The traditional answer of a "common allegiance to the Queen" disappeared in 1949; the next conventional answer of "parliamentary democracy" has worn pretty thin with the emergence of a military autocracy in Pakistan and one-party states in Ghana and Tanganyika. The rather vague (but truthful) answer that most leaders of the commonwealth have had long experience in working with (or against) British rulers is unsatisfactory to those who have traditionally thought of the commonwealth as a family united by ties of blood. This racial view of the commonwealth had little intellectual appeal, but it did strike a strong emotional chord and its disappearance has left a gap of which politicians are uneasily aware.

The fact is that the new commonwealth is overwhelmingly neutralist and anticolonial, and Britain receives support for her policies only when they fit that pattern. The classic instance was the Suez operation, when Britain and France suddenly determined to reassert their imperial role to insure "the life-line of Empire" through the Suez Canal; the new commonwealth, joined by Canada, were leaders in the opposition. Again it was pressure from the new commonwealth and Canada which forced Britain to accept the removal of South Africa from the commonwealth. Most recently Britain has been forced to choose between the African nationalists in the Rhodesian Federation and her "kith and kin," the white settlers. To hold the commonwealth together it was essential to choose the Africans, and Britain seems to be doing so.

For the "kith and kin" concept of the commonwealth, and the whole idea of the overseas possessions as outlets for emigration, has been destroyed by the new concepts of a multiracial commonwealth. In recent years there have been few attempts to maintain large European settlements in the developing world—Algeria, Kenya, the Rhodesias and South Africa are almost the only examples. In each case the European population has offered very considerable economic advantages to the African population in the hope that this would reconcile them to leaving politics predominantly in European hands. In no case has the local population accepted the offer; in the first three cases after varying amounts of bloodshed the metropolitan power has withdrawn support from its kith and kin and granted independence to the Africans, although the exact outcome in Southern Rhodesia is not yet clear. In South Africa Britain had no power, legal or physical, to change the constitution, but it did, in effect, withdraw its support by allowing the Union to leave the commonwealth. Yet in any glance at the future of Europe's relation to Africa one must take note of the time bomb still ticking away in South Africa. One day, almost certainly, the whites will be attacked by the blacks, who may also by then be reds. This will provide the great test, in African eyes, of whether Britain's (and Europe's) professions of multiracialism are as strong as their race loyalties.

Thus in political terms the sudden expansion of the commonwealth from a group of people with similar racial and political backgrounds into a multiracial body with widely differing backgrounds and prospects has greatly weakened the old political and strategic motives for support in Britain. The debates on Britain's entry into Europe, and on the Commonwealth Immigration Bill (which limited the freedom of commonwealth citizens to enter Britain) showed that there was a good deal of disenchantment with the postwar commonwealth, and a certain desire to contract out of the obligations of the relationship. Unless some new sense of purpose is infused into the commonwealth the relationship is likely to wither away for lack of support in Britain.

IV The French Community

The other world-wide empire—the French—emerged from the war in worse shape than the British. French rule had to be reasserted over most of it, except for the sub-Saharan African provinces, which had remained loyal to de Gaulle. As a result France regarded the recovery of her empire as simply an extension of the war effort; the communists who fought in Indochina were as much the enemy as the Japanese had been. Later in Algeria when the Arabs revolted they too were written off as part of the communist conspiracy, largely because of the influence of the resident settlers. In Morocco and Tunisia, where settler influence was less strong, the French government came to terms with the nationalists and gave them independence in association with the French Union.

Inevitably in these circumstances great emphasis was placed on the politico-strategic motive for empire. Even in the settlement with Tunisia the naval base at Bizerte was kept firmly in French hands, with the result that relations with Bourguiba were poisoned and

Tunisia nearly moved completely outside the French orbit. Indeed the emphasis on the politico-strategic side of the relationship, especially during the Indochinese and Algerian wars, has nearly wrecked France's relations with many of her ex-colonies, and there is today for instance very little French political influence in Asia. In response France is relatively isolationist toward Asia, though she pays her share of the Aid to India consortium. It remains to be seen whether in the aftermath of the Algerian war France will seek to or succeed in establishing any sort of close political relationship with the countries of the Mahgreb. It seems unlikely that French technical assistance and particularly French teachers will continue to maintain a close cultural link.

The real success story of the French empire postwar is to be found in her relations with sub-Sahara Africa, which used to be called French West Africa and French Equatorial Africa and is now the sixteen French-speaking republics of the area. These provinces were loyal to de Gaulle and so it was not necessary to fight to recover them, nor to emphasize the politico-strategic motive in the postwar relationship. On the contrary, France stressed first the development-cultural ties and second the commercial relationship. The result has been to establish a new and hopeful form of post-imperial relationship.

Unlike Britain, whose best efforts were always damaged by an effortless sense of racial superiority, France encouraged a small élite to become fully French and accepted them when they did so as equals. Following the Roman pattern, its provinces were allowed to elect delegates to the French Assembly in Paris, and encouraged to regard Paris as their home away from home. There were, and still are, in consequence a number of African leaders who regard themselves as fully French in culture although they are also African nationalists.

An attempt was made in the mid-fifties to build on this political foundation a sort of political federation including metropolitan France itself, which was called the French Union. But African nationalism was just too strong and the élite just too small for this to succeed. De Gaulle tried to salvage something by loosening the bonds of union into a community, in which self-government but not full independence would be granted, but again nationalism was just too strong. Guinea chose immediate independence and was ostracized by French as a result; soon its example was followed by Mali and eventually by all the constituent parts of the community.

However, France had learned something from the example of Guinea, and elsewhere withdrew its political control with good grace while maintaining all its cultural and economic aid, which is discussed in more detail below. At present therefore, while France has abandoned all overt political control, it enjoys great influence and good will among about 20 millions of people, who send sixteen delegations to the United Nations and to the numerous gatherings of African states. It is hard to identify exactly what is the intellectual or theoretical nexus which holds this "non-union" together, but it appears to be a mutual attachment to the French culture and tongue. In reality too many of the new African states are dependent, and know they are dependent, on French financial and technical assistance for their survival.

Will this last? On the French side it is a very large expenditure for a rather intangible result in a very small part of the world. But a recent poll in France showed overwhelming popular support for the existing cultural and technical assistance program whatever its cost. It even appears from some recent speeches of President de Gaulle that he is thinking of extending the program to other "Latin" parts of the world such as South America. Thus it may be possible to build a new and lasting relationship on the basis of the motives of prestige and philanthropy which played their part in the earlier colonial relationship. But it is also possible that the ex-colonies will find these attentions somewhat stifling. The ex-British colonies frequently point out that France is being neocolonialist, and whether or not the charge is true or even meaningful it certainly hurts any country anxious to prove its genuine independence. It remains to be seen whether African cultural nationalism (the concept of negritude) and La Mission Civilisatrice of France are broad enough to embrace each other.

V The Economic Changes

The nineteenth and early twentieth century view that Europe's prosperity depended on maintaining control of its colonies survived World War II. The assumption was that political control was necessary for commercial exploitation of resources. In the years after the war, when all the European economies were as closed and as managed as their finance ministers could make them, there was a belief that shortages at home could be relieved by development schemes in the colonies—for instance Britain's Gambia egg scheme and the more famous Tanganyika groundnuts plan. Though both of these schemes failed, for lack of adequate preparation, the conventional wisdom of the day remained that to lose the colonies would be to lose a great source of wealth. In the debate on Indian independence this was a recurrent theme among opposition Tories, and it was the main burden of complaint in the Dutch parliament during the legislation granting freedom to Indonesia. The historic examples of Spain and Portugal were cited to show that the fall of empire meant the decline of the metropolis, though it could be argued that both those countries were in fact exhausted by building their empires.

However the warnings have proved unfounded. In the 1950's Europe divested herself of empire and enjoyed unparalleled prosperity. The Netherlands lost its East Indian possessions at the beginning of the decade and since has steadily become more prosperous. Belgium had a less profitable fifties, lost the Congo in 1960, and in 1961 had a very favorable balance of trade in the franc zone. Portugal retained its colonies and slithered along in endemic poverty. Britain is something of an exception to the trend of prosperity accompanying decolonization. Its share of trade in her colonies and ex-colonies fell quite steadily in the late 1950's, the gainers being the United States and Japan. But this decline (which was part of the pattern of British trade generally) does not seem to have been due to the granting of independence, though it can be attributed in part to the declining value of preferences, which was itself due to rising prices and the pressures of GATT.

In general the lesson of the past fifteen years has been that colonial rule is not necessary to maintain trade. Goods flow for economic rather than political reasons; this is especially so when, as in recent years, there is a buyer's market with surpluses of most world commodities. Put concretely Britain does not need to go to the expense of administering Ghana in order that Cadbury's can buy its cocoa supplies there. It has proved harder to teach this lesson over such strategic materials as oil, but in general it is now becoming accepted that raw material supplies will flow without political guarantees.

Similarly the reverse flow of manufactured goods to colonial markets has not been interrupted by the ending of political control. The pattern of trade built up over a century has in general been maintained; traditional suppliers retain their markets because of habit without political pressure. The franc zone remains a somewhat closed system with the French ex-colonies in Africa buying the majority of their goods from France (though increasingly from the Six), but this is due to economic manipulation rather than political control. Even within the sterling area it is still true that more than half the trade of all commonwealth countries is with other commonwealth countries, but the percentage is steadily declining as Britain's trade with rich developed countries expands and that with developing countries stands still.

Here we can see one of the future dangers of decolonization—that as it is apparent that there is no commercial need for political control, the developed countries will come to feel that they can disinterest themselves almost entirely from the ex-colonies. At present trade between the rich developed countries is increasing at a far greater rate than trade between developed and undeveloped countries. To carry the principle of decolonization and removal of preferences to its logical conclusion could result in rapid disinvestment in the ex-colonies, and a free trade system which, by destroying such sheet anchors as the Commonwealth Sugar Agreement, would simply wreck the fragile economies of many territories. There are already signs that the weakening of the commercial motive is resulting in a form of disengagement from the ex-colonies. There is plenty of evidence, though few exact statistics, to show that there has been massive repatriation of capital to Europe as African colonies have approached independence (the most obvious example is the Congo). It seems almost certain that the new African countries as a whole have lost more through disinvestment and falling commodity prices than they have gained through aid and investment during the short period of their independent existence.

However, what were "colonies" are now described as "developing countries," and in spite of everything a good deal of aid is being poured into them. How far is this altering the relationship of Europe to its old possessions? In general it may be said to be diversifying the relations of the ex-colonies; where they used to deal almost exclusively with their own metropole they now deal with the whole world, East and West, and in particular with the United States.

France has to some extent swum against the tide in West Africa. Because she gives generous aid in investment and skill, the ex-French colonies do still trade largely with France. But the European Economic Community has been involved, at France's insistence, in giving massive aid to the ex-colonies of all members (predominantly French Africa and the Belgian Congo); and gradually other countries, particularly Germany, the Netherlands and Italy, are beginning to establish their commercial bridgeheads in French-speaking West Africa.

In the ex-British areas Britain has found itself unable to shoulder so large a share of the burden, and the United States is often the majority donor or investor, with Germany not far behind. As a result, in part, the Asian and African ex-empire is beginning to trade with the whole world, including the Soviet bloc. Technical assistance also being provided from all over the world, and this is not without its commercial effects, for exports tend to follow the experts. Germany—it may be noted which ceased to be a colonial power in 1918—has re-entered the "colonial" commercial world with considerable aid in capital and technical assistance not only to Asia and Africa (with special attention to Tanganyika, which used to be German East Africa) but also to Latin America; this is all closely linked to its trade drives to recover markets lost during and after the war.

To sum up, the commercial motive which was strong in building empires remains strong in Europe's relations with the new countries, though the belief that political control was a highly desirable concomitant of trading relations has been weakened. The danger is that this disinvolvement will go too far and that short-term commercial interests will dominate the relationship. For instance there is a new scramble for Africa today in which the developed countries are looking for aid projects with good commercial prospects, ignoring some of the infrastructure which is necessary for balanced development. Again there is a danger that loans for developing countries will result in enormous debts to the richer countries which cannot be repaid or even serviced without a drastic change in the pattern of trade.

In the very long run the real test of whether the commercial relationship between Europe and its ex-colonies is healthy lies not in whether there is sufficient investment, or even reasonable prices for primary products, but in whether plans are being made to accept growing quantities of the manufactured goods which will be the fruits of development first in Asia but eventually in Africa. It will prove insufficient to have brought these territories out of colonialism into our free political world unless we also consciously strive to make them part of our rapidly expanding trading world.

VI Aid and Development

The three main motives for the colonial adventure were, as we have seen, political, economic and philanthropic. The first two were largely self-regarding, the third was concerned with the welfare of the colonials. How far, now that political responsibility has been shed, will the philanthropic motive survive in the form of a drive for development? How far does Europe recognize any continuing responsibility for the future of Africa and Asia?

There is no overall answer. France seems to have disclaimed responsibility for what was Indochina far more than for Algeria; Holland seems disinterested in Indonesia; Britain seems to show more interest in the welfare of her ex-African than her ex-Caribbean territories. Yet in the last days of colonialism the concept of trusteeship was accepted, at least formally, by all the colonial powers. The question was: what were the limits of the trustees' responsibility?

Britain, in general, argued that it was to bring the new states up to the point at which they could stand on their own feet politically; France, in general, believed that its mission was to give an ever larger section of the population and understanding of civilization as epitomized in French culture. The Belgians saw themselves as being father figures with complete political control, until a large section of the population had developed into European-type citizens.

All three concepts have proved insufficient in the light of circumstances. The Belgian disaster in the Congo is well known, and it is not yet clear whether Belgium will again be able to play a continuing role in Africa. The French approach, similar to the Belgian but with the saving grace of having an outlet for African political ambitions, has proved highly successful but only in the limited backward area of West Africa. The granting of political independence there was regarded as a comparatively small incident in the process of "civilizing." The Frenchmen who had been civil servants administering and developing French Africa remained on the French payroll as before, but became automatically "advisers" to the new indigenous civil service. The teachers remained as before with their numbers augmented; most of the cost remains on the French budget. Some idea of the magnitude of the French educational and technical assistance effort can be gained from the following two tables:

Table I

Number of French Experts on Technical Assistance Missions Abroad in 1961 by Area

Morocco	10,857	47%
Africa and Malagasy	8,527	37%
Tunisia	2,198	9%
Cambodia, Laos, Vietnam	960	4%
Other countries	550	2%
Total	23,092	100

Table II

Comparison of 1960 and 1962 for Number of French Colonial Civil Servants in Africa and Malagasy

	January, 1960		July, 1962	
	Number	Per cent	Number	Per cent
Education	2,146	21	3,542	42
Administrators	1,472	15	698	8
Others	6,382	64	4,312	51
Total	10,000	100	8,462	100

This is a magnificent effort and one which undoubtedly will promote a lasting two-way cultural relationship between a part of Europe and a part of Africa. The difficulty, as has already been suggested, is that the relationship is only between parts of larger wholes, and that it may break down because of the strains thus involved. This becomes more likely the more that political and commercial motives for action are stressed by France; insofar as education and technical training are philanthropic they are acceptable to Africans—but might become difficult to justify to French taxpayers.

The British theory of colonial responsibility suffered from one major defect which still maims her relationship with her ex-colonies: the doctrine that there was a cut-off point at political independence where help became interference. This was based on the analogy of the old dominions, which achieved full independence long after they had become self-supporting; in the new African states, in particular, where political independence was given as a gesture early in the process of becoming self-supporting, the doctrine had little relevance. Yet on Ghana's obtaining independence in 1957 all the aid machinery through such organizations as the Colonial Development Corporation came to a halt. Only slowly has this error been corrected and the fact accepted that independent commonwealth countries are still economically dependent.

Similarly it was assumed that with the end of colonial rule would come the end of the colonial service, with all the vast amount of technical assistance involved (during the 1950's there were about 16,000 colonial service officers who were "experts" rather than administrators, of whom 2000 were teachers). It was quite early recognized that the immediate withdrawal of all of these experts would create havoc, but the British government resolutely refused to follow the French example and take them onto the strength of the domestic civil service and then loan them to the new governments. The best that could be devised was a system whereby London increased the salaries of some who worked on the strength of the new African governments on contract. As a result of this, and of a rather generous compensation-for-loss-of-career arrangement (charged to the new government), the technical services have run down very fast in British Africa, particularly in East Africa where they were least easy to replace. There remains the danger of a dip in the standards of life and efficiency in that area, and probably also in Central Africa as the result of this withdrawal.

Britain has of course recognized its obligation to try and replace its permanent corps of experts by technicians on short contract, and by young people at the beginning of their careers. A new Department of Technical Cooperation has been set up whose name is meant to imply that basis of equality with the ex-colonies which is their due as independent states. It has taken over the first major British effort in this technical assistance field—the Colombo Plan—which again was designed to stress the equality of both donor and recipient in the exchange and training of technical experts. In the long run this system of sending out many people for a few years, rather than a few people for many years, and sending them as partners not as masters, could improve and deepen Britain's relations with the new commonwealth. It remains to be seen whether the new men can quite take the strain of the period of transition, when expertise is so badly needed, and whether the sense of obligation and purpose in Britain is sufficient to bring forth adequate personnel.

Though the British at governmental level never placed quite the same emphasis on education as the French, the missonaries set high standards, and it remains true that the percentage of literates is higher in English-speaking than French-speaking Africa (higher still is the Belgian Congo, and highest is South Africa). About 20 per cent of the funds available under the Colonial Development and Welfare Act were usually allocated to education, but only 3.5 per cent to technical and vocational subjects. British colleges and universities also have a good record of accepting students from the commonwealth—there were some 7000 resident in 1961, and in all some 45,000 students from developing countries held places in Britain up to that time. Also some 300,000 schoolchildren a year around the world take the Certificate Examinations organized by London and Cambridge universities. This is immensely valuable work, and it has a considerable effect on the development of many English-speaking countries, but it would be untrue to pretend that there is much enthusiasm in Britain for her "educative mission." It is proving hard to get teachers at any level or to raise funds for the new African universities and schools. One difficulty is that the English language is not a British perquisite, as the French language is of France. The culture purveyed by the English language may be British or American, which is undoubtedly an advantage for those who learn it; but this fact deprives those who teach it of some sense of exclusive national pride and purpose.

VII Conclusion

With all its defects colonialism was a definite, positive and understood relationship between the metropolitan country and what is today called the "developing" country. That relationship has now ended for most European countries, and they are, consciously or unconsciously, seeking for another relationship to the developing world, with the bleak alternative of isolation never quite out of mind.

On the whole the ex-metropolitan powers feel that they cannot be indifferent to their ex-empires, but the tendency—noticeable in both Britain and France—is to carry on many of the old attitudes and actions little changed and little reconsidered. Both countries have increased their aid programs (mainly to their ex-empires) without any important public debate.

The United States, on the other hand, which used to stand aloof from the colonies and condemn colonialism, has become deeply involved in the colonial areas as they attain independence. Yet the United States is prevented from achieving a wholly satisfactory relationship with the *tiers monde* because America itself is reft by the clash of color which is part of the world scene. Europe, inoculated by its colonial experience, seems likely, in spite of Algeria and Rhodesia, to be spared an internal color problem.

Looking to the future the question arises whether a positive program of help to the developing world might not be the great unifying factor in the Atlantic Community—the main motive of the alliance in its relation to the outside world. At first this may seem a utopian dream but there are several reasons why it might prove the answer to the present discontents of the Atlantic Community.

First of all the original basis of the western alliance is beginning to wear out—ever since the death of Stalin the real fear of Russian aggression into Europe has waned, until in recent months, the Soviet threat has clearly proved insufficient to hold NATO together. The easiest substitute for a Red Menace is a Yellow Peril, to replace Russia by China. But the Chinese threat is less immediate to Europe, and the nature of the struggle must surely be different. Indeed it seems likely that to a large extent any conflict with China will be a struggle for the allegiance of the developing world.

Second, the Atlantic Community is already aware of the danger of becoming an exclusive, rich white club. Even without China's bid to become the militant leader of the underprivileged colored world, Europeans and Americans have known that they must find some way of associating themselves with a section at least of the colored majority of the world's population.

This sentiment is just as strong among the powers without a colonial past, and is found at its strongest in the new generation which has hardly known colonialism. The "Peace Corps outlook," which is to be found in Germany, Britain and France as well as in the United States, represents a new generation's uninhibited and generous approach to the problem of helping the poorer sections of their community—the world community, that is.

There are, in fact, many reasons of interest and sentiment why helping the poorer countries to develop should become a unifying and positive force in the Atlantic Community. But it remains necessary to translate sentiment into effective action. Here there is a great lacuna, for the West has singularly failed to produce any science of development. A great deal of experience is available, from the time of the Marshall Plan to the latest Indian Five Year Plan. Yet there has not been much attempt to synthesize this experience so as to save new countries from making all the mistakes of their predecessors. Nor has the West yet worked out a successful cooperative system of giving aid without rousing resentment and cries of neocolonialism, or alternatively of miserliness if the amounts are too small.

A working science of development, a reasonable system of cooperation between donors, a relatively frictionless association between donor and recipient—all these remain to be worked out. But they are not Himalayan tasks to undertake once the decision has been taken that the proper role of the Atlantic Community in the mid-twentieth century is to concentrate its efforts on raising standards in the poorer parts of the world community. Only if that decision is taken will Europe once more find a proper relationship with the world it once ruled.

ALFRED GROSSER

The Evolution of European Parliaments

EVEN the most ardent partisans of prediction and of the theory of
games agree, in principle, in recognizing that rational expectation
should be based on analysis in depth of present reality. How is it
possible to talk about the future of parliaments in Europe when the
study of their operations and their place in the political system remains in the embryonic stage? Only the House of Commons is continually the object of intelligent, detailed study.[1] What has been
written about the assemblies in Bonn, Rome, Paris and Brussels is
very slight, and comparative studies are almost nonexistent.[2] In addition, my own knowledge is very inadequate; largely limited to
France and Germany, it rules out a comprehensive treatment and,
even more, any prediction about the subject as a whole. Since I have
also not been able really to treat the subject which should be included in this collection—the future of European parliaments in
general—I have finally confined myself to certain reflections on
European parliaments which I think may clarify their present situation and enable us to perceive their relationships to other forces
in the European states. This, hopefully, should permit us to formulate a limited number of plausible hypotheses for the future.

I The Political Context

Whether institutions function well or badly does not depend
only on their machinery or on the value of each institution in itself.
The ideological orientation of a given political regime and its legitimacy are often the determining factors. By legitimacy I mean a consensus of the citizens to accept the existing institutions as the normal
framework in which to deal with their differences. Belgian institutions did not change between 1930 and 1945, or between 1945 and
1960, or even in recent years, but the "royal question" and, today,
the intensification of the language conflict have put the institutional
system itself in a precarious position.

Why has the West German Federal Republic existed from the beginning in an atmosphere of political calm, envied by many Frenchmen and Belgians, in contrast to the Weimar Republic, which was virtually never free from troubling disorder? Is it the value of the institutions—particularly parliament—as such, that is in question? Not at all. The real reasons are quite different. One is that the words "republic" and "democracy," synonomous in the 1920's with defeat, humiliation and misery, have acquired the connotation—even if they are not synonomous—of "escape from chaos" and "economic and diplomatic rehabilitation." The regime and its institutions have been reinforced, legitimized. The second reason is that the Weimar Republic was ideologically torn apart. The Communist extreme left was only a minority in the parliament, but it constituted a force of opposition to the regime. On the right and extreme right, the republic in its liberal form was vilified and attacked. Today, the Federal Republic is unanimously anti-Communist and the anti-liberal extreme right has practically disappeared. Since it had no colonies, West Germany has been spared the conflicts over legitimacy caused by decolonization. It has also up to now been able to make its institutions work on a basis of ideological unity very favorable to the regular functioning of a pluralist democracy. Parliament can discuss the most difficult questions without disrupting a kind of fundamental unanimity which affects even the most essential national interest, because the overwhelming majority of citizens prefer the continued division of Germany to any form of reunification that would not insure its protection from Communist influence.

In France, on the contrary, disputes over legitimacy have not ceased to hamper the effective operation of its institutions. In my opinion, the poor functioning of the parliamentary regime was only an accessory cause of the decline of the Fourth Republic. Its essential cause was the internal schism in France, reflecting the divisions of the contemporary world as a whole: anti-Communists against Communists, old states against new nationalisms. Italy has experienced the first conflict, Great Britain and Belgium the second. Only France has had the legitimacy of a regime established by majority vote challenged in both ways at once. There was also the challenge of European supranationalism.

Between 1947 and 1958 the Communists challenged the majority decisions in the name of peace, and the Gaullists waged a campaign against the European treaties in the name of a national legitimacy above the will of the majority. There was a moral dispute over Indochina and Algeria: a regime which violated its own principles in opposing the liberty of other peoples was thought by some to have lost its legitimacy even if the administrations were elected by a majority of the electorate. At the same time there was another opinion that could be called the national type of establishment of legitimacy whereas the precedent type was in the ethical sphere: no government, no parliamentary majority, has the right to abandon a part of the nation's patrimony or to accept a decrease in territory— notably in Algeria—or to permit the expulsion from the national community of men desiring to live in it—as was the case with many Algerian Moslems. The *coup de force* of May, 1958 that brought de Gaulle to power, and later the abortive uprisings against de Gaulle in January, 1960 and April, 1961 were inspired by this feeling.

Today quarrels over legitimacy continue; the question of a successor to Chancellor Adenauer involves merely an individual, the question of a successor to General de Gaulle involves a regime. French debates over institutions and especially over relations between the parliament and the executive are continually falsified by conflicts where what is at stake is above and beyond the level of institutions. The specific debate over the Fifth Republic and General de Gaulle should not, however, obscure the ameliorating factors that have already or soon will have manifested themselves: the absence of colonies reduces conflicts arising from decolonization, and the evolution of the Communist party transforms its doctrinaire hostility of 1947–1954 into acceptance, albeit an acceptance qualified by combativeness. For reasons deriving from changes in France and outside, the French Communist party no longer has the goal of hindering the operation of institutions as it did at the height of the cold war, and it is accepted more and more by others as a participant in the political game. This is normal in a period of rapprochement between Khrushchev and Kennedy and of alliances within France against the "personal power" of General de Gaulle. In the immediate future, it is in Belgium rather than in France that the most violent troubles arising from a conflict over legitimacy seem likely to occur. It is nonetheless true that the presence of strong Communist parties in Italy and France will for a long time yet be a decisive factor in institutional life, quite independent of the text of the constitution and of the nature of parliamentary operation.

Disputes over legitimacy are all the more important in France because the will of the majority has traditionally been considered to stand above the constitution. Constitutions are of two kinds, illustrated by a comparison between France and the United States. In France, the constitution has long been thought to be a method of operation, a technique, supposed to implement a political system founded in any case on the will of the majority. Article 91 of the Constitution of 1946 said, "the Constitutional Committee examines [the question] whether the laws voted by the National Assembly assume a revision of the Constitution." On November 6, 1962, the Conseil Constitutionnel of the Fifth Republic declared that it had no jurisdiction in the case of laws "which, adopted by the people as the result of a referendum, constitute the direct expression of the national sovereignty." In both cases, the superiority of the will of the majority over the text of the constitution is clearly affirmed.

In the United States on the other hand, the Constitution is considered the sacrosanct charter of the national life, quite literally the "fundamental law." The expression used by the framers of the Bonn Constitution show that they were referring to the American concept. Respect for the charter should be so thoroughly imposed on all the machinery of the state that the chief of state himself will be its servant and not its guardian. This latter function belongs to the judiciary. Its task is not only to declare the law. When the United States Supreme Court hands down a decision on segregation or when the Tribunal of Karlsruhe issues definitions in regard to liberty of information, it is not simply a matter of judicial interpretation of the constitution, it is a matter of rendering precise and explicit the ethic, the moral code which the national community holds as its standard.

It is partly the limited extent of a common ethical standard in France which has prevented such a charter-constitution (and a constitutional court worthy of the name) from materializing in that country. Instead, the great decisions of principle have been referred to majority opinion in parliament, and since 1958 to popular opinion through referenda, but the same lack of consensus has prevented the decisions thus reached from being really accepted by all.

Such a situation is not confined to France, however. Relations between Walloons and Flemish are not regulated by a simple majority vote but by a compromise which can only be rejected by the extremists of both camps. The Oder-Neisse line will be recognized as definitive only by a majority which would include at least the two major parties in West Germany, that is, the delegates of four fifths of the electoral body. The effectiveness of majority decisions adopted by the parliaments depends on the type of problem involved. In order to make any predictions about their effectiveness in the future, it would be necessary to make an inventory of the questions pending or possibly pending which lie outside the usual institutional or constitutional arena.

Within the constitutional systems the place of parliament depends on how popular sovereignty is exercised. All the constitutions affirm forcefully that sovereignty lies in the people, without giving this affirmation a really precise meaning. When we read in the fundamental law of Bonn (Article 20, Number 2), "All power comes from the people, who exercise it through election and through the intermediary organs of legislative power, executive power and judicial power," we see at once that the parliament in West Germany has a lesser place than under the Fourth Republic in France. Did not Article 3 of the Constitution of 1946 say, "National sovereignty belongs to the French people . . . the people exercise it in constitutional matters through the votes of their representatives and through referenda. In all other matters, they exercise it through their deputies in the National Assembly"?

The order of chapters or subdivisions in the various European constitutions is very significant in this respect. In Italy the order is as follows: I Parliament, II the President of the Republic, III the Cabinet, IV the Judiciary, V Regions, Provinces, Communes. In the Fourth Republic in France: I Sovereignty, II Parliament, III Economic Council, IV Diplomatic Treaties, V the President of the Republic, VI the Council of Ministers. In the Fifth Republic: I Sovereignty, II the President of the Republic, III the Cabinet, IV Parliament. The order of subdivisions in the West German Constitution is Bund and Länder, Bundestag, Bundesrat, the Federal President, the Federal Government. These comparative lists show us the relative importance of the different aspects of government as the framers of the constitutions conceived them. We shall have to consider whether it corresponds to the reality. In any case two observations should be made.

First, the nature of the national legislature is a function of the structure of the state, centralized or federal. The German bicameral system is justified in ways similar to bicameralism in the United States or Switzerland. The sovereignty of the people is supposed to express itself through two channels because the national collectivity rests on a double notion of equality and each must find its own means of expression. There is the equality between the citizens and there is the equality (or near equality) of the territorial collectivities. In the House of Representatives the idea of equality between American citizens is expressed, while the Senate expresses equality between states, even though they are very unequal in population. The composition of the Italian Senate reflects a much less clear-cut situation in this respect. In France, the way in which the Senate is chosen strengthens the small communes at the expense of the large ones. It does not appear to us certain that the utility of this double representation will in the long run be sufficient to justify the existence of a separate legislative chamber.

Since the upper houses based on privileged personal status, like the House of Lords, will not come back in favor, the domination of assemblies elected by direct universal suffrage will become greater unless one or the other of two possible developments takes place: either the formation of a federated Europe can revive respect for federalism and give birth to a doubly federal structure, both within the nation-state and above it; or the constantly increasing role of pressure groups (including the regional ones) will lead to the development of legislative assemblies reflecting economic and social pressure groups. We shall return to this point later.

The second necessary observation is that what is meant by parliamentary representation is not defined in the constitutions. Immediately after World War I, André Maurois could write with irony in *Les Silences du Colonel Bramble:*

So you condemn us, Doctor, to oscillate continually between brawls and coups d'état?

No, because the English people, who have already given to the world Stilton cheese and comfortable arm-chairs, have invented for our welfare the parliamentary safety-valve. Our elected champions now enact the brawls and the coups d'état in the House, which gives the rest of the nation leisure to play cricket. The press puts the finishing touch on the system by letting us take part in these clashes vicariously. All this is a part of modern comfort and in a hundred years every man, white, yellow, red or black, will refuse to live in an apartment without running water or in a country without a parliament.

This notion of the parliament as the real center of political life, with citizen-spectators and power to govern delegated by the representative assembly, already disputable at the time, is today in the process of disappearing because of the changed relations between parliament and administration that we shall analyze subsequently— and because of recent social changes. As it is not possible here to present a kind of sociology of Europe serving as a basis for institutional change, I shall confine myself to one example, which, in my opinion, is particularly important because it relates to one of the most important functions of parliament—even if this function is not spelled out in the text of the constitution—to wit, paliament's role as a transmission-belt of political information.

How does an administration proceed when it wants to inform the citizens about policy or has important news to communicate? The tradition of the parliamentary regimes gives a clear answer: a representative of the cabinet makes a statement in parliament or answers questions from the members. Subsequently the information is promulgated in two ways: the press reports the parliamentary sessions and the members, returned to their constituencies, explain to important groups and individuals how the administration statement should be interpreted.

Today this model no longer holds. This is because, first, the powerful organization of the parties often leads the administration to use the channel of the majority party, and second, and above all, because the development of the mass media (everywhere to some extent) has brought about a diminution of the role of parliament both as the representative of public opinion and as the intermediary between administration and the citizens. Radio and television permit direct contact between the governing and the governed that calls into question the very essence of representative democracy. As in other matters, General de Gaulle has simply carried to extremes a tendency discernible almost everywhere.

The American example seems to me particularly striking. Nowhere—as I hope to show—does the legislature hold a more important position or have a greater real influence on national policy or control the administration more directly; but, in the realm of information, the political system of the United States has a real institution unforeseen in the Constitution: the presidential press conference. The importance of the press conference as a test of the American Chief Executive has often been noted. It should be emphasized that the institution of the press conference makes the press the representative of public opinion and gives to the press the role of intermediary between the citizens and their government which classic theory reserved to the legislature. It is characteristic that American senators and representatives often put their questions to the President by getting friendly or sympathetic reporters to ask certain questions at a presidential press conference.

Of course, the American presidential system, with the separation of powers, virtual direct election of the President and his nonparticipation in congressional debates, facilitates this recourse to a means of disseminating information that bypasses the legislature; but the situation is a phenomenon of modern civilization and not of the institutional machinery. "The President from time to time shall report to Congress on the State of the Union." The Founding Fathers certainly did not intend this to mean only the annual message to Congress. In the Cuban crisis of October, 1962, a statement to Congress would have corresponded to the text of the Constitution, rather than a televised talk to the nation. In Europe, outside of France, the technique of radio and television statements, of press conferences and interviews has not yet been developed sufficiently to eliminate parliament as a means of disseminating information, but it seems to me that the tendency is increasingly in that direction.

In the other direction, of the government informing itself on the state of opinion, the situation is slightly different. Here there are two rivals to the legislatures as intermediaries or representatives, the press and the public opinion polls. Government depends less and less on members of parliament for information about the state of public opinion. Instead, it increasingly depends on the press, and unfortunately, in my opinion, on polls, because passive citizens, who must be sought out and then interrogated, are thus equated with active citizens who show their positions. The government uses the opinion polls to know how to conduct itself, what to say and also how to act. At the same time, especially in countries with single-member constituencies, the deputy often succeeds in maintaining his own role because he is in a position to be in contact with a psychological reality that often is not accessible to the executive branch, the other source of official information.

II The Problem of the Triangle

In classic textbooks political regimes were largely defined in terms of relations between the executive and the legislative powers, between parliament and administration. This model almost completely neglected the existence and the role of parties. The first question to ask is, "Does a dominant party exist?" The second is, "If so, what is the relation between the three vertices of a triangle formed by administration—party—parliamentary group?" A few examples will show better than theoretical considerations why this triangular problem always underlies what we will have to say about the relations between parliament and administration, and between parliament and the parties.

Can one still speak of a separation of powers in Great Britain when the parliamentary majority and the cabinet—or Government, as the British call it—both arise from the same party? It is useful to make some distinctions: when the Conservatives are in power the cabinet dominates both the parliamentary group and the party; when the Labourites are in power the influence of the party on the Government is stronger, while the parliamentary group retains important prerogatives, not the least of which is the power to choose the head of the party, as in the recent election of Harold Wilson to succeed Hugh Gaitskell. The head of the party is at the same time prime minister or shadow-prime minister, which is not always the case with the Conservatives, where the prime minister is not formally designated by the party but by the Queen, as in the case of the choice of Macmillan over Butler.

The confusion or distinction between the two roles is and will remain important in the West German Federal Republic. Since 1957 Erich Ollenhauer has ceased to be both president of the Social Democratic party and aspiring chancellor. Willy Brandt has taken his place in this second function. If the SPD wins the elections of 1965, what with the relative power of President Ollenhauer and Chancellor Brandt, whose authority is based on the elected body, much will depend on the attitude of the party's group in parliament.

The succession of Chancellor Adenauer presents the same kind of problem. From 1949 to 1963 there have been few conflicts between the administration and the Christian Democratic Union because the Chancellor was, on the whole, able to assure harmony by the fact that he personally combined the two functions. The few revolts have come from the parliamentary group, although its successive chairmen (Heinrich von Brentano, Heinrich Krone and then again Heinrich von Brentano) have never represented a real public force capable of opposing Adenauer. Tomorrow Chancellor Ludwig Erhard and the chairman of the party (Josef Dufhues or Heinrich von Brentano) will confront each other, and a new situation in German political life will be brought about. It is so new that the Christian Democratic Union had not even prepared a procedure to designate a candidate for the chancellorship. The party elects its own head in a party convention. The constitution says that the chancellor is designated by the president of the republic, but who will really propose the man to be designated by the chief of state—the outgoing chancellor, the parliamentary group, or the party organization? A kind of revolt in the rank and file of the party was required following the repeated electoral defeats, for the choice of Ludwig Erhard to be made, largely because the public opinion polls had demonstrated his popularity.

In the United States, it is the absence of tight organization in the parties that gives so much independence to members of Congress. In the Fifth French Republic the dominant party has a feeble structure, but the parliamentary group lacks independence because the real head of the executive and the party are the opposite of what they are elsewhere: while Messrs. Kennedy, Adenauer, Macmillan and Khrushchev owe their positions respectively to the victory of the Democrats, Christian Democrats, Conservatives and Communists, whatever may be their personal merits or popularity, the Union pour la Nouvelle République and its leaders owe their political existence to General de Gaulle. Thus we see why we must keep the problem of the triangle in mind even when we are referring to the traditional functions of the various legislatures.

LEGISLATION AND THE BUDGET

The legislature makes laws; the executive carries out the laws. Reality does not any longer correspond at all to this official statement. Everywhere the legislative initiative has passed into the hands of the administrations. The legislatures sometimes amend, rarely reject, usually ratify. Their members continue, indeed, to call themselves collectively "the Legislative Power" in the law books, but in most cases they merely participate in a procedure of registration. Here, for example, is the summary of twelve years' legislation in Bonn:[3]

	1949–1953 Bills Submitted	1949–1953 Number Enacted	1953–1957 Bills Submitted	1953–1957 Number Enacted	1957–1961 Bills Submitted	1957–1961 Number Enacted
By the Cabinet	472	392	446	368	401	348
By the Bundestag	301	141	414	132	207	74
By the Bundesrat	32	12	17	7	5	2

The reality is both a little less and much more serious, from the point of view of parliament, than the figures suggest. On the one hand, the federal organization of the German state does after all permit the Landtage to play a certain legislative role, although even at the level of the Land, the administration predominates. On the other hand, the administration can bypass the assemblies to a considerable extent by issuing directives. As in other spheres, the Fifth French Republic has pushed to extreme limits a tendency that is general but less pronounced elsewhere. While tradition reserves to parliament whatever is not specifically designated to the administration, the Constitution of 1958 describes the domain of the law in a limiting way, after having stipulated that "laws are voted by Parliament."

Why is the legislative function of the parliaments in decline? There seem to me three competing ways of explaining this phenomenon:

1. The nature of the law has changed. With rare exceptions, laws, which used to be few, formerly served to make more explicit the rights and duties of citizens or the organization of society, conceived as a stable whole. Civil law, criminal law and administrative law belonged in the legislative assemblies. The administration was there to direct, to administer. Except in the international sphere, did the administration even need to have a policy? It is not by chance that the constitutions framed since World War II no longer define the administration as an executive but as an initiator of policy.[4] Administrative action is destined to transform society, and the law is the privileged instrument of this transformation, but if the legislative assembly expresses its adherence to a policy in instituting an administration, does not the administration have the right to claim the means to carry out the policy? Or in other words to demand that laws be passed to provide the means?

2. The epoch of the "representative of the people" is largely over. The existence of organized parties, whenever one of them is in a dominant situation, involves a relative dispossession of the members of the legislature. Should the members of a majority party in a parliament criticize an administration proposition—or should they, on the contrary, defend it against opposition attacks?

3. The technical complexity of economic and social legislation is such that the administration, using its bureaucracy and its experts, is able to impose it on the legislature. It is no longer enough, as in the nineteenth century, to be a good speaker and well versed in the law to be an impressive legislator. We shall see why this point is even less applicable to the United States than the previous points.

Even if parliamentary resistance were strong, the administrations often have effective means of constraint at their disposal. The vote of confidence is to parliamentary life what the referendum is to the political life of the French Fifth Republic. It might be phrased, "Even if you do not like this particular text, vote yes, or you will oblige me to resign, which you do not want either."

The Constitution of 1958 has brought to fruition an inheritance from its two predecessors. In France, as it does still in the other countries, it used to require a positive vote to enact a law. Today, all that is necessary is for the prime minister to indicate that the administration is committed to a given text. "In such a case," says Article 49, "the text is considered as enacted unless a motion of censure . . . is passed." This is how, for example, the nuclear striking force, an essential element in French foreign policy, came into being without being approved by a parliamentary majority.[5] At the end of the parliamentary session where the motion of censure was being voted upon, the chairman said:

Here is the result of the vote on the motion of censure. Two hundred and seventy-seven votes are required for adoption.
For adoption, 214 (applause on the Right and Extreme Left)
Since the necessary majority was not reached, the motion of censure is not adopted (applause on Left and Center).
As a result, the law establishing the program for certain military installations is considered to be adopted . . .

The Magna Carta imposed on King John in 1215 said, "No scutage nor aid shall be established in our kingdom without the consent of the common council of our Kingdom." Since then the power of the purse, or exclusive right to tax, has constituted an essential prerogative of parliament. But is this not also more a matter of form than of substance? There are, in any case, several phenomena which suggest that this is so.

1. National budgets have become monstrously complex. What member of a legislature, in spite of simplified versions prepared to help him, can find his way in such a jungle of chapters and provisions? Furthermore, at a certain level of importance, figures lose their meaning. The famous meeting of an administrative council described by Parkinson could be reproduced in a parliamentary assembly. At this meeting it was decided to authorize fantastic expenditure for the construction of an atomic reactor, but the cost of installing a bicycle rack was considered too high. In the same way, the average deputy will dispute the subsidy accorded to a small private association but will allow tremendous military expenses to pass without much discussion.

2. The limitation of the budget to one year and the annual debates on the budget do not fit the conditions necessary for good policy or efficient administration. In practice, the basic funds are granted once and for all and are not later called into question. Other items, especially in countries which tend to long-range planning, cannot safely be changed in less than several years. What a relief it would be for the President of the United States—and for the countries receiving United States aid—if foreign aid could be granted clearly and with carefully worked out detail for a period of four or five years. Things are moving in this direction. In Europe, programs for disposition of land, industrial development and the transformation of agriculture make it increasingly necessary for budgetary commitments to be made for longer periods.

3. Pressures put on members of legislatures do not cause them to call into question the main lines of the budget, but they do cause them to quarrel among themselves over particular points. Pressure groups bring pressure either on the government or on party leaders rather than on individual deputies. The real struggle often takes place before the budget is presented to the parliament. In a hierarchy of western legislatures based on the criterion of budgetary control, the Congress of the United States would be at the top: Congress is almost as much of a force to be reckoned with by the administration after the budget has been voted as before. At the bottom of the ladder would be the House of Commons, whose lack of power is striking once the Chancellor of the Exchequer has revealed "his" budget to the public.

CONTROL

The third function of the parliaments, after legislation and consent to taxation, is the control of executive action. This is a less well defined area than the others. First, what *is* the legislature in relation to the administration? Or what is the cabinet's relation to the assembly? The physical arrangements are very revealing of the political or psychological situation. In Westminster, the Government, or cabinet, is not separated from the parliamentary group. The arrangements anticipate an exchange between a majority and a minority rather than a confrontation between the administration and Parliament. At the Palais-Bourbon, the cabinet sits in the front row of the members, facing the speaker and the chairman. Is the cabinet not an emanation of the assembly and do not persons speaking from the rostrum— even members of the ruling majority—address the cabinet at the same time (and even more) as the other members? At least this was the case under the Third and Fourth Republics. Since 1958 it would have been more appropriate to adopt the arrangements of the Bundeshaus in Bonn: the government bench, a long raised table, is placed beside the presidential armchair, slightly behind the rostrum, facing the deputies. This gives the government the air of attending as a spectator the parliamentary game it dominates.

In Europe, it is rare for a parliament to control the administration by acting as a whole. The hearings of ministers before committees cannot be compared to the hostile grilling to which administration leaders are subjected by congressional committees in the United States. The West German Federal Republic has developed an interesting technique as a result of a delicate and controversial problem. Article 45 b of the fundamental law, passed in March, 1956, anticipates the establishment of a *Wehrbeauftragter des Bundestages* "for protection of fundamental rights and as an auxiliary organ to the Bundestag in the exercise of parliamentary control." This permanent commissioner of the assembly, chosen jointly by the opposition and by the majority, received in the year 1961 alone 4380 complaints, of which 1330 were found to be entirely justified, and 296 partly justified. The annual reports of the commissioner to the assembly show the extent to which he has become a kind of parliamentary control on the military administration.

In a more general way, administrative action is controlled by means of questions posed by individual deputies. The two most usual methods at the present time are those of the written question and of the so-called oral question, which is submitted in writing but answered orally. Two points are important here:

1. In a highly centralized country like France, where, moreover, the deputy is traditionally considered to be the representative of his constituents in the sense that a traveling salesman represents his employer, a member of parliament does not ordinarily use the procedure of written or oral questions to control the administration, or more precisely to bring his weight to bear on its decisions. The

French member of parliament spends a considerable part of his time writing directly to ministers in various departments of the administration or in taking steps to hasten an administrative decision. We must remember that the financing of the construction of a village street by a savings bank in the neighboring town cannot be arranged in France until all the relevant documents have been to Paris and back.

2. In London, Bonn or Paris, if the oral question is usually a method of controlling executive management or efficiency, it can also be easily transformed—in the first two capitals—into a method of exerting political control. When M. Debré was drawing up the constitution of the Fifth Republic, he hoped to achieve the same sort of relation between the administration and parliament in France. The result has not fulfilled his intention. In vain would one search for examples of a real political dialogue arising from an administrative response to an oral question in French parliamentary life since 1959. It is true that the rules of the French parliament do not permit further debate by other members, while in Bonn the debate on the Spiegel affair in December, 1962, grew to great importance because the minister (administration spokesman) had to undergo a real crossfire of related questions and was forced to admit that he had lied in an earlier part of the discussion. From that moment his resignation seemed probable.

It is important to note that Mr. Franz-Josef Strauss had to resign because he agreed to submit himself to questions and also because the chairman of the Bundestag conducted the debate with total impartiality. The Spiegel affair proved the reality of parliamentary control in the Federal Republic, a control made possible because the minority can oblige the government to discuss a point seriously. We cannot overemphasize the point, because from the exchange or dialogue arises a political reality which is not defined in any constitutional text or regulation. At the end of a clash with the opposition the government can sometimes no longer maintain a certain decision, or it is compelled to modify a certain stand. No vote has forced the government into a change of position, however; it is a matter of purely moral constraint. For such a force to exist, the necessary and sufficient condition is that the cabinet and the majority party accept the fundamental idea of pluralist democracy: respect for the minority.

A supplementary condition should also be fulfilled. The minority must follow the rules of the game also. The French deputies in the Fifth Republic are not used to debates except those which threaten to bring down the government.[6] Between 1875 and 1958 the principal means of political control of the executive by parliament consisted of attempts, often successful, to overthrow the government by the technique of what the Germans call *Grosse Anfragen,* although other means were also used.

In France there was and still is a long debate to determine how efficient executive control could be obtained by the legislature without constantly calling into question the existence of the administration. I cannot go into the details of this debate here, all the more because the remedies proposed were extremely varied—(the establishment of an American-style regime, for instance, with a president directly elected and not responsible to the assembly and without power of dissolution; automatic dissolution of the assembly when it voted against the administration, etc.) It must suffice to re-emphasize the extent to which the situation of the Fifth Republic is unique and does not allow one to make predictions: The government is stable and parliamentary control limited because General de Gaulle, the chief of state, is so popular. In other words, if he threatens to dissolve the Assembly it gives in because the voters would choose the general rather than the majority deputies. This is what happened in 1962. With another president one might find the reverse situation: The president would not dare to dissolve the Assembly because the nation would rally to the support of the anti-administration majority. Furthermore, as we shall see later, the system of parties is undermined by the fact that the present dominant party derives its strength from the personality of the chief of state.

METHODS OF OPERATION

In the European parliaments great debates have become rare. Everywhere one hears complaints about the absenteeism of deputies from the plenary sessions. In Germany the televising of these sessions was stopped largely because of the unfavorable impression the sight of the empty seats made on the viewers. No system of coercion has so far remedied this situation, although in France theoretically deputies may not vote by proxy and in West Germany absent members are fined. The causes of this situation are profound: lack of interest or lack of professional conscience on the part of the deputies are only a part of the explanation, and not the most important part. The basic work of parliament takes place in committees. Committees listen to the members of the administration, even if they cannot summon them as do congressional committees in Washington. The committees of the Bundestag, unlike French committees, can organize hearings, and the members are quite well informed about questions under their jurisdiction. They often have the services of a staff which assembles the necessary information.

Why should the other deputies come to plenary sessions if they have confidence in the specialists of their own political group? Each group has its experts on agricultural and on social questions, and they are the ones who attend the plenary sessions, having already discussed the matter in committee. Would it not be better to give the committees the power to draw up laws or at least to reserve to them the right to amend laws, leaving the prerogative of the final vote to the full assembly? This method has been proposed and some concrete suggestions in this direction are being made.[7]

There is another possible remedy for absenteeism—to reduce the number of deputies while paying them more. Indeed, why is the United States congressman an important personage? Because he is not subject to group discipline, but also because there are few congressmen and because the considerable sums they get as perquisites and for secretarial service permit them to have a personal staff. The European deputy is not so well off, and a member of Parliament in Great Britain, in particular, is badly paid. Even the deputies of the French Fifth Republic, who have relatively good salaries, cannot afford to engage young economists or political scientists as research assistants. Furthermore, the collection of documents and sources at the disposal of the European parliaments are laughable in comparison with the resources of Congress. The result is the incompetence mentioned above. In these unfavorable conditions the European parliamentarian has only three sources of information—and each shows his subordination to an outside force: administration and cabinet, the political party, and the pressure groups who wish to enlist his aid. We must examine these dependencies more closely.

III Parliament, Parties and Pressure Groups

WHAT IS THE ADMINISTRATION?

The European regimes are theoretically parliamentary, that is, the administrations are responsible to the parliaments; but what is the administration? It is possible to give a variety of very different answers.

In the France of the Fifth Republic the government, in contrast to what the constitution says, is in fact a group. The administration is a group of ministers, some of whom are direct collaborators of the president of the republic, an executive head who is not responsible to parliament, while others work under the prime minister, himself a sort of chief of staff of the president.

In the Fourth French Republic, the administration was a kind of executive committee of the parliamentary majority, although the scattered nature of the groups permitted the president of the republic to exercise initiative in the choice of the président du conseil or premier, as in the case of Antoine Pinay in 1952. Although the framers of the constitution wanted to make the government a team of ministers under a head who was exclusively responsible for cabinet policy, in reality the ministers were transformed into delegates of their respective parties. In 1954 the Socialist party did not take part in the cabinet of Mendès-France, largely because its secretary-general, M. Guy Mollet, had refused to allow the premier to exercise his constitutional prerogative to choose his own ministers. Mollet took the position that the premier should take as ministers those whom the party considered worthy—or there would be no Socialists in the administration.

In Italy, the power to make and unmake cabinets does not belong to parliament, but to the Christian Democratic party. Only De Gasperi's eighth cabinet (1953) and Fanfani's second cabinet (January, 1959) fell as a result of parliamentary action. The fate of the others was determined by the internal struggles of the Christian Democratic party.

Curiously, the much discussed Article 67 of the West German fundamental law[8] arranges for administrative succession between two elections by means of a crisis within the coalition. Established in anticipation of preventing the negative majorities that had blocked the parliamentary system in the death-throes of the Weimar Republic, the mechanism of the constructive no-confidence motion can only function in the Federal Republic if there is a coalition government and if one of the member parties of the coalition changes sides. Up to now Article 67, or more precisely its imitation, Article 61 of the Constitution of North Rhineland-Westphalia, has only been used once, when in February, 1956, the Liberals (in Düsseldorf) left the Christian Democrats in order to form a new majority with the Socialists. Can one really say that parliament overturned the cabinet of Arnold and established that of Steinhoff?

How does one explain the fact that Adenauer's third cabinet (1957–1961) experienced no change in its entire period in office while his second cabinet (1953–1957) had internal difficulties in 1955 and 1956, and his fourth cabinet had great difficulty coming into existence in 1961 and underwent a serious crisis a year later? The answer is simply that the Christian Democrats having obtained an absolute majority in the election of 1957, the third cabinet did not depend on negotiations between parties. After the elections of 1961, on the other hand, Adenauer was forced to sign a "charter of coalition" with the Liberals, which was deeply contradictory to the spirit of the constitution. If that charter had been followed, legislative action and the general policy of the administration would have been put under the control of a special committee designated equally by the two parties.

The existence of an electoral plurality law would have been sufficient to eliminate the third party, just as the introduction of a proportional system would have allowed British cabinets, from 1932 to 1935 and since 1950, to be the expression of a coalition of parties.[9] It is not the electoral law that matters here, but the transformation that the change would have made in the nature of representation. In my opinion this is a fundamental matter.

In most of the parliamentary regimes the cabinet is no longer an outgrowth of the legislative assembly. The citizens, in voting for this or that party, understand that they are taking a hand in the selection of the executive. In Great Britain, in Belgium and in Germany one votes for or against the outgoing administration. Under the Fourth French Republic—as in the Weimar Republic—the rise and fall of coalitions forced the citizen to give a blank check to his party without knowing what cabinet the party would accept or overthrow and without having the power to pass judgment on the administrative action of the past cabinet at the following elections, because his party was sometimes in power (and never alone) and sometimes in the opposition. One of the major causes of the alienation of the French people from politics, one of the chief reasons they have several times given a plebiscite to de Gaulle and voted for the UNR in 1962, is that they had formerly disliked feeling themselves dispossessed by the parties and they are now pleased to be asked their opinion about the administration.

Parliamentary democracy thus seems to me to have changed. One of the chief functions of parliament used to be that it constituted the source of executive power. Today one might say, with hardly any exaggeration, that the freedom of the members of the legislature to choose the administration—in regimes which function well—is not much greater than that of the American electoral college in a presidential election.

THE LEGISLATOR AND HIS PARTY

In theory, a member of a legislature is responsible only to his conscience and his constituents. The reality is shown in the following figures. According to an analysis of the 288 roll-call votes taken in the Bundestag in the first two legislatures, between 1949 and 1957, deputies were overwhelmingly loyal to the decision of their parties: Social Democrats, 99.8 per cent; Christian Democrats, 94.5 per cent; Liberals, 90.5 per cent.[10] The concept of the deputy as an individual has given way to the concept of the deputy as a member of a parliamentary group which itself depends on a political party.

The mechanisms of decision in parliamentary groups have not yet been sufficiently studied. We know only that sometimes the party dominates the group, sometimes the group enjoys great freedom, and sometimes the party ministers, arising from the group, dominate the party. In France the Socialist party, the Radical party, and the Mouvement Republicain Populaire represent these three possible models of the relations of power. In Italy, Article 84 of the statutes of the Christian Democratic party says: "In all questions of a political nature the Parliamentary groups should respect the general lines fixed by the Congress [of the party] and the directives of the National Council and the Governing Board which interpret and apply the said orientation." The domination of members of parliament by the party in Italy is so real that breaches of party discipline do not occur in votes of confidence (by roll-call) but in the ordinary votes, which are secret.[11] Immediately following the elections of 1963 the political game depends even more on the relative strength of factions within the Christian-Democratic party. It is up to the dominant party to make the essential choice concerning the future orientation. But a second element has intervened: the struggle within the Socialist party in which Pietro Nenni was outvoted by the "leftists," who would have nothing to do with a pact with the Christian Democratic party. The Italian example clearly shows the transformation of the political system: the elections furnish the brute facts, that is, the numerical composition of the assembly, but this raw material is manipulated outside the assembly.

The dependence of members of parliament on the party can sometimes be explained in financial terms, especially in socialist parties, where a good many of those elected are officers of the party; but above all it stems from the simple fact that the party machinery fairly generally plays a decisive role in the designation of candidates in the elections. The voter votes for a party rather than for a man. The electoral system does not influence this phenomenon. If Macmillan were to leave the Conservative party tomorrow and present himself in his constituency against a Labour candidate, a Liberal and an unknown Smith or Jones chosen by the Conservative party, he would have only a feeble chance of retaining his seat. In France, the elections of 1962 as a whole confirmed the triumph of the label over the personality. Certain electoral systems can reinforce the deputy's dependence still further. In the West German Federal Republic, for example, half the members of the Bundestag are not really elected in the true sense of the word. In fact, the parties have a right, according to the number of votes received, to a certain number of "places on the list"; the voters do not know even the names that are on the lists.

PARLIAMENT AND PRESSURE GROUPS

Candidacies in single-member districts and the drawing up of slates in multimember districts must, of course, reckon with the interest groups the party wishes to reach. This phrase has two possible—and quite different—meanings. Interest groups may be defined as social groups, the voters of a given economic level or political orientation, considered as a group. The other meaning is, organizations whose members share the same status or political orientation. Interest groups in both senses intervene between parties and the members of parliament on the one hand and the electorate on the other. In the first and looser sense it is a question of the party or member of parliament mobilizing a sector of the electorate, of undertaking to represent its interests directly; in the second sense it is a matter of agreements negotiated between the party and the leaders of the associations or groups. These leaders wish to be the primary representatives of a given sector of the electorate; the party and the member of parliament are only its representatives at second hand.

The Conservative party in Great Britain obtains the vote of most of the middle class without having to go through a national association of "upper middle class" or "lower middle class." The M.R.P. can address itself quite directly to practicing Roman Catholics in the eastern and western parts of France, but it has to negotiate far less with the hierarchy of the Roman Catholic Church than the Italian Christian Democratic party or the Belgian Christian Social party. The German Social Democratic party would get the majority of working class votes in Germany without the existence of a powerful unified union movement, but it is in continual contact with the German Labor Union (D.G.B.), and the power relations between the two organizations may vary according to the circumstances. As for the British Labour party, it is closely tied to the trade unions by its very origins and by its constitution. Many other examples and variations could be added. Sometimes the organized groups bring pressure on the members of Parliament, sometimes the leaders of an organized group penetrate the hierarchy of a party; sometimes the party controls and dominates one or several of the organized groups; sometimes the leaders of such groups try to get commitments from several parties at the same time; sometimes there is competition between a party and an organized group to represent a given segment of society.

What is essential for our subject is to determine how members of the legislature enter into the representation of interests and to ascertain whether they actually do so. Here we might return to certain observations made earlier. It often happens that organized groups bring pressure on the government or on the parties without going through the parties' representatives in the legislature. New structures seem indeed to deprive the parliament of its classic prerogatives, as in the case of the committees of the Commissariat au Plan in France. Is it necessary, then, for the representation of interests by the organized groups to be channeled through parliament? In the West German Republic the important bill submitted in 1950 by the D.G.B. to set up co-determination at the level of the national economy would have moved in this direction. It was never passed, however. In France, above and beyond the Social and Economic Council, the plan to replace the Senate by a second economic chamber reveals the same process. Everyone has in mind the Yugoslav example.

Another solution would be to carry even further the direct action of the organized groups on the parties, as is done in the United States, where different groups confront each other within each of the two major parties, which thus become real centers of arbitration, preparing the way and making easier the task of final arbitration in Congress and in the administration.

The problem is all the more acute in Europe because the unification of Europe has already given rise to organized groups which cross national lines (in contrast to the embryonic public institutions, administrative or parliamentary, and to the feeble international organization of parties). These new supranational groups are likely to assume power themselves in the absence of a firmly established authority upon which they might act.

IV The National Parliaments and the Making of Europe

The construction of a unified Europe from the beginning of the OEEC to the development of the EEC has posed many problems to the national parliaments of the European states and, furthermore, has called into question their structure, their nature, their very purpose. Limitations of space confine me to a few observations on this matter.

1. The very existence of the European treaties and institutions limits the parliaments' sphere of action. Several years ago the French National Assembly was taken by surprise when it learned that it could not intervene in some regulation of the metallurgical industry (nor could the French administration) because, according

to a treaty ratified by the Assembly in 1951, only the high authority in Luxembourg had a right to do so. Already dispossessed to some extent by the national executive, the members of parliament have the impression that they are being dispossessed of their remaining powers by the action of the European institutions.

At the same time, much of the behavior of the deputies, especially those who have held office in the international institutions in Strasbourg or Luxembourg, as well as many parliamentary techniques, are affected by the fact that there is today a European dimension transcending the nations. The publication of the comparative study directed by Professor Max Beloff will show the transformations brought about by European institutions in the national administrations. It is to be hoped that a similar study of the national legislatures will be undertaken.

2. Deprivation of national powers by the European institutions began with the treaties themselves, that is, with texts that the parliaments could not amend. Are the legislatures then placed in the disagreeable situation of having to approve the results of negotiations made by the administration alone, without having the power to control them? The answer is affirmative only up to a certain point. Some fairly subtle procedures have been worked out empirically which will continue to permit the parliaments to express themselves before any texts which have important effects on the daily lives of the voters become final. It is precisely because of the repercussions of European treaties in everyday life that the members of the legislatures can less and less tolerate the control of foreign affairs to remain in the hands of the executive alone, while the European administrations, on the other hand, are less and less inclined to submit their international policy to real parliamentary control.[12]

3. The existence of the European institutions obliges observers, if not men in public life, to re-examine both the nature of foreign policy and the nature of parliaments. The best way to proceed is no doubt to discuss the clear-cut thinking of General de Gaulle. For him, the nation is a kind of person, acting in a world composed of other persons. From this point of view, foreign policy is the only real policy. The aim of domestic policy is to assure order and unity, to develop power which can be used in foreign policy. If we reread Volume III of General de Gaulle's *Memoirs*, we find that the state is not "a juxtaposition of particular interests from which nothing can emerge but feeble compromises, but a real institution of decision, of action, of ambition, expressing and serving only the national interest." Here de Gaulle agrees, curiously enough, with such a man as Hans Morgenthau, especially in his book *In Defense of the National Interest*. Of course, for the President of the Republic the fate

of Frenchmen is not an end in itself but a means to improve the situation of France; while for the American professor the fate of his fellow citizens as individuals is inseparable from the destiny of the United States. But both affirm two equally questionable principles: first, they assume that at every moment a perfectly discernible national interest exists from which could issue an uncontroversial foreign policy. This policy would, in the last analysis, be challenged only by traitors or stupid men. Second, this national interest would be the supreme objective of the political collectivity regrouped within the body of the state.

One has the right to believe, however, that except on rare occasions there is no such thing as the national interest, but different national interests, and that the highest function of the political game is precisely to arbitrate and settle these conflicting interests by majority decisions in which compromise certainly plays a considerable part. To paraphrase Raymond Aron, it is a question of taking into account the variety of objectives existing in every society operating as a political unit. There is not, then, especially on the European level, a basic difference between the essence of domestic policy and the essence of foreign policy. For General de Gaulle each Frenchman has, to some degree, two selves. He is a member of various groups, economic, social, ideological. As such he is represented by the parties and by the parliament. But whatever his socioeconomic status, he is also a Frenchman, with the same dominant interests as all other Frenchmen, and as such he is represented by the state embodied in the president of the republic. The parliament is thus basically incompetent in matters of foreign policy.

More than any other institution the Common Market shows the difficulties involved in such a conception. Peasants, workers in the metallurgical industries, Protestants, academics, Sicilians: each social group within each nation-state has its own special interests. Should these interests be protected by the state—in relation to the outside world? Against the states themselves in cooperation with corresponding foreign groups? Arbitration and compromise are required, but by what means? Executive, parliamentary or others? At what level—regional? national? European? How can one say once and for all that the group known as the nation takes precedence over all others if not by an ideological choice which is always controversial? I cannot go to the root of this question here, and I shall content myself by indicating its importance.

4. Assuming that the building of Europe continues on the institutional level, what will become of the national parliaments? What could a European parliament really be? Up to now the formula adopted has been to erect European assemblies composed of

delegates from the national parliaments. The powers of these assemblies are feeble; that of the Council of Europe is purely consultative, which means that it is not consulted very much. The legislative assembly of the European institutions theoretically has the right to control the embryonic European executive bodies. The rise of supranational ideological groups (Socialist, Christian Democratic, Liberal) marks, nevertheless, the beginning of a real European parliamentary movement.

Are we headed for an assembly elected by direct universal suffrage? The partisans of this idea seem to conceive such elections more as propaganda operations than as the establishment of an institutional organ of decisive importance. And is such an operation viable in view of the widespread disaffection with parliaments? To make a European parliament efficient, would it not be better to have a second assembly modeled on the United States Senate or the Bundesrat, that is, composed not in proportion to the population but by an equal number of deputies for each nation, in order to form a counterweight to the assembly elected, like the House of Representatives, according to population? Does not the nature of the Common Market involve bringing into existence a chamber based on socio-economic representation? Despite many articles, speeches and books, these questions have not yet been really seriously studied.

V Conclusion

If one defines as "parliamentary" no longer a political system where the administration is responsible to the legislature, but a system where parliament as an institution exercises an important influence on political decisions, everything I have said leads me to conclude that the European governments are clearly less "parliamentary" than the government of the United States.

The indisputable decline of the European legislatures, their disposession by the administrations on the one hand and by the parties on the other, should not be exaggerated. Their functions are still often important. To be a member of the legislature is not futile, even for the back-benchers. The dominant political ideology in western Europe has made the existence of a freely elected parliament so clearly the touchstone of democracy that the institution is in no danger of disappearing.

Nevertheless, the European parliaments are definitely in a state of crisis—precisely because the nature of the institution is at stake. Formerly, the institutionalized political power of a nation meant the legislative power and the executive power. Today, when one speaks of the government in Europe one means the administration, meaning only the former executive; whereas in the United States the word *government* continues to designate the political institutions as a group, Congress included. In Europe, the legislature has, to a great extent, become the intermediary body between the citizens and the administration, with greater legitimacy and tighter institutional structure than the pressure groups or the parties, but not necessarily more useful or more efficient in the eyes of the citizens. In Great Britain, Germany and Italy the parties have a tendency to displace the parliament as the intermediary between the citizens and the government, whereas in France it is the pressure groups that do this. Everywhere the original model of a parliamentary regime is to some extent in the process of disappearing.

Those who value the institution of parliament—like me—wish that men in public life and political scientists would investigate these changes further and ask themselves what remedies exist, if it is desirable to change the present trend.

REFERENCES

1. The small but substantial comparative manual of K. C. Wheare, *Legislatures* (Oxford, 1963) gives the most recent and most useful titles. See pp. 234–239. I would add A. H. Hanson and H. V. Wiseman, *Parliament at Work* (London, 1962), and D. J. Bartholomew, *Backbench Opinion in the House of Commons* (Oxford, 1961).

2. Some good studies: Union Interparlementaire, *Parlements* (Paris, 1961). This is a comparative study of the structure and operation of representative institutions in forty-one countries. See also "La profession parlementaire," in *Revue Internationale des Sciences Sociales*, XIII, 4 (1961), pp. 577–725. The most useful study is undoubtedly Samuel H. Beer and Adam D. Ulam (eds.), *Patterns of Government: The Major Political Systems of Europe* (New York, 1962, second edition, revised and enlarged).

3. Source: *Die Bundesgesetzgebung während der dritten Wahlperiode des Deutschen Bundestages*. Ein Bericht des Parlamentdienstes. (Bonn, 1962, 82 pp.)

4. See for example, Article 95 of the Italian Constitution, Article 65 of the West German Constitution, Article 45 of the Constitution of the Fourth French Republic and Article 20 of the Constitution of the Fifth Republic.

5. *Journal Officiel* (Assemblée Nationale of 23 November 1960), p. 3972.

6. Jean-Luc Parodi, *Les Rapports entre le législatif et l'executif sous la Vième Republique* (Paris, 1962) gives very useful examples. (Mimeographed at the Foundation Nationale des Sciences Politiques, Centre d'Etudes de la Vie Politique Française.)

ALFRED GROSSER

7. See for example the very interesting plan of Friedrich Schäfer, Secretary-General of the Parliamentary group of the Social Democratic party: "Bundestag im kleinen Saal?" in *Die Zeit* (April 12, 1963).

8. "The Bundestag can only express its defiance of the Chancellor by electing a successor by a majority vote and by asking the President of the Republic to relieve the Chancellor of his office. . . ."

9. Concerning the basis of an eventual majority system in Germany, see Bernhard Beger, "Was bringt die Mehreitswahl?" in *Die Politische Meinung* (February, 1963), pp. 26–45. For Great Britain, see D. E. Butler, *The Electoral System in Britain, 1918–1951* (Oxford, 1953), p. 188, cited with commentary in an important German study by Thomas Oppermann, *Britisches Unterhauswahlrecht und Zweiparteiensystem* (Karlsruhe, 1961, 151 pp.).

10. Gerhard Loewenberg, "Parliamentarism in Western Germay." *The American Political Science Review*, LVII (March 1961), 95.

11. See the analysis in Jean-Paul Chasseriau, *Le Parti Démocrate-Chrétien Italien* (thesis in the Faculté de Droit de Bordeaux, 1962, 2 vols.), "Le Parti et ses parlementaires," pp. 250–258.

12. On this entire question I take the liberty of referring the reader to the chapter "Le rôle du Parlement," in my book *La Quatrième République et sa politique exterieure* (Paris, 1961), pp. 79–101.

KARL DIETRICH BRACHER

Problems of Parliamentary Democracy in Europe

I The Dilemma

THE PHRASE "crisis of parliamentarism" is nearly as old as the phenomenon of modern parliamentary democracy. It is closely bound
up with the deeply rooted social and intellectual transformations in
which the process of emancipation—first with a liberal, then with a
socialistic stamp—broke the framework of constitutional government based on privileged estates, and in which the principle of full
representation and participation of all citizens in a parliament
chosen in a general and equal election was carried out. This development reached its critical peak after World War I. For the concept of parliamentary democracy the moment of apparently complete victory over the autocracies of old Europe signified at the same
time the beginning of a structural crisis which particularly affected
the newly created parliamentary democracies of Europe and which
aided the strongly antiparliamentary dictatorial movements toward
a quick rise.

With the exception of Czechoslovakia and Finland this crisis
quickly displaced and destroyed all new parliamentary democracies:
in Russia and the Baltic states; in Poland, Hungary and the Balkan
countries; in Italy, Germany and Austria; in Spain and Portugal.
Everywhere in this area the parliamentary system seemed to prove
itself unworkable; almost nowhere did it seem capable of absorbing
the political and social tensions of the "age of the masses" in a democratic order that was both stable and flexible. The transition from
the old liberal parliamentarianism of well-to-do individuals (*Hon-
oratiorenstaat*) to egalitarian party-state parliamentarianism led to
serious functional disturbances even in the tradition-bound older
democracies of Europe. In England, to be sure, it was possible to
absorb the effects of these disturbances by thorough-going changes
in the system of parliamentary rule; in France the Third Republic
was able to sustain itself, but only with difficulty. Even in the

Scandinavian countries, spared by the World War and apparently sheltered against the European crises, minority governments were often only provisionally able to contain the tensions; even they scarcely provided a proof of the workability of the parliamentary system.

The second postwar epoch of the European parliamentary democracies is of course significantly different from this first crisis period, which ended in the catastrophe of another world war. On the one hand it was still confronted with those basic problems of democratic structural change which the nineteenth century had laid in the cradle of European parliamentarianism. But on the other hand conditions had deeply changed, giving a new profile to the attempts at reconstruction or new construction of parliamentarianism in western Europe after 1945. On three levels these new perspectives were opened.

1. *Constitutional:* The experience of the twenties and thirties directed attention to possible precautionary measures and modifications in the parliamentary system for the protection of its substance and its efficiency. The West German "chancellor democracy" and even more the half-parliamentary presidential regime of the Fifth Republic in France are examples of this attempt at a limitation of parliamentarianism.

2. *Sociological:* At the same time the process of realignment and leveling of society—the product of the radical changes of the war and postwar period, a tendency away from ideologizing and toward pragmatizing of the parties—fostered the concentration of parties and finally the approach to a two- or three-party system, which was strengthened and hastened by constitutional and technical electoral provisions. West Germany was the most strongly affected by this process, in the course of the immigration and absorption of well over ten million displaced persons. But the tendency characterized much too simply as "Americanization" of party and parliamentary life was strong in the rest of Europe as well. This development seemed to simplify the formation of an administration and an opposition, to clarify political alternatives and to allow the parliamentary process to become less hindered by the formation of ideological fronts.

3. *Foreign Affairs:* The decisive phase of European political change at the end of the forties was marked by an increasingly firm opposition to the dynamics of Soviet Russia's European politics. The American politics of restraint, the Marshall Plan, the establishment of NATO placed western Europe within the framework of a broader international cooperation. It opened aspects of a supranational integration which could have an incomparably more lasting effect on

the internal politics and structure of the European states than the League of Nations had once had. The idea and the weight of a European and Atlantic community formed, first of all, a kind of protection for the new parliamentary democracies; insofar as they were still limited by powerful groups hostile to democracy—as in the case of France and Italy with their strong Communist parties—the growing interdependence meant a supplementary support.

The starting conditions for the "new Europe" thus seemed more favorable than in 1918. The attempt at a self-limitation of sovereignties had taken the place of a confusion of national ambitions, which at that time had made the rise and triumph of nationalistic dictatorial movements possible. The East-West conflict seemed to outweigh the internal explosive forces of national parliamentarianism. In the foreground stood the overlapping problems of political cooperation, economic and military networks, and the overcoming of the colonial age. In the face of such problems intrastate tensions tended to diminish in sharpness and importance or at least to recede to a deeper level of confrontations more specific and more suited to compromise. Such a prognosis seemed especially plausible from the German point of view. Had not Germany immediately after the occupation joined, as the Federal Republic, the European and Atlantic politics of alliance, within whose frame the West German parliament system could develop and stabilize itself almost without hindrance? Indeed, the experience of a parliamentary democracy operating with political and economic success was something entirely new in the history of German political thought, which had learned from the catastrophes of 1848, 1918 and 1933 to identify parliamentary politics with crisis and collapse.

But these positive perspectives reflect only the external, superficial image of the reconstruction period. They say nothing about the real stability and functional capability of the reconstituted parliamentary democracies of western Europe. Upon closer inspection it has quickly become apparent not only that the old problems of parliamentary politics continued to exist unsolved under the double protection mentioned, but also that the new conditions of the postwar period, with their revolutionizing consequences in the economic, social and intellectual areas, necessarily led to new crises of adjustment in the political system. It became a question whether and how, in the light of the changes cited, the individual parliaments would be able to carry out their role—which was still conceived in the classical sense of control and "decision-making"—in the actual practice of national politics. The increasingly complicated network of the modern industrial state confronted them with a dismaying array of new problems for which political common sense and the old parliamentary practice no longer seemed adequate. These problems threatened to undermine the competence and decision-making ability of the individual member of parliament, to strengthen at the cost of parliament the power of committees, experts and the bureaucracy of the executives and to lead toward an undermining of the parliamentary system of government from within.

As a result a series of surprisingly similar basic questions came to the fore in all of the western democracies. Is a parliament as such still capable, under such circumstances, of exercising an effective control of politics, not even to mention active participation in the formulation of political desires? Further, is it possible any longer to defend the submission of complicated economic, social and military decisions, which demand precise planning, to the tedious discussion procedure of technically incompetent large assemblies, considering that the deliberations of a small circle of committee experts are simply repeated in these sessions? And under these circumstances is it at all possible to continue upholding the classical basic principle of parliamentarianism—to combine democratic representation and the correct decision of all questions—or does not the parliamentary process become reduced to a formality in the face of the incompetence of the mass of the representatives?

A further consideration derives from the fact that precisely the supra- and international network of those technical decisions transcends the capacities of the national parliaments and at the same time must impose sensitive limitations upon them. The development of European institutions has demonstrated in recent years what a great effect this consideration has had in shifting politics from the parliamentary level to that of administration and bureaucracy. A European bureaucracy of a new character has gained a decisive advance upon the parliamentary organs in those institutions; the supranational formation of politics has been shifted extensively to an extra- or superparliamentary area of competence handled by experts and governments; in the face of this power the merely advisory function of the European "parliaments," which moreover have possessed only a derivative legitimation, not a direct one through direct European elections, has had little effect.

In view of these problems our diagnosis of parliamentarianism in western Europe will consider the following elements. We shall inquire about the model, the reality and the structural transformation of "classical" parliamentarianism, which has also been the point of departure for the parliamentary democracies of postwar Europe. We shall analyze the most important factors and arguments that form the basis of this structural change. What are their consequences: the transformation or the decline of parliamentary politics? Last, we shall endeavor to ascertain what efforts toward reform, substitute forms and future perspectives can be recognized within the national and supranational framework. Although the examination will proceed from Germany to the particular conditions of the various countries, attention will be devoted principally to the typical instances of those problems which today more than ever bear a general European character, both in positive and in negative regards.

II Structural Transformation of Democracy

The "crisis of parliamentarianism" figured, immediately following World War I, as the central theme of countless conferences of the Interparliamentary Union—in Washington, Ottawa, Geneva, Paris, Prague and Berlin. The discussion probed deeply into essentials. It dealt with the actual and necessary adjustment to the new European situation; it vacillated between a modernization or a limitation of parliamentarianism. At the same time it became increasingly clear that parliamentarianism had undergone an actual structural transformation which also needed to be put into effect constitutionally and institutionally.

Indeed the language of the constitutions and of their interpreters —insofar as it referred to the original model of the "classical" parliamentarianism, developed according to the idealistically elevated English pattern—was so far from reality that it appeared to be more and more fictitious. Whereas constitutional theory held to the concept of the independent member of parliament, responsible only to his conscience, in reality the representative found himself to be working within a network of social and political ties, a network which had become increasingly dense with the complication of modern industrial society and with the organizational consolidation and increase in importance of parties and organized interest groups. The result was that the member of parliament, contrary to the postulates of the constitutions, was subjected increasingly, whether consciously or unconsciously, to an "imperative mandate" by party interests and other joint interests. His role as representative of the people as a whole had thereby become unreal. The classical-liberal form of representative parliamentarianism gave way to a parliamentary democracy determined by plebiscite and party politics, a democracy which also brought about far-reaching changes in the process of forming political opinion and the function of the parliament as an organ for decision and control.

The interrelationship of this "structural transformation of democracy" (Leibholz) with modern party history has meanwhile been thoroughly analyzed. After World War II some of the European constitutions tried to give the new reality its due—though only in a makeshift way and rather incidentally—by dedicating a few articles to the role of the parties and their structure. Probably the most prominent instance of this was in the Basic Law of the Federal Republic of Germany, the West German constitution of 1949, in which (contrary to the Weimar Constitution) not only is the participation of the parties in determination of political policy emphasized, but their democratic structure and their agreement with the ordinances of the constitution are also specifically required. To be sure the old postulate of representative democracy was also preserved. The deputies are considered the "representatives of the people as a whole, not bound to specific commissions and directions, and subject only to their consciences" (Art. 38); thus they are supposed to be free of the "imperative mandate" to which they are in fact so thoroughly bound by the manner of nomination of candidates, electoral modes, parliamentary practice and party coercion.

The whole tension between theory and practice continues in these introverse stipulations. In other European countries the situation appears to be scarcely any different. In the merely laconic, usually meaningless reference to the parties there still prevails that "conspiracy of silence" (Loewenstein) with which the constitutions hold to the fiction of partyless parliamentarianism and the superparty parliament member. This is true of the Italian constitution (Art. 49) as well as of the French constitutions of the Fourth and Fifth Republics, even though the beginnings of a transformation are visible and in the practice of constitutional interpretation there is a growing attempt to give the political reality of party democracy its due. It is expected that this reality will be taken into account still more thoroughly by the new Swedish constitution, which has been in preparation for years with the authoritative participation of political science.

There is, however, a further aspect of that structural change which, although so far it has enjoyed less attention, has a more fundamental, comprehensive significance than the constitutional-political reform of the relationship between party, parliament and government. This is the expansion of the organized interest groups on the one hand and of public administration on the other hand. The consequence of both is that "unpolitical" experts and superparty planning confront the parliament's claim to power of decision and control with an increasing claim to primacy, attempting to undermine or even displace the parliament. The reasons for this development are as various as they are obvious. They lie in the need for continually improved, rational organization and planning in a complex, highly differentiated, sensitive society which can no more afford mere improvisation and dilettantism than can modern economics and industry.

But at the end of this development, which opposes to the political process of parliamentary democracy the greater effectiveness of the "unpolitical" experts, the objectively planning and rationally functioning, specialized bureaucracy in state and society, there appears the frightful image of a mere technocracy, a rule by the managers and functionaries, which would evade control and the entire realm of democratic-parliamentary decision-making. Thereby the balance of power would be seriously disturbed and a new form of dictatorship would be coldly brought into being. It is this opposition between highly specialized expertise and the principle of democratic participation that appears as the central structural problem of all western parliamentary democracies. To be sure this dilemma is also by no means new, however sharply it confronts us today on all sides.

Bureaucratization and specialization, no less than liberal and social emancipation movements, accompanied the development of parliamentary democracy at an early stage and continue to do so to an increasing degree. They have governed its forms and at the same time complicated them. The development of the apparatus of government has meant more than an expansion of its political functions. It has fostered the rise of the modern professional bureaucracy, which especially in nineteenth-century Germany was most closely tied to the continuation of absolutistic and authoritarian-official (*obrigkeitsstaatliche*) elements in the structure of state and society. This became especially apparent after the establishment of the Weimar Republic, which tried, with the army and the state bureaucracy, to incorporate the great, allegedly indispensable supports of political continuity into the new order of parliamentary democracy—an attempt which is known to have been a huge failure. The collapse of the first German democracy was to a considerable degree a result of the unsolved tension between parliamentary and bureaucratic-authoritarian elements of structure; this tension was already prepared for in the dualism of the Weimar Constitution; it finally ended with the victory of a bureaucratic presidial dictatorship and its pseudo-democratic manipulation and subjugation by Hitler.

To be sure, the cause for this was not simply a faulty construction of the constitution. Rather, the problems of the first German republic showed how unavoidable was a clarification of the relation between the conflicting elements. Max Weber had already recognized at the end of World War I the tendency toward bureaucratization and expertise in the leadership of the state as a dominating sign of the age; according to him there remained only the choice between bureaucratization and dilettantizing. Later Karl Mannheim saw our "period of social change" to be essentially determined by the fact that great "strains" arose "out of the contiguity of the principle of competition and the principle of regulation and planning," strains which could be solved only by a system of "planning for freedom."

This problem certainly did not apply exclusively to the democracies. The authoritarian and totalitarian regimes were also unable to solve the strain, even after eliminating the parliaments; it continued to exist almost undiminished in the dualism of state and party, especially visible in the "Third Reich." And finally it became apparent in postwar France and Germany how great an importance is possessed by the continuity and the growing weight of the elite of experts in organized interest groups or unions and in state bureaucracy as opposed to the politically-parliamentary dynamics. Only recently it was once more pointed out, by Maurice Duverger, that the bureaucracy of experts in France plays a stabilizing role that alone makes government possible. The Fifth Republic deduces from this fact the consequence—albeit a disputed one—of a restriction of parliament, which ultimately aims at a *gouvernement de legislature* in which the parliamentary and the presidial systems would be merged. This, however, could be the end of real parliamentarianism and the victory of rule by executive mandate with a plebiscitary façade.

In West Germany, which with controversial arguments held to the continuity of the political apparatus beyond the period 1933–1945, the development proceeded somewhat differently. Here the "chancellor democracy" commanded a continually growing governing and steering apparatus whose complication and indispensability in the modern bureaucratic state works against a change of government. Now that it has outlasted several parliamentary periods this apparatus is far superior in technical knowledge to the parliamentary agencies of power, which in the Bonn system are curtailed anyway. In addition there is the fourteen-year duration of the political constellation, which is modified only by the federalistic structure. Here the danger of instability of the government is averted at the cost of disempowering the parliament, whose capability for control becomes inferior to the claim to expert knowledge and the stability of the political apparatus. The head of the government himself was able, thanks to his constitutionally assured position and to the special authority of Adenauer as Chancellor and party head, to extend the executive power far into the parliament, which then converts his will into laws prepared for him by the government bureaucracy.

In both cases, even though by different courses, the consequence of the unsolved strain is a tendency toward authoritative remodeling of parliamentary democracy. Of course in both cases the concrete form owes much to a personal element. It may not outlast de Gaulle and Adenauer. But the development itself would scarcely be thinkable without the factual and structural problems which lie at the basis of the crisis of parliamentarianism in the industrial and mass state of the twentieth century.

III Between Crisis and Reform

In the following survey we shall try therefore to summarize the most important points of view and arguments which characterize the critical discussion of parliamentarianism in Europe.

In the representative system the direct contact with the will of the people is lost, since in the large modern state the parties of rank have become mass parties, and elections based on personality have become impersonal, machine elections. One consequence is the stronger demand for plebiscitary arrangements, which correspond to a more general tendency toward "supraparty" ties. Just recently de Gaulle, who set the Fifth Republic on this course, criticized the lack of such arrangements in the Bonn democracy. All the recent experiences indicate, however, that they are feasible only in the smaller framework of a direct democracy (such as Switzerland still is), if the danger of uninformed demagogy or even of a new autocracy is to be avoided.

The prestige of the members of parliament has fallen precipitously since they no longer have to resist an autocratic principality and are enjoying a career that is almost without risks. To the public they seem to be dispensable: a constitutional state and a functioning government are already insured by good organization and efficient development of the political apparatus.

The organization of parliamentarianism, originally created for political problems, is not suited to deal with the penetration of economic and social problems into the concerns of government. Lawmaking has extended its boundaries considerably. It embraces almost all areas of social existence and it makes too great demands on the abilities of the members of parliament, both technically and temporally. The results are extended periods of session and necessary specialization. The participating citizen is replaced by the professional politician, who himself becomes a bureaucrat, a functionary, without having the experience and the specialized training of the state official.

Thus the continual broadening of functions of the state threatens traditional parliamentarianism, which is thereby alienated from its real function and fragmented in its effectiveness. On the other hand, a limitation of the extent of parliamentary control, especially in the economic area, has proved fatal, the more complicated the economic and social organism of the modern state has become and the more it has called for coordination and planning. But one is confronted with the facts that the state is seldom a capable entrepreneur and that the parliament is not a good organ of control for economic undertakings, especially since in this case it will transfer its prerogatives to a great extent back to the political bureaucracy. A system of decentralization scarcely offers the satisfying solution either. Federalism can of course unburden parliamentarianism, given the appropriate historical premises (as in Germany or Switzerland) by disseminating responsibility and control more broadly. But thereby coordination and planning become more difficult and complicated.

As the expansion of the state places too great demands on the abilities of the members of parliament, it at the same time lowers their position and the importance of their activity. An elected representative cannot, by the nature of the thing, be equal to the many-sided detailed problems with which society and bureaucracy confront him. The fact that he has to make pronouncements and decisions and exercise control in these matters, as if he were an expert, contributes to the lessening of the prestige of parliamentarianism in the eyes of the public and makes the member of parliament himself vulnerable, insecure and resigned in the face of the real or alleged specialists inside and outside of the political institutions. It also does not help to make his activity more attractive to the really suitable persons. At the same time that technical and political competence is concentrated in a minority within the parliamentary parties, the representative becomes dependent on an apparatus of reporters and specialists, and parliamentary debate is reduced to a mock struggle in the foreground behind which work those anonymous and nonresponsible apparatuses upon which the member of parliament is dependent to a great extent in technical matters.

The consequence is not only a weakening of the parliamentary debates but also that loss of substance and interest which has become characteristic for the greater part of parliamentary activity, with the exception of the few debates over matters of principle; this is also especially true of that domain particularly proper to parliament, which has become so complicated—household politics. The attendance in the parliament chamber is often meager; the parties function as mere voting machines; their activity seems to the critical public to be an expensive waste and complication; derogatory remarks against the conduct of parliament, whether they come from the government and the bureaucracy or from the interest groups, fall upon fruitful ground; finally, the institution itself is no longer taken seriously and it is overridden wherever possible and led into error. Overtaxed in its assignments, the parliament limits itself to topics that have an effect on the elections and abandons important decisions in practice to the planning and formulating bureaucracy. Thus their roles are often exactly reversed. Lawgiving is transferred to the apparatus of administration and parliament loses its authority to a quasidictatorship of the executives. Finally the will of the experts triumphs over the parliamentary art of submitting technical decisions to political decision and control; the decisions have already been made.

The structural transformation into the party state has sharpened these problems still more. The advance determination of decisions in the party committees so extensively binds the parliamentary member, whose parliamentary existence rests upon the party's favor, that even without express party coercion his parliamentary flexibility is extremely limited. Discussion, the basic element of democracy, no longer takes place chiefly on the parliamentary level but in the preparliamentary area of party politics, and largely to the exclusion of the public. Parliamentary decisions are prefabricated there and become a mere matter of form, since the voices are previously counted; the minority, that is usually the opposition, is left with mere resignation—until the next election—or with increasing anger, which can become intensified to enmity toward the regime itself, to a revolutionary mood. Old and new attempts to put an end to this development—for instance by prohibiting the "imperative mandate"—are of course condemned to failure. But the consequences can be lessened, above all under two conditions: by the loosening effect of decentralization and federalism and by a greater flexibility and elasticity of the parties themselves if they are no longer strictly bound to certain classes and programs and if there is a continuation of the process of leveling and pragmatization, which is so characteristic for the postwar development, especially that of Germany. On the other hand, here as in Italy and other countries the phenomenon of the "Christian party" has been thwarting this process and has added a new chapter to the European history of the (ideological) "Weltanschauung" parties.

The selection and education of the members of parliament is not holding pace with the complication of political tasks. Even the process of selecting the candidates seems inadequate from this point of view. The central dilemma of modern parliamentarianism becomes apparent here. A strong influence of the central party leadership is the only guarantee for the nomination of objectively suited, specialized candidates for parliamentary and party work; but this method endangers precisely that immediate contact with the constituency which seems to be possible only by way of local electoral committees, through a decentralized party organization. The technical question of the electoral system is secondary to this. The point of view of the continental backers of the majority election, in so passionately supporting the reform of parliamentarianism by a "personality election," is still oriented to the older model of parliamentarianism. However, empirical observations in England have confirmed that with the change from prestige democracy to party democracy, the elections have also changed from personality elections to party elections regardless of the electoral system.

It is felt especially urgent, therefore, that the representatives to parliament be better informed and equipped. An advance technical examination of the candidates, such as has been called for again and again, can be neither politically justified nor technically realized; it seems impossible to set up suitable standards. On the other hand, an expansion of the apparatus for information and assistance is under way everywhere. Assistants, experts, forces of aid of all sorts are to see to it that the balance of power between the government apparatus and the parliament, which is supposed to control the government apparatus, does not become too unequal in the conduct of affairs. But precisely this may give rise to another problem. A second big apparatus is created which is scarcely less subject to the tendencies of bureaucratization than is the government apparatus. Such a bureaucratization of parliamentarianism once more calls up, only on a different level, the old danger that the member of parliament is overridden by or becomes dependent upon extraparliamentary, nonresponsible experts. The collaboration of government officials, experts and members of parliament in committees of experts does increase the possibilities for objective information and controls, but it also considerably complicates the course of government and committee activity and in addition confuses the executive and legislative competences. One way out is the formation of commissions of experts in the government, as they are used in England with some success; thereby the technical knowledge of the organized interest groups is drawn especially into economic and social planning. But that does not essentially foster either a solution of the control problem or the reactivation of parliamentarianism as a whole; it only shifts, and probably sharpens, the tendencies to "expertocracy."

In all of this it is the ponderousness of the parliamentary system that is especially exposed to criticism. The first principle of modern government and economy, the principle of rationality and effectiveness, is apparently contradicted by the existence and practice of the parliaments so strikingly that the critics question not only their ability to function but also their justification for existence. Important decisions—as in Germany a new penal law, the social reform or the party law expressly required in the constitution—and also a plethora of detailed tasks are often postponed over several periods of sessions or remain entirely unsettled. For the greater part of the representatives the sessions mean up to 90 per cent idle time; for the public they mean a waste of valuable working power. This too scares many a qualified person away from the parliamentary career. Therefore recommendations have been put forward again and again for the technical rationalization of parliamentary procedure, which is still in the state it was in the eighteenth and nineteenth centuries. For example, time-wasting sessions might well be curtailed by the exchange of opinion and voting in writing or by telephone, extensive use of electric brains and other methods. But there are still narrow limits set to the simplification and shortening of the procedure. It is precisely the nature of the parliamentary system, as distinct from and contrary to bureaucratic procedure, to achieve a more comprehensive basis and sharper control of political decision through more extensive proceedings.

The idea of a second chamber of experts to bridge the gap between expert knowledge and political power has been playing a significant role right up to the present. Made up on the basis of technical suitability and professional grouping from the various provinces of economic and social life, such a "parliament of experts" could contribute as an auxiliary organ of the parliament and government to the objectification of the political process. To be sure, it has proved an insolvable difficulty to decide in what way and according to what key such an institution could be recruited. All previous attempts have also either run aground in useless technical discussions, as in the economic council of the Weimar Republic, or have been misued for the purpose of deposing the parliamentary system by authoritarian regimes, as in Mussolini's *stato corporativo* and similar institutions in Greece, Poland, Austria and Portugal in the thirties. In France since 1945 and especially in the Fifth Republic the idea of an economic council has been institutionalized; but this coincides again with a threat to parliamentary democracy.

Theoretically the auxiliary function of such an agency, which makes it possible to incorporate technical-economic expertise into the political process, should be hailed as a support of parliamentarianism. But the practical realization of it appears to be incomparably more difficult than the formation of commissions and councils, which according to the English example of the royal commissions and committees would have to bridge expert knowledge and politics and simultaneously curb and channel the pressure of interest groups. A chamber of professionals and experts seems to be not only historically discredited but also a danger in the present. The interest groups' influence on politics, which is already almost too strong, would have in such a chamber an additional vehicle and instrument. Therefore as a guarantor of objectivity it would be scarcely better qualified—indeed, its members would be still more subjectively tied to particular interests than the members of parliament, who have to represent various interests at once and therefore are more pre-destined for a comprehensive manner of making decisions. The primacy of politics is also indispensable in all matters of technical decision.

An especially weighty argument of the critics is finally the lack of stability of parliamentary governments. This was especially true of the unbridled parliamentarianism of the period between the wars. The twenty-one administrations in the fourteen years of the Weimar Republic were a frightening example. Even after World War II the French Fourth Republic exhausted twenty-five administrations in the space of thirteen years. It is true that the rapid change of cabinets was mitigated by the fact that often there were only minor shifts in the personnel component. But without a doubt, not only the total triumph of Hitler (and the assent of broad circles in Germany) but also the more moderate victory of de Gaulle over parliamentary democracy are to be ascribed in no small way to discontent about the discontinuity of parliamentary state politics. This discontinuity has been particularly consequential in periods of economic and political crises, which have needed the more far-sighted objective planning and persistent execution of a course of consolidation to a greater extent. Parliamentarianism appears to be not only a par-ticularly cumbersome but also an unreliable form of government which, because it is entirely bound up with the transitory present, is incapable of demanding unpopular sacrifices for more far-reaching politics from a short-sighted "will of the people."

Thus the tendency of European democracy is toward a modifica-tion of the parliamentary system of government. Its particular goal is to lengthen the duration of periods of government and to render more difficult the overthrow of cabinets and the dissolution of parliaments. This of course has always implied the danger of lessen-ing or even blocking political dynamics, the flexibility and capability for decision of the political forces. The rigidifying chancellor democ-racy of Adenauer and the pseudo-presidential regime of de Gaulle are examples of this problem, which can result in the undermining and displacement of a lively parliamentarianism rather than in re-form. There are various forms of this modification. The Fifth Republic has established a dualistic system, which runs on two tracks by placing representative and plebiscitary execution of the popular will in a parallel position and thus producing a peculiar system of balance in which finally the presidial-plebiscitary element dominates. From the German point of view this recalls all too vividly the faulty construction of the Weimar Republic; a decision for genuine presidential democracy or for the restitution of parliamentary democracy will not be avoidable when the present special form is no longer protected by the peculiar phenomenon of de Gaulle.

But the forms of modification in the Bonn democracy are also disputed. Undoubtedly an astonishing stability of the political constellation has been brought about by the elimination of splinter parties by the 5-per-cent clause, by the officially privileged position of the parliament parties by state financing, by hindrances put in the way of the overthrow of government by the "constructive vote of lack of confidence"; at the same time the dissolution of parliament is impeded, owing to a weakened position of the federal president. But the other weaknesses of parliamentarianism enumerated above have appeared all the more prominently. And more particularly the government, the bureaucracy and the interest groups, protected by the stable parliamentary conditions, have achieved such a great weight that many clear-sighted critics characterize the Bonn democracy as an actual government by bureaucracy and interest associations. This parliamentary democracy also will not have to stand its test until the moment of a change of administration; the end of the Adenauer era leaves many questions open, even though it seems to be less dramatic than the transition to the post-de Gaulle era.

This summary of the critical points in European parliamentarianism, as incomplete as it is, nevertheless indicates the central significance of the inquiry into the relation between politics and technical knowledge with regard to the future of European parliamentary democracy. This problem should now be pursued first in the national, then in the supranational, contexts.

IV Perspectives toward a Solution

Three main directions are taken in the attempts to solve—without a loss of democratic substance—the sharpened conflict between parliamentary politics and technical planning in the expanding industrial state of present-day Europe. The first direction is pursued especially in England and in the Scandinavian countries. It is the attempt to democratize the growing phenomenon of specialists and experts by making it useful and at the same time bringing it under control within the framework of, or in association with, the apparatus of government. This attempt proceeds from the insight that the activity of the interest groups cannot be separated from the political process and abandoned or consigned to a fictitious neutrality of the experts. In England the development of the royal commissions and similar institutions is significant in this line and at the same time poses a counterbalance to the rule of an isolated state bureaucracy. To be sure, new problems are created by the expansion of such commissions, which advise the government and administration in economic, social and cultural-political questions with technical competence, but also with their own interests prevailing. The importance of the experts has been fostered, the "anonymous empire" (S. Finer) of interest groups becomes institutionalized, but the parliaments' loss in substance has progressed further while the cabinet system, which is founded on parties and the administrations, has grown stronger.

A second course proceeds by way of the attempt *to submit parliamentarianism itself to the tendencies toward technology and rationalization* which have led to the advance of the expertise-and-planning system. This course has been pursued most decisively in France by means of the unburdening of the parliament (which of course also means its loss of importance), and by means of the institutionalizing of the system of expertise in large planning commissions. Another variation of this "rationalization" of parliamentarianism is the progressive shifting of technical decisions from the plenum to the commissions of the parliament, as is especially characteristic of the German development. The plenum retains little more than the sanctioning of the decisions that the members of the commissions bring before it. Therefore the selection and incorporation of the experts into the parliamentary party groups becomes the principle content of parliamentary activity. Here too the "rationalization" results in a loss of substance and significance of the actual parliamentary discussion. The system of *hearings,* which could steer this development, is lacking in the European parliamentary democracies with the exception of the Swiss democracy, which has a different form. Substitutes such as the interrogation hour of the Bonn system, in which the ministers must answer critical questions before parliament, are hardly sufficient, although in some cases (as the Spiegel affair) it proved quite important. But the basic principle remains in danger—the principle that decision is the prerogative of the politically responsible, elected officials of the parliament and of the government, and that it is not to be relegated to the bureaucracy or to the experts, with or without an interest-group slant.

All the more important are the efforts toward a new delimitation of the altered functions of parliament, government, administration and the organized interest groups which are undertaken in view of this dilemma. Their premise is that in view of the general tendency to bureaucratization the future of democracy depends upon whether objectivity and expertise can also be exercised outside of bureaucratic areas of organization. A clear separation of political decision (parliament) and technical planning (bureaucracy) is not possible; it would finally lead to the hypertrophy of the administrative state, to the victory of the hierarchy of officials over open democracy. To equate bureaucracy with expertocracy could appear as the tempting solution to the problems. But it contains serious dangers; it implies an evasion of democratic control and creates a new gap between the state and the citizens; it sharpens their dependence and helplessness in the face of the political-social process and degrades them to subjects facing a highly specialized, uncontrollable network of rule without comprehension. The result could be indifference and resignation; the political answer could become an erroneous reaction such as that of 1933 in Germany, if in place of a political solution to the problems a bureaucratic one were to prevail.

It is indisputable that the number of the actual decision-bearers in the modern state is becoming steadily smaller and the tendency toward rule by experts is becoming steadily harder to control. Thus the future of democracy depends all the more on whether it becomes possible to open up new ways for the citizens to participate in political and social affairs and thus to rise above the role of mere observers. Parties, organized interest groups and self-rule offer possibilities to create a counterweight against the threatening depolitization; an improved political education seems to be its precondition. This is true at the same time for the expert in the planning and steering committee. His "democratization" and control is most likely to become feasible if every kind of monopoly and hierarchy of the agencies of competence is avoided and if room is made for the principle of free competition in the sense of competition for achievement.

The basis for all attempts at solving the problem is therefore the insight that there must be no necessary opposition between expert knowledge and politics, between expertise and democracy. The primacy of politics must be maintained. The question is only what place parliamentarianism is to retain here, in what form it is to be brought into accord with the changed conditions of modern state, social, economic and military politics. The parliament and the parties which support it still have the double function of first working for contact and conjunction between the various areas of expertise, interests and politics, thereby guaranteeing the openness, readiness for compromise and competition; and second of control of technical counseling and technical planning, re-examining them in the discussions between administration and opposition and relating them to concrete political reality.

For both tasks—the uniting of political determination and technical planning on the one hand; the critical examination of the interest associations and also those of the experts on the other hand —the European democracies now as before need parliamentary institutions that are capable of functioning. We have indicated what possible modifications are being discussed and also to some extent realized to reduce the disadvantages and crises of parliamentarianism and to consider the structural changes of society and state. These modifications are resulting everywhere—not only in France —in a limitation of the "classical" parliamentary rule. But at the same time they aim at an intensification and rationalization of parliamentarianism in its indispensable functions. Improvement of the channels of information, expansion of the system of commissions, more conscious policy in the selection of their own experts on the part of the parliamentary parties and incorporation of the specialists into the work of the parliament are the means of this rationalization. Its goal continues to be to work as a clearing house and counterweight to the technical claims of the bureaucracy of government as well as of interest groups, and to provide the comprehensive impetus for the primacy of political decision.

This is particularly applicable to the new problems that have been brought forward by the international network and the creation of *supranational* institutions. Today an isolated view of intrastate parliamentarianism is no longer possible. It is superseded by the comprehensive question as to how the separation of politics and planning, of democracy and expertocracy can be bridged in the sphere of the European network, and partly also in the Atlantic network. Here too only an inadequate political control by the governments confronts the forward-moving, expanding bureaucracy of administrators and specialists. Commissions and ministerial councils of the European economic community incorporate this tendency as do the other European administrative offices. And here too the parliamentary institutions have remained far behind. As qualified as some of their members are and as favorable as the supranational exchange of thought is, European parliamentary institutions have little actual weight as long as they lack legitimation through direct European elections and as long as they carry out only insignificant advisory functions. Here too it must be recognized that technical planning needs political planning and control if it is to be both effective and democratic.

The danger of self-satisfied expertocracy is heightened still more by the economic and technical successes of cooperation on the level of bureaucracy. The collapse of negotiations between the Common Market and England fits into this complex. If England can be counted as a model of a parliamentary democracy that has succeeded in adjusting to the changed conditions without a breach of the basic principles, then England's inclusion would without doubt shift the politics of European unification from the bureaucratic level to the parliamentary level. Therein—and not only in a French claim to leadership—lies one of the reasons for the resistance of de Gaulle, who may fear the disturbing effect of such tendencies on the economic-technical development of the European cooperation. But therein also lies the reason for the all too long hesitation of England, which regards with mistrust the reciprocal effect on the tested institutions of its own political system.

Not only in Italy and the Benelux countries but also in Germany these political aspects of the problem—along with the economic and military ones—have in the meanwhile come into such prominent awareness that the French standpoint appears considerably isolated. The Fifth Republic is considered a special case, not a model for the solution of the problems of European parliamentarianism. Precisely at a moment in which a Europe of reduced sovereignties is considering its strengthened role in the world, a retreat into national, or even regional, small-European isolation has become unthinkable. This is not only a question of economic and military potential. It is still more a political question. The danger that threatens the European democracies externally because of their geographical position, and internally still more because of the multifariously broken tradition of their parliamentarianism, also has not been averted by their rapid reconstruction. In the search for security and necessary reform the European states need not only close association among themselves but also with the Anglo-Saxon democracies, which command the strongest traditions and experiences in the art of the adjustment of a firmly established parliamentarianism to the new conditions of the industrial world.

V Conclusion

While there are striking parallels and similarities in the appearance and problems of parliamentarianism in present-day Europe, the differences between the national forms of its realization still seem very great. In Germany, the experience of the Weimar Republic and the causes of its fall form the exit-point for all discussions about the relation of parliament, government and bureaucracy. The pseudo-presidential experiments of 1930–1933, which led to the dictatorship of Hitler, seem to justify the widespread mistrust against all attempts to minimize the position and function of parliament in favor of bureaucracy. In France, under the impact of the failure of classical parliamentarianism in the Fourth Republic, the experiences influencing public opinion and discussion support a very different view, almost contrary to the German version of a parliamentary party state. While in both of these cases, however, the main tendency goes toward a modification of parliamentary democracy, in Italy the older type of a multi-party system still prevails, confronted with the classical problems of a parliament which is split up in many political groups hardly able to form stable coalitions.

Such profound differences in the domestic scene of the European states must be considered if the prospects of coordination and integration of the national systems into a "new Europe" are examined. Besides strong remnants of the past—including very different experiences—it is a question of how to combine strong government and executive authority with effective control, which has led to individual solutions of the problems of parliamentarianism; decentralization and federalism—as traditional in Germany—are further elements of difference. The quest for European integration may as well complicate these problems as it tends to neglect them. It is also for such reasons that the position of a European parliament as a legislative body seems still very uncertain.

If the relation between parliament, government and bureaucracy demands new answers on the national as on the supranational level, this applies even more to the role of parties, interest groups and expert commissions within the institutional framework of parliamentary democracy. Beyond all national differences, two main tendencies are discernible: the growing importance of pressure groups, tending even to a *Verbände-Staat;* at the same time, the decline of ideological parties. This process, to be sure, is modified by the existence of strong Christian parties which may work as integration factors in a biconfessional society, as in Germany; but it may simultaneously block the tendency to open two-party systems, as does the unbroken strength of Communist parties in Italy and France.

In summing up, the development of democracy in western Europe, showing so many different traits and tendencies, has posed many new questions. On the level of domestic politics, there are as yet no common answers in terms of a "new Europe." This will be the future task of interstate compromises which may result in the creation of a European parliament. In spite of the experiments of the French Fifth Republic, however, the substantial form of European governments has remained that of parliamentary democracy, though modified: a fundamental change in the direction of a presidential system seems outside of all possibilities. On this point, the difference between Europe and the United States, whose peculiar political system seems not fit for export, remains a reality which in its importance for European and Atlantic politics should not be overlooked.

ALESSANDRO PIZZORNO

The Individualistic Mobilization of Europe

I Europe as a Tired Continent

THE events leading to the formation of the image of Europe as an aggregate of stagnant societies are quite familiar. Until 1913 the principal economies of Europe had to a greater or less extent enjoyed several decades of almost uninterrupted growth.* All in all, however, the relative economic position of Europe with respect to the United States had already begun to decline. World War I, then, clearly established the superiority of American economic potential over that of Europe. The consequences of this were soon felt. Among other things, for the first time in its history Europe, a typically creditor zone, had become a debtor. But the early postwar years showed a masterpiece of historical hypocrisy: while the returning armies of victorious or defeated soldiers (it does not matter which) marched gallantly under triumphal arches—soldiers who were later to shoot down workers in their respective countries—governments struggled around their idol of sound money, the bourgeoisie wallowed in the roaring twenties, and economists ruled out the possibility of a crisis.

When the crisis did come, it came to the United States, and the United States felt it more than Europe and took more time to recover. It was an American economist, Alvin Hansen, who introduced the concept of stagnation into economic thought and who applied it to the study of the American economy. Notwithstanding this, it was by now clear to many that Europe was the really stagnant society, sick to its very roots.† The painfully slow economic recovery of the

---

* "During the period from 1880 to 1913 the total output of manufactures in a group of six countries 'fairly representative of general European trends' was growing . . . by about 2 per cent per head of population." J. Frederick Dewhurst et al., *Europe's Needs and Resources. Trends and Prospects in Eighteen Countries* (New York: Twentieth Century Fund, 1961) p. 109. The author is referring to Ingvar Svennilson's *Growth and Stagnation in the European Economy* (Geneva: ECE, 1954). It should be noted that the rate of growth of the main European economies, for the last fifteen years, has been much higher.

† For a diagnosis of the economic situation of Europe in those years, we need only quote Svennilson: "Europe was suffering from the arterio-sclerosis

265

late 1930's was an illusion based on war orders. Stripped of arms production, industrial production figures for the principal countries remained at a lower level than those of 1928.[1] In Europe they were even lower than those of 1913. Seen from a distance, World War II might appear to be no more than the internecine war of an old once powerful tribe now on the way to extinction.

This is why no one in the postwar period could even remotely predict the speedy recovery and expansion of European economies, an increase in per capita income rates never before seen for such long periods and, as a result, the spread of an affluence inconceivable thirty years ago. This is why attempts are being made—with the wisdom of hindsight—to trace the reasons for this phenomenon, to discover its effects on the social structure and above all to try to understand whether or not these causes and effects truly run deep—are durable, that is—and whether or not they have really reversed prewar tendencies and modified Europe's relative position with respect to those of other countries throughout the world. Is what we have here the tendency of a new age through which it is possible to make out the pattern of future societies, or only a momentary flash after which we can expect the return of the same old problems and impasses, the same old contradictions and conflicts? Or what else may it be?

All these are evidently not problems which can be dealt with rigorously, as one might calculate the exact relationships among variables. We can, however, point out a few phenomena which suggest better than others what the characteristics of European economic dynamism might be, and what their effects are on the social structure.

I shall particularly try to demonstrate that certain aspects of the war crisis characterize, and to some extent restrict, the importance of the social changes we are witnessing. On the one hand what we can call the renewal and the failure of ideological perspectives, and on the other hand the social and institutional breakdown following the war (naturally along with the change in the state's role in the economy which dates back to the crisis of 1929) underlie the new relationship between state and society. The phenomena of social mobility, in the very broadest sense, of the access to power and of mass consumption make it possible for us to give a better description of the nature and limits of these changes.

---

of an old-established, heavily capitalized economic system, inflexible in relation to violent economic change. Low productivity in agriculture and many manufacturing industries and widespread unemployment kept national output and income low, and blocked the road towards rapid general expansion" (Svennilson, *op. cit.*, p. 52).

I *War and Society*

After 1945 the reaction of European peoples was quite different from that which followed 1918. Historical self-deception was more difficult, because despair was more profound. Europeans in those years felt something that it would be hard to define, but something nonetheless important for all that: what we might call the ideological orientation of social goals. By this we mean that for a certain period individuals perferred to think of their own lot in terms of the lot which they imagined or desired for the collectivity. Durkheim would have called it one of those periods of collective enthusiasm during which patterns of values are formed which will indirectly continue to inspire society even in its everyday life. Like all great ideological moments in modern societies, this too was filled with egalitarian claims. Indeed, it is at such times that the contradictions inherent in the system of values of industrial societies burst forth: we have on the one hand the sanction and support of the ideal of individual success, of achievement through competition, and therefore of distinction and differentiation; on the other hand, the need to create an appreciation of equality as a basic criterion for the exercise of opportunity and as a norm of general morality, so as to make it possible to recognize and to justify individual achievement on a moral plane. In the normal course of social life, when daily goals can normally be set and achieved, the picture is prevalently that of the quest for an emphasis on distinction and differentiation. But in critical moments, when the very bases of collective life are threatened, the value of equality is posed once again.

Political programs could also be quite different: laborites or Christians, communists or even liberals, they all, at least to some extent, started from a basis of common experiences. This was the prewar experience of the depression and the failure (or at least so it seemed) of the economic system of private initiative. It was the experience which every society goes through in wartime: a paradoxical experience, because for all its hierarchical rigidity, it contains an egalitarian element, in that the individual enjoyment of social rewards is strictly controlled, and everyone is ostentatiously acknowledged as being important in his particular role. And this element was exalted when there finally came a slackening in this hierachical straitjacket. The last element orienting ideological perspectives, directly and indirectly, was the presence of the Soviet Union as an example of the total renewal of a society.

This was the particular climate of these postwar years. If one had to keep in mind only this aspect, one's predictions as to the course of European history would be quite different from what actually happened. Indeed, collective enthusiasms failed. And yet many characteristics of present-day social transformations could hardly be understood without taking into account, at least as a background element, the importance of this enthusiasm. Besides its political influence in general, its impact was particularly felt: (a) on the social role and status of political activity and profession (this is one of the points that I shall try to develop later on); (b) on the criteria adopted in the evaluation of certain social questions, essentially those of equality, political participation and power; (c) on certain individual behavior which can be understood as a reaction against this kind of collective commitment, a manifestation which I shall try to describe in dealing with the various phenomena of mobility.

Another phenomenon which makes it possible to appreciate the social consequences of World War II is that which we might call the breakdown of institutions. Let us consider the four major (from the demographic point of view) European societies: the breakdown was most violent and radical in Germany, then in Italy, then in France, and finally practically nonexistent in Great Britain. This order also holds for the gravity of inflation (which can be considered a kind of financial breakdown) immediately after the war: almost immeasurable in Germany, 41 to 1 in Italy, 10 to 1 in France, and 2 to 1 in Great Britain. Now this same order holds for the average rate of growth for the whole postwar period: assuming 1938 as a basis of 100, the gross national product in 1948 and 1958, respectively, was 76 and 225 for Germany, 93 and 161 for Italy, 98 and 170 for France, and 106 and 134 for Great Britain.[1] I am not suggesting any cause and effect relationship. But the coincidence calls for some thinking. Let us put it this way: the more complete the breakdown in social continuity caused by the war, the more it represented a challenge which society was compelled to accept.

But all this is still arguing with metaphors and seems to imply that society and peoples act and react like collective individuals—and, indeed, this mode of expression is sometimes useful in describing the atmosphere in which individuals operate and from which they absorb their values. But who are the real actors?

One of the most striking aspects of the expansion of the European economy since the war is the fact that it took place in the name of private initiative. Private initiative had been considered definitely a failure after the crisis of 1929 and the continuing depression in the years following. The need for the state to intervene more and more decisively in the economic machinery had become clear to all, and indeed state intervention had already begun to spread in the years just before the war. The ideologies which took hold during the years of the Resistance and after, the military and economic successes of the Soviet Union, among other things, led most people to believe that the end of private initiative was at hand. Yet here too these predictions were contradicted by the facts. How is that? Perhaps the simplest explanation is the best: in the general collapse of the social order, the last institutional pillar left standing was the right of property. The more everything else crumbled, the more the still-standing right of property took on a fundamental importance for the reconstruction.* The simple juridical and economic fact then became a sociological fact: around this point of reference was spun the web of confidence, was organized the delegation of authority and the system of values which are to be either explicitly or implicitly accepted; in other words, the old pattern of the ruling class was being reconstructed. In this case, too, the more serious the institutional breakdown, the more openly private groups exercised their leadership.

It is now more evident what was meant in speaking of the exceptional importance of the war crisis in stimulating the rhythm of European recovery. A typical example is Germany. The two most dramatic experiences of this country, the social and institutional collapse and the division of the national territory into two parts, were paradoxically the principal factors in its economic success. And this was so in a double sense in that it constituted a challenge and yet it was due to much more precise and measurable facts: the destruction of the war, in that it stimulated Germany industry to begin from scratch; the movements of population from the East to the West, in that they provided the necessary labor force (we will see this point in the next section). If we overlook the effort involved in recovery immediately after the war, the trend of European development looks much more normal. In fact, since 1953 the highest rate of income growth has been Italy's, along with Austria's and Greece's, and the reason is simply that these economies started from lower levels. Moreover, still higher in eastern Europe are the growth rates of the economies of Jugoslavia, Poland and Czechoslovakia.† And although

* From this we can argue that if the right of property is of secondary importance in the normal functioning of an advanced capitalist system, its impact becomes paramount during critical and decisive periods.

† We give here, in order, some index numbers of per capita product from 1953 to 1961 at constant prices (with the basis of 100 in 1958). For Yugoslavia it rose from 73 to 125; for Germany, from 76 to 120; for Italy, from 79 to 123; for Czechoslovakia, from 77 (1954) to 119; for Greece, from 77 to 118; for Austria, from 72 to 111 (1960); for Poland, from 72 to 107 (1960); for France, from 83 to 110; for Great Britain, from 91 to 108; for the United States, from 101 to 106. Source: *U.N. Statistical Yearbook* (New York, 1962), pp. 489–490. If we consider the index numbers of industrial production, for some countries, in 1961 (with the basis of 100 in 1953) we have for Italy,

Germany and France have continued to enjoy very high rates of growth compared to any other period in their history (and in the case of France the situation is still influenced by the repercussions of the end of the Algerian war), they are approaching the conditions of mature economies.

Thus the elements giving life to postwar Europe were interwoven: collective enthusiasm; institutional breakdown; the reconstruction of a capitalist class which more than others (especially more than the government structures) contrive to remain intact after the crisis and which took the lead in development, dragging most of society along toward a kind of "individualistic mobilization." How can we express all this in terms of phenomena (and not just economic phenomena) which are to some extent measurable and can give us an idea of the modifications introduced into the social structure? Let us begin by examining the whole of such apparently more "external" phenomena as "mobility."*

II Mobility and Integration

If the perfect mobility of production factors is the very essence of a successfully operating capitalist economic system, the mobility —that is, the geographic, occupational and social mobility—of one of them, labor, represents the realization of a certain aspect of the typical values of modern society. In general, it means conversion to productivistic attitudes and therefore the acquisition or strengthening of individual behavior which is congruent with and suitable for the needs of the economic system; it also means the uprooting of individuals and small groups from the social contexts to which they traditionally belonged, and therefore the loss of the old security, a striving toward new achievements and new wants.

European society, and not only the stagnant Europe of the 1930's, was habitually compared with American society and seen as lacking the mobility of the latter. Often, there was even a tendency to point out social mobility in its various forms as the secret of Americanism. "Mobility, too, is something of an explanation," wrote H. S. Commager a few years ago in describing the specific quality of American history, "a mobility that began with the movement

---

196; for Germany (excluding Saar and East Berlin), 191; for France, 177; for Great Britain, 129; and for the United States, 120. Source: "Compendio Statistico Italiano," (Rome: ISTAT), p. 347.

* The concept of mobility is one of the most equivocal concepts in the sociological vocabulary because it covers many different kinds of phenomena. But it could be useful here in order to express synthetically the prinicpal characteristics of a definite period of social history.

from the old World to the New, the trek from Virginia and Massachusetts Bay inland, and which continues to our own day; ten million people moved to the Pacific Coast in the last decade." [2] European societies did not enjoy any such fermentation. On the contrary, they suffered a continuous loss of mobile individuals, who abandoned the continent for other countries (especially the United States), where, along with their restlessness, they brought their productive power and their will to a new life.

Things changed after World War I, when the United States severely limited immigration into its territory. Emigration from the continent fell considerably.* In the 1930's, moreover, in correspondence with the general economic stagnation, the internal mobility of the various European nations sharply declined. Although the exodus from the countryside continued, it lost some of its intensity, and the growth rate of the biggest cities diminished.

During World War II, however, Europe had a dramatic experience in the movements of populations. It is calculated that from 1940 to 1943 throughout Europe, including the Soviet Union, the war caused the transplanting of about 30 million people from their home soil. Immediately after the war a shift of another 25 million people was organized.

Independently of these compulsory mass movements, new migratory currents are beginning to appear, attracted by one or another zone of Europe. By far the most notable movement, basically more political than economic, was the approximately 15 million Germans who moved from East to West Germany. Two other interesting emigrations are those from the Commonwealth toward Great Britain, and from North Africa toward France. For the first time Europe, which traditionally lost inhabitants in favor of other continents, has been almost regularly closing its accounts on the credit side in the matter of migrations. But, of course, it is not Europe as a whole which has been attracting new populations, but only certain zones. In fact this movement can be seen to come from all the marginal zones toward what may be considered the "economic heart" of Europe. Indeed, if we glance at the map of "population potentials" in Europe (including eastern Europe), we see that the zone of greatest intensity is a rhombus running from the city of London to the lower Rhine, and it includes southeastern England, Belgium, Holland, northwestern Germany and northeastern France. Around this zone

* The most significant case is that of Italy. Its emigration fell from an annual average of about 600,000 emigrants (for the first twelve years of the century) to 90,000 between 1931 and 1935. It was to rise to 270,000 between 1951 and 1955, and then fall again to 80,000 between 1956 and 1960. Source: "Sommario di Statistiche Storiche Italiane, 1861–1961" (Rome: ISTAT, 1962).

are arranged the successive contours: much denser toward the east and west, since the fall is more immediate; at somewhat greater distances from one another toward the south, so that Switzerland and northwestern Italy, for example, can still be considered fairly near the center.[3] If it were possible to prepare a map of per capita income in the same detail, it would take more or less the same form (of course, the islands represented by the big cities should be overlooked in both cases). Also similar would be the map showing the points of greatest attraction for the mobile population. Now this map, with its waves spreading from the London-Rhine center, is also, we might say, the map of successive Europes or, if you will, of successive zones of economic Europeanization. Independently of its technical value it is interesting in that it offers a picture of European dynamism according to categories different from those usually made on the basis of national incomes, a picture suggesting that there has been a kind of territorial expansion of economic Europe within its traditional geographic borders. Reduced to its own territory, Europe has this time expanded within itself, unlike the still pseudo-imperial Europe between the wars, which tried to maintain its presence in other continents at all costs.

If, however, we apply Myrdal's concepts[4] to this phenomenon, according to which for all the spread effects irradiating from the zone of expansion there are corresponding backwash effects in the more distant zones, we have to ask ourselves if these international migrations of workers are dynamic enough to effect a balance, eventually, among the various conditions (as happened in the case of the United States) and equilibrate development in all European zones, or whether the backwash effects will not end by creating even more severe imbalances.

In the first place, it should be noted that the international migrations taking place in Europe are minimum compared to those going on within the borders of each single country. This is partly due to the officials policies of various states. In fact, these policies aim at minimizing the need for foreign labor and keeping entry for such workers at a bare minimum, at restricting foreign workers to the less desirable occupations where they do not compete with native manpower, and at limiting work and residence permits to a short duration.* But, of course, there are not only institutional ob-

---

* "The Rome Treaty provides for the free movement of workers within the Community . . . but on the other hand calls for machinery to balance the demand for and supply of labor, 'in such a way as to avoid serious threats to the standard of living and employment in the various regions and industries' (art. 49). As long as there are wide differences in living standards workers in the more developed regions are not likely to accept completely unrestricted

stacles. The various aspects of cultural distance, still so very strong among the various European peoples, and above all the difficulties of the different languages and the different degrees of skill at work, are all factors which contribute to limiting the growth of this phenomenon. It is true that recently, owing to the labor shortages in many European nations, there has been a tendency for these international migrations to increase. In the main, it is estimated that in western Europe in the year 1963 there were about 2,750,000 laborers working in foreign countries. For the most part they were Italian and Spanish, but another figure shows that there were 800,000 Irish or Commonwealth citizens working in England; it is also interesting to learn that there were about 80,000 Greeks and 20,000 Turks then working in Germany.[5] This widens the circle of nations which constitute a reservoir of labor for industrialized regions; and also the circle of regions attracting populations. Sweden has for some time now been a zone of attraction; and now the industrial triangle of northwestern Italy is beginning to become one, for while they are only a few hundred, the first Greek laborers have arrived.

It is therefore likely that these international migrations will continue to increase in the near future.* But in this case, too, we must keep in mind the low capacity for social transformation that these forms of mobility reveal. This capacity is inversely proportional to the ability of the migratory currents to integrate with the host society, that is, to the willingness of the host society to offer the same opportunities granted the corresponding occupational categories of the local population. A few traditional migratory currents, like the Italians in France and in Belgium or the Irish in England, have, with the passing of generations, achieved this integration. But these conditions are still exceptional in Europe. In the great majority of cases, the immigrants remain confined to the lowest categories of the labor force, where the physical labor is hardest, and they have practically no prospects of advancement. Integration is almost impossible and, in any case, they remain only a limited number of years in the host country. With the slightest signs of unemployment,

---

immigration" (*Regional Development in the European Economy Community* [London: PEP, 1962], p. 73). It is obvious that when "wide differences no longer exist" (we are still far from it) migrations will no longer constitute a problem.

* Some forecasts to the evolution of the labor force show that the immigrants in Germany will be 2.21 million in 1970, while they will be 1.09 million in France at the same date. See H. Blanpain, "L'evoluzione della popolazione attiva dei paesi della CEE nei prossimi dieci anni," *Informazioni statistiche* (Statistical Office of the European Communities, July–September 1963), 3, 285–301.

they are always the first to lose their jobs.* This is (with the obvious exceptions) the situation, for example, of the Italians in Germany or in Switzerland, of the Poles and Spaniards in France (although these are by now rather traditional currents), of the Greeks and Turks in Germany, of the Algerians in France, and so on.

Very often these difficulties exist also for the populations in movement within their own country. This is why we can never really overrate the contribution of East Germans to the economy of West Germany, which was due for the most part to the homogeneity of the population in movement with the host population (for the very reason that the exodus was not due to economic reasons). Greater difficulties of integration are met, for instance, by southern Italians moving to the industrial zones of the northwest. They are relegated to the jobs which are the most laborious, the worst paid, the least important and which offer the smallest possibilities for social advancement. But in this case the difficulties are not such that they cannot be resolved after a certain period of time or, at most, in the second generation.

While for different reasons Germany and Italy showed the highest rates of territorial mobility since the war,† France has also had much greater movement than was expected. In fact, while for the 1956–1961 period the predictions of the III Plan calculated an annual decrease of 80,000 persons of the population actively engaged in agriculture, the most recent figures reveal that in that period actually 140,000 had abandoned agriculture each year.[6]

These forms of mobility are polyvalent in their effects on social structure and economic development, being in some cases stimulating and in others depressive. It is not my task to analyze them in detail. However, we cannot ignore one of the most important phenomena associated with them: territorial inequalities. One picture of postwar European societies would be incomplete if it did not reveal the extent of the imbalances still existing or, in certain cases, newly forming within the European territory.

First of all, the differences are still very strong among the various

* Between 1960 and 1962, in Great Britain, the unemployment among colored immigrants was 10% while the national average was 2%. The colored unemployed were 8000 in 1960 and 38,000 in 1962.

† Geographical mobility, in Italy, after the war, has been exceptionally high. Each year, 1.5 million inhabitants (that is 3% of the total population) officially change their towns of residence. This means one third of the population in ten years. Source: "Annuario di statistiche demographiche" (Rome: ISTAT, 1962).

The annual rate of decrease of the agricultural labor force was 0.7% between 1950 and 1955, and has been 2.6% since 1956. See G. Fuà and P. Sylos-Labini, *Idee per la programmazione economica* (Bari: Laterza, 1963), p. 14.

countries, each taken with its own average. If the per capita income in 1957 was $1139 in Great Britain, in France it was $1117, in Germany $1002, while it falls in Italy to $545 and to still lower levels, of course, in Greece, Spain and Portugal.*

But at times the differences within the same country are even wider. In France, if we keep in mind the per capita income of labor, we see that for the year 1955–1956, assuming the national average to be 100, the Department of the Seine, which has the highest figure, shows 167 while Corsica,[7] which has the lowest, stands at 45 (little more than a fourth). The differences between northern and southern Italy are even more striking: differences in income are not only very wide but increasing. In fact, the income of the south, which was supposed to increase from 21 per cent of the national income in 1954 to 28 per cent in 1964 (according to the predictions of the Vanoni Plan) was actually 20.5 per cent in 1959.[8] And if we wish to consider some extreme examples, there is the fact that in 1961 about 3 million inhabitants of the province of Milan showed an average income of 635,000 liras (almost $1000), which was four times higher than the average income of the 2.7 million inhabitants of the two regions of Calabria and Basilicata.[9]

Although these figures have not been presented systematically, they are probably sufficient to demonstrate that the kind of mobility we are witnessing in Europe is quite different from the mobility which once helped to form "a nation of immigrants" in North America. It would be a mistake to think that the population movements which have taken place so far, and may reasonably be expected to take place in the future, will end in a European "melting pot," a creator of new social forms, or at least a destroyer of old divisions. It is true that one of the strongholds of traditional European society, the rural world, is crumbling and that Europe, even outside the London-Rhine belt, is steadily evolving toward a totally urbanized and industrialized society; but the various new processes of integration seem, at least at first sight, to be short term in nature and to develop in a halting and petty way. Immigrants are considered little more than manpower which has come to solve temporary problems of labor shortage, when they are not actually looked on as outsiders who have come to take away work from the local population. There is no mirage of "new frontiers," but only the still ponderous weight of old frontiers, and not only political frontiers.

---

* In the same year, the average income in the United States was $2109; this means that the average incomes of these four countries were respectively 54%; 52.9%; 47.5% and 25.8% of the American average income. See R. Courtin and P. Maillet, *Economie Géographique* (Paris: Dalloz, 1962), p. 342, table XL.

Add to this that if one cannot deny the intensity of the spread effects from traditional centers of development, economic inequalities among nations and among regions will very likely give rise to tendencies to territorial separatism, however anachronistic this may seem in these times of European integration. The Flemish-Walloon controversy is only the most striking one of many we could mention. Moreover, the processes of industrialization have almost always brought along these two forms of contradictory tendencies. Tendencies to integration or to moving beyond one's frontiers correspond to the need to expand the market for new goods; tendencies to separatism and independence are a consequence of differentiations and discrepancies which inevitably become more marked during the course of development. Since the industrial revolution, Europe has known more struggles for independence than struggles for union.

Territorial migrations are obviously only one of the forms of mobility. They are the easiest to measure analytically, and this is generally the reason why they are given the most attention. However, they may be considered, at least to some extent, to include the other aspects. In fact, they are not only the most brusque and lacerating form of mobility, but we can say that when there is territorial mobility there is practically always occupational mobility as well and probably also vertical mobility. Indeed, the transition from the countryside to the city or from a small town to a big city almost always brings with it a certain rise in the social scale. This is why the figures I have given here are sufficient to give a general outline of the intensity of mobility in postwar Europe. If we could have all the data on the movement from occupation to occupation, from one to another place of work, and from sector to sector, our picture would be complete. In fact, the modernization of the European economy has been realized not only by the migrations of enormous masses of manpower from agricultural occupations to jobs in the city, but also with considerable shifts within these occupations, from sectors in decline (for example, textiles, coal and mining) to expanding sectors (chemicals, the production of durables); and moreover, from small enterprises to big organizations.* New kinds of jobs and professions have been created which did not exist before. Certain independent occupations have narrowed down considerably, and those who exercised them have become dependent on others. All this means that masses of individuals have given up their habits, their environment, their ways of work; that they have seen part of

* It is true that in many European countries, chiefly in France and Italy, very small units still contribute a high proportion in agriculture, retail trade and the building industry.

their working lives made useless and the skills they had acquired made obsolete; that, moreover, they have had to learn new skills, adapt themselves to new situations, strive toward new kinds of acknowledgement and new forms of security. But all these are no more than the well-known side effects of any intensive process of economic development and of mobility. Unfortunately, we are not in a position to say if and in what way such phenomena in recent years in Europe have been different from other typical and analogous processes; or how they have differed from country to country.

Another interesting point worth investigating, but on which there are still fewer data, is whether all these phenomena of mobility have increased the chances for individuals to climb the social ladder. There is an abundance of studies (this happens to be one of the most important problems in sociology) but a dearth of sound and conclusive data. So far it has been impossible even to raise the question—which is of more than sociological interest—as to whether social mobility is more intense in Europe or in the United States. It is known that the work of Lipset and Bendix[10] tend to demonstrate that there is practically no difference between the rate of social mobility in the United States and that in the more highly industrialized societies in Europe. The fundamental condition fostering vertical mobility would seem to be the process of industrialization and not the kind of institutional structure or of political regime. S. M. Miller's review of studies on social mobility[11] seems to make possible (but we can never be too cautious) somewhat more analytical conclusions. Italy and Germany seem to have a low rate of mobility both with respect to changing from manual occupations to nonmanual occupations and with respect to access to the elites. The United States is said to have a high degree of mobility for both cases. But all these conclusions are vitiated first of all by the fact that they are not certain and, second of all, because they describe social situations which have still not felt the effects of the exceptionally dynamic period of postwar Europe.

We may be able to reconstruct a fairly revealing image of these effects by taking into consideration two specific kinds of phenomena resulting from what we have called individualistic mobilization: the access to power and the access to mass consumption goods.

III Access to Power

The modifications in the power structure of European societies have been dealt with in another article of this issue. Here I shall only try to analyze a particular aspect of the relationship between political activity and "civil society," in the modes it has been assuming through the vicissitudes of the postwar period, owing mainly to the effects of the period in which European societies were strongly oriented ideologically.

In fact, this has meant an increase in the number of persons willing to assume public commitments and to choose political activity for universalistic motives, and not simply as one of several possibilities for employment or for a career. The circle where political personnel are recruited has grown numerically, spread socially (the attraction of political activity, in fact, has been strongly felt in widely different social strata and environments), and risen qualitatively. Moreover, the selection of this personnel, at least at first, took place in accordance with standards of total dedication to the given programs and ideologies (to the "cause," as the expression goes). Much less important were factors which usually carry much weight in other periods: one's social background, one's special competence in a particular sector of civil life, the network of "acquaintances" that a political leader can build up. Again, for related reasons, the political calling has enjoyed considerable prestige in this period.*

What have the consequences been? The chances for attaining political power have improved for individuals belonging to the middle and lower middle classes, and not only for those belonging to the classes which are the traditional reservoir of the ruling groups. The tendency to enlargement, however, has been constant although very slow, in the last few decades. In all likelihood it dates back to the introduction of universal suffrage in various countries. The periods of intense political awareness, as in this postwar era, or those in which there is an increase in state intervention in economic affairs, with a corresponding growth in the number of offices attainable by political or parapolitical means, enhance the importance of this broadening of the bases from which the political classes are recruited. All this is demonstrated by the fact that the end of the period of collective enthusiasm, and the gradual normalization of political life, have not brought with them (at least, to all available knowledge) any modification of this tendency. Broadly, that is, we

* S. M. Lipset and R. Bendix, *Social Mobility in Industrial Society* (London: Heinemann, 1959), pp. 39–41, gives evidence that in the United States the status of the civil service is lower than the status of politicians while in Europe (in France, Germany, Great Britain, Sweden and Holland), the opposite is true. Thus, in the higher political positions we find more persons with lower class background in Europe than in the USA. Rightly, they state that "this difference is probably related to many factors: to the presence or absence of labor parties and class-conscious politics, to the different structure of political parties in Europe and America, and so forth. In Europe more workers are motivated to enter politics and there is more opportunity for them to do so than in the United States" (*ibid.*, p. 39).

can say that by and large the political personnel has been increasingly recruited from the middle class, and that even the contribution of those coming from working class background, although still minimum, is not negligible.[12]

But all this holds for the political class as a whole: things change when we move on to an analysis of the governing groups in the strictest sense. The available data indicate that at the summit of political power, among those who attain government offices or the equivalent, the influence of one's social background is again strongly felt. Not only have individuals belonging to the upper classes a greater chance of attaining the very highest offices but, also with respect to those belonging to the middle class who have managed to achieve equal positions, they enjoy a much more rapid and more direct career, not being so conditioned to the filter and the obligations of routine party duties.[13] It is almost as if it were evident that they have fewer things to learn and fewer guarantees to give compared to others. The initiation of class is still the royal road to political success.

Has this situation been consolidated, or is it changing? And if so, in what sense? A number of considerations would suggest that this "closed club" of governing groups should gradually open. The influence of the much wider political class from which the governing class is still recruited, and the growing complexity of the state organization are only some of the many circumstances which should be exerting pressure in this sense.

Actually, none of the data now known confirms this hypothesis. They sometimes even contradict it, as in the case of England. After the war it seemed clear to all that the sudden rise to power through the Labour party of those who had been outsiders with respect to the traditional Establishment was no transitory matter but the beginning of an irreversible historical trend toward the abolition of the class bar. From then on, it seemed that all roads, including that to political power, had definitely been opened. After fifteen years, the figures reveal that the groups now in power in Great Britain come from a much narrower and much more class-conditioned category than those who governed before the war.*

---

* Guttsman, *op. cit.* Glass had already observed that the chances for the sons of professionals and high administrative workers of following in their fathers' footsteps were in fact thirteen times greater than would have been expected if mobility had been "random" or "perfect." See D. V. Glass and J. R. Hall, "Social Mobility in Great Britain: A Study of Inter-Generation Changes in Status," in D. V. Glass (ed.), *Social Mobility in Britain* (London: Routledge and Kegan Paul, 1954), pp. 177–217. See also D. Lockwood, "Social Mobility," in A. T. Welford et al. (eds.), *Society. Problems and Methods of Study* (London: Routledge and Kegan Paul, 1962), p. 514. On this point,

ALESSANDRO PIZZORNO

For all these limitations, however, it must be admitted that the growing importance of political activities has increased the opportunities for social mobility, for the political road gives one more chances for rising to social power than a career in business organizations. All research data confirm this. They reveal that, on the whole, even in a full period of individualistic mobilization, the traditional and socially inaccessible economic ruling class has not in the least been disturbed by what happens in the other layers of the society whose material fortunes they rule. As the author of one of the most recent studies on the French economic rulers very effectively puts it: "Nous constatons qu'ils sont presque tous issus de la bourgeoisie, et même, pour une grande part, de la haute bourgeoisie." And further on: "Peut-on alors constater une certaine évolution dans le sens d'un élargissement social du recrutement? Il semble que non. Bien que la compétence des dirigeants se soit élargie et soit moins uniquement technique, le milieu où ils sont recrutés varie peu. La haute bourgeoisie industrielle surtout constitue toujours le noyau essentiel de ce recrutement."[14] This does not hold only for France. For Italy, although studies are much less complete and sound, the conclusions seem fairly similar, and especially with respect to the fact that economic ruling groups are much less accessible than political ruling groups.[15]

As for Great Britain, there is another surprising fact: the persistent importance of hereditary wealth. A recent study, in fact, demonstrates that despite the famous system of graduated tax applied in Great Britain, the wealth that one leaves to one's heir is still a function of the wealth that that same person himself once fell heir to.[16]

Summing up, the conclusion is that despite the dynamism which characterizes the economic life of this postwar period, the group wielding the economic power remains exclusive and virtually inaccessible. This does not hold, however, at intermediate levels, or even at a fairly high level which remains outside the circle where the ultimate decisions are made. Here mobility and renewal are considerable. And that, again, confirms what one observes in other

all commentators agree: "We had all taken for granted immediately after the war that progress, whether it was rapid or slow, would be in the direction of classlessness—that the public schools would be either abolished or reformed, that careers would be thrown increasingly open to talents. In the last years the opposite has been happening," commented Christopher Hollis in his article "Power and the old school tie," *The Observer*, July 21, 1963. See also "The shape of the sixties," *New Society*, May 2, 1963.

fields: European societies have been permeated by evident phenomena of dynamism in these years; but their effects, the transformations which they imply, only go so far. Certain of the more rigid structures hold out, and it does not at all seem that their being caught up in the general movement is only "a matter of time."

The discrepancy between the high mobility found at the middle and upper middle level on the one hand, and the restricted circulation in the ruling groups on the other hand, is also interesting for another hypothesis. But we shall go into that later. For the moment it would be best to leave aside the question of the social origins of the ruling class, for it is not quite so important as political sociologists habitually make it out to be. Or rather, the real interest of the question is not that of knowing whether belonging to an upper class family gives one greater opportunities for becoming part of the ruling groups; but that of knowing, in given circumstances, what the necessary social qualities and characteristics are for holding positions of power. If hereditary transmission has for so long and in so many societies been of decisive importance in the formation of the ruling classes, this is evidently because the necessary qualities were acquired almost exclusively through family upbringing. Then, for a certain period (which, for that matter, is still going on) certain specialized institutions (Oxbridge, les Grandes Ecoles, the Ivy League) complemented the family in the job of upbringing. Still later, the mechanism becomes more complex and other elements have to be uncovered. But the tendency to characterize a ruling class on the basis of the modes and the places of their upbringing is only a short cut—it is easier to get the facts in this matter. The questions on the ruling class which seem to me fundamental, instead, regard the relationship between the modes of selection (and not merely of social origins) of the ruling groups and those of the wielding of power. In other words, what relationship exists between the qualities on the basis of which a man is selected for power, and the qualities of effectiveness in the attainment of the goals for which he is selected and by virtue of which the organization which chooses him is socially recognized and justified? Within this matter, there is another question of particular interest for the situation of contemporary European elites: what is the degree of conformity to the system of values held by society as a whole which a specific organization tends to adopt among the standards of selection of his particular ruling group? This point is indicative of the degree of pluralism, nonconformity, and innovation possible in a given society. Let us consider the case of a political party. This is often (in Europe it almost always is, and has been particularly so since the war) an organization which proposes to change certain structural elements of the society in which it operates.* If among the standards which it adopts in selecting its leaders an important place is given to the capacity to conform to the present values of the society which the organization is committed to transform, it is clear that the goals of the organization will become increasingly difficult to attain.

Let us see whether these premises are useful for understanding how things have been going on in Europe. We have seen that in the immediate postwar period political activity enjoyed considerable social prestige for a while and recruitment expanded to and beyond the middle class. Moreover, the most important social problems were defined in political terms. State intervention in the economy was another factor which strengthened this tendency toward an expansion of the political sphere and its penetration into "civil society." But it evolved differently. The needs of the reconstruction (and of economic development in general) made it necessary to give preference to such leaders as were capable of moving freely in the world of economy and private enterprise. This does not necessarily entail the acquisition of economic techniques and knowledge, but rather means that there is an ever greater appreciation of the ability to get along with those who rule the world of economy, to make their ends one's own and to know how to operate effectively within the mechanism of private enterprise. The political leader who most identifies himself with the institutional goals and programs of his organization is not so successful as the one who is better able to make and develop his contacts with "civil society." From this point of view, we can say that the role of politics in western Europe has developed in the same direction as that of the single party in the Soviet Union, which has been induced to work itself into the mechanisms of the productive organization in greater and greater detail. And this is not surprising because when economic development becomes the declared and preponderant goal of the social organization as a whole, the role of politics must inevitably be absorbed, more or less directly, by that of the economy.† A political leader (excluding the highest level, where foreign politics become preponderant) will be successful to the extent that he is able to contribute to the general efficiency of the system, and also the standards for his rise to power will be based on this element.

* We need only remember that socialist and Christian socialist reform parties have been in power in most of the countries of western Europe since the war.

† An interesting manifestation of this could be seen in the attitudes of intellectuals. After the war, as in all periods of crisis, a generation of them committed themselves to politics. In the fifties, a sort of conversion took place, and industry, through human and public relations, advertising and other means, attracted a good number of them.

As a consequence of all this, political organizations and movements tend to abandon the pursuit of ideological ends (it is the phenomenon which has been called "the end of ideologies"). But on analysis it must be deduced that this abandonment is not connected to the advancement of industrial society or to the coming of affluence, but to a specific situation which derived from a particular way of solving the problems of postwar recovery. The role of politics and of ideology is different in the United States, probably because the main task of the political leadership is world equilibrium, more than economic development.

A connected consequence is the leading role of private initiative, even with the partial modification of its characteristics in the sense of the greater importance given to the technical and managerial values. It is a phenomenon that has already raised a great deal of comment and this is hardly the place to deal with it again. But it is interesting for another question which it brings up: does this mean that the traditional ruling groups of the economy have been transformed into a new technical class or does all this simply mean that new technical-economic values (and therefore new standards of selection) have been adopted by traditional groups? Although answering this point would also involve dwelling on certain definitions, the second answer is probably the right one. In fact, I think we can say that technical-economic values now constitute effective standards of selection at middle and upper middle managerial levels, and that they are replaced by traditional criteria of "belonging" and conformity when we come to the highest positions of power. This seems to be confirmed by the data mentioned before, according to which access to managerial positions seems relatively easier, whereas the very highest positions are still exclusive.

The last consequence of all these conditions is a more and more privately oriented daily life and a growing apathy toward public affairs. But this is a subject which deserves a more extended treatment; it will be considered together with the phenomenon of mass consumption.

IV The Limits of Mass Consumption

It may seem strange to be dealing with mass consumption when our purpose is to highlight the specific characteristics of European societies. Indeed, this is a typical, and one might now say "traditional" American phenomenon; so much so that when its social consequences spread to other countries they are labeled "Americanism." But this too is only partly true. In the first place, two aspects of mass consumption in Europe make it at least partially different from what it is in the United States: it is much more limited, much less a "mass" phenomenon; again, it maintains certain more evident traditional cultural characteristics. One need only consider the difference between urban life in Europe and urban life in the United States, the greater attraction, in European cities, of the traditional city center with all the weight of its cultural overtones; and, as a consequence, the absence of the suburban atmosphere, with all its consequent socio-cultural characteristics.* But this is a subject which calls for special study; without it one risks slipping into stereotypes.

As for the question of quantitative limits, it is not merely a matter of the United States having more and Europe less, with the implicit corollary that when incomes are higher in Europe things will be much more as they are in the United States. What seems to be a matter of "more" and "less" in reality becomes a series of differences in ways of living and therefore in the relative positions of groups and classes.

Let us examine the question in the light of a few significant items, for example, the spread of automobiles, refrigerators and washing machines, the goods which most effectively characterize the new type of domestic organization and therefore the new way of life.[17] The increase has been rapid and will continue to be so in the near future. But if we consider that what we have here are *mass consumption* goods, the most widespread goods, it is interesting that in the richest country, Great Britain, at least 60 per cent of the households are not part of this "mass," but below it; in France and Germany the same thing holds true for about 70 per cent, and in Italy for 80 per cent. Around 1970 things will improve, but when the first men have landed on the moon or thereabout, almost half of the families in the richest countries in Europe will still not own an automobile. There would not be anything serious about this if it were not for the fact that the other half *will* own one, or more.

But, as we all know, the averages of such aggregates as the populations of whole countries are not very meaningful. We have not enough data to know what the differences in living standards are among the various social categories. But a few figures are enough to give us an idea of the extent of these differences. In 1954, in France, about 43 per cent of the category of professional men and executives owned a refrigerator, 23 per cent a washing machine, and 70 per

---

* It is true that in this respect differences are lessening. The sprawling of suburban life around great cities becomes a real alternative to the attractions of city centers in many European big cities. Conversely, a movement toward the re-evaluation of the city center has been growing in the United States in the last few years.

cent a vacuum cleaner. Only 6 per cent, 8 per cent and 3 per cent, respectively, of the workers owned these goods.[18] In 1960, things had considerably improved for the higher category, because the proportion of households owning these three kinds of goods had risen to 76 per cent, 49 per cent and 86 per cent. At the same moment, however, agricultural families possessing these goods were respectively 8 per cent, 16 per cent and 4 per cent.[19]

There is no need to dwell on the figures for other European countries; the discrepancies are about the same, if not greater. For Italy, for example, 1 per cent of the workers owned a washing machine in 1957 and 38 per cent stated that they would like one but did not think they would ever have one. As for refrigerators, the proportions for the same questions are respectively: 2 per cent (who own one) and 41 per cent (who would like one but did not think they would ever have one). For automobiles the figures are 1 per cent and 66 per cent.[20] But the differences between the various regions of this country (as we have already seen in the case of per capita income) are impressive. This item is enough by itself: at the end of 1958 in Piedmont, there were 48 automobiles for 1000 inhabitants, and in Basilicata, 7.[21]

These data clarify and scale down the picture of mass production civilization in Europe. Of course, certain other elements of increasing importance will have to be taken into consideration. In Europe one's economic future is not quite so unsure as it used to be. Among other things, the various integral or partial measures taken by welfare states have strengthened one's sense of security and made it possible for families to organize and plan their lives as consumers. Thus the spread of the huge oligopolistic organizations has brought greater job security than that found in an economy of small businesses. Again, there has been an increase in the sales of houses. All this has enabled families to make more and more use of the various forms of family credit and of installment buying, and to provide their homes with all the gadgets created by a new technology. The domestic unit thus becomes a technological unit of a new kind, the instrument of a vision rationalizing and, in a certain way, planning private life. All this brings with it a new cultural element, which is translated into the necessity to assume the value standards which make possible this new kind of organization of consumption and leisure: standards allowing one to choose among the alternatives offered by these new ways of living.*

* "The people of Western Europe . . . have reached the stage of making choices between one pattern of living and another; whether to live in a poor home and own an automobile or in a better home without one; whether to purchase a television set and a washing machine or to take more expensive

But these new standards take on their true sense only if they are widespread in a population and not felt as a social privilege. We can say that they stem from a cultural pattern of values which allows small differences (and therefore comparison and emulation) but not large ones. But when they discriminate against most, or at least half, of the population, the effects of these differences on the system of social relationships become contradictory.

The phenomenon of the spread of mass consumption, with the consequent tendency toward a private or home-centered daily life, therefore, is real, but it should be qualified. The new type of home-centered family based on the close union of the married couple—who organize their patterns of consumption; a couple relatively indifferent to public affairs and problems of the collectivity—has appealed to the imagination of contemporary sociologists and journalists, because this type of family is one of the most characteristic novel phenomena of contemporary living. But is this really the only new kind of family which is beginning to appear or is this only a general image covering various divergent cases?

Numerous studies carried out in England, for example, reveal a series of concordant facts which may be considered fairly conclusive.[22] The working class and the middle class (white collar workers, technicians and so on) continue to differ rather sharply not only with respect to income (although the gap is narrowest at this point), but especially as regards the different degree of job security and differences in the prospects for a career which the two categories enjoy. Even in a welfare state with relative full employment, wage earners continue to fear that the future of their jobs is insecure and could be jeopardized. Opportunities for advancement, moreover, even in an economically dynamic period (these remarks, however, refer to the English situation, which is the least dynamic in Europe) continue to be very low for manual workers.

Even when home-centeredness and domestic rationalization spread to the working class, this class remains out of touch with the typical ways of life found in the middle class, as their way of choosing friends and giving them a role in their private lives and their propensity to join associations.[23] Still very important for working class families are their networks of extended kinship, the feeling of community among neighbors and their daily friendliness with them (as opposed to the choice of friends on the basis of common interests, so typical of the middle class). On the whole, the working class family seems more isolated, less capable of bridging social distances;

vacations" (Dewhurst, *op. cit.*, p. 875). Let us say more exactly, "A part of the people of Western Europe ..."!

its social relationships are more conditioned by occasional meetings taking place within the proximity of its home. Instances of class mixing seem to be becoming rarer and rarer. Ecological segregation is much more marked in the new city suburbs of housing estates than in the old city. Even with a middle class income the working class family does not make a good neighbor for the status-seeking family. The so-called working class aristocracy produced by the welfare state and by the "affluent society" does not seem to be readily admitted among the old and the new status-conscious middle classes.

Are these distinctions of class or just of status? That is, will they lead to conflicts and then to structural changes, or just to emulation and imitation by one layer of Joneses by another Jones?

To try to give an answer would call forth a new series of studies. But let me just say that in this case another variable should be taken into account, the most important of all; and that is the role of non-European peoples. For the sake of brevity I have left out—speaking of European economic development—one of the most important factors: the impact of the world trade and the growing favorable conditions for Europe of the terms of trade with the primary producing countries. The socio-political consequence of these and of other analogous conditions is the increase in the inequalities between the industrial (that is, white plus Japan) and the primary producing (that is, colored) societies.* Will Europe (plus the Soviet Union and the United States), in the 6 billion people's world of 1990, become a ghetto of welfare states defending themselves with their atomic weapons against the starving colored masses?

With such perspectives in mind one can easily lean to other problems than those of conflicts *in* Europe. Or anyway one can easily predict that class conflict and structural changes in Europe will be a function of the policies of our societies on the issue of growing international inequalities.

V Conclusions

At the beginning of this essay several questions were put regarding the nature of the tendencies which have modified European societies in recent years, questions which, obviously, it has been

---

* In the recent issue of L'Observateur de l'OCDE, No. 5, August, 1963, Mr. Sheerwood M. Fine has comparatively calculated the growth of European and of underdeveloped countries until 1970. The average per capita income of OEEC countries will grow by 36%, while that of underdeveloped ones will grow by 9%. This means that the per capita income of the former countries, which is 14 times higher than that of the latter now, will be 17 times higher in 1970.

possible to answer only by coupling data with impressions. My hypotheses in seeking to give them some meaning were the following.

Many of the stimuli contributing to the progress of contemporary European societies are to be sought in the reactions to the war. As might be expected these stimuli have diminished and the once powerful dynamics of these societies have slackened and become normal.

The processes of social mobilization and social change have been important, but limited in the various dimensions of what Sorokin would call social space, and probably also in time. These limits regard particularly access to ruling groups and the discrepancies in living standards found among various social strata, regions and nations.

These limits and inequalities are not glaring, but remain on the edges of a general trend toward prosperity until the social groups whose aspirations have risen, and whose achievements have become consolidated, set the general tone of social and cultural life.

The fact that Europe has relieved itself of its empires and at the same time has achieved among the highest rates of development in its history should not lead anyone to imagine that this continent has become self-sufficient and that it has set in movement an endogenous mechanism of progress and renewal destined to last indefinitely. All appearances to the contrary, the mechanism is not internal and if we wish to predict whether it will continue to function or break down, the most important facts (or, if you will, the independent variables) should be considered in the light of the network of cultural, political and economic relationships which link European societies to others throughout the world.

REFERENCES

1. See Figure 4–1: "Growth of Gross National Product, by Country, 1938–1958," in J. Frederic Dewhurst et al., *Europe's Needs and Resources. Trends and Prospects in Eighteen Countries* (New York: Twentieth Century Fund, 1961), p. 112.

2. Henry Steele Commager, "The Nature of American Nationalism," in *The World of History* (New York: New American Library, 1954), p. 186.

3. See Figure 2–6: "Population Potentials in Western Europe," J. Frederic Dewhurst, *op. cit.*, p. 56.

4. Gunnar Myrdal, *Economic Theory and Underdeveloped Regions* (London: Gerald Duckworth), 1957.

5. These data are from the article "Europe's Economy is aided by Migrant Labour," *The Times*, June 20, 1963.

6. Mario Levi, "Possibilità e limiti della pianificazione francese," *Istituto Studi Economici*, February, 1963 (mimeographed paper), p. 12.

7. Institut National de la Statistique et des Etudes Economiques, "L'évolutions des revenus départementaux des particuliers," *Etudes et Conjoncture*, 6 (June, 1959), 587–622. See also *Regional Development in the European Economic Community* (London: Political Economic Planning, 1962), p. 42.

8. "Relazione al Parlamento del Presidente del Comitato dei Ministri per il Mezzogiorno," reported in *Mondo Economico*, XVIII, 28 (July, 1963), II. It is interesting to note that all the goals of Vanoni's plan had already been surpassed in 1961, three years sooner than expected. The only one which will not be attained is the shortening of economic distances between northern and southern Italy.

9. G. Fuà and P. Sylos-Labini, *Idee per la programmazione economica* (Bari: Laterza, 1963), p. 145.

10. S. M. Lipset and R. Bendix, *Social Mobility in Industrial Society* (London: Heinemann, 1959).

11. S. M. Miller, "Comparative social mobility," *Current Sociology*, IX (1960), No. 1.

12. For the data on the formation of the political elites, I have drawn from the following works: G. Sartori, *Il Parlamento Italiano, 1946–1963* (Naples: Edizioni Scientifiche Italiane, 1963); W. L. Guttsman, *The British Political Elite* (London: MacGibbon and Kee, 1963); A. Girard, *La Réussite sociale en France* (Paris: Institut National d'Etudes Démographiques, 1961); *International Bulletin of Social Sciences*, XIII (1961), No. 4.

13. See G. Sartori, *op. cit.*

14. Nicole Delefortrie-Soubeyroux, *Les dirigeants de l'industrie française* (Paris: Fondation nationale des Sciences politiques, 1961), pp. 108, 109.

15. See Sartori, *op. cit.* and *Inchiesta Shell*, No. 3, "La classe dirigente italiana," (Genoa: Shell, 1961).

16. C. D. Harbury, "Inheritance and the distribution of personal wealth in Britain," *Economic Journal*, December, 1962. About two thirds of the people who leave big fortunes received at least 25,000 pounds and half received more than 100,000 pounds.

17. Sources for the following percentages: 1955: Dewhurst, *op. cit.*, p. 266; 1970: *ibid.*, p. 1002; 1960: United Kingdom—"The Social Change Survey," *New Society*, December 27; France—M. G. Vangrevelinghe, "Quelques caractéristiques de l'équipement des ménages en avril 1960," INSEE, *Etudes statistiques*, April–June, 1961; Germany—Statistical Office of the European Communities. See "Il progresso sociale nei sei Paesi del M.E.C.," in *Corriere della Sera*, July 19, 1963, p. 6; Italy—A. Luchini, "L'évolution des niveaux de vie en Italie," *Economie et Humanisme*, January–February, 1963, p. 75.

18. Institut National de la Statistique et des Etudes Economiques, *Bulletin Hebdomadaire de statistique* (supplément), Paris, May 12, 1956.

19. "De la prévision à moyen terme. Quelques remarques théoriques et pratiques," *Etudes et Conjoncture,* June, 1962, No. 6.

20. Bollettino DOXA, January 31, 1957. See also F. Momigliano and A. Pizzorno, "Consumi in Italia," in *Aspetti e problemi sociali dello sviluppo economico in Italia* (Bari: Laterza, 1959), p. 198.

21. S. Somogyi, "Differenziazioni regionali alla luce di fenomeni socio-economici," in Atti per il congresso, *Il Progresso technologico e la società italiana* (Turin: Einaudi, 1960), p. 34.

22. See M. Young and P. Willmott, *Family and Kinship in East London* (London: Routledge and Kegan Paul, 1957); H. Jennings, *Societies in the Making* (London: Routledge and Kegan Paul, 1962); F. Zweig, *The Worker in an Affluent Society* (London: Heinemann, 1961); P. Willmott, *The Evolution of a Community* (London, 1963). Part of these results have been well reviewed by J. Goldthorpe and D. Lockwood, "Not so bourgeois after all," *New Society,* October 18, 1962, pp. 18–19.

23. T. Bottomore, "Social Stratification in Voluntary Organizations," in D. V. Glass (ed.), *Social Mobility in Britain* (London: Routledge and Kegan Paul, 1944), pp. 349–382.

RALF DAHRENDORF

Recent Changes in the Class Structure
of European Societies

Introduction

IF BY the class structure of a society we understand the relationship of its members to the exercise of power, there are above all four groups which demand our attention: (1) those who, by virtue of their position in a given country, are able to lay down the law for others in both the literal and the metaphorical sense (*the ruling groups*); (2) those who assist the ruling groups in their legislative task by executing and adjudicating law as well as by advising and generally helping those in power (*the service class*); (3) those who are subject to the power of the rulers as well as their servants, even if their citizenship rights enable them occasionally to make their voice heard (*the ruled or subjected groups*); (4) and finally, those who stand outside this whole structure of leaders and led, the "free-floating intellectuals," "those who"—in Bertrand Russell's words—"withdraw" and who therefore "do not fit readily into the social structure, and in one way or another . . . seek a refuge where they can enjoy a more or less solitary freedom" (*the intellectuals*).[77]

If there is any formula to describe the change in the interrelationships among these groups with which I am above all concerned in this essay, it would be the enormous expansion of the service class at the expense of all others and—even more significantly perhaps—the infusion of the values characteristic of this class into the behavior of all others, including even the ruling groups.* Thus the

* If there is any criticism of this essay which I should find it hard to defend myself against, it would be that I have left the notion of European societies as vague as it is in everyday language. Throughout, I am referring to western Europe. Most of the materials used are German, French and British; only occasionally are Scandinavian, Belgian, Dutch, Italian and Swiss data introduced. Some other countries of western Europe are referred to in passing. Foolhardy as it may be, I shall nevertheless claim that the conclusions presented in this essay apply to most of the countries of western Europe.

service class and its properties will be the focus of our attention in this essay.

Emphasizing the paradoxical trend toward an increasingly dominant position of a class, which, owing to its membership, cannot be dominant is of course no new discovery. Possibly there is no other occupational group which has been dealt with as extensively in the last decade by sociologists everywhere as the service class of "white collar" or "blackcoated workers"; and more or less dramatic notions such as that of a "white collar revolution" or that of the "bureaucratization" of all social organizations have been current for some time. Rather than describe the increasing importance of the white-collared helpers of those in power in every walk of life, I shall be concerned therefore with some analysis of the causes of this trend, of its uneven progress in different countries and of its ramifications for the social, economic and political condition of Europe.*

I The Demise of the Old Order

THE OLD ORDER: MYTH AND REALITY

If anything confirms Kant's epistemology, it is traveling: the traveler can always recognize in reality the categories which he brings to it. Nineteenth-century Europe was undoubtedly characterized by flagrant inequalities and, more particularly, by a rigid division of societies into rulers and ruled; that is, a small group at the top and a very large one at the bottom of the power structure. Even then, there were two types of this dichotomy of power. There was the old feudal division into the very rich and powerful and aristocratic on the one hand, and the very poor and powerless and nameless on the other; and there was the new inequality of power based on control or subordination, property or poverty, in the new organizations of industry. At least in theory, the distinction between these two inequalities is extremely important, the double dividing line between them being formed by nothing less than the French and the Industrial Revolutions. In reality, of course, the French Revolution was never complete in France, nor was the Industrial Revolution in England, and even countries like Spain and Italy did not remain entirely unaffected by both. The conjunction "and" in Marx's simple formulae of "capitalists and landowners," "workers and peasants," conceals the fact that here two very different ages and types of social structure are lumped together which in historical fact presented a complex crisscrossing of lines of power in most European countries, with England perhaps closest to the purely industrial, and Spain closest to the purely feudal types.

Nobody can be surprised to find that traces of both these dichotomies of power are left in most European countries even today. It is for this reason that the twentieth-century traveler has little difficulty in discovering the nineteenth century (and earlier ones) in Europe. The only undisputed difference between the present and the time at which Marx wrote is probably that the frontier of industry has been pushed further ahead everywhere. Except in the marginal countries of Spain, Portugal, southern Italy and Greece, pre-industrial types of dependence are today confined to islands within what are often called industrial societies. What is more, no economist or sociologist has yet come up with the assertion that these islands of feudalism and regions at the margin of Europe will remain forever as they are today. In fact, the grip of industrialization can already be sensed in most of them. Insofar as the old inequalities of power survive, they are thus almost always of the industrial type: divisions between the owners and controllers of the machinery of a modern economy, and the others who are wheels in this machinery without being able to determine its course or speed. Of all sociological models, Marx's theory of two antagonistic social and political classes emerging from the economic conditions of industrial production would alone seem applicable.

There is some evidence in political reality as well as in social research that this kind of division into two classes is still a fact in most European countries. In the political systems of Europe, the vis-à-vis of conservative and socialist, that is managerial and labor, parties has become almost universal, at the expense largely of the liberal parties of an earlier period of political history. Moreover, studies in several countries have shown that what the Polish sociologist S. Ossowski called "la vision dichotomique de la stratification sociale" is still very widespread in Europe, and more particularly among those who think of themselves as being placed "below." [25, 44, 68, 71, 72] But, of course, parliamentary disputes between conservatives and socialists are rather unlike a revolutionary class war, and the dichotomous view of society bears little similarity to the increasingly hostile class consciousness envisaged by Marx, to say nothing of the fact that "conservative" and "socialist" are labels that require much closer inspection, and that by no means all of those interviewed by sociologists displayed a dichotomous image of their social environment. Generally speaking, the Marxian notion of a society split into two antagonistic classes growing out of the property structure of the economy is no longer a correct description of European reality. The European Nightmare has become as old-fashioned as the American Dream. Perhaps the European and American societies have grown closer together; in any case, a new type of class structure is emerging in Europe which differs in many respects from the old.

A generalization of this kind, even if it is shown to be plausible (as I shall try to do in this essay) is bound to leave many individual cases unappreciated. Today, as in the nineteenth century, there is a great deal of crisscrossing of class lines in all European countries. There are some in which a roughly Marxian view would still seem applicable to many areas: nor are these confined to the southern parts of Europe, as those who identify North and South with developed and underdeveloped regions seem to believe.* Thus, the north of England and industrial Scotland still display many features of the traditional class antagonism which has already given way to new strains and structures in Orpington and elsewhere in the south of England; in fact, Britain as a whole may be somewhat "lagging behind" this time by comparison to many continental regions from Copenhagen to Milan. On the other hand, it is evidently true that the countries described as marginal before are also still at a point of social development to which not only the dichotomous view of society, but also a notion of two increasingly antagonistic political classes are applicable. Insofar as these countries have representative government, the strength of Communist parties may be taken as an index of this "lag"; in Spain and Portugal, the sentiments channeled into Communist support elsewhere remain a seed of revolution so long as they are suppressed. But for Europe as a whole, the society described by Marx is by now an Old Order. Insofar as this is the case, its demise was effected, or at least accelerated by three sets of factors: social, economic, and political. Let us turn, therefore, to some examination of these factors and their effect in the various societies of Europe.

THE SOCIAL MIRACLE

It is often not realized that in 1913 there was hardly a country in Europe in which suffrage extended to more than 25 per cent of the population, but many in which (if they had popular elections at all) fewer were entitled to vote, including Great Britain (17 per cent).† [85] Of those who had the right to vote, only a portion

---

* The extent to which the identification of the North-South dichotomy with that of development and underdevelopment is becoming fashionable even among social scientists was particularly striking in the discussions of the General Assembly of UNESCO in 1962. The simplicity of this identification is attractive, but its social geography is clearly dubious.

† The main problem of these figures is in the fact that the percentages are calculated on the basis of total populations, that is, including children, so that

actually did, so that the conclusion is borne out by evidence that, before World War I, only between 10 and 15 per cent of the population of Europe had a realistic chance to take part at all in the political life of their countries. Moreover, this state of affairs was a recent achievement at the time. If we go back another thirty years, Italy is by no means untypical, with suffrage extending to 2 per cent of the population, and only half of these actually going to the polls. Even in Britain, often described as the classical instance of modern representative government, barely 4 per cent of the population took part in national elections before the reforms of 1885. Curious as it may seem, in terms of suffrage, the German Empire was among the most progressive countries of Europe at this time.

The factual situation in the United States was not altogether different from that of Europe. In the presidential elections of 1912, for example, little more than 16 per cent of the total population took part, as against more than 50 per cent in the somewhat comparable countries of Australia and New Zealand at the same time. But then, people in the United States have until recently never taken much interest in political affairs, at least on the federal level, so that there suffrage and voting are rather less symptomatic of social inequalities than in Europe. For the point I want to make in quoting these figures is that while in the United States the notion of citizenship had a practical significance ever since the Declaration of Independence, if not before, its realization was still in its initial stages in Europe 120 years after the French Revolution. The abstract creature of liberal political theorists, common man, was in fact a highly privileged social being: man, not woman; older than 25 years; property owner, and not wage or salary earner; often, owner of land rather than renter of a flat or even owner of a house. In the family history of most Americans who are not Negroes, there are those whose names stand out because of their decision to leave their country of origin and emigrate to the United States. In Europe, however, the emergence from the nameless darkness of history was for most a long and much more gradual process. While the ideas of the French Revolution and the half-hearted measures of 1848 may have given to the extension of citizenship rights to all persons their pathos and much of their impetus, it was not until a century later—and, possibly, in large measure due to the effect of the intellectual and political force of socialism—that for the majority of Europeans, these rights acquired reality.

"One man, one vote" has become a powerful slogan for all the

---

different demographic structures of countries must necessarily result in different percentages. However, this shortcoming cannot, in my opinion, destroy the interest of this type of analysis.

underprivileged peoples of the world. But the slogan, as our reference to the development of suffrage and political participation, points to a symptom of the development of equality of citizenship rights rather than to its entire substance. Citizenship is the social institution of the notion that all men are born equal. Its establishment requires changes in virtually every sphere of social structure. Apart from universal suffrage, equality before the law is as much part of this process as is universal education, protection from unemployment, injury and sickness, and care for the old. Representative government, the rule of law, and the welfare state are in fact the three conditions of what I should describe as the social miracle of the emergence of the many to the light of full social and political participation. For it is a startling fact, peculiar to modern societies, that in certain important respects everybody counts for as much as everybody else; and while one hesitates to use the notion of progress in our time not only because of its naive abuse in the late nineteenth century, but above all in the face of Auschwitz and Buchenwald, the conclusion is forced upon us that in recent decades most European societies have experienced tremendous progress in the effective realization of basic equality for all citizens.

This is not to say, of course, that social differences, including differences of class, have ceased to matter. For one thing, the social miracle has not by any means reached every part of Europe yet. Once again we have to remember the great national and regional differences within Europe (which, from this point of view, coincide fairly accurately with the North-South slope). Secondly, one is almost irresponsibly overstating the case if one asserts that the social miracle of generalizing equality of citizenship rights has already occurred. In every country of Europe—indeed, in every country of the world—these rights are still restricted by traditional dependencies, social and even legal barriers, and new differentials of social position. For this is the third and most important comment to be added to the general thesis of this section, that citizenship does not abolish differences of class.[62] There are certainly fundamental differences between the slave, the vassal, the subject, and the citizen, but even the citizen cannot do away with the realities of power. In fact, Orwell's bitter dictum might almost be taken as a serious description of social reality everywhere: in a society of citizens all men are equal; but it remains a stubborn fact that some are more equal than others, that is to say, that some occupy positions which enable them to lay down the law for their "equals." The extension of citizenship in European societies has certainly changed the basis and the ramifications of the old dichotomous structure of class; but a new class structure has emerged on this new basis.

THE ECONOMIC MIRACLE

There is one change in the social face of Europe after World War II which cannot escape even the passing traveler from abroad, and which is itself the source of many other transformations: namely, Europe's economic development. More appropriately, this development must be described as an explosion or—with a term originally applied to the Federal Republic of Germany, but often extended to other countries now—a miracle. Once again, I am not using the word "miracle" to indicate that it would be impossible to explain this development; I am using it rather in a figurative sense to emphasize the almost incredible order of magnitude involved. Since in this context we cannot and need not go into a detailed examination of European economic development, these assertions must remain unproven. However, some brief considerations may at least help to make them plausible and to provide a basis for the analysis of their social consequences.

Economically, the interwar years were a period of stagnation. For the older industrial countries, 1913 marks a year of especially high production.[82] For the following thirty-seven years, however, industrial production fluctuated without at any point reaching much beyond the level of 1913. The low points of this fluctuating development were, of course, the two postwar periods and the great depression of the 1930's, the high points the late 1920's and the late 1930's. In the less industrialized countries of Europe, the interwar years were a phase of very slow development, so that here too we may speak of a period of stagnation.

However, while the economies of most European countries were fluctuating between depression and recovery, individual real income underwent an almost continuous process of increase. Thus, what appears as a period of stagnation was also a period of redistribution, that is, of internal changes in the economic structure of many countries. This is particularly true of the years before the great depression in which the real income of industrial workers very nearly doubled by comparison to 1913. In the 1930's, this development was arrested for obvious reasons, although at the same time the expansion of social services increased indirect incomes considerably in some countries.

European economic development took a completely different course after World War II. Production expanded at an unprecedented rate and, in some countries, within a decade reached three times the volume it had had in 1913. Although this expansion has slowed down in the last few years, the trend has not been broken. What is more, in the postwar era the development of total industrial production went hand in hand with increasing personal incomes for very nearly all social groups. In almost all countries of Europe, the real incomes of industrial workers have at least doubled since the end of the war, and while not all groups have kept pace with labor, increasing prosperity has been a general phenomenon.

Once again, regional differences within countries and differences between countries must not be overlooked. Socially, the most relevant distinction is probably that between countries for which the postwar boom is the result of the first impact of industrialization, and those others which are now undergoing what is sometimes called a "second industrial revolution." It is in the latter that changes in the class structure as a result of prosperity are perhaps most marked. The "second industrial revolution"—a rather imprecise term except that it indicates the radicalness of the development in question—has meant not only expansion but also certain well-known and often discussed changes connected with what W. Rostow calls the phase of mass production: [76] the increasing importance of the so-called tertiary sector of industry and employment; the extension of semi-automatic or fully automatic mechanization to ever new occupational spheres, including the office; the rediscovery of human skill as a necessary ingredient of economic success and its impact on the place and substance of education; to say nothing of the new patterns of consumption adopted by most people, which are inextricably linked to the future development of the economy.

Through the social miracle people have become citizens with a definite set of rights in which they are equal to all others. But it may be surmised that this development would have remained rather abstract and unreal had it not been followed by the economic miracle. Higher incomes and shorter working hours enable more and more people to make effective use of their citizenship rights. More, they place in the reach of many the chance of a life of which their grandfathers would hardly have dared to dream. It is not surprising that under these conditions old ideologies of class are increasingly losing their grip on people, and new and more complicated structures are emerging.

CHANGES IN THE STRUCTURE OF POWER

But class is about power. While social and economic status affect the relations of power, these have their own peculiar characteristics and laws of development. By power, we shall mean what John Locke meant when he said: "Power, then, I take to be a right of making laws with penalties of death, and consequently all less penalties, . . . and of employing the force of the community in the execution of such laws, and in the defense of the commonwealth

298

from foreign injury." [58] To try a somewhat more modern formulation: power is the right to make laws, that is, norms binding upon those subject to them by virtue of the sanctions attached to them, as well as the right to execute these laws and to enforce the sanctions. This "making" of laws thus involves all three of the classical branches of government.

I find Locke's definition rather more useful than all modern attempts to define power in terms of "control over others," "the chance to find obedience," and the like.* But in quoting Locke, I have left out three short phrases which require brief comment. One is Locke's concluding optimistic requirement: "and all this only for the public good." It is hard to share this optimism today. Second, Locke specifies the making of laws by the addition "for the regulating and preserving of property." At least from Locke to Marx, property was the prime mover of all things social—and very nearly an obsession —for most social analysts. To us, it seems not only unlikely that it is property that moves the world, but also evident that laws can be made for many other purposes. Third, Locke is not really trying to define power in general, but, as he says, "political power." In our context, political power is only one—if the most general—of many aspects of power; it is power as it affects people in their position as citizens. But as clerks (in their occupational or economic organizations), as laymen (in their religious organizations), as members of tennis clubs (in voluntary organizations), and in many other organizational contexts people also make laws that are sanctioned and executed; and it is a question of great empirical relevance how political power relates to that in other institutional orders of a society.

Regarding the structure of classes in contemporary Europe, four trends in the recent history of power require our attention. The first of these is closely related to the advancement of citizenship in the last half century. It is the transformation (in Max Weber's terms) of *Macht* into *Herrschaft*, that is, of personal power into institutional power.† Strictly speaking, personal power does not come under Locke's definition. It is not a right, but simply a capacity to make others do what one wants them to do. The relation of dependence

---

* Among sociologists, the most widely quoted definition of power (*Herrschaft*) is Max Weber's: "Herrschaft soll heissen die Chance, für einen Befehl bestimmten Inhalts bei angebbaren Personen Gehorsam zu finden." (*Wirtschaft und Gesellschaft*, 4th ed., Tübingen, 1956, p. 28) This is not the place for conceptual discussions, but one of the disadvantages of this definition seems to me that it describes power in too personal a fashion ("command," "obedience").

† Unfortunately, terminology is not settled here in English. Numerous concepts—power, authority, rule, domination, dominion, imperative coordination, and others—compete, so that it seemed wisest to me to express the trend in question by adjectives.

constituted by personal power is tied to the individuals involved; thus, in a sense, it is not a social relation at all. Yet there have been such relations of personal power throughout history. Where they have taken the form of "charismatic rule" they have involved not two but hundreds and often thousands of people; perhaps there is an element of personal power in the genesis of every form of institutional power. However, there is a general trend in politics as well as in all other social organizations today to reduce the unbounded potentialities of control inherent in personal power to power vested in positions and incumbent on persons only for the duration of their occupancy of such positions. (As a consequence, the claim to charismatic rule becomes increasingly unlikely in modern social organizations.*) At no time could the powerful really "do what they want"—as many would have it—although this notion is akin to that of personal power; but in modern Europe, their radius of action is much more limited still by the comparative neutrality of power exercised only within well-defined roles associated with social positions.

This domestication of power would of course not be very effective if it were not coupled with the development of mechanisms to control the exercise of power more effectively than can be done by unchanneled expressions of protest or agreement. The generalization of the "rule of law" is the second relevant trend in our context. Hobbes had, if not logic, then at least probability on his side when he claimed that the sovereign is exempted from the laws which, after all, he himself has a right to make. In actual fact, it can still be demonstrated by many instances that the law—that is, those who execute and enforce it—tends to become more lenient with people as they occupy positions closer to the source of the law. Prime ministers are unlikely to get tickets for speeding. At the same time, Laski was right in observing that the very paradox of the sovereign—the legislative, executive, and judicative—who is subject to his own law has come true in modern societies. The courts are open to all; and that means that everybody can find himself on either side of their disputes.[43, 52] Possibly, the rule of law is only part of a syndrome of control to which elections, parliaments, a free press, and other institutions of modern representative government also belong. In any case, the extension of these controls to most—though not all—European countries has changed the nature of class and class conflict profoundly.

* Weber himself has often discussed the mutual exclusiveness of charisma and bureaucracy. However, I am here using Weber's so-called "types of power" in a rather different sense than was intended by Weber.

A third modern development of power, although no less significant, is of a somewhat different kind. There are several reasons why,
in the phase of industrialization, economic and political power tend
to coincide in the sense of being held by the same group. In nineteenth-century Europe, industrialization created huge instruments
of power in a sphere of life where many people had to spend almost
the whole of their waking life, and at a time when the influence of
the state was largely restricted to the tasks prescribed by Locke,
that is, to "the regulating and preserving of property." Thus, the
economically powerful tended to be all-powerful by the same token,
and of course vice versa. Industrialization in the twentieth century
is invariably the result of vigorous and direct action by the state.
Thus, the politically powerful tend to be all-powerful, and vice
versa. However, insofar as European societies have passed through
this first stage of industrialization—whichever of the two forms intimated here it may have taken—neither of these coincidences holds
true any more. Instead, everywhere there is a large, relatively independent machinery of political administration; and those who
have power in other institutions, whether economic organizations,
churches, universities, trade unions or women's clubs, act as influence groups in the penumbra of political decision-making. Clearly,
some of these influence groups are able to exert more pressure than
others. This is true notably for the military and for the leaders of
industry and labor; but none of these is exclusive in a world in
which people's lives are no longer confined to one and only one
sphere of organization.*

I have described the machinery of political administration as
being large and relatively independent. In fact, the fourth important
trend in the nature of power in European societies today is the
seemingly ever increasing division of labor in the business of making, enforcing and executing laws. Where a comparatively small—
and thus easily identifiable—group of people controlled the classical branches of public and private governments a century or even
half a century ago, numerous positions of partial power have since
come into being, many of them so apparently subordinate that it
is hard to discover their relation to the exercise of power. The
analogy to the division of labor is striking: in the exercise of power,
too, one process has been subdivided into so many contributing
part-processes that it is hard to discover the whole in any one of

* Few theses of my book on *Class and Class Conflict in Industrial Society*
(Stanford-London, 1959) have been more widely criticized than that of the
"institutional isolation of industry and industrial conflict" in the modern world
(pp. 267 ff.). Perhaps the preceding formulations can help to clarify this discussion.

its individual parts. Just as in a modern shoe factory it is hard to answer the question, "Who makes the shoes?" it is hard to tell who, in the bureaucratic administration of a modern enterprise, church, trade union or state, holds the reins and in this sense has the power.

This last observation is indeed the main source of an interpretation of society which is today almost equally widespread among sociologists and ordinary citizens. In a word, this interpretation amounts to saying that the peoples of Europe have once again turned into "tribes without rulers." Since it is hard to localize power, power itself has disappeared. There is no longer a ruling class but only a market of veto groups, or the reduction of power to administration, or the transformation of power over men into power over things, or simply the power of the law. This of course is also David Riesman's conclusion with respect to the United States.[73] But, in one form or the other, a number of European scholars have followed Riesman or advanced similar interpretations on different grounds—although it is a striking fact that these are more numerous on the continent than in England, and, again, more numerous in German-speaking countries than in all others.[79] I shall try to show that the alleged disappearance of power is as much of a myth as its opposite, the tightly-knit, conspiratorial "power elite" à la Mills.[67] But if there is any conclusion to be drawn already from this cursory analysis of some trends which have changed the structure of class in many European societies, it is that this structure has become rather more complicated today than it was as described by Marx and seen by many people throughout much of the last century. Class in Europe is no longer a matter of the antagonism of a small group of all-powerful rulers and a large mass of powerless subjects. Indeed, Europe can no longer be properly described as a "fairly rigid class society."

But these remarks can do little more than set the stage. Let us turn, therefore, to the principal characters in the new drama of class and power.

II The Classes in Perspective

THE RULING GROUPS

Upon closer inspection, even Africa's "tribes without rulers" turn out to recognize some positions of power.[65] It would be very surprising indeed if this were different in contemporary Europe. As a matter of fact, our definition of power makes it quite clear where to look for the rulers; they are evidently those who have a say in the making, carrying out and enforcing of laws. For the purpose of the present analysis, I should like to restrict the definition of the ruling groups even further to those who, above all others, participate in making laws, and in making those laws which concern every citizen as such.[9] Probably no more than about two thousand people in any given European society can be described as belonging to these groups. Among these, the following categories may be distinguished. (It must be understood that these distinctions are introduced purely for purposes of identification and are not meant to indicate lines of cleavage within the power elite.)

    a. Incumbents of formal political positions of political power; that is, members of both houses of parliament, cabinet ministers, other ministers, undersecretaries of state (or their equivalent) insofar as their position is regarded as "political" in the sense that they are tied to a given government.

    b. Incumbents of formal administrative positions of political power, including the highest civil servants as well as generals, diplomats and judges of the Supreme Court (or its equivalent).

    c. Incumbents of other positions of political power.

    d. Incumbents of positions of political influence.

What is the social origin, what is the recruitment of the ruling groups of contemporary European societies? If there is any general answer to this question, one of three first posed by Ramond Aron [3] it would resemble the heading of a section of one of M. Dogan's studies of the French political elite: "from the republic of dukes to the reign of the middle class and lower-middle class." [32] Not all European countries are of course republics, and from the evidence we have there is some doubt as to the importance of the lower middle class as a reservoir of the ruling groups in our restricted sense, but the general trend observed by Dogan is certainly confirmed by studies in many countries. Throughout the last decades, there has been an increasing trend for the upper two thousand to be recruited from fathers in professional and commercial occupations rather than from the older agricultural and often aristocratic groups.*

Among members of parliament, this trend has had two complementary components. While the total figures given, for example, by M. Dogan for France and W. L. Guttsman and G. D. H. Cole for Britain, M. Knight and H. Schmidt for Germany, demonstrate the increasing importance of the urban middle class,[17, 32, 40, 41, 51] their breakdown by parties shows a more complicated picture. It seems clear that among the conservative groups (the "right"), the proportion of deputies of aristocratic origin has declined fairly con-

---

* Since D. R. Matthews published his little booklet on *The Social Background of Political Decision-Makers* (Garden City, 1954), there has been an ever increasing number of studies of this subject. At the same time, the question has rarely been asked what precisely these studies tell us. Thus we really know very little about the ways in which social background determines political behavior.

sistently in favor of what is generally called middle class origin. At the same time, a recent study by W. L. Guttsman in Britain indicates that the leadership of the Labour party has changed also. A slight decline in the proportion of Labour members of Parliament recruited from working class families was accompanied by a remarkable increase in the number and proportion of Labour M.P.'s whose own occupation must be described as middle class and who have received secondary or university education.[41] If this observation about the "left" is confirmed in other countries—as seems likely —it would indicate not only that politicians in general "follow a career pattern not dissimilar to that of other professionals," [32] but also that parliamentarians of all groups have contributed to the invasion of "the middle class" (or its children) in positions of power.

However, parliamentary groups are only part of the ruling groups in our sense of the term. In fact, the studies cited themselves show that, in general, cabinets tend to consist of people of higher social origin than parliaments. In France and Germany at least, this would also be true for higher civil servants, diplomats, generals and judges. A certain degree of "democratization" is, however, discernible for these groups also. Among the higher civil servants of Britain, for example, 18 per cent were, in 1950, recruited from the manual census categories III, IV, and V, as against a mere 7 per cent in 1929.[47, 48] In Germany, this trend was not quite as pronounced.[1] In fact, the administrative elites appear least affected by the social and, more surprisingly perhaps, the political changes since the 1920's. Thus, the trend toward recruitment from middle class families, while present everywhere, can be asserted only with reservations for Europe's ruling groups as a whole.

This conclusion is accentuated if we try to render the highly general term "middle class" more concrete. In many studies, this term has in fact replaced the older labels of "upper" or "ruling class" —a procedure which may in itself be symptomatic of the changing interpretation of status and power in Europe. In fact, the "middle class" that forms the main recruiting ground of the power elite of most European countries today, often consists of the top 5 per cent of the occupational hierarchy in terms of prestige, income and influence. From a study of over 2000 eminent people in France, A. Girard concluded that "plus de 68 pourcent des 'personnalités contemporaines' se recrutent dans 5 pourcent de la population, ou encore 81 pourcent dans 15 pourcent." [39] The same study shows that this conclusion holds *a fortiori* for the political power elite. A series of similar studies in Germany has consistently yielded the same result.[5, 27, 29] "Middle class" as the reservoir of ruling groups generally means fathers in one of the occupations included by M. Janowitz in the "upper middle class" of his stratification model (a category which, in the Federal Republic of Germany, comprises 4.6 percent of the population): "professional occupations, higher civil servants, independent businessmen with large enterprises, higher salaried employees." [46] In other words, the recruiting ground for the ruling groups of today is what we shall call the service class.

Which are the qualities that seem to assure success, and what are the modalities of the career? The transition from upper class to "middle class" origin—the answer to Aron's second question—would seem to imply a transition from ascribed to achieved status as the basis of personal success. For instance, the proportion of "dukes" with hereditary privileges has declined fairly consistently in the political elites of all European countries. Apart from the occasional "cabinet of barons" (Hitler's first cabinet in 1933), and of the permanently renewed peerage of Britain, aristocratic origin does not seem an advantage to speak of in the top power positions of Europe today. Once again, incumbents of formal administrative positions of political power are the most conservative group in these terms.[17, 32, 88]

This also holds for a new type of ascriptive status less easily recognizable but equally effective: self-recruitment. In Germany, 7 per cent of all judges are the sons of judges, 8 per cent of all professors the sons of professors, very nearly one third of all higher civil servants are the sons of higher civil servants.[27] Girard's study in France confirms this conclusion, and Guttsman found in Britain that there is a considerable number of what he calls "political families" where political activity is inherited (although their number is apparently rather smaller among non-aristocrats than among aristocrats). [39, 40] Without doubt, the degree of self-recruitment varies from country to country as well as in the different segments of the power elite. It is not likely to be as great among members of parliament as it is among generals or diplomats. But self-recruitment— that is, the invisible hand of the family—certainly plays an even larger part in the careers of top people than it does in society in general.*

However, emphasizing this point should not make us overlook the fact that an increasing proportion of the members of Europe's ruling groups acquire their position by their own achievement, and that generally means by education. Nowadays, the road to the top almost invariably leads through a successful university career, or

* All mobility studies since D. V. Glass's *Social Mobility in Britain* (London, 1954) confirm the conclusion that throughout society (with the deceptive exception of peasants, in whose case only one son can succeed his father) the most likely status of sons is that of their fathers.

at least a secondary education. Of a sample of 250 members of the ruling groups in Germany in 1955, a mere 14 per cent had received primary education only, and 23 per cent either primary or secondary education, all others having at least started university studies.[88] Of the much larger sample studied by Girard in France, 5.1 per cent had received primary education only, 10.4 per cent secondary education, and no less than 84.5 per cent a "higher education." [39] In England, a university education is socially regarded as rather less important, but here too "the rise of the meritocracy"—as M. Young, an English sociologist, has called it—is unmistakable.[17, 86] The school is replacing the family as an avenue to the top.

To understand the modalities of the career of top people, reference to the importance of a "good" or higher education is, however, too general to be of real interest. The important question is: is there any particular kind of education which helps the ambitious to make a success of their careers? While there is no type of education which guarantees entry to the upper reaches of the power structure anywhere in Europe, there are two types of institution which—with varying weight in the various countries of Europe—make success very probable, to say the least. One of these consists in especially prestigious schools, of which the English Public Schools are perhaps the outstanding example. Even today, the overwhelming majority of all conservative members of the British Parliament, and a not inconsiderable minority of Labour members, has been educated in Public Schools.[41, 64] While the proportion of Public School boys has been decreasing among higher civil servants in the last decades, almost two thirds of all British higher civil servants had attended such schools even in 1950, and one out of five had been to one of the twenty best known and most expensive schools.[10, 47] There is no real equivalent to the Public Schools anywhere on the continent, although the four grandes écoles in France play a somewhat similar part.[39] But the real continental equivalent to the Public School as an avenue to power is the study of law. Dogan demonstrates that lawyers are the most numerous occupational group in most European parliaments.[32] For entry into the higher civil service a law degree is, in many continental countries, an essential condition. Even among captains of industry, it is not unusual to find lawyers, so we may conclude that a law degree is the most helpful single achievement for those Europeans who aspire to a place at the levers of power.[28]

From W. L. Guttsman's study of British Labour leadership, it would appear that the most frequent career pattern of Labour cabinet members between 1924 and 1950 was "working-class background, with a career as an official of a trade union or other working-class organization." [40] Outside socialist groups, this kind of pattern has of course never been typical. But even so far as these groups are concerned, it would appear that the educational system, and more particularly the study of law (and in Britain, attendance of a Public School) is the new road to positions of power.

What is the rate of circulation or exchange of personnel in given elite positions; in other words, how much "job security" do members of ruling groups enjoy? I would like here to insert a question of my own among Aron's. "One of the essential characteristics of a legislative career is its insecurity." M. Dogan backs up his conclusion by solid evidence: "To sum up, 2,400 deputies out of 4,300 . . . or 55 percent, finished their legislative careers in electoral defeats." [32] The figure seems surprisingly high, and one would think that it did not hold in all political systems and at all times (although Dogan suggests that electoral systems other than that of the French Fourth Republic are even more sensitive to small shifts in voting preferences and, therefore, even more likely to unseat deputies). The rate of turnover of members of ruling groups is relatively high everywhere in Europe if we compare it with a time at which most top positions were held for life. (G. K. Schueller's study of *The Politburo* suggests that, in a thwarted fashion, tenure for life is still prevalent in totalitarian countries, where liquidation and death are the main causes of circulation.) [80] At the same time, there are clearly great differences between various elite groups as well as between times and countries. Not surprisingly, a circulation index developed by W. Zapf and applied to Germany shows a relatively high rate of turnover among political leaders, as against a very low one among what he (somewhat misleadingly) calls the "feudal elite groups," meaning church dignitaries, generals and large-scale entrepreneurs.[34, 35, 87]

In discussing the turnover of members of European political elites, we cannot omit the fact that most European countries have undergone, in the course of the last decades, at least one more or less violent change of political regime. Not all these changes have been as violent as the Spanish Civil War or military occupation, but in our context Mussolini's March to Rome and Hitler's rise to power in 1933, as well as the transition from the Fourth to the Fifth Republic in France, are no less important. In the last decades, relative political stability such as has been enjoyed by Sweden, Switzerland or Great Britain was the exception rather than the rule in Europe. Changes of political regime invariably involve changes of leading personnel. At the same time, it is not always a "counterelite" that replaces its predecessor entirely when political systems change. W. Zapf, who has studied samples of German ruling groups in our sense of the term in 1925, 1940, and 1955, has been able to show that: (1) there was rather less change between 1940 and 1955 than between 1925 and 1940, that is, less change between the Nazi elite and the present ruling groups than between the leaders of the Weimar Republic and the Nazis; (2) in both periods, change was most marked in what Zapf calls the "political elite," while there was considerably less turnover among both the "administrative elite" and the "economic elite." Clearly, these changes were of a very much higher order of magnitude in countries that had known "Quisling" regimes under German occupation during the war. Here, presumably, Dogan's conclusion can be generalized: "Two-thirds of the (French) deputies elected in 1951 and 1956 were also former members of the Resistance." [31, 34, 35, 88] In any case, the job insecurity of European men of power has been due as much to political upheavals as to patterns of circulation characteristic of the normal process of political development.[32]

What is the manner of thinking, what is the conception of existence characteristic of this category? While there are numerous studies of the social origin and career patterns of elites in many countries, there is comparatively little evidence that bears immediately on Aron's last two, and perhaps most significant questions. Interview studies of leaders are as rare as interview studies of workers are frequent in Europe. Rather than trying to piece together a more or less literary image of Europe's rulers from scattered sources and materials, let me emphasize, therefore, two features suggested by sociological studies, both of which seem to me highly characteristic of trends in the social self-image of Europe's ruling groups. They are, of course, largely guesses which will have to be tested in further research.

When A. Girard asked his sample of French leaders to which factors they themselves ascribed their success, by far the most frequent answer was "hard work." No less than 78 per cent of those asked replied in terms of "travail, persévérance, tenacité, volonté, énergie." [39] Perhaps the result of a similar survey a hundred years ago would not have been altogether different. It is evidently more pleasing to ascribe one's success to one's own effort than to factors outside one's control. Yet it seems to me an evident fact that the ruling class of Europe is no longer a leisure class, and that with ever shorter working hours for labor, the traditional relations between the working and the leisure classes have been reversed. In any case, a modern prime minister can hardly afford to stay in his castle (if he has one) for months at a time without bothering about the business of government, as Bismarck did; nor can a modern industrial manager spend half the year traveling around the world for fun before his retirement. Ambition and hard work are features characteristic of the ruling groups of today and their outlook on life.

Possibly this is one of the reasons for a second change in outlook suggested by recent studies. When M. Janowitz gave a sample of over 3000 Germans the choice to ascribe themselves to the upper, middle, working or lower class, only 1.9 per cent placed themselves in the upper class. Of these, no less than half must have done so in order to mislead the interviewer, since their actual occupations ranged from the small shopkeeper and the postman to the unskilled laborer. Of the 4.6 per cent placed by Janowitz in the "upper-middle class" on occupational grounds, more than 70 per cent preferred to describe their status as "middle class," and an additional 10 per cent as "working" or "lower class." In short, people at the top seem reluctant today to admit that they are at the top.[46] In fact, everybody who is "at the top" in terms of status, income or power is sure to know somebody else who, in fact or at least in his opinion, is placed even higher. Those who are by many workers described as "they," as being "above," themselves tend to think of society as a long ladder with many steps. And while without doubt they realize that they stand somewhere near the top of this ladder, they do not believe that they have reached the very top, and they would probably be as hard pushed as sociologists are to describe that peak of all ambition. In other words, the ruling groups of Europe today tend to be a rather self-conscious elite.

What is the coherence, what is the consciousness of solidarity among the members of this category? Several years ago, the English weekly *Spectator* started a discussion about the question of whether Britain is ruled by a small Establishment—a coherent set of powerful people—or not. If I am not mistaken, most English intellectuals seem inclined to believe in the reality of the Establishment and thus to subscribe to a variant of the conspiracy theory of society according to which a few invisible hands pull all the strings and monopolize the roads to power. The outside observer, on the contrary, is inclined to regard the very discussion of the Establishment as a symptom of the dissolution of the old upper class of British society. Yet it remains probable that the two thousand people with whom we are here concerned are a more coherent and solid social category in Britain than in most other European countries. Many of them have attended the same, or the same kind of, school and university; many of them belong to the same clubs, follow the same pastimes, meet and talk regularly, and feel part of the same "set." In this sense, the ruling groups of Britain do in fact tend to what might be called the "established" type.

Near the other end of the scale, we have the German case. The ruling groups of West Germany today are an almost perfect example of the "abstract" type: their unity exists nowhere except in the minds of some social analysts. In actual fact they are a highly heterogeneous and heteromorphous category. A career characteristic of a member of an established elite which leads him successively to being a university professor, director-owner of an investment trust, brigadier general and cabinet minister, and who may yet become an ambassador or director-general of the BBC, would be unthinkable in Germany, where every one of these "estates" has its own standards, interests and, above all, well-guarded boundaries. It is for this type of elite that the plural "ruling groups" is particularly appropriate, for ruling classes of this kind consist in fact of a plurality of competing and often hostile groups, the members of which are separated by great social distance.

In summarizing the evidence presented in this section, I would contend that the abstract type of elite, in Europe, constitutes the ruling class of the future. There are of course still remnants of the established elites of pre-industrial Europe, especially in countries like Spain or Portugal. There are also new kinds of establishment brought about, for example, by similar educational biographies (the "meritocracy"). But by and large, there is little indication that the ruling groups of the majority of countries in Europe really form coherent classes. They are anxious rulers, divided among themselves, uncertain of their position, and too hard-working to enjoy its rewards. In many ways, they have become indistinguishable from those one or two or three steps below them on the ladder of success, the service class.

THE SERVICE CLASS

To a generation of politically minded social scientists whose image of modern society and its development was almost invariably painted in Marxian colors, the most striking development of this century was the emergence of the "new middle class." This was the name given by E. Lederer and J. Marschak—the first to study this development extensively in the early 1920's—to the new occupations whose names are as numerous as the group involved is many-faceted and hard to describe: clerks, blackcoated workers, salary earners, white collar workers, employees, and their brothers and sisters in many other languages. The emergence of this group was, and continues to be, disturbing to all those who believed that the polarization of classes predicted by Marx was bound to occur. In general, this was clearly the reason for the interest of social science in the white collar worker in the 1920's and 1930's.[37, 53] Since then, however, a new generation of scholars has come up which, although much less under the spell of Marx's predictions, seems hardly less puzzled by the phenomenon of the white collar, especially since this category continues to grow. However, the new interest stems from a different source. Every one of several hundred studies of the white collar published in Europe since the war is somewhere inspired by the intention to place this category in the whole of modern society, and thereby to furnish a reasonably coherent image of the social world in which we are living. Ever since most scholars have given up, readily or reluctantly, the Marxian theory of social development, there has been a vacuum in social analysis which scores of empirical studies could not, and ambitious attempts at analysis did not fill. Invariably, the white collar category and its placement was and is regarded as the test of such analyses. The present essay is no exception to this rule.[6, 18, 19, 20, 49]

By the end of the nineteenth century, the category of white collar employees in public or private employment amounted to roughly 5 per cent of all persons gainfully employed. There were differences between countries, of course, but by and large the similarities in both the starting point and the extraordinary rate of growth of the white collar group since the beginning of this century are more startling than the differences. By 1910, the proportion of blackcoated employees had reached 10 per cent, in the developed countries, by 1930, 15 per cent; and some of the more recent figures given by the International Labour Organization are 35 per cent for Sweden (1950); 32 percent for Austria (1951); 28 per cent for Germany (1950); 27 per cent for Belgium (1947); 25 per cent for Britain (1951). Other sources give somewhat lower figures for all these countries, but they confirm the same trend.[6, 18, 19]

This is clearly an extraordinary rate of growth. But if there is any conclusion on which all students of white collar are agreed, it is that figures such as those quoted here are all but meaningless, since they lump together the most variegated groups, the postman and the manager of a large enterprise, the assistant secretary and the salesgirl, the union secretary and the chauffeur, etc., etc.* In fact, there is general agreement that "white collar employees," "blackcoated workers," "Angestellte," "salariés," as well as "new middle class" not only describe what D. Lockwood called a "non-class," but a social non-entity.[59, 61] In order to become an entity, even if only for purposes of analysis, the new middle class has to be broken up into its significant components. Once again, there have been

---

* It must be remembered that we are here concerned only with the "new middle class," so that shopkeepers, peasants, etc. are excluded from the present discussion.

many attempts to do so. But few of these explicitly take the power structure as their point of departure, so that only a segment of the literature can be of any assistance to us here.

Let us take a set of occupations usually described as belonging to the "new middle class," say, postman, bank clerk, senior civil servant, shop assistant, secretary general of a football club, waiter, tax official, chauffeur. I suggest that in terms of their relation to the exercise of power, these occupations fall easily into two categories. There are, on the one hand, those jobs which might be more properly described as "new working class" (if this term was not generally used in a different context, as later in this essay), that is, the purely subordinate positions in the vastly expanding new industries of the tertiary sector of the economy. In this group belong the shop assistant as well as the waiter, but also the older service occupations of chauffeur and postman; the proportion of women in it is especially large. All these people may receive salaries; they may be insured as *Angestellte* (or, in the case of the postman, even *Beamte*); they may not regard themselves as workers; but they are in fact in no way part of the power structure of their occupational contexts except as subordinates. In terms of power at least, their position is the precise equivalent of that of workers in the secondary sectors of employment.

On the other hand, the bank clerk, the senior civil servant, the secretary general of a football club and the tax official, as well as the army of public and private bureaucrats, may not strike one as a power elite if one compares them with the kings and nobles of the Middle Ages or even the ruling groups of today; but in some peculiar, though definable way they do in fact take part in the exercise of power. This is the group with which we are here concerned, and although these terms do not cover all of them, we may describe its members for the time being as bureaucrats, or, more generally, as administrators.

It is of some interest to ascertain the approximate size of this category in European societies today. Since official statistics are not broken down by the criterion employed here, we have to rely largely on estimates. In West Germany, the public bureaucracy (*Beamte*) comprises today 5 per cent of the employed population. If we follow a plausible argument of Geiger's in his analysis of German census figures in the 1920's, about one fifth of all *Beamte* "have to be ascribed to the lower-qualified wage- and salary-earners," that is, belong to the group excluded here, for which the postman is an example.[37] A similar breakdown of the category of private employees (*Angestellte*) is less easy. However, in the Federal Republic, nearly half the salaried employees work in commerce and communications;

exactly 50 per cent are women. Furthermore, a recent study by D. Claessens and others suggests that a large proportion of all *Angestellte* in private industry can hardly be counted among the industrial bureaucracy either.[16] In the light of these and other facts, I should suggest that only about one third of all *Angestellte* in Germany, or roughly 8 per cent of the employed population, can be described as bureaucrats, so that the group under discussion would comprise about 12 per cent of the gainfully employed in the Federal Republic. Considering general similarities in occupational structure, this figure can at least indicate the approximate size of the group elsewhere in Europe as well.[13, 14, 17]

But of course, even this 12 per cent is an obviously heterogeneous category. It includes the foreman as well as the managing director, the junior official behind the counter as well as the permanent undersecretary. Is it not rather nonsensical to include in one class the numerous ranks characteristic of every administrative hierarchy? The skeptical question is understandable. Indeed the foreman and the managing director would probably both deny that they are members of the same class. Yet here I should insist that it does make sense to lump them together. The top of the ladder may be far removed from its bottom—this is certainly true for modern bureaucratic hierarchies—but in terms of the exercise of power it is more significant that top and bottom are both steps on the same ladder. More precisely, the hierarchical internal structure of the category under discussion is in itself its primary characteristic. Bureaucracy means a hierarchy of well-defined positions in a systematic rank order which is at the same time the order of promotion, as Max Weber so clearly pointed out.[4, 22, 70]

The growth of the "new middle class" has often been attributed to the expansion of the tertiary sector of employment. While this may explain the development of the categories excluded above, it is only partly relevant for the process of bureaucratization. Here the division of labor of power described earlier seems more important (although, of course, this is a process itself in need of explanation). In a number of publications, Croner has advanced and defended his "theory of delegation," according to which white collar occupations have, at least historically, grown out of entrepreneurial, that is, power positions.[18] Croner himself points out that this theory is even more clearly applicable to *Beamte,* the public bureaucrats. For the latter, Chapman has described this process of dividing the labor of political power in some detail in the "historical introduction" to his *Profession of Government.*[15] Although by his own testimony Croner did not mean to do so, I think that this historical description can be turned into a real theory of the position of bureaucrats, according to which they all contribute, to whatever small extent, to the exercise of power in their social contexts, and are therefore an appendix of the ruling groups rather than an addition to the ruled groups.* It is amusing to note that it was a Marxist, the Austrian sociologist and politician K. Renner, who first gave clear expression to the significance of this trend in a little-known essay on modern social changes: "Zu all den Wandlungen, die bisher dargestellt sind, kommt eine andere, nicht minder bedeutsame. Der Kapitalist . . . bedient sich als solcher bezahlter Helfer, die ihn . . . in seiner Funktion allmählich ablösen . . . Zum Vorbild dieser Regelung hat dem Kapital der öffentliche Dienst (public service) gedient. . . . Nach diesem Vorbild besoldet der fungierende Kapitalist seine Helfer, und soweit er ausser Funktion tritt, seine Ersatzmänner, sowie die Helfershelfer, die ausführenden Organe, die er mit Recht nicht als Arbeiter, sondern als 'Angestellte', als Beamtete oder Bedienstete bezeichnet. . . . *Neben die Arbeiterklasse* (im streng technischen Sinne) *ist die Dienstklasse getreten.*" Renner's language is that of the Marx-trained socialist, but it testifies to his stature as a scholar that he was open to notice the very un-Marxian changes of European society as well ("Es ist sonnenklar, dass dass tatsächliche Substrat, der gesellschaftliche Unterbau, sich seit hundert Jahren völlig gewandelt hat . . ."). Moreover, he gave one of the most significant of these changes a name which indicates its significance more tellingly than any other I have found in the literature by calling the new element in the class structure of European societies a *Dienstklasse*, a service class.[75]

In describing the social role of members of this class as we have now defined it, it has become almost commonplace in the sociological literature to quote what M. Crozier calls the "célèbre chapitre de *Wirtschaft und Gesellschaft*" [83] on bureaucracy with its rather colorless list of attributes of bureaucratic organization ranging from "defined rights and duties" to "fixed monetary salaries." [22] In part, these attributes are—as studies by Bahrdt, Pirker, Crozier and others show [4, 22, 70]—no longer correct descriptions of service class membership; above all, they leave implicit what seems to me the most important single feature of bureaucratic roles. The main expectation attached to service class positions is the administration of laws, whether public or private, formal or sanctioned. This involves their adaptation to individual cases, their reformulation, their publication, their enforcement. The service class provides a bridge between

---

* This does not apply to what Lockwood (*The Blackcoated Worker*, London, 1958), following Weber, calls the "market situation," the "work situation," or the "status situation" of most bureaucrats. It may be argued therefore that Lockwood's approach to class leaves out some very important considerations.

rulers and ruled. But the direction of the road does not and must not change on this bridge. More than any other social category, the service class is committed to the ruling norms which it administers without having made them; more than others the members of this class tend to be "conformist" (if this pseudo-sociological expression is permitted here). The member of the service class has no choice but to be "other-directed." He has to take his cues from elsewhere—that is, to be more precise, from "above." The judge and the military officer, the departmental manager and the senior clerk, the income tax collector and the secretary of the football club are all expected to be the epitome of the values of their respective organizations—and the expectations are usually not disappointed.

But by mentioning the judge and the military officer, as well as other obviously influential people, it becomes quite clear that the service class is by no means as unimportant as its name might suggest. The very fact that it administers and thereby defends the values of its social context makes it a strong conservative force. In order to introduce change into bureaucratized social organizations, one has to convince, if not to transform, the service class first. While it is not part of the role of this class to inaugurate policies, it can and in fact does do so by the inertia of its conservative role, and by the possibility to pervert a law in the process of its application. Here is the truth of Riesman's otherwise somewhat misleading statement, "While it may take leadership to start things running, or to stop them, very little leadership is needed once things are under way." [74] Crozier suggests that this is one of the aspects of service class behavior in which there are considerable national differences within Europe.[21] In any case, both the traditionalism and what national variations there are have political implications to which we shall return.

Despite some claims to the contrary by its members, the economic miracle has of course not bypassed this class, whose members in the past could often be characterized by the combination of poverty and status ambition.[37] They can no longer be described as a "proletariat"; nor is the clerical worker who foregoes the necessities of life for the sake of the appearances of status a reality any more. This conclusion is clearly borne out by studies of white collar consumption patterns in several countries.[11, 19]

At the same time, prosperity has not diminished the preoccupation of the service class with matters of prestige and status. Here it appears that the occupational context of bureaucracy has determined its general attitude to society: "authority relations between positions which are ordered systematically," "appointment and promotion which are regulated and based on contractual agreement," "technical training (or experience) as a formal condition of employment" (to quote Max Weber's celebrated chapter [83] once again) are translated into what both Popitz and Willener call a "hierarchical image of society," [25, 68, 71, 72, 84] and generally great attention is paid to matters of status. The symbols of status have changed; but the two-tone car and the holiday in Mallorca are no less effective insignia of status for people who, in Europe as in the United States, may well be described as "status seekers."

Status, for the service class, is not a static notion. Hierarchy always implies the possibility of promotion; social mobility and the service class belong inseparably together. There are no service class occupations which do not enable their incumbents to move ahead a few steps if they are capable and punctual, although there are quite a few cases of "blocked" and "once-for-all mobility," to quote Kelsall, Lockwood and Tropp, and their number may be growing.[49] It is also of more general social significance that mobility within the ranks of public or private bureaucracies is greatly facilitated by education. Experience helps one move ahead to the next barrier, but this can as a rule be overcome only by formal education. As a consequence, many administrators spend a good deal of their leisure time in trying to acquire "entry tickets" to new positions by evening classes and other types of further education; and there is evidence from several countries that members of the service class tend to spend an exceptional proportion of their income on the education of their children.[19]

As far as the social origin of the members of the service class is concerned, Bolte has compared a number of (largely German) studies. His main conclusion is that since World War I the proportion of clerical workers recruited from the "old middle class" of independent businessmen and craftsmen has decreased (from over 50 per cent to less than 25 per cent), that of working class origin has increased (from 20–25 per cent to 30–35 per cent), but the bulk of the service class is recruited today from service class families (40–45 per cent).[11] It may be assumed that the latter figure hides a great deal of upward mobility within the ranks of bureaucracy, for the general conclusion seems indicated that social mobility in contemporary Europe often requires in the first place that some member of a family get his foot on a rung of the ladder of service, and that more than half of the members of this group in most countries of Europe today have risen socially. If any class bears witness to the comparative openness of European societies, it is the service class.

At this point, the last and most difficult question about the service class must be raised: what is its political orientation? If our analysis is correct, we should expect its members to be somewhat conservative in orientation, and to support the parties of the moderate right.[12, 26, 36, 37, 42, 56] There are no survey figures of the social stratification of the electorate of different parties in the 1920's. But on external evidence it seems likely that the "new middle class" was one of the main sources of support for the Nazis, and possibly for the Italian Fascists too.* On the other hand, membership in labor unions, or indeed radicalism of the left, is rare among bureaucrats, if we except their own estatelike organizations and interesting, but isolated, instances like the French teachers. Thus there appears to be a general trend to the right in the political orientation of the service class; but dependent on the national context, this trend takes the form of supporting either moderate conservatives or authoritarian extremists.

Quite a few explanations of the apparent political unreliability of the "new middle class" have been offered in the literature. Some of these are at least implied by our discussion of the role and status of the administrator. But the question to which such explanations invariably return is: is it a class, that category of bureaucrats and administrators, or is it not?

Among the groups discussed in this essay, the one under review in this section is the only one which I have described as a "class" in the title of the section. At the risk of appearing extremely confused as well as confusing, I now wish to offer the conclusion that of our four groups, the service class is in fact the one which is quite clearly not a class in any terminologically strict sense. In terms of social position, this is so since this group must be described as an appendage of the ruling groups. In one possible usage of the term "class," ruling groups plus service "class" might be called the ruling class of a society. In terms of the social characteristics of the service class, there is one further fact to be considered. Class involves a certain amount of class consciousness and political solidarity, if the term is to make any sense at all. The members of the service class, however, are, in Crozier's words, a "classe sans conscience."[21] Instead of feeling cohesive, they all stand in a relation of individual competition to each other. Of course, not every bureaucrat competes with every other one. In fact, Bahrdt has shown that even that minimum of communication which is a prerequisite of competition is generally missing along the horizontal line of bureaucratic organizations.[4] But for the bureaucrat, advancing his status is essentially an individual achievement. He has little to hope from collective

* By "external evidence" I mean here the analysis of election figures, coupled with plausible assumptions about the social sources of support of various parties.

action which would leave his status exactly where it was in relation to those with whom he compares himself, that is, to all others who have stepped on at least the first rung of the ladder of service. In the service class, individual competition takes the place of collective solidarity. But individual competition is a strenuous and, at times, an ugly type of behavior, especially if it pervades the entire life of a person. Even on general psychological grounds, it may seem likely that a price has to be paid for this kind of life—a price which may be private and make the person mentally or physically ill, but which under certain historical conditions may also become public and lead him to support a romantic movement of "community" (*Gemeinschaft*), of which fascism is a prototype in the modern world.

THE RULED GROUPS

In all society no boundary is probably more cruelly felt by those involved than the one between those who stand just above and those just below the line dividing power from impotence.[37] R. Hoggart's description of the borderline is very much to the point: "So often their (the working people's) contacts are with the minor officials, with those in the lower grades of uniformed and pensioned jobs. Again, as with the police, they may be to the other classes servants, but to the working classes they seem the agents of 'Them' and are mistrusted, even though they may be kindly and well disposed. If they are ill disposed, they can display to working-class people all the insolence of minor office, the brusqueness of the pettily uniformed. . . ." Hoggart also goes some way to explaining the cruelty of this boundary: "They tend to be sharp towards the working classes because they would like to feel more securely separate from them; they know in their hearts by just how little they are separated and do not like to think of dropping back."[44] Even today, it would be useless to deny that in terms of power there is this boundary, and that its existence testifies to the potential of class conflict all over Europe.

But the actualities of class conflict are nowadays determined less by the clear line that divides rulers and ruled than by the blurring of the lines between people of differing social status. In other words, there is many a compensation for those who are excluded from the exercise of power in contemporary European society. While those "below" may still feel the superiority of the policeman and other petty officials who can push them around, there are spheres of life where they are and feel equal to at least many of those in power, or where distinctions of power do not seem to matter at all. The dichotomous image of society is still there, but it is no longer an image of resentment and boundless hostility toward "them." The studies by Popitz and Willener confirm other observations in their finding that even among industrial workers in most European countries only a dwindling minority adheres to a Marxian view of a revolutionary class struggle.[25, 68, 71, 72, 84] Let us look at some of the reasons and symptoms of this change which apply to all those who are not in power, before we inspect briefly the component parts of the evidently rather summary category of "ruled groups."

In the first place, it is important to remember that when one speaks of those who have no share in the making of laws in contemporary Europe, expressions like "impotence" or "subjection" are really no longer applicable. Apart from countries with authoritarian or totalitarian regimes, and regions or social institutions in which feudal or military types of rule still obtain, the status of citizenship defines for most Europeans a "floor" of social position, below which they cannot fall. Within the economy, what Marshall called a "secondary system of citizenship" is in the process of coming about, so that in their occupational context, too, most people are protected from arbitrary and personal power.[62] Systems of industrial relations, and in some cases institutions of "partnership" and "co-determination," today give the subjects of an earlier period of industrial development effective rights of control over their superiors.

In the second place, a combination of factors, some of which have been discussed in the first part of this essay, have provided many of those who have no share in political power with a "second chance" in other institutions: economic, educational, voluntary. There is no longer any one social position which determines all others, as was the case with occupation for many in nineteenth- and early twentieth-century Europe. As working hours get shorter, the world in which people live grows larger, and with it the probability of compensating gratifications for the deprivations inevitably inherent in the quasi-military discipline of industrial production. It has become fashionable in Europe to describe the condition I mean here as "pluralism," that is, a competitive plurality of institutional contexts within which the social life of the individual is patterned. Reports of refugees from East Germany show that the wider chances of a pluralistic society provide one of the main incentives to leave a rigidly organized totalitarian country.

Discussions of power are nowadays often confused by the introduction of arguments in terms of status. Undeniably, however, a third significant aspect of the position of ruled groups is that there is a great deal of overlapping between their socio-economic position and that of the service class especially. The scales of power, prestige and status do not coincide any longer, if they ever did. There is many a working man who earns more than the man in the office who can push him around.[11, 19, 46] Repeated surveys of occupational prestige invariably place the skilled mechanic above the policeman, and other qualified workers above routine clerks.[11, 45] Technological changes bring the actual work tasks of salary and wage earners closer together.[6, 16] In modern light industries the working man is indistinguishable from the office clerk during as well as after working hours. If this overlapping between rulers and ruled has been widely observed as far as the working class part of the ruled groups is concerned, it is *a fortiori* the case for those others who are even "officially" described as middle class.

Probably the most important single symptom of the changed position of the ruled groups in European society is the extent of social mobility. Sociological studies of mobility are as plentiful as they are uninformative. Their underlying scales of status are of dubious relevance, their interview data not always impressive, and the measures they use at times downright false. But if we survey individual studies as well as the two important comparative analyses by Miller and by Bendix and Lipset, certain basic conclusions are inescapable.[57, 66] It appears that in all European countries where mobility studies have been conducted since the war, about one out of three sons of industrial workers now rises into one of the "nonmanual" categories. (Among the sons of peasants this proportion is very much higher, for obvious legal as well as general social reasons.)* [46] While it is impossible to break down existing data by the groupings used in this essay, there can be no doubt that the line between rulers and ruled no longer provides an insurmountable barrier either. In fact, we have seen earlier how large a proportion of the service class is recruited from working class families; and while this proportion is very much smaller among the upper two thousand, mobility from low parental status is by no means exceptional even here. The effects of social mobility on class consciousness and solidarity are considerable. If it is possible for oneself or at least for one's son to cross the all-important boundary of power, one's feelings about one's own position are not likely to be so bitter than as if the worlds of rulers and ruled are caste-like prisons.

All these factors and symptoms go to support a fifth feature of the ruled groups of contemporary Europe, the often-noted "diffusion du modèle de conduite des classes moyennes" (in Crozier's words).[21] In the work situation of industrial laborers as well as routine salaried employees and small independent businessmen or peasants there is

---

* Where only the eldest son can inherit, all others generally leave the country. Armed with a middle class ideology, they rarely "drop" into manual occupations.

really no place for the kind of status-consciousness, prestige-interest and ambition that goes so well with bureaucratic hierarchies. Yet these tend to become pervasive attitudes throughout society, which by implication is further proof of the assertion that occupation is no longer the all-important social position. Time and again, when opinion research institutes in all countries ask people whether they regard themselves as upper, middle, working, or lower class, about equal proportions place themselves in the middle and working classes, with very small groups at the extremes.[17,46] If we assume that only about 12 per cent of the population has any relation to the ruling groups, it is clear that the term "middle class" itself has become an ever more general status symbol. The belief in mobility by education (if not for oneself, then for one's children) is spreading rapidly. While the suggestion of some German social scientists that the new "middle-class society" has abolished all social differences seems a little surprising in the face of still considerable differences in income and prestige (to say nothing of power),[79] it is true that in Europe, too, the old symbols of inequality are being replaced by new and more subtle ones. The question is no longer whether one has a car, a motorcycle or a bicycle, but which kind of car one has. Whether, from the point of view of the individual, the new kind of differentiation is less cruel than the old one seems to me at least an open question.

Throughout this survey of social classes in Europe, we found "groups" which have the same relation to the structure of power to be in fact highly heterogeneous aggregates of competing individuals and groups. This is no less true for the ruled groups than for the rulers and their servants. In this section, we are concerned with about 85 per cent of the people of Europe. Even the crudest of distinctions has to recognize among these three vastly different social categories: (1) the "old middle class" of small independent craftsmen, shopkeepers, and—above all—peasants; (2) those parts of the "new middle class" which we have not included, on account of their power position, in the service class; and (3) the working class. What has been said so far in this section was meant to apply to all these groups, if perhaps in varying degrees. But even if we stick strictly to our main line of argument, some of the striking peculiarities of these groups, and their own subgroups, cannot be left unmentioned.

It was of course the "old middle class" which Marx had in mind when he predicted the polarization of society into two classes. To the present day it has remained a nice topic of argument among Marxists and Marxians, whether this prediction has come true or not. In statistical fact, the proportion of self-employed people is between about 15 per cent and 25 per cent in all European countries—with the single exception of Britain, the country which provided Marx with most of his data, where only about 7 per cent are now self-employed. The largest single bloc within this census category is in most countries that of the peasants. But here again, variations are great. In Italy, Portugal, Spain, Austria and France, agriculture is still the largest of eight standard categories of employment, whereas in Belgium and Holland it comes third, in Britain sixth (and, for comparison, in the United States, fourth).* Generally speaking, sociologists have not paid as much attention to these groups as to the elites, industrial workers and the "new middle class." In the more highly industrialized countries, such as Britain, Holland, Belgium, Germany and to a lesser extent the Scandinavian countries, there is some evidence that the attitudes described here as characteristic of the service class have reached the countryside as well.[23] But for France, Italy, Austria, Spain and countries with similar proportions of peasants and agricultural workers, our conclusions must be taken with more than one grain of salt, and point at best to possible trends of the future.†

As far as that larger part of the "new middle class" is concerned which we have left aside so far, our general conclusion can be adopted with much greater confidence. Despite the almost meaningless generality of the term "new middle class," most studies of the subject do not distinguish between its bureaucratic and its purely subordinate components, so that many of the results discussed above apply to both these groups. What we have called the political unreliability of the service class probably holds *a fortiori* for the non-bureaucratic sections of the "new middle class"; for here we find a clear contradiction between the work situation of subordination, the status of low income and prestige, and the description as *Angestellter*, *salarié*, white collar, and, therefore, middle class. If there is any reason to qualify this conclusion, it is in the fact that these are also the occupational groups among which the proportion of women is largest. The statistical data gathered by Bolte and Croner suggest

* For figures, I have used here the appendix "Internationale Übersichten" to *Statistisches Jahrbuch für die Bundesrepublik Deutschland 1958* (Stuttgart, 1958), T.C. 2. The eight standard categories are: agriculture and fishing; mining and quarrying; manufacturing industries; building; electricity, gas and water; commerce; communications and transport; service occupations.

† At this point I have to confess ignorance. Evidently the shortlived Poujade movement, or the so dramatically abolished original electoral law of the French Fifth Republic with an electoral college consisting of the "70,000 mayors," document the importance of the old middle class in France. Similar observations have been made in other countries. To explain these and other relevant phenomena, one has to be more familiar with this problem than I can claim to be.

that about one half of the people in the category in question here are women.[11, 19] To the present day, however, the social status and the class position of women are not as "serious" as that of men. For the unmarried woman's social status, her father's occupation is as important as her own, and in the case of married women the same is true for their husbands.

Even today the largest section of the ruled groups of European societies consists of the industrial "working class." Moreover, it is the changes in the position and in the outlook of industrial workers that have occupied European sociologists above all. In Europe, sociology grew up as the study of working class life, and as late as the 1920's there was an element of truth in the naïve identification of "sociology" and "socialism." Insofar as this is true, the discovery of the "new working class," that is, of industrial workers who no longer conformed to the radical expectations of the intellectual socialists of the 1920's and 1930's, came as something of a shock to social scientists. There are numerous studies in the postwar period which may be understood as an attempt on the part of their authors to explain to themselves what they regarded as the sudden advance of the *embourgeoisement* of the working class.*

Not all these studies managed to follow D. Lockwood's precept and guard against "the mistake of comparing the most prosperous and least socially distinctive sections of the working class of today with the least prosperous and most socially distinctive sections of the working class of yesterday."[60] Sociologists still like to invent their history so as to lend profile to their statements about the present. But the very discovery of "sections" within the working class—of the skilled, the semi-skilled, and the unskilled, for example—was one of the achievements of postwar research in Europe. It was soon discovered also that these skill groups had had rather different histories in the course of industrialization, and that they differed in their social and political attitudes as well.[24]

The internal differentiation of industrial labor came out most tellingly in the study of the social stratification of voting. In France, for example, about 70 per cent of the electorate of the Communists consists of industrial workers, but even in 1951 and 1956 less than half the working class cast its vote for the Communist party, and in 1958 this proportion had dwindled to 36 per cent, with 45 per cent

* European sociology after World War II started with a large number of studies in industrial sociology. Most of these were devoted to the working class and betray the disappointment on the part of their authors with this class. If M. Stein could write a highly perceptive history of American sociology under the title of *The Eclipse of Community,* "the eclipse of the working class" might be an appropriate analogue for Europe.

voting for "other parties," for example, de Gaulle.[33] In Britain and Germany, working-class consciousness is, if anything, less pronounced. Here, between one third and one half of all working class people give their vote to the Conservatives and the Christian Democrats respectively.[12, 36, 42] Such findings have led some sociologists to dissolve the seemingly unified bloc of the working class into several "types." Two of the most impressive typologies are those by M. Dogan in France and by H. Popitz in Germany (which display, moreover, striking similarities). Dogan distinguishes, on political grounds, six types: "l'ouvrier revolutionnaire," "l'ouvrier protestataire," "l'ouvrier réformiste," "l'ouvrier catholique," "l'ouvrier conservateur," and "l'ouvrier indifférent."[33] If we reorganize the order of Popitz's typology, his two most frequent types—"progressive order" (type 2) and "dichotomy as a collective fate" (type 3)—seem to bear some resemblance to Dogan's "ouvrier protestataire," who votes for the Communists without accepting their ideology or, in terms of the German context, who experiences society as dichotomous and supports progressive organizations of the left, but is no real radical. Among six hundred workers interviewed by Popitz, only six subscribed to an ideology of "class war" (type 6), and only twelve to a radical reformist view (type 5). By contrast, the number of conservatives (type 1, "static order") and that of workers who experienced the dichotomy of society as an essentially personal problem (type 4) was much larger, with sixty interviewees in each of these categories. Of course, there is in all countries a large number of "indifferents"; the figure given by Popitz is 20 per cent.[71]

R. Hoggart adds to his description of "Them" and "Us" the significant reservation "the 'Them/Us' attitudes seem to me strongest in those over thirty-five. . . . Younger people . . . here inhabit a different atmosphere from that their fathers grew up in: at least, the atmosphere has a different emotional temperature."[44] The much less cautious terms in which the Austrian author K. Bednarik described the young worker as a "new type" have caused an extensive discussion on the European continent.[7] In the course of this discussion, many have come to agree that the young worker feels no longer a worker at all, and that he has in fact become indistinguishable from his middle class peer, but above all that he displays no feeling of class solidarity, and aspires to individual happiness and success instead. Studies by H. Kluth, U. Lohmar and R. Tartler among young German workers lend strong support to this thesis which would seem to imply that service class attitudes have gained a hold on at least the younger sections of the working class as well.[50]

Our thesis in this essay is not that the economic miracle has by itself converted class-conscious workers into bourgeois conservatives. We have placed great emphasis on the social miracle and on changes in the structure of power which may be of much greater importance than a decade of prosperity. Above all, the crucial change in attitude seems to me to lie in the fact that feelings of solidarity and of the desirability of collective action have given way, for many workers, to the desire to advance their position individually. For the individual, this means piecework earnings and "moonlighting," but also evening courses and the wish to be promoted; for his family, mobility by education becomes increasingly important (although, in this respect, the North-South slope is once again unmistakable in Europe). But we cannot conclude this section without referring once again to Lockwood's rather skeptical analysis of the "new working class."[60] To aspire to the values of those "above," to display these values credibly, and to be accepted as one of "them" are certainly three very different things, of which the last at least is still a distant dream. Despite all changes in their social position and attitudes, the ruled groups remain such, and many of their members realize this fact and behave accordingly.

THE INTELLECTUALS

No discussion of class is complete without referring at least in passing to the intellectuals. The very fact that they are hard to place in the structure of power (to say nothing of an additional fact that the analyst himself is usually one of them) adds to their interest. When K. Mannheim and A. Weber described intellectuals as "free-floating," they had two features of their social position in mind.[38] One of these relates to their social biography: intellectuals have often undergone a series of breaks with the groups to which they belonged. The other aspect concerns their actual position: intellectuals are neither rulers nor ruled nor, of course, servants. At least, it is under these conditions that they display that mixture of belonging and estrangement which may be the prerequisite of the critical task often ascribed to them. All this would not be true for "intellectuals" or the "intelligentsia" in the comprehensive French or Russian sense, which makes this group almost coextensive with white collar, and certainly with professional people. But if we use some notion like Lipset's, according to which intellectuals are those who "create, distribute, and apply culture," the above description would apply.[55] The position and attitude of intellectuals in this sense are indicative of the class structure of a society in that they betray its rigidity or looseness, its stability or explosiveness, and often its neuralgic points.

At the risk of seeming unduly insistent on one point, the first observation to be stressed about the position of intellectuals in Europe today is that they are often no longer as "free-floating" as the celebrated model of their social existence would have it. With the generalization of social mobility by education, specialist knowledge is no longer the prerogative of any one group, and breaking with one's primary group has become an almost normal feature in the social biographies of rulers and their servants. As far as occupational position is concerned, almost all intellectuals in Europe are striving for a secure position in some organization or other, and on the whole they are doing so successfully. If we look at the positions they occupy, many of them resemble closely those of the upper reaches of the service class: the university lecturer, the newspaper editor, the manager responsible for job training in an enterprise, the government-employed town planner, etc. In many organizations, the distinction between "staff" and "line" may give the intellectual rather more independence than those along the line can enjoy; but this distinction is not, in reality, always as clear as organizational charts would have it. Thus, many intellectuals all over Europe have not only come to resemble the service class in their profession and general outlook, but they have become members of this class (or, rather, non-class), that is, individuals competing with others for a place in the sun.[30, 54]

But nowhere are national differences quite as marked as with respect to the position of intellectuals. In France—or, to be more precise, in Paris—there is still a large number of intellectuals of the old school: "free-floating" in terms of origin and position, not prepared to accept any authority as valid, critical of everything that is happening, radical in temperament, and left in conviction. Perhaps their number, and, probably, their influence are on the downgrade too. The days of the Spanish Civil War are forever gone, and even if we have not reached the "end of the ideological age," there has come to be something pointless about an intellectual existence such as that intimated here.[2, 8, 78]

Britain used to be unique in its capacity to produce what one might call "part-time intellectuals," that is, men who for long periods of their lives occupied positions of power, who were part of the ruling groups, but who then withdrew either temporarily or permanently to a position of critical detachment. It is clear, however, that at least since the Fabian origins of the Labour movement, this has not been the only type of intellectual in Britain. More recently, the "angry young men" testify to a change that has brought a good, possibly even a Public School and "Oxbridge" education to many without automatically leading them into the inner circle of the Establishment. The paradox in the outlook of American intellectuals exposed by Lipset—their political egalitarianism and their personal desire for a privileged social position—is not confined to the United

States.[55] In looking at the British scene, one might be tempted to go even further and claim that intellectuals tend to become more "radical" and "Left" (or "New Left," as it is now the fashion to call it) as society around them, and with it their own position, becomes more egalitarian.

The history of German intellectuals is different from both that of their French and their British brethren. German intellectuals have for a long time tended to become either collaborators or emigrants, that is, either servants of those in power, or so desperate about the condition of their country that they preferred to leave it, if they were not forced to leave. Even in the Federal Republic, both these attitudes can still be found. Only very gradually does a third attitude of critical participation develop, and as it becomes a little more frequent, anti-intellectualism grows as well.[31, 26]

I am not suggesting that the three intellectual conditions sketched in these paragraphs are exclusive types. All three of them are changing. Every one of the countries mentioned has intellectuals of many kinds; there may be completely different intellectual types in countries not mentioned here. This is the case, for example, in the rigidly organized Communist countries of Europe. Here, the intellectual has been forced entirely into the service class. But the society which I am trying to describe in this essay has its own rigidities, even if it is more liberal in its political organization. Permanent competition between individuals for the next rung on an endless ladder of status does not make for freedom and openness, and it remains to be seen how much it advances the greatest happiness of the greatest number. Under these conditions, it may well be argued that the critical intellectual has rarely been as necessary for the welfare of society as he is in Europe today. Let us hope, therefore, that Cole (and the many others who share his analysis) will continue to be right in his somewhat optimistic statement: "The 'intellectuals,' *as ever*, are difficult to place in the social hierarchy." [17]

III Toward the Service Class Society?

A NEW PHILOSOPHY OF LIFE

It is not difficult for the traveler to find his preconceptions confirmed in the countries he visits. When introducing the changes which have transformed the social climate of Europe, I have used this assertion to claim that it is quite conceivable to see contemporary Europe through the dark glasses of its nineteenth-century past. But the assertion cuts both ways. The American traveling in Europe today may also find much that is familiar to him. In fact, many Europeans believe that what they like to call the "Americanization"

327

of Europe has made rapid progress everywhere, and continues to advance. To late nineteenth-century Europeans, England seemed the model toward which all other countries were tending. In the middle of the twentieth century, the United States—or what is widely believed to be characteristic of its society—has taken the place of England.

Underlying the so-called materialism of Europeans, and more particularly young Europeans today, however, there are certain kinds of motivation, ways of looking at life and society which for most of them are a relatively new acquisition. One of these is the emphasis on individual happiness rather than, say, national grandeur or group community.* And closely related to the discovery of individual happiness is the emphasis on individual success as the road that leads toward it. It is a short distance from these values to the social institutions which support them, that is, above all, to the whole system of social mobility by achievement. While some parts of Europe are still a long way from having removed all barriers of individual advance and happiness, these barriers are breaking even in the most traditionalist regions of the continent.

It is not surprising that, at a time at which the gross inequalities of life chances have given way to a common basis of citizenship, the universal social necessity of inequality is expressed in other terms and areas of life. Status has become a matter of prestige rather than of rights and privileges; prestige itself is increasingly attached not only to occupations but also to consumption patterns and leisure time activities. Suburbia is growing fast, and with it the advantages of easy living and the anxieties of keeping up with the Joneses. If one cannot be promoted in one's job, one can at least rise in the eyes of one's neighbors—and, of course, send one's children to secondary schools and universities which are as useful for their personalities as they are for one's own status.

Sociologists have given many names to this new society: post-capitalist and managerial, leisure-time and consumer's, advanced industrial and mass society are but a small selection. It cannot do much harm therefore to add one further name and claim that Europe is well under way toward a service class society. Although only a fraction of the population can be counted among the service class proper, the values of this category have spread to all other groups. Paramount among these values is the replacement of cohesive feelings and groupings by individual competition. In the past, progress was a matter of immense public interest; in the present, progress

---

* The acquisition of these new values is still somewhat tenuous, as occasional complaints about a "lack of goals," and the political success of a man like de Gaulle, show.

has become a private affair or, rather, a matter of the abstract sum of innumerable advances in individual happiness.

THE POLITICS OF SERVICE

Much has been and more should be said about the structure and climate of the service class society. As a general proposition, it seems to me desirable that such analyses should lose some of the snobbish temper of *Kulturkritik* which they so often have today. But this essay is about class, and class is about power, and power is about politics. And it is in the sphere of politics that the service class society displays its most problematic face.

Our image of the history of representative government is obviously too neat to be correct. Yet there remains an element of truth in it despite the somewhat unexpected figures about the development of suffrage mentioned at an earlier stage: representative government worked, for the first time, at a time at which the two conflicting parties were the Conservatives and the Liberals, representing an old society of social and economic privileges and a new society of free enterprise, respectively. Toward the end of the nineteenth century—that is, with the progress not only of industrialization, but also of universal suffrage—Conservatives and Liberals merged into a new conservative group which from now on was opposed by the new progressives, the Socialists. Ever since, representative government has meant, in many countries, some variant of the competition for power between the newly privileged and the newly underprivileged, or those who felt that they belonged to either of these groups.

In the service class society, however, this social basis of representative government is giving way. This does not, to be sure, affect the strength of the traditional conservative position (although its platforms have undeniably changed as well). But where there was the progressive party, the Liberals, and later the Socialists, there tends to be a great vacuum today; and since representative government lives on the productive antagonism of inertia and progress, its very foundations are in danger.

To be sure, all the countries of Europe still contain Socialist parties. In some of them, these have been, or are government parties. But I think it is fair to say that most of these parties are Socialist only in name—a generalization which is correct to the extent to which the service society has come about. In terms of their political platforms, the parties of the traditional right and left in Germany, the Scandinavian countries, Holland, and Belgium have become virtually indistinguishable. In England and France, this is not quite true as yet, but there are clear tendencies in the same direction. All political parties are trying to become "people's parties," that is, non-ideological election machines appealing to all sectors of the electorate alike. In this way, the value of individual competition is translated into politics. To many voters, it is no longer the party that matters, but the individuals it offers for choice as ministers or members of parliament. Studies of political behavior in many European countries show an ever increasing volume of the floating vote: one no longer belongs to one party, but one supports the most appealing candidate.

Of course, there are still vested interests and pressures on governments and parliaments. In fact, the situation I have in mind tends to favor even minor pressure groups. For the majority of voters no longer seems to have any clear set of economic or social interests which are translated into political decisions—with the single exception of one overriding, if negative, desire, and that is, not to be pushed about, not to strengthen authority, not to see the sphere of individual enjoyment reduced in any way. Perhaps this is one of the reasons for the apparent revival of old-fashioned liberalism in several countries of Europe, the struggle of "Orpington man" vs. the State. With the exception of this concern, however, appeal seems to count for more than interest, personality for more than program.

The absence of a progressive political force is the result of the absence of a suppressed class in the classical meaning of this term. When the sense of solidarity gives way to individual competition, there is little hope for radical political groups. This development has many an advantageous aspect both for the individual and for the political system. The individual can fill the horizon of chances, which is all that politics can ever bring about, with his own personality. The political system is no longer threatened by groups which intend to transform not only society but its constitutional foundations as well. At the same time, representative government becomes singularly ineffective in this pacific world. In the absence of a progressive force, the powers that be, and above all the inert force of bureaucracy, keep things running without ever changing them. This is the world in which Parkinson's laws become almost laws of nature immune to human intervention, even if it takes the form of control by elected parliaments. In the service class society, representative government lies dormant, and a very uninspiring kind of bureaucratic conservatism dominates the scene. Whatever has been started, goes on and on and on.

Postwar elections in many European countries testify clearly to this new conservative mood. Three or four successive electoral victories by the same party, and possibly even victories with increasing majorities, are simply not permitted by the classical theory of representative government.* Yet this conservatism is not the ugliest consequence of the pervasive influence of the service class. The mood in question also means that most people take but little interest in the world of politics, which is after all always to some extent a world of solidarities. Lack of political interest, however, is the historical concomitant of authoritarian rule. To be sure, in the past it was the authoritarian rulers who prevented the many from taking an interest in politics, whereas in the present it may be the indifference of the many that produces and supports authoritarian rulers. But the difference is not as great as it may seem. In the service class societies of Europe, the political situation is often not unlike that described so brilliantly by Marx in his *Eighteenth Brumaire of Louis Bonaparte*:[63] there are large numbers of individuals who cannot form solid political groups and represent themselves. They have to be represented, and they love the man who pretends to do so without actually hurting what few concerns and interests they have. The inability to form cohesive organization was, in Marx's analysis, based on a lack of communication among the small peasants of France. Today, it is based on the diffusion of service class values. But in either case, the social situation favors developments like Gaullism in France, or the "Chancellor democracy" of Germany.

The course of history is not predetermined. Nothing is further from my intention here than to suggest that the development of a new authoritarianism by way of a new conservatism is "historically inevitable," or that it will go on forever. It is equally uncertain whether the relations between classes will remain as relatively peaceful as they are today. The service class society may be a passing phase of development, a brief interlude between clearer lines of class and political cleavage, or it may be here to stay. For the present, however, the theory of the prevalence of the service class and its values seems to me to provide a reasonably good explanation of such diverse phenomena as the success of the Liberals in British by-elections, the French Fifth Republic, and Adenauer's four electoral victories in Germany.

Conclusion

Whoever has been patient enough to follow our course of argument up to this point is sure to conclude that this essay is either too long or too short. It is too long to make a point as concisely as any point worth making ought to be phrased; at the same time it is too short to convince by the weight of evidence and argument.

* From J. S. Mill to A. Downs (*An Economic Theory of Democracy*, New York, 1957), the emphasis has been on the overwhelming probability for the incumbents to be defeated by a coalition of groups alienated by their decisions.

But then, it is perhaps the peculiar charm of an essay that is simultaneously too long and too short: long enough to give food for thought, but too short to satisfy the hunger for knowledge. If this is regarded as an impermissibly personal remark in what is supposed to be a scholarly piece of work, I think the objection can be answered. By answering it we may suitably conclude these considerations.

One of the striking political and social developments of the postwar period has been the increasing reality of Europe as a unit, as against the assembly of often hostile nations that filled the same place on our maps in the past. Despite occasional stoppages of this trend, such as the rejection of the European Defense Community in 1954, or that of Britain's application to join the Common Market in 1963, western Europe, including Britain, is today more than a geographical concept. But this political fact must not deceive us about the variations within the continent. Even within a single country there are some social differences as large as those between, say, Sweden and Ghana. This is all the more true as we move across the boundaries of nations and languages. It is one of the melancholy shortcomings of any generalizing sociological analysis that it tries to make us believe that living in Palermo is really much the same as living in Bordeaux, in Graz, in Amersfoort, Preston, Göteborg or Darmstadt.

Again, I believe that the trend toward the service class society is a fact in many parts of Europe. What is more, I think that it marks the road of the immediate future. But there is an element of cruel neglect of human detail in a generalization of this kind. The world of Danilo Dolci has as little in common with the service class society as that of the declining textile industry areas of Lancashire or that of the ancient feudal relations of lower Bavaria. Fortunately, human society is always more complicated than our simple theories make it appear. At least three historical structures of class compete with each other in the Europe of today: the pre-industrial conflict between feudal landlords and their dependents, the classical struggle between capitalists and wage labor, and the anxious peace of the service class society.

Finally, class is clearly only one of many vantage points from which to survey the scene of European society. In some European countries, conflict between town and country, North and South, Flamands and Walloons, Protestants and Roman Catholics is far more important than that between people of different class positions. In all countries of Europe such other lines of cleavage cut across those of class and serve to complicate further a picture which is in any case more complex than our historical consciousness would have it.

No monograph could afford to neglect these and many other qualifications of the thesis advanced in this essay. But an essay is, by comparison to the monograph, a personal venture. I have singled out one aspect for discussion which seems to me important, and neglected many others which may seem important to others. It is for my critics to decide where the truth lies.

BIBLIOGRAPHY

Numbers correspond to reference numbers in the text.

1. M. Albrow and W. Zapf: Unpublished data gathered under the supervision of the author, available at the Sociological Seminar of the University of Tübingen.

2. Raymond Aron: *L'Opium des intellectuels* (Paris, 1955).

3. _____: "Classe sociale, classe politique, classe dirigeante," *European Journal of Sociology* I/2 (1960).

4. H. P. Bahrdt: *Industriebürokratie* (Stuttgart, 1958).

5. W. Baur, W. Mersch, W. Zapf: Unpublished theses and dissertations in Tübingen.

6. H. Bayer (ed.): *Der Angestellte zwischen Arbeiterschaft und Management* (Berlin, 1961).

7. K. Bednarik: *Der junge Arbeiter—ein neuer Typ* (Stuttgart, 1953).

8. D. Bell: *The End of Ideology* (Glencoe, 1960).

9. *Berichte aus dem Soziologischen Seminar der Universität Tübingen* 1 (1963).

10. T. J. H. Bishop: Unpublished Ph.D. dissertation, University of London.

11. K. M. Bolte: "Angestelltenfrage," in H. Bayer (ed.), *Der Angestellte zwischen Arbeiterschaft und Management* (Berlin, 1961).

12. J. Bonham: *The Middle Class Vote* (London, 1956).

13. [British] General Register Office: *One Per Cent Sample Tables* [1951 Census].

14. [British] General Register Office: *Classification of Occupations 1950.*

15. B. Chapman: *The Profession of Government. The Public Service in Europe* (London, 1959).

16. D. Claessens, J. Fuhrmann, G. Hartfiel and H. Zirwas: *Angestellte und Arbeiter in der Betriebspyramide* (Berlin, 1959).

17. G. D. H. Cole: *Studies in Class Structure* (London, 1955).

18. F. Croner: *Die Angestellte in der modernen Gesellschaft* (Frankfurt-Wien, 1954).

19. _____: *Sociologie der Angestellten* (Köln-Berlin, 1962).

20. M. Crozier: *Petits fonctionnaires au travail* (Paris, 1955).

21. _____: "Classes sans conscience," *European Journal of Sociology* I/2 (1960).

22. _____: "De la bureaucratie comme système d'organisation," *European Journal of Sociology* II/1 (1961).

23. *Current Sociology*: "Rural Sociology," VI/1 (1957).

24. Ralf Dahrendorf: "Industrielle Fertigkeiten und soziale Schichtung," *Kölner Zeitschrift für Soziologie* VIII/4 (1956).

25. _____: *Class and Class Conflict in Industrial Society* (Stanford-London, 1959).

26. _____: "Demokratie und Sozialstruktur in Deutschland," *Gesellschaft und Freiheit* (Munchen, 1961).

27. _____: "Deutsche Richter. Ein Betrag zur Soziologie der Oberschicht," *Gesellschaft und Freiheit* (Munchen, 1961).

28. _____: "The Education of an Elite: Law Faculties and the German Upper Class," to be published in *Transactions of the Fifth World Congress of Sociology* (German version published in *Der Monat* 166 [1962]).

29. _____: "Eine neue deutsche Oberschicht? Notizen über die Eliten der Bundesrepublik," *Die neue Gesellschaft* IX/1 (1962).

30. V. Deneke: *Die freien Berufe* (Stuttgart, 1956).

31. K. W. Deutsch and L. J. Edinger: *Germany Rejoins the Powers* (Stanford, 1959).

32. M. Dogan: "Political Ascent in a Class Society: French Deputies 1870-1958," in D. Marvick (ed.), *Political Decision-Makers* (Glencoe, 1961).

33. _____: "Les clivages politiques de la classe ouvrière," in L. Hamon (ed.), *Les Nouveaux Comportements Politiques de la Classe Ouvrière* (Paris, 1962).

A. Downs, *An Economic Theory of Democracy* (New York, 1957).

34. L. J. Edinger: "Post-Totalitarian Leadership: Elites in the German Federal Republic," *American Political Science Review* LIV (1960).

35. _____: "Continuity and Change in the Background of German Decision Makers," *Western Political Quarterly* XIV (1961).

36. E. Faul: *Wahlen und Wahler in Westdeutschland* (Villingen, 1961).

37. Th. Geiger: *Die soziale Schichtung des deutschen Volkes* (Stuttgart, 1932).

38. _____: *Aufgaben und Stellung der Intelligenz in der Gesellschaft* (Stuttgart, 1949).

39. A. Girard: *La Réussite sociale en France* (Paris, 1961).

D. V. Glass: *Social Mobility in Britain* (London, 1954).

B. Gleitze: *Wirtschafts- und Sozialstatistiches Handbuch* (Köln, 1960).

40. W. L. Guttsman: "The Changing Social Structure of the British Political Elite, 1886–1935," *British Journal of Sociology* LI/2 (1951).

41. _____: "Changes in British Labour Leadership," in D. Marvick (ed.), *Political Decision-Makers* (Glencoe, 1961).

42. W. Hirsch-Weber and K. Schütz: *Wähler und Gewählte* (Berlin, 1957).

43. Th. Hobbes: *Leviathan* (London-New York, 1934, new ed.).

44. R. Hoggart: *The Uses of Literacy* (London, 1957).

45. A. Inkeles and P. Rossi: "National Comparisons of Occupational Prestige," *American Journal of Sociology* LXII/4 (1956).

46. M. Janowitz: "Soziale Schichtung und Mobilität in Westdeutschland," *Kölner Zeitschrift für Soziologie* X/1 (1958).

47. R. K. Kelsall: *Higher Civil Servants in Britain* (London, 1955).

48. _____: "The Social Background of Higher Civil Service," in W. A. Robson (ed.); *The Civil Service in Britain and France* (London, 1956).

49. R. K. Kelsall, D. Lockwood and A. Tropp: "The New Middle Class in the Power Structure of Great Britain," *Transactions of the Third World Congress of Sociology* (Amsterdam, 1956).

50. H. Kluth, U. Lohmar and R. Tartler: *Arbeitersjugend gestern und heute* (Heidelberg, 1955).

51. M. Knight: *The German Executive 1890–1933* (Stanford, 1952); H. Schmidt, article in *European Journal of Sociology* IV/1 (1963).

52. H. Laski: *Grammar of Politics* (London-New Haven, 1934, 3rd ed.).

53. E. Lederer and J. Marschak: "Der neue Mittelstand," *Gundriss der Sozialökonomik* IX/1 (Tübingen, 1962).

54. R. Lewis and A. Maude: *Professional People* (London, 1952).

55. S. M. Lipset: "American Intellectuals: Their Politics and Status," *Political Man* (Garden City, 1960).

56. _____: "Fascism—Left, Right, and Center," *Political Man* (Garden City, 1960).

57. S. M. Lipset and R. Bendix: *Social Mobility in Industrial Society* (Berkeley-Los Angeles, 1959).

58. John Locke: *Second Treatise of Civil Government* (Chicago, 1955, new ed.).

59. D. Lockwood: *The Blackcoated Worker* (London, 1958).

60. _____: "The 'New Working Class,'" *European Journal of Sociology* I/2 (1960).

61. _____: "Der Angestellte: Eine international vergleichende Darstellung," in H. Bayer (ed.); *Der Angestellte zwischen Arbeiterschaft und Management* (Berlin, 1961).

RALF DAHRENDORF

62. T. H. Marshall: *Citizenship and Social Class* (Cambridge, 1950).

63. K. Marx: *Der achtzehnte Brumaire des Louis Bonaparte* (Berlin, 1946, new ed.).

64. D. R. Matthews: *The Social Background of Political Decision-Makers* (Garden City, 1954).

65. D. Middleton and D. Tait: *Tribes Without Rulers* (London, 1958).

66. S. M. Miller: "Comparative Social Mobility," *Current Sociology* IX/1 (1960).

67. C. W. Mills: *The Power Elite* (New York, 1956).

68. S. Ossowski: "La Vision dichotomique de la stratification sociale," *Cahiers Internationaux de Sociologie* XX (1956).

69. J. C. Papalekas: In H. Bayer (ed.), *Der Angestellte zwischen Arbeiterschaft und Management* (Berlin, 1961).

70. Th. Pirker: *Büro und Maschine* (Tübingen, 1962).

71. H. Popitz et al.: *Das Gesellschaftsbild des Arbeiters* (Tübingen, 1957).

72. _____: "Zum Begriff des Klassengesellschaft," *Hamburger Jahrbuch für Wirtschafts und Gesellschaftspolitik* Vol. III (1958).

73. David Riesman: *The Lonely Crowd* (New Haven, 1950).

74. David Riesman, N. Glazer and R. Denney: *The Lonely Crowd* (Garden City, 1953).

75. K. Renner: *Wandlungen der modernen Gesellschaft* (Wien, 1953).

76. W. W. Rostow: *The Stages of Economic Growth* (Cambridge, 1961).

77. Bertrand Russell: *Power: A New Social Analysis* (London, 1960).

78. H. Schelsky: *Ortsbestimmung der deutschen Soziologie* (Dusseldorf-Köln, 1959).

79. _____: "Die Bedeutung des Klassenbegriffes für die Analyse unserer Gesellschaft," *Jahrbuch für Sozialwissenschaft* (1961), XII, 3.

80. G. K. Schueller: *The Politburo* (Stanford, 1951).

Statistisches Jahrbuch für die Bundesrepublik Deutschland 1958 (Stuttgart, 1958).

M. Stein: *The Eclipse of Community* (Princeton, 1960).

81. F. Stern: *The Politics of Cultural Despair* (Berkeley-Los Angeles, 1961).

82. F. Sternberg: *Kapitalismus und Sozialismus vor dem Weltgericht* (Hamburg, 1951).

83. Max Weber: *Wirtschaft und Gesellschaft* (Tübingen, 1956, 4th ed.).

84. A. Willener: *Images de la société et classes sociales* (Bern, 1957).

85. W. L. Woytinsky: *Die Welt in Zahlen* (Berlin, 1928), Vol. VII.

86. M. Young: *The Rise of the Meritocracy* (London, 1958).

87. W. Zapf: Unpublished doctoral dissertation, University of Tübingen.

88. _____: In *Berichte aus dem Soziologischen Seminar der Universität Tübingen* I (1963).

SEYMOUR MARTIN LIPSET

The Changing Class Structure and Contemporary European Politics

DURING the 1950's commentators on both sides of the Atlantic began to depict western society by terms such as "The End of Ideology," "the post-industrial society," and the "post-bourgeois society."[1] While emphasizing different themes, these commentators agreed that the growth of bureaucracy and "affluence" in western industrial democratic society has made possible a social system in which class conflict is minimized. Domestic politics has become the politics of collective bargaining. True, an argument does remain as to the relative income at any given moment of the rural sector, of different groups of workers, of private corporations and so forth. But each group accepts the others' right to legitimate representation within the structure of representation and discussion.

Such a pattern in European society is relatively new. Much of the history of industrial society was a story of class-conscious politics and violent controversy between proletarian and bourgeois ideologists. Marxists viewed such tensions as inherent in a capitalist culture. That the United States, the most powerful capitalist state, lacks a strong socialist movement was viewed as a cultural lag, an inheritance of the period of an open land frontier that served as a "safety valve" for the tensions of industrialism. Presumably once this safety valve was gone, the European model of class-conscious politics would emerge.

In fact, history has validated a basic premise of Marxist sociology at the expense of Marxist politics. Marxist sociology assumes that cultural superstructures, including political behavior and status relationships, are a function of the underlying economic and technologi-

I would like to express my thanks to Joseph Strotgen and Ruth Ann Pitts for assistance. This paper has been written as part of the program of the Research and Training Group on Comparative Development of the Institutes of International Studies and Industrial Relations of the University of California at Berkeley.

cal structure. Hence, the most developed industrial society should also have the most developed set of political and class relationships. Since the United States is the most advanced society technologically, its superstructure should be more likely to correspond to the social structure of a modern industrial society than the "less" developed economies of Europe. In addition, one might argue that the absence of a traditional feudal past should mean that the United States has been most likely to develop the pure institutions of a capitalist industrial society. Hence, as an unpolitical Marxist sociology would expect, instead of European class and political relationships holding up a model of the United States' future, the social organization of the United States has presented the image of the European future.

The linkage between level of industrial development and other political and social institutions is obviously not a simple one.[2] Greater economic productivity is associated with a more equitable distribution of consumption goods and education—factors contributing to a reduction of intra-societal tension.[3] As the wealth of a nation increases, the status gap inherent in poor countries, where the rich perceive the poor as vulgar outcasts, is reduced. As differences in style of life are reduced, so are the tensions of stratification. And increased education enhances the propensity of different groups to "tolerate" each other, to accept the complex idea that truth and error are not necessarily on one side.

An explanation for the reduction in the appeal of total ideologies (*weltanschauungen*) as simply derivative from the social concomitants inherent in increasing economic productivity is clearly oversimplified. T. H. Marshall has suggested that such extreme ideologies initially emerged with the rise of new strata, such as the bourgeoisie or the working class, as they sought the rights of citizenship, that is, the right to fully participate socially and politically. As long as they were denied such rights sizable segments of these strata endorsed revolutionary ideologies. In turn, older strata and institutions seeking to preserve their ancient monopolies of power and status fostered conservative extremist doctrines.

The history of changes in political ideologies in democratic countries, from this point of view, can be written in terms of the emergence of new strata, and their eventual integration in society and polity. The struggle for such integration took the form of defining the place in the polity of the old preindustrial upper classes, the church, the business strata and the working class. The variation in the intensity of "class conflict" in many European nations has been in large measure a function of the extent to which the enduring economic struggle among the classes overlapped with the issues concerning the place of religion and the traditional status structure. Such controversies usually were perceived in "moral" terms involving basic concepts of right versus wrong, and hence they were much more likely than economic issues to result in sharp ideological cleavage and even civil war. The continuance of extremist movements in nations such as Germany and the Latin countries of southern Europe may be traced to the force of moral sentiments inherent in concerns for traditional status or religious privileges. Where such issues were resolved without becoming identified with the economic class struggle, then as Marshall suggests intense ideological controversy declined almost as soon as the new strata gained full citizenship rights.

Still a third factor related to the general decline in ideological bitterness has been the acceptance of scientific thought and professionalism in matters which have been at the center of political controversy. Insofar as most organized participants in the political struggle accept the authority of experts in economics, military affairs, interpretations of the behavior of foreign nations and the like, it becomes increasingly difficult to challenge the views of opponents in moralistic "either/or" terms. Where there is some consensus among the scientific experts on specific issues, these tend to be removed as possible sources of intense controversy. As the ideology of "scientism" becomes accepted, the ideologies of the extreme left and right lose much of their impact.

But whatever the long-run sources of the reduction of the appeal of total ideologies (and there are short-run factors as well, such as the impact of wars both hot and cold), the fact remains that there has been a reduction in the intensity of class-linked political struggles in most of Europe. This paper surveys developments in the economies, social structures and political parties of European societies which are relevant to an analysis of such trends. Within the context of a broad comparative analysis it also deals with the sources of deviations from these trends. The analysis thus seeks to define the elements in the changing structures which make for a lessening or persistence of class ideologies in different parts of Europe.

I Class and Political Consensus after 1945

The "miracle" of the postwar economic growth of Europe has been well documented. A combination of circumstances—the depression crises, prolonged experience with state economic intervention and planning under fascism or wartime regimes, the sharp increase in approval of socialist or welfare state concepts during and immediately following the war and the need for some years after the conflict to plan for and even furnish the capital for capital investment— resulted in a far greater amount of planning and government involvement in spurring economic growth than had existed in any democratic state before 1939.[4] The nationalization of businesses in France under the first de Gaulle regime surpassed the most grandiose ambitions of Third Republic Socialists, and systematic planning emerged in the early fifties.[5] The Austrian economy is characterized by large-scale government ownership. Italy retained and even expanded the considerable government economic sector developed under Fascism. In Germany, the numerous dependent war victims and the presence of refugees from the East, comprising more than one quarter of the population of West Germany, involved the state in welfare and other expenditures that took a large share of the gross national product for many years.[6] And in Britain, the Labour government undertook an elaborate program of nationalization and welfare expenditures.

In almost all of these nations, therefore, two general events of considerable significance for class behavior have occurred. On the one hand, many of the political-economic issues that occasioned deep conflict between representatives of the left and of the right were resolved in ways compatible with social-democratic ideology. On the other hand, the dominant strata, business and other, discovered that they could prosper through economic reforms that they regarded a decade earlier as the rankest socialist measures. The socialists and trade unionists found that their formal structural objectives, in many cases, had been accomplished with the cooperation of their political rivals. The need for government planning for economic growth and full employment was generally accepted; the obligation of the state to provide welfare services for the ill, the aged and other dependent groups was viewed as proper by all parties; and the right of the trade union and political representatives of the workers to participate in decisions affecting industry and politics also was increasingly coming to be accepted. Domestic politics in most of these societies became reduced to the "politics of collective bargaining," that is, to the issue of which groups should secure a little more or less of the pie.

The transformation in class attitudes as reflected in political and interest group behavior is most noticeable in northern non-Latin Europe and among the socialist and Roman Catholic political parties. Large-scale extremist or avowedly authoritarian parties have almost completely disappeared north of France and Italy, with the exception of Finland and Iceland. The Norwegian and Austrian socialists who subscribed to a relatively left-wing Marxist view before World War II are now clearly moderate social-democratic parties.[7] The latter take part in what has become a stable coalition regime with the bourgeois People's party. The parties of the three German-speaking nations, Switzerland, Austria and Germany, have given up any adherence to Marxism or class war doctrines and are little concerned with any further expansion of the area of state ownership of industry.[8] The 1959 Godesberg Program of the German party explicitly revoked the traditional policy of public ownership of the means of production.[9] An indication of the mood of European socialism may be found in a description of an international socialist conference:

In July, 1958, the socialist international held a congress in Hamburg. The name of Karl Marx was mentioned exactly once. The old slogans of the class struggle and exploitation had disappeared. But the words "liberty," "democracy," "human dignity" came up again and again. . . . The principal theoretical speech was made by Oscar Pollack [famed theoretician of prewar Austro-Marxism]. His theme was, "Why is it that we cannot get the working classes excited about socialism any longer?" The answer that Pollack gave is that their lot is so improved, in a way which would have been incredible to nineteenth-century Socialists of any variety, that they are no longer easily moved by the slogans of class struggle and socialism.[10]

On the right, one finds that those parties which still defend traditional European liberalism (*laissez-faire*) or conservatism (social hierarchy) are extremely weak. The Scandinavian Liberals and Agrarians now accept much of the welfare state. Many Scandinavian bourgeois politicians, in fact, propose that their countries adopt Swiss and Austrian political practice, a permanent coalition of all parties in which collective bargaining issues are fought out and compromised within the cabinet.[11] The Roman Catholic parties, on the whole, have accepted the welfare state and economic planning, and have even supported increases in government ownership. They willingly participate in coalitions with socialist parties in many countries. Roman Catholic trade unions, once the bitter rivals of the so-called free or socialist unions in most Roman Catholic countries, either participate in the same unions as the socialists, as in Germany and Austria, or cooperate closely with the socialist unions, as in the Benelux nations. Issues concerning the relationship of church and state, particularly as they affect education and family legislation, still separate the left wing of the Roman Catholic parties from the Socialists, but these are not of grave moment as compared to their agreement on economic and class matters. In Germany the traditional base of the opposition to a democratic regime, the regions beyond the Elbe, the homeland of the Junkers and feudal social relationships, is no longer part of the nation.[12] West Germany today is physically and socially largely comprised of regions and classes which historically have shown a willingness to sustain modern socio-economic and political systems. Although once playing a

major role in politics, the civil service and the army, the old aristocracy today participate little in these institutions.

Reactionary parties in postwar Europe have tended on the whole
to be peripheral movements based on the outlying regions and strata
which have not shared in the rapid economic growth, which find
themselves increasingly outside of the new cosmopolitanism and
which have lost out in the relative struggle for influence and
status.* [13] Thus in Norway the Christian party, which seeks to further traditional values, is clearly a provincial party based on the
lower middle classes of the rural and provincial communities.
Poujadism was the classic case of a movement appealing to the
ressentiments of declining strata; its base was the backward parts of
France which had been losing population, and the petit bourgeoisie
whose relative position in French economy and society had worsened
with the growth of the metropolis and large business and government. In Italy, the Monarchists and Neo-Fascists have recruited
strength from roughly comparable groups, a pattern that has also
characterized the support of the Austrian Freedom party. [14]

* Parenthetically, it may be noted that similar processes are operative on the
left. The only significant exceptions within European socialism to increased
political moderation have been the enhanced strength of "radical wings" within
the socialist and labor movements of Great Britain and Belgium. These movements have long been among the most moderate in the European left, and their
dominant tendency has not changed, so that the growth in left strength is not
very important. However, it should be noted that the growth in "militancy"
within these parties and unions seems to constitute a form of proletarian
Poujadism. Both nations lag behind the other industrialized nations of Europe in their growth rate, their standards of living have increased more slowly
than those of most other European countries, and the felt need to renovate
their economies—these are the two oldest industrial countries—by building new
plants or changing policies in old ones poses serious threats to the established
way of life of many workers and union leaders. In Wallonia, the ancient
industrial section of Belgium, the socialists and unions waged a major general
strike in 1960–1961 designed basically to stop the shutdown of marginal coal
mines, and the location of new and efficient factories in Flanders. Since the
strike, the "left-wing" socialists have formed the Walloon Popular Movement
seeking to divide Belgium into a federal state with two autonomous regions,
an action which would enable a Walloon government to defend the Walloon
economy. Similar Poujadist processes have occurred in Britain, although their
impact is not as visible, since the background sections of the British economy
are not concentrated within one ethnic-linguistic region as they are in Belgium.
The powerful resistance among many British union leaders and members to
Britain's entry into the Common Market is, to a considerable extent, motivated
by their fear of the possible effects on their jobs and unions resulting from the
modernization of the national economy which would be necessitated by the
need to compete within the Market. As in Wallonia, this essentially Poujadist
reaction has taken the form of an alliance between trade union leaders and
"left-wing" intellectuals who formulate the opposition on traditional left socialist
grounds.

Not unexpectedly, studies of the attitudes and behavior of the entrepreneurial strata in various parts of Europe suggest that the managerial groups in the traditionally less developed countries of Europe, such as France and Italy, have been the most resistant to yielding their historic autocratic and paternalistic view of the role of management. "In general, France and Italy have been characterized by a large number of small enterprises, looked on by the family as a source of personal security and conducted in an atmosphere of widespread absence of trust."[15] The resistance to accepting trade unions as a legitimate part of the industrial system is greater in these nations than anywhere else in democratic western Europe. And consequently, the presence of extreme views of class and industrial relations among leaders of workers and management has contributed to resisting the pressures inherent in industrialization to stabilize such relationships. The available evidence would suggest that Italian industrialists may be more resistant to accepting a *modus vivendi* with trade unions and the planning-welfare state than are the French, although, as shall be noted, the relative situation is reversed among the worker-based Communist parties of these countries.[16] It is difficult to account for these variations other than to suggest that Fascism as practiced in Italy for two decades conditioned many Italian businessmen to a pattern of labor-management relations that they still long for. Conversely, however, Fascism spared the Italian Communists the experience of having to repeatedly purge the various levels of leadership of a mass party. The party could emerge after World War II with close intellectual links to its pre-Fascist, and more significantly pre-Stalinist, past and with a secondary leadership and rank-and-file whose major formative political experience was the Resistance rather than the Comintern.*

Class conflict ideologies have become less significant components of the political movements supported by the middle classes in Germany, Italy and France. In Germany and in Italy, the Christian-Democratic type parties, with their efforts to retain the support of a large segment of the unionized working classes, have made a transclass appeal in favor of moderate changes. As compared to pre-Fascist days, they have gained considerably at the expense of older, more class-oriented, more conservative parties. The classically liberal Free Democratic and Liberal parties receive about 7 per cent of the vote in each country. In France, the Christian Democrats (MRP) were not able to retain the massive upper and middle class conservative vote which the party inherited in the first elections of the Fourth Republic, as a result of the traditional right's being dis-

* The differences between Italian and French Communism are discussed in more detail below.

credited by its involvement with Vichy. And large-scale anti-labor and anti-welfare state parties arose in the late forties and fifties. The Gaullism of the Fifth Republic, however, has replaced such parties in the affections of the conservative and business part of the electorate. Gaullism is oriented to a trans-class appeal designed to integrate the lower strata into the polity, and it supports economic and social reforms which foster economic growth and reduce class barriers.

Looking at the policies of business toward workers and their unions, it would appear that Germany first, and much more slowly and reluctantly, France and Italy, in that order, have been accepting the set of managerial ideologies characteristic of the more stable welfare democracies of northern and western Europe.[17] Curiously, the one country for which research data exist which bear on the relationship between degrees of modernization and bureaucratization of industry and the attitudes of industrial managers is contemporary Spain. An as yet unpublished study of the Spanish businessman by Juan Linz indicates clearly that the larger and more modern a factory, the more likely is its manager to believe in, or accept, modern personnel policies with their denigration of the particularistic rights of *patrons* and their assumptions concerning universalistic treatment of subordinates. It is interesting to note that whether a manager is an owner or not seems to have little bearing on his attitudes on such issues. If the Spanish pattern occurs in the other Latin countries as well, it would suggest that those who argue that significant changes are occurring among managers in France and Italy are correct. As yet, however, little systematic comparative data exist on the subject, and many of the available analyses rely heavily on published statements of, or interviews with, the officials, that is, ideologues, of business associations. The latter tend to mouth, and probably even believe, the traditional *laissez-faire* and anti-labor ideologies which many of their members no longer follow in practice.

II The Integration of the Working Class

But if the evidence drawn from developments in various parts of the continent suggests that the secular trends press for political moderation, for the politics of collective bargaining, it is also important to note that these trends do not imply a loss of electoral strength for working class-based parties. In fact, in all European countries varying majorities of the manual workers vote for parties which represent different shades of socialism. As the workers have become integrated into the body politic, they have not shifted from voting socialist to backing bourgeois parties. If anything, the opposite seems to have occurred. In the Scandinavian nations, for example, "all evidence indicates that social class explains more of the variation in voting and particularly more of the working class voting than some decades ago. This has occurred simultaneously with the disappearance of traditional class barriers. As equality has increased the working class voters have been more apt to vote for the worker's own parties than before."[18]

A comparative look at the pattern of working class voting in contemporary Europe reveals that with the exception of Holland and Germany, the leftist parties secure about two thirds or more of the working-class vote, a much higher percentage than during the depression of the 1930's.[19] The two exceptions are largely a by-product of the Roman Catholic-Protestant cleavage in their countries. The traditionally minority German and Dutch Roman Catholics have considerable group solidarity, and the Christian Democratic and Roman Catholic parties in these countries secure a larger working class vote than occurs anywhere else on the continent. Close to 70 per cent of German Protestant workers vote Socialist, as do "humanist" and moderate Calvinist Dutch workers, as opposed to the conservative Dutch Calvinists, who are more like the Roman Catholics. The leftist working class-oriented parties have increased their strength in much of Europe during the 1960's. It is clear, therefore, that the easy assumption made by many, concerning American as well as European politics, that greater national affluence would mean a weakening of the electoral support for the left is simply wrong. Regardless of how wealthy a nation may be compared to its past, all democratic countries, from the still impoverished lands of the Mediterranean basin to Sweden, Australia or the United States, remain highly stratified societies in which access to education, economic opportunity, culture and consumption goods is grossly unequal. The nature of such inequalities varies greatly; in general the poorer a country, the greater the gap in the standard of consumption between the classes. However, in all countries the more deprived strata, in income and status terms, continue to express their resentments against the stratification system or perhaps simply their desire to be represented by politicians who will seek to further redistribute the goods of the society, by voting for parties which stand for an increase in welfare state measures and for state intervention in the economy to prevent unemployment and increase their income vis à vis the more privileged strata.

Greater national wealth and consequent lower visible class differentials, therefore, do not weaken the voting strength of the left as compared with the right; rather, their effects become most evident in the decline of ideological differences, in changes in the policies advocated by different parties. The leftist parties have become more moderate, less radical, in the economic reforms which they espouse. A look at the political history of Europe indicates that no mass lower class-based political party, with the single exception of the German Communists, has ever disappeared or significantly declined through losing the bulk of its votes to a party on its right.*

The loyalties once created in a *mass* left-wing party are rarely lost. The most striking testimony to this has been the ability of the Finnish Communist party to retain mass support and even to grow since World War II, in spite of the Russian invasion of the country in 1940, the subsequent war of 1941–1945, and the Russian annexation of Karelia. The Communists are able to secure a quarter of the vote even though 10 per cent of the population are refugees from the Russian-annexed territory. The support for the Communist party goes back to the Finnish Civil War, which followed the Russian revolution, when the Social-Democratic party, the largest party under Czarist rule, divided into two roughly equal groups in reacting to Bolshevism. And although the Communist party was illegal for much of the period between the wars, it seemingly lost little backing. In recent years, it has grown somewhat during a period of rapid economic development and a sharply rising standard of living.

But if workers have remained loyal to the parties of their class on election day, they show much less commitment to these parties the rest of the year. All over Europe, both socialist and Communist parties have complained about losses in membership, in attendance at party meetings and in the reading of party newspapers. Such changes attest to the growth of what French intellectuals are increasingly coming to describe as the problem of *dépolitisation*.[20] Another phenomenon illustrating these trends is the growing tendency of all the working class organizations to place less emphasis on traditional *political* doctrines and to put more stress on representation of concrete interests. Roman Catholic trade unions also are increasingly reluctant to intervene directly in politics.

In discussing the implications of changes such as these, a number of French political analysts have argued that what is occurring in France, and presumably in some other countries as well, is not so much a decline in political interest (*dépolitisation*), as of ideology (*déidéologisation*). Thus René Rémond, in introducing a general symposium on these issues, points out that while political parties

---

* Although the German Communists secured about 16% of the vote in 1932, they were never as large as the Social-Democrats. The latter always retained their status as the predominant party of the workers. Hence even the German case is not a real exception.

have suffered a considerable decline in membership, this has not been true of other French associations; that in fact there has been a considerable increase in the number of voluntary associations in France. Such groups, while nonpartisan, play important roles in politics in representing the specific interests of their members. André Philip has even suggested that contemporary France finally is developing the social infrastructure recommended by Tocqueville as a condition for stable democracy, widespread support for secondary associations. He suggests that this is another consequence of modernization, since the pattern of commitment to one group which represents the individual totally is a characteristic of the early phase of development. In a modernized society, any given group or party will report a relatively low level of direct participation by their members or supporters since the segmentalized individual involved in many roles must support diverse groups, and hence seemingly takes on the role of spectator in most of them.[21]

It would seem as if much of France has taken the plunge of finally dropping its historic commitments to total *weltanschauungen* and seeing the problem of progressive social change as a pragmatic and gradual one. And insofar as Frenchmen are able to see some of the changes and policies which they advocate being adopted, even by a government which many of them distrust, their motivation to continue to participate in such pragmatic parapolitical activity continues.

There are many ways in which the more pragmatic orientation of Europeans manifests itself, but the changes in trade union behavior are most noticeable. As already noted, in a number of countries socialist and Roman Catholic unionists are cooperating as they never did before World War II. The fact of such cooperation reflects the extent to which both have moved away from ideological or political unionism toward pragmatic or even, in the American sense of the term, "business unionism." In Italy and France, the trend toward a *syndicalisme de controle* is furthered by the emerging patterns of plant unions and supplementary factory contracts.[22] Such organization and negotiation for the first time involve the unions in dealing with the concrete problems of the factory environment such as job evaluation, rates, productivity and welfare.[23] The pressures in this direction have come primarily from the non-Communist unions, though the Communist unions have also increasingly come to accept such institutions, more in Italy than in France.[24] The increase in economic strikes as distinct from political ones, though often resulting in an overall increase of the strike rate, has been interpreted by some observers as reflecting the integration of the workers into the industrial system; an economic strike is part of a normal bargaining relationship with one's employer. Some have suggested that the Italian strike wave of 1961 and 1962 was perhaps the first of this type since the war in that country.[25]

The two major strikes of 1963, those of the coal miners in France and of the metal workers in Germany, are also notable for the extent to which each resembled a typical American strike flowing from a breakdown in collective bargaining. Each strike was ended by a negotiated settlement in which the unions secured more than they had been offered initially. Neither turned into a political strike, though the governments were directly involved in the negotiations. Essentially there was general recognition on both sides that the strike was a normal part of the collective bargaining process, although de Gaulle showed some initial reluctance to concur. Note further that in France the Communist-controlled CGT initially called for a two-day protest strike, while much less politicized miners' unions affiliated to the Socialist *Force Ouvrière* and the Roman Catholic CFTC called a trade union strike, one that would last until settled by negotiation. The Communists were forced to change their tactics, to shift from a political protest to an economic strike. These strikes in Italy, Germany and France may signify the beginning of a new era in labor relations—one in which strikes are recognized as part of the normal bargaining relationship rather than an embryonic civil war the outbreak of which is threatening to leadership on both sides.[26]

The relative weakness of traditional leftist ideology in western and southern Europe is suggested also by various attitude surveys. These studies indicate that the actual sentiment favoring a "socialist solution" to economic or social problems is much lower than the Socialist or Communist vote. It again demonstrates that people will vote for such parties without commitment to the once basic ideological values of these parties.

In Britain today, where public opinion polls and local election results indicate that the Labour party has an overwhelming lead over the Conservatives, only 18 per cent of the electorate say that they favor more nationalization. Among Labour party voters, 39 per cent support increased nationalization, 46 per cent would leave things as they are, and 15 per cent would actually favor some denationalization. Conversely, only 43 per cent of the Conservatives advocate denationalization.[27]

A comparative analysis of attitudes toward ownership of industry in seven European countries based on interviews in the spring of 1958 reported strong sentiment favoring public ownership of industry only in Italy, the nation which has the largest support for radical ideologies in the form of large Communist and left-Socialist parties.[28]

In France, where about half the workers have voted Communist in most postwar elections, with another 20 per cent going to the Socialists, and a large majority voting for the Communist-controlled CGT trade union federation in Social Security Board elections, opinion data suggest that the workers are not as hostile to the existing institutions as this record might imply. A detailed survey of French workers in 1956 reported that 53 per cent thought there was "confidence" in the relations between employees and management, as contrasted to 27 per cent who said there was "distrust." Over four fifths believed their employer was doing his job well; nine tenths thought the quality of the work done at their plant was good; only 13 per cent thought there was a great deal of waste in their firm; 57 per cent stated that they had a chance for a promotion at their work; and 86 per cent reported they liked their jobs. Though the Communists had secured the vote of a majority of French workers shortly before this survey, only 12 per cent of those interviewed stated they were very much interested in politics, about the same percentage as that which reported strong interest in trade union activities.[29] And when asked in which country "the workers are best off," 54 per cent said the United States as compared with 14 per cent who answered the Soviet Union.[30]

How many of the French Communist voters actually adhere to a class war perspective and a generally Communist view of politics is a question that is impossible to answer. French experts who have examined the available evidence from studies of workers' attitudes differ in their interpretations. Thus Raymond Aron suggests that the polls indicate that about two thirds of French Communist supporters are "convinced Communists," while Mattei Dogan believes that less than half of them think of political action and the class struggle in the Marxist sense of the term.[31]

The weakness of a sharp class conflict view of politics in Germany is borne out by a 1960 opinion study which asked a sample of the electorate their opinions concerning class solidarity and party voting. Less than one fifth took a purely class view of voting behavior, that is, that workers should always vote for the Socialists, and middle class people always for the non-socialist parties.[32] The majority agreed with the statement that workers or middle class people might vote for either tendency, depending on the political situation and the issues involved. Over three fifths of those in middle class occupations, although predominantly non-socialist in their voting habits, agreed with the opinion that the division between the bourgeoisie and the workers was no longer strong and that a doctor or a professor might vote either Christian Democratic or Social Democratic, depending on the particular issues of a campaign.

Conversely, only 30 per cent of the workers thought that a worker must always vote for the Social-Democrats, while half of the worker respondents agreed with the statement that a worker should choose between the parties according to the issues.[33]

The ideology of the "open society" in which competent individuals can succeed seems to have permeated much of Europe, a phenomenon which may also contribute to a reduction of class tension. Thus surveys in a number of countries which inquired as to the chances of capable individuals rising socially in their country found large majorities which reported their belief that the chances were good. The percentages of respondents saying that chances were good were 90 in Norway, 88 in England, 72 in West Germany, and 70 in Belgium. The one European country covered in this study in which the proportion of those who were optimistic about mobility was less than half was Austria, but even there the positive answers outweighed the pessimistic ones, 49 per cent to 34 per cent. Italy and France were not covered in this comparative study. However, another set of surveys which inquired as to careers one would recommend to a young man found that the Italians ranked second only to the English in suggesting high status professional occupations (62 per cent). The strongest French preference seemed to be for careers in the civil service, an orientation which distinguished them from all other European nations except the Belgians. It should be noted also that the Italians and the French were least likely among the citizens of eleven European countries to recommend a career as a skilled worker or artisan to a young man.[34]

There is some direct evidence that modernization results in a positive attitude by workers toward their occupational situation. A French study of the consequences of modernization in textile factories in northern France brings this out clearly. The author notes that the workers view the effects of technological innovation as a "good thing," that they see it as resulting in an increase in employment, greater possibilities for social mobility and increased earnings.[35] The findings of French factory surveys with respect to worker reaction to modernization are paralleled in a report on the comparative strength of the Communist party in five large Italian factories which varied in their degree of modernization. The less modernized the plants the larger the proportion of workers who belonged to the Communist party, holding size of plant constant.[36]

But if workers react positively to working in modernized, more bureaucratic work environments, if they see these as offering greater opportunity for higher earnings and mobility, if job satisfaction is actually higher in many of these, the fact remains that when one looks at the sources of left-wing strength, either in voting or in union membership, and in the extent to which men agree with "anti-capitalist" attitudes, such strength is to be found disproportionately in the larger factories and the larger cities.[37] This seeming contradiction points up an interesting relation between the variables linked to the overall characteristics of a national political class culture and the same variables operating within a given society. As noted above, nations with a high level of industrialization and urbanization tend to have a low level of ideological conflict. But within nations, whatever the level of intensity of political controversy, larger factories and cities tend to be the strongholds of the left politics dominant in the country, Communist, Socialist or Democratic.[38] Trade unions also are generally stronger in large factories in large cities. It would seem that while greater industrialization and urbanization with consequent greater national wealth make for a more stable polity, *within* any system these social factors are conducive to fostering working class political and trade union strength.

How might we account for this? In part it may be related to the fact that the large factory environment sustains fewer informal relations between members of different classes, reducing the possibility that the members of the lower class will be influenced personally by the more conservative and more prestigeful members of middle and higher classes such as owners, managers and supervisors. And the more concentrated the members of a lower class are in a social environment, the easier it is for common class attitudes to spread among them and for representatives of class-oriented parties or other organizations to reach them and activate their anti-elitist sympathies.[39]

But though the emergence of large social environments that are class homogeneous facilitates the spread of lower class-based movements, the same factors operating in the social structure as a whole become linked with other tendencies operating to reduce class friction. On the working class level these involve a rise in standards of living, educational levels and opportunity for upward social mobility within industry. In all countries with large Communist movements (Italy, France and Finland), within any given structural environment, the better-paid workers are more moderate in their political views than the poorer ones. Modernization reduces the sources of worker hostility to management by altering the sources of managerial behavior. These trends involve a decline in the family-owned corporation and in the domination of the economy by the *patron* type who sees himself as all powerful, and the rise within the management strata of a corporate leadership characterized by a division of labor and by the requisite of formal higher education. Accompanying the growth in large systems is a consequent increased emphasis

351

on universalistic and achievement values, on judging individuals on the basis of their specific roles as worker or manager. As management's resistance to formalizing the labor-management relationship gradually declines, union labor's commitment to an ideological view of unionism, as distinct from a business or pragmatic view, is also reduced.

III The New Middle Class—The Base for Employee Politics

The emergence of the new middle class—the increasingly large layer of clerks, salesmen, technicians, middle management, civil servants—has served to introduce as a major factor in the European polity a group which itself is so exposed to conflicting pressures from the left and the right that it can contribute to stabilizing class tensions. A broad middle class has a mitigating position because it can give political rewards to moderate parties and penalize extreme parties on both sides—right and left. Its members wish to obtain more for themselves and their offspring; they advocate universalistic equality in the educational and other aspects of the status-allocating mechanisms; they often uphold the extension of the welfare state. Yet their position among the relatively privileged in status and possession terms makes them supporters of political and social stability, of the politics of collective bargaining. And the larger a proportion of the electorate and the labor force formed by the new middle class, the more both the left and the right must take this group into account in determining their own policies. The political and trade union influence of the new middle class is largely thrown on the side of pressing for greater opportunity, not greater social equality. The unions of the middle class are interested in maintaining, or even extending, the income gap existing between themselves and the manual workers. They often abstain from affiliating to the same central federation as the manual unions, and many of them are led by men who back "liberal" rather than labor parties. In some countries of Europe, and in Israel in recent years, there have been strikes by unions of salaried professionals in order to widen the gap between themselves and manual workers.[40] However, interest in income differences apart, these rapidly growing new middle classes press the political system toward consensus because as employees they favor many of the same statist policies that were long advocated by the representatives of the manual workers. Otto Kirchheimer in fact has argued that it is the very growth of these strata, who form the mass base of the "bourgeois" parties, that is largely responsible for the decline of ideology.[41]

It is important to recognize that the bourgeois parties are no longer bourgeois in the classic sense of the term. That is, the proportion of those who are self-employed, or who have close ties to the self-employed on the land or in the town, is an increasingly small part of the electorate. Most large parties now represent employees, manual or nonmanual. And while these strata differ in their orientations to many issues, they are also united on many welfare concerns. Recent Swedish political history is an apt illustration of this point. The dominant Social-Democrats were experiencing a secular decline in support, largely, according to survey analyses, because the white-collar segment of the population was growing relative to the manual sector. The party introduced a major reform, an old age pension of 65 per cent of salary, in large part because their electoral researches had suggested such a proposal would be popular not only with their traditional manual supporters but with many white-collar workers. The proposal ultimately carried in referendum, and the party increased its national vote substantially. Even more significant, perhaps, is the fact that the Liberal party, which accepted the general principle of the enlarged pension, gained enormously at the expense of the Conservatives, who took a traditional position against high taxes and against increases in the functions of the state. This suggests that the political struggles of the future will increasingly take place between parties representing the status concerns and economic interests of the two employee strata, and that the parties drawing heavily from the self-employed will continue to lose influence.[42]

IV Communism Resists the Trend

The dominant structural trend in Europe involves the final triumph of the values of industrial society, the end of rigid status classes derivative from a pre-industrial world, and increasing emphasis on achievement rather than ascription, on universalism rather than particularism, and on interaction among individuals in terms of the specific roles played by each rather than in terms of their diffuse generalized statuses. The heightening standard of living of the masses gives them greater market power and enables them to affect much of culture and societal taste. All these changes imply the emergence of a somewhat similar social and political culture, one which increasingly resembles the first advanced industrial society to function without institutions and values derivative from a feudal past, the United States. And as has been indicated earlier, this should mean the end of class-linked severely ideological politics.

Yet there is one major force which in a number of countries has rejected this view of European social change and which has done its best to block these trends—the Communist party. It is clear that the very existence of powerful Communist movements in countries like France and Italy has been a major force perpetuating the institutions and values of the old society. In countries in which the Communists are the largest working class party, in which they secure around a quarter of all votes, it has been difficult to elect a progressive government to office. If governments must secure a majority from the non-Communist three quarters of the population, they have to rely in large part on the conservative and traditionalist elements. The fact that one quarter of the electorate, constituting one half or more of the social base of the "left," have been outside of the political game inevitably gives a considerable advantage to the conservatives. In effect, by voting Communist, French and Italian workers have disfranchised themselves. Thus not only does a mass Communist party serve to fossilize the ideological orientations characteristic of a pre-industrial society among the working class, it contributes to preserving pre-modern orientations on the right.

A series of political developments—the revival of French Communist support recouping most of the electoral losses it suffered between 1956 and 1958 as a result of the Hungarian revolution and the Gaullist coup, the continued massive strength of Finnish Communism and the fairly continuous slow growth in the vote of the Italian Communists—each of which has occured during long periods of prosperity and economic growth—would seem to contradict the thesis that economic growth and an improvement in social conditions enhance the prospects for political stability.[43] In these countries economic modernization has seemingly not been followed by a reduction in ideological tensions.

The countries with large Communist parties, however, remain among the less modernized of the big nations; their industry tends to be less centralized in large plants. Thus in the mid-1950's the proportion of German employees in plants with more than 1000 workers was twice as high (38.9 per cent) as it was in France (17.6 per cent), while only 12 per cent of the employed Germans were in plants with fewer than 50 workers, in contrast to 37 per cent of the French.[44] Note too that the European countries in which Communism is strongest are among those with a relatively small proportion of their total population living in metropolitan areas.[45] The rank-order correlation between the proportion of Communist votes in a nation and urbanization as of the early 1950's was —.61, while the comparable correlation between left extremist voting and an index of industrialization was —.76.[46] Insofar as the general pattern of politics, class relations and other social attitudes is affected by the degree of bureaucratization of industrial and community life, it is clear that the nations with large Communist movements are on the whole among the less developed in these respects of the nations of Europe.

The comparative analysis of the consequences of economic growth on class relationships in relatively industrialized societies is further complicated by the fact that processes endemic in such improvement affect those workers who are accustomed to the industrial system differently from those who are drawn into it. For the former, increased bureaucratization of industry should make for improvement in income and the conditions of work, and thus should serve to moderate their propensity toward extremist politics. For the latter, the experiences of dislocation inherent in social and geographic mobility, particularly the shift from rural or small-town background to crowded urban slums, and from the pace and discipline of rural work to that of the factory, may increase their potential for support of political radicalism.[47] The need to adjust quickly to new social conditions and cultural norms makes individuals receptive to new values and ideologies which explain the sources of their discontent in revolutionary terms.[48] It should also be noted that the decline in the number of the chronically unemployed—from 2,500,000 in 1950–1951 to around 800,000 in 1962—in Italy may have increased rather than decreased the vote available to the extreme left. There are two empirical generalizations about the political behavior of the jobless and the formerly unemployed that hold true in a number of countries. First, the unemployed are much more likely than those regularly employed to be uninformed and apathetic about politics. Their insecurity would seem to reduce their availability for any "outside" interest, including the act of voting. Second, employed individuals who report a past experience of unemployment, or areas which were once centers of high rates of unemployment, are much more likely to exhibit leftist voting propensities than those with more fortunate economic histories.[49]

The most comprehensive analysis of the sources of, and changes in, the support of a mass European Communist party, that of Erik Allardt in Finland, strongly suggests that economic growth in the less industrialized regions of a rapidly developing nation heightens the possibilities for extremist class-conscious politics. He points out that the characteristics of Communist strength in regions in which Communism has gained greatly since World War II, the north and east, are quite different from those in the areas in which it has always been strong, the south and west. The latter are the original industrialized sections of the country. His detailed statistical analyses point to the conclusion that *"increase in Communist strength in all areas is related to changes which in one way or another are likely to uproot individuals."* [50] Ecological analysis indicates that increases in the per capita income of the poorer regions are correlated highly with gains in Communist support. Allardt's analysis also suggests some of the factors underlying the continuation of Communist strength once attained. Stable Communist strength, that is, little fluctuations up or down, is associated with the older industrial areas in which the party has been strong since the Russian revolution and which also give strong support to the Social-Democrats. In such regions, the Communists have erected an elaborate network of party-linked voluntary associations and leisure activities, so that, as in parts of France and Italy, one almost has a functioning Communist subculture unaffected by political events.

As already noted, it is doubtful that structural changes alone will result in the decline of a mass Communist party.[51] Where the party is strong, it endeavors, as in Finland, to isolate its base from serious influence by non-Communist sources. There are plenty of social strains inherent in the situation of the worker or poor peasant to reinforce acceptance of leftist doctrine, and a mass movement can claim that any improvements are the result of its agitation. The Communist sector of the electorate will join the democratic political game in the foreseeable future only if their party, as a party, does it. There is little doubt that if the various European Communist parties were genuine national parties—that is, if their behavior were largely determined by experiences within their own countries—they would have evolved in much the same way as the European Socialist parties. And consequently, it is necessary to recognize that any predictions about their future behavior must be part of an analysis of developments within the Communist-controlled nations. If the break between the Soviet Union and China permits genuine autonomy for all national Communist parties, then the pattern of independence from Russian control emerging in Italy will probably occur elsewhere as well.

The doctrinal base for such a change in the role of Communist parties has already been advanced by various Yugoslav and Italian Communists.[52] The former have argued that there is a world-wide pressure for socialist innovations which is inherent in the nature of large-scale capitalist economic institutions. They accept the proposition that Communist movements and ideologies as they emerged in eastern Europe and Russia are appropriate for underdeveloped countries which have not had the experience of large and legally instituted labor, political and union movements nor the experience of political freedom.[53] The more developed nations not only can avoid the experiences of the less developed Communist societies, but they can and are moving toward socialism while preserving political freedom. It has even been suggested that in the United States, socialist adjustments and institutions exist even though Americans refuse to accept the term socialism to describe the changes occurring within their society. Co-existence is possible, say these Yugoslavs, not only because war is impossible in an atomic age, but because there is no basic cleavage between the Communist and the capitalist world, since the latter is ceasing to be capitalist in any traditional meaning of the term. Hence Communists in the developed countries will not have to make a revolution or come to power in their own right. By collaborating with other "progressive forces," they can hasten the emergence of socialist institutions.

The Italian Communist party has gradually modified its ideology so that some sophisticated observers would now describe it as a left social-democratic rather than a Communist party. Like the Yugoslav party, it no longer sees a fundamental dichotomy between capitalism and socialism, but rather argues that "there exists in the capitalist world today an urge towards structural reforms and to reforms of a socialist nature, which is related to economic progress and the new expansion of the productive forces."[54] And its leader, Palmiro Togliatti, has gone on to argue the need to "correct" Lenin's position that "bourgeois state apparatus cannot be used for building a socialist society," in the light of "the changes which have taken place and which are still in the process of being realized in the world."[55] It denies the need for one-party dictatorship in Italy, and it has accepted Italian membership in the Common Market. Communist municipal office-holders work closely with business groups in fostering the interests of their cities, and party-controlled labor unions play a somewhat more responsible role in collective bargaining and Italian life generally than has been true for Communist unions in the past.[56] The Chinese Communists correctly point to the Italian party as the foremost example of reformist heresies among the nongovernmental parties. If the Italian electorate has not turned away from the Communists, the Communists have moved to the right. Thus the effect of a reduction in social strains among sections of the Italian workers may be reflected in the changed behavior of their party and unions.[57]

But if the experiences and the behavior of the Italian party suggest an adaptation to the emergence of stable political institutions and economic modernization in Italy, the French Communist party simply did not behave in the same way and its policies until very recently seemingly challenge the underlying interpretation here.[58] The French party also had to react to the end of Soviet domination of party life and to economic modernization in France. But where the Italian party and its union federation, the CGIL, modified their programs and explicitly decided to cooperate "with what they termed the representatives of neo-capitalism," the French party refused. It continued to insist that capitalism could not reform itself, that the workers could not make long-term improvements in their social situation, and that the unions must remain primarily political instruments. The Italian party decided to join forces with modernization, the French party to resist it.[59] The reasons for the differences between the parties are complex and I cannot detail them here.[60] Briefly, they would seem to relate to the fact that the French party was Stalinized and proletarianized in its leadership and membership during the 1930's and 1940's, while Fascism enabled the Italian party to escape some of these consequences; after 1944 it recruited and retained many non-Stalinist intellectuals in its organizations. Palmiro Togliatti, the leader of the Italian party, though an official of the Comintern during the 1930's, more closely resembles the pre-Stalin leaders of Communism than those like Maurice Thorez, who won and maintained leadership as a result of following Stalin's every turn.[61] The variations in the Italian and French political systems have meant that elected local Communists have had more real power and involvement in running municipalities and other institutions in Italy than in France.[62] The Italian Socialists, in part because of their long and mutual Fascist experience, have been much less hostile to the Communists than have been the French Socialists. Hence the Italian party has never been as isolated from non-Communists as the French. These differences between the French and Italian Communist parties may be related to the facts that the Italian party has lost fewer members than the French (both parties have lost a considerable portion of their membership as compared with the post-war high point), and that the Italian party has done better at the polls.[63]

Communist parties without a Moscow-centered world party would be like national Roman Catholic churches without a pope, without the need to follow a dogma decreed from a single source. And many observers predict that the individual parties will follow the road of Protestantism, of deviation, of variation, of adjustment to particular national conditions, much as the Social-Democrats did half a century or more earlier. Those parties which operate within democratic societies will be under constant pressure to modify their totalitarian structures, as in fact the Italian party seems to be beginning to do.[64]

Given the history of the Communist movement, the training which its leaders have received in totalitarian methods and the use of conscious deception, the acceptance (even though now critical) of the experiences of one-party regimes as a positive model, no one who cares about freedom can accept a Communist party as an equal player in a parliamentary game. On the other hand, the possibility that changes in the Communist world are permitting sufficient independence and variations among Communist parties to allow some of them to react to the forces which press them to act as regular participants within political democracies should not be ignored. The more positively involved are Communists and their *followers* in a political system which in fact is paying off socially and economically, the more difficult it will be for a given Communist party to renew an alienated stance among its supporters should the leadership decide to do so. Hence the possibility may be held out that the vicious circle of Communist-reactionary resistance to modernization in Latin-Europe may be breaking down, not only as a result of the decline of the reactionary groups, but because of changes within Communism. Even Communism may be yielding to the pressures making for a decline of ideology and of class war.

V *Continuing Sources of Strain*

There are many sources of political strain within stable democratic societies. The stratification systems of all inherently involve a grossly inequalitarian distribution of status, income and power. Even the very "affluent" United States contains a large minority living in poverty by its own standards.[65] A look at consumption standards for Europe finds that very large minorities or majorities in different European countries still lack many items which are available to all but a few in the United States.[66] Status inequality would seem to be experienced as punitive by the lower classes in all systems. But while all societies present some ideological justification for enduring consumption and status inequalities, the concept of mass citizenship that arose with the industrial revolution undermines the stability of class systems because it implies, as T. H. Marshall put it, that "all are equal with respect to the rights and duties with which the status is endowed." [67] Hence he argues that modern democratic industrial society is historically unique in seeking to sustain a system of contradictory stratification values. All previous societies had class systems that assumed inequality, but they also denied citizenship to all except a small elite. Once full and equal political (manhood suffrage) and economic (trade union organization) citizenship was established, the equalitarian emphasis inherent in the concept sustains a successful and continuing attack on many aspects of inequality. Much of democratic politics involves the efforts of the lower strata to equalize the conditions of existence and opportunity.

The tension between equality and inequality is endemic in modern industrial democratic society. The dominant strata will continue the attempt to institutionalize their privileges, to find means to pass on to their kin and offspring the privileges they have gained. This conflict, however, does not mean that one or the other tendency must triumph, or that the strain will destroy or even necessarily weaken the social fabric. The predominant character of modern industrial democracy, as a free and evolving society, is in part a result of the chronic tensions between the inherent pressures toward inequality and the endemic emphasis in democracy on equality.

The current wave of writings that somehow see in the growth of affluence in the western world the emergence of a peaceful social utopia—which will not require continued political struggle between representatives of the haves and of the have-nots—ignores the extent to which the content of these very concepts changes as society evolves. As Marshall has pointed out, ever since the beginning of the industrial revolution almost every generation proclaimed a social revolution to elevate the lower strata. "From the 1880's to the 1940's people were constantly expressing amazement at the social transformation witnessed in their lifetime, oblivious of the fact that, in this series of outbursts of self-congratulation, the glorious achievements of the past became the squalid heritage of the present."[68]

But in spite of the progress leading one generation to proclaim the significance of recent social improvements, only a few years later others are arguing that the present conditions of the poor, of the lowly, are intolerable, that they cannot possibly be tolerated by free men who believe in equality.[69] And as Marshall indicates, such phenomena do not "mean that the progress which men thought they made was illusory. It means that the standards by which that progress was assessed were constantly rising, and that ever deeper probing into the social situation kept revealing new horrors which had previously been concealed from view."[70] One may ask with Marshall whether the concept of the affluent society will have any longer life than some of its predecessors.

In large measure, the problem of the lower strata is now seen as that of "cultural deprivation." It is clear that in all countries, variation in participation in the intellectual culture serves to negate the dream of equal opportunity for all to mount the educational ladder; consequently, access to the summits of the occupational structure is still grossly restricted. In Sweden, for example, in spite of thirty years of Social-Democratic government providing free access to universities together with state bursaries, the proportion of working class children taking advantage of such opportunities has hardly risen. Few commodities are distributed as unequally in Europe as high school and university education. The simple improvement in economic standards of living, at least at its present pace, does little to reduce the considerable advantages held by the culturally privileged strata to perpetuate their families in an equally advantaged position.[71] And socialist parties in a number of countries are beginning to look for ways to enhance the educational and cultural aspirations of lower class youth. Here, then, is the most recent example of the conflict between the principles of equality inherent in citizenship and the forces endemic to complex stratified society that serve to maintain or erect cultural barriers between the classes. The latter operate as a consequence of the differential distributions of rewards and access to culture, and must be combatted continually if they are not to dominate.[72]

In conclusion, this survey of economic and social developments accompanying the modernization of European society has shown compelling evidence for the moderation of ideological differences in Europe as a consequence of the increasing affluence of European nations, the attainment of economic as well as political citizenship by the workers, the gradual absorption and assimilation of the remnants of European society still living in feudal or otherwise underdeveloped economic and social conditions. The changes in parties of the left, especially Communist parties, to a more moderate orientation toward capitalist society and class conflict have been shown to be also related to broad changes in the international Communist world, as exemplified by the thesis of polycentrism and the reinterpretation of Marxism concerning the possibility of a rapprochement with capitalism. But it has also been pointed out that industrialization does not automatically remove sources of tension. These sources are endemic to an industrial society which permits a relatively open struggle for the fruits of individual effort and which does not automatically give access to opportunity for individual advancement to those on the lower rungs of the status ladder. Finally, it has been shown that much of the anachronistic ideological politics of the "Poujadist" left and right is a response to anachronistic orientations and forms of industrial organization still present in some sectors of European society, as among some peasants and small businessmen in France, or a result of the preservation of outmoded forms of production and extraction, as in Britain and Belgium. In the latter two nations ideological left working class politics, in part, has taken the form of opposition to modernization which might threaten the present security of some categories of workers and their unions in the interests of improvement of the total economy. In the long run, however, the remaining bases of ideologically intransigent politics will continue to decline due to the contradictions between reality and their definition of the situation, and because of the irrelevance of their call to action in terms of a situation which will no longer exist.

As a final comment, I would note that not only do class conflicts over issues related to division of the total economic pie, influence over various institutions, symbolic status and opportunity, continue in the absence of *weltanschauungen*, but that the decline of such total ideologies does *not* mean the end of ideology. Clearly, commitment to the politics of pragmatism, to the rules of the game of collective bargaining, to gradual change whether in the direction favored by the left or the right, to opposition both to an all powerful central state and to *laissez-faire* constitute the component parts of an ideology. The "agreement on fundamentals," the political consensus of western society, now increasingly has come to include a position on matters which once sharply separated the left from the right. And this ideological agreement, which might best be described as "conservative socialism," has become *the* ideology of the major parties in the developed states of Europe and America. As such it leaves its advocates in sharp disagreement with the relatively small groups of radical rightists and leftists at home, and at a disadvantage in efforts to foster different varients of this doctrine in the less affluent parts of the world.

REFERENCES

1. It is difficult to establish credit for the origin of this concept. Raymond Aron certainly deserves recognition for having presented it in the form which was widely followed by other writers in the West. See Raymond Aron, "Fin de l'age ideologique?" in Theodore W. Adorno and Walter Dirks (eds.), *Sociologica* (Frankfurt: Europaische Verlaganstalt, 1955), pp. 219–233, and *L'Opium des intellectuals* (Paris: Calmann-Levy, 1955), pp. 315–334. However, it should be noted that two major European scholars, T. H. Marshall and Herbert Tingsten, enunciated the same basic thesis without using the term in the late 40's and early 50's. Tingsten's early writings on the subject were presented in various articles in the Stockholm newspaper, *Dagens Nyheter*, while Marshall elaborated on the theme in his now almost classic essay, "Citizenship and Social Class," first presented in 1949 and recently reprinted in his volume *Sociology at the Crossroads* (London: Heinemann, 1963), pp. 67–127. See also Edward Shils, "The End of Ideology?" *Encounter*, 5 (November, 1955), 52–58; Herbert Tingsten, "Stability and Vitality in Swedish Democracy," *The Political Quarterly*, 26 (1955), 140–151; S. M. Lipset, "The State of Democratic Politics," *Canadian Forum*, 35 (1955), 170–171; Otto Brunner, "Der Zeitalter der Ideologien," in *Neue Wege der Sozialgeschichte* (Gottingen: Van den Hoeck und Ruprecht, 1956), pp. 194–219; Lewis Feuer, *Psychoanalysis and Ethics* (Springfield: Charles C Thomas, 1955), pp. 126–130; Otto Kirchheimer, "The Waning of Opposition in Parliamentary Regimes," *Social Research*, 24 (1957), 127–156; Stein Rokkan, *Sammenlignende Politisksosilogi* (Bergen: Chr. Michel-

sens Institutt, 1958); Daniel Bell, *The End of Ideology* (Glencoe: The Free Press, 1960), esp. pp. 369–375; and S. M. Lipset, *Political Man* (Garden City: Doubleday, 1960), esp. pp. 403–417. Daniel Bell has written of the "post-industrial society." See his "The Post Industrial Society" (mimeographed, 1962). Ralf Dahrendorf describes comparable phenomena as the "post-capitalist society." See his *Class and Class Conflict in Industrial Society* (Stanford: Stanford University Press, 1959), esp. pp. 241–318, and Gunnar Myrdal, *Beyond the Welfare State* (New Haven: Yale University Press, 1960). George Lichtheim has commented on many of these ideas under the heading of the "postbourgeois" society. See his *The New Europe* (New York: Frederick A. Praeger, 1963), esp. pp. 175–215; see p. 194.

2. For an excellent article on this subject see Val Lorwin, "Working Class Politics and Economic Development in Western Europe," *American Historical Review*, 63 (1958), 338–351.

3. See Simon Kuznetz, "Economic Growth and Income Inequality," *American Economic Review*, 45 (1955), 4.

4. For systematic data on government ownership generally in Europe, see John O. Coppock, "Government Expenditures and Operations," in J. Frederick Dewhurst, John O. Coppock, P. Lamartine Yates, and Associates, *Europe's Needs and Resources. Trends and Prospects in Eighteen Countries* (New York: Twentieth Century Fund, 1961), pp. 436–442. See also Massimo Salvadori, "Capitalism in Postwar Europe," in *ibid*, pp. 746–758.

5. On the nature and extent of planning in postwar France see Pierre Bauchet, *La planification française. Quinze ans d'expérience* (Paris: Editions du Seuil, 1962).

6. In "Germany in 1952, something like 37 per cent of the stock of industry was State-owned." Roy Lewis and Rosemary Stewart, *The Managers: A New Examination of the English, German, and American Executives* (New York: Mentor Books, 1961), p. 233. The figure is probably lower now.

7. See Hubert Ferraton, *Syndicalisme ouvrier et social-democratie en Norvège* (Paris: Armand Colin, 1960) for a detailed analysis of the transformation of the Norwegian Labor party from a radical oppositionist to a moderate governmental party. For a detailed account of the general changes in Norway see Ulf Torgensen, "The Trend Towards Political Consensus: The Case of Norway," *Acta Sociologica*, 6, Nos. 1–2 (1962), pp. 159–172. For analysis of the changes in the Austrian parties, see Alexander Vodopivec, *Wer regiert in Österreich?* (Vienna: Verlag für Geschichte und Politik, 1961).

8. For a detailed account of the changes in the approach of the Swiss Socialist party, a movement rarely discussed in social science political analysis, see Francois Masmata, "Le parti socialiste suisse" (thesis for the Doctor of Research degree, École Politique, mimeographed, Paris: Foundation Nationale des Sciences Politiques, Cycle Supericur d'Études Politiques, 1963).

9. See Jossleyn Hennessy, "Productive Unrest in Germany," *New Society*, 1, No. 15 (January 10, 1963), pp. 21–23. For the text of the new program which favors competition, see *Die Zeit*, 22 (June 7, 1963), 14.

10. Bertram D. Wolfe, "A Century of Marx and Marxism," in Henry L. Plaine (ed.), *Darwin, Marx, and Wagner* (Columbus: Ohio State University Press, 1962), pp. 106–107.

11. See Dankwart A. Rustow, *The Politics of Compromise* (Princeton: Princeton University Press, 1955), pp. 219–223.

12. Theodore Schieder, *The State and Society in Our Times* (London: Thomas Nelson and Sons, 1962), p. 121.

13. Discussions of the problems of British and Belgian economies may be found in Michael Shanks, *The Stagnant Society* (London: Penguin Books, 1961); A. Lamfalussy, *The United Kingdom and the Six* (London: Macmillan, 1963); A. Lamfalussy, *Investment and Growth in Mature Economies: The Case of Belgium* (London: Macmillan, 1961). On recent trends in British politics see C. A. R. Crosland, *The Conservative Enemy* (London: Jonathan Cape, 1962) and Norman Birnbaum, "Great Britain: The Reactive Revolt," in M. A. Kaplan (ed.), *The Revolution in World Politics* (New York: John Wiley and Sons, 1962), pp. 31–68. On Belgium see Val Lorwin, " 'All Colors But Red': Interest Groups and Political Parties in Belgium" (mimeographed paper: Center for Advanced Study in the Behavioral Sciences, Stanford, California, 1962); Marcel Bolle de Bal, "Les sociologues, la conscience de classe et la grand grève belge de l'hiver 60–61," *Revue de l'institut de Sociologie*, 34 (1961–3), pp. 541–579; and Ernest Mandel, "The Dialectic of Class and Region in Belgium," *New Left Review*, 20 (Summer 1963), 5–31.

14. On Norway see Stein Rokkan and Henry Valen, "The Mobilization of the Periphery," *Acta Sociologica*, 6, Nos. 1–2 (1962), pp. 111–141. On France and Italy, see Mattei Dogan, "Les Bases sociales des partis politique en France et en Italie" (mimeographed paper presented at the Fifth World Congress of Sociology, September, 1962), pp. 13–14.

15. See the various studies reported in Frederick Harbison and Charles A. Myers, *Management in the Industrial World. An International Analysis* (New York: McGraw-Hill, 1959). On Italy see also Joseph L. Palombara, "La Confindustria e la politica in Italia," *Tempi Moderni*, 4 (October-December, 1961), 3–16; on France see François Bourricaud, "Le 'Jeune Patron' tel qu'il se voit et tel qu'il voudrait être," *Revue Économique*, 6 (1958), 896–911; Lewis and Stewart, *op. cit.*, esp. pp. 165–187; Harbison and Myers, *op. cit.*, p. 123.

16. See La Palombara, *op. cit.*, and Bourricaud, *op. cit.*, pp. 901, 903.

17. "Paradoxes of the French Political Community," in Stanley Hoffman, et al., *In Search of France* (Cambridge: Harvard University Press, 1963), pp. 61–62; see also Laurence Wylie, "Social Change at the Grass Roots," in *ibid.*, p. 184. For a detailed analysis of the problems of analyzing the complexity of French economic life see Raymond Aron, *France Steadfast and Changing* (Cambridge: Harvard University Press, 1960), "Myths and Realities of the French Economy," pp. 45–77.

18. Erik Allardt, "Traditional and Emerging Radicalism" (mimeographed paper), p. 5.

19. See Mattei Dogan, "Le Vote ouvrier en Europe occidentale," *Revue française de sociologie*, 1 (1960), 25–44.

20. See especially the various articles in Georges Vedel (ed.), *La Dépolitisation, mythe ou réalité?* (Paris: Armand Colin, 1962).

21. Colloque "France Forum," *La Démocratie à refaire* (Paris: Editions Ouvrières, 1963), "La Dépolitisation de l'opinion publique," pp. 15–74. The relevant comments of Rémond are on pp. 26–27; Philip's statements are on pp. 38–39.

22. See Jean Maynaud, "Apatia e responsibilita dei cittadini," *Tempi Moderni*, New Series 5, No. 9 (April–June, 1962), pp. 30–38.

23. See Arthur M. Ross, "Prosperity and Labor Relations in Western Europe: Italy and France," *Industrial and Labor Relations Review*, 16 (1962), 63–85; see also Vera Lutz, *Italy, A Study in Economic Development* (London: Oxford University Press, 1962), pp. 222–223; and Joseph A. Raffaele, *Labor Leadership in Italy and Denmark* (Madison: University of Wisconsin Press, 1962), pp. 291–293.

24. See Serge Moscovici, *Reconversion industrielle et changements sociaux* (Paris: Armand Colin, 1961), pp. 127–128.

25. E. A. Bayne, "Italy's Seeds of Peril, Part IV," *American Universities Field Staff Reports Service*, Southeast Europe Series, 10, No. 4 (July, 1962).

26. See Club Jean Moulin, *L'État et le citoyen* (Paris: Editions du Seuil, 1961), "Vers le syndicalisme d'enterprise," pp. 271–279, for an analysis of the structural pressures changing the nature of French unionism.

27. *Gallup Political Index*, Report No. 38, March, 1963, p. 34.

28. See studies completed by Affiliates of International Research Associates and reported in DIVO Institut, *Umfragen: Ereignisse und Probleme der Zeit im Urteil der Bevölkerung* (Frankfurt: Europaische Verlagsanstalt, 1959), p. 77.

29. "The French Worker: Who he is, how he lives, what he thinks, what he wants." *Réalités*, 65 (April, 1956), 8–18.

30. The findings of a study conducted for *Réalités* by IFOP, the French Gallup Poll; see also Charles Micaud, *Communism and the French Left* (New York: Frederick A. Praeger, 1963), pp. 138–139.

31. Aron, *France Steadfast and Changing*, pp. 39–40; Mattei Dogan, "Il compartamento politico degli operai francesi," *Tempi Moderni*, 9 (April, 1962), 26–27. Dogan reports that in 1952 the majority of workers supporting the Communists told interviewers that "the doctrine of this party was not the main reason for their vote" (*op. cit.*, p. 25). See also Micaud, *op. cit.*, pp. 140–141.

32. The most recent German opinion polls (March, 1963) indicate a large Social-Democratic lead (47%) over the Christian Democrats (41%). Quincy Howe, "World Press Comment," *Atlas*, 5 (1963), 324.

33. Viggo Graf Blucher, *Der Prozess der Meinungsbildung dargestellt am Beispiel der Bundestagswahl 1961* (Bielefeld: Emnid Institut, 1962), pp. 73–75. See also Heinrich Popitz, Hans Paul Bahrdt, Ernst August Jures and Hanno Kesting, *Das Gesellschaftsbild des Arbeiters* (Tubingen: Mohr-Siebeck, 1957), p. 233. Similar findings are reported in Alfred Willener, *Images de la société et classes sociales* (Berne: Stämpfli, 1957), pp. 153, 206. See also Ralf Dahrendorf, "Burger und Proletarier: Die Klassen und

ihr Schicksal," in his *Gesellschaft und Freiheit* (Munich: Pieper, 1961), pp. 133–162, esp. p. 175; Rainer M. Lepsius, "Zum Wandel der Gesellschafts-bilder in der Gegenwart," *Koelner Zeitschrift für Soziologie*, 14 (1962), 450; Hansjurgen Daheim, "Die Vorstellungen vom Mittelstand," *ibid.*, 12 (1960), 252; and Renate Mayntz, *Soziale Schichtung und Soziale Wandel in einer Industriegemeinde* (Stuttgart: Ferdinand Emke, 1958), p. 103. For a poll of workers, see Institut für Demoskopie, *Jahrbuch der Öffentlichen Meinung, 1947–1955* (Allensbach: Verlag für Demoskopie, 1956), pp. 265, 267.

34. DIVO Institut, *op. cit.*, pp. 120, 124.

35. Claude Durand, "Positions syndicales et attitudes ouvrières à l'égard du progrès technique," *Sociologie du travail*, 4 (1960), 351.

36. Mario Einaudi, J. Domenach and A. Garoschi, *Communism in Western Europe* (Ithaca: Cornell University Press, 1951), pp. 43–44.

37. Dogan, *op. cit.*, p. 26. For reports of opinion data on characteristics of working class vote, data on traits of union members and their attitudes drawn from a secondary analysis of the IBM cards of a survey of French workers completed by the French Institute of Public Opinion (IFOP) in 1956, see Richard Hamilton, "The Social Bases of French Working-Class Politics" (unpublished Ph.D. thesis, Department of Sociology, Columbia University, 1963).

38. See Lipset, *Political Man*, pp. 263–267.

39. German data indicate that the larger the plan a man works in the more likely he is to discuss politics with his fellow workers in the factory. Wolf-gang Hartenstein and Gunther Schubert, *Mitlaufen oder Mitbestimmen* (Frankfurt: Europaische Verlanganstalt, 1961), p. 25. Conversely, the larger the size of the work unit, the fewer the workers who report that they chat informally with a higher-up. See Juan Linz, *The Social Bases of West German Politics* (unpublished Ph.D. thesis, Department of Sociology, Columbia University, 1959), p. 397.

40. On the behavior of white-collar workers in various countries of Europe see Michel Crozier, "Les attitudes politiques des employés et des petits fonction-naires," in M. Duverger (ed.), *Partis politiques et Classes sociales en France* (Paris: Armand Colin, 1955), pp. 85–99; *Petits Fonctionnaires au Travail* (Paris: Centre National de la recherche scientifique, 1955); "L'ambiguité de la conscience de classe chez les employes et les petits fonctionnaires," *Cahiers Internationaux de sociologie*, 28 (1955), 78–97; "Les relations de pouvoir dans un système d'organisation bureaucratique," *Sociologie du Travail*, 1 (1960), 61–75; "Classes sans conscience ou préfiguration de la société sans classes," *European Journal of Sociology*, 1 (1960), 233–245; "Le rôle des employés et des petits fonctionnaires dans la structure française contemporaine," *Transactions of the Third World Congress of Sociology* (Amsterdam: International Sociological Association, 1956), III, 311–319; "White Collar Unions, The Case of France" (to be published, 1964); Roger Girod, *Études sociologiques sur les couches salariées* (Paris: Marcel Rivière, 1961); Fritz Croner, *Die Angestellten in der modernen Gesellschaft* (Frank-furt: Humbolt, 1954); John Bonham, *The Middle Class Vote* (London: Faber and Faber, 1954); David Lockwood, *The Blackcoated Worker* (Lon-

don: Allen and Unwin, 1958); E. Dahlstrom, *Tjanstemännen, Naringlivet och sämhallet* (Stockholm: Studieförbundet näringsliv och Samhälle, 1954).

41. Kirchheimer, *op. cit.*, p. 148.

42. It is interesting to note that a similar pattern has emerged within the United States. See Herbert J. McClosky, Paul J. Hoffman, and Rosemary O'Hara, "Issue Conflict and Consensus Among Party Leaders and Followers," *American Political Science Review*, 54 (June, 1960), 406–427.

43. Source: E. A. Bayne, "Italy's Seeds of Peril," I, *American Universities Field Staff Reports Service*, Southeast Europe Series, 10, no. 1 (June, 1962), p. 7, and "Unions on the March Again," *The Economist*, April 13, 1963, p. 137.

44. For Germany see the *Statistisches Jahrbuch*, 1959, p. 179, and for France in 1954 see Institut national de la statistique et des études economiques, *Mouvement Economique en France de 1944 à 1957* (Paris: Presses Universitaires, 1958), p. 42.

45. See Jack P. Gibbs and Kingsley Davis, "Conventional Versus Metropolitan Data in the International Study of Urbanization," in Jack P. Gibbs (ed.), *Urban Research Methods* (Princeton: D. Van Nostrand Co., 1961), pp. 422–424.

46. William Kornhauser, *The Politics of Mass Society* (Glencoe: The Free Press, 1959), pp. 143, 150. The degree of urbanization was measured by the proportion of the population living in cities with over 20,000 population, while industrialization was measured by the proportion of the labor force in nonagricultural occupations.

47. The change in the Italian occupational structure has been dramatic. See Bayne, "Italy's Seeds of Peril," II, no. 2 (June, 1960), p. 6.

48. See Edvard Bull, Jr., *Arbeidermilje under det industrielle gjennombrudd. Tre norske industristrok* (Oslo: 1958), as cited in Stein Rokkan and Henry Valen, "Parties, Elections and Political Behavior in the Northern Countries: A Review of Recent Research," in Otto Stammer (ed.), *Politische Forschung* (Koln: Westdeutscher Verlag, 1960), pp. 107–108, 110; Lipset, *Political Man*, pp. 68–71. See also John C. Leggett, "Uprootedness and Working-Class Consciousness," *American Journal of Sociology*, 68 (1963), 682–692. Leggett also cites various historical studies which point to the link between "uprootedness" and radicalism.

49. Lipset, *Political Man*, pp. 187, 198, 236; see also S. M. Lipset, *Agrarian Socialism* (Berkeley: University of California Press, 1950), pp. 176–177.

50. Allardt, "Traditional and Emerging Radicalism," p. 21. In an earlier study Allardt has demonstrated that areas with the highest proportions of unemployed during the depression gave the highest support to the Communists in 1951–1954. See Eric Allardt, *Social Struktur och Politisk Aktivitet* (Helsingfors: Söderstrom and Co., 1956), p. 84.

51. Greece may be an exception to this generalization. See Marcello Dell' Omodarme, "Greece Moves Toward Dictatorship," *Atlas*, 3 (1962), 301–305 (translated from *Communitá*, December, 1961).

52. An analysis of the similarities in the approaches of the Yugoslav and Italian Communists may be found in Francois Fejto, "Le parti communiste français et le 'polycentrisme,' " *Arguments*, 6 (1962), 69–70.

53. See Walter Z. Laqueur, "The End of the Monolith: World Communism in 1962," *Foreign Affairs*, 40 (1962), 362.

54. Quoted in The Editorial Department of Hongqi, *More on the Differences Between Comrade Togliatti and Us* (Peking: Foreign Languages Press, 1963), p. 13.

55. Togliatti's report, *op. cit.*, p. 130. (Emphasis mine.) For a discussion of some of the issues underlying the question of Marx and Engels' original position, the influence of the Paris Commune on them, and Communist revisionism, see S. M. Lipset, "The Sociology of Marxism," *Dissent*, 10 (1963), 59-69. This is a review article on George Lichtheim, *Marxism: An Historical and Critical Study* (New York: Frederick A. Praeger, 1961). This book must also be read in this context. Lichtheim argues that Marxism as a revolutionary doctrine is appropriate only to countries in the period of early industrialization.

56. In Italy see Giorgio Galli, "Italy," in Walter Laqueur and Leopold Labedz (eds.), *Polycentrism: The New Factor in International Communism* (New York: Frederick A. Praeger, 1962), pp. 127–140; and Giorgio Galli, "Italy: The Choice for the Left," in Leopold Labedz (ed.), *Revisionism* (New York: Frederick A. Praeger, 1962), pp. 324–336.

57. For an indication of the diversity of opinion and level of open debate which exists among the leadership of the Italian Communist party, see the translations of the report published in *L'Unità*, the organ of the party, of a two-day debate within the central committee. Perry Anderson, "Debate of the Central Committee of the Italian Communist Party on the 22nd Congress of the C.P.S.U.," *New Left Review*, Nos. 13–14 (January-April, 1962), pp. 151–192. For the history of open debate within the Italian party, see Guglielmo Negri and Paolo Ungari, "La vita dei partito," in Alberto Spreafico and Joseph La Palombara (eds.), *Elezioni e comportamento politico in Italia* (Cremona: Edizioni di Communitá, 1963, pp. 175–180.

58. But for a different interpretation, see Lichtheim, *op. cit.*, p. 180.

59. See Pierre Fougeyrollas, "France," in Laqueur and Labedz, *op. cit.*, pp. 141–151.

60. An excellent analysis of the differences between the Italian and French parties may be found in Fejto, *op. cit.*, pp. 66–72. A similar point is made by Laqueur, *op. cit.*, p. 369.

61. See Ignazio Silone's essay in R. Crossman (ed.), *The God That Failed* (New York: Harper and Bros., 1949), pp. 106–112, and Antonio Gambino, "Togliatti's Balancing Act," *Atlas*, 3 (1962), 126–127 (translated from *L'Espresso*, December 31, 1961).

62. See Michel Crozier, "La France, terre de commandement," *Esprit*, 25 (1957), 790–792.

63. See Hamilton, "The Social Bases of French Working-Class Politics," p. 59. See also Crozier, "La France, terre de commandement."

64. Richard Lowenthal, "The Rise and Decline of International Communism," *Problems of Communism*, 12 (March-April 1963); see also Laqueur, *op. cit.*, pp. 371–373.

65. See S. M. Lipset, *The First New Nation* (New York: Basic Books, 1963), pp. 321–335.

66. A quick glance at any statistical table reporting on income or consumption standards in Europe suggests the extent to which European affluence is considerably below that of the United States. See J. Frederick Dewhurst, "Consumption Levels and Patterns," in Dewhurst, et al., *op. cit.*, pp. 146–147, 161–162; P. Lamartine Yeates, "Household Operations," in Dewhurst, et al., *op. cit.*, pp. 266, 267, 1005; Report of DOXA, XV, No. 16, August, 1961, p. 2; and "Tableau général de la consommation des français de 1950 à 1960," *Consommation*, 8 (July-December, 1961), 5–174.

67. T. H. Marshall, *op. cit.*, p. 87.

68. *Ibid.*, p. 268.

69. See Howe, *op. cit.*, pp. 325–326. See also John Goldthorpe and David Lockwood, "Not So Bourgeois After All," *New Society*, 1, No. 3 (October 18, 1962), p. 19.

70. Marshall, *op. cit.*, pp. 269–270.

71. See H. Bouterline Young, "Detection and Encouragement of the Talented in Italian Schools," *The British Yearbook of Education, 1962* (London: Evans Brothers, 1962), pp. 275–280. See also Christiane Peyre, "L'Origine sociale des élèves de l'enseignement secondaire en France," in Jean Floud, et al., *Ecole et société* (Paris: Marcel Rivière, 1959), p. 10.

72. See Mark Abrams, "Social Class and Political Values" (paper presented to the British Sociological Association, Scottish Branch, Conference in Edinburgh, May 3–4, 1963), pp. 13–14.

ALAIN TOURAINE

Management and the Working Class in Western Europe

I Introduction

THE concept of social class acquired its practical importance in a specific historical context: the beginnings of large-scale industry in western Europe. This happened not because it was here that large numbers of workers were assembled in mines and factories for the first time—this would explain the new forms of social stratification but not the development among workers of class consciousness and class action based on the idea and experience of social exclusion. These two ideas arose from the fact that in Europe economic development took place with a minimum of access to power or even to modern forms of consumption for the new working class. Social control of economic activity was held almost exclusively by those who brought about industrialization.

It seems an exaggeration to say that the play of political forces was at that time reduced to a conflict among leading economic groups, especially between landed interests and industrialists; but the necessary corrections—which Marx himself considered—of this oversimplified image should not conceal the fact that the economic transformation of European societies took place within a system of limited democracy based on property qualifications. This early industrial society, although sometimes troubled by popular uprisings or Bonapartist movements, was easily able to withstand them. This was especially true in England, where the entry of the new labor and urban forces into political life, achieved through the electoral reforms of 1832, 1867, 1884–1885, and finally 1918, was very gradual. Full democracy, based on universal suffrage, lagged far behind the progress of mass production.

There was also a lag between mass production and mass consumption. Even though there were important changes in the workers' standard of living, especially in periods of prosperity, their style of life remained traditional, even after the commercial concentration introduced by the first big department stores. This historical lag between capitalistic accumulation and industrial development on the one hand and the slow progress of democracy and mass consumption on the other explains why the working class at first conceived itself to be proletarian, excluded both in and out of work from all control of economic development.

In the middle of the twentieth century these characteristics peculiar to European industrialization have, on the whole, disappeared. The political influence of industrial workers is extensive, and even when not in possession of power they have, to use Lipset's classical distinction, an important access to power. Mass consumption has been introduced more slowly, but it is one of the obvious characteristics of social evolution since the end of World War II. Should one therefore conclude that the "European" sense of the concept of social class belongs to the past and that the situation of industrial workers, like that of all other socio-occupational groups, ought to be defined in terms of their possession of social goods, such as money, education, power or prestige? One might add—and we will return to this later—that the situation of workers, like that of white-collar employees or farmers, is less and less homogeneous, sociologically speaking. For example, an important proportion of workers have an economic level or a level of technical competence superior to that of those in certain occupational categories, while these same workers remain more strictly subjected to authority than do white-collar workers or civil servants, have a lower level of education and, according to Halbwachs' analysis, remain on the outskirts of society, further removed from the symbolic centers of social life.

But it is impossible today to claim that one can define the conditions of the working class in terms of social exclusion, continued proletarianization or absolute pauperization. In any case, the proletarian conception of the working class was introduced here only to avoid overhasty conclusions. If in fact one adopts such a concept, then the disappearance of the exceptional historical situation which created it and gave it importance must necessarily cause us to acknowledge certain facts: the end of ideologies, of the revolutionary class struggle, of the intellectually and politically conscious avant-garde of the workers' movement; and at the same time their replacement by systems of inequality with tensions and demands inevitable in an industrialized hierarchical society organized bureaucratically.

Both conceptions, opposed to each other though they are in tenor, share the common idea that class action is the expression of a certain degree of participation in the operations of society. Ostracism from society is only one extreme; the other would be perfect integration, a complete coordination of the interests and opinions of the workers on one side and the organization of society on the other, such as great utopians like Fourier dreamed. The utopian theme is no more absent from contemporary industrial societies than is the "proletarian" theme. One finds examples of a concept which, recalling Rousseau as well as Lewin, seeks, in view of the gains made in terms of social and economic rights, to raise democracy to the level of primary relationships and informal groups—an idea which has resulted in a faction within the French Student Union movement—thus continuing a long tradition derived from anarchism and sometimes from Trotskyism.

Whether one takes a position at one extreme or the other or on the more realistic middle ground which is the analysis of social stratification, one does not approach directly the study of social movements, of social classes as "agents of history," elements of socio-political dynamics. To stress the possibility of another mode of analysis is in no way to underestimate the importance of studies of social stratification. But first this other mode must be briefly defined.

II Proto-industrial Class Relations

Class consciousness, as the term is used within this other mode of analysis, occurs when one socio-occupational group, basing its claims on the economic necessity of its own role in production and conscious therefore of its participation in an organized system whose aim is technological and economic rationality, comes into conflict with another social group which seems to be opposed (through its private interests) to the public interest—that is, to "progress"—in both the economic and the social spheres. Class consciousness therefore exists only when a conflict of private interests is seen in the context of the whole social system and when at the same time it emphasizes fundamental values—in this case the economic and technical development of production. If one is willing to accept such a definition, one must first recognize the existence in western Europe of social forces involved in conflicts more elementary than those based on class consciousness.

Some workers, especially skilled workers, oppose management's profits by the defense of their craft. The conflict therefore arises from two equally private principles, work and capital, without the least reference to industrial society and to economic development as such. This sort of conflict is more common when craft unions have continued to exist in spite of the development of industrial unionism. The printers as a group still represent this defense of workers' autonomy and try to control and reduce the supply of labor in order to strengthen their bargaining power with the employers.

If these workers focus their consciousness of themselves and of society on the defense of their occupational role, others are more fundamentally sensitive to the dependent position in which they find themselves. The miners are the most striking example of such awareness. They do not struggle, like the printers or the masons, to defend their craft, since their activity is defined primarily in terms of hard work and output. It is not their work but their capacity to work that is involved, and that is, according to them, exploited by the employer. The principle of opposition is more basic for them than the principle of identity, but no more than the former group do they think of themselves in relation to the concept of industrial society. The context in which they see themselves is not the abstraction of economic development; it is the nation or the region, that is, a concrete social or cultural community. This orientation is all the more clear cut as management itself is less engaged in a policy of development, either because it lacks "production-mindedness" or because of unfavorable economic conditions. Thus it is in Belgium, in the basic industries of the Walloon districts, that a workers' movement characterized both by economic opposition and by appeals to the nation has best maintained itself. The writings of A. Renard immediately after the war clearly show the continuation of protest unionism seconded by an appeal to the national interest against the domination of the banking class. This recalls the point of view of Jaurès, formed in the Carmaux mines, which united in the same way social claims and an appeal to the national conscience. Socialist on one side of the Franco-Belgian frontier, Communist on the other, this type of workers' consciousness is today modified by a new situation—the relative decline of these old industries and the difficulties of their adaptation—but it nevertheless continues also to operate in its traditional form.

It was in the industries where technological progress, scientific management and concentration of business and market controls had developed most vigorously in the latter part of the nineteenth century, that is, in the mechanical and electrical industries—especially in the big companies—that skilled workers first united the defense of labor and the opposition to management within the context of an industrial society. They were looking to the future. Their occupational status in itself did not wholly explain the workers' action, but it determined their basic attitudes toward labor and industry and it fostered the growth of class consciousness. In France, the large-scale strikes of June, 1936, many of them sit-down strikes, are still remembered by the workers as the most important movement and the greatest victory of the century. We shall soon see why contemporary workers' attitudes are shifting further and further

373

away from this framework of crisis, but in those countries where crisis was most strongly manifested without being dominated by a totalitarian regime, it remains a model often cited with hope and nostalgia. The union leaders of today grew up under the influence of conflicts largely fed by class consciousness; their personal experience affects the whole labor movement.

A common factor unites these three types of labor attitudes: none of them is directed toward the company. A more or less strong relationship is established between the class or workers' group and the nation or capitalist regime, and the only role left for the company is that of providing the marketplace where the opponents meet and agree or fight; it is rarely considered an organization in itself. That is why the type of conflict to which we have referred involves only a frail unionization within the company and therefore leaves great freedom of action to management, which behaves in a technocratic, a paternalistic or an essentially capitalistic manner.

When the workers' attitudes are organized around the craft, the employees are primarily concerned with the market. The absence of rational mass production obliges them to work to order; concern with competition, with finding capital and customers, absorbs all their energy. Their attention rarely turns to the business itself; it is satisfied to provide a purely regimented system of authority. These employers rarely become modern entrepreneurs. Hardening their management policies, they come up against labor class consciousness reinforced by the old defense of workers' autonomy.

In the case where labor is defined in terms of work and output and where workers' action is dictated by direct and often personal hostility against the bosses and their representatives, management fights back by an attempt to organize labor, sometimes in the form of direct pressure, sometimes by indirect pressure and especially by building company towns or by other paternalistic measures. These measures are the more effective as the worker is closer to his rural origin or as he was recruited at a distance from industrial centers. German and French steel mills and coal mines have offered and still offer today many examples of such policies.

Finally, just as labor's class consciousness can be linked to the initial stages of rationalized mass production, management can be composed of men who are at the same time capitalists and organizers. Often this type of employer comes into being through the transformation of the paternalistic type, giving rise to a curious mixture of paternalism and rationalization.

Class relations in these "traditional" situations are nearly always limited to those which link and oppose management and workers.

The rural world is a society apart, still more archaic than the first of the three industrial types described. The chief conflict in rural society is between producers and merchants, or sometimes between producers and absentee owners in a region of large estates. It is not possible here to discuss rural problems, which belong only indirectly to the analysis of economic development and of the social transformation of societies already industrial. As for civil servants, they appear either as a bureaucracy in the Marxist sense, that is, as the instruments of political domination in the hands of the ruling classes, as white-collar workers not directly involved in economic life, or finally as allies of the industrial proletariat.

III The Wage Earner in a Technological Society

It is quite clear that this industrial society no longer corresponds to anything but archaic socio-economic relations in contemporary Europe; therefore one should stress first not its decline but the aspects of social change that reinforce it. Western Europe, with the exception of Great Britain, weakened and disorganized by the war and its aftermath, is more a region of reconstruction and growth than it is an affluent society. It is not yet what Riesman calls a post-industrial society, and its social problems in recent years have continued to be strongly affected by the priority given to rehabilitation and industrial growth. The importance of industrial workers within the working class has increased considerably since the beginning of the century. The primary sector, which constituted 60 per cent of the labor force in France in 1850, today absorbs less than 25 per cent. If the number of independent farmers has diminished, that of salaried farm hands has fallen even faster; in France, from 1,200,000 in 1946 to 750,000 in 1954. Domestic services are also declining—by 16 per cent in Germany between 1938 and 1956. Finally, transportation (which is sometimes classed in the secondary, sometimes in the tertiary sector) has either declined in manpower, as in France from 1946 to 1954, or progressed less rapidly than the rest of the labor force, as in Germany. Western Europe is becoming predominantly industrial. Although Europe had 7.2 per cent of the world's labor force in 1958, it furnished only 2.4 per cent of the world's primary employment, while accounting for 11.9 per cent of the tertiary sector and, most important, 14 per cent of the secondary sector.

If one considers only the wage earners, one observes that between 1948 and 1956 in Germany their number in the tertiary sector increased from 5,3000,000 to 6,800,000, that is, by approximately 28 per cent, and in the secondary sector it increased from 6,600,000 to 10,900,000, that is, by approximately 65 per cent. The rural exodus, especially in Italy, and the small increase in the labor force in transportation, trade, banks and insurance companies strengthens the position of the industrial worker. In France the development of the tertiary sector is due fundamentally to the growth of the public services—especially teaching and the professions. It should be particularly stressed that commerce and the hotel business accounted for the same proportion of the tertiary sector in France in 1954 as in 1906 (about 35 per cent) and that the proportion in transportation is the same as in 1896 (about 14 per cent). Similarly, in England, the proportion of trade in total employment was the same in 1951 as in 1911 (13.5 per cent). Employment in banks and insurance companies has greatly increased in Germany since the war, and in France between 1954 and 1962. This increase is an aspect of the growth of big business, whether industrial, commercial or administrative, rather than an aspect of growth in the tertiary sector as such.

More generally, the secondary sector in Great Britain represented 47 per cent of the labor force as against 44 per cent in the tertiary sector in 1901; in 1951, these figures were about 49 and 46 per cent. Contrary to certain forecasts made at the end of the war, the secondary sector is in no way on the decline. It is reasonable to expect that the distribution of the labor force in western Europe will tend in the future to approach that of the United States, but such a generalization tends to gloss over certain important characteristics of contemporary Europe as a region in the process of industrial development.

The observations are also affected by the framework in which they are presented. Without denying the validity of the classic division of labor into primary, secondary and tertiary sectors, I prefer a classification that distinguishes between (a) the production of primary consumer goods, especially food and clothing; (b) production and the maintenance of human and material elements essential to the growth of production; and (c) services to individuals and groups.

The first of these categories, whose essential elements are agriculture and the clothing and leather industries, is in clear decline. The second category, which includes power plants and manufacturing industries as well as education, health services, banks and insurance companies, is developing rapidly. The third category, which includes commerce, administration and leisure-time activities, is progressing less rapidly in the present phase, a fact which proves the "industrial" character of the western European nations, where production remains more important than consumption. Activities most directly connected with economic growth are those which are progressing most rapidly. Above all, an increasing number of jobs outside of the traditional domain of industry, can be defined by their role in economic and technical growth. This evolution is particularly evident in two sectors of employment.

First, clerks employed by private companies or by the state, whose function used to be primarily part of a chain of command defined by a certain degree of delegated authority, are in the process of becoming more like "technicians" or "workers." This is caused by the mechanization of office work—especially well described by H. P. Bahrdt—and administrative concessions to economic preoccupations and duties, as shown by the researches of M. Crozier and J. P. Worms on the transformation of prefectoral administration in France. Second, technicians and engineers, becoming more numerous in the modernized industries, which are in turn increasingly dominated by both technical imperatives and collective bargaining, consider themselves less as supervisors and more as technicians, even as professionals. The entry of these groups into the labor movement is clear in the most advanced industries, as O. Benoit has demonstrated in his study of technicians in a French company manufacturing electrical equipment. Public opinion in France was astonished by the active solidarity—formerly unthinkable—of the mining engineers with the striking miners early in 1963 and even more by the leading role of technicians and engineers in industrial conflicts in companies such as Neyrpic or Thompson-Houston, which operate on a high technological level.

If it is legitimate to speak of the substitution of wage earners for the proletariat, it is not only in order to define the wage earner in terms of his type of income. Much more important is his direct connection with production in an increasingly mechanized society. The survey of Italian white-collar workers by Anfossi in the collective study *Lavoratori e sindacati di fronte alle trasformazioni del processo produttivo*, edited by F. Momigliano, shows that they consider themselves primarily to be "dependents" of industry and not an occupational category fundamentally different from the other workers. This feeling of inclusion in production and in relations of social dependence is also often found at the opposite end of the scale, among workers of agricultural or rural origin. These workers, subjected to an often brutal transformation of their occupational, social and cultural life, usually begin on the lowest level of industrial work. Living in the city slums or in the shantytowns on the outskirts of the large cities, they may react as a marginal group, easily manipulated by demagogues and responsive to revolutionary unionism. This attitude is linked to their awareness of entering an "open" economy and labor market but not into a society whose organization is profoundly transformed by their arrival. One extreme case of considerable importance in numerical terms, especially in Switzerland but also in Germany, Belgium and France, is that of workers who come from Italy, Spain, Portugal, Greece, North Africa and more recently black Africa and who constitute the lowest socio-occupational group, the "lower-lower class." Their foreign origin and their frequent desire to return after a few years to their native country place them on the fringes of a society which is not modified by their arrival but which has only acquired a new lowest level. If their social status is less marginal, movements of revolt, both industrial strikes and peasant uprisings or "Jacqueries" may develop, but industrial growth weakens these movements by assuring new jobs and a virtually guaranteed wage.

When there is a greater continuity between the milieu of departure and the milieu of arrival, permitting the newcomer to consider his migration as a personal step forward and not only as an occupational change, these workers of rural origin have a strong self-consciousness and hope of upward mobility. They remain on the outskirts of the workers' group and of the business in which they find themselves temporarily placed and think only of leaving it unless they are forced to acknowledge failure, in which case their withdrawal from society becomes even greater (see O. Ragazzi and A. Touraine, *Ouvriers d'origine agricole* [1961]). However, there is a third situation of greater importance in Italy than in the other countries: the new members of the labor or white-collar groups, partly because they are numerous and concentrated in one area, are aware that they are transforming older patterns of social relations. They represent the "new nation," as was the case in Argentina, where the new workers who came to live in greater Buenos Aires during the principal phase of economic development, between 1930 and 1945, constituted the chief support of the Peronist movement. In Italy, the mass arrival of new workers has contributed directly— and even more indirectly—to the development of a consciousness of the importance of economic growth; it has also shaken the traditional unwillingness of the older working class to think and act in the context of economic growth.

The attitude of the new workers, therefore, depends not on what could be called their degree of participation in the definition of goals and in the social relations of the occupational sector into which they come. Here we touch upon one of the main principles of our analysis. Social movements, and therefore the existence of social classes as "agents of history," cannot be defined by a simple change in the composition of the labor force or in the worker's standard of living. They must be defined primarily in terms of the kind of relations in which different categories of workers stand to the values of industrial civilization, that is, to the rationalized development of production. Social relations differ according to whether a society's economic development is planned or haphazard.

IV Neo-liberal Society

The characteristics of industrialization inherited by Europe from the nineteenth and early twentieth centuries have been aggravated by the fact that the exclusion of the working class from the social controls over economic activity was reinforced by a very solid traditional class structure. Owners and workers conceived of themselves in terms of ascription more than of achievement, that is, as social and cultural groups providing their members with specific aspirations and opportunities from the start. Each group was an "estate" whose existence was determined not by an occupational role but by the place it occupied in a social order itself determined by non-economic values. The great strides made by the industrial wage earners mentioned above meant, in western Europe as in all industrial societies, a decline of the concept of social classes as "subsocieties" and their gradual replacement by socio-occupational categories organized in hierarchies.

Given the past power of the bourgeoisie in Europe, the most striking feature is the continued evolution of management. Harbison and Burgess, in *The American Journal of Sociology* (1954), emphasized the fact that employers kept the business "in the family," especially in France and Italy, and that they maintained the principles by which E. Goblot defined the bourgeoisie in 1925: "barrier and level." H. W. Ehrmann, in *Organized Business in France* (1957), recalled the desire on the part of French employers for stability, the protection of small marginal firms by the big—who preferred to insure their profits in this way, rather than to extend their production—and the determination of the employers to maintain for themselves and their descendents a certain standard of living. M. Duchemin, head of the Confédération Générale du Patronat Français, has drawn a naïvely complacent portrait of these employers (*L'organisation syndicale du patronat en France* [1940]), which still portrays accurately some sectors of management. Faced with the economic transformations of the postwar period, these employers, especially the small and middle-sized ones, turned from mere conservatism to a reactionary point of view. Their attitude approached a Poujadism of the small businessmen, craftsmen and professionals whose individualism is directly threatened by economic concentration and technological progress.

The big companies, on the contrary, are headed more and more by leaders recruited not from the hereditary class but clearly from the middle or upper socio-occupational categories, who rose to the top by their own efforts and who enjoy a freedom increased by the growth of self-finance, by the decline of the capital market— especially conspicuous since the war—and by the growing complexity of the internal problems of the various companies, whether financial, economic or technical.

In Italy especially, the rapid and thorough transformation of the economy has diminished the importance of heredity in the choice of senior executives. Even though the categories in the survey made for Italian Shell (*La classe dirigente italiana* [1961]) are too broad, since it includes both economic and administrative leaders, one notes that only 13.3 per cent of these leaders are sons of industrialists. Sons of professionals make up 23.3 per cent; 13.5 per cent are sons of white-collar workers, 14.1 per cent sons of small businessmen, 11.1 per cent sons of civil servants or teachers. It is their parents' level of education that is most important in the recruiting of these leaders; the ratio between their level of education and that of their parents is approximately 1, whereas for members of the clergy the ratio is about 2.92 and for politicians about 1.75, which indicates that the parents of the latter groups were, on the whole, of a much lower educational level.

Especially in Great Britain and in France, nationalization of industries has created a new type of management, naturally anxious to defend the company against the demands of the state but aligned with it in its fight against certain financial or industrial groups. The name of E. Mattei has become the symbol of these industrial leaders who favor the national development of industry and who desire at the same time the strengthening of big business as the center of economic decisions. The role of these industrial or administrative "promoters" is variously combined with that of the financial and industrial groups. In Germany and in Holland the economic initiative belongs to big industrial corporations which frequently extend beyond national boundaries. It is within these corporations that the role of the new executive develops. In Belgium more than in the other European countries, some big banks, especially the Societé Générale, continue to manage a large sector of the economy directly and thereby considerably reduce the field of operation open to "new" executives. In Italy and especially in France the role of the state in economic development is more direct, a fact which has given rise to a more autonomous group of industrial executives without, however, eliminating the other types of industrial leaders. In a more balanced manner, Great Britain contains examples of all three types.

The growing role of the executive is therefore not directly tied to a decline in traditional class relations, since that role seems to be more conspicuous when there is great conflict between the effort toward economic development and the weight of traditional society and its institutions. For the moment we will draw only one conclusion from this observation: the decline of the old class relations is more evident when economic expansion is directed by big private companies in the form of a "social market economy," in Professor Erhard's definition. This conclusion parallels Lipset's observations when in his brilliant analysis of "Political Man" he examines the conditions of the existence and strength of democracy.

When economic power is concentrated in business, management tends to consider the workers as members of the company first occupationally, by adopting—in Germany and Italy more than in France—systems of job evaluation, that is, by substituting evaluation of a job's level for evaluation of a man's skill, and by emphasizing training, promotion or occupational upgrading; second economically, by discussing wages and working conditions with union representatives; and finally in a social sense, through a policy often called "human relations," one of whose effects is to break down the hierarchical traditional relations fraught with class connotations and to give the social relations within the business greater autonomy compared to those which continue to exist in the society at large. It is one of the main principles of company policy during economic expansion to intervene in workers' affairs in as limited and specific a way as possible. The decline of traditional class relations is thus connected to the transition from extensive action on the worker as a "whole man" to intensive action in terms of his occupational role.

In this type of social situation, more important in Germany than in Great Britain, in Great Britain than in France, trade union strategy follows the same general "neo-liberal" path, and R. Dahrendorf has clearly analyzed the practices of the German union movement as opposed to its unworkable ideology of codetermination.

The most important fact encountered in all industrial societies is the fragmentation of the workers' grievances the moment that traditional class consciousness, and still more the proletarian consciousness, is weakened. The situation of a worker in mass-production industries can be analyzed in terms of constraining pressures, some growing out of the technological organization, others associated with management administration, others depending upon the system of decision making in the economic and social policy of management. A differentiation is created between those who are involved directly in the manufacturing process and those who intervene from outside or who are allowed a certain initiative. Sometimes a substantial group of workers shares along with the technicians in the control, maintenance or planning of the production process. A generally bigger group continues to be mere manpower judged on its output, whether it tends machines or watches for signals to operate the machines from afar. In the same way the economic and social goals of production (especially when it provides consumer goods or fills the exacting needs of scientific and technical specifications) appear to many as socially unquestionable, whereas in other cases the notion of profit comes between workers and management in an obvious manner. Finally, the internal organization of the firm—industrial, administrative or commercial—increases or diminishes the intensity of those conflicts inherent in every large organization which is rationalized and technologically complex.

We do not mean to say here that the working class, as a socio-occupational category, is more heterogeneous now than it was. One could easily maintain the contrary; but an assertion of either proposition would confuse two kinds of problems, those of socio-occupational stratification and those of social class. In this light, heterogeneity in the working class continues to grow in proportion as the workers conceive of themselves more in terms of their situation in the plant rather than in terms of their occupational, social and cultural characteristics. Workers naturally carry these characteristics into the business, but they cannot be defined in relation to its operation. The well-known and growing gap between life at work and life away from work is added to this fragmentation of social problems within the plant. Industrial areas are increasingly being separated from residential areas, and the worker spends a proportionately greater time commuting to his job, particularly in the big cities.

One may add, as suggested by a survey made in France, that in those big cities where tertiary activities are extremely numerous, the proportion of families composed entirely of industrial workers is diminishing. Not only in the mining regions but also in the average industrial towns, where office work and commercial activities offer few opportunities to white-collar workers, it is usual for the family to live exclusively on the worker's wage, which is sometimes supplemented by the products of a small vegetable garden. However, in cities like Paris the women find many opportunities for employment outside industry, a circumstance which contributes to the breakdown of the social and cultural unity of the working class family.

Finally, it is useless to insist that the democratization of comfort and the progress of mass consumption will reduce the gap between workers and nonworkers. Even if the former have on the whole a lower level of consumption than other groups, and even if a large proportion of European workers live on the margin of poverty (especially where housing conditions are poor, as in France and Italy) it is still necessary to recall that a rise in the standard of living or the diffusion of automobiles or television sets cannot in themselves cause a disappearance or even a weakening of industrial conflicts. These conflicts spring neither from scarcity nor from the mode of distribution of wealth, but from the ratio—considered unsatisfactory and unjust—between technological and economic progress on the one hand and social progress on the other. The most serious conflicts break out when management seems unable to foster economic progress and passes on to employees the burden of unemployment while displaying its own conspicuous consumption in contrast to their employees' poverty.

In neo-liberal societies conflicts tend to be no less sharp, but they are more limited than in other societies. Instead of there being a great distance—with concomitant acute tension—between a centralized system of economic decision making on the one hand and consumption defined in terms of different styles of life on the other, these two factors meet on the intermediary plane of the company. Conflicts then arise from the relatively underpriviledged situation of one group, whose criteria of underprivilege become more and more varied. The assembly-line worker wants to be paid more in return for his fatigue and his boredom; the worker in a leading industry wants a higher wage because wages represent only a small part of the total cost of production. The growing complexity of types of jobs and of their criteria of evaluation increases the likelihood of conflicts which take place within a system of organization which is not itself challenged. This produces a situation which allows hope for a better standard of living and which brings about a softening of the conflicts as well as a simplification of negotiations because they are more directly economic. In France, where no big union accepts such a neo-liberal situation as a matter of principle, sharper and sharper tensions break out between the militant union leaders of the growing and most modern companies, eager to increase as much as possible their economic bargaining power, and the local, regional or national labor leaders more interested in a general social change. More than in the CFTC, it is in the FO, and particularly in the metallurgical and petroleum industries, that this tendency

383

manifests itself; it is the same in Italy, where this tendency is stronger in the UIL than in the CISL, and there still more than in the CGIL.* It is in this context that one may speak of the end of ideologies and more generally that one may discern distrust of "positions of principle." An optimistic empiricism is developing, bent on destroying the cumbersome ruins of the centralized and administrative state, of the traditional system of education, and of the hierarchical social doctrines inherited from the beginnings of industrialization. This "realism" opposes the sentimental involvement of the intellectuals and advocates a pragmatic, nonphilosophical and nonpolitical study of economic and social problems.

V Social Contracts

Social reality can depart from this neo-liberal model only in two contradictory ways at the same time, or rather by facing the contradiction that a planned advance of society toward economic development is tied to the upholding of social barriers and archaic institutions. It is the break with the past that propels one toward the future. But it was out of the question, in western Europe during the postwar expansion, for such a movement to take on revolutionary form. It was during the period immediately after the war in Italy, and especially in France, that revolutionary strikes broke out whose purpose was to undermine conservative forces both politically and economically, and more generally to modify the traditional society. Even if one forgets for a moment the determining role of international conflicts in the evolution of social situations in nations, the state and the big companies—by insuring the economic recovery of all the western countries—allowed the general characteristics of industrial civilization we have mentioned to develop while avoiding the revolutionary question of a "general crisis" and of the insolvable contradictions inherent in a capitalistic society which is increasingly dichotomous. The twofold movement we have mentioned has been defined since the 1920's as "structural reform," but usually in terms of a pure economic theory that conceals its wider social implications.

In the neo-liberal situation analyzed in the preceding section, the two factors, of group concern for economic development and labor's attempt to control working conditions and employment without being subject to the employer's personal power, are not widely separated. These two goals—economic development and social control—seem to be tightly connected at the company level,

* Confédération Française des Travailleurs Chrétiens; Force Ouvrière; Unione Italiana del Lavoro; Confederazione Italiana dei Sindacati Liberi; Confederazione Generale Italiana del Lavoro.

because the solution of social problems is a necessary condition for the efficient operation of the organization. Such a solution is even imposed by the necessity to avoid a harsh disparity between the improvement of living and working conditions of labor and the expansion of the economy.

The situations we are considering now are those in which both the workers' wish for economic development and their desire to exert control over working conditions encounter great obstacles. In theory, one can distinguish three very different situations. In the first, economic growth which is considered adequate is accompanied by the continuation of traditional social relations, especially the autocratic power of management. In the second, on the contrary, considerable power on the part of the union, usually supported by the state, is accompanied by relative economic stagnation. In the third, workers come up against the weakness of both the economic system and a society characterized by traditional class relations.

Here it will suffice to equate roughly the first two types in order to distinguish them more clearly from the third type. We will try thus to oppose first a "reformist" situation and then a situation which in certain cases may have revolutionary possibilities to the neo-liberal situation described above. First we shall consider the reformist situation, in which both aims of the labor movement—economic and social—meet partial obstruction. Two types of industrial relations can develop. The first type attempts to maintain at the level of the company the conflict existing between participation in economic development on the one hand and the demands for social rights on the other. At first glance, this method appears rational; in most European countries since the end of the nineteenth century a whole arsenal of social legislation has protected the workers and lessened the dominant power of the employers. But these rights and unionism itself have penetrated business only slightly. It should suffice to recall that in French or Italian industry even today, the union local has no legal existence—and the defense of this existence, in one of the rare cases where it is recognized in France, in the Neyrpic factories, was an important aspect of the conflict that burst out there during the autumn of 1962. Under these circumstances, it was only through the pressure of the state, or at least of forces outside the business, that the personal power of management could be broken and at the same time that some information about the business and thus a certain participation by the employees in the decisions of the business could be assured.

Today, however, it is justifiable to say that the systems of participation by workers in management have, on the whole, failed.

Even in the case of Germany, T. Pirker and R. Dahrendorf have shown that the results of the *Mitbestimmung* were on the one hand only a development and a modernization of personnel management, which in this field gave Germany a big lead over France, where the director of personnel only painfully and with much difficulty replaces the traditional chief of personnel, who is responsible particularly for the application of administrative regulations and social laws. On the other hand, the *Mitbestimmung* resulted in an increase in the bargaining power of the unions. In Great Britain, several studies, those of W. H. Scott and his Liverpool group in particular, have shown the very limited success of joint consultation, both distrusted by the unions—which do not wish to relinquish their power to discuss wages—and held to minor duties by management, which considers it to be an adjunct of administration and not a feature of workers' representation. In Italy, however, the *commissioni interne*, when not serving as tools for the company to weaken unions by developing company unions, are the means of legal action for the union. The *comités d'entreprises* in France, of which the majority either do not function at all or are reduced to the role of administrative social work, were used by the CGT almost exclusively as a platform for the class struggle, which removed them completely from their stated official role.

The inadequacy of these attempts to have wage earners share in management arises from the fact that they do not assume or involve any "political" change in the company. Union action can operate with sufficient strength in relation to management only if (1) it concentrates entirely on exerting economic and social pressures on behalf of the wage earners—without concerning itself with problems of management—thus restoring neo-liberal social relations, or (2) it can at the same time exert pressure on a higher level than that of the company, either through contracts or through legal methods.

It is logical that the conflict between participation in economic expansion and demands for social rights should manifest itself in a relative divorce between the two kinds of union action, and this conflict represents the second type of "reformist" industrial relations. On the one hand, the action takes place at the level of the national economy. In France the unions are represented in the Economic and Social Council, in the specialized Committees of the Planning Commission, in the Commission Supérieure des Conventions Collectives, in the Commission des Comptes de la Nation, on the boards of directors of nationalized industries, etc. On the other hand, the unions try to obtain by direct—or, more successfully, by indirect—pressures social advantages such as guaranteed wages, supplementary retirement pensions and extension by law of paid vacations. By direct rather than by indirect means they try to obtain wage increases, fringe benefits or a shortened work week.

Sometimes, in Sweden or in Holland especially, the relations between the two aspects of what we call "control unionism" are well and solidly established. Union participation in economic policy at the national level is supplemented by opposition to management within the company. The wage drift in Sweden and England shows the full scope of such a combination. This double aspect of union action corresponds to the double nature of management itself, that is, as a center of decision making and as a tool for the rationalization within overall economic policy, whether public or private. It is accompanied by the active continuation of a certain class structure which can take the form of sponsoring important movements for popular education, as in the Scandinavian countries, or that of less concentrated action aiming on the one hand at the democratization of education, and on the other at the organization of mass movements more or less closely connected with political and union groups. Social relations in the company are not conceived merely as economic negotiations. They coincide with the concept of industrial democracy which, in all its forms, aims to introduce into business decision making mechanisms analogous to those of the political order. The most up-to-date theorists, like F. Bloch-Lainé in *Pour une réforme de l'entreprise* (1963), also seek to reconcile the necessary stability for management with representation of economic and social forces by acknowledging the fact that the legislative function of stockholders' meetings, or even governing boards, has become a fiction. Such conceptions of industrial democracy also assume that the unions will abandon the attitude of overall opposition at the company level. This is possible only if they possess a real access to power at a higher level—proof that the modern forms of industrial democracy, like the older formulations, correspond to a "reformist" situation, that is, *both* active participation of the social forces in economic development *and* a recognition of the necessity for concerted action to overcome social and economic obstacles encountered.

VI Policies of Economic Development

When the workers come in conflict with a weak economic system and traditional class relations, their actions tend to overturn the social system as a whole; the transformation of social relations is associated with new modes of economic direction. Nationalization of industry and the growth of state machinery must destroy both the weakness and the privileges of management. This theme, highly important between the wars, constituted a point of departure for the evolution of the labor movement in Italy and in France especially. The force of the Communist party in these nations reflected the resistance of old social and economic structures to the formation of an industrial society. As a reaction, the workers and white-collar workers and especially the civil servants who already possessed greater guarantees in relation to work and wages—usually thanks to the intervention of the state—tended to stand apart from the revolutionary tendency and to concentrate essentially on improving their conditions of work and chances of promotion. Thus the split among unions becomes a quasi-permanent characteristic of the labor movement, as a result of the continuing strength of the pre-industrial elements. The much smaller proportion of wage earners in the active population in France made it difficult to form a social-democratic or labor party like that of Great Britain. Only for brief periods of time, especially when the extreme right was strong, could a liberal middle class group, represented by the Radical party, join the working class parties and assure the triumph of a "front," which was unstable and heterogeneous but which was still capable of piercing a hole in the "wall of capital." This situation continues to this day to a considerable extent, especially at the level of official organizations and of ideology. But economic expansion has profoundly modified the conditions and significance of social movements in nations which are just becoming highly industrialized. The labor movement, and more generally what one may call the left, are actually suffering from contradictory tendencies.

The revolutionary tendency has contributed to economic development and social change. Even more than particular social and economic reform, the weakening of the classical right and the disappearance of the traditional extreme right and of the Fascists directly after the war have made possible the elimination of the former management elites and have facilitated true cooperation between the new labor movement and the new business leaders, who are especially aware of the necessity for social and economic rationalization. Nationalization of industry on the one hand and economic intervention by the state on the other gave the workers control over their jobs and the new business leaders a wide field of action at the same time. Opposition between union members and the proponents of rationalization was lessened by the memory of their joint action in the Resistance, by their shared opposition to the old management and by the necessity for economic rehabilitation in the immediate postwar period.

But as economic rehabilitation progressed, the revolutionary group became less realistic and it retreated to feeble opposition based on theoretical considerations, while simultaneously (and largely as a result of the international situation) the so-called moderate forces regained favor and were even able to come back to power. Hence the serious crisis experienced especially by the Italian labor movement. Faced with a Communist movement which stubbornly expected catastrophe in the West, the large, dynamic industries enjoyed considerable freedom of action and tried to "integrate" their workers in various ways: sometimes in a violent manner by persecuting militant union members and by creating company unions; more often by drastic limitations on the power of the unions and by creating in the occupational sphere, as in the wider economic and social sphere, new forms of dependence upon the company for industrial and white-collar workers.

The movements for union reform have struggled to resolve the problem of how to maintain the goal of an overall social change while at the same time operating within the big corporation where the major decisions are' actually made. The most spectacular effort was that of the members of the Italian CGIL and their French followers. For them the new forms of economic and social organization of labor could and should reinforce the old struggle to bring the working class to power. Since real economic power lies in big business, the demands of labor, provided that they are strong and therefore united, should logically be broadened into general economic and political action and even to democratic planning.

The very substantial result these reformers obtained was to refocus union action on the company instead of letting it exhaust itself in futile attacks on an economic system which, to say the least, does not seem to be dying. But can one escape in this way the apparent contradictions? It becomes increasingly clear that this company-oriented unionism works for relatively privileged categories, that is, for skilled labor, white-collar workers and technicians who participate directly in economic expansion and who are in a strategically favorable position. Alongside of their action, very new but very limited, two quite different types of labor action continue or are developing. One consists of the demands of groups which suffer from the unfavorable consequences of economic change and which do not profit from expansion; the other is the opposition, anarchosyndicalist in type, of the new workers, often of rural origin, who demand direct and immediate job control and who are supported by small groups of skilled workers and intellectuals faithful to the old forms of revolutionary hope. The great strikes in the Fiat factory show how great a distance separates the new company-oriented unionism from the old aspirations for worker-management. In France there is less separation between these two types of labor action than in Italy, a nation much further removed from industrial civilization right after the war and consequently much closer to the revolutionary tradition of the pre-fascist period, which was reinforced by the dominant influence of Gramsci.

In France it is not so much company-oriented unionism as democratic planning that has constituted the principal theme of renewal in union action. Proposed to the congress of the CFTC in 1959 by Declercq, taken up by minorities in the CGT and the FO and discussed in many meetings, it also meets difficulties which clearly appear just as soon as the problem of a national policy of income distribution arises, such as, can one pursue such an objective without having, at the least, a substantial access to power on the level where economic and political decisions are made? Is it not more realistic, before undertaking a general policy, to build a force of pressure and social action at the company level, bringing to an end the traditional weakness of French union organization in the shop itself? On the other hand, would this not mean a return to neo-liberal collective bargaining and the abandonment of all hope of structural reform? Here again the contradiction would appear to be insurmountable if there did not exist a proper political solution: to unite the two tendencies in a single opposition (qualified or absolute) to the Gaullist government and to its concept of union action in particular.

Our object here is not to predict the evolution of unionism in the nations where workers' participation in industrial decisions has been lagging but to observe its twofold and contradictory tendency. It is not sufficient to say that at the present time the means employed in former union gains constitute checks on economic development and social progress by reinforcing the rigidity of the machinery of the state. Such a conclusion belongs directly to the overall conception that in my opinion must be criticized. According to that view, industrial nations in the West differ from each other only by their unequal degree of participation in a single model of industrial society. European industrialization, however, has not always followed the neo-liberal model, nor does its present progress necessarily lead to a single type of affluent society. The Italian and the French labor movements, as well as German management, are still attached to older models of action, but they are not only resisting change. They are trying, in various ways, to maintain the necessary relationship between progress and integration, between the functional and structural necessities of all industrial society. Awareness of economic and political responsibilities on the part of various social groups is the positive aspect of an action whose negative aspect is a partial attachment to old forms of management or of social demands. The lure of prosperity should not lead us to dream of utopias which lead to a very inaccurate interpretation of contemporary social movements.

To try to solve the crisis of unionism by a return to economic demands alone is as unacceptable as the belief that this crisis can be easily overcome by an ideological reconciliation between the neo-liberalism of big business and the traditional will to power of the working class. These two positions have the great advantage of giving the labor movement a single orientation, but we are forced to recognize that this advantage is visible only on the ideological or theoretical plane. In practice, labor's action can be explained only by a contradiction between the desire for economic development and the necessity for the workers themselves to control the conditions of labor. The greater the obstacles to industrial development, the greater is the conflict between these two tendencies and the more the conflict takes place at a higher level, that is, in society as a whole rather than at the company level. The requirements of this large-scale perspective are often likely to exceed the real means of union action. Labor is caught between the desire to intervene generally and the well-founded fear of being obliged to participate in negotiations without having sufficient influence to make its views prevail or even to negotiate effectively at the highest level. Management, on the contrary, takes on big social and economic problems with more confidence. The great silence after the war of disorganized and uninfluential French management has given way to a willingness to take positions on the widest possible variety of subjects, if not on the part of management as a whole, at least on the part of a fairly well defined group of business leaders, organized in the Centre de Recherche des Chefs d'Entreprises and in the group Prospective. The optimism of the new leaders and their will, less for reform than for social change, is one of the newest characteristics of social life in France and in Italy. This interest goes far beyond the collective bargaining level characteristic of the first neo-liberal type of industrial society and even beyond the concern for in-plant industrial democracy, for the "social contracts" typical of the second type of industrial society.

Two problems assume special importance: education and regional planning. In both cases, indeed, discussion is undertaken explicitly in the context of economic development. Economic growth demands a growing number of technicians, a fact which makes it impossible to recruit them only from certain limited groups of the population, as was formerly done. Economic growth also requires that the human and material resources of the nation be efficiently used. No one now seriously postulates that there is a mutual opposition between education and economic organization; there is a common objective for all—social rationalization. But differences arise over what "social rationalization" is and over the means of achieving it. The chief problem is to define the conditions and terms of effective discussion of these problems, that is, to separate what all the parties concerned have in common which opposes them to conservative or reactionary forces from that which separates them from each other. Management attempts as much as possible to reduce social demands to those necessitated by economic development. The weakness of workers' movements is that in maintaining the priority of social reform, they underestimate the support that economic expansion itself gives them. Management seeks obstacles to change in order to eliminate them; labor seeks to work out complete programs of action, an effort which is more ambitious but which supposes greater power of decision making. In nations that are both confident of their capacity for development and conscious that traditional social relations offer obstacles to such development, conflict arises between these two forces, between the organizers and the reformers.

On the highest level, the debate crystallizes around the idea of planning. For management it is, according to M. Massé, a "reduction of uncertainties," and the aim of the planners should be especially to educate, to inform, to organize, to avoid the obstacles that stand in the way of the "living forces of the nation," to help them to negotiate among them. For labor, planning should be a socially clear choice of certain goals and it should possess the necessary means to realize these goals. The differences of opinion between M. Massé and M. Francois-Perroux recently underlined both the differences between these two positions and their common orientation.

VII Toward a New Class Consciousness?

In an advanced, rapidly developing society, defensive labor movements supported by the most underprivileged categories—or by those most exposed to changes they must endure without being able to control it in any way—can lead to actions of great scope or even serve as a basis for important political undertakings. Yet they cannot have that total significance on which Lukacs so rightly insists—they do not have a meaning in themselves but can be used in very different ways, sometimes even in opposite ways. In France the Communist party's campaign for the defense of the craftsmen and small businessmen threatened by big business joined the Poujadist opposition, at least in some cases and for a short time. It is impossible to imagine autonomous and creative popular movements, that is, ones giving birth to consistent social action, other than those which, in the name of workers' rights, are based on a will to promote economic development (which, in the present situation of expansion, has no sense unless it recognizes actual development) and at the same time are based on total opposition to the system of power and control which directs this development. But the strength and degree of these two objectives depend on factors in great part mutually contradictory, in my opinion, and this opposition dominates the entire field of social movements within an industrial framework.

First, awareness of economic development is greater when the connection between economic growth and social change is more evident, and this link is concealed as much by the continuation of traditional class relations as by the violence of political or, more generally, institutional crises which accompany the rapid transformation of society. France offers an extreme example. The majority of workers interviewed in surveys taken between 1954 and 1957, that is, during a period of economic expansion and rising standards of living, gave clearly pessimistic answers about the progress of the working class, answers which hardly differed from the impressions of many foreign observers conscious of the chronic crisis of the "sick man" of western Europe. This was at a time when important economic expansion and transformation were taking place in France —in many ways under somewhat unhealthy conditions. Inflation, colonial wars, governmental instability, underdevelopment of public services and administrative techniques—all these factors, which cannot here be analyzed in themselves, explain the obvious disparity between the growth of production and that of society. They explain why the expansion was not experienced as a development. One can therefore advance the hypothesis that awareness of development grows weaker as one passes from the first to the second and finally to the third type of industrial society that we have distinguished. More precisely, the closer one comes to the third type, the more the awareness of development is restricted to the limited occupational and social categories which are most directly involved in technical and economic expansion, that is, public or private executives, junior executives and technicians, and highly skilled workers in leading industries. These are all categories which are relatively privileged, professionally and economically, at least compared to the rest of the wage earners.

Second, industrial conflict tends to take place at higher levels when development is more deliberate and organized. In situations of the first type it concerns mainly working conditions and private consumption. In situations of the second type it concerns mainly the organization of the company on the one hand and the life of the working man on the other, and aims to secure guarantees on all sides. It is in the third type that it is more likely to concern the system of decision making itself. Here one first thinks of Italy, the occupational migrations having brought about in Italy a very lively awareness of the changes in society, whereas the rural exodus in France has rarely inspired conditions other than those favoring individual upward mobility.

The result is that conditions encouraging the appearance of one of the two principal components of "class-conscious" social movements—the awareness of development—are least favorable to the appearance of the other—concerted action directed against the power system of the society—and vice versa. One can admit that in the first type of society a generalized awareness of development and an elementary level of social demands (which do not rule out its considerable power) involve considerable integration of the technicians and supervisors in a more flexible kind of organization more sensitive to the requirements of professionalization than to those of discipline and traditional hierarchy. At the same time, labor constitutes a mass movement led by union leaders who are negotiators rather than innovators. In a situation of the third kind, on the contrary, it is the most highly skilled workers who initiate the most original social movements, thus playing the same role as the skilled workers in the metal industries in the early industrial period. The participation of intellectuals, as can be seen in Italy, is important in this type of social movement. In the intermediary situation the lead is taken chiefly by executives in big business, in the unions and in government service. The conditions that determine the formation of social movements in industrial societies are therefore more directly political as one approaches situations of the third type, that is, as the obstacles to development inherited from the past are greater. This is certainly the main problem. Social movements in the name of a particular class which is fairly clearly defined economically, culturally and even ecologically are no longer possible, at least where there exist important obstacles to economic development. In a way that is only superficially paradoxical, it is in the most "Americanized" situations that the theme of the "labor movement" is maintained, that social conflicts develop most easily within a society without challenging the general direction and organization of that society. The further one goes from this type of situation, the more national problems assume importance.

Even though it is not possible to enter into direct discussions of these problems here, it is also impossible to define the problems of the contemporary labor movement apart from their increasingly close connection with those of international politics, especially in terms of the unification of Europe. Indeed one cannot conceive of social movements of the type we are considering here except in a real political unity, that is, within an autonomous political system of decision making. Let us recall that this necessity becomes stronger as economic development becomes a more deliberate policy and when there is a determination to overcome the obstacles, be they economic or social. The interest shown in the construction of Europe by the German and Dutch labor movements bears this out. The difficulties are much greater for the majority factions within the French and Italian unions. In the case of France the situation is confused; union opposition to Gaullist nationalism merges with distrust of a neo-liberal Europe integrated in an Atlantic community.

In the present situation the result is that unionism is less likely to constitute a social movement for the whole society in which it wishes to operate, in proportion as its will for economic and social development and its sense of political responsibility are greater. French unionism, tempted after 1958 to take the place of the weak political parties, has very clearly resisted this temptation, recognizing the primacy of political action and organization even while suffering from the present weakness of the left. In Italy, throughout the whole period of the "opening to the left," the CGIL has remained solidly faithful to the alliance of the PCI with the PSI which is basic for the Italian labor movement.

The more difficult it is to form a concrete principle of "totality," the more what we have called the principles of identity and opposition tend to become separated. The principle of identity, which can no longer be centered on the traditional awareness of the craft, takes an increasingly corporative form, that is, defense of an occupation, of a legal status, of guarantees. The principle of opposition is stronger as an occupational category participates less directly in economic progress, and this participation depends on the organization of collective bargaining even more than does the nature of the job. It is therefore easier for these two principles to become allied in distrust and resistance than in what Y. Delamotte has called *participation conflictuelle*. In France it is in the public sector that this combination comes about most easily because it is there that the best established "statutory" regimes, that is, civil servants, miners and public transportation personnel, are found together with the most inadequate system of collective bargaining—inadequate because the management of public services enjoy very little independence.

The importance of the conflicts—sometimes chronic—which break out in this sector do not reflect merely the inability of the traditional state machinery to handle modern social and economic problems; more basic is the weakness of labor and its inability to organize itself in an overall movement oriented toward social and economic development. Such concern certainly exists, but because of insufficient access to power it cannot become a central principle of action. These conflicts therefore represent the dysfunctional aspect of a certain system of social relations. The difficulty is much less acute in situations of the second type, where the principal conflict is between both labor and management leaders on the one hand and the rank and file on the other. The latter maintain at the company level certain forms of conflict and of direct pressure.

To summarize: one may consider with Harbison and Myers, in *Management in the Modern World* (1959), that there exists a type of management and therefore also a type of working class and of industrial relations appropriate to the fully developed industrial society, and that progress toward this type is variously hampered by the existence, in the various nations, of more or less cumbersome obstacles which embody the resistance of a traditional society in both it patrimonial and administrative aspects. France and Italy are generally chosen as good examples of this kind of resistance, a factor which explains the archaism of these countries and their difficulties in becoming industrial societies. Speaking of French management, for instance, people recall the importance of small-scale family firms, more interested in stability than in progress, and it is usual to mention only in passing, as deviating from this model, the role of certain large companies or nationalized industries and planning organizations. However, one is obliged to note that these countries have not, in recent years, demonstrated a marked economic inertia. We are thus led to present an analysis somewhat different from the preceding one. We first distinguished three types of industrial societies in the process of change, and we admit that when the legacy of the past is heavy it is more likely that progress will take form in the third type rather than in the second or, still less, than in the first. But in such a case which can be defined as being both more and less advanced than the first type, important conflicts and contradictions develop. These often tend to be overcome if (1) management happens to be of the third type, concerned with progress and conscious of general social problems and thus close to what one might call state capitalism; (2) if the unions, on the contrary, tend at first to limit themselves to an attitude which results in opposition and conflict at the lower level of work and wages; and (3) if the state, faithful to its administrative role, attempts to fulfill that of arbitrator and legislator.

If the lag to be overcome is not so great, two cases must be distinguished. This lag may be primarily economic because of the relative obsolescence of industrial machinery, whereas the workers and their unions have already obtained and continue to hold on to important social gains. In this situation, the conflict between the past and the future is the least marked; continuity seems complete, for the three elements which make up the system of industrial relations—union, management and the state—are of the second type. It is then that the idea of industrial democracy—of extending political institutions to the economic field—and the idea of "constitutional" management triumph.

Second, on the contrary, the lag inherited from the past may be more social than economic, as is often the case in countries where industrialization was promoted by the state or the traditional ruling classes. It is predictable that in this case management will establish itself on the highest level; the unions, desirous of obtaining social rights within the company, on an intermediary level; and the state on the first level, playing only a limited part, possibly because it is preoccupied by political problems that weaken it. This case shows as great a lack of balance as when the lag to be overcome is both social and economic. In these two cases, a self-confident management, believing itself to be the major dynamic force of society, dominates the situation, but in one case it must take into account the unions' "contractual" policy and in the other case it encounters more initiatives on the part of the state.

Finally, if the past has not left any major lag but rather an economic dynamism and advanced social democracy, the society in process of development evolves naturally and logically at the first level, a factor which does not predetermine economic results but makes society deal with essentially economic problems, as is natural in a neo-liberal society.

This is only the outline of an analysis which should lead to a study of the internal characteristics of the company, its decision-making system, its industrial relations policy and its type of management. It might be useful to recall, however, that the development of rationalization in the company and in the economic system, held back by the conservatism of family firms and the state's administrative role, is made easier where social and political conflicts are dealt with on a more inclusive level (which is the case of the French and Italian, as well as of the German types) thereby leaving beneath them a vast area where rational criteria can prevail rather than business policies in which rationalization and private economic interests tend to be confused or to come into conflict.

VIII Conclusion

The novelty of the situations, problems and conflicts arising from the conflict between old methods and new solutions allows one to speak of a "new working class," not in order to designate new occupational categories, highly skilled workers, technicians, designers or others, whose importance is in fact growing, but in order to define probable new orientations of social action. The working class is "new" to the extent that its action no longer rests on the defense of the job and the craft as factors of production, but on a *conflictual participation* in the values of economic development. The same metamorphosis is occurring in management, which does not at all mean that industrial conflict is replaced by integration or codetermination, but simply that the conflicts are of a new type. This change is only one aspect of the formation of a new type of industrial society. We are finally in a position to see that the beginnings of European industrialization did not provide a prototype of this new industrial society, but only an exceptional form of transition from traditional society to industrial society.

Just as the most important fact in industrial evolution is the change in the social problems of organizations, halfway between occupational problems and the more specifically economic problems of the labor market, so industrial relations are more and more dominated by the growing role of technicians and professionals, that is, to use the phrase of A. Pizzorno, of those who through their technical or professional knowledge possess new principles of "accumulation."

Their role is all the more important in that deliberate orientation toward development, both public and private, is more evident. This situation is also that in which the distance appears greatest between the centers of economic decision making and political power—still widely influenced by traditional social forces and forms of action. On the contrary, the closer one comes to what we call the first type of industrial society, the more the centers of economic decision making and political power seem linked—without thereby forming a unified power elite—and the larger and less restricted political and union coalitions conceal the real role of the "new stratum" of technicians.

The nature of the social categories on which sociological analysis must be based depends, therefore, on the process of formation and on the type of industrial society considered. But in all cases it is impossible to retain the simple dichotomy between a working class and a politically and economically dominant ruling class which justifies the weakening if not of the traditional organization of the workers' movements, at least of their ideology.

Today in Europe, at the same time that people often refer to the end of ideologies, one can see that doctrines and ideologies are developing whose diversity recalls those accompanying the beginnings of European industrialization. Some people are at first amazed by the change in customs and institutions and by the development of mass society, as Tocqueville was, and they worry about the dangers that this new democracy may hold for liberty. Others see mainly the immense progress in scientific and technical knowledge; they refer to the "era of producers" and dwell no more on the conflicts between managers and workers than did the Saint-Simonians. Still others, in trying to understand the new conflicts, revive the combined social and humanitarian ideals of 1848 and wonder what type of social analysis could today have the power exerted in the past by the analysis of Karl Marx.

Given the economic expansion of western Europe, its achievement of mass consumption and the international stress which has broken, divided or disorganized the working class organizations in several countries, it is natural that public opinion should be most influenced by neo-Saint-Simonian ideas or by the anxious confidence in mass society of Tocqueville's followers. Both of these schools of thought are well able to describe and criticize the extraordinary disparity between theory and practice in unions, the persistence in certain circles of the intelligentsia of an outdated and quasi-mythological image of social relations and conflicts, and the vague and excessive optimism of management's theoreticians, who just barely escaped many of their own "great fears" and who are glad to look to a brilliant future rather than to a past full of bad memories.

Finally, it must be recognized that trade unionism, historical force of primary importance since the beginning of mechanized large-scale industry in the late nineteenth century, is at present no more than an instrument of limited negotiation in which the employees take part more and more indirectly and in relation to only some of their occupational roles. The economic conflict between employers and employees, far from remaining the main principle of social change and organization, is no longer more than one of the important but hardly dominant problems. At the time when western Europe had just gone through the misery and proletarianization accompanying the beginnings of industrialization, the contradiction between labor and capitalistic profit justifiably appeared to be "the social question," the explanation of all social problems. Today, this unifying principle has vanished; we speak more of social problems in the plural, of such and such a type of conflict in such and such a sector. But the disintegration of old problems and old social movements must not be interpreted as anything other than the transition from one society to another. Europe, swept by misery a century ago, has recently been afflicted once more by wars and concentration camps; it is dominated today by the atomic threat. Thus through new forms of terror, new problems appear which do not always create unbearable tension or exclude in any way a sense of progress and well-being, but which at least require new types of analysis. Social conflicts were at first related to the economic organization of production; today they bear directly on the political organization of society. It is not impossible that in these new industrial societies movements as profound as the advance of the working class for half a century may appear, but it is certain, in any case, that they will not repeat past forms. The study of social movements and of the historical process will not disappear in the study of the functioning of the social system, if it can only—once and for all—break with the ideas and images inherited from the pre-historic stages of industrial society.

MANLIO ROSSI-DORIA

Agriculture and Europe

UNTIL 1914, greater Europe, from Gibraltar to the Urals, "had a kind of inner unity,"[1] and it would probably not be arbitrary to see much of the reason for this in the development of its agriculture. Even if it seemed natural to distinguish between western, eastern and southern Europe the agricultural evolution of each of these three groups of countries in the last century followed patterns that were similar. Rapid population growth was everywhere accompanied by a conspicuous increase in agricultural production. It was this and not the expansion of industrial activity —very modest until the last quarter of the nineteenth century everywhere except in England—that made it possible for a doubled population not only to live, but also to eat far better than it had ever done in the past.[2]

The paths that led to the expansion of production were everywhere the same: progressive breaking down of the remnants of feudalism, the spread of cultivation over more and more of the land, the introduction of better technology and organization. Naturally, the rates and characteristics of development differed from country to country. But every episode of liberation and progress was, as it were, echoed and shared by all the countries of Europe, for all equally and directly experienced the necessity and difficulties of the way. Common experience created reciprocal bonds and helped to form, side by side with the national consciousness, a kind of European consciousness as well.

Contradictory as this may seem, the national and nationalistic movements themselves, which were most directly responsible for Europe's distintegration, were the ones that for a long period of time contributed the most to the growth of a sense of European unity. This was true because these movements had their common roots and support in agriculture and in the peasantry. National movements proudly and romantically coupled national independence with the peasant's freedom on his own land. This made it

401

natural for them to participate in what was, at the time, called the "green rising"—a movement that, in all its various manifestations, always had a strong supranational, "European" component.[3]

It is my impression that we could push very far this search for the agricultural roots of the growing inner unity of Europe up to 1914. There is, for example, the European spirit that pervaded the rural socialist movements, whether they turned into Communist revolutions or continued as democratic reform movements. One could also look into the international ties that linked all the groups and endeavors which worked for the improvement of rural life in each country—whether by spreading education and services to farmers or by helping to found cooperatives to meet many of the farmers' needs.

Two central events in Europe's agricultural history contributed, in an extraordinary way, to this feeling of a common destiny and to an awareness of the need for unity among Europe's rural areas. These were the common participation in the great migration and the overwhelming experience of the terrible agricultural crisis of 1875-1895.

Of the sixty million Europeans who, in a century and a half, crossed the ocean in search of a temporary or permanent new home, the majority were farm people who left their countries because of the growing disparity between resources and population or because of the upheaval caused by national and social conflicts in the countryside.[4] Coming from many different countries, these emigrants became acutely aware of their common fate; those who were left behind were scarcely less conscious of it.

The agricultural crisis,[5] which lasted for two decades, revealed to all European farmers—after years of high prices and uninterrupted development—the real precariousness of their condition. It made them aware of the threat of competition from overseas producers. They became conscious of their dependence on an economic system dominated by industrial interests, and of the resulting, inevitable contrast between agricultural and industrial states and regions. Finally, they were brought face to face with the structural weaknesses of their own agricultural production. The crisis provoked a chorus of protest. It brought investigations and proposals. A common defense of agriculture appeared so necessary that, from the start, the ferment of ideas surmounted all national barriers. The concept of unity was strengthened and the first ideas regarding real unification were born.

On the eve of the First World War, these ideas were fairly widespread in European rural society. With emigration and growing exodus towards the towns, social tension diminished in the countryside; prices were rising and there was increasing international trade in agricultural produce; there was a new wave of technological progress and a relative abundance of cheap credit and capital; the benefits of better organization among farmers began to make themselves felt. All these things canceled the memory of the agricultural crisis and kindled hopes for peaceful economic evolution in Europe which would permit a progressive integration between industrial and agricultural states.[6] The First World War broke out just as some were boldly beginning to proclaim that the unification of Europe was close at hand.

I The Disintegration of Europe

When peace came, at the end of 1918, Europe had lost every sign of inner unity. The separation of eastern Europe, although not yet complete, was already apparent; there were early signs of the isolation that awaited the countries of southern Europe. Even northwestern Europe's unity, shattered by the war, appeared difficult to reconstruct. The period between the two wars confirmed the worst of these expectations and completed what may be called the disintegration of Europe.

To understand this opposing trend, it is again useful, in my opinion, to look at the agricultural side of the story. With Russia broken away, the other countries of eastern Europe found no solution to their economic and political instability. Absorbed in their own national and agrarian revolutions during the first ten post-war years, they found it very difficult to consolidate their status as new, sovereign states. The economic structure of these newly independent countries was weak because it rested mainly on agriculture. Despite attempts to correct this organic weakness through agreements in the "little entente" and outside it, the great crisis of 1928-1930 dealt a more crippling blow here than in any other area. After a resistance which was often heroic by the combative leaders of "agrarian democracy" movements, the political regimes became more or less openly fascist. Their economies, on the German and Italian example, became closed in artificial autarchic or corporative structures. Well before the end of the Second World War and before the iron curtain shut them off from the rest of Europe, the great depression and their common political destiny had, in effect, already cut them off.[7]

The isolation of the southern countries, between the two world wars, was no less complete. Emigration and freedom of trade had given these countries a measure of economic relief and had intensified their contacts with Europe and the rest of the world. The war and its aftermath pushed them back into their poverty and backwardness. Greece and Turkey exhausted themselves in national conflicts and population disputes; Portugal soon succumbed to a squalid form of corporatism; Spain was torn apart by civil war; the people of southern Italy were forced to give up their traditional agricultural exports and were barred from emigrating. In all these countries, which were almost exclusively agricultural, the effects of renewed poverty, overpopulation, and arbitrary totalitarian power, were felt most acutely in the countryside.[8]

The breaking apart of western Europe was a more complex process, but even here agricultural developments were significant. Economic recovery had just begun when uncontrolled inflation cancelled its effects everywhere. Inflation played havoc with the whole class structure of European society, but it had a particularly devastating effect in rural areas and on the relations between town and countryside. The depression of 1928, which first appeared in the guise of an agricultural crisis, broke the last vestiges of unity. International trade was gradually extinguished and the economies of the different countries became more or less explicitly autarchic systems. These reached their most complete expression in so-called "policies to defend the national agriculture." Such policies, as we shall see later, had a lasting effect on the structure of agriculture and left a heritage so burdensome that it is still appropriate to refer to agriculture as "la grande malade." [9]

II National Agricultural Policies

Since the present problems of European agriculture, with which this article is particularly concerned, derive directly from situations created and consolidated by agricultural policies within each country between the wars, it is time to look at what these policies were and what their lasting effects proved to be. The outspokenly autarchic character that animated them arose, not so much from a desire to defend the farmers' interests—although every effort was made to convince them that this was its purpose—but from preoccupations with foreign exchange and food supply. The First World War had shown that a harsh fate awaited countries that did not, in time of need, possess an adequate agricultural production to rely on. Monetary instability, caused by a precarious balance of payments, made it necessary to reduce imports; those that were not destined for productive investment or armaments—such as food were the first to be cut.

The defense of agriculture, as a consequence, assumed forms that were more insidious and complex than what had once been common with simple, old-fashioned customs tariffs. Quotas and other discriminatory restrictions within every country forced agricultural production into abnormal patterns; these accorded neither with natural conditions nor with technical and economic requirements. They permitted small groups of producers, who happened to be more fortunate or better organized, to profit from the situation and to strengthen their political position at the expense, not only of consumers, but also of other producers, mainly those who would have been interested in exporting their products.[10]

It is worth considering what effects these policies had on self-sufficiency, trade, output, productivity and agrarian structure. While the effects were different from country to country, there was much in common between them. The goal of self-sufficiency, for example was undoubtedly achieved for many products,[11] but, under protectionist systems, it meant artificially high internal prices, which limited food consumption and discouraged further expansion of production.[12] The barriers to inter-European and international trade were effective. They arrested agricultural development in countries most directly interested in exporting. Denmark, Holland and the countries of southern Europe were immediately affected; they were most vulnerable to falling and unstable prices.[13]

The gravest consequences of protectionist policies were a slowing down of progress in technology and organization, a small reduction in costs and a negligible rise in productivity. Obviously, European agriculture made some progress in this period, but it was slight compared to what was accomplished elsewhere, for example, the United States.[14] Behind the barrier of protectionism and relatively high prices, the weaker farms continued to survive and even multiplied. Since their technical and productive levels were low, they violated all the requirements of modern agricultural development.[15]

III The Economic Miracle

The economic miracle that has been taking place in western Europe since the Second World War is all the more surprising when considered against the background of previous stagnation and disintegration. Not only has it, in fact, provoked rapid social transformation in the western countries, but it has also finally given a decisive impulse to the revival of southern Europe. Considering that it has been accompanied by a similar process in Russia and the other countries of eastern Europe, it is probable that historians of the future will look on it not merely as a western phenomenon —although it originated in the West—but as something that has, once again, affected "greater Europe" as a whole.

The dimensions of the economic revolution now in progress are well known. In the group of countries belonging to OECD, gross national product increased between 1950 and 1960 by 56.8 per cent, gross national product, per man employed, by 39.6 per cent, industrial production and services by 65 per cent and agricultural production by 25 per cent. These increases, varying from country to country, were significantly higher in some, such as Germany and Italy. The impulse given to the economy is such that it is safe to assume that very similar rates of growth can be maintained from 1960 to 1970.[16]

These simple figures are enough to explain why the problems of agriculture, since 1950, have become very different from what they were in the past. The very categories into which our present agricultural problems fall—rural exodus, technological progress, expansion of production and evolution of policies—enable us to understand that we are confronted with a real revolution which will require difficult adjustments.

IV Rural Exodus

Increase in productivity—greater outside than inside agriculture—accounted for a significant gap in the past between agricultural and other income in all European countries. The long period of economic stagnation and the accumulation of excess population in the countryside caused this gap to widen until, and in some cases past, 1950. While unemployment and uncertainty of employment prevailed everywhere, and while incomes outside agriculture increased slowly and remained uncertain, the gap did not provide more than a slight incentive to leave the countryside. When, however, economic development entered its present rapid and dynamic phase, the difference between agricultural and other income increased to a point where farmers felt compelled to make a choice: either transform and modernize their operations, or abandon agriculture for other activities which were finally opening up to them.

This dilemma affects different groups of farmers in different ways. Those with good land who can, without too much trouble, draw upon a reserve of new technology, are able to accept the challenge. They find it possible to reorganize their farms so that the income they derive is equal or superior to what they would realize if they invested their capital, labor and entrepreneurial skills elsewhere. There are farmers of this type in every country and, in certain regions, they may be the prevailing group. They benefit from the flight of the weaker operators to enlarge their farms and to increase their productivity. In the overall situation, however, they are a minority: a large minority in some countries and a small one in others, depending on environmental conditions, agrarian structure and organization, degree of technical progress, the quality of services available to them and the soundness and effectiveness of policies on which they depend.

At the other extreme, there are, everywhere, farmers and full or part-time hired laborers, who having always lived in poverty, have taken quick advantage of the opportunity to emigrate. They have in large part accounted for the first and most legitimate wave of the rural exodus movement.[17]

The majority of farmers fall between these two groups. Their traditional, medium-sized, family-type farms have a modest economic capacity. Most of them have resisted until now, but all of them are worried. They know that they must, sooner or later, face the problem of reorganizing their farming operations and commit themselves to joining other farmers in much more organic, robust and modern organizations than have existed to this date. This alone can permit them to continue. A few have already given up and have moved to other occupations; a growing number of the younger generation have decided that the low incomes of farming are unacceptable, and they are rejecting the whole rural way of life.

This rural exodus, while natural and beneficient if kept within certain limits, may assume proportions that go far beyond both the necessary and the convenient, threatening to leave not a less populated, but a ruined and abandoned countryside. In such cases, we must consider the exodus not only "physiological" but pathological, for it leads to the rapid collapse of entire rural societies that might, with sufficient time and some assistance, find a new and satisfactory equilibrium. Some of the most beautiful and "civilized" areas of Europe—central Italy is a good example—are menaced in this way. They point up, in new and dramatic terms, how the problems of agriculture are also the problems of safeguarding the social texture of large areas of Europe.

The negative aspects of exodus are even more serious where disintegration of agriculture and of traditional rural communities is not accompanied by industrial and urban development in the near vicinity. To leave the countryside in these circumstances can mean only to emigrate. This is happening today in the poorer parts of southern Europe, which are being abandoned by a growing number of the active male population. These men are as unprepared for the life that awaits them elsewhere as their predecessors were during the great overseas migrations. The employment they find

407

during the first years is usually temporary or insecure and they generally leave their families behind in the old villages. These villages have lost all signs of life and are rapidly becoming a sort of concentration camp for women and children, for the old and the weak. More often than not, the type of assistance that is greatly needed here is altogether lacking.[18]

Those of us who have been watching these processes have had to recognize that if their adjustment is left only to the free play of economic forces or to existing institutions, the problems they raise will become more serious every year and will lead to useless waste and suffering. What answers can the people of Europe find to this problem? If they decide to act, what form should their action take? This is one of the questions that economic development is raising for agriculture.

V Technological Progress

If we turn now to consider the second class of problems we spoke of earlier, problems relating to technological progress, we find the new situation characterized by no less disturbing developments and phenomena. During the twenty-year period, 1930-1950, —despite the noteworthy precedents set by many European countries in the application of science to agriculture, in technology (particularly in the area of animal breeding) and in the field of cooperative organization—the stagnation of agriculture and the chaos wrought by war created a serious technological lag between Europe and the United States. In the United States, agriculture was emerging at this time from a period of important scientific, technological and organizational revolution. Initiated in the areas of mechanization and plant and animal genetics, the revolution was extended to all fields, its rationalizing principles being everywhere applied. It was accompanied by a thorough revolution in the methods of organization of agricultural enterprises and of industries and services relating to agriculture.

When, therefore, around 1950, the better equipped among the European farmers were in a position to resume their forward progress, they found at their disposal, in addition to their own experience and skills, a vast new wealth of knowledge, experience, technical inventions and organizational models all ready to be put into practice, if they could only find the resources to master the situation of stagnation and disintegration which restrictive agrarian policies and wartime economic upheaval had left in their wake. The technological transformation of European farming, though limited to only a fraction of her agriculturalists, developed in consequence

408

with extreme rapidity. In a few years it attained surprising and unhoped for levels of production and organization. If we compare the mean for the two five-year periods, 1949-1953 and 1954-1958, for the countries of northwestern Europe—notwithstanding the fairly uneven distribution of the development and the fact that agriculture had already lost about 20 per cent of its labor force— we note, over this cultivated area, an overall increase of 15 per cent in agricultural production and an increase in productivity of over 30 per cent.[19] This result was obtained by the combined use of an impressive number of machines and more abundant fertilizers, and through better strains in the plants and animals raised.[20]

In addition to these changes directly bearing upon production, consideration must be given to changes effected in the structure of markets and industries connected with agriculture. In this respect, there occurred in Europe after 1950 developments similar to what had already taken place in the United States. The growth of co-operatives and of horizontal and vertical integration in agriculture profoundly modified the structure and efficiency of agricultural markets. The tremendous development of the processing indus-tries and of industries turning out production materials for agri-culture created, alongside European agriculture in the true sense —whose importance in the general economy did not cease to de-cline—a powerful "agribusiness," whose importance continued to grow.[21]

These are facts of general knowledge; they nevertheless pose a series of problems whose novelty lies, if nowhere else, in their new dimensions. We must consider first of all that the application of modern technology and the exploitation of its possibilities call for a very different type of farmer from the one traditional in Europe: technically prepared, solidly organized and well supplied with capital or at least sure of easy access to credit. This means that, in the beginning, only in a few countries and regions and only among certain groups is it feasible that farmers will be ready to advance along the road of technological progress. For the over-whelming number—faced with the difficult dilemma of resisting on their farms or abandoning them—technological progress is condi-tional upon a long and arduous process of education, organization and waiting, which all are not capable of facing. The result is that the rate of exodus from the land is accelerated.[22]

In the second place, it is obvious that the adoption of a great part of modern technology is practicable only where a farm has at its disposal an acreage and physical plant of sizable dimensions. It calls therefore for the elimination of farms not in a position to achieve these dimensions, and for the consolidation of lands thus freed for the formation of larger undertakings. This is precisely what is occurring spontaneously at the present day. It remains to be seen at what rate this process will take place and whether abandonment may not, in many cases, be more rapid than reconstruction.[23]

It is, in the third place, apparent that, since technological progress involves an agricultural production based on much higher "inputs" than has been the case in the past, farmers are considerably more vulnerable to the fluctuations of markets, both with regard to their products and to the production materials on which they depend. Their risks are increased not only by seasonal variations, but also, and especially, by price instability. Thus, not only is every form of "autoconsumption," all subsistence farming—which in the past represented a none too negligible proportion of European agriculture—destined to disappear, but an agricultural policy capable of assuring effective stabilization of agricultural markets and of coping with the growing tensions between agriculture and industry is made even more indispensible.

Will the countries of Europe succeed in finding solutions to the three types of problem raised by the technological revolution: the education of farmers, the reorganization and expansion of agricultural enterprises, and the stabilization of markets? If they prove themselves capable of coping with each of these, what are the chances that the steps will be taken in time, that is, before the processes of agricultural disintegration gain the upper hand? Also, will they not prove too costly for the community at large?

VI The Building Up of Surpluses

The third group of problems is directly bound up with the preceding ones and will tend to overshadow them in the near future. The increase in agricultural production, though proceeding at a substantially slower rate than industrial production, is still such that the supply of agricultural products is in danger of exceeding the corresponding demand, thereby creating serious problems with respect to the disposal of surpluses. Also, problems are created in the area of international trade, where Europe runs the risk of assuming the role, no longer of an importer of foodstuffs, but of a potential exporter.

We have already observed how, thanks to the preceding developments and to policies of an autarchic nature, many European countries had already attained or were near attaining self-sufficiency with regard to many products, though not always at completely satisfactory levels of consumption. The surpassing of pre-war production figures before 1950 and the overall increase of 25 per cent in production in the ten-year period, 1950-1960, considerably aggravated the situation. Not only—as is well known—was the point of absolute rigidity reached in the demand for cereals, flour and potatoes, but also—at least in the chief European countries—in the demand for milk and cheese products. Predictions of a further overall increase of 25 per cent (for the European countries included in the OECD) make it apparent that—unless there is some change in current policies—the problem of food surpluses in Europe cannot be avoided.[24] The problem of surpluses is, indeed, obviously connected with that of prices, which, in turn, is bound up with the problem of farm income, and the farmer's ability to persevere.

VII The Common Agricultural Policy

It is beyond the scope of this article to illustrate the complex interaction of national agricultural policies of the post-World War II period; the long and complicated sequence of events and negotiations that led ultimately to the institution of the Common Market and the so-called common agricultural policy; the substance of the agreements already reached and of the discussions in progress. I would like, however, to draw attention to a few salient facts; they bear, respectively, on national agricultural policies, on the stage reached by the community policy with regard to control of the market for various products and the stage reached in discussions of so-called structural policy.

With regard to the national agricultural policies, we may state simply that—inasmuch as they are in essence a continuation of the corresponding policies in effect between the two world wars, although modified to suit the new economic conditions—they present the same defects as did the former policies and constitute at the present time the greatest single obstacle to the achievement of a common agricultural policy.[25] Though they differ from country to country, we may, however, for our purposes here, divide them into two main groups: the first comprising the agricultural policies of the more highly industrialized countries; the second those of the sparsely industrialized countries of southern Europe (including Italy and, in part, France). The distinguishing feature of the latter is the prevalent recourse to traditional instruments: restrictions on imports, various emergency provisions, subsidies to farmers and a few survivals of corporatist or wartime regulations. As a consequence, they have failed to stabilize farm prices or to get under way any concrete policy of structural reorganization of agriculture.

The outstanding feature of the more industrialized societies is that they have moved consistently—albeit along different paths —toward the creation of a system of farm price stabilization at levels designed to bring farm incomes as close as possible to so-called parity (corresponding to approximately 75 per cent of extra-agricultural incomes).[26] The result of these policies has been to consolidate a system of prices for the various products in each country, prices that differ substantially from those prevailing on the international markets and from those operating in each of the other countries. At the same time, a policy of structural reorganization has been adopted which has the same ends in view and is attempting to bring about a progressive reduction in costs.

With regard to the policy of the community on the subject of markets, we should mention that, after overcoming every conceivable kind of resistance and incomprehension, a complicated system of control of trade in farm products has been adopted, variously adjustable according to the nature of the products themselves. The hope has been that this may help to stabilize prices. It is also expected that it will pave the way for the gradual creation of a common market made up of the six countries (or nine, should Great Britain, the Scandinavian countries and Greece become members) within the time-limit laid down by the Treaty of Rome. Many of the specific regulations concerning products or groups of products have already been approved or are on the way to being approved.[27]

While there still remain grave doubts about the practical operation of such a complex, bureaucratic and delicate system,[28] we should bear in mind the fact that the basic problem of the Common Market policy, that of determining the final level of common prices, has not yet been faced for any product, despite the imminent expiration of the allotted time-period. An initial discussion on the fixing of this common level for cereal prices ran into very marked disagreements and resistance. The question, therefore, of just what type of common market can be created is still an open one. Will it be such as to close off the European market in a new agricultural protectionism not very different from that which characterized previous national agricultural policies? Or, will it represent one of the central nuclei of a world-wide reorganization of the farm product market?[29]

Finally, with regard to the common agricultural policy insofar as it relates to questions of structure, matters have not for the moment gone beyond a primary statement of the issues involved and the declared intention of entering upon such a policy. The matter is still entirely in the hands of national agricultural policy-makers who continue to pursue methods and objectives differing greatly from country to country.

When we consider, then, the current status of the common agricultural policy, we can only conclude with the words that Mr. Sicco Mansholt, its chief promoter and guiding spirit, never tires of repeating: "What we have achieved so far in the Community in the field of agriculture is only a beginning."

The nature of the fundamental problems which must be faced by the European Community if it is indeed to create in Europe a situation of balanced economic development, leading eventually to broader-based agreements, calls for decisiveness, political courage and clarity of vision of a very different order from those evinced so far.

VIII *The New Viewpoints*

Resting our case on the facts summarily indicated above, we may conclude not so much with solutions to the fundamental problems discussed, as with new viewpoints from which they must henceforth be considered. First and foremost, the European experience tells us that, while the problem of agriculture can no longer be viewed within closed national limits, neither is it possible to consider it within the closed limits of a Europe made up of six, nine or however many countries participate in an expanded Common Market. In fact, the more the market expands, the more we are compelled to consider it in relation to the so-called third-party countries, who in practice amount to the whole world, from the Americas down to the underdeveloped countries and even to those countries governed by socialist regimes. A common agricultural policy in western Europe must therefore be regarded—as is implicitly admitted by Mansholt and the more intelligent European observers—solely as a course of action leading eventually to international regulation of agricultural markets, and not as a fresh obstacle to the attainment of this goal.

Secondly, the examination of the problems shows that, at least as far as agriculture is concerned—the economic activity that at one time seemed best adapted to the system of free enterprise—the phase of free competition is definitely over and the phase of planning, on both the international level and within the individual countries, has begun. After decades of injurious and unstable restrictive planning of national agricultural policies, we have entered the phase of planning for large areas and of international economic agreements. What we must now discover are the types of regulation

413

and organization best suited to reconcile planned stabilization of prices, and hence planned supply and manipulation of products, with autonomous responsibility in individual or associative farming enterprises. This alone will make for real and continuous agricultural progress, as has already been proved beyond a doubt by the negative experiences of the socialist countries in the field of agriculture.[30]

The recent evolution of agriculture in the countries with the most advanced economic development has, in the third place, shown that agricultural activity may be accompanied by incomes comparable to those enjoyed by other business enterprises provided that all the labor force employed at lower rates of productivity is eliminated. In other words, this depends on the rural exodus, within certain limits, being encouraged, the size of agricultural enterprises increased, capital and high job productivity placed within reach of the farmer and lands unfitted to ensure this high level of productivity abandoned or utilized extensively.

Since the present state of agriculture in all the countries involved is very far from satisfying these conditions and since spontaneous adjustments through natural and gradual processes would prove too slow, or even impossible, all the countries are faced with the necessity of imposing a policy that would ensure: first, assistance in the difficult exodus phase for farmers who decide to transfer to other activities; second, reorganization of agriculture by way of territorial development plans; third, the localizing of a considerable proportion of extra-agricultural activity in rural areas which, though suited to stable human settlement, are not able to survive on agriculture alone.

Without the intervention of assistance and planning of this kind, in fact, there is a danger that the flight from the land and the transformation of agriculture may create very serious economic and social situations. On the other hand, interventions of this kind must, if they are to be valid, be effected in such a way as to ensure full respect for the autonomous responsibility of the individual and of individual and associative enterprises.

Finally, the formation of product surpluses in European agriculture, as had already occurred in America, calls attention to the urgent and pressing nature of the problem, not of preventing their accumulation, but rather of finding a way to make systematic use of them on a large scale to alleviate the serious deficiency of foodstuffs that exists for most of the populations of underdeveloped countries, now living under conditions of starvation and undernourishment.[31]

Agriculture and Europe

The viewpoints from which we must henceforth consider agricultural problems make us realize that men can no longer escape the responsibility of profoundly rethinking many of their most cherished ideas. The fact that such a conclusion arises naturally out of the analysis of the most remote and the most recent developments of European agriculture, and that it is now shared by some of the most responsible leaders in the economic and political renewal of Europe, shows how rich in vital ferment is the transformation which the old continent is at the present moment undergoing.

REFERENCES

1. See Folke Droving, *Land and Labor in Europe—1900-1950* (The Hague: M. Nijhoff, 1958). On page six of this comparative survey of recent agrarian history, the author writes: "At the beginning of the period here considered, Europe had a kind of inner unity. An essentially common ideological framework and many resemblances in past social history formed the background for the pros and cons of public debate. Despite great differences, conditions seemed basically comparable from one country to another. Manifold contacts all over the continent created a consciousness of unity and common ways of expression. In many respects, the differences were smaller than they are now, and the idea of comparative surveys of Europe might perhaps have seemed more natural then from a static point of view."

    After having said that this book discusses, with reference to agriculture, ". . . how this unit came to fall apart," he adds: "One of the most fascinating problems is why the social and economic disparities in Europe should have become ever greater. This is the explanation for a comparative enquiry on our continent, while the presence of widely varying yet comparable social patterns as well as contrasting trends of development, make it a model subject for a comparative analysis, from which conclusions, which are generally valid, might emerge."

2. Including the countries of the present Soviet bloc and Yugoslavia in the eastern European group, Portugal, Spain, Greece, Turkey and southern Italy in the southern group, and the remaining countries in the western group; the distribution of territory and population among the three groups was as follows in 1960:

	Territory (in thousand sq. miles)	%	*Population* (in thousands)	%
Western Europe	1,084	27.1	242,743	41.3
Southern Europe	336	8.4	69,174	11.8
Eastern Europe	2,571	64.5	275,806	46.9
Total	3,991	100.0	587,723	100.0

Population growth, between 1800 and 1900, was approximately as follows:

	1800 (in thousands)	1900 (in thousands)	Index 1800=100
Western Europe	94,000	191,000	203
Southern Europe	28,000	53,000	189
Eastern Europe	65,000	156,000	240
	187,000	400,000	213

In the same period, the number of those employed in agriculture presumably grew from 25 to 35 million in western Europe (40 per cent), from 8 to 13 million in southern Europe (62 per cent), and from 20 to 42 million in eastern Europe (110 per cent).

3. The term "green rising" was used to describe the victorious peasant movement in eastern Europe immediately following the First World War. See David Mitrany, *Marx against the Peasant* (Chapel Hill: University of North Carolina Press, 1951), pp. 137 ff.; and William B. Bizzell, *The Green Rising* (New York: The Macmillan Co., 1926). The origins of this movement, which succeeded in imposing land reforms, reached further back in each country, precisely to the last decade of the nineteenth century, when the ideologies were stated, the first organizations created, and the future political leaders of the movement formed.

4. 60 million is the number indicated by Imre Ferenczi, "Migrations: Modern" in *The Encyclopedia of Social Sciences* 1935, Vol. X, pp. 429-440 for the period 1800-1924 and repeated by the *Encyclopedia Britannica* 1960, Vol. 15, p. 465 for the period 1800-1940. According to immigration statistics, the greatest number of immigrants to the United States (following those from the British Isles at the beginning of the preceding century) came from Italy (9.5 million), Spain and Portugal (together 6 million), and the eastern European countries, both within and outside the Russian and Austro-Hungarian empires (over 10 million). Ferenczi writes: ". . . modern mass migration was a voluntary movement of free wage earners, tenants and small farmers. . . . During the entire century these migrations helped to solve the problems of unemployment and overpopulation and at the same time acted as a political safety valve."

5. A large contemporary literature exists on the agricultural crisis of 1875-1895, but there is no recent critical history. The best available sources are provided by German agricultural economic literature, and particularly: Max Sering, *Agrarkrisen und Agrarzölle* (Berlin: W. de Gruyter and Co., 1925); S. V. Strakosch, *Das Agrar-problem in Neuen Europa* (Berlin: P. Parey, 1930); and Constantin von Dietze, *Die gegenwärtige Agrarkrisis* (Berlin: Junker und Dünnhaupt, 1930). All three of these works, however, deal also with other and broader topics. The crisis was slow in developing and affected grain in particular, causing the price of wheat in England in 1894-1895 to drop to 43 percent of its average price during the period 1851-1875. Other sectors, for example, wine and grapes, were also hard hit. It was generally in this period that some of the traditional measures for the defense of agriculture originated, such as protective tariffs, as well as some of the most solid European farmers' organizations.

6. The idea of a European federation took more concrete forms only after the First World War, but it had entered people's thinking long before that. One of the books that gives an impression of what deep roots this conception had for those who had seriously studied the continent's economic situation is Wladimir Woytinsky, *Tatsachen und Zahlen Europas* (Vienna: PanEuropa Verlag, 1930).

7. The history of the non-Soviet eastern European countries between the two world wars is among the most dramatic and one in which agriculture and its problems most directly determined political events. Much of Mitrany's book (*op. cit.*) is devoted to these events, but the most complete account is given by Hugh Seton-Watson, *East European Revolution* (London: Methuen, 1950). With regard to the land reforms that dominated the immediate postwar years in these countries, see Mitrany's excellent summary in the *Encyclopedia of Social Sciences*. Other, even more complete analyses can be found in the studies of the International Institute of Agriculture (particularly the volume, *The Land Tenure Systems in Europe*, which the Institute prepared for the European Conference on Rural Life in 1939). Other works on single countries during the same period include the studies by the International Conference of Agricultural Economists, and the book by F. Dovring (*op. cit.*).

8. Although a vast literature has since been accumulating on the problems of southern Europe, the most complete and objective study remains the one prepared by the Research and Planning Division of the Economic Commission for Europe: "Economic Development in Southern Europe," published in *United Nations, Economic Survey of Europe in 1953*. (Geneva: 1954). Southern Europe was also included in the *FAO Mediterranean Development Project* (Rome: 1959), which, as stated in the subtitle, deals particularly with "the integrated development of agriculture and forestry in relation to economic growth." The countries included in both studies are Spain, Portugal, Greece, Turkey, southern Italy and Yugoslavia.

9. On the evolution of European agriculture between 1930 and 1950, see: U. N. Economic Commission for Europe and Food and Agriculture Organization, *European Agriculture: A Statement of Problems* (Geneva: ECE, 1954); Ingvar Svennilson, *Growth and Stagnation in the European Economy* (Geneva: ECE, 1954); Ruth Cohen, *Survey of National Measures for Controlling Farm Prices in Western European Countries* (Rome: FAO, 1953); Organisation Européenne de Coopération Economique, *Les politiques agricoles en Europe et en Amerique du Nord* (a series of five reports, Paris: 1956, 1957, 1958, 1960, 1961). Worth particular note is what Svennilson writes at the beginning of chapter five of his work, "The Agricultural Background" (*op. cit.*, p. 82): "It is not surprising that agriculture did not make any great contribution to the long-term growth of the European economy. Factors which can be regarded as strategic in the generation of economic growth, such as innovations in methods of production, a high level of investment, or the opening of new outlets for exports were not characteristic for agriculture in this period. On the contrary, agriculture showed many of the signs of a depressed industry— indeed, the major depressed industry of Europe—and its effect was mainly to slow down the expansion of the European economy as a whole."

10. Svennilson, *op. cit.*, pp. 89-90, writes, with regard to agricultural policies between the two wars: "Agriculture is the outstanding example of the new policy of national welfare. In no other part of the European economy was the protection of one section of the community at the expense of the rest of the nation carried so far. The farming community had suffered severely, first from the direct effects of the war and subsequently from the world economic crisis. The various national policies of agricultural protection were designed to mitigate the most catastrophic effects of this crisis, but they could not prevent agriculture in most European countries from showing many of the symptoms of a "depressed industry": low wages, low farm profits, a slow rise in output and productivity, and a wasteful use of manpower."

11. In the five years preceding the Second World War, the European countries (except Great Britain) were completely self-sufficient with regard to milk, meat, cheese, butter and vegetables, 86 per cent self-sufficient for sugar and fruits, 85 per cent for wheat, 82 per cent for other cereals (see tables on pages 38-39 of the FAO/ECE study, *European Agriculture* (*op. cit.*). It need hardly be pointed out that these figures are based on an entirely different situation, with regard to income and prices, than exists at present.

12. FAO/ECE, *European Agriculture, op. cit.*, p. 37. "Most of the western European countries (with the exceptions of Denmark and the Netherlands as well as the eastern and southern European countries) were large importers of agricultural products and protectionist policies had, for a time, favourable effects on the volume of their agricultural production. The limits of these possibilities of expansion became apparent the nearer self-sufficiency is approached: the high prices paid for the protected home production limit consumption, and the expansion of output tends to slow down and come to a halt when there are no more imports to be replaced. At this stage, import restrictions and high prices hamper the growth of production not only in countries that have been, traditionally, net exporters, but also in those that have been net importers of agricultural products."

13. *Ibid.*, p. 70. "The restriction imposed against agricultural exports from Denmark and the Netherlands in the thirties brought no lasting setback to these two countries, which were already sufficiently industrialized to be able to react by proceeding further with industrialization, substituting home production for the manufactured imports they could no longer pay for and, at a later stage, reducing their employment in agriculture.

"For eastern and southern European countries, and for many overseas countries as well, the limitation of agricultural exports in the thirties had far more serious consequences. The loss of export markets severely handicapped industrialization and contributed to the accumulation of surplus population in agriculture."

14. Svennilson, *op. cit.*, p. 90. "The exclusive nationalistic character of these protective policies also prevented proper specialization between different countries so that national advantages and disadvantages tended to be neutralized in the same way as between different parts of the same country. National wheat farming, milk and butter production, or wine growing were protected against competition from abroad even if domestic condi-

tions for this kind of production were unfavourable. In no other field was economic nationalism such a striking success to the detriment of general European efficiency. Yet in no other field of comparable importance to Europe as a whole were natural conditions so different and the potential advantages of trade over national frontiers so great. In a period when transport by road and the technique of canning and freezing were great innovations, the advantages of intra-European trade in agricultural products were increasing. These possibilities were, however, far from being exploited to the point which would have offered advantages for the European economy as a whole. The contrast with the enormous cross-country transport of grain, dairy products, fruit and vegetables within the wide United States market is striking.

"From a productivity point of view, the protection of agriculture before the war thus suffered from a double weakness. On the one hand, it was never able to restore the prosperity of the farmer to a level which would have given a stimulus to rapid modernization. On the other hand it prevented—by maintaining incomes derived from less efficient production—an increase in productivity through elimination or regional specialization."

15. FAO/ECE, *European Agriculture, op. cit.,* p. 18. "The size of farms in Europe influences to a considerable extent the pattern of production. Millions of small farms which have come into existence either by inheritance or by land redistribution are too small to provide productive employment for a family in ordinary farming of the type normal on larger farms in the same area. Wherever possible, they therefore specialize in labour-intensive products. In the South this specialization is mainly in horticulture, tobacco and wine; in the North, mainly in animal production. Many of these specialized small farms both in the South and North are very high-yielding and give a good income to their owners, but most of them manage to be competitive only because the owners accept lower earnings for their own labour than the rate for hired labour in the same area.

"However, the majority of smallholdings in Europe, particularly in the East and South but also in most northwestern countries, are not specialised farms with high yields but subsistence farms producing the base necessity of life for the farmer and his family with only a very small surplus left over to sell. These farms conceal a structural labour surplus in agriculture in some cases simply because the farmers are idle for a considerable part of the year, but more often because they perform work of a very low productivity and use more time-consuming methods than those employed in farms without a labour surplus."

16. These figures are reported by OECD for countries included in that organization. They serve as the basis for the working paper submitted to the Third FAO Regional Conference for Europe held in Rome, October 8-13, 1962, entitled, *Agricultural Policies in Europe in the 1960's: Problems of Agriculture in a Growing Economy* (*Monthly Bulletin of Agricultural Economics and Statistics*), p. 4. With respect to the next decade (1960-70), the report states: "Much has already been written about the economic prospects of the nineteen-sixties but one feature is common to all the crystal-gazing, namely that growth is expected to continue. For example, recent projections for the European OECD countries suggest that gross national product may increase by 42.5 per cent (average of two hypotheses) compared with the

56.8 per cent increase recorded during the nineteen-fifties. Similarly, gross national product per man employed is projected to rise by 30.5 per cent compared with 39.6 per cent in the past decade. In the planned economies of eastern Europe a continuance of rapid economic growth is intended."

17. A complete and current count of the real reduction of manpower in agricultural activity is still lacking and would, in any case, continually have to be brought up to date. According to the FAO/ECE study *European Agriculture in 1965* (Geneva: 1960), in the ten countries of northwestern Europe the number of agricultural workers fell by over 30 per cent with respect to the pre-war period and by 22 per cent with respect to 1950—in other words, diminished from 17 million in 1950 to 13 million. Successive developments probably brought the total number involved in the exodus up to 5 million. To this must be added the exodus from agriculture in the southern European countries, including Italy, which has greatly accelerated during recent years. On the basis of various indications, this exodus amounts to another 4 million workers. The percentage of workers employed in agriculture would, therefore, be reduced from 44 per cent to 32 per cent in the southern European countries and from 21 per cent to 15 per cent in the northwestern countries.

18. The disruptive effects of the rural exodus are becoming more evident every day in many of the rural areas of Europe. This, and the specific work of assistance that is needed on behalf of the remaining rural population in these areas was discussed at the Third Congress of the European Society for Rural Sociology (St. Wolfgang, Austria, September 1962). See proceedings of the conference in *Sociologia Ruralis*, Vol. II (1962) no. 1-2.

19. In the FAO/ECE study, *Towards a capital intensive agriculture* (Geneva: 1961), it is estimated that the production per work unit expended in agriculture—where the corresponding mean for the period, 1950-1952, is made equal to 100—was, in 1956-1958, equal, in West Germany to 157, in Belgium to 150, in Denmark to 145, in Great Britain to 140, in Holland to 138, in France to 128; and the mean for the twelve countries of northwestern Europe (not including Italy) was equal to 138.

20. According to the data of the FAO/ECE *European Agriculture in 1965* (Geneva: 1960), the average yields for cereals went up by 30 per cent since the pre-war years for the whole of the countries of northwestern Europe. The mean milk production per cow increased by 23 per cent. On the other hand, it should not be forgotten that these production increases were obtained at the cost of a substantially more extensive use of technical devices. As is shown by the other study of the FAO-ECE, *Towards a capital intensive agriculture* (Geneva: 1961), the number of tractors in northwestern Europe (not including Italy) rose from 300,000 units in 1950 to 1,580,000 units in 1960 (a more than five-fold increase); the use of fertilizers during the same period rose by 58 per cent and the use of prepared feeds, selected seeds and breeders by 67 per cent.

21. The term "agribusiness"—which is well suited to describe what is happening in Europe as well as in America—was introduced by J. H. Davis and R. A. Goldberg, *A Concept of Agribusiness* (Cambridge: Harvard

University Press, 1957), to designate the aggregate of economic enterprises, in addition to agriculture in the true sense, which are directly associated with agriculture. So far as I have been able to ascertain, there exist no figures which would permit us to measure its importance in Europe. For America, the estimates cited in that text showed that, while in 1910, 54 per cent of the final market value of products of agricultural origin was represented by the added value produced in the farm plant; in 1954 this constituted scarcely 17 per cent of the final value at consumption. These proportions have assuredly not been reached yet in Europe, though it is nonetheless apparent that the importance of "agribusiness" is such as to represent a figure considerably larger than the plain value of agricultural production as reported in national accounts.

22. There are increasingly vast and more complex organizations devoted to the education of farmers in preparation for the new demands of modern agriculture. The OECD has done an excellent job in the international coordination of these enterprises. See in particular: OECD, *Agricultural vocational training in Europe and North America* (Paris: 1962) and OECD, *Intellectual investment in agriculture and economic and social development* (Paris: 1962).

23. Farm expansion is taking place on a large scale throughout Europe and is being encouraged by ever more extensive legislation and public action. The same is true also of "land consolidation." For these topics, see especially: E. H. Jacoby, *Land Consolidation in Europe* (Wageningen: FAO, H. Veenman, 1961).

24. The FAO's forecast, which takes into account accurate computations of the elasticity of the demand for the various agricultural products, is that, even if the national income were to increase by 42.5 per cent by 1970, the increase in foodstuff consumption might be as low as 17 per cent and would not, therefore, be in a position to absorb the anticipated 25 per cent increase in production that we have noted. "This of course is an average for all countries and the figures for individual countries may be very different, but there will be few countries who will not experience difficulties in the marketing of one or more of their agricultural products." (FAO, *Agricultural Commodity Projections for 1970* (Rome: 1962); and *Agricultural Policies in Europe in the 1960's* (Rome: 1963.)

25. In the FAO publication previously mentioned (*Agricultural Policies in Europe in the 1960's, op. cit.*, p. 7), it is said in this respect: "Existing agricultural policies and many of the laws on which they are based are a legacy from the past and a number of their principal features were appropriate to the circumstances of earlier decades. They are still influenced by the idea of promoting higher production and conserving labour on farms. To obtain these objectives, high prices for farm products and the maintenance of small, intensively operated farms were appropriate methods. . . . Yet nearly all European countries are in the position of having more agricultural land than they need, using present techniques, for supplying their national food requirements and consequently, it is no longer useful to continue measures which deliberately stimulate higher production. Similarly certain measures which were designed for keeping marginal farmers in business today cease to have justification when chronic labour shortages exist in other sectors."

26. The same goal has been pursued by the various policies of northwestern Europe, though along different lines. We may thus distinguish policies of the "English type," constructed upon the direct payment to the farmer by the state of a specific compensation, making up the difference between price received and price guaranteed; policies of the "Swiss type," based upon rigorous protectionist control of international trade and a complicated system of internal price adjustments; policies of the "Dutch type," established on the basis of rigorous self-discipline among the producers, organized into cooperatives, and of capillary interventions on the part of an intricate and scrupulous planned economy, and so on.

27. For the present state of negotiations regarding the common agricultural policy, see especially two recent publications—the brief but indispensible FAO, *Agricultural Commodities and the European Common Market* (Rome: 1962); and "Agriculture and the European Common Market," *International Journal of Agrarian Affairs*, Oxford University Press, Vol. III, Nos. 5-6, pp. 237-371. For the subsequent development of this policy, that is for the basic problem of price fixing, see the fundamental report prepared by a group of experts (published in the four languages of the EEC in the series *Studies* (Agricultural series) no. 1 (1962). "Effects of a lowering of farm prices in the area of the common agricultural policy of the European Economic Community upon the incomes of agriculture in the German Federal Republic."

28. This point of view has found many articulate supporters, though not all of the criticisms have been as radical as those expressed recently by Colin Clark in "Agricultural Economics—The Further Horizon," *Journal of Agricultural Economics*, Reading, England, Vol. XV, No. 2 (December 1962), pp. 218-231. "The agricultural policy, on which the Common Market countries were supposed to have reached agreement is quite hopeless, without any redeeming features. The policy at present announced continues to protect all the most uneconomic and highest cost producers in the Common Market area, without imposing any restrictions to their output. No wonder that such a foolish and internationally unacceptable policy has to be wrapped up in such obscure verbiage."

29. The danger of the common agricultural policy following the first of the two courses is still far from past. In this respect, the comment made on the initial plans for a European "Green Pool" in the FAO/ECE report cited above (*European Agriculture*, Geneva, 1954, p. 69) remains true: "The desire to stimulate trade in agricultural products among western European countries through some kind of regional discrimination is understandable enough in view of the difficulties encountered in reaching agreement on a broader international scale. Nevertheless, the creation of one more area of regional discrimination would be a substitute of doubtful value for a far-reaching reduction of trade barriers and a mitigation of the regional discrimination already existing."

Fortunately, the Vice-President of the European Community, Mansholt, appears to be quite convinced of this danger. He said recently in a speech at the Third Regional Conference for Europe, Rome, FAO, October 1962: "It is our conviction that these agreements should be the beginning, the basis, of an organization of world markets. Indeed it must be so. Once the Community accounts for practically half of world imports and acquires a certain form of central direction that will result from the common agricultural policy, it will no longer be necessary to organize the world market."

The most recent and accurate analysis of the tendencies toward agricultural agreements on a world and not a regional level is contained in an article by J. H. Richter, "Towards an International Policy on Agricultural Trade," *Kyklos* (1963) fasc. 2.

30. The need for programmed action is clearly sustained by Mansholt. In the speech quoted above, he declared: "We must all cooperate as closely as possible in working out a program for Western Europe as a whole. For there is no doubt about it, a program is needed; we must know where we are going, we must have a clear idea of the size of the farm population we hope to arrive at, of what steps are necessary to achieve this and of how we can finance them. If each of us goes his own way, Europe, for want of a single plan, will remain where she is today, so that by 1975 we shall be up against insurmountable difficulties."

31. Along this line of thought too, the most recent developments are extremely promising. We are all aware that the UN/FAO World Food Program is gaining ground daily. A new and courageous vision of the dimensions that can and must be assumed by such a program, if it is to contribute also to the solution of the agricultural problems of highly developed countries is given in the recent study sponsored by the Atlantic Institute with the collaboration of many American and European specialists. See the Final Report written by Pierre Uri, *Dialogue des continents: un programme economique* (Paris: Plon, 1963.)

In the speech already cited, Mansholt made the following remarks in this regard: "Our planning must be guided by the fact that there is an enormous need for food products in the world—indeed, this must be the cornerstone of our policy. We do not want to be misjudged for restricting production when there is a chance of raising nutritional level elsewhere in the world—yet we also know that we are still not able to solve the problem. To do so we must, in the first place, organize ourselves at the European level."

ERNESTO N. ROGERS

The Phenomenology of European Architecture

EUROPE is unique, owing to the particular character of its history and the influence that this has exerted on the expressive form of its cities and monuments. No other continent in the last 2000 years has had such a variety of political events and such a complex cultural pattern. Europe is the producer of original cultures and the mediator of other far-flung cultures; a study of the origins of European architectural terms inevitably leads outside Europe to a recognition of the immediate and intermediate influences of other civilizations; this occurs whether we examine ancient, medieval or modern architecture. If we draw up a balance sheet of this give-and-take of European architecture, we can state, without any fear of being taken for chauvinists, that in this dramatic exchange of experiences Europe has played a leading role because nothing taking place outside its territory can escape its influence, while all styles entering this territory have been unmistakably colored by its character. Such is the variety and the difference between the French and the Italian Gothic, to choose random examples, or between Italian and Scandinavian Romanesque, that all European events require a qualifying adjective in order to specify—although in a rather general way—their historical and geographic value.

What, then, does it mean to talk about European architecture in comparison with that of other continents?

Essentially, it means rediscovering a particular accentuation of figuration, as a result of which the religious and civic history of every age was fixed in spatial representations which could not have arisen elsewhere because they are all conditioned by one fact: that Judaic, Mongol, Arab and other cultures filtered into ours through Christianity; this set up a common measure for the various aspects of things, in idioms and in all social structures.

But it must be added that the very nature of places has a determinative dimension, since it is more easily referable to the human scale. In Europe there are no rivers with indefinable horizons, where

424

the waters run between shores so distant as to seem those of immense lakes or even the sea; nor are there any mountains with inscrutable peaks like the Andes or the Himalayas or infinite deserts like those in Africa; nor does Europe pullulate with men, like China or India; nor are there any rarefactions of communities as in the Pampas or in Australia. The relation with a human scale can always be grasped, just as the sense of social organization can always be perceived; therefore, this continent, so much smaller than others, has the greatest density of culture and the richest variety of combinations of the various elements making it up. This centripetal melting pot of civilization has the greatest centrifugal energy for influencing zones at great distances from its territory, and even today, in this critical moment of its political history, all comparisons show the leading role played by Europe.

It is no mere chance that the greatest danger of world war, despite the fact that the poles of dialectical tension are in the United States and Russia or China, is to be found in Europe; for while Europe is in itself not sufficient to cause such a war, should that war break out here it would quickly spread to every corner of the globe.

In dealing with the specific subject under discussion here, town planning and architecture, one must consider what is produced in one zone in order to understand what is happening elsewhere. The history of the past is actively present in all European cities, just as the development of modern thought and technology deeply influence them as well. Therefore, the first problem is to examine the relationships between the ancient and the modern, as the problem is seen on our continent.

The generations of architects who were still young "between-the-wars" and who came to maturity after World War II have taken on the task of revising the development of the *Modern Movement* in architecture, accepting its fundamental and irreversible tenets while enriching its detail in a process of continuous transformation. Only those who have understood this movement in a formalistic way have fallen into the error of following its initial expressions, accepting as a "style" the very movement which, by rejecting the notion of style as emanating from the figurations of the past, had implicitly denied the possibility of any prefigurative style and therefore all the more so of any codification of a "modern style."

It is always difficult to create an active harmony between what one accepts and what one refuses, because although a person may try to discover his own truth within himself and isolate it from all he has acquired from previous experiences, he cannot help being to some extent influenced by them: revolution cannot be completely divorced from tradition, even when it is only that part which makes the revolutionary aware of his role of opponent. A historically valid action must necessarily contain, to some extent, also a reaction: the dangers of the extremes are easy to make out, because on the one hand there is a modernism which is acritical and not differentiated with respect to the problems of culture; while on the other hand there is a conservatism which is insensible to the contributions of an evolution in the field according to which all works of art, being the interpreters of the moment in which they are executed, should represent that moment with expressions typical of the moment itself.

If, in our works, we wish to represent the totality of the culture which we necessarily share in, we cannot possibly ignore the contributions of the past. This concept has been at the base of much of the architecture which has developed since the period of functionalism. But many have failed to appreciate its value as essential continuity and are disappointed by what seems to them an involutional or even reactionary trend; but those who have grasped the more profound significance of this investigation into the past perceive its fundamental logical coherence and its cultural enrichment. This historical method may be applied equally successfully to the larger scale of the environment and the urban setting. This concept is decisive for evaluating new quarters worked into zones destroyed during the war and, in general, for the whole immense operation of restoration, as well as for the even more general work on settlement of an unusual size, whether in unsettled zones in the open country or limited to urbanized areas. Europe has been faced with two orders of problems, and on a scale much vaster than anything known before: very serious questions of a historical and sentimental character and also of a technical and social nature; the formulation of these problems inevitably leads to diverging solutions which only strong cultural action can integrate into a unit.

If we consider European cities in particular, which for the most part developed in keeping with an order which could be called evolutionary, it must be acknowledged that the huge and very rapid wartime destruction and the urgent need to construct and reconstruct have produced an actual break in the historical system. The mending of this break is insufficient owing to an overlapping of negative conditions of various kinds but all necessarily concomitant with the work of new design. The profound revolution in architecture occasioned by the Modern movement had not even fully matured when architects were summoned to translate thought into reality. Theoretical studies to establish productive systems adequate for meeting the exceptional market demand had in very few countries been subjected to the test of the building yard before being integrated, no longer as an experiment, in the practical field of large urban quarters. I am referring particularly to the conditions of prefabrication, a system which, although acknowledged by many even before the war as the system needed to transform the production of housing from the artisan to the industrial level, was still not fully and concretely seen in actual practice. Thus, the idea of rejecting formulations of a stylistic character had just begun to persuade vast numbers of individuals, by then aware of the need to plan not on the promptings of taste but in accordance with a scientific methodology, when, lacking experience of this kind even with constructions on a modest scale they were suddenly called on to deal with enormous problems.

This immaturity had the effect of turning the Modern movement against itself; freezing it in preconstituted forms deriving from stylistic formulas. These figurations, which embodied contradictions in terms with the very principles with which the Modern movement professed to be inspired, were in themselves inconsistent and such as to give little spiritual life to the reconstruction and an instrumentality not entirely satisfactory even on the practical level.

But the real failure of this movement is to be found in a widespread uncertainty of an intellectual character. This uncertainty does not enjoy the benefits of a systematic doubt or of a still unresolved series of problems, but it arises from a confusion of different ideologies, each of which is in turn seeking a plausible resolution for itself. Consequently, although the pressing need for housing is in itself a stimulus, it has resulted in neither a maturity of expressive modes, nor an adequate technology, nor any thinking capable of taking the responsibility for giving Europeans integrated environments again. Results may be acceptable and in a few instances even admirable, but it is still not where technology becomes one with art and art represents the sum of our ethical requirements. Therefore, against all our convictions that nothing can be considered valid unless it is such as a totality, we have to accept a few examples which we would consider a sample, an earnest or promise of the universality (dynamically dialectical and not dogmatic universality, of course) to which we aspire, for these examples contain the seed of the whole or, at least, they are conscious of this whole for the very reason that they betray their incompleteness.

With the end of the last war European architects had abandoned hope that they could direct the ever more chaotic and empiric expansion of urban centers. On considering the more advanced countries (England, Holland and Scandinavia) in which it was possible to work inside industrial and residential development by individuating case by case the best solution, architects agreed to accept the economic and political trends of a changing society; since they considered that abstract schemes (merely technical ideologies) had forever fallen from grace, they convinced themselves that their work could still be useful when they took action where it was still possible, keeping their choice within the limits of a number of concrete occasions and actions.

Indeed, while the architect was credited with having abandoned "drawing-board" projects and capricious poses, he risked more and more being accused of accepting inadequate measures and organizations: of having reduced his contribution to a very limited diagnosis of what was instead a much deeper and more general crisis throughout society. Consequently, the resulting cure, even when it was of some worth, did not affect the great problems of giving the city a new pattern.

It was within these terms that the figure of the architect of the second generation (in his fifties) began to take shape and, following him, that of subsequent generations. One can therefore readily see— I am talking about Europe but there are similar cases on all continents—why modern architects, through a process of elimination, have been narrowing down the terms of their research as with the passing of time they have had to wake up to reality; nor can the fact be avoided that it has been in this phase, during which the problems entrusted to them have been shrinking, that they have characterized and often even developed their artistic personalities, especially in countries in which contact with socio-economic reality has been most desultory, indeterminate, and less positively influential. In fact, countries with much more solid traditions in social questions and in town planning, where a slow but continuous reform has been going on for years, have been much less generous in cultivating rising personalities and tendencies in conflict with current architecture.

Instead, nations undergoing a transformation, with profound contradictions in their economic structures and a slow and difficult evolution in their political institutions, have more often produced exceptional architectural solutions and exemplary results. We need only mention Japan, Latin America and Italy.

It would be well to remember that this has not always been an exterior experience, a matter of taste: only in a few cases was it the result of true self-criticism applied in the hope of not losing contact with reality. The continual growth and urgency of work did the rest: every scheme had to be continuously fitted into reality and then partially modified; as a result it acquired a more and more characteristic and exceptional physiognomy.

Take, for example, Italian architecture, which has been accused of deviating from the Modern movement. This "deviation," however,

428

is true only to the extent that Italian architects have refused to fully accept all the hypotheses demanding a total break with the past advanced before and reproposed after the war by a few of the masters of modern architecture. These masters have always believed (and unfortunately they are not alone, for the ranks of their slavish imitators are swelling) in imposing a structural revision of dwellings and human collective living from above, through the soul-searching which presumably society would spontaneously undertake in the face of their great and brilliant intuitions. In this they are ideally not unlike the great utopians of the last century, predecessors who make them smile: unbending, full of hope and romantic optimism, continually disgusted with reality, ready to protest against the exploitation of man by an inhuman civilization, but incorrigible in their hope to save him through "technology" (or simply "aesthetics") and always ready to delude themselves as to the availability of means for achieving this goal.

After release from the academic manner imposed by schools like the Ecole des Beaux-Arts, a release effected by the Modern movement, the figure of the architect relapsed into what was recognized, both in Europe and in the United States, as a state of crisis. From the concept of the architect as the designer of façades averse to any deeper or more socially conscious intervention in the phenomenon of construction, we have moved on to the figure of the architect conceived as the demiurge of the whole historical process, the architect who believes in the cathartic role of architecture as being in itself sufficient for progress.

As this kind of architect with his curious illusions was firmly persuaded that his work could by itself substitute political renewal, he believed that he could identify the struggle for a new expression with that of a total revolution; this gave him the role of missionary (witness Wright, Le Corbusier and, in the field of teaching, Gropius). But he ended, especially in the case of his numerous followers and mannerists, by alienating these groups from any more direct intervention in the political-economic structure, or rather by confusing one struggle with the other and by blocking all clarification as regards the instruments to be used and the fields where this revolution was to be carried out. A typical attitude is that of Italian rationalist architects who opposed the rhetorical architecture of the Fascist regime with their own architecture, which was certainly much sounder and more progressive, without even trying to be real anti-Fascists and tear the system out by its roots. They came to condemn the regime actively only during its last years, when it was understood that modern architecture could hardly triumph as the expression of a free society until society itself was delivered from the oppressive restraints of the dictatorship. This is how modern Italian architects took on the role of conspirators and had their martyrs: the martyrs of a faith in art which had been transformed and had become identified with a much more efficacious political ideology. Pagano, Banfi and young Labo were slaughtered by the Germans because of their underground activities after militating in the ranks of the renewers of architecture.

Most modern architects who had survived the war and who were therefore faced with the task of carrying architecture on to deal with the problems of reconstruction were in many respects deficient in their cultural backgrounds and were clearly uneasy when they had to take part in the processes of production where sensibility in art was not sufficient but had to be reinforced with a thorough knowledge of the economic and social problems involved in the choice of technological means. The architect's area of professional competence was suddenly expanded beyond the normal limits of the works carried out in the recent past, to embrace such responsibilities as that of counsel in the use of financial elements; again, from his more limited duties as the creator of art, in architecture, interior decorating and design the architect had to take part as an active member in the teams charged with carrying out socio-economic research which would give rise to the expressive forms of architecture. Consequently, from the town planning activities traditionally carried out by the architect, he moved on to the configuration of large territories.

It was in this climate that the largest European cities (London, Stockholm, Rotterdam, Hamburg) developed plans which were modern in concept and based on integrated units of dwelling, work and recreation, but which ended by accepting the pyramidal structure of the city, progressing from a dense center heavy with overlapping functions to the most recent urban expansion. Also to be found in this picture was the revival of the "autonomous quarter," which proposed to enlarge the city by means of closed rings in equilibrium with one another and similar in process of dilution. This concept also made a certain contribution to the architect's culture in the framework of a general redemption, but in certain respects, in considering technical problems as the only real problems of structure, and in highlighting sectors of production and life in a purely schematic way, it ended by turning inward on itself. It deeply affected the generation of architects who graduated after the war and, for the very reason that it was so desperately schematic, caused several complex destructive trends toward formalism, routine professionalism and agnosticism, inasmuch as it based its presuppositions on technocratic or sentimental thinking and rejected all possible concepts of historical development of national conditions.

Before considering the great cultural alternative now winning the support of the better qualified architects in Europe, it would be advisable to get a clear picture of those sources which are its natural premise. First there was the greater thoroughness of studies on territory undertaken in the more advanced countries (the United States, England and the Soviet Union) even before the war and in recent years culminating in hypotheses anticipating future developments in urban centers. It should be noted, however, that these studies, which were carried out in an essentially scientific way, sector by sector (economy, statistics, sociology, etc), completely abstained from making any suppositions as to the factor of space in the future urban fabric and from making any conjectures as to the future development in the architectural unit, in the sense of an expressive and tangible manifestation of the qualities of a town plan.

The planning of a house, a school or the "heart" of a city under the public and private conditions still imposed today amounts to no more than the disintegrated reform of a few elements of the total pattern characterizing the complex reality of European regions. If the conservation of old centers is dictated only by sentimental impulses it amounts to no more than embalming, which runs against the vital stream of the historical process. But this kind of "activism" is equally deplorable when it is believed, in keeping with a rather short-sighted view of utilitarianism, that the works of the past are obsolete and, in consequence, one sets to work with criminal fervor on the demolition of old buildings, with the excuse of traffic requirements or other pretexts of this kind. Absurd as they are in themselves, these excuses are seen to be even worse when, under this trite justification based on pseudo-technical thinking, one discovers the avidity for money underlying so much capitalist speculation of this kind. The solution to the problem of historical centers, which unquestionably should be respected, takes on a positive meaning when viewed in organic relation to the more recently developed periphery; reciprocally, instead of being left to become a desolate and inhuman no-man's land, the periphery must be regarded as part of a whole of which the historical center may represent one of the essential components.

From the residue of any experience, if we wish to absorb it fully in our own individual or national existence, we can draw only the essential value, the active germ still capable of reproducing vitality, but not such aspects as are conditioned by the historical and physical environment, which are in all places determined by very specific causes.

The adventure of Palladian architecture, for example, holds for all others because no other style spread so far and lasted so long, and yet no other was so precisely characterized in the cultures that adopted it. Even Inigo Jones, for the very reason that he was more Palladian than Palladio himself, left his own unmistakable mark on all the works he derived from that master, despite his reverence for Palladio.

The value of Palladio, or of any great artistic expression, is such that it can nourish, without being consumed, other men or historical periods of great creative capacity, when they are able to accommodate their own world to the experience of history without being overwhelmed. The mark of the practical interpretation of Palladio persists in the British Isles and can be recognized beyond the middle of the eighteenth century in the works of the Adamses, who, although not neoclassicists in the true sense of the term, would not have been classical-romanticists in the way they were without the profound reciprocal influence of empiricism and Palladianism already intuited by Inigo Jones. Their example, if we overlook chronological matters, is a useful comparison for understanding Palladian architecture in the United States, a subject already discussed in a lucid critical analysis by Lewis Mumford (*The South in Architecture* [1941]). Here, this phenomenon is seen from another angle and again expresses a great variety of original developments of which I shall mention only two distinct cases: that of Thomas Jefferson, who was much more concretely Palladian and representative, and that of the decidedly more "democratic" instance of the architecture of dwellings in Virginia and New England. The latter are a Palladio qualified by the practical necessities and technical limits to which architects were subject in those regions at that time.

Palladio is an example of the centrifugal power of European genius, but I should like to mention the assimilation of Frank Lloyd Wright in Europe to illustrate the European centripetal capacity for assimilation. For all his dialectical opposition, Wright had assimilated the essence of Europe through Sullivan, as he had absorbed certain other lessons from Japan. Some of Wright's fundamental principles have been circulating in European culture and influencing it since he gave his great 1910 exhibition in Berlin. One need only consider these words of Mies van der Rohe (*The Museum of Modern Art* [1947]) to be convinced: "at this moment, so critical for us, the exhibition of the work of Frank Lloyd Wright came to Berlin. This comprehensive display and the exhaustive publication of his works enabled us to become really acquainted with the achievements of this architect. The encounter was destined to prove of great significance to the European development." And even more directly persuasive is, for instance, the German Pavillion at the 1929 International Exhibition at Barcelona, the work of the same Mies van der Rohe.

Wright's theory and realizations of continuous space, which have not only aesthetic but also symbolic and social significance, underwent a long elaboration of acclimatization here, and it is no paradox to state that the conception which was originally organic was profoundly transformed into a rationalist key by European culture. And it is not a matter of contamination, but of a true translation expressing with fresh energy the deepest generating essence of the phenomenon. To offer another example of architectural interchange between Europe and the United States, it is said, in this case by Leo Grebler (*Journal of the American Institute of Planners,* November, 1962) that "For many decades the United States looked to advanced European countries for models and guidance in the development of housing policies and the improvement of city planning. In the case of urban renewal, the shoe is on the other foot. It is not much of an exaggeration to say that the evolution of an articulate national program for the renewal of its cities and towns since 1949 has placed the United States in a position of leadership. Most of the Western countries on the European continent are only now on the threshold of national renewal programs. A few have adopted legislation in the past few years, and others are busily engaged in preparation. But more are involved than mere precedence in time. The legal and financial tools of our program have set a pattern for adaptation in other nations and are under intensive study by European specialists and governments everywhere. Our experience is being keenly watched. The stream of influence has been reversed. Instead of United States experts travelling to Europe for inspiration and instruction on housing policies, Europeans now come to our shores to look into urban renewal."

This statement is substantially true provided that we set concrete limits to this balance sheet of give and take and remove its somewhat mechanistic aspect. One can and one should always learn from everybody, without presumption; but one must also, and without timidity, bring to the union of peoples and individuals one's own contribution, especially the part of it which is original and specific and not an immediate thing for persons of different cultural position.

If there is anything inherent in the European spirit (God keep me from making racial distinctions!) it is a feeling for history, for the simple reason that Europe is the laboratory of history. Indeed, the most sensitive and, actually, the most modern Americans do not come to Europe to improve their technological knowledge, which only in exceptional cases is less advanced than our own, but to admire our public squares, the relationships of our urban organisms, and to become one with their essence. An old square may very well seem odd if it is considered only in the light of "practical" parameters, as it most assuredly would be if it were taken out of its natural context. But this is something beyond the mere forms that they take, for to this day the old square is still the essence of a way of life, and it is only the ultimate truth of this way of life that can be exported, for the purpose of giving substantially new appearances to those forms, appearances inherent in places greatly different from our own.

The great transformations which Europe needs are to be understood also in consideration of the dimensions of new technological means (traffic, for instance). This I have already mentioned, as well as the difficulty of achieving a valid synthesis in which there meet, driven by equal forces of necessity, both the technical and the humanist, understood not as irreconcilable antinomies but as indispensable parts of the dialectical process of history.

It may be useful here to point out a few examples, in one sense or the other, in order to demonstrate the real conditions of the European process in its concrete manifestations. Without pretending to formulate exhaustive conclusions, I should like to mention a few typical instances and turn our critical attention to the history of this postwar period, during which one must at least acknowledge the efforts made by many countries to renew themselves.

The most salient example is England, with its more than century old traditions in the problems of town planning and with its traditions growing from a more consummate experience of democracy, despite all the contradictions discovered not only by the theorist intent on ideal goals but even by any superficial observer who considers the substance of things. It can be said that in English democracy the pragmatic spirit has left its mark on the abstract ideal, so that this democracy has acquired highly specialized characteristics during a slow but sure reform of structures still burdened with conditions which would be unacceptable elsewhere; for the moment these structures guarantee the civil evolution of this country.

English town planning is a true mirror of the society which produced it, for it contains the qualities and limits of that society, even though these limits are for the most part absorbed and left behind in the almost inexorable march of its history. The over-all picture of city development in England compensates for its contradictions and makes them less obvious in a general blurring of the whole which if it discloses no negative protrusions, discloses nothing particularly positive either. The strongest criticism of the new towns has come from the English themselves (an authentic instance of self-criticism): they have admitted that despite the efforts to create a new town pattern, these towns have not achieved the self-sufficiency which their authors intended. Nor is their architectonic expression exemplary, because the English, for centuries so intelligent in organization, did not reveal an equally high talent for representing themselves in sufficiently valid images on the plane of figuration. The emblematic value of these images is certainly lower than their civil content. But all this effort, even if considered from a severely critical viewpoint, cannot fail to win our respect, and even our admiration. After the war the Labour government laid down the fundamental social structures, for example England's numerous schools, which are probably the best and the most complete, if not the most beautiful, in the world. But neither that government nor any that followed was able to give these new residential settlements any validity in terms of sensitive collective living, where the form directly expresses the validity of the content. Perhaps it was just this content which was formulated within much too narrowly empiricist and, for that reason, nonunified systems.

France is dominated by the figure of Le Corbusier, by far the greatest living architect in the world. The French do not particularly like or understand him, but they have nevertheless been unable to throw off his influence by an act of rebellion capable of offering substantial alternatives to his message. Le Corbusier's town planning and architecture are everywhere present, like a demon with magical powers whose influence must be passively obeyed with automatic gestures, unconscious to those who make them and therefore lacking any charge of authenticity such as might justify them. The Unité d'Habitation, and the urban vision which developed from it, is like a model which no one wants to accept but everyone ends by imitating in pale copies. And yet French work in prefabrication, carried out by highly intelligent but somewhat insensitive technicians, is one of the few European (and extra-European) experiences verified by many years of trial and error that is seriously moving toward better prospects.

Norway, Sweden and Denmark have achieved an equilibrium between the civil structures and the urban environments containing them, but they are small nations (Switzerland could also be included here) which are not useful as models for much bigger countries where the complexity of the components raises problems of quite a different magnitude, just as the experience gained by navigating in a lake would be of little use to those who have to face the winds and waves of the ocean.

As for Finland, we could more or less say the same thing as we said for France. Here the figure of Alvar Aalto is so outstanding that it has put his peripheral country in the very center of world attention. He personifies the confluence of organic culture and rationalist culture in all the objects he produces, from the teaspoon to the house and the city. Unlike Le Corbusier, who has produced only a train of mannerists, Alvar Aalto may be considered as truly the head of a school, even though many of his disciples are unaware that they are such, or (*nemo propheta in patria*) even deny that they are such. On the civil plane Finnish architecture is an excellent instrument for interpreting and forging reality, with many courageous openings for its evolution.

Although small and admittedly provincial, Holland is one of the European countries which carries out, especially at the level of vast concepts of town planning, among the greatest number of valid works because its way of life has found the juridical expression and practical way of being translated into concrete realizations.

Moreover, the tradition of modern architecture is also a national tradition for the Dutch, since they forged some of the most coherent branches of the movement. Here we need only mention De Stijl and a few aspects of expressionism to acknowledge the vitality of that people in the cultural and artistic debate, even though today one cannot credit them with as much prestige in their development of part of these earlier theories. For both in theory and in its formal consequences, the Dutch have taken to imitating themselves. The center of Rotterdam (Lijnbaan), which is the "heart" of the highly accurate reconstruction undertaken after Hitler's total bombing, betrays something frail in its figuration, in consequence of which the expression seems poor in content. The same can be said of Amsterdam, even though the coherence between the plans and the tridimensional reality of the new quarters makes it a model of a very honest civil scheme.

Germany, which bled itself of its own best architects, who went into exile during Naziism, has undoubtedly suffered from their absence, so that although a great many important international names were called on and produced good results in Berlin's "Interbau," this work lacks unified direction and is hardly the model of an organic quarter it was planned to be. On the other hand, the reconstruction of the center of Frankfurt, which was supposed to restore its courtly environment while respecting modern requirements, becomes despite the simultaneousness of its architectonic and urban character a phenomenon of a merely culturalistic nature. For the truth of an old environment cannot be repeated and the new requirements have not been expressed.

Characteristic of Yugoslavia's activities is careful choice in the policy and economy of planning. Although this is a socialist regime, we find a counterbalancing of the eastern world and considerable

436

TORRE VELASCA, MILAN (1956–58)

Architects: Lodovico B. Belgiojoso, Enrico Peressutti, Ernesto N. Rogers

"If . . . we wish to represent the totality of the culture which we necessarily share in, we cannot possibly ignore the contributions of the past."

APARTMENT HOUSE, VENICE (1957)

Ignazio Gardella

". . . Italian architects have refused to fully accept all the hypotheses demanding a total break with the past . . ."

DEPARTMENT STORE, ROME (1961)

Franco Albini, Franca Helg

"The generations of architects who . . . came to maturity after World War II have taken on the task of revising the development of the *Modern Movement* in architecture, accepting its fundamental and irreversible tenets while enriching its detail in a process of continuous transformation."

HAMBURG: THE NEW OST-WEST STRASSE

Part of the reconstruction of the city

"Germany . . . bled itself of its own best architects, who went into exile during Naziism . . ."

MARSEILLE:
UNITE D'HABITATION

Le Corbusier

"France is dominated by the figure of Le Corbusier, by far the greatest living architect in the world."

THE CONVENT OF "LA TOURETTE" (1959)

Le Corbusier

". . . The French do not particularly like or understand him, but they have nevertheless been unable to throw off his influence by . . . offering substantial alternatives to his message."

OFFICE BUILDING, HELSINKI (1961)

Alvar Aalto

"As for Finland . . . the figure of Alvar Aalto is so outstanding that it has
put his peripheral country in the very center of world attention."

WHOLLY PREFABRICATED MANSIONS, WARSAW (1962)

"After the suffocating climate of Stalinism . . ."

LOUGHBOROUGH ESTATE, LONDON (1952)

London County Council

"After the war the Labour government laid down the fundamental social structures . . . But neither that government nor any that followed was able to give these new residential settlements any validity in terms of sensitive collective living . . . the pragmatic spirit has left its mark on the abstract ideal . . ."

profiting from the experiences of the western world. In Zagreb expansion is provided for in very precise directives, even though the architecture amounts to no more than a rehash of early rationalist schemes.

After the suffocating climate of Stalinism, Poland reacted with a strong charge of feeling only in its reconstruction of Warsaw. But even this is historical despite the anti-historical character of its forms, which are supposed to represent a souvenir of its past beauty and an accusation of the invaders who destroyed it.

Today, many young people deeply opposed to the cultural tendencies of the recent past have been looking to European experience, as is characteristic of their history, and are particularly interested in the figurative trends and technological means (prefabrication) worked out in France.

I have mentioned Italy also several times in this essay, either directly or indirectly. To sum up, it is to be hoped that however painful Italy's troubles have been in the various sectors, social, economic, and specifically urban-architectonic, they will not have been in vain if we retrace our way back through the years during which we shed a number of heavy ideological chains and then move on to much broader and freer concepts. From such early realizations as the small town of Matera in southern Italy, sprung of a popular myth garnished with a bit of abstract moralism, we have come to the San Giuliano quarter near Venice, where Italian town planning roots itself in the matrix of the territory, starting from the reality of the moment and moving on to programs of integrated action on a much larger scale.

Besides this we have the projects for the city center of Turin, which seem to propose great city parameters, based on the intuitions of regional and national programs as well as on a more consummate vision of space in architecture. The relationships between these various functions have been constantly present in the minds of the planners. But there is still much to do: we need a modern law to release land from speculation; we have to redress the imbalances existing between the homes of the privileged and the many hovels still inhabited on this peninsula; in the schools we have to offer teaching designed to prepare architects capable of dealing with the concrete problems of the country, rather than clever routine professionals who indifferently take on either public or private commissions equally lacking in a human vision of problems.

If this is Italy, however, if these are the many other European countries whose many shortcomings I have pointed out, why did I say that Europe is still the leader? And why did I add that there is again hope? Perhaps the real reason for my optimism is that nowhere else (for all the errors of others) do I find so much uneasiness: this may not be a sure sign, in general, but it is sufficiently symptomatic of an actively critical state of mind, of a mature awareness of shortcomings and a will to overcome them with new means, new research and, if necessary, with new struggles. What we Europeans have to do, each within the context of the culture for which he is responsible, is to transform this anxiety into a propulsive force which will take the form of concrete works. This transformation will have to take place by way of a process of choice, while we turn to tradition even up to the very recent past in order to absorb it fully and keep our views fresh for the future; the choice will have to be intentional and set goals, even if on contact with reality they prove to be an unattainable conquest which arouses our hunger and thirst, Tantalus-like.

Of course, we shall have to fully penetrate the architectonic-urban phenomenon as it reflects on the man who has to live it and on the environment in which it arises: in the sociological environment and with the technological instruments by means of which it is realized both physically and aesthetically.

Our European history, if it is to continue its evolution progressively, must aim to transform all policy into culture and to base its actions on the necessity of this culture; for without it we shall slip into mere technology, a technology which would not serve our ultimate purpose because our technology would not be even comparable with that of countries technologically more developed.

FRANK BOWLES

Education in the New Europe

THE changing patterns of European society offer a design that can
be seen nowhere else in the world. In no other region is it possible
to observe so many stages of development, ranging from the most
complex modern society to unchanging simplicity, and from stunning
change in some aspects of European life to little or no change in
others.

There is no easy explanation for the patterns which have appeared in recent years, nor for the rapidity with which they have
developed. However, they can be studied by identifying the main
components of European life and setting them on a continuum which
covers the range from change to no change.

In making placements on such a continuum, it would probably
be reasonable to assign the position of greatest change to the component of transportation. Certainly, to take only one part of this
component, the expansion of the automobile industry, particularly
in the production of small cars—the 2 CV's, the Fiats, the Volks-
wagens, and the Dauphines—has brought about something very
much like a revolution. In fact, it is not one revolution, but many—
a revolution in transport, another in patterns of family living, another
in mass production and another, hidden under the surface, in credit
financing.

If transport be taken as one end of the range of the continuum,
then, one remove along it, there is the change in distribution. There
are the new products, including the unbelievable plethora of red and
yellow plastic in every imaginable and unimaginable form; new
abundance of products pouring across the lines where the customs
barriers once stood; new packaging, new marketing, new advertising and, plain to see, the supermarkets elbowing in among the
hereditary shop keepers, preparatory to elbowing them out of existence.

Housing, like distribution and transportation, has fallen into the
pattern of mechanization and mass production. Some of the largest

and noisiest machines in the world are tearing down European cities, while others are putting together huge building blocks into slab-sided buildings picked out in bright squares of color, which lift themselves under the long-necked cranes that are the contemporary form of the conjurer's wand.

There is newness in the fields and the villages. The red and green tractors have plowed deep in more ways than one. The fields are well tilled, but, save in the smaller holdings, they no longer have the patina of hand labor. The contrast with the older farm economy is so complete in some areas that it goes almost unremarked, but its effect in loosening the bond which has for so long held families to the farm can be measured in the number of children of farm families in upper grades of the schools, in the universities, and in the business offices in the cities, as well as in the statistics which show the declining farm population.

There is change in the factories too—combined with a curious lack of change. The new equipment, improved design, the acceptance of new product ideas such as washing machines and refrigerators, gives an impression of industrial revolution which stands oddly beside the fact of the continued tradition of family business and the pace of production which so often lags behind demand. Here, as in so many of the other phases of the continuum, the change is more important for what it may or will mean than for what it has meant.

In this successive placement of structural elements of European society along the line which stretches from major change to no change, the elements of transportation, production, distribution, commerce, mechanization and related activities at one end of the scale are a family of components which, having undergone major change, have combined to produce the image of "New Europe." At the other end of the scale, where the image of "Old Europe" remains strong and sharp, it is striking to the point of apparent paradox that education appears to find place with those other components which support the older image through resistance to change and maintenance of traditional patterns and functions.

The paradox, real or apparent, is heightened by the fact that European economists, planning experts and educators, through the Organization for Economic Cooperation and Development (OECD) and other study groups and consultative bodies, have been among the most assiduous students of the conditions required for economic change and technical development. In their studies they have concluded that there is a necessary relationship between educational development and economic growth. In fact, the basic theory of national development evolved by OECD states: "In a complex industrial society, economic strength derives from technology—in particular, the application of science to industry. This, in turn, is based on the creative capacity of man and his education." [1] In other words, the achievement of a complex industrial society rests upon a technology resting in turn upon an educational system which can develop the technology. This implies a continuous reciprocity of development as between science and technology on the one hand and education on the other, supporting a steady expansion of the industrial society.

Such a reciprocity of development has, in fact, taken place in both Russia and the United States. It began during the 1930's in both countries with expansion of technical, technological and professional education on the levels of secondary and higher education, followed by economic changes which were, of course, accelerated by the war, in turn stimulating further educational changes.

But no such sequence of relationships can be traced in western Europe to account for the changes which began in the mid-1950's and which by 1962 had produced the phenomenon of the New Europe. The prewar educational system was carried over to function as the postwar system, and it still functions, in outward appearance, largely unchanged. The outward appearance does not, of course, mean that European education has been static since before the war. But it does mean that the entire development of the New Europe has been built upon the education established by the Old Europe.

This fact is central to any examination of the present state and probable development of European education, for it instantly establishes three fundamental questions as the framework of such examinations. The first such question is:

What has been the relationship between the European educational system and the economic and technological developments leading to the emergence of the New Europe?

In answering this question, it is necessary first to establish the nature of the system of European education, which, as observed above, has been maintained without substantial change for many years.

Two basic facts control education in all countries of western Europe. The first is that education is supported by the state at all levels, free of cost, or at most at nominal cost, for all pupils. This means that, at least in theory, there are no financial barriers in the path of any student seeking education at any level. The second is that any level of education is open to any student who can qualify for it, it being understood that examinations control all movement from one educational level to the next. Thus, anyone who chooses may elect to try for the highest educational rewards, but he can attain them only through competition, and the competition becomes more severe as the upper levels are approached.

The base in this system is formed by a guarantee of education for all children up to age 14 years, or in some countries up to age 16. This guarantee means that on completion of primary school, usually at age 12, the student has a choice of three courses of action. He may continue general education up to the school leaving age and then leave school; he may enter preparation for higher education; or he may enter technical or vocational education to prepare for a specific occupation. This represents a wide field of choice, but the true breadth of opportunity is perhaps not as wide as it seems, for as of 1960 it was still true in western Europe that more than half of all primary school students dropped out of school at or before age 14. In this sense the presumed base of universal primary education becomes something very like a ceiling for most of the school population. There are also great differences between the two forms of education which carry beyond primary school.

The opportunity to enter preparation for higher education represents the maximum of educational opportunity. This form of schooling is actually a part of the university line, for it is entered by examination and taught by university-trained teachers using university methods, the programs of instruction are prescribed by the universities, and the final examinations are the university entrance examinations. University education itself means education in the arts, the sciences, the humanities or the liberal professions, preparing for careers in university teaching, in high government service or in professional life. The achievement of such education opens membership in the group which takes responsibility for policy and decision in all sectors of European life, as well as for scholarship and research, a group which essentially sets the intellectual, social and educational standards by which Europe is guided. The standards are severe. Ultimately less than 5 per cent of an age group enrolls in European universities.

The other form of educational opportunity beyond primary school is in the form of a separate and complex system for training artisans, certain types of teachers—including, in many countries, primary school teachers—technicians and professional workers, categories which cover such fields as social work, librarianship, nursing and surveying, as well as specifically industrial and technological fields. This is a system which offers an alternative to general secondary and university education. It does not provide for higher education for those who enter it, for, as noted above, higher education is strictly defined in terms of programs offered within university institutions. Nor does it provide for any real opportunity for entry to the university line for those who desire to change the course of their education, even though technically such opportunities do exist and are utilized by a few exceptional students. What it does provide is a service training which carries reasonable assurance of secure employment. It is a training which has made for highly competent artisans, mechanics, technicians and professional workers but which has had little commerce with the higher reaches of the educational system.

The marked differences between educational opportunities available in different parts of the European system have been realized for many years. They formed the basis for what may be described as a prophetic dialogue on the need for educational change which began in England during World War II. This resulted in the Education Act of 1944, which introduced a form of universal secondary education and raised the school leaving age to 15 years. In another set of significant actions at the same time, England also introduced specific encouragement for students of high ability in the form of a large national scholarship program to assist them to prepare for and to enter universities.

Carried over to the continent at the close of the war, this movement was picked up and developed on the theme that the existing educational structure was not democratic. As pointed out in an article on "The Reform of Education in France," [2] the existing educational system was in reality two sub-systems, one for the bourgeoisie and one for the people, essentially different and very difficult to fuse. (In fact, as the description of the system has already shown, the two component sub-systems had only primary education in common, and separated at the point of entrance to secondary schools.) Secondary education preparing for the university was viewed as perpetuating classical culture, and as therefore having been given priority over modern education. The enlargement of popular education had not, in fact, made secondary (and higher) education any more accessible, nor had it effectively improved the quality of primary education.

Entirely aside from these organizational considerations, a new point—democratization as an ideal—was presented in social terms:

There is a new factor—aside from war devastation—which stresses the need for reform: our awakening consciousness of the needs of a true democracy, passing beyond simple constitutional affirmations into the depths of social living, and into all the relationships between man and man. Social entity and the full respect for the individual—these two terms must be made closely complimentary and schools must become the pattern and instrument of true democracy.[3]

443

Two years later, the report of the Langevin Commission, evaluating French education, produced four principles which may be taken as the precepts of democratization: (1) social justice, by which every child was to be assured of opportunity to achieve the maximum development his personality and aptitude could permit, without social or economic barriers; (2) a reclassification of real values to equalize social tasks, whether manual, technical, artistic or intellectual; (3) provision for general guidance in the schools followed by vocational guidance, so that "every worker and every citizen will be directed to the kind of work for which he is potentially best fitted" [4]; (4) provision for general education. "If education must yield a larger and larger place to specialized education, the training of the worker must, nevertheless, not jeopardize the development of the man." [5]

The movement which thus early acquired the name of democratization and a formally stated philosophy in England and France actually developed simultaneously in every European country. It took the very direct form of a substantial enrollment increase in primary and secondary schools. This increase was not traceable to change in either the structure or the standards of education as offered in those schools. It was, rather, due to what appeared to be a widespread and spontaneous decision by parents of school children that their children should remain in school longer, complete the level of education in which they were enrolled and, if possible, proceed to the next higher level of education. Thus, a larger percentage of primary school pupils completed primary school, a larger percentage of those completing primary school went on to some form of secondary education and a larger percentage of those entering secondary education stayed on to completion. This piling of increased percentage upon increased percentage, even without increase in the size of the age group, inevitably produced a mushrooming effect on enrollments at all levels. The effect of this phenomenon has been presented and projected by the French publication *L'Explosion Scolaire,* which pointed out that "In 1900, for an average of 800,000 annual births, there were 6,000,000 pupils in all types of schools. . . . Now, in 1970, education enrollments will reach the figure of 11,-000,000, that is to say, from a birth rate essentially the same as that of 1900, nearly double the enrollments of 1900." [6]

An appraisal of the results of the democratization movement is difficult to make. It is essentially a statement of social goals which was made simultaneously by a number of people at about the time that a major economic change was in its early stages of development. Under such circumstances, an examination of enrollment figures for European education in 1950 and 1960 provides general information on enrollment patterns but no very clear indication as to whether changes were due to educational reforms or economic development. What is of interest, however, is the fact that clear patterns of enrollment change do emerge, and that in general they conform to the goals stated by those urging democratization.

The source of information for the following statistics on enrollment in European countries, at the several levels of education, is the UNESCO *World Survey of Education.* Volume II of this series gives data for the period 1948–1950 and provides a basis for comparison with the figures for the period 1958–1960 which appear in Volume III. (All figures have been rounded.)

Type of School	Number of Schools		Number of Pupils	
	1950	1960	1950	1960
Primary	285,000	328,000	30,000,000	32,000,000
General Secondary	16,500	26,000	5,000,000	6,800,000
Terminal Secondary	23,000	24,000	4,700,000	7,100,000
Higher Education	194	224	690,000	970,000
Totals			40,390,000	46,870,000

Examined first in terms of general patterns, these figures show an increase in the number of primary school students which mainly reflects population increase at the primary school age level. The increase in numbers of schools shows a major improvement in educational facilities. More important is the fact that in 1950 only one European child in three went beyond primary school, while in 1960 the proportion had risen to better than two out of five.

Secondary school enrollments increased from 9,700,000 to 13,-900,000, reflecting the increased movement of primary school students on into secondary schools. But even more interesting than this general increase was the shift in direction shown by the figures. In 1950 more than half of the students entering secondary education had gone into the line leading to higher education. By 1960 the proportions had shifted and it was the vocational, teacher-training, semiprofessional—in short, the technical terminal line which attracted more than half of the students.

Of the one primary school student in six who in 1950 entered the line of secondary education leading, presumptively, to higher education, one in five would expect to enter higher education and, beyond this, one in two would finish some program of studies within higher education. Restated in terms of final products, these figures mean that one in thirty primary school students might expect to enter universities, and that one in sixty would finish a program of studies. In 1960 these ratios remained substantially the same, although the numbers of students had, of course, increased. There had also been a substantial increase in the number of schools, representing what has unquestionably been an expansion of opportunity to enter the university line as the favored area of education.

With respect to the terminal-technical line, it will be observed that slightly better than one out of seven primary school students entered that line in 1950, but that in 1960 the ratio had changed to better than one out of five (better than the 1960 ratio for students entering the higher education line). These programs in general have been less demanding than those in the university line and, of course, they are shorter since they do not carry students into the third level of education. It can be estimated that one in three of those entering these programs would finish a program and receive some form of qualification. This meant that in 1950 about one primary school child in twenty could expect to receive such a qualification, while in 1960 the number would be one in fourteen. This substantial increase in numbers of students has not been accompanied by commensurate increase in numbers of schools. This situation, compared to the sizable increase of facilities in the university preparatory line, is difficult to explain, although it may well be that schools in this line have been relatively uncrowded and therefore had substantial room for expansion. But, whatever the reasons, it would seem that the enlarged enrollment in the technical-terminal line was unexpected and, on the whole, had not been prepared for. This would suggest that the movement for democratization of education may have been taken more seriously by parents and students than it was by the planning authorities in ministries of education.

The number of students enrolled in higher education increased by 280,000, an increase over ten years at about the same rate as the increase of enrollments in the university preparatory line, indicating that the percentage of students in primary education planning on and ultimately achieving entrance to higher education, remained fairly constant, despite increases in numbers.

The small increase in the number of institutions of higher education relative to the large enrollment increase indicates that expansion has been taken care of largely by putting more students into existing institutions. In fact, the increase in the number of institutions is overstated, because about one third of the new ones exist only on paper, or are just beginning their work. Even assuming that all are operating at full capacity, the size of the average European university has gone up from 3550 to 4330 students, an increase of 20 per cent over ten years.

The higher education enrollment figures include a certain number of enrollments in higher technical education, but it is difficult to say how many, since this is not defined as higher education in many countries. If the figure were available, it would be an important indicator of the effects of economic and technical change on educational enrollments. Since it is not available, it is necessary to estimate. Starting with the fact that the Grandes Ecoles in France and the British Colleges of Advanced Technology fall into this category, as well as higher technical schools in some other countries, it would appear probable that the number of students in this field is about 100,000—a sizable number, but well short of a movement.

The system which included preparation for higher education, and the corpus of higher education itself, probably produced in 1950 about 85,000 graduates of universities and 100,000 secondary school graduates who had finished university preparation but who had dropped out of schooling before completing any university program. By 1960, these numbers had probably risen, respectively to 90,000 and 110,000, a relatively modest rate of growth.

The system of technical-terminal and professional education probably produced in 1950 about 100,000 individuals who had attained technical, professional or teaching qualifications and about 150,000 who had qualified via the apprenticeship route as skilled workers. By 1960 the comparable figures would probably be 175,000 with technical or professional qualifications, and 200,000 skilled workers coming out of the apprentice training programs. This must be counted as a rapid rate of growth in this form of education.

These figures, unfortunately, are no more than estimates, for neither in 1950 nor in 1960 were there any statistics available on the total annual product of European education. Nor is it possible to estimate the value, for European society, of the large numbers of students who continued their studies beyond primary school but did not complete any further qualification.

Insofar as can be judged from this meager evidence, there was no sign within the European educational system, prior to 1950, of any development such as the enlargement of technical education, which might have been construed as preparing for a major technological development. Indeed, the limited size of the technical education establishment and, despite its ease of access, its actual unpopularity as compared with the path to higher education could have been taken as indicators that the system would have difficulty supporting a major development resting on applied science and technology.

The 1960 figures indicate an increased rate of enrollment at all levels of education with a strong emphasis on technical and professional programs. This emphasis did not indicate any shift away from interest in university entrance, for this continued at the same rate as before, but rather a marked increase in interest in education beyond the elementary level, which accepted technical and specialized education as the best available opportunity. This is a significant shift which represents the first stage in the establishment of the reciprocity between educational and technological development postulated by the OECD statement already quoted. However, this shift, although important for the developments it foreshadows in the future, does not affect the fact that emergence of the New Europe was accomplished from the educational base supplied by and for the Old Europe.

This opens up a puzzling question, for while there are no sure criteria for testing whether an educational system is producing enough trained individuals to support an economic and industrial revolution, it would have seemed clear that the European system as described could hardly have been doing so. In fact, the system at the close of World War II and for some years thereafter was obviously doing exactly what it had been organized and developed to do—to provide new cadres of trained individuals each year in the numbers required to maintain the existing social and economic organization. However, against this statement must be placed the fact that the economic and industrial revolution did take place, and that it did so without giving any advance notice detectable within the educational system. This fact leads directly to the second fundamental question on the present state and probable development of European education. This is:

How has it been possible for evident and large-scale economic, political and social change to take place in Europe during the last ten years without obvious change in educational systems?

The answer to this question requires an examination of the most obvious of the factors on which the development of the New Europe has rested.

Probably first in importance among these factors is what may be described as the unblocking of industry. The use of the phrase involves three points—that European industry has long had the equipment and manpower for mass production and distribution; that it had not until recently had the opportunity to apply them to those ends; and that changes in European life since the close of World War II have opened those opportunities and changed the orientation.

A brief statement of the basis of these comments begins with the observation that the close of the first war left Europe with an immense task of physical reconstruction, with a heavy external debt to the United States, with one of its largest markets shut off by the American Smoot-Hawley tariff, with a heavy commitment for the support of colonial empires which in hindsight may now be seen as economic liabilities, and, above all, in a state of political readjustment. The difficulties of the 1920's were followed by the depression and political turmoil of the 1930's and the tragic war of the 1940's. Only after the war, with the re-entry of the United States into world affairs, the massive infusion of capital into the European economy, and the reopening of world markets, did European industry have the opportunity to realize on its potential. This realization was delayed until the mid-1950's only by the time required for readjustment —actually, the ten years elapsed after the close of the war represented a surprisingly short time for the effective beginnings of industrial expansion.

The second of the major factors was the series of changes which took place with the rationalization of agriculture. The large-scale introduction of agricultural machinery and of modern methods of agriculture increased yields to the point where the feeding of Europe could be done from less land and with the employment of less labor than ever before. In consequence, much poor land was driven out of use and a substantial part of the agricultural labor force was freed to become part of a labor pool for industry.

A third major factor was the development of a large pool of inexpensive labor, drawn in part from labor released by the rationalization of agriculture; in part refugee labor from eastern Europe; and in part from labor from Italy, Spain, and Portugal, where the pace of economic development was notably slow during the decade after the war. The existence of this pool has operated effectively both to hold down labor costs and to make labor quickly available for new enterprises or for expansion of existing productive capacity.

A fourth factor has been a consequence of the first three. Rising employment has contributed to rising incomes, rising standards of living and rising consumption, so that a substantial internal European market was generated to support rising production. Concomitantly, these developments contributed to bring about a sharp expansion in the third or service sector of the economy, which had been relatively unimportant in the slow-moving economy of the prewar and early postwar period.

A fifth factor contributing to increased production and improved distribution has been the movement for the integration of certain sectors of the European economy. Beginning with the critical areas of fuel, power and steel, it moved circumspectly toward the economic areas, eventuating in the creation of the Common Market. This community, with the lowest internal tariffs in the world, became automatically the largest unified market in the world in terms of population and resources, linked by excellent communications systems and

449

open by preference to the products of Europe's expanding industry and agriculture.

In addition to the five factors named, all of which contributed directly to economic change in Europe, there are two other factors which have an important but indirect bearing on the change.

The first of these, and the sixth among important factors in European development, has been the loss of European colonial empires. This loss, which according to older economic theories should have been disastrous to Europe, has actually proved a blessing in many ways. It has removed the problems and the burdens of colonial governments and has made former colonial administrators and colonists available in their home labor markets. It has ended the drain of colonial troubles, including some wars of considerable size. It has brought nations into existence which have been eager to enlarge their trade and which have actually created new and larger markets to replace the limited colonial markets. It has shifted the money paid out for the support of colonies into loans to independent nations, and even though many of these loans may in time be canceled, they have nevertheless had at least the temporary effect of trade stimulus and the opening of new investment opportunities. And, what may in the long term be more important than anything else, it has brought about revolutions in the educational establishments of the former colonies, increasing the educational opportunities they offer and producing in many cases closer intellectual ties with the former mother country than had existed during the colonial period.

A seventh factor, also indirect in its effects and particularly difficult to evaluate, has been the development of technical competence and political longevity in government. Essentially, this has been the result of a rise in administrative power within governments and the extension of administrative responsibilities into the field of political decision making. The difficulty of analysis here lies in the fact that administration by bureaucracy has always been an important feature in European government. It provided a stability which balanced the volatility of parliamentary government and was at the same time responsive to parliamentary control. It maintained its position by being nonpolitical, which meant, first, that the bureaucracy did not support any one political party against the other and, second, that it left political decisions to political parties. However, with the development of industrialization and the moves toward European integration, the position of the bureaucracy changed in two respects. One change was the rise of an industrial bureaucracy to a size and power comparable to that of governmental bureaucracy, with the significant difference that industrial decisions were often of such scope as to have the political effect of forcing the government in the same direction. The other change was the creation of inter-governmental technical bodies to administer the new supranational agencies. These bodies produced technical recommendations which, in their complexity, went beyond the capabilities of parliamentary government. They therefore required technical action within govern-ments which then had the effect of political actions. Their approval by parliaments became formalities which ratified the cession of political power to the technical experts and which, in turn, held the experts in office as the persons best qualified to deal with the in-creased technical responsibility of governments.

The list of factors which brought about the development of the New Europe is by no means completed with the seven that have been discussed. However, it seems evident that these seven cover most of the major items that ordinarily figure in economic develop-ment, and equally evident that they are independent of educational change. Rather, they have depended on education and training already accomplished, upon the existence of basic industrial capacity, technical knowledge, management skill, a supply of trainable labor, waiting markets and active government commitment to industrial development. Given these basic conditions, only a few triggers were required to set the production-consumption mechanism in motion.

The triggers themselves took many forms but, generally speaking, they probably fell into two groups of actions which had more or less immediate effects upon the European economy. The earliest actions, taking place well before the signs of the emergence of the New Europe, were in the form of Marshall Plan aid and the planning and administration which developed around it, accompanied by the actions establishing the planning and coordinating agency which was to become the OECD, and in the early moves toward integration of specific sectors of the European economy. These were all actions which tended to support and coalesce the factors which did touch the economy, and to point a direction for movement.

Following these moves, the slow decline in political tensions and the development of decolonization during the middle years of the 1950's created conditions favorable for government support of industrial development, for joint planning and eventually for eco-nomic integration on a scale larger than has even been tried before. These triggers were essentially psychological, creating an atmos-phere and eventually a confidence and a concentration which were indispensable for development, once the movement had started.

The accumulation of evidence now makes it clear that, at least in the Europe of the 1950's, educational change did not precede tech-nological and economic development, which amounts to saying that

451

the existing system for all its problems and presumed faults was strong and flexible enough to support major change. However, this does not mean that there is no need for change to support the continued growth of the European economy and to consolidate the social and political gains that have been made during the past decade. This observation leads to the third of the three questions as to the present state and probable development of European education. This is:

What changes in European education appear to be necessary to support the continuation of the economic and social developments which have created the New Europe?

The examination of this question begins with a further consideration of the factors already listed as largely responsible for the changes which have taken place in terms of the educational consequences which they have produced.

1. The unblocking of industry, having opened the way to industrial expansion, has obviously been responsible for a number of changes, of which three have important educational implications. These are:

a. A sharp rise in urban population resulting from the increase in the size of the industrial labor force and its concentration in industrial centers. This, in turn, has resulted in new concentrations of markets and new patterns of consumption. It has also resulted in new patterns of communal living which, in turn, have made possible a concentration of educational activity.

b. The rationalization of industrial production following upon increased size of industrial plants and increased concentrations of industrial labor. These factors have eroded the foundations of small enterprise in many fields and forced industrial concentrations to the levels of medium and even larger enterprise.

c. A rising demand for technical personnel resulting directly from the rationalization of industrial production, as a direct product of increase in size of production units and use of modern equipment and facilities. In particular, there has emerged a demand for the type of senior technician capable of assuming supervisory and management responsibilities which in smaller enterprises were dealt with directly by the proprietor in his role as manager.

In the first stage of industrial expansion, it has been possible to meet this demand by using either experienced foremen or trained engineers. However, in the long run the supply of experienced foremen trained through apprenticeship is not large enough to meet continued expansion of demand, and the services of trained engineers are too difficult to obtain and too costly to be devoted to what are essentially the tasks of technicians. Since, as already observed, European education does not in general provide for the training of senior technicians, this demand has proved difficult to formulate, and has so far elicited little response.

2. The rationalization of agriculture has also produced several results which bear upon educational changes. These are:

a. The reduction in the size of the agricultural population required to maintain food production contributing to the urbanization trend already mentioned which, in turn, has made possible a concentration of educational activities which was simply not possible in sparsely populated rural areas.

b. Improved methods both increasing the quantity and holding down the costs of agricultural products, adding considerably to the attractions of urban life, as well as increasing the flow of agricultural income.

c. The enlarged productive capacity of agriculture, depending in large measure on technical improvements, bringing pressure on agricultural education to add a professional level to the vocational and technical levels at which it has been offered until recently.

3. The large labor reserve pool which existed in western Europe after the close of the war was, as already suggested, an important factor in supporting industrial development. However, it had quite an opposite effect on educational development. By supplying mature individuals who were unskilled, or semiskilled, and who could be trained as skilled workmen on the job—that is to say, in apprentice type training—it tended to perpetuate and even enlarge apprentice training and to mark the need for change in methods for the formal education of industrial workers. These effects were relatively long lived, for the training methods still persist.

The pool, however, is drying up, in part because of the closing of frontiers in eastern Europe, partly because of economic improvements in western Europe which have cut down on worker migration and partly because much of it has been absorbed into the active labor force.

As it dries up, two interesting results of its existence become clear. The first is that the apprentice method of training can no longer be supported now that its base of cheap labor, which has tended to depress all labor costs, is dissolving, for with this base gone, the system emerges as costly in time and in production results. The second is the need for an extension of the existing patterns of technical and vocational teaching to provide for more general education and more advanced training in specialities—a natural consequence of the need to replace cheap labor, no longer available, with the combination of modern equipment and workers capable of operating it.

4. The enlarging class of industrial workers and the developing service force have created a new demand for educational opportunity. This demand, which is evident from the enrollment statistics presented earlier, is conveniently matched to the demand for more and better trained workers, and, what is of real importance, it brings political pressure as represented by the workers' votes to the support of evident educational needs.

5. Demands of the developing technology for more scientific knowledge as a base for further expansion and more technical skills to make the expansion possible have emerged as, essentially, demands for increased research activities.

Such demands have already posed serious problems. Europe has always had, on paper, an imposing array of research enterprises. However, most of these have been small, consisting often of a small research title and an office attached to a professor or to a group of professors, and their product has been limited by their scale.

But present requirements for equipment and research personnel which can deal with major problems are such as to require large support. In some areas, notably that of atomic energy, the costs involved are beyond the reach of many governments and can be met only on an intergovernmental basis, which has meant moves toward European integration on the research level. One handicap in research expansion has been a developing shortage of personnel, outstripping the present output of universities.

A further factor should be mentioned as of an intergovernmental nature. This is the planning and evaluating activities conducted by OECD and other agencies which provide yardsticks for the measurement of changes that have taken place and goals for activities in progress. There can be no doubt that they have had a direct influence on provisions for educational expansion.

6. The decolonization of the European nations is a factor which has so far received relatively little public attention as a factor affecting European life, and it is therefore difficult to assess in terms of its implications for education. It is clear that it has contributed to the increase of the European labor force, both directly by the return of colonists and indirectly by the reduction in military establishments which it has made possible. However, its direct educational effects may well be limited to the responsibilities that most European countries have assumed with respect to their former colonies. These include the foundation and support of universities, the development of secondary, technical and vocational education, and assistance in the expansion of primary education. These are, of course, considerable activities, and they do have a traceable influence on the educational system.

7. The increasing political longevity of European governments and the developments of technical and administrative competence which have gone with it have provided still another form of demand for highly qualified technicians to support what may be termed a rising level of technical discussion. The phrase refers to the fact that actions required to deal with the European problems which are now, in some areas, superseding national problems require approaches which are broader and, at the same time, more technical than had been employed before. The result is the continuous and highly practical training of technicians of the highest level, accomplished by drawing engineers out of industry, administrators out of business and economists, demographers, sociologists and scientists out of universities into direct participation as technicians in governmental and intergovernmental decisions. This method of recruiting and training has given a new meaning to the term "technician" and, in so doing, has made it possible to think of the education of technicians as a reasonable activity for the universities, which in the main have, until now, turned away from it.

These pressures on education, developing out of the factors which have changed the European economy, have generated certain specific requirements which European education must plan to meet. In terms of three levels of education, these are:

For higher education:

To enlarge the capacity of present university programs to increase the number of teachers, scientists and administrators that can be graduated from universities to meet increased requirements for such trained individuals. The existing system of universities, if it does not add any new programs of study, must double in capacity by 1970 in order to meet these requirements.

To create by 1970 a new sector of technical higher education to provide programs for the training of senior technicians and professional workers who are now trained at the level of secondary education. This form of education now exists on only a limited scale, but by 1970 it should be as large as the university sector if it is to meet developing demands.

For secondary education:

To double the enrollments in the general secondary line, leading to university entrance, to support enlargement of university enrollment.

To improve both the general education offerings and the preparation in basic science within what is now technical secondary education and double the size of the improved programs in order to supply the students required for expanding higher technical and professional education.

To phase out apprentice-training, replacing it as rapidly as possible with full time vocational schooling carrying to age 16 years, or, in some areas, to ages 17 or 18.

For elementary education:

To plan on an increased flow of students from elementary school into all forms of secondary education in order to support enlarged secondary school enrollments.

To give particular attention to talented or unusually able students and to urge them on in the educational system.

These requirements may be related to the estimates of OECD that there will be an increase in school attendances over the next decade of 18 per cent of the 5–14 or elementary school age group; of 94 per cent of the 15–19 or secondary school age group; and of 83 per cent of the 20–24 or higher education age group.

It is not possible to predict the extent to which these requirements as stated will actually be met, for the variables within the problem are numerous and powerful. However, a recent report supplies information on developments of the past several years which indicate that the democratization movement has now developed strength and has had considerable influence on primary and secondary education. Evidence as to developments in higher education is less conclusive but indicates that considerable expansion of size and some enlargement of function are under way. The report supplies specific information on the following points:

1. The extension of compulsory education. ". . . extension of compulsory schooling to the age of 16 and even sometimes to 18 is an object of common concern to nearly all countries. Some have already put it into practice (France, Sweden); others are planning to do so in the near future or have already introduced it experimentally (Federal Republic of Germany, Austria, Denmark, Luxembourg, and several Swiss cantons), and others are now considering it in connection with their plans for educational reform or are attempting to introduce it by encouraging voluntary continuation of studies beyond the age limit for compulsory school (Belgium, Spain, Ireland, Italy, Great Britain, Norway, the Netherlands, and Turkey)." [7]

2. Easing of requirements for admission to secondary education. "There is a general tendency to abolish the examination hitherto required for transition from the primary to the secondary period. Moreover, coupled with the extension of compulsory schooling, there is in most countries a desire to postpone by some years the age at which pupils must make a choice with a view of specializing in certain subjects. Henceforward, instead of deciding on a child's future

once and for all . . . on the results of a transitional examination, a number of countries plan or have already put into effect, measures for placing pupils under observation for one, two, or three years at the end of the primary period in order more accurately to assess whatever inclinations, ability and aptitude they may have for some type of specialized education." [8]

3. Easing of movement between programs. ". . . in nearly all countries, steps have been or will be taken permitting pupils who have been guided into unsuitable channels or whose intellectual qualities or manual dexterity reveal themselves at a later age, to pass without difficulty from one type of specialized instruction to another." [9]

4. The reorganization of the secondary period hitherto confined to "classical" studies and its division into "streams" for all types of education. "Until quite recently, the humanities (classical secondary studies) had a prestige value stemming from the fact that they were the sole means of access to the liberal professions or to posts of leadership. Today, as a direct result of the progress of science and technology, (secondary) education in these branches holds an equally, if not more, esteemed place." [10]

5. The placement of vocational and technical education as one of the options during the lower level of secondary education. The distinction between technical education and general secondary education remains strong in many countries, but a number of countries are experimenting with multilateral schools from which the students may move after completion of a first cycle of studies into the type of studies best suited for them.

This summary indicates that the expansion and even the reform of secondary education has received careful attention in European countries. However, it is not possible to make the same statement with respect to higher education.

Generally speaking, all countries anticipate increased enrollments in higher education and foresee a particular need for strengthening scientific and technical education. England, France, the Netherlands, Norway and Sweden are making detailed plans in terms of doubled enrollments within a decade. Austria, Belgium, Germany, Italy, Portugal, Spain and Yugoslavia are engaged in studies of varying scope and depth as to the needs and problems of expansion. But, as an OECD report remarks, "A survey of all these plans gives the impression that expansion is more stressed than reform." [11]

The data presented in the preceding paragraphs complete the tally of available data as to the present state of educational development in Europe and its relation to economic development. The findings that can be drawn out of these data are sparse. There had been before 1950 little educational change in Europe which could be identified as related to technological and economic development. By 1960, some such developments could be identified on the levels of primary and secondary education. By 1963, a study had found significant change under way within secondary education, and another study had detected stirrings in the field of higher education.

The data, or the lack of them, underline the problems which European education faces. The urgency for change lies within higher education, but the response reflects no sense of urgency. There are signs of expansion of traditional forms of higher education, but as yet the universities, even as they expand, are unwilling to accept technical and technological education, including education in the service professions, as higher education.

The university resistance to such acceptance is not negative in the sense of blind opposition to change, but affirmative and vocal in the defense of broad and leisured learning, or scholarship and of intellectual community, in short, of long-established standards versus the hurried demands of mass education. However, the motivations which support the block are beside the point. The point is that the effectiveness of the block creates and supports the illusion that the present system is adequate and that there is no need for change. In fact, the present situation in education parallels the 1950 situation of industry. A block exists, concealed but firm. By its existence, it establishes immobility at all points. Removal of the block opens a completely new pattern of movement in which even the oldest immobile elements take on new life.

In this context, it does not matter whether universities take on and develop the new sector of education or whether, as was done in the United States by the creation of the land grant colleges, an independent sector of education is established and given support for development. The point is that the block must be removed if the sector of education is to develop. Once removed, it will expand rapidly and standards will rise, until the parity with existing programs of education becomes self-evident.

It must be observed that it is not inevitable that the block will be removed. European universities are so strong and their control over the channels of education so complete that they may continue, perhaps for a generation, their indifference toward problems of education for an industrial age. In that case, other channels will be found. It is fully within the power of industry to establish its own school systems for the training of its needed specialists. In fact, more or less formally, an extensive network of such programs evists already. This will not be the same thing as provision of educational channels for the newer forms of specialization, but it will be an answer. Unhappily, the answer will contribute to the alienation of industry from education—always a danger under any system, and a certainty when education refuses its support to industry.

The sum of the matter is that education in the New Europe is now on the knife edge of decision. It may choose to accept new tasks, or it may refuse them. Refusal would be, certainly, from the best of motives—the determination to hold fast to basic values. Yet, in the act of such refusal, there would be the tragic loss of the richer opportunity to establish anew the validity of those values against the changing background of our time.

REFERENCES

1. OECD, *Forecasting Manpower Needs for the Age of Science* (Paris, 1960), p. 4.

2. Henri Wallon, *France, New Plans for Education* (London: New Education Fellowship, 1946), p. 5.

3. *Ibid.*, p. 5.

4. Langevin Commission, "La Réforme de l'Enseignement" (Paris, 1947), p. 9, as cited by A. E. Meyer in "Langevin Plan for Reform of Education in France," *School and Society*, July 10, 1948, p. 19.

5. *Ibid.*, p. 19.

6. Comité Universitaire d'Information Pedagogique, *L'Explosion Scolaire* (Paris, 1961), pp. 13, 14.

7. Jean Thomas and Joseph Majault, *Educational Problems Common to European Countries,* report to the Third Conference of Ministers of Education (Rome, 1962), p. 13.

8. *Ibid.*, p. 14.

9. *Ibid.*, p. 14.

10. *Ibid.*, p. 15.

11. OECD, *Policy Conference on Economic Growth and Investment in Education* (Paris, 1962), II, 59.

FABIO LUCA CAVAZZA

The European School System: Problems and Trends

I Introduction

IN comparing the school systems of the United States and western Europe, one cannot help but notice the much higher output of the former as compared to that of the latter. It is even more surprising to note that at the beginning of the century no substantial difference in output was observable. How does one account for the divergent developments of the two systems?

It seems to us that it was in the period between the two world wars that the difference in the respective rates of expansion became most dramatically pronounced. If one views the school system as a necessary (though not sufficient) condition for the formation of the leading class; if one looks, in the last analysis, to the formation of a large class of leaders, one notices two main factors as causes of this interwar divergence of the positions of Europe and North America.

First, in the United States, industrial output per worker has increased (in spite of the great depression) more rapidly than in Europe, because the large dimensions of the United States' internal market allowed it better to overcome the limitations represented for the development of international commerce by the end of the gold standard. For our purposes the output per worker is a very significant index, because insofar as production depends on technological innovation, it requires a proportional increase of technical personnel. Increase of productivity is the fruit of an enlarged heritage of knowledge and must in turn be sustained by adequate cultural institutions—schools of various kinds and levels. A general increase of productivity has as a necessary condition the existence of a good school system equally strong at both the base and the vertex, that is, of a school system which makes its selection from the largest possible part of the social body.

Second, the pattern of the national state in Europe has favored the centralization of its politico-administrative services, and therefore it has tended to limit the size of the leading classes. Since there was no need of a particularly large leading class, it was not felt necessary to make selections from the whole social body. The student body came to be selected instead from among the more or less well to do—those who could actually hope to reach the higher levels of education.

Let us use a comparison to illustrate these remarks. While in the United States the number of graduate students quintupled between 1919 and 1935, in the same period the number of university students was halved in Germany, and in France, Holland, England and Italy it increased in proportions varying from only 15 per cent to 60 per cent.

Beginning with the postwar reconstruction and economic reconversion, Europe began to gain ground, expanding its industrial production both in absolute terms and in relation to the number of workers. The causes of the economic development of western Europe are many and difficult to isolate, but we may list briefly only those which are most closely connected with the increase of productivity. The main ones are the reconstruction, with more modern equipment, of war-destroyed industries; the liberalization of exchange and the impulse which this gave to international commerce; and the creation of the European Common Market—a fundamental factor in recent years.

The effect of these causes on the educational system has made itself felt only after a certain delay. As a matter of fact, in the postwar period the reabsorption into peacetime production of military personnel and of those who had become unemployed as a consequence of the reconversion of war industry delayed recognition of the imbalance between the ever increasing demand for qualified personnel and the supply of such personnel which the educational system could offer. Also one must keep in mind that in the immediate postwar period, in areas such as Italy or Germany the excess of labor made it convenient to still hold to relatively obsolete production methods, and that this fact contributed toward making the demand for qualified personnel less pressing.

In those years there was a great deal of talk about humanism and technology, about "homo faber" and "homo sapiens," but the connection between the educational system and economic development continued to go unnoticed. As always happens in such cases, however, after a certain critical point the problem of the expansion of the school structure began, for a number of reasons, to make itself felt. We may locate in the year 1955 the watershed between the old and the new conceptions of the school problem.

At that time it became evident that a larger proportion of the young population was enrolled in the schools. This is due to a number of factors: a higher rate of employment, and consequently the increase of income of many families; the subsequent increase of the amount of income destined for investments with delayed returns (for example, educational expenses); the increase of social mobility, characterized, in its most evident form, by urbanization and by the shift of agricultural workers to secondary and tertiary activities; the inducement of the lower income groups by the "demonstration effect" to model their behavior on patterns set by the higher income groups and, in particular, to send their children to school in order to guarantee for them a better future; finally the formation of the larger body of qualified personnel required by industry.

At that point school administrators, scholars and politicians began clearly to see the problem of the schools as a general political problem. Called upon to satisfy an ever increasing number of collective needs, the state was called upon to concern itself above all with the continuity of economic development. Regardless of any change in political ideology, the state was therefore compelled to augment recruitment for its own leading classes, for in a world characterized by ever growing productivity and increasing organization of work, it felt the need to increase productivity in its own services and thus the qualifications of its own leading class. The particular problems of some countries accentuated the need of those governments to intervene in the formation of a larger leading class, and therefore to devote a larger part of the national income to educational services. Consider, for example, the problems that Italy has had to face in the modernization and industrialization of the south— problems that it could not solve without stimulating the creation of a new and large group of leaders. Again, consider the large personnel required by France in order to effect its economic planning program. In brief, the state on the one hand and industrial expansion on the other increased the rhythm of growth of the European educational structure, giving to it that impulse which was almost completely lacking between the two world wars.

But at this point the first bottlenecks are becoming clearly apparent. Schools and educational facilities, teachers to meet the demands of expanded enrollments, universities to furnish the necessary teachers as well as the other members of the leading classes—all these are lacking in great numbers in almost all European countries. The European petty and medium bourgeoisie no longer have enough children to sustain in an almost exclusive manner, as they did until the immediate postwar period, the growth and turnover of the leading classes. At this moment the old European educational structure decisively enters a period of crisis.

This crisis emerges simultaneously with the stupendous and very rapid European economic reconstruction after World War II. In the space of a few years war ruins have been reconstructed. The European citizen, with the memories of the economic strains of the 1930's still alive in his mind, has entered the disturbing and fascinating first stages of a mass consumption economy. The social stratification systems, which had evolved during the past century, have been very deeply affected. Vast population movements, a rapid decline in the percentage of the labor force employed in agriculture and the emergence of new social classes have taken place at a pace unprecedented on the European social scene. These phenomena had never before so urgently attracted the attention of the sociologist. Even less had they been the object of choices and decisions on the part of politicians.

At present, opinions, beliefs and values are discussed and shared by an ever increasing number of citizens. This widening of the national debate inevitably implies a transformation and a reassessment of these same opinions, beliefs and values as the face of Europe changes. A process of development is not only a quantitative fact measurable with indexes and diagrams; it is also a qualitative fact insofar as social classes which were previously passive take now an active role in the life of the country. Every citizen becomes involved in a new reality and is forceably made aware of the transformations that have shaken the long-established social structure.

The educational structure has a task of primary importance: to transmit the values of the past together with the newly formed ones to the sons of the new era. The crisis, therefore, while it is quantitative in nature, at the same time deeply influences the quality, that is the substance, of the educational organization. The problem of quantity is that of modifying the school structure in order to enable it to give a basic and common education to all European citizens up to the age of 14 or 15 years, and to meet the increasing demand for qualified manpower at all levels which comes from all the productive sectors of society. The problem of quality, on the other hand, is to form a citizen patterned after those values in which the society believes and after which the society is modeled.

What kind of person will emerge from the transformations presently under way in the European school system? We are witnessing two crises which are, so to speak, parallel but distinct. Every discussion concerning the quality of the schools which will be established by the revolution presently under way must necessarily be preceded by a careful analysis of the European educational structure from the quantitative point of view. Such an analysis gives us the necessary clues to the understanding of the complexity of the problems which face European educators. For this reason, I shall put my emphasis prevalently on the "quantitative revolution" which is now under way in Europe and which is affecting educational structures that are several centuries old. An examination of these structures will be helpful if we are to understand the causes of this educational crisis.

II The Spirit of European Educational Structures

If it is not easy to survey the European educational system, it is even more difficult to do so within a short compass, since it presents widely different configurations each rooted in a century-old tradition. In France and in Italy, for example, the educational system is to this day faithfully patterned after the Napoleonic model. It is highly centralized; it is strictly dependent on a national legislation which establishes uniform teaching programs throughout the country; and one might call it—if Riesman's well-known term is applicable to institutions as well as to individuals—other-directed. The Anglo-Saxon model, which prevails in England and Germany, on the other hand leaves greater autonomy to local communities and local agencies as well as to the teacher's own judgment in matters of programs and methods.

Much as the various educational systems differ from country to country, however, they still share a broad pattern: their common derivation from a situation where there existed, on the one hand, a *school for the elite*—the real school, the educational school, aiming at knowledge for its own sake—and on the other hand a *school for the people,* a second-class school with modest aims of its own, to defeat illiteracy and to impart an elementary preparation to the future members of the working class. At a certain point in European history, however, the increasing complexity of the organization of contemporary society and its mounting requirements made mandatory a higher level of education and a higher average length of time devoted to schooling. This led to the expansion and greater specialization of the people's school rather than to its integration with the elite's school, which remained the only avenue for access to higher education. Let it be remarked in passing that this pattern of development was not due to a diabolic machination of the conservative groups. In fact, up to the end of World War II even the working class movement and the parties of the left showed very little interest in the problems of secondary education and directed their educational policies toward the expansion and improvement of primary and trade education (the people's school). Their misdirected maximalism, in other terms, led them to accept the logic of the conservatives to the extent of becoming its prisoners. To quote an Italian example, *L'Avanti!,* one press organ of the Italian Socialist party, wrote in December, 1907 in an article on the elementary school:

We have torn one grade from the series of theoretical studies and added it as the fifth to primary education, and another grade (the sixth) will be set up due to our efforts. . . . Let them do as they please with the secondary schools, but the primary school ought to be left alone. In the fifth and sixth grades the primary school must have an exclusively working-class orientation.

We believe this shows quite clearly and concisely how mistaken was the educational policy of the Italian left.*

What may have been originally a conservative pattern, at any rate, became more and more nearly a reactionary pattern in the presence of evolving historical conditions. In the nineteenth century the populace might be allowed, or forced, to seek merely a primary education and some further technical training exclusively designed for the working class; but as the secondary and tertiary sectors of the economy developed at a faster and faster pace, the ruling political groups were inevitably led to seek for ways to confront the new problems thus being created.

Increased technological requirements made it impossible for the traditional leading groups to fill all the new positions which were being created at the managerial and executive levels. There arose, therefore, institutions for technical training of a new type, culminating in schools at the university level, albeit often arising apart from the traditional universities. In Italy until about thirty years ago the "upper schools" of engineering, of business, of agriculture and of

* Professor Pierre Jaccard, Head of the School of Social and Political Sciences of the University of Lausanne, in his book *Politique de l'emploi et de l'education,* recalls the thesis of a well-known French trade unionist which, though expressed in more openly ideological terms, coincides with the assertions of the Italian socialist paper: "At the end of the last century the trade-unionist Albert Thery strongly asserted the opinion that science not only is a bourgeois monopoly but also that it is so permeated with bourgeois spirit that it cannot but corrupt the workers' youths. The workers' youth should therefore refuse to enter classist secondary and higher institutions of learning the expansion of which would only perpetuate the enslavement of the proletariat. This strange theory which is an absurd and illogical expression of the social inferiority complex whose strength is too often underestimated, has certainly favored the development of post-elementary schools. In the milieu of French elementary school teachers it has long been thought that the institutions of primary education would take the place of the traditional secondary schools created by the revolution to the exclusive advantage of the bourgeois class." Pierre Jaccard, *Politica dell'impiego ed educazione* (Rome; Armando, 1963), pp. 204–205. Translated into Italian by Umberto Massi.

veterinary medicine did not depend on the ministry of public education but on the corresponding ministries of industry or of agriculture,
and they were not a part of the university system. The educational
pattern followed by these schools was tainted in fact with the serious
sin of a "vocational orientation"; this was enough to deprive them of
the full legal status and academic prestige which were enjoyed by
the traditional university curricula (law, humanities, natural science,
medicine and surgery). This separation between the traditional universities on the one hand and the "polytechnical" and business
schools on the other is still a feature of some educational systems in
western Europe; but it is no longer meant to underline the greater
status of the traditional university studies. If one may even today
observe a separation between technical and classical studies, one
ought to bear in mind that this state of affairs developed first in
social and political terms, and then in cultural terms.

The superiority of the elite's school was taken for granted, and
this tradition was in fact backed by this school's longer history and
by the rather formidable tradition behind it. Without attempting to
substantiate it, it remains a fair judgment that the educational system of the European continent was the heir of the Jesuits' schools.
The various classical lyceums and gymnasiums are descendants in a
direct line from the Jesuits' *ratio studiorum,* and all other types of
secondary schools were born from the same source, even when they
were meant as improvements upon it. All schools of this type, be
they called lyceums, gymnasiums or athenaeums, share the basic
pattern, the general spirit, the teaching methods of the classical
lyceum, and only their curricula show minor differences. Greek may
be taken out and more physics and mathematics added; or both
Greek and Latin may be removed and business techniques, accounting, technology, quantitative chemical analysis or chemical plant
design may be added. But the basic pattern remains the same, all
the more so if one considers that very often the teachers of the technical subjects themselves—those which have taken the place of Latin
and Greek—had gotten to the university by way of the lyceum.
A further factor by which the various schools are shaped after the
pattern of the mother school is the academic and abstract orientation
of the teaching methods, whatever the subject matter. It is important
to emphasize that the ruling upper strata traditionally elect the
classical studies for their new generations, thus determining—apart
from any consideration of intellectual skill and actual aptitude for
learning—which school gets what type of pupil. This ruling class also
determines the function of the schools where the classical subjects
are taught. That the leading groups are systematically educated in
these schools does not happen because they are the better schools,

but because those who have access to them already belong to the leading groups.

Such are the reasons behind the attraction of the classical schools and the prestige which the humanities enjoy as a model for the educational system. Such is the mechanism which makes of the classical school the elite's school. No wonder, then, that similar conclusions are reached by Ottaway's analysis of a type of school whose traditions do not go back to the Jesuits' *ratio studiorum,* that is, of the English secondary school:

The secondary schools would imitate the public schools with their academic, classical and linguistic fixations; with their games, their monitors, their colors, and their old school ties; a whole repertory of social distinctions and of aristocratic mentality. Thousands of students crowded into the secondary schools seeking the possibility of becoming wealthier, of reaching a loftier social position. The prevalent aims were always the same, and the pedagogical principles accepted by the members of the new professions and of the suburban white collar groups were those of the upper classes. What did it matter whether the teaching did or did not correspond to the actual requirements of their future careers? As long as attending the secondary schools means to get better jobs, the parents are willing to let their children learn anything, provided that they pass their exams and earn their diplomas.[1]

Even more cogently, the Spens report of 1938 asserts:

The tradition was so strong that when the state, on the basis of the education act of 1902, undertook for the first time the overall organization of the secondary schools, the old classical school, local or not local, became the almost exclusive model for the secondary schools.[2]

To fully understand the separation between classical and technical education, or between elite's and people's schools, one must grasp the idea (or indeed, in a changed situation, the prejudice) which lies at the root of that separation. For all the difference between the Napoleonic and the Anglo-Saxon models, for all the peculiarities in the historical development of each national educational system, all European systems share the same basic premise: the constrast between "liberal" and "servile" occupations, to which must correspond that between a "liberal" and a "servile" education. The former aims exclusively at training the intellect to perform the operations and attain the achievements of knowledge for its own sake—knowledge, that is, which is free and frees man's creative energies by virtue of not being bound to any practical demand; or, to employ the plain and appropriate definition of the Oxford Dictionary, "liberal" education is such as "befits a gentleman, a general literary education rather than one of the technical type."

On the other hand, to the "servile" occupations there corresponds

FABIO LUCA CAVAZZA

a "servile" education, which aims solely at training people through practical exercises to handle tools, to produce goods and to perform services. Actually this objective did not even require a particular form of education, if this word is taken in its broad modern meaning; it was enough to possess rather modest technical or manual skills, such as could be acquired with a minimal intellectual effort but with great application, and above all through the continuous repetition of a certain number of acts requiring a great deal of physical labor. This contrast between the two types of education, which has its roots in Greek thought, has today become anachronistic in that the requirements of both democracy and industrialization work against it. In spite of this, that same contrast still influences quite strongly the European educational systems which owe to it their present pattern and inspiration.

If one wishes to examine against this background the transformations undergone by the western European system, two basic phases need to be brought to mind: the phase of educational expansion, which has taken on truly remarkable proportions in these last few years; and the phase of the democratization of education.

It would be wrong to consider these two phases as being clearly distinct from one another. As a matter of fact, the expansion of educational facilities, when it goes beyond certain limits (one might say, a certain "threshold"), unavoidably brings with it a transformation of the social structure of the school population and tends to transform correspondingly the educational system itself. As an increasing proportion of youths from the less privileged social strata attend the older schools, which had been designed for the scions of socially homogeneous upper groups, a number of consequences begin to develop.

Several factors concurred in giving the old educational structures a definite and consistent internal configuration (albeit an aristocratic and subtly reactionary one). The schools which traditionally led to the universities were well integrated with the social groups which normally had access to it; the cultural patterns which inspired teaching were consistent with those to which the great majority of the pupils were socialized in the family; students and teachers shared a common language because of their similar social origins, the abstract and "cultured" language in which classes were taught. This situation reflected itself not only in the upper secondary schools which immediately prepare their pupils for the universities, but also in the lower secondary schools, since right at the end of the four to six years of elementary education the selection began of those who would later have access to the institutions of higher learning. There were even cases where this selection took place, formally or not, since the first year of school: at times, in fact, the very first rudiments of reading and writing were taught in the same building and under the same school administration where older students were going through their lyceum. Witness what *Esprit* wrote in its September, 1962 issue: "les enfants des milieux aisés ont souvent accompli la scolarité elementaire dans les classes primaires des lycées (on les supprime periodiquement sur le papier, mais elles ont la vie dure)."

Yet, as the expansion of the educational system reaches youths from relatively underprivileged strata and from recently formed relatively well-to-do strata, the inner configuration of the traditional educational structures undergoes a serious crisis. There emerges a lack of integration between the social origins of the great majority of pupils and those of the great majority of teachers. The abstract and "cultured" language which is normally in use in the schools is no longer compatible, especially in the lower secondary schools, with the type of "culture" to which the majority of pupils have been socialized. The cultural patterns upheld in the schools progressively lose their meaning, since they are accepted only for expediential reasons, for the sake of conformity.

In sum: educational expansion, to the extent that it reaches new sections of the population, brings about a crisis of the traditional structures and some sort of democratization. For this reason one ought not to separate too clearly educational expansion from democratization of the schools. However, the democratic impact of expansion is limited and half-hearted; its results are mostly a negative threat to the old aristocratic structures. But whatever the connections which hold between expansion and democratization of the educational system, it is more expedient, for the sake of our argument, to examine these two phenomena separately.

III Characters of Educational Expansion

We shall try to show, if only briefly, the dimensions of the process of expansion of the educational systems in a few European nations over the last eight to ten years. We shall not take into account the data concerning "primary" or "elementary" schools, since they correspond very closely to demographic trends. In other terms, since almost all of the population of elementary school age does actually attend school, there is a rather close fit between enrollment and population growth.

However, in the various European countries, at about 14 or 15 years of age the proportion of the population at each age level which is enrolled in school begins to drop. It is therefore from this age on, or rather from the grade levels which pupils attend after this age (that is to say, practically all upper secondary schools), that one may sense an expansion of school enrollment not directly due to demographic variables, but rather to the increasing access of new social strata to those medium-upper secondary schools from which they were previously excluded.

The statistical data which we have been able to employ are not particularly abundant. In fact, the OECD report "Targets for education in Europe in 1970," presented to the Policy Conference on Economic Growth and Investment in Education at Washington, D.C., in October, 1961, also points out that there are very few reliable, significant and comparable statistical data on educational enrollment in the various countries.[3]

Taking into account primarily the lower and upper secondary schools, Italy and France are the European countries where the educational system has expanded most rapidly over the last decade. In absolute terms France holds the record, since the number of regularly enrolled students has more than doubled, going from 1,204,000 students in 1951–1952 to 2,562,000 in 1961–1962—a 112.8 per cent increase in ten years. In Italy in the same period of time the enrollment in the secondary schools has gone from 1,225,000 to 2,400,000 —a 96 per cent increase.

It may be interesting to note that in both countries the rate of expansion has gone up in the second part of the decade, which means that the process is not yet slackening. Between 1951–1952 and 1957–1958, in fact, the cumulative increase in enrollment has been equal to 41.9 per cent in France and 38.2 per cent in Italy, while in the four years between 1957–1958 and 1961–1962 the increase has been 49.9 per cent in France and 41.8 per cent in Italy.

If one wants to look more deeply into the comparison between France and Italy on these counts, one may remark that since 1946 the birth rate has progressively decreased in Italy, while it has gone up in France. Thus from 1957–1958 on, the "lower-middle" French schools were getting their enrollment from larger and larger school age populations, whereas in the corresponding Italian schools the opposite was taking place. In view of this consideration, if the school enrollment is calculated for each age bracket, it becomes evident that the rhythm of expansion has been grossly the same in the two countries over the last ten years.

An increase in enrollment (even though not as marked as the one just mentioned) has made itself felt in both countries also with respect to the so-called "maternal schools" or kindergartens. In this case the increase is more substantial in Italy, and for the following reason. The expansion of maternal schools is fundamentally connected with the process of urbanization and with the increase in the number of women who enter the national labor force, which is in turn an effect of industrialization. The fact that these developments have taken place later in Italy than in France accounts for the more marked rise in maternal school enrollment in the former country: 9.1 per cent between 1951–1952 and 1957–1958, 9.2 per cent between 1957–1958 and 1961–1962 as against 7.0 per cent and 5.3 per cent in France in the same time.

Another important aspect of the expansion of the European educational systems is the increasing proportion of girls in the school population. The most marked increase in this proportion is shown by the statistics for Italy, Germany and France. At the university level the percentage of women in the total enrollment has increased in Italy from 19.5 to 27.5 per cent between 1938–1939 and 1955–1956; in France, in the same period, from 30.5 to 36.2 per cent; in Germany, finally, from 12.2 to 17.8 per cent. The proportion of women has therefore increased by 41, 19 and 46 per cent respectively. In view of these figures, and of the fact that the comparable data for England and the Netherlands show a much less marked increase, one cannot help noticing that the highest percentage increases have taken place in Germany and Italy, that is in two countries which have changed from an authoritarian rightist regime to a democratic one. Apparently the factors involved are attendant not only upon the economic development but also upon the wider social mobility which characterizes the democratic regimes.

The increase in women's enrollment is a rather eloquent index of the profound transformations which the educational systems are undergoing. That an increasing number of women go to school is due not only to the increasing equality between the sexes (a phenomenon which undoubtedly characterizes modern society), but also to a changing appreciation of the utility of education. As the enrollment of all types increases, what takes place is not merely an attack on some typical prejudices of the archaic and patriarchal societies; what happens, above all (although the legislatures seem to take no notice and do not try to adapt the educational systems to the new requirements of the times) is a radical change in the school system and particularly in its upper reaches. The system ceases to be an instrument for the selection of elites and becomes one for the education of the masses.

In view of these reasons and as a symptom of other aspects of the current developments, the trend of enrollment by female students is rather significant and deserves some further comment, especially with reference to Italy. In the latter country, indeed, cer-

471

tain changes take place in a more obvious and telling way than in the other western European countries for the very good reason that among them Italy represents the lowest stage of development.

In the Italian classical lyceum—the Italian school with the most glorious traditions; a typical elite's school, and for this very reason one which has felt the educational expansion of the postwar period less markedly than the others—the proportion of enrolled girls has gone up from 27.1 to 38.1 per cent between 1938–1939 and 1959–1960. Within the same period the boys' enrollment has gone up by 10.2 per cent and the girls' by 90.7 per cent.

An even more marked increase in the girls' enrollment can be noticed in the so-called professional schools and technical institutes. The professional schools and institutes are schools of upper secondary education whose pupils have previously gone through eight years of compulsory education. Their curricula last for from two to four years according to the occupation for which they train students, but upon graduation the latter cannot go to the university. In the professional schools between 1938–1939 and 1959–1960, the proportion of female students has gone from 15.5 to 31.5 per cent, corresponding to an increase of 879.5 per cent as against an increase of 335.6 per cent for the male students.

An even more spectacular development is brought out by the data concerning the so-called technical institutes. These are also vocational schools, but their graduates can now go to the universities, provided that they enroll in such departments as engineering, mathematics and natural sciences, agriculture, business, and modern languages. These schools have witnessed a more marked increase in enrollment than any other type of school, and this has been even more noticeable as regards the enrollment of girls. This is quite remarkable if one considers that more schools of this type, such as the nautical, agricultural, surveyors' and industrial technical institutes, train their students for what have traditionally been male occupations. Yet the enrollment of girls, which represented only 8.3 per cent of the total enrollment in 1938–1939, was 23.3 per cent of the total by 1959–1960. Enrollment by girls has gone up, over the same period of time, by 1205.8 per cent, whereas the male enrollment has gone up by 291.0 per cent. In the latter years the increase in the enrollment of girls has been even more marked than the one we have related for the same period. In the four years between 1955–1956 and 1959–1960, the enrollment went up by 32.6 per cent for male students and by 64.7 per cent for female students. A similar trend, although not as marked, is noticeable in the data concerning others among the aforementioned types of school: an indication that the ongoing transformation of the Italian educational system has not yet lost its momentum.

The other European nations are also undergoing comparable developments. In Germany, for instance, while in 1939–1940 the girls' enrollment in the upper secondary schools was 29.3 per cent of the total, it reached 40.3 per cent in 1955–1956. It may be interesting to remark that before the advent of Naziism this statistic was 36.2 per cent—further evidence for the fact that the rate of female enrollment varies not only with industrial expansion but also with prevailing political conditions. In the French lower secondary schools between 1950 and 1960 the enrollment of girls has gone from 46 to 51 per cent of the total enrollment, thus becoming greater than the male enrollment in absolute terms. (This is due also to the fact that a greater number of them finish compulsory schooling at the primary level.) In the Dutch lower secondary schools the enrollment by girls has gone up from 45.7 to 50.4 per cent of the total enrollment between the prewar years and 1961. In the upper secondary schools the same statistic has gone from 31.5 per cent in 1938–39 to 39.9 per cent in 1960–1961. Between 1938–1939 and 1960–1961 male enrollment in the lower secondary schools has increased by 142.1 per cent and female enrollment by 249.5 per cent. Furthermore, also in the Netherlands the enrollment of girl students increased at a faster pace than the enrollment of boys: in the four years between 1956–1957 and 1960–1961 the male enrollment has gone up by 38.9 per cent and the female by 47.3 per cent.

The most decisive developments in the educational systems of the various European countries brought about by the increasing school population may, however, be viewed only by taking into account the institutions of higher learning. The university in Europe is placed at the summit of the educational system not merely as a matter of prestige and glamor, but because it is in the university that the leading social groups are consecrated after having been selected and partly formed through pre-university education. Leaving aside for the moment the question whether the terms of access to the European universities have become more democratic, let us take a look at the extent to which university enrollment has expanded. In Germany in the last fifty years the number of students per 10,000 inhabitants has tripled, in the Netherlands it has quadrupled, and in France and Italy it has quintupled. The significance of this increase can be grasped only if one bears in mind that the legal structures of university education are basically still the same as at the beginning of the century and that the number of universities has increased only by a very small amount.

The critical factor, however, that has had the greatest actual impact upon the university structure is not as much the quantitative increase in enrollment as the qualitative developments that go with it. It is the access of new social strata to university education, in fact, which brings about the increase in enrollment. Although one may not maintain that talent and skills of individuals vary with the social stratum to which they belong, it is at any rate true that in the education of the younger generations an important role is played by the culture of the social setting of their everyday life, that is the language in which they have originally learned to express themselves, the types of reading to which they are exposed or not exposed, the things which are positively or negatively evaluated by those around them. Students are attending today a type of university which, in its basic organization, is still that of the last decades of the nineteenth century. Having been created as an elite school and with a view to promoting scientific research and to supplying the scientific preparation needed for the practice of professional careers, the university receives today a great number of young people who are not asking these goals of it. Very few are concerned with scientific research (and it could not be otherwise); many aspire to a diploma which would qualify them for professional practice; many more, especially in the humanities departments, are seeking a diploma which would (in strictly formal terms) qualify them to compete for civil service jobs or for positions in private employment. There exists, therefore, an extremely marked gap between the cultural patterns which the university has traditionally made its own and the type of training which most university students demand of it. This gap causes a crisis in the university; it initiates a *de facto* transformation and makes even a *de jure* reform mandatory.

IV Aspects of the Democratization of the Educational System

Expansion, as we have said, is but one aspect of the transformation of the European educational system. Democratization is another. On this, however, the conclusions that can be drawn from a survey of the developments in the last decades are not so satisfactory. What has taken place in Europe is basically only a *quantitative* expansion, spontaneous in most countries, since only in France has economic planning been in use since 1946, and only in the past six to eight years has there been an effective educational planning program. As a general rule, one can say that most European countries have expressedly concerned themselves to provide only some of the conditions for educational expansion. Similar conclusions were reached in the above quoted OECD report to the Washington Conference, which concludes as follows its analysis of the perspectives for educational development in Europe in the next ten years:

A survey of all these plans gives the impression that expansion is more stressed than reform. There is, however, a certain awareness that expansion will of itself bring about a change of content.

One of the most interesting consequences of educational development can be seen in the fact that some countries seem about to attempt planned, as against natural and spontaneous, expansion of their school systems. Taken in itself, educational planning represents merely an instrument for the rationalization of public activity in the field of education. Thus, *per se*, educational planning is neither intrinsically democratic and "liberal" nor intrinsically coercive and socialistic. In fact the western European country with the most advanced economic and educational planning happens to be France— that is, a country which has often seemed to pursue the ideal of a paternalistic technocracy, especially in constantly reducing the functions of parliament and of the political parties.

It is, however, true that as far as concerns the democratization of the educational system, planning represents some amount of progress over spontaneous expansion. Since it operates in a socially and economically heterogeneous setting, spontaneous expansion tends to deepen the existing imbalances. It affects above all the urban centers, and only on quite a minor scale the rural areas. Even in the cities, it tends to slacken as it reaches the lower income groups, since the latter find it less easy to direct part of the family resources toward an investment, such as that in education, whose benefits are deferred over a period of time. Furthermore the lower income, or at any rate the less well-to-do, groups are often penalized by the selective processes taking place within the educational institutions, for the following reasons:

The lower the socio-economic level the more tenuous school-family relationships tend to become. Lower income, or at any rate socially underprivileged, families are materially incapable of lending much support to the school's educational efforts, because of insufficient cultural resources, inadequate availability of time, and lesser understanding of the educational process.

The lower the socio-economic level, the poorer the verbal resources tend to become and the harder the process of learning as it develops in the European schools.

The two previous phenomena bring about an even more damaging one, that is, a lower degree of mutual understanding between teachers and students in those schools where the majority of pupils come from lower socio-economic strata. The traditional academic formation of the European teachers tends to worsen this situation.

Scholastic failures discourage more grievously those families for which keeping their sons in school already represents a relatively serious economic burden. In these situations families are more easily induced by scholastic failures to give up and to turn to the possibilities for gainful employment already open to their sons.[4]

Educational planning, at least in a democratic country, to the extent that it limits the impact of the free play of spontaneous forces on educational expansion, cannot treat these aspects of social inequality as permanent, much less strive to maintain them or make them deeper. Unavoidably it will seek to correct those imbalances, both because the political leaders on whom planning depends tend to equalize opportunities as a matter of democratic policy, and because the experts in charge of planning seek to make the educational system more functional for the productive system by setting up a selective process which covers the whole population and thus ensures that all available talent will be properly employed.

Only France possesses today educational planning in the proper legal and juridico-administrative meaning of the term. Barring radical transformations in its political conditions, Italy ought to be the first country to follow France's example by giving itself its first school plan in the next five years as an integral part of its economic plan. The last pre-election cabinet has fairly committed itself on this point, and it has appointed a committee of experts. The third Italian legislature, moreover, has created a Study Committee of sixteen members of parliament and fifteen experts in the educational, economic and social fields. This committee has already investigated the school problem and made a number of suggestions on which the future legislation on educational planning and reform may be based.

In the other western European countries various agencies and committee of experts are putting forth proposals for the reorganization and the coordination of the various school systems. The same demands are often espoused by groups of educational scholars who try to win over political forces to the cause of educational planning as the ideas and the demands which lie behind the conception of educational planning are becoming more and more widely accepted and recognized. The programs for educational development which are in the making in various countries constitute the first success of this general idea. It is thus easy to forecast that during the 1960's educational planning will be widely adopted throughout Europe. This is the natural outcome of a number of factors all of which press for the adoption of some type of educational planning: the increasingly important role of the schools in the various national societies; the increasing share of the national income which is invested in education; and finally, the European tradition which gives the state primary responsibility for the organization of the educational system.

Let us stress, however, that educational planning is a mere instrument, and if it is to contribute to democracy it must operate within democratic forms and in view of democratic objectives. From this viewpoint the overriding commitment ought to be that of making university education truly available to everyone. Today, unfortunately, the European universities appear as inverted images of their countries; they are so like one another in this respect that any statistical data are superfluous. Everywhere young people from the workers' and peasants' world are extremely underrepresented. Everywhere the sons of professionals of industrialists, and of high public and private officials, although constituting only a very small part of each generation, are preponderantly represented. This is also true of England, in spite of the fact that it gives more financial assistance to its university students than does any other European country, 80 per cent of whom receive some sort of scholarship.

But the fact is that assistance given to university students changes the situation very little, since its effect becomes felt only after the process of social selection has already taken place in the upper and lower secondary schools. It is in the secondary schools that the European educational authorities must intervene in a decisive way. Mere expansion of the school system has in effect lessened the effects of a selection which, in the last analysis, is inspired by social Darwinism. But the fact remains that the biggest selection takes place between 10 and 15 years of age and tends to eliminate those from the lower economic groups. It is clearly understandable that, as we have already said, expansion of the schools has been possible only insofar as they have reached out to incorporate new groups. Thus it is also true that the present composition of the student body of European universities is more differentiated and heterogeneous than it was in the prewar period. We are, however, still very far from an effective democratization of the university.

If we are to attain this goal several structural and socio-economic obstacles must first be removed. In Italy, for example, up until 1963 the young people, after five years of elementary school, had to make a choice between enrolling in the *scuola media* or in the *scuola di avviamento professionale*. The latter usually precludes entrance into the university; it is thus a "dead end street," chosen only by those who know that they cannot aspire to the longer and more expensive pre-university schools. This is an example of a typical structural obstacle which formally is juridico-administrative in nature, but which in fact selects young people not only when it is still too early for their aptitudes and abilities to be adequately assessed, but also on the basis of socio-economic criteria. It is clear that the *scuola di avviamento professionale,* which offers no relevant outlet for further education, is categorically excluded by those parents who have ambitions for their children. Although certainly not by law, it is a school reserved primarily for children of the worker, peasant and artisan classes whose parents cannot afford to renounce a part of their income for very many years and who neither adequately appreciate the advantages and benefits offered by education nor desire their children to receive an education much better than their own. It is interesting to note in this last connection that in France, as Marcel Bresard points out, the majority of low income self-employed workers, especially small farmers (89 per cent) and commercial artisans (85 per cent), declare that they do not desire for their children an education much higher than their own.[5]

In Italy, the premature choice between *scuola media* and *scuola di avviamento professionale* excluded, at the age of 11 years, half of the children who continued to attend school after the five elementary years. In the other European countries the proportions are different, and doubtless the percentage of young people who enroll in pre-university schools is greater than in Italy; but in all of them, and always very prematurely, the young people are faced with two alternatives, one of which leaves all possibilities open and the other of which precludes almost all of them. In Germany the same kind of choice must be made immediately following the first four years of elementary school. On the one hand there is the *Gymnasium* and on the other the *Mittleschule, Realschule* or *Volksschul oberstufe.* In Belgium after the first six years of elementary school the child must decide between the schools of classical studies which open all paths (*ecole moyenne, athénée, lycée, collège*) and technical, professional, and post-elementary schools. In France the choice presents itself after the first five years of elementary school. A selection must be made between the post-elementary course (*collège d'enseignement général*) and the other three kinds of school (lyceum, complementary courses, and technical institutes). The first type of school, the "dead end street," is attended by 77 per cent of the school-age population between ages of 11 and 14 years. This 77 per cent is, therefore, barred from the university as early as eleven years of age.

This is the first obstacle to be overcome: a premature choice which precludes, as early as preadolescence, the possibility of better future developments. Of great importance, in this connection, is the reform launched a few months ago in Italy which unifies the various branches of early secondary education, postponing until after 14 years of age the decision which formerly had to be made at 11. This allows a better evaluation of aptitudes and abilities, eliminates a premature selection that is actually made, as we have seen, on the basis of social criteria rather than on merit, and strikes at the roots an old aristocratic prejudice.

Presently in France there are strong pressures toward the same sort of solution. But even if in other countries the Italian example were to be followed, the problem would merely be postponed for three or four years. In spite of the undeniable improvement over the old system, neither the structural nor the socio-economic obstacles would cease to make themselves felt in the upper grades of the secondary schools. For example, in Italy until two years ago the technical institutes (the better attended schools of higher secondary education) did not, except for the department of business, give access to the university. Though this limitation has recently been overcome, another structural obstacle still stands in Italian higher secondary education: the professional schools and institutes still may not send their graduates to the universities, while in other European countries departments of engineering may, with certain difficulties, be entered by way of professional schools. In Italy these schools have not yet succeeded in gaining full academic acceptance. This is the heaviest inheritance which remains from the old contrast between liberal and servile occupations. One may hope, however, that just as in recent years the most serious obstacles have been removed, this one also will finally disappear.

Because of the financial burden which it implies, the most difficult problem to solve is that of giving economic assistance to deserving and needy pre-university school students. For those who reach the university the problem has, during the last year, been opened to a solution with the introduction of the so called "pre-salary," a modest monthly stipend given, under certain conditions of scholastic merit, to less well-to-do young people. But, as we have said, the selection of students is made before the university; and it is therefore before the university that the greatest effort must be concentrated. For the present we must rely mainly on the indirect effects of a state of full employment, toward which Italy has decisively and speedily begun to march.

Even bearing in mind the already mentioned limits, it is still certainly the case that the framework of the old European school system has received its first decisive blows. It is not by chance that the opening of the universities to the graduates of the technical institutes has met with strong opposition in parliament, while the unification of the lower secondary schools has engaged the parties of the present coalition government (Christian Democrats, Social Democrats, Republicans and Socialists) in a hard-fought parliamentary battle.

When we speak of blows delivered to the old European school, we naturally do not intend to imply that there is not a tradition, indeed a glorious one, to maintain. On the contrary, it should be stressed that there are many things which, in the course of the present transformations, must be saved and even given greater expression. We mean to say only that the aristocratic prejudices rooted in the school system and challenged by postwar scholastic expansion must finally be exorcized. Equally important is a resolution of the misunderstandings concerning the dichotomy between humanism and "technology" (with a derogatory implication), a dichotomy which has been challenged by modern science.

It is the democratization of education that sets the conditions for overcoming the equivocal aristocratic pattern after which all European school structures are more or less modeled. The dichotomy between humanism and technology must be overcome by a new cultural synthesis which accepts modern science (giving due weight to technology) as the most conspicuous fruit of a better humanism, a fruit which, however, modifies the very tree from which it grows and from which it cannot be detached.

Expansion of the schools provided the impulse necessary to make the European political and scholastic authorities aware of the old equivocations and of the necessity of resolving them along the indicated lines. It is not by chance that in the last six or seven years discussion of scholastic problems has become more concrete and more compelling.

Scholars and political figures in ever increasing numbers are realizing that the structural obstacles must be removed; that the weight of socio-economic obstacles must be made less pressing, especially in the higher grades of the secondary schools, by giving substantial aid to deserving but economically underprivileged students; and finally, that dignity and cultural seriousness must be accorded to every type of study without preclusions which, although rooted in old academic traditions, have no justification in the context of a modern conception of culture and professional activity. One thing is certain, that in Europe a renovation along the indicated lines is taking place.

If the example of Italy, a country less developed than the other western European nations, means anything, it tells us that the spirit of school reform now arising in old Europe will not leave things unchanged.

REFERENCES

1. Cf. A. K. C. Ottaway, *Education of Society. Introduction to the Sociology of Education.* We quote from the Italian version *Educazione e Società. Un introduzione alla sociologia dell'Educazione* (Rome: AVIO, 1959), p. 94. Translated by Paolo Massini.

2. The Spens Report (London: H.M.S.O., 1938), p. 12.

3. OECD, Policy Conference on Economic Growth and Investment in Education, Washington, D. C., October 16–20, 1961, "*II. Targets for Education in Europe 1970*," Paper by Ingvar Svennilson in association with Friedrich Edding and Lionel Elvin, cf. p. 60.

4. Cf. Umberto Paniccia, "Verso la scuola del 1975," *Il Mulino*, 104–105 (June–July, 1961), p. 412.

5. Cf. Pierre Jaccard, *Politica dell'impiego ed educazione* (Rome: Armando, 1963), p. 204. Translated into Italian by Umberto Massi.

STEPHANE HESSEL

Is Europe Facing Its Educational Problems?

THE western European nations are discussing their common problems in all conceivable fields, sometimes in a spirit of defense of values questioned in other parts of the world, more often with the ambitious design of regaining jointly the leading positions they have individually been forced to relinquish. Much depends, as regards the outlook in each field, upon the relative position western Europe still occupies in the postwar world. This is sometimes quite difficult to define.

Militarily, the polarization of East and West and the rapid breaking up of colonial empires have resulted in a steep decline of power. No European nation is liable to exercise effective military leadership, neither Germany in spite of the possible motivation of reunification, nor France in spite of its "atomic fighting force," nor Great Britain, nor even—or so it seems—a United Europe which probably could not build up rapidly the major centers of thermonuclear production that exist outside, and which furthermore would not wish to contain them.

Politically, the leadership of the United States as the major decision-making center of the western world has been challenged, occasionally by Great Britain, more frequently and with greater combativeness by France; but up to now western Europe, as such, has not shown a manifest intention of becoming a separate, semi-autonomous center of political decision-making. This intention, however, is clearly in the minds of many of the most outspoken and lucid protagonists of a united Europe, whose influence may be the more predominant among the youth as a policy of "summit compromise" becomes apparent between Washington and Moscow.

Economically, on the other hand, the period of withdrawal, of defensive barriers and search for outside assistance has now definitely come to an end and the very encouraging results already achieved have been reached through joint enterprise, breaking up the traditional structures of national economies, through OEEC, and more powerfully still through the Common Market.

If we turn to the fields of science and education we are faced with a more complicated situation. Most Europeans still believe that the cultural level of their population is higher than that anywhere outside. The challenge has not been clearly felt up to now. The field itself is one of extreme diversity: at least four of the main currents of scientific and cultural achievement have their origin in Europe: the Anglo-Saxon, the Franco-Latin, the Germanic and the Slavic, each with its offsprings in other geographical areas, each burdened with tradition and ritual, not easy to reconcile or to combine.

Simultaneously, since the First World War and more evidently during the Second, spectacular progress has been made outside of Europe, and some of the centers of scientific research and advanced learning have moved away from western Europe to the United States and the Soviet Union. Meanwhile the once unchallenged concepts of selective training through the channels of primary, secondary, technical and university education have been questioned, both outside of and within the European area. New models described until then in Europe as inferior imitations attract growing attention. Could it be that modern industrial civilization tolerates or even demands a type of education more cooperative than competitive, producing a growing level of information and participation for all and a less distinctly marked hierarchy of intellectual schooling? These questions have been asked for the past thirty years in most European nations, but until about 1950 the answers have been sketchy, unrelated and superficial.

During the past ten years things have changed quite considerably, forcing observers from outside to revise their judgments and to admit that the economic and demographic vitality of the western European nations may have a counterpart in education and research. The process may be described rather similarly: a growing consciousness of the weight of antiquated structures; attempts by individual nations at replacing these structures by revolutionary new ones; failure to do so individually and gradual combining of forces among Europeans. Such organizations as the Council of Europe, the European Atomic Energy Authority (EURATOM) and the Organization of Economic Cooperation and Development (OECD), until quite recently indifferent to school, university and other forms of education, have now entered this field of activity: reports have been drafted on common problems in the field of education; institutes and universities have been planned; research has been conducted jointly by several nations; the prospects of a common European education have been explored.

If we wish to ascertain, however, how far and how deep western European cooperation has reached into the realities of educational habits and traditions, shaping them into the new molds of western society, it may be preferable to select a small number of specific aspects in which the impact of the new trends and the stimulus of cooperation across frontiers are already becoming apparent.

I The Search for a More Democratic School

It is one of the basic tenets of the European faith in democracy that education—free and compulsory—is a right that should be granted to every boy or girl, every future citizen. Whether the state assumes full responsibility as in France, or whether this responsibility is shared according to various methods between state, local authorities and churches as in England or Germany, the right as such, alive in democratic consciences and spelled out in democratic constitutions, is neither questioned nor seriously examined. And yet it is an important question to know what is meant by "education" considered as a right of man. Does it mean that children must learn to read, write and count or that they all should know Latin, physics and Roman history? Does it mean that a common modicum must be provided for all, leaving it to the choice of parents to have them pursue elaborate and drawn-out studies or to turn quickly to a limited training for their professional life?

The European concept has been relatively clear until World War II: schools are there to encompass everyone, to test his or her abilities, not to let anyone escape without a fair knowledge of his language, his history, his surroundings and general morals prevailing in his community—the content of primary education; to make it possible through appropriate examinations to select the better gifted and have them continue to absorb a large amount of general knowledge about literature, classical languages, science, history and modern languages; to turn the less gifted ones toward technical schools, where they will be taught alongside their trade a great deal of subjects of general interest, and gradually to eliminate through all types of competitive examinations those children who cannot hope to reach the upper strata of conceptualization and formulation required for university studies. In other words, the pyramid of learning had remained in accordance with its traditional profile: democratic education would enable any child lucky enough to possess a mind geared to the profile of that pyramid to ascend its degrees without too many financial or social qualms.

Let us add, in order to be fair, that a vast amount of experience and understanding had been invested in building up primary schools throughout Europe. The inventions and intuitions of great educators had been combined to turn out, at the age of twelve or fourteen years, youngsters with a real comprehension of their destiny and environment, already equipped with a sense of freedom and a command of verbal expression and communication for which adolescents of other areas may well envy them.

This system, however, has become terribly obsolete in the face of a fundamental change in the vision of democracy as molded by the exigencies of the second industrial revolution. Strangely enough, this fundamental change has been experienced pretty much simultaneously in most parts of western Europe during the decade following World War II. It is variously analyzed and accounted for in other articles contained in this volume, dealing with class structure, economic upheavals and deep modification in the international framework of European life.

As far as its effects on education can be categorized, demographic, technical and political factors may be distinguished. The pressure of a disproportionately voluminous generation born between 1944 and 1956 has put a quick and heavy stress on the traditional school systems, forcing all European nations to set up vast school building programs and plans for accelerated teachers' training, in the wake of which quite naturally the content and impact of traditional teaching have been questioned.

The development of industrial relations and their requirement of manipulative skills rather than technical crafts have jeopardized the traditional distinction between professional or vocational training and secondary education, with the result that these two functions have been integrated and jointly assigned to the guardians of the commonweal, whether state, municipal or regional. How far-reaching a change this means for educational systems with a traditional focalization upon "classical" schooling it is too early to assess, but judging by the daily battle those responsible for the carrying out of these new plans have to fight, it is bound to have a significant effect upon the whole concept of education.

Finally, the gradual awareness of a wider than national political and therefore civic setting for the education of young Belgians, Dutchmen, Swedes, Swiss or Italians has greatly increased the demand for a wide open, comprehensive and cosmopolitan form of teaching which will in the time of a generation result in a fundamentally different conception of world affairs—far less idealistic, much more practical and matter of fact—in the minds of the young. Working, as all human minds do, along the lines of future-loaded projects, the prestige and greatness of their national community will no longer be the plausible background of their capacity to digest and to reinvest educational material.

European governments have been faced with these facts and

with the outlook they command, since 1945 or longer. And yet it has taken more than ten years after the end of World War II to overcome the resistance of self-satisfaction and tradition and to reap the full meaning of compulsory schooling to the age of fifteen or sixteen years that is presently instituted or planned in most European countries.*

The main cause of these resistances lies in the influence of secondary and higher education upon the stable hierarchies of social groups in most European countries. The whole area may indeed be characterized by the priority it confers, among distinguishing factors in society, upon the cultural factor.

The history of the nineteenth century, during which revolutionary changes have been mainly concentrated within Europe, could be analyzed as a succession of blows dealt to the various elite-groups, other than the intelligensia, at the hands of rationalist-reformers, idealist-revolutionaries or merely events. First the birth-grounded elite, then the land-based, then the money-founded and finally the high-income-bracketed, have been demystified and set aside. By the end of the century, after Babeuf, Comte, LaSalle, Marx and Engels, neither birth nor fortune nor economic status any longer played their traditional roles and the authority derived from diplomas, university titles or degrees and, more subjectively, the handling of a heavy scientific and cultural "baggage" was matched by no other.

Quite naturally, therefore, the ruling groups in society had a tendency to reserve for themselves or to grant only to those whom they wished to associate to their endeavors the means to achieve such a valuable education. The war has shaken their feeling of pride and satisfaction; the technological revolutions have made them realize more clearly the lacunae of their *culture générale;* and the demographic pressure has blown the lid off the nicely arranged system where the criteria from above reached down toward the best adjusted youngsters of the lower strata.

But the change involves a new style: if we are reminded that, for instance, Italy in 1970 will scholarize 80 per cent of its fourteen-year-olds as against 30 per cent of that age group in 1955; that in France 100 per cent of sixteen-year-olds will go to school in 1970 as

---

* The Thomas-Majault report on common problems in European countries in the field of education indicates the following compulsory school ages for various countries; 16, certain *Länder* of Germany, France, Switzerland; 15, Belgium, United Kingdom, Iceland, Norway, Netherlands, Sweden; 14, other *Länder* of Germany, Austria, Denmark, Spain, Ireland, Italy, Luxembourg, Turkey; 12, Greece. It is remarkable that in practically all these countries extensions have been voted during the last three or four years.

against 50 per cent in 1958 and that in England in the past three years the number of children continuing up to sixteen years of age has risen from 10 per cent to 30 per cent of the age group, there can be no doubt that programs, methods and examinations will be deeply modified by the event.

One very important effect is the change in the meaning and objectives of primary school. This is no longer an end in itself but the groundwork for further progress. Moreover the line is no longer sharply drawn between primary and secondary schools. Sometimes, as in Sweden and Norway, the nine-year cycle is self-contained for all; in other cases (Germany, Italy, Belgium, Luxembourg) a long-drawn-out primary cycle is subdivided into two or three sections, the last or "terminal" one being closely related to the first half of the secondary cycle. With surprising speed these structures that had seemed unalterably linked to the social background are being shifted and re-examined by boards no longer composed of educators only, but through which administration and industry are making their influence felt.

With the primary school thus brought into new focus, no longer as a framework for elementary knowledge but as part of an overall education leading to as complete information as possible on nature and society, together with as solid training as available of intellectual and technical processes, all European countries are finding it necessary to concentrate, during that early period of the child's schooling, on a limited number of major subjects: the national language and at least one foreign modern language—which is to be taught in the future much earlier and with greater emphasis on its practical use than it is at present—history, civics and social institutions, observation of nature, arithmetic, manual and artistic activities and physical training are the common elements of almost all European children today.

As for the selective process which makes it possible to determine what child should attain what level of intellectual or scientific education, or what child should be led to exercise other abilities, this is considered by European reformers and legislators as a continuing one, no longer confined into examination periods or tests, but subject to the constant observation of pupils by teachers. One of the most striking common aspects of the dozen or more sweeping educational reforms passed in European countries between 1956 and 1962 is the generalization of an orientation or school guidance period between the ages of eleven and fourteen years, during which pupils are under special observation from the staff of the school in order to determine their aptitudes and advise parents as to the continuation of their studies. No longer does the traditional image of the ladder apply, where many ascend the two or three first rungs and few reach the top.

Fewer examinations, a greater personal care by the teacher for the aptitudes of each pupil, a less competitive and more explorative spirit in the classroom—all this leads undoubtedly to a massive influx of eighteen-year-olds into the still very narrow channels of higher education and universities. The widening of these channels and, even more, the fundamental modifications to be introduced in the student-professor relationship and the necessary integration of higher education into the new structures of industrialized societies involve specific problems not unrelated to those we have encountered in the process of democratization of general education. But they are of such magnitude that I desist from approaching them here. Suffice it to say that all western European nations realize that these problems are to be given top priority during the crucial years to come, when the number of students will be multiplied in each one of them by two and sometimes by three in less than five years.[1]

May we draw, from this rapid picture, the conclusion that the search for a more democratic school system has succeeded or that it is at least moving in the right direction? Strangely enough, a feeling of uneasiness as regards educational reforms of the type described in the Thomas-Majault report submitted to the Rome Conference of European Ministers of Education of 1962 exists among many observers, whether teachers, parents or administrators. There is no doubt about the will to democratize. But how will the structures bend and bear the impact? What qualitative effects are to be expected? Will the new generation be forced to dispense with the type of culture, communication and comprehension that were the normal concomitants of the *Abiturient,* the *bachelier,* the *baccilerato?*

Obviously it is neither to be expected that the far greater numbers will be granted the same type of schooling that was previously the privilege of the fewer, nor to be acknowledged that a general lowering of standards is the necessary counterpart of democracy. Much rather do the optimists expect the new "middle" schools to produce the well-adjusted citizen, the modern *honnête homme,* capable of handling the actual, not the artificial, problems of the century, while the pessimists foresee the prevalence of the conformist, the superficially well informed and deep-inside indifferent type of human being.

Education for what purpose? is the question that requires an answer and that no amount of research into structures and techniques can allow us to forego. Since the very principle of democracy forbids to search for any other main way to change the social tissue of a nation than education, it is of the utmost importance to make sure that the social ideals and the historic vision of a given community be exactly kept in mind throughout the mechanisms and conceptions of its educational system.

As major links between past and future, teachers at all phases of the educational process must be aware of the goal, of a challenge for which they prepare the youth entrusted to their care. Nationalism and a bourgeois class structure with a specific role set out for the proletariat have provided such a goal and have animated the teaching of the period of industrial revolution in Europe. At the present time, world-wide internationalism and a pluralistic society where several socio-professional groups share equally the responsibilities of defining and controlling the progress of the community are the new goals that have been made attainable by the second industrial revolution.

Education for these goals should mean a much more diversified process, not hierarchically organized but composed of a variety of parallel streams all leading to similar levels of comprehension, none entirely "classical" and none entirely "technical," but each a well-thought-out blend of the manual and the intellectual, the active and the contemplative, the practical and the theoretical.

All the knowledge accumulated by child and adult psychology over recent years must be put at the disposal of the distribution among these parallel streams of the much more voluminous flow of children. Through guidance, constant observation and close association with the family, the schools and universities can be made to develop in each the highest possible level of individual readiness to participate, to understand, to adjust and to call upon his or her peculiar sources of energy and creativeness. However, such a renewal of the content and outlook of education cannot be achieved in an atmosphere of distrust where the "academics," divorced from the political leaders of their community, look upon the destiny of their fellow citizens with a mixture of pity and skepticism.

This is where Europe can play a decisive role. The new horizon, which is not yet "existentially" lived but which dawns in the projects of the youth, may well counteract efficaciously any loss of confidence in the values of education and culture. A most encouraging example to that effect is the success of "European schools" promoted by the member states of the European Community and of which half a dozen are in existence and as many more under consideration. In Brussels, in Luxembourg and elsewhere, in the neighborhood of centers of international institutions or activities, children belonging to various European nationalities are being taught a combined curriculum by a multinational and plurilingual staff, leading to a diploma, the *baccalauréat européen,* created in 1957. The rapid acceptance by a dozen and more European countries of this title in full equivalence with their national entrance requirements to universities has been a happy surprise for all those acquainted with the particularisms of higher education in Europe. Moreover, after a few years' experience and some struggle by M. Van Houtte, the Belgian champion of the idea, against skepticism and the normal fear of heavy expenditure, the development of European schools has become part of the expansion program of most European nations.

It would be greatly exaggerated to say that this still very limited feature is already influencing the general trend of secondary schools in Europe, but it is an important indication of a gradual process from which I am convinced there is already no turning back: the firmly expected qualitative change in the dimensions and objectives of education will be facilitated and oriented by its taking place in the revolutionarily renewed context of integrating Europe.

II The New Outlook for the Teaching of Science

No adult European will admit that there is anything above his or her national university level in the fields of arts or law. But most of the same group will complain that modern science, with its vast requirements of rapidly obsolescent equipment and hard to train teamworkers, is being taught and conducted with more efficiency and better results outside of Europe. I am not sure that either of these impressions is any longer confirmed by the facts. Let us leave aside for the time being the question of the financing of scientific research, where undoubtedly the order of magnitude of available budgets in European nations is dangerously diminutive as against the United States or the Soviet Union. But as far as the teaching of science in high schools, universities and national schools of higher education is concerned, the past ten years have witnessed a marked popular awareness, carried forward by the active leadership of science professors in each of the European countries.

Any statistical data available show a definite change in the choice of students away from the liberal arts toward science and technology as well as a new attitude of European parents as early as the orientation period at the very beginning of secondary education, testifying to the growing attraction of scientific studies. This phenomenon could have been passed off as a vogue if it had not lasted as long as it has. But it could also have bred bitter disappointment if it had not been supported and guided by the energetic efforts of small groups in France, Germany, Great Britain and the Netherlands, usually composed of young and brilliant mathematicians or physicists alarmed at the growing gap between what was taught at the universities and what was needed to keep abreast.

In France, the Mouvement National pour le Développement des Sciences enlisted in the years 1954 to 1957 the active support of the most prominent professors and scholars, among whom is the present Dean of the Paris Faculty of Science, in an effort to re-equip and remodel the whole of scientific teaching in French institutions of higher education. A similar movement has been at the root of British plans for the development of new universities. The common purpose is to provide the nation with a network of selective institutions producing the new type of scientific mind and mental approach capable of coping with the overwhelming need for top research in the not yet explored realms of natural and social phenomena.

These movements and associations deny the practicability of merely adding to traditional scientific curricula the time and space required to catch up with the most recent theories and discoveries. They emphasize the need to re-examine the curriculum in its entirety, to determine the various degrees of scientific aptitude in youngsters and accordingly select and train them, to adapt the pedagogic methods of science teaching to these aims and particularly, in the field of mathematics, to extend the dimensions of the basic principles taught to include their ever more widely varied forms and formulations. At first decried as an unjustified sophistication, these new methods have been found to come closer to the original common sense of the child or adolescent than the more traditional ones, and although here too the road toward generalization is still long and arduous, a definite step forward can be witnessed since 1956 throughout western Europe.

Two factors happily combined to give a wider scope to the efforts of these relatively small groups of pioneers. One is the demographic wave over most European countries gathering momentum since the end of World War II; the other is the very process of unification, economic, cultural and political, for which no less than fifteen intergovernmental or nongovernmental organizations share the ever renewed responsibility. The first factor makes it imperative for all governmental or non-governmental authorities in charge of education to draw up vast plans for new installations, new equipment, the training of new staffs, the publication of new textbooks. They are consequently tempted quite naturally, before they proceed, to acquaint themselves with the most recent, most forward-looking ideas on the subject instead of merely to repeat or to enlarge upon what was said and done before.

The second factor introduces a typically European element of competitive cooperation. The conferences, seminars, working parties or expert groups convened by the various European organizations, notably the Council of Europe and the OECD, to examine such problems as the teaching of physics, of chemistry, of mathematics, the comparison of levels and curricula, the equivalence of diplomas, the use of educational material and other items of mutual interest, all allow for a similar process: the most advanced team in a given country—quite possibly not yet recognized by the prevailing "authorities"—has a chance to meet partner teams from neighboring countries. Experiments which are not yet widespread in any country are checked against each other and a selection is undertaken at a relatively high level of critical appraisal. The procedures or inventions thus selected spread with far greater ease throughout the educational systems not only of the competitor countries but even of the inventor country than they would have otherwise.

How may we assess the results already achieved? Judging by the complaints of students and the discontent of professors, by reports of delays in construction as well as training of personnel, by the yearly budget struggle when the ministries of finance and the treasury departments curtail the university expenditures in each country according to different rules and traditions, the new approach to science teaching is still nothing more than an outlook. If, on the other hand, we look at the reports submitted to the Committee on Higher Education and Research recently set up under the auspices of the European Council of Cultural Cooperation, another aspect of the problem becomes apparent: the era of unrelated growth of learning, teaching and research is past. The teaching of science and training for research is an integral part of educational development in the plans of all European governments.

In 1958, when the OECD launched a series of studies on the development of scientific training and research in member countries, the top ranking officials entrusted with each individual report had the difficult task of interviewing a vast number of sometimes quite independent institutions and authorities, none of which, in several instances, were in a position to give them an over-all view of plans in progress. Three years later the same countries could explain their national policy and foretell its projected results over a period of five or ten years. What had happened in the meantime was not very apparent in the way of a social or cultural revolution; it was rather the spread of a new outlook as to the respective parts to be played in the shaping of generations by individual freedom and by common planning. It cannot be stated too strongly for any American reader that it is at present this delicate balance, this constant readjustment between knowledge about common objectives and compliance to their imperatives on the one hand, and knowledge about individual capabilities and full expansion of the potential they contain, on the other, that is taking the place in the political vision of Europeans so long occupied by the outmoded conflict between capitalism and socialism. The faith in man's ability to meet this challenge and to enforce this balance, albeit against the deep-grounded resistance of privileges of all kinds, has dislodged and replaced the faith in a social revolution.

III Investment in Education

When the ministers of education of the sixteen member nations of the Council of Europe last met in Rome in October, 1962, they came to the common conclusion that education in Europe is no longer a consumer good but a part of national production. From this surprising and somewhat paradoxical statement they drew the consequence that expenditures intended to increase the educational facilities and equipment of a modern country should be considered as productive investments and charged to the general program of productive equipment of the country, not to the inevitably limited program of social investments.

This may seem like a trivial matter of budget technique, but it is not unlikely that its effects will change the prospects of school and university expansion within a foreseeable future. All modern countries suffer from the combined pressures of growing demands by public opinion for social and cultural amenities, and of fears that an imbalance between productive and unproductive expenditures will subject the general economy to inflationary trends. When a community expresses the need for a playground, a hospital, a theater, a school, a cultural recreation center and a day nursery—it all adds up to an impressive amount of heavy investment and costly maintenance. If, on the other hand, it is clearly realized that the training given to citizen A in school and university will in time increase the productive capacity of A so much above the productive capacity of citizen B, who has had to go without it, that the difference compensates for the expenditure of the school or university, then we are faced with a new situation. The building of schools becomes an anticipation of future gains for the economy and its cost can be drawn from resources normally devoted to the anticipation of such gains, resources the amount of which has become, in our industrial societies, incomparably larger than the equipment budget of public services. Moreover, by injecting the preoccupation with schools and universities into the context of planning for development, the governments of western Europe are quite naturally led to examine this problem as part of their common problem of economic cooperation.

As soon as this is said, there is a general raising of eyebrows among the champions of culture and of the traditional values of liberal education: they find it difficult to admit that the right of every boy and girl to learn and study and acquire the fundamental knowledge on which to base their quest for further learning and studying, in accordance with their personal choice and inclination—this very essence of a free people—should be subjected to the speculations of technicians responsible for the increase of production. This, they feel, would be the victory of materialism and the negation of the true European spirit. However, since it is no longer possible to identify national production with industrial output; since the requirements of an expanding economy cover not only the material but also the intellectual and cultural achievements entering into the composition of the market; since the world our planners have to prepare through an appropriate investment policy is not a world of massified needs for material goods but one of highly diversified demands for all types of satisfactions of body and mind, it is quite illegitimate to deny them the right to include education—this most basic component of the most eagerly looked for instrument of expansion: man—into their previsions and calculations. Obviously, such planning, if it is to be convincing, must be undertaken by carefully selected persons whose conception of education is appropriate to the highest requirements of our times. During the past five or ten years this requirement has been more and more successfully fulfilled in western Europe.

Difficulties arise—greater in countries like Germany with its federal structure, England with its complete independence of universities from the ministry of education, Belgium with its double sector, half state half church; somewhat lesser in the highly centralized countries where education possesses a well defined quasi-administrative status, such as France and Italy—when it comes to adjusting the development plans of a variety of institutions, at various levels of teaching and research, which contribute to the national effort to increase the cultural and intellectual level of the population. Any accurate description of the "educational apparatus" of one of the European countries makes the economist shudder. Any streamlining of that apparatus makes the intellectual wince. Thus we are far from the goal, only at the beginning of the road. A deeper understanding of the intricate ways in which knowledge may be gathered, unfolded and transmitted has to be acquired by the economist, while the scholar will have to realize much more clearly the general movement and overall desires of modern societies and the manner in which his no longer isolated task may contribute to their fulfillment.

But if on the national level the struggle between rational finances and the free pursuit of research and teaching has not yet come to a balance, internationally, and again particularly among European nations, great progress has been made in coordinating the most expensive forms of scientific research so as to achieve the maximum results with the minimum investment. The best known example of this type of coordination is CERN, the European Center for Nuclear Research, the basic convention of which, signed in 1953, has enabled all partner countries to set up and make use of equipment for research which none of them could well have afforded singly. More recently the European Space Research Organization has opened up similar possibilities in a field where the most modest experiment involves millions of whatever currency one wishes to choose. The late Director of Higher Education in France, Gaston Berger, has given his name to a more ambitious plan which has not yet come into being, although the basic texts were drafted two years ago and have met with a certain enthusiasm from the six members of the Common Market. This would consist of the creation of European research institutes in all fields of investigation, lerning and teaching, designated by common agreement of the partners, either among existing institutions endowed with the attributes of a European destination or in new fields in centers still to be set up. All partners would agree to concentrate research in these institutes, appoint a multinational staff, encourage research workers to join and students to apply for training. Costs would be equitably shared and results, of course, made available to all. Other nations would be encouraged to participate, either in the scheme as a whole or in individual institutions.

Does not such a plan—like all other forms of cultural cooperation among European nations—raise a very difficult problem of boundaries? What countries may be considered as European and why? Why should non-European countries be excluded? How can the objectives of science and learning be combined with any geographical limitations? When the Italian government suggested in 1959 the founding in Florence of a European university, all the universities in Europe (including the Italian universities) declared emphatically that they all were not only European but universal, since science, truth and arts admit of no frontiers. And yet such objections do not meet the true intention of the promoters of European cooperation for scientific research. The truth, the science, the cultural values sought in such joint institutions are obviously universal, but the logistics are European. Instead of each nation calculating for itself what it can spend to promote research in certain particularly expensive fields, the group of nations already aware of its common historic situation, the Six or perhaps the Sixteen, join forces and establish a common evaluation of what they feel they can spend.

This elementary and fundamental operation engenders by itself the most genuine confidence in the future of European science and education, for the sum is very large indeed. But the confidence and will to cooperate are strengthened still further by the consideration of what effect a planned concentration of European skills on jointly operated experiments may have upon the results achieved. No single nation in the world and probably no other group of nations brought together can yet match that level of potentiality.

IV Education in the Age of Leisure

All of these measures and projects, however, still appear to the most forward-looking groups of citizens in European countries to be not much more than the extension and completion of concepts that have been elaborated during the nineteenth century. The radically new aspects of the second industrial revolution, for which the works of the American school of sociology provide what may be looked upon in Europe as a prophetic description, seem to them to require an even more drastic reconversion of the methods and objectives of education.

In this perspective, schools and universities are no longer the only major instruments of education. The distinction between a period of learning and training—beginning at the age of reason and protracted as long as social and economic circumstances of the family will permit—and one of work until retirement age, is rapidly becoming obsolete. In practically no field of service or production is it either necessary for the active worker to devote his whole time to his job or possible for him to satisfy himself with the mental and technical knowledge gathered during his training years.

Education is becoming an ingredient of production and the communication of new acquisitions a component part of the responsibilities of every active person. No educator I know has more aptly expressed this new dimension of human endeavor than Professor Bertrand Schwartz, Director of the Nancy Ecole des Mines, and one of the most energetic participants of the group "Prospective," an association of brilliant French educators, industrialists and engineers, very much European in its outlook and devoted to the fundamental task of casting their eyes and minds forward into the shaping of our societies. Professor Schwartz not only popularized the introduction of active educational methods into the sanctuary of higher technical schools but also suggested ways by which the acquisition of any kind of specialized knowledge could be accompanied by the acquisition of techniques of expression and communication enabling the trainee to become a trainer throughout his professional activity. This can be considered the new key to a meaningful program of adult education.

A Committee on Out-of-school Education set up in 1961 is examining such new trends within the cultural framework of the Council of Europe. Its members find it easier, in fact, to reconcile in this field the initiatives and expectations of European youth than in the more heavily structured and geographically differentiated field of formal education. Indeed, throughout Europe the growing importance of extra-scholarly influences on child and adult—the ambiguous but tremendous impact of television and radio, the rapidly expanding volume of travel and tourism and of holidays and special leave for additional training—have become a major preoccupation of governments, educational authorities and civic or political groups.

But there would be a real danger in any isolation of the various components of education, any building up of a separate construction for outside-of-school transmission of knowledge, any keeping apart of the functions of teacher and those of adult educator. Recently at a seminar where specialists from various European countries and in various disciplines had come together to discuss the teacher-parent relationship, I have witnessed how concerned we all were with the growing number of technicians in the innumerable fields of child psychology, tests, aids against dyslexia, dysorthography, family handicaps and malajustments, besieging the parent and ignoring the teacher. Much rather should the training of educators, without neglecting the acquisition of a very solid and balanced culture, be aimed much more than in the past at the transmission of methods and techniques intended to adjust school instruction to the needs of the general comprehension of the realities of life and work.

It is by no means easy to circumscribe the efforts and changes required to turn the well built and impressive pyramids of European educational institutions into the smooth and complex machines needed to deal with the much broader problem of permanent education of the modern citizen. The temptation for Europeans merely to imitate the American model is much stronger in fact than is apparent from speeches and articles on the subject. It should nevertheless be resisted.

If the so-called age of leisure is to produce a new type of culture, much must be brought into it of the tumultuous experience gathered by the nations of Europe during their long and never quite successful fight against scarcity and overwork. Forces are in abeyance among the young generation in Europe which may, if properly mobilized, complete the dialectical process that would enable us to retain within the movement of constant training and retraining the exigency of a deep-set structural understanding of the meaning of our destiny.

V Education and International Understanding

It could have been said until very recently with only a modicum of sarcasm that the European spirit and the awareness of common objectives for all western European nations were fostered by all types of activities with the single exception of education. In school and university the emphasis was and to a large extent still is on the national language, the national literature, history, and geography, the national civics and institutions. A child becomes deeply French, or English, or German or Dutch not so much through his family surroundings, sometimes permeated by a growing international awareness, as through his school life and his formal education. The concepts and formulation common to all children of his own school, and to all children of the similar schools of his country, give him the mental structures and expressions that will singularize him as the member of a given national group. It is hardly conceivable, as long as national governments exist in Europe, that the requirement for just that task to be performed by the educational apparatus of each country could be given up. Does it then make any sense at all to try to combine school education with the wider and more ambitious objective of education for international understanding?

I believe there are two very different aspects to this problem. One has been underlined throughout its past activities by the United Nations Educational, Scientific and Cultural Organization, under the obligation set out in its constitution. It consists in revising school and university programs in all countries in order to eliminate anything in them that could foster hatred or distrust between various national groups, and to include wherever possible the type of information that may give pupils or students a better knowledge of and understanding for other communities, races and civilizations, in addition to some instruction in international organization and its aims and structures, with special emphasis on the criminality of violence in international life. Obviously the way in which these member nations react to such criteria is closely dependent upon the historical and political situation of each. Even the very newly independent may agree to deprive their youth of the strong meat of anticolonialism, but they will scarcely admit to reduce the content of nationalism, indispensable for a still fragile sense of community within a young nation. On the other hand, even the most perceptive educational authorities of a Scandinavian country will be inclined to present their past history under an angle which condones or at least gives some plausible explanation for the violence that has accompanied the growth of the nation. But in spite of such more or less minor difficulties, it may well be said that modern education throughout the world pays its respects to the ideology of international understanding and the equal value of all cultures and races.

As far as Europe is concerned, however, there is another quite different aspect to this problem: not only because of the secular rivalries, battles, wars and mutual hostility in which European history and literature is steeped, but also because the aim, in this case, should be much more ambitious. Children should be led, very early in their school life, to realize that the international entity to which they will contribute their activities reserves a special and common part to be played by Europe as such—by western Europe as a "neither this nor that," or by continental Europe as a guardian of very specific cultural and human values, or by the European partner of the Atlantic world as a distinctive component of the great common democratic venture to solve the problems of freedom and equity, or by any other concept of Europe as a unit or as a part of a larger unit, as a defender of values to be preserved or as a conqueror of new hopes for mankind.

All ambitious believers in European unification fight for one or the other of these objectives and frequently express regrets at the lack of real contribution toward their attainment from schools and universities. Various organizations, intergovernmental or nongovernmental, have made generous efforts to define some sort of European civics on which all educational authorities might agree and which could then be taught throughout our countries. But some doubt has spread in recent years as to the efficiency of such attempts.

Perhaps it would be more sensible not to start from any *a priori* in a field where diversity of opinions and the general motto "beware of dogmatism" seem to offer the most solid common ground. I am personally much more confident that a converging and constantly challenged growth of educational institutions in neighboring European countries, together with the ever more explicit feeling of a fundamental solidarity of this alert and undespairing group of nations, will bear the fruit of a new philosophy. Of this new philosophy we should say nothing in advance until it has stuck its roots into the rich but yet unexplored soil of the crowded young generations. Whether this soil will bear disorder and despair, or the neo-Hellenic design of a well-balanced human being, can at best be a guess in the dark.

STEPHANE HESSEL

REFERENCES

1. The elaboration of the Robbins report and the more recent designation in France of a *commission de reforme de l'enseignement supérieur* are interesting examples of the complexity of this problem and the international spirit in which it is being everywhere considered.

ALEXANDER KING

Science and Technology in the New Europe

Introduction

THE NEW measures of economic cooperation and integration in
Europe and the political consequences inherent in them are closely
tied to the explosive development of science and technology of the
past few decades. Contemporary industry, based on a complex technology derived in turn from scientific research, can operate only
through large units of plant and organization and requires resources
of research and development which, unless above a specific threshold value, are uncompetitive on a world scale. In other words,
modern technology can be productive only in terms of large markets
which an economically and politically fractionated continent is incapable of supplying. Measures of economic harmonization and integration are thus inevitably demanded by a highly developed and
rapidly growing technology.

Equally, however, the closer political and economic ties which
are now being created between neighboring countries provide conditions propitious for accelerated scientific growth, and it is inevitable that the new economic arrangements in Europe will directly
influence the extent and vigor of scientific effort in the countries
concerned in much the same ways as the size, political unity and
economic strength first of the United States and later of the Soviet
Union have produced massive research and development.

For such a development, the European countries possess at the
outset an enormous asset in their scientific tradition. The natural
sciences have in fact their origin in western Europe, and until after
World War II by far the greatest proportion of significant scientific
discovery came from European laboratories. The argument behind
"Science, the Endless Frontier," which Vannevar Bush submitted
to the President in 1945, was, in fact, that the United States had
until then relied too much on the scientific product of western
Europe and had need therefore to make a relatively much greater
effort in fundamental scientific research.

In Europe the industrial revolution was caused by the same spirit of inquiry which marked the beginning of contemporary science. This approach, based on the experimental method, was indeed a delayed flowering of the Renaissance and had a strong flavor of universalism in it. Yet, in reality, early science was able to contribute little to the industrial revolution, which depended essentially on empirical invention; and during the nineteenth century science and manufacturing technology grew further and further apart until the natural sciences had accumulated a substance of fact and principle sufficient to found the science-based industries of the present century. During much of this period European science, despite its strength and its glory, often tended to be somewhat remote from everyday life and from practical application, while on the other hand European industry as a consequence of tradition and of its very success was often less ready to incorporate new scientific ideas. This situation, in spite of many notable exceptions, persisted until World War II; in some countries industry was much less competent than that of the United States in the development phase of innovation typified by the engineering prototype and the chemical pilot plant. This deficiency, contrasted to American mass production techniques, was undoubtedly encouraged not only by the smaller domestic markets of the various European countries, but also by the prolonged success of traditional European products on the world market, a success which appeared to make innovation unnecessary.

This phase of industrial history is past. Contemporary European industry, with its prospects of larger "domestic" markets and its new managerial consciousness, is well prepared for a full exploitation of technology. Furthermore, European industry is open to change to an extent unthinkable during the last century and a half. The coming into existence of the Common Market has necessitated the abandonment of many long-held ideas and has brought about a willingness on the part of managements, workers and the public at least to consider new concepts, new approaches, new methods—a change perhaps more significant for the future than all the immediate mercantile consequences of economic integration. In science as in industry, extensive changes are taking place, through the building of greater research resources, government encouragement and a rapid expansion of universities that reflects not only the increasing levels of education needed by the economy but greatly enhanced social demands.

The extent, organization and objectives of science in Europe are thus moving very quickly as a result of the particular political and economic development on that continent. They are perhaps even more influenced, however, by the inherent changes in the nature of science itself as it develops throughout the world. It is this double influence which is bringing about the fundamental changes in European research and scientific education today.

To understand the evolving scientific scene in Europe, it is necessary to examine these world trends and then to consider them in terms of the European environment.

I World Trends in the Position and Functioning of Science

The great extension of research activity of the last few decades, its evident and direct importance for economic advancement and defense, its prestige value and its high costs, have completely changed the position of science and of the scientist in national and international life. Yet the organizations of science, while gradually modifying to meet the new circumstances, are in most countries largely based on long established tradition suited to conditions of scientific research of fifty years ago, and on institutional models long since outmoded. In order to understand how these institutions are evolving, it is necessary to enumerate some of the circumstances and trends in scientific work today which render such development necessary.

A public image of science has emerged as a power compounded of good and evil. There is general comprehension of its role in both war and peace which has given rise to widely different and even contradictory attitudes. Science, the creator of the hydrogen bomb, intercontinental missiles and potential space weapons, has naturally enough produced a violent popular revulsion against the misuses of discovery. Yet there is widespread recognition of its importance for human well-being and of its decisive role for the future of the race. It is unfortunate that it has been the more dramatic developments of technology, with their potentialities for both destruction and human welfare, that have raised the prestige value of science in the eyes of the public and of its governments, rather than the multitude of less dramatic but in the aggregate more solidly useful contributions to national and individual life.

The political prestige as well as the obvious economic and defense value of science and technology make it increasingly difficult for the scientist to work quietly in the corner of his laboratory without excessive interest being focused on his actions by governments and industrialists. Indeed the large funds which he requires for his experiments have in many cases produced cracks in the ivory tower; many individual scientists have shown little reticence in commenting on the political consequences of their work. This situation is but another example of the difficult balance of privilege and responsibility which will have to be established through good sense and understanding on both sides if circumstances propitious to the maintenance of scientific creation are to be preserved with long-term advantage to those who enjoy its fruits.

Equally important is the influence on science of economic pressure for improved technology. The arising of the science-based industries has already changed the pattern of the economy and of trade quite brutally and has made accessible new materials, drugs, equipment and devices of all kinds which have altered the daily lives of men and women throughout the world. Meanwhile, industry generally is becoming technologically much more complex, highly capital-intensive, requiring large units of production for economic operation and large research efforts to ensure the future; the gap between discovery in the laboratory and application in production is rapidly diminishing.

This increasing technological complexity throws a great burden on management and necessitates the presence of scientific and engineering skills in the board room as well as in the production shop. Industry is in fact entering a new phase of development which succeeds the earlier stages, first of invention, and later of application of the physical sciences, for innovation is now determined not only by discoveries in the laboratory but also by a complex of economic and sociological considerations. In many aspects of automation, for example, not only is basic scientific discovery sufficient for considerable practical advance, but opportunity for technological development is equally ripe. Increasingly in the future, social and economic factors are likely to be equally important with new science as determinants of change, and much development of research in the social sciences will be necessary if the prerequisites of innovation are to be understood and its social consequences intelligently allowed for.

Increasing recognition of the value of science for industry will tend toward the acceptance of research expenditure as a normal company investment requiring as careful assessment of possibilities, selection between alternatives and sound management as any other investment item. It will also have an increasing influence in Europe, as in the United States, on demands for supporting fundamental research.

Science has potentially as great contributions to make to the developing as to the underdeveloped areas of the world. Problems of raising living standards in the underdeveloped regions of the world are essentially those of making possible greatly increased rates of technological innovation, whether these may take the form of a simple improvement such as the replacement of the wooden plow by a steel instrument or the introduction of a degree of industrialization. Scientific discovery has the greatest importance for such areas through agricultural improvement, the conquest of disease and the availability of new forms of energy. As in industrialized societies, more primitive conditions still call for a balance of technological, economic and social forces for effective change, and transfer of technology from advanced to subsistence economies demands much more than conventional technical assistance. Science can and will provide an impulse to rapid development in these areas, and this development is likely to require the skills of a quite considerable proportion of the scientific and engineering manpower of the donor nations in the next few decades. It becomes increasingly more clear, however, that such help can be effective only when it is conceived in terms of integrated economic development, the growth of societies, the evolution of permanent local institutions and, above all, a coherent and balanced educational plan.

Help in development will become an increasingly important political necessity and will require much more than conventional financial and technical aid. Real progress from the subsistence level can be achieved only through industrialization, which the advanced countries will have to encourage without reserve. This will mean a change in the pattern of their own industries away from the traditional; and the simpler manufacturers will have to encourage the production of complex products of high added value in skills and research.

The amount of scientific research undertaken is increasing very rapidly not only in the highly industrialized areas but throughout the world, so that there is likely to be much less dominance in the future by the scientific achievement of any one region. Nevertheless, areas of high industrialization and high per capita income, such as Europe, are well favored for the still further extension of their scientific resources, particularly if these are developed with a sensible balance of effort in the context of a deliberate national policy.

Not only is the total amount of research increasing, but the cost per unit of research is becoming very high, owing to the need for special instruments and equipment, especially in fundamental research fields such as high energy physics and radio-astronomy. In an increasing number of cases, including those just mentioned and still more for space research, fundamental research relies on the development of highly complex and costly technologies which may not have any direct utility for the economy, thus reversing the normal chain of events in which fundamental scientific discovery precedes applied research, which in turn leads through technological development to production. In some fields, the demand for expensive equipment is already excluding the smaller political units by economic limitations from participation altogether, except where means for international cooperation and cost sharing are available. This difficulty will become increasingly serious until certain activities become possible only in terms of total world effort—and even then the limits are in sight.

Fashions in science are as dominant as in other realms of activity and may, through prestige considerations, distort the balance of scientific advance to the extent that some countries can neglect the less glamorous subjects and give insufficient attention to subjects on which national well-being depends. It is most unfortunate that excesses of scientific fashion should be encouraged by the highly science-based countries with regard to the development of new nations to which such luxuries, although even less easy to afford, are tempting for reasons of international status.

There are profound changes in research work itself. It is widely recognized that the breakthrough discoveries of fundamental science are due to a very few men of scientific genius whose creative ability can never be replaced by regiments of more pedestrian workers, however well trained and competent they may be. It is realized as important by all political systems that such pioneers of the future must be provided with facilities to work in the directions chosen by their genius and given conditions which preserve their creativity. Rapid advances of knowledge have, however, greatly encouraged specialization, so that few universities can longer pertend to universality in their teaching. Furthermore, progress in many of the new fields of discovery lies on borderlines between different sciences and can be successfully assured only by teams of scientists from different disciplines. Conditions of scientific work are changing in many other ways: for example, in activities which require very expensive equipment, their technology will necessitate an understanding of the basic engineering problems posed by research needs, and the research leader will have to work in harmony with those who develop and maintain his equipment. In such cases too the approach to a scientific problem can often not be easily modified once the work has begun, because of the extremely heavy capitalization necessitated by the scientist's cerebration. We know very little as yet as to the influence of such change on the emergence and maintenance of the creative research worker.

II The Institutions of Science

While it is generally agreed in Europe, as in the United States, that the university provides the best environment for fundamental research, and that applied research for industry is most effectively carried out by the individual enterprises, great differences exist nevertheless between the patterns of institutional organization which have developed in different countries. These differences result from factors of history and environment, or they have a political origin.

Among features of the European scene which have helped to shape the nature of European scientific organization are the long tradition of academic freedom and status derived without a break from medieval learning; the great influence of academies and learned societies which help to maintain and extend this tradition and to enhance the status of fundamental research; the existence of massive concentrations of industrialization, often all too inbred; the strong and sometimes centralized authority of government frequently determining educational policy in detail and operating its own research facilities; and above all the high degree of political and economic fractionation which has persisted until now. These circumstances explain many features of the European institutions; a few of them will be subject of brief comment.

During the earlier phases of scientific history, the individual scholar, the research worker and indeed the university were largely supported by rich or noble patrons. The social changes which followed the industrial revolution gradually altered this system, although the emergence of large foundations financed by the fortunes of rich and successful industrialists is to some degree an extension of the individual patronage of earlier centuries. Until recently, however, foundations have not had as important a role in Europe as in the United States, although since the war the Nuffield Foundation in the United Kingdom and the Gulbenkian Foundation located in Portugal have made their mark, while the new Volkswagen Foundation in Germany may well be important for scientific development. The great increase in expenditure on science has taken it quite beyond all reliance on private patronage. There is indeed no alternative to major financing of science by governments and by industry. The very term "patronage" disappears, of course, as soon as these expenditures are regarded as investments, and the concept must be replaced by considerations of enlightened self-interest. In education too, with increasing costs, inflation and rapid expansion, university endowments are grossly insufficient and have had to be augmented massively with government funds.

In Europe therefore research and scientific education have become recognized as aspects of national investment. Already during the first decade of this century, governments began to appreciate the practical consequences of research and assumed responsibility for institutions such as the Kaiser Wilhelm Institute in Germany and the National Physical Laboratory in England. The 1914–1918 war gave a great impulse to this movement and encouraged governments to promote industrial research and to set up their own scientific institutions for specific fields. These activities increased markedly between the two world wars, to the extent that government influence and operation have now become a dominant feature in the organization of science in Europe.

At present, all European countries with the exception of Austria, Switzerland and Greece possess central national scientific organizations of some sort. These vary greatly in character, function and influence from country to country. In some instances they are great and powerful organs of the state, operating networks of national laboratories; in other instances their function is largely advisory or their main task may be the distribution of government funds in the form of fellowships and grants for research to individual scientists or to academic institutions. They form, in some cases, part of the conventional civil service; they may be largely government financed, but advised and managed independently for reasons of efficiency and of easier contact with the academic and industrial worlds. They may concentrate exclusively on the support of fundamental research or they may cooperate with industry in the promotion of applied research and development. History plays a great part in shaping scientific organization, and those countries which have large defense commitments necessarily have a more complicated scientific system. In the United Kingdom and France, for example, military research contracts have greatly helped to build up electronics and precision engineering industries—for civil as well as for defense products—while in countries such as Austria, where defense science plays little part, the place of government in science remains ambiguous.

The existence of central research councils and similar bodies does not avoid the creation, in most countries, of scientific organizations both separate and attached to individual departments of government; the following survey indicates the wide range of functions in science which the average European government has assumed.

(a) *Science Education*

Primary and secondary education being accepted as a universal human right, they become a central charge on government, while a large proportion of the finance for higher education also comes from central and local governments. Education is regarded still mainly in terms of basic social and cultural objectives and only secondarily in terms of its vocational importance to the individual and its economic function in creating the necessary scientific and engineering manpower for future national needs.

(b) *Research in Universities and other Centers of Higher Learning*

In many countries such research is made possible as part of general university financing by the state or by regional bodies through the provision of fellowships to enable a substantial number of graduate students to be trained in research, although the extent of such support varies greatly from nation to nation. The dual objectives of such support is to provide trained research workers for the government's own purposes and for industry as well as to contribute to the extension of knowledge.

(c) *Defense Research*

Only governments can assume responsibility for the complex military technology of today, and in Europe it is mainly carried out in defense science laboratories, although at the development stage much is done by contract in industry. In the United Kingdom, defense research forms a very substantial proportion of the total effort, as in the United States. It is also important in some other countries, such as France, but it is proportionately much less significant in most of the other European countries.

(d) *Research for Public Utilities*

Since in the modern state government activity is so extensive, it requires the undertaking of research and development work in fields where the government is a direct user of the results. Examples are forestry, geological survey, water resources and their purity, prevention of air pollution, road research, fire preservation, loose-bed hydraulics, and insect control. In European countries such topics are generally the concern of governmental or semigovernmental institutes.

(e) *Medical Research*

Although much medical research is done in universities and their medical schools in close proximity to great hospitals, many governments support special medical research councils, such as that in the United Kingdom, which maintains central laboratories and achieves a balanced research effort by financing research units for particular topics in hospitals and universities.

(f) *Industrial Development and Research*

In many European countries a great many sectors of the economy are nationalized, particularly the railways and other transportation services; coal, iron and steel; and gas, electricity and nuclear energy. In addition particular industrial enterprises such as Renault in France are state owned. All of these undertake research in much the same way as the ordinary industrial corporation under private enterprise, that is to say with little direct state intervention. Outside the government's own productive effort, however, there is much influence on industry, and industrial policies are often framed in such a way as to encourage development and technological innovation. Fiscal policies are important instruments to this end but can, if badly conceived, have a contrary influence. There is also a tendency, only now becoming important, for the stimulation of industrial change by the granting of research contracts for firms, or groups of firms, to undertake particular developments deemed to be in the national interest, in much the same way as for defense technology.

A further industrial preoccupation of many governments is to speed up the development of scientific discoveries in the laboratory, through applied research and development, to production; some governments have therefore set up special organizations to scan the output of national science, to select topics of potential economic importance and to facilitate their exploitation. The National Research Development Corporation of the United Kingdom is a well-established and successful organization of this type. It is an independent organization with government capital and a board of industrialists, bankers and professors, expert not only in technological forecasting but in the legal and organizational problems of facilitating development. Through international cooperation among European countries, there is a healthy exchange of experience on this subject, which becomes increasingly important with ever greater research expenditures of governments.

Many governments undertake directly background research of utility to industry as a whole, such as experimental investigations related to the maintenance of standards of weight, electricity and radioactivity, and provision of reference materials such as exceptionally pure chemicals; many often conduct researches on metallurgy, corrosion, etc. Increasingly too, governments undertake research for industries where the average unit of production is very small, such as in agriculture and building; where the individual firm or the small contractor respectively cannot be expected to undertake their own research; and where, even could they do so, the result would be excessive duplication and waste. Such production elements are unable in most cases even to select and apply relevant research done by others, and hence most countries have created for such sectors a complex network of specialist research institutions and extension services.

The role of governments in stimulating research activity on a cooperative and sector by sector basis has been particularly important in Europe, and it is described on page 447 in relation to industrial research in general.

A particular feature of many European countries is the extent to which governments are content to delegate responsibility for the expenditure of national funds to specialist groups. This is particularly true of the universities. European universities, which in some countries are directly under ministries of education, or which in any case receive most of their funds directly from the state, have for long maintained a very high level of academic attainment, and they enjoy an honorable status in society. Their long traditions, together with the relatively small proportion of Europeans who have until recently had the privilege of higher education, have enabled the universities to pursue for the elite their aims of scholarship and to resist a too narrowly vocational education. Nevertheless, in the engineering, medical and other schools and as a result of the pressures exerted by a rapid expansion, much instruction of a directly utilitarian nature, albeit of a high quality, has crept in. European universities have striven hard to maintain their levels of quality despite their very rapid postwar expansion, and they have very largely succeeded. High uniformity of attainment is controlled in many instances by systems of examination determined nationally or by the use of examiners from sister universities, who are able to insist on enforcement of the generally recognized standards. There is in fact little in the way of a pyramid in European higher education to compare with that of the United States, with what appears to many Europeans to be an excessive variety of institutional methods and quality, or with that of the Soviet Union, where a large proportion of higher education is carried out by institutes for particular subjects such as agriculture, mining or medicine, which, although teaching at a very high level are admittedly vocational in their objectives.

Further, considerable expansion of the universities is envisaged in the next decade, and there is every reason to question if this will or indeed should permit the maintenance of uniform standards and academic bias as at present. There are many indications of change and of greater flexibility in European university planning, and of a more practical orientation. The last few years have seen a very marked tendency, discussed on pages 453–454, to attempt to relate educational investment to long-term economic needs and social objectives. The increasing demand in economic activity for the services of large numbers of educated persons is leading to a new concept of education, planned to benefit the individual and yet in the joint interest of himself and of the economy, to make sure that such education (and to a lesser extent, higher training) is suited to future employment patterns.

Technical high schools of great achievement have existed for years, especially in Germany, Switzerland, Holland and Scandinavia, and it is interesting to note recent decisions for example in the Netherlands, where new technological universities are being planned as consequences of national policy to intensify industrialization. In France too demographic changes, technological advance and social pressures are leading to radical modification of the educational structure. For example, fourteen colleges of science and seven of arts have recently been set up to relieve the pressure on the already too large University of Paris. These are mainly restricted to the preparation for short-term (two-year) diplomas, specially created. Many long held traditions of French education are being questioned in relation to their suitability to meet contemporary needs, and in the engineering schools, for instance, openings are provided, much as in Russia, for candidates from factories and workshops. Interesting experiments are being made in many other places, such as in Yugoslavia, where a novel three-cycle system is being tried out to provide the pyramid of skills needed by the economy and at the same time designed to provide the elite of scholarship and research.

It should not be assumed that these changes will result in a narrowly utilitarian concept of education. Attempts to relate the educational process to long-term economic objectives (or, as far as the individual is concerned, employment prospects) give great importance to the adaptation of a man's knowledge and skill throughout his career to the quickly changing tasks which result from a dynamic technology. This continuous learning process will be fruitful only if the initial, formal education is sufficiently developed and focused on principles, and above all if it develops permanent equipment to allow for learning at later stages. Paradoxically then, really enlightened approaches to vocational needs stress true education in contrast to training for immediate tasks.

European governments generally accept the university as providing the best environment for fundamental research and for long maintenance of the creative ability of scientists. In spite of the inclusion of a healthy proportion of fundamental investigation in government and industrial laboratories, therefore, by far the greatest effort remains in academic surroundings.

Increased costs of research and particularly of equipment in fields such as nuclear physics and radio-astronomy have also led in most countries to the provision of special funds for the purchase and often the maintenance of such equipment, which can hardly be provided through normal university budgets without causing grave unbalance among different fields of learning. Government support of research in European universities is mainly in the form of fellowships and grants rather than as contracts for specific research projects, as is so common in the United States. There is, in fact, a strong feeling in Europe that the best way to encourage research is to back well-established research leaders and young scientists of promise and to discourage project research since, however germane it may be to the normal work of a university institute, it tends to inhibit the creative development of research which depends so much on the free choice of the professor to follow the lines of his own genius. On the whole much greater importance is given in Europe than elsewhere to the right, and indeed to the duty, of the professor to choose his own research topics undiverted by the attractions of research projects offered by government departments, military or civil, and by industry. This, of course, encourages the trends of fashion; and in some countries a corrective has been applied to assure the investigation, in the national interest, of important research fields not at the moment à la mode. This has been achieved in France by the National Center for Scientific Research, and in Great Britain by the Medical Research Council by the insertion of special research units associated with, but financially independent from, existing university research departments. Such units offer great advantages over other forms of aid for oriented fundamental research in that they involve no new institutions or capital equipment; if they are successful, these units gradually become assimilated into the university research fabric.

The extent and cost of research in the natural sciences also present many problems of balance of discipline, and the increasing extent of specialization renders true universality, within a single university, impossible. There are as yet few centers of university cooperation for research on expensive topics on the Brookhaven model, but international institutions such as the European Council for Nuclear Research (see page 518), have somewhat the same function although they are intergovernmental, rather than interuniversity, in character. An interesting "growing points" scheme is being attempted in Scandinavia, where a number of specialized science institutes of the universities of the three countries have been selected by the research councils of the countries concerned to receive priority support and to serve the needs of the whole area for the specializations concerned. This experiment is of general significance because of the attempt of too many European universities to provide too wide a coverage of subjects, with the result that for some subjects, research centers are too numerous and individually too weak.

European industrial research also differs greatly from that of the United States, mainly for a pattern of industry reasons and because of the existence of so many small political units. European industry is extremely heterogeneous in character, ranging from huge corporations of the most advanced type with operations throughout the world and generally supported by sound and extensive research programs, to small family-controlled business often survivals from the successful industrialization of the middle of the last century. On the whole, however, industry in Europe has been technologically less agressive than its American counterpart, less concerned with the dangers of obsolescence and often quite indifferent to needs for innovation. This attitude was understandable during the long period when possibilities of economic expansion ceased to be discussed, and it was entrenched by an accumulation of marketing tradition, ingrown management tradition, product range and process stability which had been successful for so long.

Management in many European countries has been until recently dominantly mercantile in its approach. In some areas control has been firmly in the hands of the accountant and of the lawyer, although in Germany the engineer has played a big part—a sign of the success of the technical high school system. Science in European industry has been usually "on tap"—although only at a trickle, and seldom "on top"—with the consequence that in too many instances new scientific and technological ideas were unable to penetrate the financial sanctity of the board room.

This situation is rapidly breaking up; wartime destruction rendered inevitable the replacement of old buildings, old machinery, and often of old managements. Social change, the broadening of education, the general prestige of science, completely new managerial attitudes with technological awareness infiltrating from the large science-based corporations and through association with the United States—these things and the general hurricane of change which economic integration or its threat is blowing through all the board rooms of Europe, and also, it should be whispered, through many of the trades union headquarters too—are producing an expansive and forward-looking industry in Europe, likely to be aggressively competitive and fully aware of the possibilities offered by the application of science.

In the process, research resources are being built up and, what is even more important, technological appreciation is becoming widely evident at board level. Attitudes to research in industries such as chemicals, pharamaceuticals, electronics, and the precision engineering sectors are much the same in Europe as in the United States, while in some countries, such as the United Kingdom and France, defense science contracts have speeded their building up. The lowering of trade barriers with consequent prospects for larger "domestic" markets is encouraging association among firms in different countries of the Six for research and design cooperation or for the exchange of technical ideas, a very necessary movement in view of the rising thresholds of research expenditure above which alone investment yields from science are statistically likely to prove profitable.

The high degree of density of industrialization in much of western Europe, which has led to the concentration of many firms engaged in the same type of manufacture in a particular area, has encouraged the evolution of cooperative research schemes which are a uniquely European growth unlikely to find extensive emulation in the United States, if only for the practical reason of the much greater distances there between industrial units. In Great Britain, for example, there are upwards of fifty research associations for particular industries undertaking cooperative work to raise the general technological level of the sector in question. This system, which had its origins at the end of World War I, is in fact a financial partnership between government (through the agency of the Department of Scientific and Industrial Research) and industry, and represents a significant part of British industrial research. Not only is research successfully undertaken for an industry as a whole, and its results made available to the contributing member firms, but great stress is laid on the communication to the individual firms of relevant new scientific and technological information, including know-how from sources throughout the world by means of information services, field liaison schemes, demonstration methods and the like. Similar schemes exist also in the Netherlands, France, Germany and Belgium, while in countries such as Norway, novel schemes of government-industry cooperation for research have been created which are adapted to particular national conditions.

The cooperative research movement is particularly successful for the more traditional sectors such as textiles and the metal industries and is much less important in newer branches, where large firms with their own highly evolved research facilities dominate. It is generally found that in an industry where the research association is strong and aggressive, the scientific activities of the individual member firms build up quickly with the initial role of enabling use to be made of the technological experience from the association. The cooperative research approach should therefore be regarded as a stimulus and complementary to, rather than as a substitute for, the competitive research of the individual enterprise. Some research associations, particularly those of the Dutch TNO Organization, conduct research under contract for individual firms in addition to their broader cooperative work; and it seems that confidential work, which becomes the property of the firms which buy it, is compatible within the same institute with cooperative research leading to results which are commonly owned. Since the war, a number of private or nonprofit-making industrial research institutes have sprung up in Europe, while some of the United States-sponsored research organizations, such as Batelle, have established overseas branches. These initiatives have met with some success, but this type of system has not grown as quickly as was initially expected.

III International Cooperation in Research

The rising costs and astonishingly quick growth of scientific research make it difficult for any country to keep abreast of scientific development along the whole extending frontier of knowledge. This is especially the case in those fields of fundamental research where unit equipment costs are beyond the possibilities of the smaller countries. Nevertheless, bridging the gap between the promise held out by science and the resources available to undertake it is gradually becoming a general and more difficult problem. It has been argued in some quarters, and has even become national policy in a few instances, that smaller countries should rely for fundamental scientific discovery on the outpourings of the great research efforts of the United States, the Soviet Union, and the larger western European countries. This is, however, a doubtful policy in the interest of a nation, since applications of productive value from such research can be very great and in quite unexpected directions. Furthermore, unless a country possesses scientists with some experience in new specializations and novel techniques, the applied research and productive technology of the future can be acquired only slowly and with difficulty. This means in effect that all countries with ambitions of progressive industrialization are tempted to undertake research work on a broad front and to deploy their limited scientific resources over too many subjects.

This problem is particularly acute in Europe as a result of high levels of industrialization and small political unit size. The basic overheads of science have to be met separately by each state, with the result that there is much useless duplication and subthreshold effort. The situation is much the same as if, in the United States, each state of the Union were to attempt individually to provide the whole apparatus of the contemporary scientific effort. This problem can be solved satisfactorily in Europe only by some degree of political integration, but in the meantime much has already been achieved through cooperative effort. The close proximity of European countries and a considerable identity of objectives make the growth of regional cooperative research particularly attractive, and in fact they present the only means at present available for small progressive countries to participate in some of the newer and most quickly advancing fields of scientific investigation. This movement has already proceeded to the extent that some of the smaller countries expend a considerable proportion of their total research budgets on cooperative research undertaken beyond their frontiers; on the other hand they may receive in the form of international research contracts more money than they disburse. There is thus gradually emerging among European countries, it would seem, a "balance of payments" position for scientific effort.

It must be admitted, however, that participation in such schemes, important and costly as it may be, is often a matter of individual enthusiasms or of prestige rather than a decision of policy. The extent and direction of this international movement is of sufficient interest for other areas of the world for some of the major institutions to be described.

Apart from the United Nations specialized agencies, such as

UNESCO, which have world membership and are more and more preoccupied with the problems of underdevelopment, there exist for European countries a number of important intergovernmental organizations with a practical interest in science, or at least in its promotion, each of which has different general objectives, different membership and quite different approaches to the problems of science.

One of the most important of these is the Council of Europe, with sixteen members, which, in addition to its important parliamentary assembly, receives annual reports on the scientific work of other European bodies. This organization has an important cultural program supervised by a Council for Cultural Cooperation. Important problems of university development, equivalence of university degrees and improvement in the teaching of particular subjects are discussed here. The Council of Europe also provides the Secretariat for occasional conferences of the European ministers of education which are organized independently. In quite a different category is the North Atlantic Treaty Organization (NATO), whose thirteen European members, together with the United States and Canada, are bound by defense treaty obligations. NATO operates an important Science Committee concerned with the general health of European science, and not specifically with defense problems. Its main science activities are to operate a large fellowship scheme, which in 1963 will amount to two and a half million dollars, the support of summer schools in European universities on advanced scientific topics and the provision of grants for university research. The strength of NATO science lies in its Atlantic constitution; its weakness in the absence of "neutral" European countries such as Sweden and Switzerland, which nevertheless contribute greatly to the fabric of the European security effort.

Yet another "Atlantic" organization which has scientific interests is the Organization for Economic Cooperation and Development (OECD), which has eighteen European members (including the "neutrals"), the United States and Canada, with Jugoslavia as an associate; it will shortly accept Japan as a full member. OECD is concerned with objectives of high rates of economic growth and the encouragement of economic development. It has two scientific committees, one for Scientific and Technical Personnel, and one for Scientific Research, whose work is directly related to these purposes. Each committee has a substantial program of operation, the first including important studies and actions to make possible planning of educational investment in relation to future economic and social needs, programs for the reform of secondary school science and mathematics curricula and the introduction of new educational technology; the second committee, among many activities, is encouraging the provision of national research and development expenditure data, studying the relationship between research investment and economic advancement and organizing cooperative research between member countries on specific topics, mainly of an applied character. This functional approach to research cooperation allows groups of institutions interested in a specific subject to plan a comprehensive program for which each laboratory takes responsibility for a particular element. The object is to obtain a much higher research yield from a particular effort, and it is only in exceptional cases that new research institutions are advocated. This network of cooperation is growing rapidly and at present includes the work of well over 1000 researchers, the overhead costs being trivial.

OECD also possesses a semi-autonomous agency for nuclear energy (the European Nuclear Energy Agency, or ENEA), which was set up to encourage the development of nuclear energy for peaceful purposes in Europe. ENEA has created a number of joint undertakings in research and development, such as the Halden (Norway) boiling heavy water reactor project, the Dragon (U.K.) high temperature, gas-cooled reactor project, and the Eurochemic Company in Belgium for the reprocessing of irradiated nuclear fuels. In each instance, the scheme is financed by a group of countries specifically interested, without commitment to participate in other ENEA schemes. Although each undertaking is independently managed from the scientific and technical point of view, connection to the parent body is maintained on matters of general policy and financial negotiation.

The six countries of the European Economic Community have not yet created permanent machinery for general research purposes, but the two sister organizations have important activities in research, development and dissemination of technical information as well as discussing social and economic implications of their research. Euratom, which employs a research staff of nearly 2000, runs a Joint Nuclear Research Center with branch establishments in Italy, Belgium, Germany, and the Netherlands; it has also placed some 250 research contracts and has been responsible for plans to create a new European University at Florence.

In addition to the above examples of international cooperation within intergovernmental organizations of a general character, western European governments have come together to finance a number of specialized research bodies, some of which are of considerable importance. The oldest and most striking of these is the European Council for Nuclear Research (CERN), situated at Geneva, with a membership of fourteen European countries. CERN undertakes research on high energy particle physics of a fundamental scientific character and has no concern with applied nuclear energy. Its main projects are a 25/28 GeV proton synchroton and a 600 MeV synchrocyclatron, together with work on theoretical nuclear physics, cosmic ray research, etc. The main arguments for the establishment of CERN were economic, and its common facilities are certainly far beyond the financial possibilities of most of its members working separately. The enterprise, which has been particularly successful, has furthermore demonstrated that the intellectual cross-fertilization made possible by the working together of scientists from different countries under a dynamic leadership is in itself ample justification for international cooperation.

Two additional independent organizations of considerable magnitude have started work more recently. The European Space Research Organization (ESRO), housed in Paris, is an attempt to organize major programs of space research which are well beyond the means of the individual members. It is unlikely that ESRO will develop a large central establishment of the CERN type, but it is more favorable to the concept of promoting its work in a group of institutions devoted to various aspects of space technology, data processing, etc. The European Launching Development Organization (ELDO), a complementary body which includes Australia as well as western European countries, has as its objective the development of suitable rocket vehicles for the launching of European satellites.

This enumeration, which is greatly simplified, indicates that the growth of cooperative scientific activity in Europe is considerable in scale, somewhat haphazard in conception, and valuable both in itself by making available entry to research fields which would otherwise be barred to many countries, and as a large-scale experiment in international technique with many lessons for the future. Many governments are beginning to be confused and even irritated by this random growth, which is exaggerated in some instances by the fact that national policy is communicated fractionally and in contradiction through different departments of state—education, science, defense, economic, and finance—frequently without sufficient coordinative machinery to enable coherent national views to be sought. The bills which are regularly presented are becoming bigger each year, amounting to a considerable part of the research budget of some countries; furthermore some members, and especially the smaller countries, feel that they have little control over the expansion and direction of these international activities which demand so high a proportion of their national research budgets. Some rationalization will certainly be demanded before long, but the whole problem is dominated by overall political uncertainty—will scientific cooperation in Europe be on the scale of the Six, of the greater Europe, on an Atlantic level, or on a world basis? In fact, all are necessary. Needs vary from case to case according to the nature of the problem, its scale, cost level, adequacy of existing resources and other factors. Problems which involve the environment of the whole earth, as in oceanography or meteorology, are most intelligently attacked on the full international scale; other problems are, for practical purposes, most conveniently handled between a group of neighboring countries.

Scientific cooperation in Europe is no longer a marginal activity; it represents a major and perhaps the only means for the smaller countries to keep in touch with the rapid advances of science, especially in expensive fields. The present arrangements are in rapid transition; through them much is being learned as to techniques of collaboration. Rationalizations will come about through evolution; the primary need is for a policy.

IV Education, Science, and the Economy

An important feature of the new Europe is increasing interest in economic planning. Most countries have now moved far from their initial repugnance to this idea, which after the war was regarded essentially in doctrinaire terms. The success of the French Commissariat au Plan has gradually built up a conviction that a degree of planning through consultation is possible, and even desirable, in a liberal society, and that indeed the scale and complexity of the modern, technological economy renders unsafe a too easy reliance on laissez faire. The Swedish concept of a labor market policy closely integrated with the changing nature of the economy is another instance among many. Planning is gradually being recognized as a technique and not as a dogma. This trend is greatly encouraged by the acceptance of the concept of economic growth and the examination of the various factors which control its rate. The decision of the OECD ministers at the end of 1961 to aim at a 50 per cent increase in the gross national product of the region by 1970 is germane.

These ideas have, of late, become quite important when considering questions of education and research policies. The *quality* of the two input factors of the economy—capital and labor—is of the greatest significance in producing high growth rates, and this quality is largely a matter of the education and training of individuals and of optimum innovation decisions. Such thinking throws great importance on the investment aspects of education and research and, since both are essentially long-term processes, on the need to plan them many years ahead and in terms of overall national needs, including economic projections, technological promise and social aims.

Much attention has been paid in Europe, during the last two years, to education and science as national investment items which are vital and related elements of economic and social progress representing a commitment on national resources as necessary as investments in factory buildings and machinery. This concept is not to be understood in any narrow or technocratic sense, nor is it in any way incompatible with appreciation of the need to develop education and science in their own right for the cultural and general benefit of the individual as well as his society. In this sense education, as research, is one of the main beneficiaries of economic growth, and long-term arrangements are desirable in order that the appropriate share of growing national resources are allocated to it. A manpower study on "Targets for Education in Europe in 1970," made by Professors Svennilson, Edding and Elvin, was the basis for a policy conference of OECD educational and finance policy representatives held in October, 1961, which considered the dimensions and the principal characteristics of the task facing education in the next decade to meet the needs of social and economic progress in the area as well as to be effective in answering requests for help from the underdeveloped countries. There was general agreement with the order of magnitude of the proposed targets for educational expenditure which represented a very great expansion during the next decade, necessary if advantage was to be taken of economic possibilities.

Practical and detailed planning of such investment needs up to 1975 has now been undertaken in six countries of the Mediterranean —Greece, Italy, Portugal, Spain, Turkey and Yugoslavia—in terms of demographic trends, economic plans and evolving social policy, and a start has also been made to similar assessment of technological and research needs. This Mediterranean Regional Project of the OECD has been undertaken by groups of planning economists of the countries concerned, reinforced by consultants from abroad and by frequent meetings of the directors of the various national teams to exchange experience and to develop a common methodology. It is expected that this activity will assist governments and particularly ministers of education in establishing or strengthening the educational planning function on a continuing basis, whereby detailed proposals based on demographic, economic, social and cultural considerations can be translated into practical plans for educational development. The corresponding studies of technological and research needs are designed to assist on the achievement of more rapid and systematic innovation and to throw light on how techniques can be more quickly and soundly transferred from industrialized to less developed economies. This investment approach of educational planning with its basically dynamic approach was discussed by the European ministers of education in October, 1962, and was unanimously endorsed by them. The Mediterranean experiment has attracted much attention and activity along the same lines as is being undertaken in a number of the more industrialized countries of Europe, both separately and in consultation with one another.

The corresponding approach to the investment value of research is as yet only at its beginning. There are no research and development statistics which enable accurate comparisons of effort between countries to be made, although agreement among the OECD countries as to definitions on which such statistics might be collected has recently been achieved. Furthermore the economic significance of research expenditure is confused by the large military and space budgets of some countries in contrast to their absence in others. Broadly speaking, countries with a high per capita gross national product have a substantially higher research ratio than those with a low per capita GNP. Advanced, industrialized countries typically spend more than 1 per cent of their GNP on research and development, while underdeveloped countries spend less than one quarter of 1 per cent; high rates of economic growth appear to be accompanied by high increases in research budgets. These matters are now receiving much attention, especially in relation to national economic plans.

V *Science and Policy*

In the complex mosaic of the European scientific and educational scene, with all its new experiments and changing attitudes, the dominant feature is a recognition of the great promise for individual and national well-being offered by science, and at the same time the insufficiency of resources to exploit these possibilities to the full— a world problem indeed, but aggravated in Europe by political fractionation. Both within each country and among all of them, there is a compelling need to establish policies with regard to science. These are required in three senses: policy within each country on the allocation of science resources of trained manpower and of finance to provide the best possible balance of effort in the broad national interest; policies for a more rational augmentation of the total resources of the region through international action; and, finally, a continuing and systematic review of the impact of evolving scientific knowledge on other elements of national policy.

So far, the greatest attention has been paid to the first of these; the science policy function is recognized in a number of countries, for instance by the creation of a ministry for science in the United Kingdom, France, Germany and Italy, and the establishment in Belgium and Sweden of Science Policy Councils under the chairmanship of the prime minister. In some instances, the European science bodies are insufficiently strong to evolve and enforce a thorough coordination and balance among different elements of national science activity, and even that of different departments of government; methods of scientific and technological forecasting, of establishing a balance of effort which favors an optimum rational development are scarcely developed; the relations among scientific effort, educational development and general economic development planning are understood as yet in only the most general terms. In spite of these inadequacies, however, the concept of a national science policy and the thinking processes of the bodies set up to create it is utterly different from the working of science councils a decade ago with their simple task of distributing relatively small government funds for fundamental research on the single criterion of scientific promise.

The science policy of the contemporary industrialized state is then a matter of determining broadly the extent and balance of its research effort, scientific manpower plans and technological development schemes in terms of long-term economic, social, defense, and cultural objectives. The establishment of such a policy will require much background data—comprehensive statistics of research and development expenditure, knowledge of other elements of national policy and planning and of raw material possibilities, energy reserves and other assets, and information concerning existing or planned legislation, fiscal or otherwise, which may influence research or innovations. Those concerned with such a policy would have to possess a deep understanding of the way research works, an appreciation of the fact that fundamental research, probably the most important investment of all, is essentially long-term in its unfolding and requires special conditions of freedom of choice, of protection against the compulsion to consider directly the practical value of its fruits. It is not easy for the authorities to understand that much fundamental research has no direct practical product, but that its addition to knowledge may throw back the frontiers of human understanding in directions not to be envisaged at the outset, with economic possibilities in directions which could not possibly be guessed when the original research was begun.

There is no necessary conflict between the acceptance of a comprehensive and intelligent policy for science aiming at a general balance of effort and the freedom of the individual research worker in fundamental science to follow the lines of his own scientific interest and intuition within it; no well-advised government would attempt to regiment the work of university laboratories and other fundamental research institutions. Nevertheless, the relationship between the work of the creative scientist on the one hand, and national or general human needs on the other, is an increasingly complex matter requiring understanding and tolerance on the part of both scientists and governments. If the scientist is to accept the responsibilities which accompany his privileges, governments must equally respect the nature and demands of research from which they can expect so much if they are willing to throw their bread upon the waters. These are compelling reasons for science itself to assume the initiative in the creation of the science policy of each nation.

The development of international or regional science policies is much more difficult to achieve. The creatively haphazard state of the European scientific organizations, useful as it has been in finding new ways of effective collaboration, will inevitably have to approach some degree of rationalization. This is unlikely to succeed in isolation, and it will probably have to await the evolution and simplification of the political structures themselves. For this purpose OECD convened a meeting in October 1963 of the ministers of its Member countries responsible for science policy or co-ordination. Under the able chairmanship of M. Theo Lefèvre, Prime Minister of Belgium, those present discussed and exchanged experiences on national science policy and ways to achieve a reasonable balance of effort in each country to meet the several and varied national needs. There was general acceptance of the importance of maintaining a significant level of fundamental research activity as the best long-term investment of all and of preserving freedom of choice and direction necessary for such work. Much attention was paid to international scientific co-operation and the need to consider it in terms of the expansion it can provide to existing national resources. Consequently, national decisions on international research must be considered as part of the total science strategy. The ministers also discussed the relationship between science and economic policy and reviewed a number of important issues on which study or action is required. They decided to meet again within two years and in the meantime to invite their senior officials or advisers to continue the policy talks. The chief significance of this meeting was the general acceptance it achieved at the highest political level of the need to consider science in policy and resource location terms.

The most significant result of the strivings of the last decade

Conclusions

European science with its long tradition is an essential element in the construction of the new Europe. The vitality of fundamental research in Europe remains, and although the fractionation of the continent into small political units has made it difficult to provide sufficient resources for some important—and expensive—fields of rapid development, resources are in general increasing and institutional methods of international cooperation are being found which can enable it to make a major contribution in these fields also. In applied research and development, progress is very rapid and adjustment is being made to the needs of the economy and of the evolving social structure. In science education too, experiments of all kinds are in train, and institutions of new types are being built up, combining new thinking with an inborn respect for learning.

The most significant result of the strivings of the last decade toward a closer relationship among European countries is probably not to be found in the halting approaches to a new political pattern, or even in tariff reduction and the economy expansion it may bring, but in a new-found openness and willingness to look at new ideas. Through the desperation of war and the subsequent reconstruction of the continent, the average European has had to cast off much in the way of backward-looking tradition and complaisancy. Whether politician, civil servant, industrialist, or trade unionist, he has had to face up to major change, and he continues to be able to do so. This new attitude is reflected in European science and its institutions, the development of which is inextricably linked with that of Europe itself.

ERIC LARRABEE

Transcripts of a Transatlantic Dialogue

EUROPE and America are the inventions of one another. America could not be called "discovered" until the idea of it had been invented, nor could the Old World exist as such until the New came into being. Physically speaking America had always been there, and Europeans (Columbus not alone) kept stumbling over it on the way to somewhere else. But they made no sense of what they found —or, rather, made sense of it wrongly—until they were able to conceive of America's existence, quite contrary to Revelation and sound reason, as a separate land mass apart from the known and long accepted Island of the Earth. Until then, as the Mexican historian Edmundo O'Gorman writes in *The Invention of America*, the so-called "discoveries" of the navigators were meaningless. Only with the *Cosmographiae Introductio* and the Waldseemüller map of 1507 does America take shape in the European mind's eye, and only then does it acquire a name.

Once America was assumed, the notion of Europe as the past four centuries have known it—as the metropolitan source and center of a world civilization—became possible. The emergence of America profoundly altered the European consciousness, for with it western man's adventure as shaper of his material destiny could begin. If America existed, then the universe was not a fixed and circumscribed place, and neither was man's place in it. In O'Gorman's words: "the world having ceased to be considered as a sort of cosmic jail, man was able to picture himself as a free agent in the deep and radical sense of possessing unlimited possibilities in his own being, and as living in a world made by him in his own image and to his own measure." The availability of a New World inflamed the energies of the Old, giving them both fuel and scope, an expectation of return for effort and an extended arena for its exercise. The European imperial hegemony—not to speak of European ascendancy in science and the arts—acquired its historic role and the backdrop of its heroic drama.

The image of Europe as mature and sophisticated, as well as fecund and original, further requires both America's youth and its derivativeness as standards of comparison. The Europe of worldy wisdom, of ruins and refinement, of a dark and inviting acceptance of the human comedy, is not only a typically American invention but an obsession of the American mind. An innocent abroad, the American stands perennially transfixed, appalled and fascinated by the rich and sinful complexity of the continent from which his forebears fled; and so doing he has become a stock figure in the mythology both Americans and Europeans find necessary. Each has an equity in the set of polarities by which each can in turn feel flattered—callowness *vs.* experience, vigor *vs.* decadence, vapidity *vs.* taste, the future *vs.* the past.

Not least is the New Europe an American conception. It is first of all a fixation of Americans that what serves them must serve others equally well; hence what could be more natural than a United States of Wherever? In the American vocabulary "balkanization" is a pejorative term; thus there is also an implication that Europe by uniting might become a less fertile breeder of wars. Furthermore, prosperity is desirable in and of itself, if only as a preventative of such troublesome conflicts (a theory the Americans may have learned from Montesquieu) so that they have consciously been willing to underwrite the costs of postwar economic reconstruction, and with it Europe's subsequent prosperity. It seems to be an American temperamental preference to deal with equals; they are uncomfortable in the presence of an insignificant adversary (such as Cuba) whose very insignificance denies them a fair opportunity for a sporting contest. Contrary to their apparent self-interest, they have therefore been prime movers in the effort to make Europeans—often contrary to *their* apparent interest—come together in combinations of increasing political viability and commercial force.

Now the New Europe is beginning to loom in the American imagination with the same preoccupying power as the Old, an ideal to be pursued at the same time it is used to frighten and instruct. Already Americans speak of the New Europe with near-parental pride and chagrin, as of the fledglings about to fly the nest: "They can get along without us." (It sends a delicious shiver down the American spine, that does.) The sense of heightened competition goes hand in hand with the belief that competition is good for everybody. Writing in *Horizon* about what he calls "The Fifth Europe," Edgar Ansel Mowrer ends his article: "They will be gratified if we choose to co-operate with them on equal terms but not heartbroken if we decide otherwise. My guess is that we shall have to run very fast to keep up." Something of this same enthusiasm for what should presumably be viewed as an affront can be found in most American reactions to the Common Market; it stands for federalism and expanding production, and must therefore be a Good Thing.

But what of Europe's culture, or what Mowrer calls "the common market of the mind"? Here the American response is no less ambiguous, but in a different way. The two continents differ profoundly in the intellectual styles they favor, so that on this subject the same words will not be similarly understood at home and abroad. The European style is competitive, strenuous and sharp-edged; the American is ironic, elliptical and endlessly polite. Writing as an American I am constantly made aware of my own elaborate deference toward Europe, and of my reluctance to express openly any disdain which may privately accompany it. It must be understood first of all that vis-à-vis Europe in matters cultural America still suffers from an inferiority complex, most of it justified. The basic American assumption is that anything requiring trained aesthetic or intellectual skill will be found better and cheaper in Europe. There craftsmen and performers of all kinds are not only more generally available, they also have higher standards and lower expectations of reward. Where the problem is one of acquiring sustained experience—whether as a chef, a scholar, or an opera conductor—Europe offers the wide and steady base of regular activity which must exist for certain kinds of talent to mature.

The result is the familiar phenomenon of Americans, individually and in concert, repeatedly turning to Europe in a posture of suppliance for what Europe offers as a matter of course. American publishers go to Europe for their four-color photo-engraving; American musicians go to Europe for the status and reception denied them at home; American tourists go endlessly to Europe for the dazzling feast spread before them of all the cities, famous buildings, historical associations and elegant food and drink they have been carefully educated to consider as the ultimate in discrimination and pleasure. Who can resist? Europe is savor and flavor; it is the genuine as opposed to the fake, the thing to have tasted if you want the real model to measure by. In the jet age the good American not only goes to Paris when he dies, he goes there as often as possible on vacation. This past year, of my immediate colleagues in an office in New York, one was vacationing in Majorca, one in Italy, and two (each just a slip of a girl) were bicycling in the Dordogne.

What charms Americans about Europe, on the other hand, is what a modern European will often find most exasperating—the deadly presence of the dead past. The New European may often outdo the American in zest for the future, and for change. To the extent that he has emancipated himself from sentimentality, he will be impatient of his fellow continentals who refuse in the name of sacred tradition to modernize themselves and their environment, and disdainful of visitors who admire what to him is merely archaic and artifically preserved, like flowers under glass. The Frenchman or Italian who feels the weight of centuries bearing down upon him, in other words, cannot be expected to think of Paris or Rome as quaint, or have any great regard for Americans who do. The Latin-culture intellectual who has looked to the Anglo-Saxon world for humanistic nourishment may well be more tolerant of modernity than the Anglo-Saxons are themselves. The Europe which looked for a model of a future self has sought it, or at least the outlines of it, in the golden West from which everything new and alive (at least since the 1930's) had been coming. "None of us can reject America," writes the London theater critic Alan Brien, "without rejecting our own youth."

The assumption, shared by both sides of the argument on both sides of the Atlantic, had been that America was the way Europe was going. In our era the experiment of mass democracy combined with industrialism was presumed to represent the far-out, leading edge of the human enterprise. One might deplore the onslaught of the automobile on the overtaxed streets of European towns, or welcome the impact of mass marketing on European cartels, but the presumption remained that only by following the American example could the older nations emulate American power and prosperity. America was the best available exemplar of what a mass culture might conceivably be like. It was the image of what could have happened to Europe, if . . . if the persisting heritage of feudalism had been discarded, if the industrial revolution had been carried through to its logical conclusion, if the lower middle class had been lifted out of its ancient dreariness to receive, at long last, a material sufficiency and the dangerous prerogative of personal choice.

All of this the New Europe both confirmed and unexpectedly transformed. The confirmation came from the upward-trending statistics; Europe was going beyond the Point of No Return in its pursuit of productivity. There comes a level above which you commit yourself to the central proposition, in Samuel Gompers' word, of "more" for those who work—so much more that the recipients will never afterward be satisfied with less. Since 1958 the purchasing power of total European wages and salaries, according to the Chase Manhattan Bank, has risen by almost 20 per cent; the average hourly wage of European workers went up nearly 10 per cent in 1962. In that same year Paris department stores sales ran 15 per cent ahead of 1961, and French automobile production more than 20 per cent.

Italian refrigerator manufacturers expect to make more than 20 per cent more units this year than last. And so on.

The sound you hear is that of Europe entering the twentieth century. Having scorned the American version, it is now about to experience its own. Having ridiculed the American cult of the automobile, for example, it is now enthusiastically busying itself to commit all the same old errors—building superhighways, widening streets, enlarging parking spaces, and turning its major cities into traffic jams that make the American equivalents seem tame by comparison. Such developments could have been predicted, and indeed were, but what had not been foreseen—not, at least, by many Americans who have begun to wake up to it within the past year or so—was that with revived vitality would come a reassertion of historical independence, a denial of the inevitability of mass society, and a rejection of the example of the United States (often coupled in this connection with the Soviet Union) as binding.

What the New Europe is saying, or what one says by asserting its existence, is that civilization of the European sort can not only survive but can form the only valid base for any future civilization worth preserving. The New Europeans are claiming, in effect, that they can build a modern society without sacrificing their traditional luxuries and limitations—the luxury of idiosyncratic individualism for a few, the limitation on too much democratizing self-indulgence by the many. They propose to be, not simply a "third force," but a historical alternative. America and Russia, however different otherwise, can be seen in this view to have sacrificed for the sake of smooth social organization too much of the inner tension and complexity on which "culture," in the best European sense, depends. Thus the New European position is not merely a negative attempt to stand fast, but a banner flung at the wind with the message that history for years to come will still be generated somewhere between the Pyrenees and the Elbe.

The responses of Americans to the challenge now tendered them are likely to be as contradictory as individual Americans are themselves ambivalent about Europe as the fount of "proper" culture. Not only is vigor thought to be admirable for its own sake, but one cannot help admiring (at the same time one deplores) the bravado of Europeans in regarding as settled all the questions Americans have found to be baffling and intractable—principally those of how the arts and the life of the mind are to be kept vital and relevant in an industrial democracy without depriving them of impact or starving them to death. The American experience is that the traditional European solutions, given a world which smiles upon the aspirations of common people to cease being common, will not work. Implicit in the New Europe are American doubts about it; a transatlantic dialogue is one of its preconditions. If the polarities are to be reversed—if Europe is to be the future and America the past— then at long last the New World can take over from the Old the privilege of dispensing sage counsel and tugging ruefully at its graying beard.

There seem to me to be two cultural categories in which Europe and America can usefully be compared: (1) the psychology of the individual artist or intellectual, and (2) the more general area of high culture's social context—specifically, how are the arts to be economically supported? Americans and Europeans are members, so to speak, of the same family and enough like one another to make comparison possible. Yet we differ in precisely those qualities which concern Europe's implicit act of aggression against the American imperium. The issue is joined. The American intellectual must learn to do without the European model, while the European must take account of the wider range of perspective and concern that Americans have opened up to him. The European's guiltily tentative love affair with cultural democracy must not be allowed to stand as the only possible ending to that story, no more than can American inhibitions at considering art a legitimate economic enterprise be allowed to prevail indefinitely.

The European intellectual (I include Great Britain in Europe) is one of God's marvels. If he did not exist, he could not be invented. He is the cultivated symbiotic product of brutal rearing in youth and soft indulgence in maturity, the end effect of which is an exceptional self-confidence. His training hones intelligence to fineness, radically eliminates those who fail the pace and fortifies the survivors with all they will need in the way of intellectual machinery—the names and dates, apt quotes and appropriate sentiments, the themes and tone of voice which will thereafter serve as password and countersign with which to recognize, and be recognized by, their kind. Of all happy humans, these know who and where they are. While young they have been forced to contend for a prize which, when old, they find to have some substance. Of all humans gulled by fate, these are among the least cheated.

Given economic independence and sufficient motive, it would be possible for a cultivated European of the present generation to have seen, read and heard everything he had been raised to think of as culturally significant. (Sacheverell Sitwell is supposed, world-wearily, to have remarked this of himself.) One lives amid the monuments. They have been studied, labeled and gone over in such exhaustive detail that few thoughts about them have not already been thought. One moves in an atmosphere in which cultural verdicts have authority; which is a masterpiece, and which not, are judgments rendered long ago. The language becomes habitual, an automatic bow before the received opinion. "He's really wonderful," the intellectual Steiner says of another writer to Marcello, in Fellini's film *La Dolce Vita*. "He has written dozens of books—you know their importance—and yet he still has the freshness of a child." Everything comes marked and weighed, like the entries in a guidebook: Trevi fountain, three stars; Villa Medici, two stars; Vatican grottoes, one star.

Accreditation is the crux, and once one is accredited all good things follow. One can be a bad boy and a bad student, provided one is Winston Churchill; but for others less favored the hurdles of competitive examination (and no appeal thereafter) rise on an even and monotonous curve, until eventually only the most gifted and adaptable prevail. Here the prizes for pure competence may be great; Europe is blessed with its openness to merit, provided you are willing to concede that merit is what the public school, the *lycée*, or the *gymnasium* define as meritorious. Those who make the grade will find that they can move among the mighty. A. L. Rowse, who like a "Tudor" Englishman came up by his own exertions, has described in his book *Appeasement* how remarkable it was for him, in the years before World War II, to sit at the dinner table of All Soul's with the Foreign Secretary, or the editor of the London *Times*, and dispute the fate of nations. Certainly nothing within the range of the American imagination can even approach the mixture of protected isolation and immanent power which adheres to the very walls and ivy of the ancient British universities.

As a consequence, however, the European intellect may often find itself in a state of mind both paralyzing and final, complete in its summations and consequences, but quite opaque to the American understanding—namely, boredom. The Americans know the boredom of their own Madame Bovary in *Main Street*, or the Russians that of their own des Essientes in *Oblomov*, but neither nation knows as yet the daily boredom of having tasted its fantasies in full. What can one do when everything is made available, or at least everything one thinks essential? At some point of satiation all the depth and copiousness of the European mind turns against itself and drives the aesthetes into exquisiteness, the exiles into flight, and the healthy who remain into disconnected contests with someone else's windmills. The luckiest Europeans are those who still have something which actually exists to rebel against, like the brainy women of moderately good family who can draw sustenance from their hatred of the heavy bourgeois tyranny in which they were nurtured; to see a French middle class family coming into a restaurant for lunch, palpable in its sullen self-satisfaction, is to understand Simone de Beauvoir or Françoise Sagan.

The virtues of the cultivated European mentality are self-evident, even to the American observer: tenacity, reverberation, sharpness of discrimination. There is a greater daring, a greater toleration of the heterodox, a greater verve and prodigality. All that one misses is relevance. The minds of modern Europe are nothing if not mobilized. The geniuses have been identified and located; the cultural circles of the major capitals are small enough to permit putting the most successful of the circus acts under a single tent; and the winds of doctrine blow powerfully enough to flap the canvas and remind the acrobats that the higher the wire, the farther the fall. But given all that is grand and perspicacious about the European intellectual, he still seems to engaging in a side show; his condensed perceptions seem yet to be brought to bear on the place, to use an American expression, where he lives. If the voice is willing, the audience is weak. The French sociology of leisure, in the hands of men like Joffre Dumazedier, is as lively and disciplined as the American, but little recognized in either country. The British city planners, despite having invented the term "New Brutalism" and deployed their considerable ingenuity against it, have been unable to prevent far worse postwar building being done in Westminster than on Manhattan Island.

This feeling of helplessness is the American intellectual's natural medium; he swims in it as though it were all he knew. One way or another he has had to declass himself in order to become a writer or artist or whatever he is; and he (in Thomas Wolfe's phrase) "can't go home again." He has cut loose from his origins and arrived at a place where there are no moorings; there is no cultural class in America as such. With rare exceptions (Edmund Wilson? Lewis Mumford? Alfred Kazin?) no Americans practice successfully the profession of the independent man of letters. Most who might do so choose instead to camouflage themselves as academics, journalists or publishers, where they are unprotected by their high but hidden aspirations. There are no convertible privileges; a doctoral degree, a professorship and a book or two make no particular impression on the civic authorities. Having no sense of fixed location, the intellectual is shoved to and fro by the demands that others make on him, then by those he makes on himself. He is one of the first victims of what the Spanish philosopher Julián Marias has called the "climate of veracity" in the United States—the requirement that words and facts be not too far apart. In some corner of his mind is an irreducible residue of the obligation laid upon the

"American scholar" by Emerson, to be not merely a thinker but "man thinking." He must reconstruct each morning, so to speak, the validity of his mind's bent upon the universe.

Where the European is force-fed in youth and indulged in maturity, the American intellectual is coddled in youth and in maturity exposed to all the harsh cross-winds that beat around his unresolved position. His typical state of mind is anxiety; he feels beleaguered as naturally as he breathes. No wonder he talks so much about "anti-intellectualism," a phenomenon he was the first to identify and the last to recognize for what it was: the flattering acknowledgment that he himself existed as an effective member of society. The need to be outwardly both effective and disinterested are but symbols for the conflicting needs he has absorbed within himself. If he is an academic, he has not met a payroll; if he has met a payroll, his scholarly standards are too low. But the interior conflict is worse, between the need to cultivate the mind in tranquility, and the need to exercise it fully and truthfully on the existing world. In short, he is unable to take culture for granted; he has to be prepared to defend it, if only in privacy to himself, as a valid and valuable social process. He cannot use it as a prop to his own status and ego, as a ceremonial ornament of membership in the genteel tradition, or as a device for being eternally one-up in his daily commerce with his peers.

To be sure, there are American intellectuals who are simply European intellectuals in disguise and who have managed to achieve, however precariously, the state of necessary self-esteem. But what comes naturally to the European comes artificially to them. Too much energy is required by their efforts to take themselves more seriously than their society does, and too high a price is paid in estrangement from society's underlying rhythm. To be an intellectual at all is to be off-beat, in every sense of the word, but the American ideal is a kind of syncopated tension based (as in jazz music) on the certainty that a fundamental beat is there. It is also a question of how much reality to let in. The outspokenness of the European is one of the luxuries of a closed society; the American by contrast is often elliptical because he can imagine a far wider circle of listeners—the audience of evidently divergent classes and origins in which he has been reared from childhood.

The stance of the American intellectual is therefore likely to be wry, self-deprecating, ironic. Trying to take account of a greater range of possibilities, he has not only a heightened sense of his probable ineffectiveness but also of the mind's fragility and loneliness on its long adventure. His view ought properly to be called tragic, despite the common typology which allocates optimism to

America and pessimism to Europe. The American may be no less bitter, but it is curious how often his bitterness is missed or misinterpreted by Europeans when it appears as irony or satire. For example, William H. Whyte, Jr., the author of *The Organization Man*, once wrote an article for the business magazine *Fortune* called "The Case for the Universal Card," in which he argued that the testing and scoring of American businessmen should be carried to its logical conclusion by having all relevant data on every executive coded so it can be entered on a card, all the cards for the whole country to be kept on file in a central repository. As a fairly broad hint, Whyte signed the piece: "Otis Binet Stanford." What shocked him most was not the number of his American readers who fell into the trap (some writing straightforwardly that they would like to go into the universal card business with him), but that the British humorous magazine *Punch* ran an article quoting him, dead pan, as yet another example of American boorishness.

What we are dealing with is of course a contrast between the condition of culture in a hierarchic society where it has enjoyed a privileged place, and in an open, fluid society where its place is far from settled. Perhaps it is the good fortune of intellectuals in America to inhabit, relatively speaking, a cultural wilderness, since wilderness conditions induce a marvelous clarity of motives. It becomes much easier to judge whether any given gesture of allegiance to culture is genuine, or simply another gambit in the games of vanity and careerism. The fact that the place of the arts in American life is a debatable topic also implies that it is an alive one, and that those alive today may play a part in the debate before it closes. The purpose of introducing the comparison here is to ask whether the debate ought not also to be going on in Europe, where, with results so admirable in so many ways, it ceased some years ago.

The most conspicuous of all dissimilarities between the positions accorded culture on two sides of the Atlantic is the European custom of governmental subsidy. It is too deeply entrenched in most countries there to be called anything but a custom. It takes various forms, from grants to individual writers (as in Italy) or aid to artists and musicians (as in France) to the partial underwriting of the expenses of publishing (as in Austria and Greece) and direct subsidies covering the major costs of theaters and operas (as in West Germany in particular but nearly every other nation as well). Austria—according to Henry Lee Munson, who surveyed seven European countries for the National Cultural Center in Washington—spends more on its five national theaters than on its entire foreign service. West Germany spent $67 million in 1960 to meet two thirds of the budgetary needs of 128 theaters and operas—topping this off the year after with the supremely contemptuous gift of $2.5 million to the Lincoln Center for the Performing Arts in New York City.

The effect of the cold figures on the page, translated into practice, is a completely different climate for art. Culture costs less in the first place, and more of the costs are paid by the state; *ergo*, more culture for more people. America puts an economic pressure on the arts to compete in the same market with necessities. Consider theater. The relative cost of productions (as of New York against London or Paris) is in a ratio of ten to one: $80,000 to $150,000 as against $7,500 to $15,000. At the same time, in Great Britain the Arts Council makes grants to Covent Garden, Sadler's Wells, the Old Vic, and so on; while in France the Ministery of Culture subsidizes the Opéra, the Opéra Comique, the Comédie Française, the Théâtre Nationale Populaire, the Théâtre de France and dozens of other regional and private theaters. The result is a fantastically lessened burden on the ticket buyer. The Metropolitan Opera in New York must cover 85 per cent of its costs by ticket sales; the percentage for operas in Europe is never over 30 and often as low as 10. A ticket to Vilar's T.N.P. in Paris costs approximately the same as a movie.

Under the circumstances it is ridiculous to pretend that America provides an environment for traditional culture remotely comparable to that of Europe. Virtually every symphony orchestra in the United States is operating at a deficit, and even so it is a commonplace that the musicians must take other jobs to earn a living. The current American enthusiasm for "cultural centers" (some eighty are said to be in prospect) has so far manifested itself as greater interest in real estate and construction than in supporting the "culture" they are intended to contain. (The architect Louis I. Kahn has described a cultural center as "an office building with an auditorium attached.") What distinguishes America on this point is the reluctance to be committed as to what is, and is not, art. Our separation of church and state, which implies a certain reverence, is matched by a separation of culture and state which implies a certain respect. To build a temple to culture is a neutral act; to write the liturgy is an act of assertiveness as yet beyond the range of the American ego.

The trouble with Europe's generosity to art, judged by American standards, is that it subsumes a frozen definition of what art, or indeed culture, is. Culture is what was regarded as cultural in western Europe in the late nineteenth century. It consists in large part of arts created for an aristocratic clientele which have since become prohibitively expensive, such as grand opera or the ballet. The question might well be asked whether these are not now economically and socially obsolete, yet they receive a very high proportion of European governmental aid (the British Arts Council has allotted from two thirds to four fifths of its annual budget to Covent Garden and Sadler's Wells). Who is to decide? Often the choice is made by bureaucrats, as in Italy, where the writers to receive grants are picked by officials in the equivalent of the American copyright office, and, so it is said, novelists such as Silone and Moravia have never been among those selected. The Establishment giveth, the Establishment taketh away. Blessed be the name of the Establishment.

Europeans tolerate cultural monopolies to an extent that an American as yet cannot. They are able to take in stride a degree of cynicism about culture as an outlet for connivance and self-interest which an American would find incredible. The English, for example, seem able to ignore the dominance of their literary world by a tiny clique split between London and the Universities, just as that clique itself can ignore the outrageous conduct of its members—as when a year ago the first novel of Auberon Waugh was absurdly overpraised by his father's friends. By the same token, the French tolerate a Parisian literary world almost unmatchable as a playground for influence peddling and political infighting. I do not wish to maintain that Americans are more moral, but only that in matters pertaining to man's highest action—his art—they are more easily shocked.

What we fear of the New Europe is that it will be only a veiled attempt to rehabilitate the Old—a kind of clean-up operation like Malraux's washing and whitening of Paris, startling and delightful to look at, but fundamentally of no significance as a new event in the world. Economically, we fear a Europe that will be only a white man's club, an alliance among the imperially disinherited mainly intended to console them for the loss of their colonies by excluding the former colonials from future prosperity. Culturally, we fear *for* a Europe which tries to preserve its culture as an offshoot of privilege, cold and perfect, beautiful to look at but dead. For the Europeans to preserve the best of their past and yet remain capable of the future would be a contravention of the American dogma. Absurdly enough, an American can wish them only well.

CHARLES FRANKEL

Bureaucracy and Democracy in the New Europe

ONE OF THE commonplaces of political discussion these days is that the spirit has gone out of democratic politics and that traditional political ideas are played out. I suspect that these reports of the death of politics and political theory are grossly exaggerated, but one of the reasons why they are widespread is particularly interesting. It is the remarkable vitality of the Europe that has emerged since the war. For that vitality seems to have been achieved more or less independently of democratic politics and political ideas—at any rate as these are normally construed.

Europe's population has grown rapidly, and its composition has become increasingly youthful. There has been a massive organization of scientific institutions, an unprecedentedly systematic application of technical knowledge to the economy, and an augmentation of the economic product per individual. A larger number of people enjoy an economic status approaching that once enjoyed only by members of the professional classes, and welfare measures and guarantees of individual security have been built into European economies which have changed the relationship of workers to the property system. Side by side with these developments there has emerged—most notably in France—a kind of economic planning remarkable for its subtlety and novelty. It fits none of the old categories and is justifiably an object of interest and envy in those two backward areas of the world so far as planning is concerned, the United States and the Soviet Union.

Nor have these events changed Europe only on the material plane. The old ideologies have lost much of their old appeal. Forty years ago, in an essay on liberal society, George Santayana wrote, "When the lists are open to all, and the one aim of life is to live as much as possible like the rich, the majority must needs be discouraged . . ."[1] But while the differences between social classes remain in Europe, the majority need no longer be so thoroughly discouraged. It can enjoy good enough imitations of what the rich enjoy to take some of the rancor and bitterness out of class hostilities. The ideology based on the belief in an international working class with a revolutionary consciousness and mission has in consequence declined. Those who still cling to it are doing so more in loyalty to tradition than in hope for the future. And the symbols and ideologies of nationalism have also receded. If the nationalistic spirit remains, it must now come to terms with the advancing sentiment for European union.

Yet these very events—events which most liberal and democratic observers would regard as happy events—have raised questions about the character and prospects of democratic institutions and aspirations in Europe today. Liberal democracies have had failures which have hurt their confidence in themselves. What hurts now is at least in part their success, for that success seems to have been brought about in ways that do not fit democratic categories. The initiative and the steady, controlling influence with respect to the decisions that have shaped the new Europe have not laid with parliaments and the political parties; they have laid with the state bureaucracies and permanent administrative services. And the main exceptions to this generalization are those in which an outstanding personality, swinging free from "the regime of parties," has taken great power into his own hands.

The genuineness of democratic institutions in Europe, their vigor, their relationship to the classic notions of democracy inherited from the eighteenth and nineteenth centuries, have in consequence been thrown into question. On one side parliaments seem to be, at best, merely watchdogs and critics and the authorizers of actions that have been taken. The flow of parliamentary business, the issues discussed, the lines that are drawn, have an epiphenomenal character. Like the blast of a steam engine's whistle, they are signs of deeper movements below, but they are not indices to the actual character of these movements, and they seem to have no causal efficacy with regard to them. On the other side, the citizens of European countries seem at once increasingly politicized and depoliticized. They live more steadily and consciously in the presence of government than ever before. But their primary experience with government is not with their representatives in parliament, or the courts, or infrequent election campaigns; it is with administrative officials.

What does this movement of bureaucracy and administration to the foreground of affairs mean for the nature and prospects of democracy in the new Europe? I propose to consider this question first, by examining it against its historical background in democratic theory and practice; second, by re-examining the idea of democracy as it applies to present conditions in Europe; and third, by considering some of the emerging practices and problems which give some indication of the possible direction of events. My interest, however, is not in prophecy; it is in raising questions which seem to me to deserve attention if basic democratic aspirations are to be served.

I Bureaucracy and Democracy in Theory and Practice

The notion that "democracy" and "bureaucracy" stand for inherently antagonistic tendencies has a long history but an uncertain intellectual foundation. If we look at the historical practice of parliamentary democracy in Europe, the relation between bureaucracy and democracy has by no means been one of simple antagonism. The present power of state bureaucracies is not a new phenomenon; it is an extension of the power they have had in the past. And despite the often equivocal commitment of the administrative services of European countries to the idea of democracy, these services supported the growth of democracy in many ways. They contributed to the industrial advances which provided the base for the intensification of democratic aspirations and the progressive satisfaction of these aspirations, and they served democratic governments by providing them with a large part of the programs and policies that any government must have if it is to meet the problems it confronts and retain the support of those it governs. And from the theoretical point of view, the relations between bureaucracy and democracy also appear to be complementary and not only antagonistic. Bureaucracy stands for the development of explicit standards and the impartial application of these standards to individuals; it gives implicit support to the notion that social hierarchies ought to reflect differences in competence and objective performance. In recompense, the "democratic principle" also tends to support the "bureaucratic principle." The spread of a democratic ethic, with its emphasis on social status as something to be acquired rather than inherited, and with its tendency toward the universalization of basic rights and responsibilities, creates a climate that is favorable to the further rationalization and refinement of bureaucratic methods.

Why, then, is the notion so conventionally taken for granted that bureaucracy is inherently antagonistic to democracy? One of the simplest reasons, I think, is that the democracies that emerged in Europe during the nineteenth century took over the administrative services inherited from the monarchical and mercantilist past. In France, to take perhaps the most dramatic example, the administrative services, which were taken over practically intact from the pre-revolutionary era, have persisted continuously, with their own traditions and *esprit de corps*, through five republics and two empires. The fidelity of these services to what they have conceived to be French interests has been constant. But the administrative services have never been identified by the French left, and have never unequivocally identified themselves, with the democratic idea. A persistent and rooted theme in the intellectual tradition of the French left, on the contrary, has been that the parliament speaks for the democratic tendency in the country and the bureaucracy for the oligarchy and plutocracy.* [2]

Other reasons for the notion that there is a conflict between bureaucracy and democracy are the consequences of inherited intellectual principle. Modern democratic theory, particularly on the European continent, came into the world with the mark of a self-confessed utopianism upon it. Rousseau's *Social Contract* is dotted with arguments on the incompatibility of the principle of popular sovereignty with the practical conditions for governing large states. [3] Modern democratic theory, in general, has reflected—and idealized—the experience of small, homogeneous communities, such as ancient Athens, Geneva, or the independent congregations of seventeenth-century England and New England. There has therefore been a continuing conflict between modern theories of democracy and the actual characteristics of democratic government in the modern era. The persisting problem of modern democratic theory has been to reconcile a conception of popular government based on models drawn from small communities with the imperatives of government in large nation-states. The conception of democracy as a recurrent popular aspiration recurrently betrayed has been one reaction to the existence of this problem.†

* In this respect, it should perhaps be noted, there is a difference between the European and American traditions. In Europe, the administrative services have always played a major role in government; in the United States they played a much less significant role until thirty years ago. And while, in countries like France, intellectuals have not usually thought of government bureaucracy as a major instrument for extending democracy, in the United States major initiatives for the extension of democracy have often come from the executive, and the sense of indentification of democratically oriented intellectuals with the administrative branches of government has been stronger than their sense of identification with Congress.

† From our present standpoint, and given the advantages of hindsight, a major weakness of most nineteenth-century political philosophies is their tendency to ignore the problems of bureaucracy, and of the relationship of specialists to laymen. Conservatism stresses the significance of leadership, but it conceives of leadership in terms of tradition, class, and property, and not in terms of technical expertise. Marxism conceives the problem of government administration as one that must disappear when the state disappears. Lenin,

Moreover, democratic theory has of course been formulated in the main by intellectuals, and for intellectuals the principal instrument for gaining the adherence of others is verbal persuasion.[4] At least one of the elements in the ambiguous idea of "the general will" is the conception of a community held together by rational argument rather than by coercion. Traditional projections of the character of a democratic society have not usually given systematic attention, therefore, to the place within a democracy of hierarchical forms of social organization and of nonrational methods for achieving agreement and concerted action. When these characteristics of actual democracies have been given systematic attention—for example, by twentieth-century theorists like Michels—the inference has usually been drawn that democracy, in Michels' words, is a "desperate enterprise."

Finally, the continuing disparity between democratic theory and the facts of democratic practice has also been a consequence, perhaps, of the intimate connection, for much of modern history, between the idea of democracy and the idea of revolution. I mean "revolution" in the simplest sense—a violent process in which new people take power and redefine the rules under which the holding of power is legitimate, and in which wealth, power and deference are deliberately reallocated to new groups and classes. (One of the prejudices of the Anglo-Saxon world is that revolution, in this plain and definite sense, is a continental specialty, and that the English and Americans prefer to accomplish their purposes more patiently and firmly in the slow muddle of time. But the first archtypical revolution, modern style, was of course the Puritan revolution. It was the model for later revolutions, like the French and Russian, prefiguring their style and the quality of their aspirations, and it fixed on the modern consciousness the idea of revolution, and the strategies, symbolisms, and ideals of revolution.) The ever present possi-

---

who worked on Marxist theory in the hopeful days before World War I, is responsible for the pronouncement that once communism was achieved, the state and its bureaucratic apparatus would wither away, and the citizens themselves would handle the day-to-day problems of administration directly. Liberal democratic theory, on the whole, was probably more, rather than less, sensitive to the issues raised by the need for specialized knowledge and professional leadership than either conservatism or Marxism in their nineteenth-century forms. Still, in its traditional form, liberal democratic theory characteristically conceived of the relationship between governors and governed as a contractual relation in which, in return for obedience to them, the governors agreed to carry into effect the already formed and informed popular will. Of all the major social philosophers of the nineteenth century, only Comte, who held democracy in contempt, and Tocqueville, who feared where it might lead, may be said to have given the problem of bureaucracy systematic attention.

bility of revolution, and the concept of the truly radical revolution which cuts away the roots of error and injustice, which liberates "the people," and which makes a new order for mankind possible, are major themes of modern history. And revolution, so conceived, has been a principal paradigm of deliberate, and of "democratic," social change. In consequence the practical problems surrounding the relation of leaders to followers, and those involving the role of administration, in the postrevolutionary world have often been treated as subordinate issues by democratic theorists.

As much as anything else, the decline of the idea or the myth of revolution is responsible, I suspect, for the spread of the opinion that political ideas are exhausted. The political ideas and political theories which have guided and encumbered Europeans of the modern era (at any rate on the Continent) have almost without exception been allied to the advocacy of popular revolution or else to its prevention. But the ideas that are now moving the western world—not its passions, but its machines, its armies, its industry, and its governments—are not the ideas of revolutionaries or counter-revolutionaries. They are the ideas, limited, specific, specialized, of administrators, officials, scientists, and technicians. "The world of today," Friedrich Dürenmatt, the Swiss playwright, has complained, "is unintelligible because it is anonymous and bureaucratic. Creon's secretaries close out Antigone's case."

II The Idea of Democracy

Against this background, it is plainly necessary to try to be clearer than we ordinarily are about the idea of democracy. The word, of course, has many meanings. But in its central meaning, I suggest, it refers to one particular way in which the authority to govern is acquired and held. A man may be said to hold authority democratically when he has been freely chosen to hold such authority by those who must live under it, when they have had, and will have, the alternative of choosing somebody else, and when he is accountable to them for the way in which he exercises this authority.[5]

Now if "democracy" is construed in this way, certain consequences follow. The first is that no society can in fact be democratic in every domain; nor would any reflective partisan of democracy wish otherwise. The administration of justice by the courts, for example, cannot be made to depend on popular opinion if the interests of justice are to be served. What we know as "liberal" or "constitutional" democracy stands for the principle that there are limits to the democratic principle, and that legal and institutional safeguards have to exist to protect other values besides democracy itself. Indeed, the preservation of the conditions for the exercise of democratic choice cannot itself be made to depend on the decision of the electorate.

A second implication of the notion of democracy that has been offered is that the democratic principle, even where it properly applies, can at best only be approximated. As a sheerly abstract issue, a completely democratic system is one in which every man would be equal to every other man in power and influence.* But this state of affairs is an obviously unlikely one; least of all is it likely in large and complicated modern societies, where the effective coordination of human activities requires that considerable powers be exercised by people in certain key positions. For this reason it is possible to say, as Raymond Aron has said, that "all democratic societies are hypocritical, and cannot be anything else."[6] But this is to put the matter, as M. Aron makes quite plain, in an intentionally paradoxical way. We cannot call a system "undemocratic" simply because some form of social stratification exists within it; such a procedure does not condemn the system but simply exposes the uselessness of the political standards we have chosen to use. In practice, the standards we employ have to make explicit room for the inevitability of some form of hierarchy in society, as well as for the fact and necessity of leadership.

Accordingly, the working touchstone of a "democratic" system of authority is simply the degree to which it gives individuals legitimate instruments for reaching those who make the decisions that affect them, and for bringing influence to bear upon them. A system is more or less "democratic" depending on the number, availability, and effectiveness of these instruments, and on the proportion of the population entitled and able to use them. Programs aimed at the more general distribution of wealth, the extension of educational

---

* I have slid rapidly from the notion of democracy as government resting on the free choice of the governed to the notion of democracy as equality in power and influence. The examination in detail of the connection between these two elements in the idea of democracy would require a long digression; I can only suggest the connection very briefly here. "Democracy," construed as government resting on the free choice of the governed, refers to a specific kind of relationship between a government and a collectivity—namely, "the people," "the citizens," or "the electorate." But this collectivity, of course, is composed of individuals, and if we look at democracy from the standpoint of the individual, then the democratic ideal calls for the individual to live under an authority which he, as an individual, has participated in freely choosing. This means, in abstract principle, that the alternatives should not be forced on him by others, and that his choice should not be subject to external coercion or to various forms of illegitimate influence, such as control of the information available to him. For this state of affairs to exist in a pure and perfect form, however, each individual must be equal in power and influence to every other individual.

opportunity, the improved communication of information and opinion and the lowering of barriers of caste and class are, from this point of view, instruments for the increased democratization of political authority.

Two further points should be added. First, this conception of democracy, it should be noted, does not, in and by itself, imply any particular political mechanisms such as elections, the separation of powers, or a parliamentary system. It is abstractly conceivable that the people's choice of leaders could be expressed in some informal, spontaneous and yet unequivocal manner, as sometimes happens in small groups. It is equally conceivable in the abstract that competition for positions of leadership should not exist. In large and heterogeneous societies, however, it is mere common sense to recognize that there will be diversity of interests and competition for power, and that if the people are to express a free choice, rather elaborate conditions for their doing so have to be defined and safeguarded. Normally, therefore, democracy is that special system of competition for leadership in which the victory depends upon an appeal to an outside public which expresses its opinions in free elections. An electoral system, however, is only one element in a system of democratic control. If influence is to be exerted by the electorate on the choice of candidates or on the decisions of those in office, there must be independent resources in the hands of the electorate, such as newspapers, journals, and voluntary associations, which allow the citizens to make their views known and to bring effective pressures on their leaders.

Secondly, there is nothing in this conception of democracy which makes it necessary to retain the classic injunction of Locke that "in a constituted commonwealth, there can be but one supreme power, which is the legislative, to which all the rest are and must be subordinate . . ." There may or may not be good reasons to insist on this principle in the *formal* organization of democratic governments; but the legislative branch is in no large democracy today the supreme power in fact, and to insist that it should be is to confuse one particular device for achieving democracy with the idea itself. And for similar reasons, there is nothing in this conception of democracy to make bureaucracy as such incompatible with democracy. In contrast with older conceptions of democracy, the view that has been stated here makes leadership central, concentrating on ways of checking and controlling leaders, but also assigning to them the responsibility to lead, to formulate the main issues, and to make the final decisions. And it is plain that political leaders cannot today discharge their tasks competently and intelligently without the advice and assistance of large corps of specialists, whose tenure of office is not dependent upon elections and whose loyalties are presumably given equally to any government.

Two interconnected problems, however, are posed for democracy by this situation. First, are the political leaders who are theoretically in charge of the administrative services in fact in charge? What leverage do democratically chosen officials retain when they depend on giant organizations staffed by people who have their own *esprit de corps,* and who know that they will still be around when the political figures go? Second, along what avenues can the citizen move if he wishes access to those whose decisions govern his life? When the power of bureaucracies is so great, do not these avenues become too long, too crowded with barriers, too filled with signs and sounds in a strange and wearisome language, for the citizen to travel along them successfully? "That the citizens have the right to participate in the conduct of affairs, that they be able to put this right to practical use, and to employ it intelligently, such might be said to be, in sum, the first demands of every democrat." So states the Club Jean Moulin in its *L'état et le citoyen.*[7] Surely neither of these problems is new in kind; but they are enormously new in degree in Europe today. They raise the question whether the democratic forms that have been retained are not simply giving a cloak of legitimacy to decisions that are not democratic in the actual manner by which they are reached. For perhaps the most serious internal peril to democracy today is that the appearances of democracy can be so easily retained—but only the appearances.

III "The Liberties of the Moderns"

In order to treat these problems at all precisely, however, it is advisable to avoid approaching them in a global manner. There are different levels of popular control and participation. There is the level at which individuals have sufficient powers to guard their personal rights and freedoms; the level at which they can intervene with some effect in the conflicts among those seeking positions of leadership and in the competition between different social interests and social ideas; and, finally, the level at which they can take a direct hand in the making of collective decisions. Before we can estimate the kind and degree of democracy that exists, or the kind and degree of democracy at which we wish to aim, we have to be clear about what level of popular control and participation we have in mind. Let us begin with the first.

It is often forgotten that there is a rather considerable difference between the "liberty" of which Rousseau spoke and the "liberty" which European democracies have ever actually afforded any large number of their citizens except under unusual circumstances. The "liberty" of which Rousseau spoke was "the political liberty of the ancients." And as Benjamin Constant pointed out more than a century ago, the "liberty of the ancients" was the liberty to take part in the management of public affairs, an "active and continuing participation in the collective power." Such liberty could go hand in hand, not simply with the existence of a large class of enslaved or unenfranchised people, but with close surveillance of the personal lives of citizens. In contrast, the "liberty of the moderns" consisted, according to Constant, in "the peaceful enjoyment of private independence" and the "guarantees afforded by institutions to these enjoyments."[8] What are the prospects for this kind of liberty, which has been the special achievement of modern democracies, in the new Europe?

It is, surely, not an unimportant kind of liberty. Many reasonable men would think it all that anyone can reasonably expect from a government, and if they have no taste for the political fracas they may desire nothing more. Indeed, if the citizens of a country are very jealous of their personal liberties and know how to enjoy them —the French are a good example—they may well be disinclined to take too active a part in the public business. For doing so can mean that they will have less opportunity to enjoy their private liberties. It is possible, in short, to make a distinction between *démocratie gouvernée* and *démocratie gouvernante*, and to prefer the former to the latter. The degree of popular control that is wanted will then be only that degree that is sufficient to protect citizens in their natural or fundamental rights.

If this is the objective, the prospects of European democracy are assuredly not dispiriting. Even if we take the bleak view that the decision-making process in the European nations is democratic only in its external forms, these forms fortify personal liberties. An independent judiciary, free institutions of inquiry and education, and private associations struggling for public favor may not be politically very efficacious, but they create a vested interest in maintaining constitutional guarantees of liberty. Moreover, however reduced the powers of initiative possessed by parliaments may be, these assemblies can continue to serve the important function of airing grievances against the system.[9] Indeed, we can very easily overlook the principal functions of democratic forms and procedures, which are latent rather than manifest. The manifest political function of competition between parties, the existence of voluntary associations, and the safeguarding of individual liberties is to produce governments that are subject to popular control. But free association, individual liberties, and the open competition of ideas and interests are not, after all, simply means to the attainment of a desirable political goal; they are desirable in themselves. From this point of view, the democratic political process can be construed as an instrument which helps to protect these ends, and which may serve this function even if it does not produce governments over which popular control is very great. And it need hardly be added that if there is voluntary association, individual liberty and open competition between different groups, the possibility of increasing the degree of popular control over the decisions of government is at least likely to be enhanced.

Still and all, a host of issues are undoubtedly created by the increasing power of administrative bodies, and by their steadily closer contact with individual citizens. Administrative agencies, unlike the courts, do their work under conditions that are more or less hidden from the trained scrutiny of professionally equipped critics. When they are capricious or arbitrary in their dealings with individuals, the individuals concerned are likely to be anonymous and the injustices invisible. One reaction in Europe to this danger has been the invention of the office of Ombudsman, which has been introduced in the Scandinavian countries, and which may shortly be introduced into Britain. The Ombudsman is a special parliamentary commissioner who receives complaints directly from aggrieved citizens and who has the power to investigate these complaints and to seek remedies. Like any other political device the Ombudsman system raises complex questions. But it indicates that the importance of the issue of personal rights vis-à-vis administrative authority has begun to receive recognition in European countries, and that political imagination is being exercised to deal with the problem.[10]

The greatest danger to personal rights in the new Europe, however, is probably atmospheric. The state, directly and indirectly, controls larger and larger sections of the economy. A strong executive, particularly in times of crisis, has many means at his disposal for making life difficult for his critics and opponents, and for abusing civil liberties. Moreover, major military and diplomatic decisions are made in private, and with the expansion of international economic planning, the same may be increasingly true in other areas. Such developments do not in themselves mean that personal rights and liberties will be denied. But they mean that the practical usefulness of these rights and liberties can be progressively restricted, and that the lively interest of the individual in having these rights and liberties may in consequence decline. Moreover, these tendencies are further reinforced by other developments, such as the tendency of majority parties to remain in power for long periods, and the emergence of the new technique by which the supreme executive bypasses intermediate groups and takes his case directly to the electorate. Neither of these developments is in principle inconsistent with democracy, but the first tends to take the sense of urgency out of political debate, and the second tends to give that debate the character of a monologue. Under such circumstances, it is conceivable that the psychological underpinnings of liberty can be weakened. Liberty will not be formally abolished. It will simply not be used.

To project this possibility, however, is to point to perils, I believe, and not to probabilities. Europe's culture and traditions, the vigor of its intellectuals, artists and scholars, the power of its independent cadres and associations, and the discrediting of authoritarianism and totalitarianism, are only some of the more obvious reasons for thinking that the concern with liberty is not likely to decline. Considering the circumstances of its birth, General de Gaulle's regime, for example, could well have been a right-wing, reactionary government; despite some serious abuses, it has maintained the main fabric of personal liberties in France, and has done so while fighting insurrection and pursuing a war. Assuming that the problem of the succession to power can be solved in countries like France or Germany, the prospects for personal liberty are surely better than they were when the European economy was in crisis, when ideological bitterness heated up the atmosphere, and when the countries of Europe were not so tightly linked and could not exercise moderating influences on one another.

IV Representative Democracy, Parties, and Parliaments

At the end of Constant's list of the liberties enjoyed by moderns, however, there is another specific liberty—the liberty of everyone "to exert some influence upon the performance of public officials, by participating in the choice of all or some of these officials, or by making representations, petitions and requests which the authorities to some extent have to take into account." As our discussion suggests, the first level of popular control, the level at which men can protect their personal liberties, cannot be easily separated from the level at which ordinary individuals, not professionally engaged in politics, can nevertheless have access to the decision-making process and exercise some control over it. What are the questions which the emerging forms of government in Europe pose with regard to this level of popular control?

The parties and parliaments have traditionally been regarded as the principal agencies of popular representation. We may begin by noticing a small but not unimportant point about their present situation. One of the explanations that is most frequently offered for the decline in the influence of the political parties, particularly in countries like France and Italy, is that they are locked into place by old ideological commitments and antipathies and cannot therefore form the combinations of power and interest that might give them greater influence over the decision-making process. True as this observation is, it points to the fact that the parties and parliaments continue, in their way, to have a representative function. The divisions between church-oriented and anticlerical parties persist, for example, because they reflect continuing divisions in the population at large. The observer may regret that "outworn" issues drain off so much of the energies of the parties; nevertheless, the fact remains that the parties represent interests which large numbers of citizens of European countries continue to think are vital interests, and that they are fairly effective guardians of the ramparts they have been assigned to watch.

A second reason that is also given for the decline in the importance of the parties is worth a moment's attention as well. In both Germany and Italy, only one party has been in power for fifteen years; in England, the Conservatives have held power almost as long, and it is only now that they are running into serious difficulties; in France, the Gaullist party is the shadow of the president, and no effective competitor is on the horizon. A multiparty system in which there is fairly frequent rotation of power does not seem to be functioning vigorously in the major countries of Europe. As a result, it is pointed out, the parliaments no longer serve their classic functions of airing the larger moral and social alternatives before the nation and of working out the agreements and mutual concessions within which major choices of direction will be made. Yet it is not entirely the case that these debates and negotiations no longer take place, or that the parties have no part to play in them; it is simply that the locus of these debates has changed. They may take place, for example, within the circles of the majority party. Italy offers a striking illustration of this state of affairs. The consolidation of power by the Christian Democratic party has been attended by the growth, within the party, of organized factions, representing a broad spectrum of opinions and interests, which contest with one another at party congresses and at meetings of the National Council. This, plus the fact that the Christian Democrats must keep their "opening to the Left," and must therefore negotiate with minority parties, turns the party into a shadow parliament, not quite so representative as the traditional parliaments, but more representative than the traditional parties whose members sat in these parliaments. A not dissimilar situation can be found within the Conservative party in Britain. In both Italy and Britain the rise to power of party bureaucracies has given the parliaments more and more of a rubber-stamp function; but the parties themselves have developed, in recompense, a dialectic of their own.[11]

Yet these functions still performed by the parties are obviously limited in their significance. The decision-making process has drifted steadily away from the arenas in which, according to traditional democratic doctrine, the fundamental decisions about policy are supposed to be made. In their place, new arenas for consultation have been formally created, such as the Conseil Economique et Social and the Commissariat au Plan in France, and the National Economic Development Council in England. These bring together civil servants and leaders in the private sector and allow an exchange of ideas more relevant to the issues that have to be decided by government, and more influential in determining the policies that are ultimately evolved, than most party platforms or parliamentary debates. The constituencies represented are definable and organized; the opinions of the participants in such discussions are informed; their power to implement or to obstruct the decisions that are taken is significant. And beneath such agencies there has developed an elaborate infrastructure of scientific commissions and technical committees, unofficial groups of civil servants, specialized consultants, and well-placed people, all of whom exercise a decorous but increasingly decisive influence on the formulation and resolution of public issues.

In the face of these developments, it is tempting to say that European democracies have simply demonstrated their resilience and adaptability and that they have successfully created new institutions of democratic discussion. One difficulty with this view, however, is that there are manifest dangers in a situation in which the actual facts of a political system diverge too widely from the official theory of that system; the authority of the system tends to be undermined.* Another difficulty is that the discussions that are carried on within these new institutions are not commonly conducted in public and are at considerable remove from the sanctions of the electoral process. It is with such considerations in mind that M. Mendès-France and others have proposed constitutional reforms

---

* The dangers are all the greater because, in countries like France and Italy, there is a long memory of elections that have been episodes only in a game of musical chairs, and that have produced minor changes in the distribution of high positions and nothing else. Men have voted in these countries in the frustrated conviction that their votes were unlikely to decide anything of great substance, and generally without knowing for whom they were voting as premier. It is this memory which is the most immediate reason for the doubts that are so widely entertained in these countries about the significance of political parties or their genuineness as instruments of democratic government.

CHARLES FRANKEL

that would establish a second parliamentary chamber representing organized social groups and professional interests.[12] In this manner, it is held, the official forms of parliamentary democracy would register the actual facts of democratic practice. This is not the place to consider the merits of such proposals, although it should be said that those who make them are aware of the dangers of "corporatism" and hope to erect safeguards against these dangers. The interest in this sort of proposal to bring "les forces vives de la nation" into the explicit constitutional structure does indicate, however, that the limitations of the old system of geographical representation and ideological parties are coming under increasing scrutiny.

It is conceivable, too, that other constitutional developments will also help reinvigorate political parties. It is difficult to predict the evolution of the new presidential system in France, which is so closely identified with the personality and program of an individual. Still, it is not beyond the bounds of possibility that the creation of a supreme executive, chosen directly by the electorate, will not weaken the parties but in the end will strengthen them. It offers a great prize as an inducement to the development of permanent coalitions; it is conceivable that it will contribute to the growth of a two-party system in which the political parties function, not as representatives of discrete ideologies or interests, but as agencies of negotiation and synthesis for large blocs of interests. The continuing control of a large vote by the Communist party and the persistence of old disagreements such as that between clerical and anticlerical parties are, however, obstacles in the path of such an evolution.

In the end, the reinvigoration of parties and politics, if it does take place, is less likely to come from constitutional reforms than from other developments. Indeed, it is conceivable that the reinvigoration of democratic politics will not come from the revival of political parties in the old form, but from the emergence of new types of political association whose outlines it is as yet difficult to foresee. Outside the parties there are growing up in the new Europe groups whose potential importance may be considerable. They are still relatively uninfluential, but they are new in style and type. In the past, movements on the Continent involving large-scale popular participation have usually revolved around global themes like peace. Today smaller groups, concerned with more limited issues of public importance, are popping up. And there are also emerging new centers for political discussion, like Il Mulino in Italy or the Club Jean Moulin in France, whose immediate purpose is not to mount a political program but to ventilate all the issues freshly. They are serving as foci for the evident interest in redefining political aims that is present in Europe, especially among the young; and it is in these movements, perhaps, that the seeds of future political growth in Europe may be found.

Finally, the general spread of better economic conditions, which has already softened the old ideological divisions, is creating the possibility for new and more meaningful political formations. The struggle for the redistribution of wealth may lose its old shape and take on a new one. It may become a struggle not over the distribution of packets of well-being to individuals, but over the relative proportion of the national product to be allocated to social or collective goods as against those goods that individuals can pick up for themselves and carry home. The beginning, although just the bare beginning, of such a debate can be discerned in the United States. In Europe it has much deeper roots, for it raises the old questions about the gospel of technology, productivity, and efficiency that have long occupied European minds. What has stood in the way of such a debate is the pressure of poverty and the rigidities of ideological disagreements. Now that these barriers are gradually disappearing, that debate may take shape. If it does, political alignments with greater relevance to the issues confronting European governments may emerge.

V *Representative Democracy and Bureaucracy*

It is quite another question, however, when we turn from parties and parliaments to bureaucracy, and ask what it is that political alignments, old or new, can in themselves do to affect the general course of events in Europe. The cry, "*A bas les technocrates!*" is an expression of fear and not a program of action, but it points to the problem of bureaucratic power, and it is a problem that cannot be solved by the repetition of comforting formulas. "To believe that we can exhume the ideal schema of a government that makes the choices and an administration that simply carries out these decisions would be pure hypocrisy. . . . It is evident that the role of the administrative services is preponderant."[13] Nor does it do much good to take the opposite position and proclaim that the age of politics is dead and the age of administration is at hand, and that we would do best simply to drop our old illusions about democracy and accept the managerial revolution.

This comfortingly pessimistic view is no more plausible today than when Plato first put forward a different version of it. It assumes that the members of a technical elite will actually agree on a single, common solution to a problem; that they have by themselves enough independent authority to put this solution into effect without the help of people who are not specialists; that they are free

553

from special pressures and temptations emanating from interest groups in the larger community. None of these assumptions is true. The individuals who compose a given technical elite do disagree, and different elites disagree with each other; the questions with which specialists deal spill over into areas where they are not specialists, and they must either hazard amateur opinions in these areas or ignore such larger issues, which is no better; today the administrative services, much more than the parties and parliaments, are the principal targets of interest groups; and by training, background and daily association the members of the civil services, particularly in the higher echelons, speak the language of the better-placed classes and groups in the nation and tend to be the informal and inadvertent representatives of these classes and groups. In short, the political game remains very much alive. And there are some particularly sturdy reasons today for desiring that this game be conducted under democratic conditions. For a major function of the democratic method is to prevent decisions from being taken which are based on narrow definitions of the interests and issues at stake—definitions which serve the interests of administrative or intellectual convenience, but which leave out vital aspects of the problem. There is a special kind of structural immorality which our bureaucratized societies tend to create and encourage; it is the immorality of the specialist or official who takes refuge in his narrow competence and passes the moral buck to others. Democracy today is more, not less, necessary than it has been before.

To say that it is necessary, however, is not to say that its existence is assured. The problem posed to democracy by bureaucratic power is to find ways of bringing bureaucratic decision-making into the open where it can be surveyed and controlled, and of placing the wielders of bureaucratic power under pressure from visible and significant competitors. To some extent, these ways already exist, at least in principle. One way, interestingly enough, is to multiply bureaucracies, to control them by countering them with others. Thus the parliaments, and both the majority and the minority parties, can have attached to them separate corps of specialists of their own; quasi-independent planning groups, outside the regular administrative hierarchy, are another device; the creation or encouragement by special forms of aid of totally independent planning groups in the private sector is another.

There is, however, another instrument for the control and democratization of bureaucratic government which is so fundamental in its significance that it cannot be called a "device." This is the broadening of the system of recruitment to the administrative services, so that they become more representative of the various sectors of the population. Such a program depends, it need hardly be said, on a change in the educational system of the major countries of Europe. Considerable discussion of this problem has been taking place in Europe for some years, and various steps have been taken, such as the broadening of scholarship systems, the strengthening of provincial universities, and the establishment of the École Nationale d'Administration in France.

It cannot be said, however, that these efforts have as yet produced significant changes. In France, for example, of those who passed the presumably "new" examinations for entrance to the École National d'Administration between 1945 and 1951, 65 per cent were from families in the business, professional, managerial, and high civil servant families. Approximately 25 per cent came from the petite bourgeoisie, which represented some expansion in the opportunities available to this group. But only 3 per cent were from agricultural and industrial working class families. Since that time there has not been any considerable change in this situation. The factors that contribute to it, of course, are many, but the largest single factor is undoubtedly the general pattern of educational opportunity in the nation as a whole. Nine children in ten can count on extended education if they come from the professional or managerial class; one in ten if they come from worker or peasant families.[14] And what is true for France is also true, *mutatis mutandis,* for other countries of Europe.

The reform of the educational system must undoubtedly be the principal item in any effective program for strengthening political democracy in Europe. Quite apart from its potential impact on the composition of the bureaucracies, it can strengthen the principle of popular control in general. For the evidence is strong that the desire to participate in public affairs and the ability to use the resources of the political system effectively vary directly with the number of years the individual has been in school. No other factor, indeed, appears to have a comparable significance.

VI Participant Democracy

So we come, by a natural progression, to the final level of popular control and participation—the level at which the individual who so desires can take a direct part in the control of public affairs. There is, undoubtedly, a fetish of participation, which is the legacy of democratic theories descended from the past and which fits neither the imperatives of contemporary government nor the desires of many democratic citizens. It is easy to forget that while the costs to the individual of political nonparticipation can be high, the costs of participation can also be high. It is even easier to forget that greater economic and social equality, and the extension of the rights and powers of citizenship to much larger sections of the community, make the ideal of full and continuing participation by any individual citizen harder rather than easier to achieve; they remove the slaves, leisure and amenities that made such participation possible. As Giovanni Sartori has pointed out, the full absorption of the citizen in the public business created in Greece a profound and unhealthy disequilibrium in the various necessities and functions of associated life: "To the hypertrophy of the political life there is inevitably attached the atrophy of the economic life."[15]

Still, one of the most notable aspects of the present scene in Europe is the growing strength of the demand for participation, for an experience with government in which the individual can be an agent and actor and not simply an observer, beneficiary, or victim. The appeal of this ideal shows itself, for example, in the remarkable reception that has been given to M. Mendès-France's book, which places such stress on this theme. And it shows itself more broadly in the steadily more insistent discussion of the need, the possibility, and the opportunity in the Europe that is emerging for the large-scale decentralization of governmental functions.

For perhaps the most striking feature of Europe today is that the two great secular political trends that dominate it—the movement toward planning and the movement toward European union—have quite equivocal implications. Planning, obviously, can increase the power of governments and reduce the powers of citizens. But planning has other possible implications, and while the notion that planning is inherently antidemocratic exists in Europe as it does elsewhere, the opinion that it can be a tool for the strengthening of political democracy is becoming noticeably stronger. Planning, which can provide a clear framework within which individuals can make their choices, does not necessarily increase the number of specific interventions by the state. On the contrary, it can integrate and simplify the process of government regulation, reducing the number of *ad hoc* interventions and of special committees and bureaus. Planning can make the citizen aware of a definite set of larger, social purposes in his everyday life, and give him a sense of meaning and direction as he goes about his affairs. It can clarify the economic costs of political, cultural or religious choices. It can highlight, if there is public discussion of it, the noneconomic costs of economic choices that are now made in the name simply of productivity and efficiency. Last and most important, a plan can express choices in fairly clear terms; the debate over a plan offers a nation the chance to confront self-consciously the alternatives before it. In this way, a plan can reactivate the interest in democratic discussion and give it an obvious purpose. The movement toward planning, and the very large amount of communication and consultation that now accompanies this process in Europe, offers a matrix for the growth of a vigorous political life. It can be used, if the will to do so is present, to bring larger numbers of people into closer and steadier touch with the public business.

The movement toward European union has comparable possibilities. For neither industrialization nor bureaucracy explain the very high degree of centralization of European political systems. The thrust toward centralization, the ideal of centralization, in most places preceded technology in time and were major factors in the growth of state bureaucracies. They are largely the products of the European state system and its continuing rivalries. If that system is receding, if the principle of European federalism is advancing, it is permissible to think that room for maneuver is emerging and that a theory and practice of regional and local autonomy can be developed. It is in such a movement—if it takes place—that aspirations for self-government are most likely to be fulfilled. The "big decisions," to be sure, would be made by the professional makers of decisions, hopefully under a system of democratic controls. But their execution at the local level could be in the hands of local officials; and the "little decisions"—the decisions that are likely to loom largest in the lives of the ordinary citizen because they most quickly affect his immediate environment—could be made by the active citizenry on the spot.

The analogy between the integrated Europe that is slowly and painfully coming to birth and the small country of Switzerland may seem to be a strained one, but, as Herbert Luethy has observed, it is nevertheless instructive. "Switzerland," he remarks, "is not very impressive because it has no splendid capital, but on the other hand, it has no neglected, sluggish, or enfeebled provinces. The life of the country is not concentrated in one favored area; it circulates throughout the whole, and this amply makes up for what is lacking."[16] In 1913, Élie Halévy remarked that Europe was faced with the choice between "a universal Swiss Republic and bellicose Caesarism." It is only speculation that the integration of Europe and the progress of the federal principle can foster this movement toward decentralization and local democracy. But it is a speculation which has begun to fascinate some Europeans and which is leading them to think about ways to make it come true. For it is through the steady and direct experience of democracy close at hand that an entire democratic system acquires its tone.

Such an aspiration toward a more fully democratic experience, indeed, marks off contemporary Europe from the Europe of the past. The citizens of European nations live on a steady diet of politics today; more of them expect equality; and when they feel cut off from their governments, they do not take this as a matter of course but complain that they are being denied a natural right. It is important to keep this change in mind when the problems posed by the influence and excellence of bureaucracy and the administrative services are examined. For they are not new problems; and if they seem more severe today, this is not only because bureaucratic powers are greater than they have been. They also seem more severe because the context has changed, because Europe today permits and requires its citizens to think about a kind of democracy which, in its quality and extent, Europe has not known before.

REFERENCES

1. George Santayana, "The Irony of Liberalism," in *Soliloquies in England* (New York: Charles Scribner's Sons, 1922), p. 186.

2. A recent expression of this point of view, together with an effort to adjust it to the need for executive power, can be found in Pierre Mendès-France's *La république moderne* (Paris: Gallimard, 1962).

3. "There is in all bodies politic a certain maximum of force which they cannot exceed, and which they only lose by their aggrandizement. The social bond is enfeebled by extension. . . . Not only does the government have less capacity to enforce the observance of the laws, . . . but the people have less affection for the chiefs they never see, and for their country, which seems like the world to them, and for their fellow countrymen, with the greater part of whom they have no acquaintance." (*Social Contract*, Book II, Chapter 9.) "Imagine that the State is composed of ten thousand citizens. . . . Thus . . . each member of the State has but a ten-thousandth part of the sovereign authority, though he is entirely subjected to it. When the people amount to one hundred thousand, the situation of the subject does not change, but each is equally under the entire authority of the laws, while his vote is reduced to the hundred-thousandth part, and has ten times less influence in the formation of the laws." (Book III, Chapter 1.)

4. For a discussion of this point see, for example, Bertrand De Jouvenel, "The Treatment of Capitalism by Continental Intellectuals," in F. A. Hayek (ed.), *Capitalism and the Historians* (Chicago: University of Chicago Press, 1954).

5. See the rather similar analysis offered by John Plamenatz, in Richard McKeon (ed.), *Democracy in a World of Tensions* (Chicago: University of Chicago Press, 1951). See also Joseph A. Schumpeter, *Capitalism, Socialism, and Democracy* (New York: Harper & Brothers, 1950), and Robert A. Dahl, *A Preface to Democratic Theory* (Chicago: University of Chicago Press, 1956).

6. Raymond Aron, *Dix-huit leçons sur la société industrielle* (Paris: Gallimard, 1962), p. 87.

7. Club Jean Moulin, *L'état et le citoyen* (Paris: Editions du Seuil, 1961), p. 188.

8. Benjamin Constant, *De la liberté des anciens comparée à celle des modernes,* in C. Louandre (ed.), *Oeuvres politiques* (Paris: Charpentier, 1874), pp. 268–269.

9. Mr. D. N. Chester has recently documented in detail the degree to which this function continues to be served effectively by the institution of Parliamentary Questions. See D. N. Chester and Nona Bowring, *Questions in Parliament* (Oxford: Clarendon Press, 1962).

10. For a detailed analysis of the Ombudsman system, see Donald C. Rowat, "An Ombudsman Scheme for Canada," *Canadian Journal of Economic and Political Science* (November, 1962).

11. See Leicester Webb, "La démocratie italienne en 1970," *Futuribles,* No. 807, Supplement 2 (Paris: Société d'études et de documentation économiques, industrielles et sociales, 1ᵉʳ janvier 1962).

12. Pierre Mendès-France, *op. cit.,* pp. 91–108.

13. Club Jean Moulin, *op. cit.,* p. 134.

14. *Ibid.,* pp. 30–31, 137–141. See also Nicholas Wahl, "The French Political System," in Samuel Beer and Adam Ulam (eds.), *Patterns of Government* (New York: Random House, 1958), p. 324.

15. Giovanni Sartori, *Democrazia e definizioni* (Bologna: Il Mulino, 1957), p. 159.

16. Herbert Luethy, "Has Switzerland a Future?" *Encounter,* Vol. XIX, No. 6 (December, 1962).

HANS KÜNG

Theological Currents in Europe Today

IF THE "new Europe" is going to be still, in a real sense, "Europe," it will have to be something more than an economic and political entity; it will have to be a spiritual entity as well. The spirit that made the old Europe great was (in combination with classical antiquity and the Germanic heritage, but in a different way) the spirit of Christianity. Now a new Europe is rising from the ruins of two world wars, growing slowly but perceptibly towards a new economic, political and social unity, and thus, we hope, towards a new peace; is this new Europe also going to be stamped with the spirit of Christianity? We do not propose to answer this question here. Two things are certain: (1) The new Europe is not going to be "the Christian West" in any romantic, medieval sense. The time is past when the faith and the Church could let themselves be identified with any particular social system. The fact that the makers of the new Europe—Konrad Adenauer, Alcide de Gasperi, Maurice Schumann, Charles de Gaulle, and others—have been practicing Catholics, and that the reconstruction—a magnificent piece of work, despite all its shortcomings—has been led by parties bearing the name of "Christian" must not mislead us concerning the degree to which Europe is secularized and dechristianized. (2) The new Europe is not going to be purely a technocrats' economic zone, devoid of values, the faith and the Church having abdicated spiritually within it. There are too many signs, in the diaspora situation prevailing in the new Europe, of a new Christian vitality in all fields. We are limiting ourselves here to one single sector of church life: one which may well be less easy to get hold of and observe than, say, the life of individual parishes, the activities of religious organizations, or the initiatives of church leaders, but one which is of fundamental importance for an understanding of the religious situation and the whole spiritual situation of Europe: the sector of theological studies. Theology in the new Europe has the advantage over theology in other continents to the extent that on the one hand it is rooted in a unique way in two thousand years of theological tradition, from which it can continually draw strength, while on the other it has been somewhat ruthlessly shaken out of its smug placidity by the spiritual crisis of the two world wars and confronted with the real needs and problems of present-day humanity.

It is not only the Catholic Church that has been roused to attention by the Second Vatican Council in Rome. The world could hear that a new note was being struck: not mere self-satisfied proclamations and moralizings, not mere condemnations and ex-communications, but critical self-examination, a hopeful willingness to reform and renew the Church, a new readiness to understand and encounter other Christians, a new openness towards the questions, problems, needs, solutions and hopes of the modern world. Has all this newness been produced out of nothing? No one should belittle the epoch-making impetus given by John XXIII. But that impetus would not have been possible, or at any rate it would not have achieved its effect, if it had not been for all the work that has been going on now for decades, tirelessly and per-severingly, in very varied fields, but certainly including—indeed most fundamentally—the field of theological study. The Council has brought visibly into play something which is otherwise easily overlooked in the whirl of modern ecclesiastical organization and administration, something which is not always taken seriously enough in its importance for the Church's everyday life: the silent labor of theologians.

I Renewal of Public Worship

We will here pick out one example which takes us straight to the heart of one of the most important sectors in current European theology: liturgical studies, oriented towards a renewal of the Church's worship in accord with the present age and with the nature of the thing itself.

Catholic worship, the Roman liturgy in particular, has a great and long tradition behind it. Century after century of the Christian era has gone to the construction of this mighty edifice, reshaping it and multifariously adorning it. But with the passing of time this multiplicity of arrangements and rearrangements had obscured the groundplan of the Roman Mass, for instance, and rendered it unintelligible to modern man. The Second Vatican Council has ap-plied itself energetically to the task of shaping the liturgy into something that the man of today can once more understand and in which he can join: the liturgy, the Church's worship, is not merely to be admired from the outside but to be understood by all and actively celebrated by all together in communal thanksgiving, praise and petition, communal singing and participation in the meal. For this reason the liturgy is to be simplified and its basic intention and basic lines clarified.

But how are we to recognize clearly these basic lines, when history has done so much to obscure and displace them, unless we have exact *historical knowledge* of how the whole of the liturgy, and the Roman Mass in particular, has developed in the course of the centuries? A vast and meticulous work has been done during the last few decades by Europe's liturgical historians, by which the whole evolution of the Catholic liturgy has been scientifically reconstructed. The crowning fruit of all this labor, especially in regard to the Roman Mass, is J. A. Jungmann's monumental work *Missarum Solemnia. Eine genetische Erklärung der römischen Messe* (2 vols., Vienna: 1949; English translation, *The Mass of the Roman Rite, its Origins and Development,* 2 vols., New York: 1951), which has now been translated into all the principal languages. Since its appearance we know with complete precision what the Roman Mass was like in each different century; what changes there were between the liturgy in a Roman house in the second or third century and that in a Roman basilica of the sixth or seventh; which profound alterations were caused by the transplanting of the Roman liturgy into the Frankish empire and which arose in the high Middle Ages. We have exact knowledge of the abuses in the liturgy in the late Middle Ages, and of the attempts at reform made by the Council of Trent. Today we can say of every element in the Roman Mass, however small, why it occurs just where it does, when it was inserted, what its original position was, and what its original meaning was.

For the point about all these studies is by no means a mere archaeological or aesthetic investigation of external rites. The point is to get at the *inner meaning* of each particular rite, which has all too often been forgotten or buried in the course of history. What is the meaning of the different stages in the rite of baptism? What does confirmation signify? What is meant by the absolution of sins? What, actually, is the point of the Mass? What was its original, basic structure? Today we know that the Mass was originally a simple eucharist, that is, a thanksgiving, a prayer of remembrance and thanks by the whole community for the good things done to us by God in Christ, at which the account of Jesus' last supper was repeated and the gifts of the memorial meal were eaten in faith. Thus we know today why, because of the original meaning of the Mass, it is absolutely necessary to have as much resemblance as is reasonably possible to the supper of Jesus. We know why all the faithful should play as active a part as possible in the liturgy, why the word of God should be intelligibly read out and relevantly expounded, why the Church's liturgy should be adapted, outwardly and inwardly, to the different nations and their mentalities. We are once more aware today of the missionary and pastoral, the catechetical and didactic character of the liturgy. And above all, we are once more aware today that all these ideas are not new discoveries but belong to the most ancient tradition of our Church, with enormous significance for current dogmatic theology, particularly in the doctrine of the sacraments.

The fact that we are once more aware of all this today is essentially a result of the liturgical labors of central European theologians; this work made a definite beginning at the time of the Enlightenment and reached its completion, particularly in Germany, between the two world wars.* During the Nazi persecu-

---

* As regards the liturgy, the tendency of the Council of Trent was to carry out a restoration rather than a constructive and creative reform; its reforms consisted in removing, on the one hand, the worst of the existing abuses and in re-establishing, on the other, the *status quo* as it had been in the Middle Ages. The rigid, formal prescriptions laid down for the various rites ushered in "a period of stagnation and rubricism" in the liturgy. The triumphalist, splendor-loving spirit of the *Baroque period* was alien to the spirit of the original liturgy. The people were no more than passive, silent spectators at the Mass. The turning point came in the period of the Enlightenment. In the second half of the eighteenth century and the first half of the nineteenth, there were numerous churchmen, especially in Germany (such as I. H. von Wessenberg) who realized once more that the celebration of the liturgy should be common to all and understood, and that there were practical consequences to be drawn from this: the whole parish should gather together for worship in the parish church, where there should be no more than one single Mass going on at a time; that the reading of the gospel should be followed by the sermon, and the communion of the priest by that of the people; that the whole people should actively celebrate the service together, with community singing and community prayer corresponding to the prayers being said by the priest. As early as this, such demands were being put forward as introduction of the vernacular, and of chant in the vernacular; deprecation of the practice of publicly reciting the rosary during Mass; reduction in the number of altars, and having the altar facing the people; concelebration; restraint in exposition of the Blessed Sacrament; more frequent communion, etc. We can recognize all of these bold demands today as having been completely in the spirit of the liturgical renewal being carried out by the Second Vatican Council. But at the time they were pushed into the background and partially overlayed by a movement of restoration, in part the product of the Romantic movement, emanating especially from the Benedictine monasteries of Solesmes (Dom Guéranger) and Beuron. It focused attention on the great liturgical traditions (especially the liturgical year and the so-called Gregorian chant), but its thinking was to a large extent on aesthetic, traditionalist and Roman-centralist lines. But after Pius X's call in 1903 for "active participation" (*actuosa communicatio*) by all the faithful in the liturgy, it was above all the powerfully

tion, in all the terrible distress of the Second World War, and in the refugee world of the immediate postwar period, the liturgical movement proved its worth; to a Church that found herself deprived of many of her opportunities for external action, it offered a new sense of religious community and a profound religious renewal, especially in regard to preaching, catechetics and pastoral work. Inevitably there were reactionary traditionalists who rose up in violent opposition to all this "innovation." But fundamentally these sharp controversies were settled in a positive sense by the German bishops, who set up in 1940 a liturgical commission of bishops and liturgical and pastoral experts, and by Pius XII in 1943. In France in 1943 the Centre de pastorale liturgique was founded and began to send out waves of extraordinary vigor through France, which had till then been liturgically backward; it was followed by the liturgical institute of the German bishops at Trier in 1947, and by liturgical institutes for Holland at Nijmegen, for Italy at Genoa and for Austria at Salzburg. Liturgical periodicals (*Maison Dieu, Liturgisches Jahrbuch,* etc.) and liturgical series such as *Lex Orandi* helped in the spreading of ideas. There was a flood of Liturgical Days and Liturgical Study Weeks all over Europe after the war. The result was not only a liturgical renewal in individual parishes but at the same time fruitful and manifold cooperation at the international level, resulting especially in the great international liturgical congresses at Assisi, Lugano and Nijmegen. Also in 1947, Pius XII gave the liturgical renewal its *magna charta libertatis* in his encyclical *Mediator Dei.* In various subsequent measures he gave a lead to liturgical reform (the introduction of evening Masses, renewal of the Easter liturgy, mitigation of the law of eucharistic fast, and others). The general reform of the liturgy was put into the hands of the Second Vatican Council by John XXIII. If the work of the liturgical preparatory commission has been outstandingly good, this was made possible only by the fact that it called upon the cooperation of those leading liturgists whose combined work at an international level had for

---

influential work of Lambert Beauduin of the Benedictine abbey of Mont-César in Belgium, and of Pius Parsch in Austria, which led the way to renewed efforts to achieve a genuine people's liturgy. A decisive factor was the linking up of the liturgical movement in Germany after the First World War with the youth movement (Romano Guardini), the great youth associations (L. Wolker) and thus with the majority of the younger clergy. Added to this were the influence of the Leipzig Oratory, of Casel's "mystery theology," of the call, especially from Innsbruck, for a "kerygmatic theology" (H. Rahner, J. A. Jungmann), of studies in liturgical history (J. A. Jungmann) and of general theological attention to the liturgy and the sacraments. Such was the dawn of the age of new developments.

long proved its worth. The Second Vatican Council has made the matter of comprehensive liturgical renewal, which began as an awakening in a few alert minds and hearts in Europe, the concern of the whole Catholic Church throughout the world. And precisely through a renewal of Catholic liturgy, so as to make of it a genuine people's liturgy, the Catholic Church is seeking to carry out long-standing and justified demands of the reformers. She is thus coming to meet the liturgical renewal which is also taking place today among Protestants, especially Lutherans; this is especially to be seen in the revised order of service (agenda) for Lutheran churches and communities.

II Concentration on the Scriptures

The liturgical renewal could not have achieved its development in this way without at the same time a new focusing of attention on Holy Scripture, from which liturgical scholarship must derive the meaning, the archetype and the norms of ecclesiastical worship, not only at the present time but ever more increasingly in the future. It was not till after the Second World War that Catholic exegesis in Europe finally emerged from the condition of crisis and stagnation into which, after some hopeful new departures at the beginning of the twentieth century, it had been plunged as part of the anti-Modernist reaction.* The decisive impulse was

---

* Catholic exegesis has passed through many vicissitudes during the modern period. The period from 1500 to 1650 is regarded as the "golden age" of Catholic exegesis, remarkable for the large number of exegetes (especially Spaniards, Portugese and Italians) and of works produced, though it must be admitted that Catholic-Protestant controversy did more to damage than to promote a comprehensive understanding of the Scriptures. This springtime was followed by a period of stagnation and apprehensive traditionalism. The outstanding figure in this second period was the Oratorian Richard Simon (d. 1712), who was far ahead of his time and consequently attacked and persecuted from all sides. He was in fact the founder of historico-critical Biblical scholarship; he was to a special degree a pioneer in textual criticism and Biblical introduction (criticism of the Pentateuch); he tried to pave the way to a historical understanding of Old Testament religion. His method was taken up by the Protestant rationalist J. S. Semler and subsequently by the whole school of modern Protestant exegesis; in Catholic circles it remained for long unproductive. Well into the nineteenth century Catholic exegesis remained apologetical in character in defense against the rationalism of Protestant exegesis. Only towards the end of the nineteenth century did an upsurge begin, especially in France, Belgium and Germany. In 1890 J.-M. Lagrange founded the École Biblique in Jerusalem and threw the whole weight of his towering authority not only on the side of geographical and archaeological research in Palestine but also of the historico-critical method in exegesis. With Lagrange were associated F. Prat in France, A. van Hoon-

given by Pius XII's encyclical on the Bible, *Divino afflante Spiritu* (1943), which has been called the "liberating encyclical." In contrast to Benedict XIV's encyclical *Spiritus Paraclitus* (1920) and to the decrees of the Biblical commission in the early years of the century, this encyclical explicitly recognized the historico-critical method as appropriate and necessary in relation to the Bible: the necessity of getting back to the original text, of textual criticism, of archaeology and other auxiliary sciences, of oriental studies; the necessity for research into the literal meaning, into literary forms, into the theological significance of the text. It is only an unintelligent zeal, said the encyclical, that combats from the outset everything that is new, or that regards it with suspicion.

The appearance of *Divino afflante Spiritu* did not, indeed, mean the extinction of representatives of the "narrow school"; there are on the contrary some among them who have been none too particular in their choice of means when trying to attack the reputations of their more openminded colleagues. But seen as a whole the progress in Catholic exegesis in Europe since the war is undeniable. Whereas in the "golden age" of Catholic exegesis it was Spaniards, Portugese and Italians who were in the lead, nowadays it is chiefly the French, Germans, Dutch and Belgians who head the movement. Difficult questions such as the problem of the Pentateuch in the Old Testament, the synoptic problem in the New, the problems of form criticism and of the development of tradition, are now discussed with an objectivity and a lack of inhibition totally different from what prevailed in the days when even such reputable Catholic exegetes as J.-M. Lagrange and F. von Hummelauer were forced to resign their teaching posts temporarily or permanently. Even though the atmosphere of theological freedom and scholarly integrity in the sphere of Catholic exegesis still leaves much to be desired, yet the change of climate is obvious. Regarding Protestant exegesis we are no longer content with defensive apolo-

---

acker at Louvain, and in Germany F. von Hummelauer, N. Peters, the *Biblische Zeitschrift*, edited by J. Goettsberger and J. Sickenberger, and other exegetes besides. This progressive element had constantly to defend itself against a backward-looking conservative element. At the beginning of this century, the fight, justified in itself, against Modernism, one of whose foremost champions was the French exegete A. Loisy, led to a somewhat un-Catholic heresy hunt and an atmosphere of paralyzing fear. This meant a severe setback to Catholic exegesis. The Catholic exegetes of the first few decades of the twentieth century, taken as a whole and in comparison with Protestant exegesis, did little critical and constructive work; they were exaggeratedly cautious in statement, avoided the really burning questions, and took refuge in platitude. It was only slowly that a turn for the better began to establish itself.

getics and negative criticism, but we have broken through to constructive discussion in mutual understanding. Catholic and Protestant exegetes take part together in the great congresses of Old and New Testament scholars. In New Testament exegesis, despite definitive differences in such matters as the understanding of New Testament ecclesiology, we can discern an important drawing together, both in method and in results; while in Old Testament exegesis we can go so far as to state that today confessional differences are no longer crucial at all. Both in the Old and the New Testaments, Catholic exegesis has not only learned an enormous amount from Protestant exegesis; it has been able, in the most recent period, to make important contributions to the progress of exegesis in many different fields.

Catholic exegetes are making definitive contributions to the critical edition of the Göttingen Septuagint, the Greek translation of the Old Testament (J. Ziegler); to the critical edition of the original text of the New Testament (H. J. Vogels, A. Merk); to the classical Latin translation, the Vetus Latina (at Beuron); and to the Vulgate (at Rome). It has been predominately Catholic scholars who have discovered the remains of the Greek Bible commentaries preserved in Byzantine catena-manuscripts. Catholic exegetes have made important contributions not only in research into later Jewish religion (J. B. Frei, J. Bonsirven), but in excavations in Palestine and the whole field of study opened up by Qumran. Both the École Biblique at Jerusalem and the Pontifical Biblical Institute at Rome are doing outstanding work. Since the war, new Catholic Biblican lexicons have appeared (*Supplément au Dictionnaire de la Bible,* H. Haag's *Bibellexikon,* J. B. Bauer's *Bibeltheologisches Wörterbuch,* Léon-Dufour's *Vocabulaire de théologie biblique*); new Catholic commentaries and series of commentaries (in Germany the *Echter-Bibel,* the Regensburg New Testament, Herder's *Theologischer Kommentar zum Neuen Testament,* in France the revised *Verbum Salutis* series and the *Bible de Jérusalem,* in Holland *De Boeken van het Oude Testament* and *De Boeken van het Nieuwe Testament,* and others); new Biblical series (*Lectio divina, Témoins de Dieu, Bonner Biblische Beiträge, Studien zum Alten und Neuen Testament, Biblische Beiträge*); new Biblical periodicals (*Neue Folge der Biblischen Zeitschrift, Bibel und Leben, Evangile, Bible et vie chrétienne*); new Biblical theologies of the Old and New Testaments (P. van Imschoot, M. Meinertz, J. Bonsirven).

What is particularly important is that the Bible today is not only a book for a few esoteric scholars but is becoming more and more the book of the Christian people. What had been begun in Germany in the period between the wars was continued in France after the war, often with greater freshness and vitality. There are many different periodicals, series and introductions to the Bible which bear the character of *haute vulgarisation* for clergy and laity. In innumerable Bible Circles in parishes, societies and youth groups in Europe today the Bible is being read, studied and discussed. Biblical Study Days and Study Weeks draw crowds of participants. Preaching and catechetics are today being fertilized by the Bible in a new way and thus display a different quality from what they had at the beginning of this century. Europe's new catechisms, especially the French "unity catechism" (1940, second edition 1947), and the German bishops' "Catholic Catechism" (1955), which was translated into twenty-two languages in its first five years, are to a quite different extent from their predecessors (though still not enough) molded by the Bible. On the other hand, it is clear that exegesis is having more and more influence on systematic theology (fundamental theology, dogmatics, moral theology). We are slowly losing the habit of treating the Bible as a source from which to quarry arguments in favor of preconceived scholastic theses. Proofs from Scripture are being built more and more on the results of modern exegesis. Slowly but perceptibly the perspectives, dimensions and emphases of Scripture are becoming once more the determining factor in systematic theology, in matters great and small.

Exegesis itself has to work on two fronts: first, it is concerned with the *historico-critical study* of Biblical texts. It has to reckon fully with the fact that the writers of Scripture were completely and totally men: men of a particular time, a particular mentality, a particular culture. The Semites of the Near East lived in a different world from ours; they did not, for instance, distinguish in the same way as we do today between historical and non-historical. Infinite pains have to be taken in order to work out today, thousands of years later, what the writer of that time himself meant by each individual sentence in any of the various writings. Added to this, the books as we have them are in many cases a compilation of many different documents from different traditions, and it is by no means easy for critical exegesis to establish the original chronology; the earlier and later traditions; the parts played by the individual author, by the community, and by the final editor; the various influences of cult, catechesis, politics, morals, whether of Israel and the surrounding peoples or of the primitive community; the different literary forms used in individual passages; and the changes in meaning of individual words. All this needs to be done seriously and thoroughly in scientific exegesis today if the word of God manifesting itself in words of men is to appear in all its complexity and richness.

568

Second, exegesis is concerned with working out the *theological meaning* of the Biblical texts. Today we are very far from thinking that the task of exegesis is complete once the detailed work in the fields of philology, history, archaeology and comparative religion has been done. Theological work is not merely the complement of historico-critical study but its goal and its meaning, in that the books of the Bible are not mere historical sources but depositions of faith, writings written from faith and addressing themselves to faith. Insofar as the writings of the Old and New Testaments are theological sources, only theological exegesis can do full justice to them. Faith starts from the position that in these human words it is not only men but God himself who has spoken, that we are here concerned not only with human words but with the word of God.

The last three decades have seen the appearance of a mass of studies in Biblical theology, especially in Germany and France, in which the historico-critical method is applied theologically, and which enter into lively discussion (including a large measure of agreement) with corresponding Protestant works. The work of J. Bonsirven, L. Cerfaux, J. Guillet, C. Spicq, P. van Imschoot, M. Meinertz, K. H. Schelkle, H. Schlier and R. Schnackenburg can be mentioned here as representative of many more.

The call to a theological understanding of Scripture was sounded from a quite different direction by those French theologians such as H. de Lubac, J. Daniélou and L. Bouyer, who approached it from a deepened understanding of the Fathers of the Church. The Patristic revival, especially in France, would call for a chapter in itself: it is displayed not only in an abundance of Patristic works (such as the outstanding theological series *Théologie* and *Unam Sanctam*) but also in new commentaries and editions of texts (*Sources chrétiennes* and the vast sourcework *Corpus Christianorum*, which is expected to run to 175 large volumes in its Latin series alone). A new world of theology, full of vitality, depth and closeness to its origins has been opened up before the eyes of theologians too long accustomed to deriving their problems and solutions solely from neo-scholasticism. When exegetes were called upon from this direction to penetrate the "spiritual sense" of Scripture, the demand was not meant, by the leading minds in the movement, as a belittling of the historico-critical method or of the literal sense, but rather as a call for a penetration of the fullness of God's word in human words. The Biblical revival and the Patristic revival, historico-critical exegesis and theological exegesis, must not be separated one from the other.

Catholic exegesis, with the other theological disciplines in its train, has made great strides in recent decades towards an understanding with Protestant theology. On the other hand it must still be recognized that Protestant exegesis maintains its lead (Catholic exegesis has produced nothing on a par with the many volumes of that great work of Protestant exegesis, the *Wörterbuch zum Neuen Testament,* edited by Gerhard Kittel) and to a large extent provides Catholic exegesis with its problems, its methods and its solutions. This applies especially to the problems, so much disputed among European exegetes today, of "form criticism" and "demythologizing," and to the whole question of "existential interpretation" in Rudolf Bultmann's sense.

III The Church and the World

The layman has in general no idea of how extensive and complex theology is and how long this survey would have to be if every important discipline were to be given any treatment at all. What a great deal, for instance, has been done in *church history,* which again includes a number of specialist disciplines—history of dogma and theology, archaeology, history of art, iconography, hagiography, religious folklore, provincial and diocesan history, missionary history! Despite ever increasing specialization, the urge towards synthesis has been making itself felt since the war. The work of pulling together the material, yielded by countless pieces of close research, on the early centuries, the Middle Ages and the modern period is being done chiefly in great collaborative multivolume histories of the Church, such as the projected twenty-six volumes of the Fliche-Martin *Histoire de l'Eglise* in France, and in Germany the *Handbuch der Kirchengeschichte,* edited by H. Jedin. A five-volume history of the Church by an international body of contributors has been announced, which will appear simultaneously in German, English, French and Dutch, and subsequently in Italian and Spanish. Among important works of synthesis, besides a revision of the history of the Popes by F. X. Seppelt, there have appeared in particular books on individual Ecumenical Councils: Chalcedon (A. Grillmeier and H. Bacht), Florence (J. Gill) and Trent (H. Jedin). The announcement of the Second Vatican Council brought about an intensification of work on conciliar history, with interest strongly concentrated, of late, on the Ecumenical Council of Constance, representing as it does, against the background of conciliar theory, the opposite pole to that represented by Vatican I and its definition of papal primacy. Here too we see the connection, which has lately been receiving increased attention, between church history and doctrine concerning the Church (ecclesiology), which is the central theological theme of the Second Vatican Council.

It is when we turn to the field of systematic theology that post-war theological writing in Europe breaks all manageable bounds. Even if we had very much more space than is available here, it would not suffice to give even a moderately adequate survey of the work that has been done, for instance, in the traditional tractates of dogmatics: on the doctrine of God in general, the doctrine of creation, Christology and the doctrine of redemption, ecclesiology and sacramental doctrine, eschatology. . . .* Themes in fundamental theology (such as revelation, Scripture and tradition, the historical Jesus, the credibility of the Church and the teaching office, etc.) and in moral theology (ethics grounded in the Bible or in the natural law; law and conscience; situation-ethics and norm-ethics; and also questions of sexual morality and birth control, war and peace, atomic weapons, etc.) have also been receiving particular emphasis in current discussion.

On the negative side, we must observe that there still persists a great lack of studies in the history of dogma and theology in all fields. Catholic theology has still not achieved a comprehensive presentation of the history of dogma to take its place beside the great Protestant histories of A. von Harnack, R. Seeberg and F. Loofs. The *Handbuch der Dogmengeschichte* by M. Schmaus, J. R. Geiselmann and A. Grillmeier, which began publication in 1951, is exclusively concerned with tracing the history of individual dogma, but it has so far hardly got past the beginnings. Yet Catholic theology does possess today, in this very field of history of dogma, some extraordinarily helpful theological *encyclopedias*. Besides the projected seven volumes of the French encyclopedia *Catholicisme* (1948 ff) and the *Dictionnaire de Théologie Catholique* (monumental, but already out of date in many respects, especially exegesis), begun in 1923 and completed in 1950, we must single out as a magnificent achievement of European theology the soon to be

---

* Since it it not possible here to cite individual works, we will list the following names which represent centers of energy in European systematic theology since the war, particularly in the ecumenical dialogue: Karl Adam, Roger Aubert, Heinrich Bacht, Hans Urs von Balthasar, Louis Bouyer, Marie-Dominique Chenu, Yves Congar, Jean Daniélou, Georges Dejaifve, Christoph Dumont, Pierre Fransen, Heinrich Fries, Josef Rupert Geiselmann, Aloys Grillmeier, J. C. Groot, Robert Grosche, Jérôme Hamer, Hubert Jedin, Josef Andreas Jungmann, Otto Karrer, M. J. Le Guillou, Peter Lengsfeld, Joseph Lortz, Henri de Lubac, Gérard Philips, W. H. van de Pol, Karl Rahner, Joseph Ratzinger, Olivier Rousseau, Thomas Sartory, Henricus Schillebeeckx, Gottlieb Söhngen, Pierre Teilhard de Chardin, Gustave Thils, Maurice Villain, Hermann Volk, Wilhelm de Vries.

completed ten-volume *Lexikon für Theologie und Kirche* (Second edition, edited by J. Höfer and K. Rahner, 1957 ff), which is in all respects the equal of such corresponding Protestant works as *Religion in Geschichte und Gegenwart* and *Evangelisches Kirchenlexikon*.

The subject matter of the new problems in systematic theology, which seems to be operating in a tension between the two focal points of the Church and the world, is something with which we cannot deal in this survey. We can only give a few categories to indicate the questions which are being vigorously disputed today:

The idea of the Church. What exactly is the Church: a supernatural officialdom or an amorphous union of religious individuals, something set up by God or a free association of believers? To what extent is it the People of God, the Body of Christ, built up in the Holy Spirit, the community of believers? What is the relation between the People of God of the New Covenant and that of the Old Covenant? To what extent is the Church, united though she is with Christ, yet not identical with her Lord and Head but ever subordinate to him and his Gospel? To what extent does the unity of the Church include diversity and multiplicity? What is meant by catholicity as adapted to the various peoples, races, cultures, mentalities and languages within the one Church? What is the theological relationship between the individual community and the universal Church? To what extent does the holy Church, being a Church of human beings, manifest herself constantly as a sinful Church? Why is reform of the Church an ever recurrent necessity? Which Church is truly the apostolic Church? Why are absolutism and totalitarianism contradictions of the image of the Church in the New Testament? What is the meaning of freedom in the Church and in theology? Who belongs to the Church? What is the theological character of the relationship of the Catholic Church to the other Christian churches? What is the significance of the historical character of the Church? What is essential and what nonessential in the Church, her teaching and her constitution? To what extent does the Church proclaim God's kingdom and to what extent is she herself (in her waiting, praying, pilgrim state) still *not* God's kingdom?

Ecclesiastical office. To what extent is the Church a society with a definite kind of structure? Whence does she derive her structure? What is the right way of understanding order in the Church? What is the relation between the Church of law and the Church of love? Why does there need to be ecclesiastical office? What is the distinction between those who bear office today and the apostles? Whence do they derive their authority? To what extent are those who hold office representatives of their communities? To what extent is ecclesiastical office the basis not of a ruling class, not of a special status in the Church, but of a special form of service to the Church? Is every development that has appeared within the structure of the Church's hierarchy a matter of divine law belonging indissolubly to the essence of the apostolic office? What is a bishop? What, theologically, is the relationship between the offices of a bishop and of a priest? What is the significance of the Petrine office as a service to the universal Church? Why do we need a Pope? What is the relationship between the Petrine office and the bishop's office? Why must there be no devaluation or depletion of either of these by the other? Why is it that the episcopal office has been declining, relatively to the Papacy, and now needs revaluing? How is the individual bishop related to the college of bishops, and the college of bishops to the Pope? How far must we distinguish between the need for a center in the Church and ecclesiastical centralism, between the Pope and papalism? How far do there exist, alongside the offices in the Church, free charisms which must not be extinguished by office? What is the significance of the prophetical element in the Church today? What is the relation between authority and conscience, authority and freedom?

The laity. How far are the laity not merely an appendage of the Church but the Church itself? How far is the relationship of office to laity in the Church *not* simply the relationship of government to subjects? What are the rights of the laity in the Church? What are the tasks of the laity in the Church and in the world? How is their task of serving the Church and the world carried out in terms of witness and confession? How far are the laity the universal priesthood? In what way do they share in the priesthood, kingship and prophetical office of Christ? How far do they all enjoy "spiritual" status? How far do they share in the mission of the Church? What responsibility does the layman bear, as a Christian, for the world? How far are the laity the realization and representation of the Church in the world? Where is the line to be drawn between what lies in the competence of the clergy and what lies in the competence of the laity? Is there a specifically lay piety, lay spirituality? What does it mean to live in the world according to the gospel?

Development of dogma. What is a dogma and what is its meaning? Are dogmas of faith an end in themselves: is definition (that is, delimitation) to be done for definition's sake or for the sake of defending the Church? How is a formula of belief itself affected by the defensive, polemical character of such a formulation? How far can we distinguish between the content and the form, the substance and the vesture of a dogma? How far is the Church's dogma binding on each individual in the Church in a way that cannot apply to the opinion of any theologian? How, within dogma, is the individual Christian's freedom of conscience safeguarded? How far is the Church's dogma an entirely human formulation, and so, like all human statements of the faith, as Paul says, fragmentary, partial and obscure? How far can the one faith be expressed by varying, differing and occasionally even contradictory formulas? What is the relevance of the human and historical character of formulas of belief to the concept of the Church's "infallibility"? What, in the light of the real dialectic between truth and error in the human sphere, is meant by this difficult concept? What is meant by the concepts of heresy and schism? Can they be used today in just the same way as they were before the great Eastern Schism and the Protestant Reformation? Is the function of heresies exclusively negative? What bearing do dogmas have on the unity of the Church?

Understanding of the world. What is the relationship between the Church and the world? What is the relationship of the Christian to the things of this world? What is meant by "the world," anyway? What meaning do the accounts of the creation of the world and of man have in the age of science? What part is played by miracle in our faith? What relevance do the findings of comparative religion have to theology? What is the relation of the Church to the great world religions? How can the principle "Outside the Church no salvation" be meaningfully expounded today? What has theology to say about the evolution of the cosmos, of life, of man? How are we to characterize the relationship of the Christian to matter and to technology? What is his relationship to the body and sexuality? What is the future of man and the cosmos? What is the significance of Christ as the beginning, the center and the end of time? What can the return of Christ and the consumation of the world mean to us today? What is meant by God's lordship over the world? What is meant by "the coming of the Kingdom of God?" How are theology and cosmology, theology and myth related to each other? What is the relationship between revelation and history?

IV Problems of Protestant Theology

If one looks through these questions, to which a great many others could be added, what strikes one is that they express problems not only of Catholic but equally of Protestant theology. Many of them would perhaps be posed by a Protestant theologian in a different way and with a different orientation. But the discovery that is being experienced more and more clearly, despite all difficulties, in European theology is this: the basic questions, even when they are looked at from two different sides, are common to us both; we have also to seek in common for common solutions. Naturally, a Catholic theologian's assessment of the situation takes more account of the position in the Catholic world; sometimes, because of the movements taking shape as a result of the Second Vatican Council, the Catholic Church occupies a special position in the center of general interest. But in the sections we have had here on renewal of the liturgy, concentration on Scripture, and problems of the Church and the world, we have been dealing with questions and problems which are questions and problems for the Protestant world as well. At least as intensive work is being done on solutions to these problems in Protestant as in Catholic theology, if with different emphases. This applies equally to exegesis and to church history, to systematic and to practical theology. Since what has been happening since the war, especially in Protestant exegesis and church history, and largely in systematic theology as well, has not been so much a matter of new departures as of progress in a long-established scholarly tradition—consider, for instance, the great Protestant commentaries on the Old and New Testaments—it is not necessary in this survey to go into too much detail on individual scholarly contributions.

The newly begun postwar Catholic-Protestant dialogue, for which the foundations were laid in the bitter experiences shared under National Socialism and the Second World War, has brought to both sides the joy of discovering that today it is possible for Catholics and Protestants to talk together about many things which formerly could not be discussed; that dispute no longer arises today over many things which formerly gave rise to it; that we can understand each other over many things today on which understanding formerly seemed impossible. Consider—to take just one example—the doctrine of the justification of the sinner, widely regarded in Protestant theology and in the Evangelical Church as *articulus stantis et cadentis Ecclesiae,* and advanced again by Karl Barth, for instance, with the utmost polemical fury against the Council of Trent, the Council of the Counter-Reformation: now there has been a Catholic discussion with Karl Barth, marked by understanding and penetration, which has shown that between the Catholic doctrine of justification, rightly understood, and Barth's doctrine there are no differences *such as need cause a division of churches;* and Barth himself has acknowledged this result. Must it not be possible to achieve over other difficult points at issue the same result as has been achieved over the doctrine of justification? On both the Protestant and the Catholic sides there is today all the readiness that is needed to carry on the discussion both critically and constructively.

Protestant theology in postwar Europe is still dominated, as before, by two names acting as two poles within one field of force, no third star of comparable attraction and brilliance having yet manifested itself beside them: Karl Barth and Rudolf Bultmann. The Lutheran renaissance, which rediscovered Luther and his doctrine of justification at the beginning of this century (J. Ficker, K. Holl), in spite of producing notable names and important achievements (P. Althaus, P. Brunner, W. Elert, H. J. Iwand, E. Schlink), has not established itself visibly in postwar theology to the same extent. But it is by no means to be overlooked that this strict Lutheran theology has had a very strong influence both at parish level and in church leadership, and finally in the World Council of Churches; and that it has also been particularly active in engaging in the Catholic-Protestant dialogue.

The name of Karl Barth* stands for the rejection of the basic principles of that theological liberalism which dominated the nineteenth century in systematic theology from F. Schleiermacher to A. Ritschl and A. von Harnack and in exegesis from D. F. Strauss to J. Wellhausen and H. Gunkel—not, indeed, without making impressive achievements in the field of historico-critical study. The catastrophe of the First World War, which marks the beginning of the twentieth century in theology, meant the collapse of

---

* Born in Bâle in 1886, Karl Barth studied at Berne, Berlin, Tübingen and Marburg. He emerged from the university as a liberal theologian and in 1909 was pastor in a parish in Geneva. In 1911 he became pastor at Safenwil, where he experienced not only the pressing nature of the social question but also the dire state of preaching. These experiences during the First World War impelled him to a new look at the whole of theology: in 1919 he published his *Römerbrief*, second edition 1922 (*Epistle to the Romans*, translated from the 6th edition, Oxford, 1933). He held professorships at various German universities, and finally at Bâle. After the production of various works, great and small, in 1932 Barth published the first volume of his *Kirchliche Dogmatik*, which marks the beginning of a new period in his theology. Eleven parts have appeared so far on Prologemena or doctrine of the word of God, doctrine of God (doctrine of predestination and foundation of ethics), doctrine of creation, doctrine of reconciliation; the last volume appeared in 1959. Still to appear are one volume on reconciliation and volumes on ethics and eschatology. The parts that have appeared so far run to about 10,000 pages. (English edition: Vol. 1, parts 1 and 2 [Doctrine of the Word of God], Vol. 2, parts 1 and 2 [Doctrine of God], Vol. 3, parts 1–4 [Doctrine of Creation], Vol. 4, parts 1–3 [Doctrine of Reconciliation], Edinburgh, 1936–1962.) The best known theologians of Barth's school are H. Diem, H. Gollwitzer, E. Thurneysen, O. Weber and E. Wolf. A special position alongside Barth must be allotted to the Zurich dogmatic theologian Emil Brunner.

rationalist self-confidence, optimism and belief in progress. The time was ripe for a theology which would once more confront man radically with God's revelation: God's revelation, which man cannot construct for himself but which comes to him as an event from without by God's word in Christ. The hidden God is here recognized as the utterly Other, the God who justifies sinful man. To this God and his word which is judgment there is nothing that corresponds on man's side but faith alone. Karl Barth's *Römerbrief* with its theology of revelation was nothing short of a bomb exploded under the theologians who had been busying themselves with moral idealism and pietist individualism, with "natural theology", and the quest for the "historical Jesus." Jesus Christ now appears as the "paradox of faith." Historico-critical exegesis is not rejected but it is pushed back within its limits: what is called for is a theological understanding of the Biblical message, which is to be applied to men of the present day. The original demands of the Reformation are taken up and asserted once more, albeit by a mind that has passed through the school of Plato and Kant, Dostoievski and Kierkegaard, Overbeck and Nietzsche.

This emphatic reassertion of the infinite difference between God and man, against the liberal leveling out of God and man on the same plane, this "crisis theology," or "dialectical theology," was not Barth's last word. He has indeed maintained the basic intentions which were his from the beginning: he is, as ever, concerned with the sovereignty of God, his revelation, his word. In the churches' fight against the Nazi régime, Barth's theology proved a strong support to the Christian resistance. Back in his native Switzerland after his banishment from Nazi Germany, Barth devoted decades of tireless labor in exegesis, history of dogma and systematic theology to the production of his vast *Kirchliche Dogmatik,* that magnificent and comprehensive work which stands alone in Protestant theology of the twentieth century as Schleiermacher's *Glaubenslehre* did in the nineteenth. In comparison with his original "dialectical theology" a complex new orientation has made its appearance: instead of a somewhat abstract consideration of God's sovereignty in language with a strong philosophical coloring, a christocentric synthesis emerges orientated in Christ towards the concrete word of God; the sharp denigration of the created order has been succeeded by a new appreciation of God's good creation; together with God's divinity, God's humanity in Christ is also seen; God's revelation in Christ does not extinguish all other sources of knowledge but illuminates them. Karl Barth's *Dogmatik* is not yet finished. It is to be hoped that it will be granted to him to write that part which still remains, the "Doctrine of the Last Things," not, like Thomas Aquinas, in heaven, but here on earth.

Parallel in time with the development of Barth's theology, the school of *form criticism** has been carrying on the work on exegetical problems produced in the nineteenth and early twentieth centuries by the school of historical criticism and comparative religion. Building on the achievements of H. Gunkel and J. Wellhausen regarding literary forms and chronology, K. L. Schmidt, M. Dibelius and R. Bultmann have investigated the preliterary processes in the formation of the traditions whose precipitate is found in the gospels. Before the gospels there was the gospel, the kerygma, which took shape in various traditions. The written gospels are the result of this oral preaching of the faith. They are thus not simply historical or biographical documents about Jesus of Nazareth, they are testimonies of the faith of the primitive Church concerning this Jesus as the Christ. What was constructively put forward as a program by Dibelius has been worked out analytically by Bultmann, starting from the totality of the material provided by tradition: the shape of the history of the individual fragments, the small units, in the gospel traditions.

The method of form criticism has proved useful not only in classifying the material and investigating the history of the *form* of the tradition, but also in investigating the *content* of that tradition. Rudolf Bultmann† has here decisively broken fresh ground. Right at the beginning, Bultmann joined with Karl Barth in his

---

* Karl Ludwig Schmidt, *Der Rahmen der Geschichte Jesu* (Berlin, 1919); Martin Dibelius, *Die Formgeschichte des Evangeliums* (Tübingen, 1919); Rudolf Bultmann, *Die Geschichte der synoptischen Tradition* (Göttingen, 1921).

† Rudolf Bultmann, born in Wiefelstede (Oldenburg) in 1884, has been professor at Marburg since 1921. Bultmann's theology, strongly influenced by the thought of Kierkegaard and Heidegger, rests firmly on an extraordinarily wide basis of exegetical and historical learning. His chief works, all of which are highly influential, show the whole imposing range of his theological scholarship and interests: his great work of research in form criticism, *Die Geschichte der synoptischen Tradition* (Göttingen, 1921), his *Jesus-Buch* (Tübingen, 1926), his exegetical commentary on the gospel of John (Göttingen, 1941), his study in comparative religion, *Das Urchristentum im Rahmen der antiken Religionen* (Zurich, 1949; *Primitive Christianity in its contemporary setting*, Toronto, 1956); and, crowning his whole work, *Die Theologie des Neuen Testamentes* (Tübingen, 1953; *Theology of the New Testament*, New York, 1955). Fundamental to any understanding of demythologizing and existential interpretation is Bultmann's hermeneutical program as set out in his essay *Neues Testament und Mythologie*, in *Offenbarung und Heilsgeschichte*, Volume 7 (Munich, 1941). Bultmann's initiatives are being followed up—sometimes in highly critical discussions with the master—by G. Bornkamm, H. Braun, G. Ebeling, H. Conzelmann, E. Fuchs and E. Käsemann.

protest against liberal theology and the hunt for the life of Jesus. He too declared for a living understanding of revelation, for its existential power and stature, and for the necessity of an unconditioned, undemonstrable faith, without foundation outside itself, in God's decisive act in Christ. But whereas for Barth what comes more and more to the fore is, in the event of revelation, the one who reveals himself—in the act of revelation, the God who acts; in the Christ-event, the person of Jesus Christ; in the act, the content of revelation—in Bultmann there is a radicalization of the actualism itself: revelation, the word of God, remains a pure event, in which all that is important is the That, never the Who or the What. The person of Christ disappears behind the Christ-event, faith as the content of belief behind faith as act, as consummation, the consummation of existence.

Every utterance of the New Testament is aimed ultimately at the consummation of man's existence. Bultmann is convinced that the mythical picture of the world and the mythical salvation-event which are superimposed in the New Testament on the actual proclamation, the kerygma, are something which modern man, with his scientific habits of thought, can no longer be expected to accept. Man can no longer conceive of the world as a three-story structure of heaven, earth and hell; nor can he enter into the New Testament belief in demons or the ascension. If the New Testament kerygma is still to find belief today it will have to be understood afresh, *translated* into the modern world picture and modern man's understanding of himself. The negative formulation of this is "demythologizing": the mythological elements in the New Testament are to be not simply excised but interpreted unmythologically; this is called for by the nature of myth and of the New Testament itself. The same idea is expressed positively as "existential interpretation": the mythological concepts of the New Testament must be interpreted existentially; that is, not objectivized in the sense of ideas but interpreted in that sense of man's understanding of his existence which lies at the heart of the myths.

Bultmann's demand for a translation of the New Testament kerygma into this modern age is one that no serious theologian will deny; he will, on the contrary, take it very seriously indeed. There can be no doubt that the liberation of modern theology from notions of the world and of humanity which belong to antiquity and to the Middle Ages has not gone far enough, either in exegesis or dogmatics or preaching or catechesis. But the question which is being violently disputed in Europe, the question which has given rise to the most passionate theological debates of the postwar period, is this: Are not demythologizing and existential interpretation, as proposed and carried out by Bultmann on the basis of certain philosophical positions taken over from Heidegger and of a hypercritical skepticism in regard to the sources, leading to a substantial truncating and emptying out of the New Testament kerygma?

But here we must call a halt. We have only been able to deal with a few questions, briefly, generally, and in rough outline; many more remain. But the account given here, incomplete though it is, should be enough to show that there is a "new Europe," full of spiritual vitality, fertility and energy, in theology and the Church as much as elsewhere. But it should also have shown, equally clearly, that this new theological Europe cannot suffice to solve all the questions and problems that have broken out: that it must look more than ever for intellectual help and scholarly support to the rest of the world—to America, and, in a different way, to Asia and Africa. If European theology is to go on working fruitfully in the Church for the world, it cannot afford, any more than anything else, to overlook the fact that this has become one world.

ERIC WEIL

Philosophical and Political Thought in Europe Today

WHAT is going on in European political and philosophical thinking? The question looks as natural as natural could be. Can it be answered? Of course, it can: as the Schoolmen said, and quite rightly, from the reality of a thing you can always infer that the thing is possible; and articles, books, talks, lectures on The Present Situation are offered everywhere. But is there an objective answer, an answer whose truth can be proved in the ordinary ways of proving a point, a thesis, a theory? Where are the facts, the documents, and, above all, where is that consensus which constitutes and expresses what we are used to call truth? Maybe such an objective approach could be found; we might try to analyze books, articles, declarations, we could measure their relative importance, for example, by comparing selling figures, audio-visual appeal, student preferences for this or that teacher, this or that subject, and so on. But unfortunately all these means would not be of much help. People who are in the public eye as a rule belong to generations not educated during the period under review, books need a long time, not only before they are written and printed, but also before they start to act, and tests are particularly suspect in a field where values fundamental for those who believe in them must be proclaimed and must become, before they are proclaimed, what they ordinarily are not, that is, conscious.

It is probably true of all history which pretends to something more than chronological tables and sound calendars of state and other papers that, even ideally, it cannot attain objectivity in the meaning the term has in the so-called exact sciences; in any case, the thesis would apply to present-day "history" and, signally so, to the "history" of present thought. The argument is old, and it has very often been overstated: if there is no total objectivity in history, there is a concept and there are criteria of lack of objectivity, of falseness, of pious and other frauds; it suffices to show in any given case that relevant facts and phenomena have been left out, misrepresented, wrongly appreciated, etc. To do that is the task and content of discussion. The present author hereby admits that he wants above all to start such a discussion. Nobody knows his time, but nobody will ever know anything about it unless discussion brings out what it is and is not; in other words, unless somebody begins to propose something, although he knows quite well the limits of his, and even of all possible knowledge in this field.

A first view of the European scene will unavoidably leave the impression, at least as far as the Continent is concerned, that nothing has changed since the last war, or even since the last years before the war. Marx and Freud remain heroes and leaders, Husserl and Heidegger are being discussed everywhere, Nietzsche and Kierkegaard exert an ever growing influence. The momentum of this influence stems from prewar days, and it is far from being spent; even existentialism, whatever that term may mean, could easily be considered as nothing but an offspring of rather old families. Religious, economical, social problems—there is no lack of them and they certainly are not forgotten and repressed. But excepting the first bubbling years after hostilities had come to an end, there is an astonishing absence of things new and felt as new. It would be difficult, unless one would want to put in this line the first books of Sartre and Camus in France, to quote one single work which has had the decisive influence of, for instance, Wittgenstein's *Tractatus*, Heidegger's *Time and Being*, even Bergson's *Two Sources of Morals and Religion*, the work of the Vienna Circle, or, in another field, the publications of Durckheim, Pareto, Max Weber, Keynes. The old great men, living or dead, dominate the scene to such an extent that the only new, relatively new, movement, existentialism in its French form, is receding before older, sometimes very old, currents. Existentialism survives only in the field of political discussion, a field whose structures are characterized and determined by other concepts, other vectors, other problems than those of existentialism proper. No young man is really interested in knowing if his comrades are existentialists; what he wants to know is if they are Marxists or not, and if Marxists, if they are "orthodox" Communists or "deviationists" and "revisionists," if they put their trust in planning and social organizing, if they are believing and practicing Christians and, if so, if they think they can be at the same time real Christians and real "progressives" and/or real Freudians.

That is the way it looks at first. But nobody who has known Europe before 1939 will be able to suppress an uneasy feeling before such a statement. Something is changed; what is it? The best word, if any single word can be sufficient, might be *demythization*.

The term has originated in the theological field, and its meaning has to be slightly modified for our purpose, since in the land of its origin it signifies the attempt to free the Christian tradition from contents which, "natural" in their time, have become inadmissible for the "scientific" thinking of our contemporaries, but whose religious significance can be maintained as opposed to their, for us, magical or mythical form. In this strict sense the concept could not possibly be applied to philosophical and political thinking. Theories do not rely on events, and when they are abandoned they grow "obsolete," "narrow," "only partially true," and so forth; but on the other hand they can loose what one may well call their mythical appeal, the place they occupy as the bottom layer of value systems, as the last presuppositions, the axioms wherefrom all other values are established or refused, all other theorems deduced, and which, quite evidently, are neither in need or capable of demonstration. The "big theories" have lost this kind of appeal. Everybody is a Marxist if somebody is a Marxist simply because he insists on the paramount importance of economical, social, historical factors, or does not think that preaching alone will heal or hide the ills of this world; but there are not many left whose whole life is guided by the star of transhistorical hope. And the same applies in other cases.

It would be tedious to dress a list of all the creeds, theories, value systems which have suffered this fate, this dreary fate, if you look at it through the eyes of a "true" believer. Anyhow, we shall have to mention different developments of this kind, and their meaning. Generally speaking, though, it is everywhere the same thing: ideals are not dead, they are not even forgotten, certainly not repudiated; but rare are the people who act on them. They sometimes make themselves felt in a negative manner: I can't do this, I can't admit of that, because my whole way of thinking (and in most cases, it would be better to say "my whole past") goes against it. But conversions are exceptional, and so are splits and schisms of any importance. True, there have been and always are schismatic tendencies in the Communist movements of western Europe. It concerns mainly the intellectual fringe of the Party; and it is less directed against the fundamental tenets than against their dogmatic interpretation by the authorities of the church (which authorities, by the way, don't hesitate to call one another schismatic and heretical). The phenomenon could be compared to one of these squabbles among specialists—as they happen, for example, between different denominations of psychoanalysts, anthropologists, economists—were it not that there is a very real Communist church, or some such churches, all of them gifted not only with good strong voices, but also with good strong teeth which they are not afraid of using.

There is no real danger when you leave the Italian or French Party, but in other places such betrayal would be rather bad for you: the consequence is that even outside the pale when people protest they feel like heroic and slightly anxious Luthers.

There is then no deep or general yearning after martyrdom. It might be said that there never was: a martyr is somebody who suffers because suffering is the only means he has to further his party. The objection is quite pertinent, but it does not refute the thesis, it confirms it. If there are no martyrs, the reason is that there is not much persecution. The people who could persecute other people don't like to do it and are afraid that martyrs might once again sow positive convictions. They prefer to act on the assumption, very rarely belied, that opinions do not matter for them as long as they don't trouble peace and order. And they don't as a rule. There have been cases, as during and after the fighting in Algeria; but on one side the convictions, old and traditional ones, meant something only to the most traditionalistic milieux and the uprooted, while on the other hand a group of romantic youngsters was torn between an extreme form of nationalism and a revolutionary pacifism ready to fight for other nations' nationalism.

But these are exceptions, and they are less inspired by dogmatic theories than by an antidogmatic revolt, unless they originate in the small and quickly disappearing traditionalistic circles. The results are sometimes quaint: General de Gaulle is probably a believer, and the people voted for him. But they did not vote for Greatness, Independence, World Politics; they liked the man who had ended the bad business of the Algerian war, had subdued the (religiously) nationalistic army officers, and established order and sound finances. If it is a question of creeds, the situation might be compared to the conditions prevailing after the Wars of Religion: at long last people had found out that convictions had to become personal affairs so that they might be kept out of the field of politics and social life. (Those who did not understand it, like Louis XIV, had to pay for it.) The comparison, as most comparisons, is only partially correct. There have been political earthquakes in Europe after the war, but no civil strife—not even the Hungarian uprising—for reasons of conviction. The fact is that governments, and not only in western Europe, do not go in for that sort of conflict, and contemporary public opinion, perhaps the greatest force in democratic countries, is not easily scandalized, not to say that it has become unscandalizable as long as it is a matter of creeds and opinions and teachings.

So there is no great desire or much opportunity for martyrdom of the dogmatic species. The restriction is important—of the dogmatic species—for it would be easy to find people going in for heroic deeds and self-sacrifice, but rather against orthodoxy as such, whatever its contents, than in favor of a new orthodoxy (we shall have to consider this phenomenon under the heading of existentialism). If what older generations called ideas and ideals are at stake, it would be hard to discover the kind of acting and fighting faith old Marxists possessed, or old liberals, agnostics, religious sectarians. The general feeling is that something can be said for every opinion, and something against it: the proof of the pudding is in the eating. The point is probably best illustrated by the lip-service paid to the poor old "last values" by *all* parties. Everybody is for freedom, justice, democracy, equality, progress, order; so people quite understandably ask themselves if this touching unanimity does not empty the hallowed words of all content and meaning. They prefer to discuss concrete proposals instead of ideas. There always are ideological families, but no Salvation Armies.

But ideological families do exist. They are even very much alive, in spite of demythization; if we don't live according to our convictions, our ideas will interest us all the more, to the point of forming the center of our intellectual occupations. That is quite understandable. On the one hand, we need something to occupy our minds; on the other, what has been called here demythization remains a new development.

The statement, though, needs some rather important qualifications. The development is new. In fact, it is the result far more of European reconstruction and construction than of the war. On the contrary, immediately after the war, during that period of social trouble, misery, starvation, new frontiers, violent or simply illegal changes of government, the mythic (or if you prefer the ideological) factor was probably more prevalent than it ever had been. And even if we think only of Europe's present face, it would not be true to say that "demythization" has been absolutely victorious: there are many people in France or Italy who believe in Communism, believe in the sense that they stick to the dogma as long as dogma is being talked about and live like most other people the remainder of their time (which explains that these countries have had no more, perhaps even less, and less grave, social unrest than countries where Communism is practically nonexistent). There are people in Germany who believe in economic liberalism in exactly the same way, protesting against state intervention on principle (and as long as it works rather in the other man's interest) and forget easily that their own business would not go so well if the state did not intervene all the time in order to protect them against crises and slumps and did not, to quote only one concrete example, maintain from public means the whole of agriculture and the corresponding part of buying power. There are even people who believe in monarchy for France, neo-naziism for Germany, a renascence of fascism for Italy. But then new things are new only as long as the old things are alive: nobody but a historian of science would call Galilei's physics new since the old physics has disappeared. Demythization is a new trend, which means that it is neither the only one nor, statistically, the dominating one; it is simply characteristic of our time as far as it is modern.

Even circumscribed in this way the thesis does not mean that the great words have lost every kind of appeal. "Reaction" remains always a bad thing, "progress," "liberty," "justice," "rationality" are good ones. The change lies elsewhere. It consists simply in this, that not many people in Europe would follow a leader who promises them freedom or justice or whatever else without telling them in what precisely the new freedom or the greater justice would consist. Europeans have become wary; not of words, but of what the man who uses them really does mean—"really" meaning practically. What they want is not so much liberty or greatness or abstract equality; they are out for better living standards, freer access to cultural goods, more security for their families and for their old age. A good proof can be found in the recent attitudes of the two biggest international (or supranational) forces, the Communist movement and the Roman Catholic Church. The Roman Catholic Church insists more and more on the necessity of positive relations with other denominations, on the importance of social problems, and on the need for ways to penetrate social strata which have lost, if they ever had, every relation to the faith and its representatives. The Communists, at least the European kind (and in this context Russia is a part of Europe) proclaim more and more clearly, even emphatically, the necessity of material, in contradistinction to ideological, motivations and incentives, to the point that in Mr. Khrushchev's eyes the struggle between the two big world systems comes to a simple competition in efficiency. The victory of his system is unavoidable in his view, not because the stars or the course of History (with a capital H) have preordained that outcome, but because his way will lead to the production of more and more goods at ever lower prices in human toil and privations and will so convince all convincible people and simply outbid the people who refuse to see, not at all the absolute truth of Communism, but what is good and profitable for them and theirs.

If this is true of movements whose very origin and fundament has always been the conviction that they possess *the* truth and which have succeeded because they were, nothwithstanding facts, able to convince their adherents that they were right, if one may say so, *essentially,* if their leaders speak in this manner (the NCO's, as always, are often a bit slow), it is not surprising if other organizations have dropped their last ideological drapings. Of revolutionary syndicalism there remains nothing outside some parts of Spain, and the often small differences on points of dogma which separate every ideological party from its neighbors to the left and to the right don't play an important part in political life any more. It may be tactics if the French Socialists and Communists are not refusing a priori every kind of understanding with the defenders of denominational schools; if Italian left wing socialists are favoring a government which supports the European Common Market and NATO; if German Social-Democrats have practically renounced, perhaps not their whole Marxist credo, but at least its revolutionary implications and do not consider as impossible political collaboration with Christian Democrats; if the Holy See does not refuse all contact with unholy Moscow. All that may be tactics, as well as the recent offer by the French Communist Party of an alliance with the Socialists even if a Socialist government stuck to the Atlantic Alliance and went on working for a unified Europe. It may be tactics, but it would be quite a remarkable coincidence if no deeper changes were at work behind this identity of tactics; and it would be impossible to explain the still more important fact that these tactics are being followed by the people, which would scarcely be the case if they seemed inadmissible to them.

Considered under this angle, the situation looks as if a new kind of "Americanization" were taking place, not simply the old one of more and more efficiency, more and more productivity, better and better living standards, but another one, on an ideological, or rather anti-ideological level. Political thought is becoming increasingly realistic, governments are judged not according to their fidelity to the faith but according to their results; political parties are no more parties in the continental sense of the word but are changing into that type of indeterminate associations which Americans know under that name: rather different families than different thoughts, rather different ways of going to the same end than a difference of ends, rather a question of temperament and tradition—what the English, with a term unfortunately dropped by our political language, called a "connection." Even political thought and thought on politics seem to follow American precedent: the same kind of scientific, statistical analysis; the same patient, painstaking, efficient group work; the same sticking to particular events and factors ("the elections of . . . ," "the political geography of . . . ," "political choices and income groups, religious convictions, instruction," "mass media and their influence," "decision making," and so on and so forth); the same shyness before subjects like "the State," "Society," "Authority" if they are taken quite generally (or philosophically); the same absence of new gospels and new utopias; the same down-to-earth realism.

All that is perfectly true. But, as it happens so often, the same phenomena are the result of very different forces, and their significance, for that reason, is not the same here and there. Americans, above all when they are looking at European "intellectuals" and ideological movements, are priding themselves upon their sense for realities and for really relevant issues. Europeans, as a rule, are rather ashamed if they have to come down to facts, statistics, practical questions—to the level, in other words, where compromise is a natural necessity. In fact, at least in the present writer's opinion, European realism, though hidden, perhaps because hidden, goes far deeper than the American species. Not only words and ideas, but those fundamental attitudes which seem to influence very strongly American opinion and political life are without any effect in Europe. Nowhere in Europe would the rule of law or the sacred character of the Constitution bring the people to their feet otherwise than for simple cheering; and even writers who, from deeply felt convictions, publish incendiary tracts in defense of individual rights would not be prepared to lead even a campaign of passive obedience (or disobedience), not in any case with the slightest hope of even relatively widespread support (there have been isolated cases, for example, in France during the Algerian trouble). Voluntary associations do of course exist, but the French or Italian factory and office worker does not like to pay dues (things are different in Germany, Belgium, the Netherlands, and the northern countries). Strikes are therefore rather numerous (and a nuisance) than long lasting and economically and technically formidable. On the one hand, it needs a lot of provocation, on the other, near desperation, to unleash a serious movement. The last big strikes in the Walloon part of Belgium and in the French coal fields found their strength in roots of a noneconomical nature and lasted because important parts of the nations and influential groups not directly involved supported the strikers morally and financially. But strictly political strikes are outdated, and the more than seven years of fighting in Algeria never permitted even the Communist Party to make an essential issue of this question and to militate in favor of "freedom for the oppressed," nor did the cry of "defense of the rights of France and of the French settlers" touch more than the settlers and part of the army. (The issue was a "moral" one for Italian and German writers far more than for political—as opposed to literary—opinion in France.) Examples could be multiplied *ad infinitum;* there has been no fight over de-

colonization in the European countries, none for national independence in the economical field (not even in the case of the "neutral"
countries), none over public ownership of industries or obligatory
health insurance. As long as things are going reasonably well people
worry in their declarations but are not prepared to pay from their
pockets for a "good cause," not even to vote for it as long as more
"serious" problems are coming up.

It may not be superfluous to say once more that all this does not
necessarily apply to all situations and to all people. It applies only
to what we may call the most modern parts of Europe and in its
different countries to the most advanced regions and social groups
(to whatever stratum of society these belong). It is a question of
trends, not of statistical facts, although statistics seem to confirm
the thesis. But even if only partially true, the description cries for
an explanation. How has it been possible that precisely Europe, the
mother country of all great political ideas and ideologies, has become what to an American could easily seem cynical?

The answer lies probably in the decisive difference between what
Americans on the one hand, Europeans on the other call "administration." In the United States, the term designates in fact the
government, preferably, if not exclusively, the federal government—
this government which at every election may change with all its
advisers, chief executives, ambassadors, leaving only in place certain technical services, such as the forestry or the engineering services, etc. In Europe, administration (*amministrazione, Verwaltung*)
is separated from the government and in principle, most of the time
in fact, is independent from it in its own sphere, the sphere of technical deliberation and preparation on one hand, of execution on the
other. It is politically neutral, which means as well that it is permanent
and protected against political intervention. (That such interventions, as well as other pressures, occur in fact, goes without saying,
but does not invalidate the rule of tenure, that is, independence. It
only leads to specific safeguards against administrative arbitrariness
and partisan attitudes.) Historically speaking, this type of "administration" has been built up from the seventeenth century onwards,
by the rulers in their fight against the feudal elements of their
societies, and has been transformed into a weapon against abso-
lutist princes and leaders when the bourgeoisie took over. Its
raison d'être, precisely because religious and ideological fighting
was so prevalent, was and is that there must be a space left for
technical discussion of technical questions and for technical solution
of political problems which do not give in to direct treatment by
prohibition, constraint, and force (the best instance is probably the

introduction of administrative and neutral social insurance in Germany by Bismarck during his political fight against the Social-Democrats). The basic decisions are up to the government; but it is, real crises excepted, the administration's task to formulate the questions, to indicate the presuppositions and consequences of all the possible choices, and to translate into concrete measures the decisions taken by the government.

It is evident that in its long history the administration has not always found favor with all parts. As long as it was royal, it was considered autocratic by the mounting industrial and commercial class; it was bourgeois in the eyes of the workers when they entered the field of political and social fight. The important point is that this distrust has disappeared. People, groups, parties may think and declare that the administration is not up to its tasks, that it ought to be reformed, streamlined, rejuvenated; but nobody would consider the possibility of abolishing the system or only of changing the personnel while maintaining the structure. Administrating has become a job for qualified men and, to a lesser degree (excepting in primary and secondary schools), women. Not only the postman and the railway worker (all of them state employees), but also a director in the ministry, let us say, of finance or public instruction, will do his job as well for a socialist as for a capitalistic government, or according to the orders of a minister with ecclesiastical leanings or to those of a free thinker. He might, of course, try to influence his political chief, in rare cases even to obstruct certain decisions which were in his judgment contrary rather to specific administrative traditions than to personal preferences (particularly if the impression is that administrative impartiality is at stake). But in the main, the system works according to its historical specifications.

The result has been that the citizen, consciously or without knowing it, has come to rely on administrative action and administrative help. In the main he has seldom been disappointed, while the disappointment has been profound for all who had put their trust in ideologies and purely political remedies. It is often forgotten that no revolution has taken place in Europe in the wake of the last war and that in every case where a new system of government and economy has superseded the old one, the event has nowhere been the result of spontaneous uprisings, but of foreign actions. The very rare revolts, unless appearances are misleading, were not meant to overthrow the established system, but were directed against its manners and methods. It is more than dubious that the East German workers and the Hungarians wanted to abolish state owenership in the means of production; they wanted better living and working conditions and more personal security against arbitrary political pressure. In other words, less of politics and more of neutral and competent administration.

The problems which preoccupy people, if this analysis is correct, are therefore in themselves of a technical, that is, administrative, nature. Life on every level has become, if not too complicated for understanding, in any case too complex for individuals and groups to handle it. Persons and pressure groups have their desires and complaints; but they do not go for direct action and do not think of helping themselves, being convinced that all problems hold together and can be solved only from the center, where a global view becomes possible. Direct action exists in situations which the interested people consider as desperate; but its end is to get a hearing by acquiring a sufficiently great nuisance value. The job itself has to be done and will be done not so much by the government, who no doubt decides, but above all by the administration, the people who really understand what it is all about and who alone are able to propose concrete measures.

This trust in administration has gained much, perhaps decisive, influence through the success of planning—planning openly called so, for example, in France, or at work under other names, of which the *ferrum ligneum* of *soziale Markwirtschaft* is probably the most enjoyable one. European conditions after the war were such that only centrally taken decisions could prevent a lasting, after a catastrophic, breakdown. The Marshall Plan was in fact the first step, and other kinds of planning, national, supranational, international have followed, all of them eminently successful. It would be astonishing if the results of this purely administrative action had not reacted on attitudes and outlook. The citizen and the interested groups do not so much want to look after their interests (private or group health insurance, for instance, when and where it plays any part, is only a supplement to obligatory insurances) as they try to get them acknowledged, rather by proclaiming that things are not as they ought to be than by insisting on their own positive proposals. No wonder if political ideologies and battles of principle are out of fashion.

The French have created a word for it: *dépolitisation*. The term could easily be misunderstood, if it were taken to mean that there are no politics any more. But it can be quite useful to characterize a development of the meaning of the word politics, from ideologies and the pursuit of absolute ends to the pursuit of limited objects. Now, such rather profound changes leave their traces in fields where they have not been willed, even in fields whose structure seems to be hostile to precisely this kind of transformation.

It has already been mentioned that recent European thinking in politics has not produced many ideas of general, philosophical pretensions. There remain certain not very numerous exceptions; but, significantly, they discuss classical theories in their present-day forms and rarely try to do independent research concerning the meaning and present importance of the old questions which lie at the bottom.

It is all the less of a wonder if one looks at the way the old game of politics is being played today. Politics is no more a noble enterprise, a thing great and valuable in itself; it is no more, to present another aspect of the same thing, in the hands of people who believe in greatness and fame. (There are some who do, General de Gaulle being the most important and the most conspicuous among them; but, as pointed out above, they are influential not because their faith is shared by the electorate but because the public considers them useful for its own, far from idealistic, purposes.) It has become a question of competent administration, or, to be more precise about it, of an administration which regards state and nation as going concerns and quite consciously applies business criteria to its work: they planify. No group believes in its own independence, above all on the economical level. A clear, understandable, far-looking coordination of all factors and forces is a necessity in everybody's view, and the blueprint for that has to be the work of an independent planning authority. Evidently there remains a place, and an important one, for political decisions: planners can do their job only when they know what they are planning for. But the reverse is true as well: if the choice of means depends upon the ends, ends depend no less on means and techniques. In that sense everything comes back to planning, and the budget, the real budget, is not any more a problem for specialists of finance and taxes, it is becoming more and more a part of an all-embracing kind of logistics, an account of real produce and forces, of material and intellectual riches, not simply of dollars and cents. The thing is not new, and money never was a value in itself. What is new is that everybody in Europe nowadays knows what for a long time was either a secret or the main content of heretical doctrines. Individual enterprise and competition have not come to a stop for that reason; it is rather the opposite, and planning very often is being conceived of as a necessary defense of competition. (It is curious to see how for years the U.S.S.R. has been doing everything to reintroduce competition between concerns, all of whom are state owned.) But industrialists, workers, peasants, merchants, not to mention state employees, do not rely on political programs; they are defending their interests in a continuous discussion with the planning authorities, with which they are sometimes in legally established permanent contacts. They turn to, or rather against, the political authorities only when they have the feeling that the planners have been unduly influenced by extratechnical considerations forced upon them by "politics" and have been prevented from doing their job the way they would have done it if not disturbed.

This is not the place to go into the organizational questions related to planning, nor to speak of the ever growing and changing possibilities and responsibilities of states whose role as owners of great parts of the industrial and, as in France, financial system is perhaps more important than most people at present understand. Nor is this the place to distinguish between the different forms of planning and public ownership and their relations in different countries. Sometimes, where both are relatively old, as in France, both are very visible. Sometimes planning may be hidden, let us say, under names of ministries of works or economics, etc. Sometimes, as in Germany, public ownership and control go without saying, while planning is being practiced and at the same time disavowed as a devilish contraption. Sometimes again, as in Great Britain, public ownership goes without modern (logistical in contradistinction to financial) planning control. This is not the place, either, to discuss the very complex and highly interesting interaction between private, national, international, and supranational planning. Suffice it then for the present purpose to observe that everywhere the gradual shifting of responsibility and power from political authorities to administrative instances has been and always is going on, a change manifest for instance in a situation like that after the breakdown of the Brussels discussions between Great Britain and the Common Market Organization. The "political" people themselves were most afraid of breaking up what had been built by the "executives" above or beneath politics, but anyhow outside of what was politics even after the end of the last war. Nations conceive of themselves as concerns which must be kept going by good management, and when they find out that they are not big enough and the best management cannot make them bigger than they are, they pool their resources with other firms and forget that for centuries they had fought or despised or disliked one another and even at present do not approve of their neighbors' way of eating, talking, working. These developments cannot but have their repercussions on the feelings, the attitudes and the ideas of our whole tradition and therefore on present-day thought, which they influence all the more since they are taken for self-evident and for granted. Not even the field of history of political thought is much being plowed, and there is a dearth on the Continent of good historical works on, for example, English and American political theory, practice, institutions.

It would seem only natural if the same applied in philosophy generally speaking, that special topics were being studied, positive and, in the widest possible meaning, positivistic attitudes carried the day; that, for instance, theory of science, logic and formalism on the one hand, precise historical inquiries of a learned, strictly scholarly character on the other predominated to the exclusion of general problems, metaphysical questions, moral worries. The exact opposite is the case. Profoundness is at a premium, even if skeptics may think that the profound can be as empty as the superficial, and even if the thinkers of the past are treated as contemporaries and forced to answer questions they probably would not have understood. There is next to no positivism except in Scandinavia, the Netherlands, Belgium, all of them strongly influenced by Great Britain (or rather England). But even there logical and linguistic analysis looks as if it were on its way out. Modern formalistic logic belongs to, and is considered more and more a part of, mathematics, and English philosophers in increasing numbers and of increasing weight seem to come to admit—the posthumous writings of Wittgenstein and the late Professor Austin's theory of *performative statements*, to quote only these names, are cases in point—that language cannot be studied in itself, but is related to attitudes and situations of a non-, or not essentially, linguistic character. At the same time metaphysics begins to lift up her head again, be it only in the guise of history of philosophy. It is perhaps significant that Professor Ayer, one of the most radical logical positivists, is editing a series, and a very good one at that, of books treating the great thinkers of the past for their intrinsic interest, not only to refute them.

This is not the only paradox in the situation. One would, things being what they are, look then for big "constructive" undertakings, for new "systems." There is not much of that either, or, more precisely, if and to the extent that it exists, it certainly does not prevail nor does it give the philosophical atmosphere its flavor. So the question will be asked: what is there?

It is not easy to give an answer, because the negative factors seem to be more important under these conditions than the positive ones; and it is difficult to characterize what there is *not*. Existentialism, to begin with it, was and remains, as far as it survives, a reaction against that kind of nineteenth- and early twentieth-century rationalistic optimism which was counting on intellectual and scientific progress to solve all problems. For existentialism, there is nothing eternal (atheistic form) or, if there is, it is accessible only by means of a jump out of the world and every worldly experience (Christian and other theistic forms); there are no essences which explain why you are what you are. You have to *assume yourself* in the meaning-lessness of your existence (unless you stipulate, but outside the field of philosophy, a reign of grace). You engage yourself, freely, under your own responsibility to yourself; you cannot rely on any pre-determined sense of History or of Nature. Sisyphus is always rolling his stone uphill, knowing full well that he will never arrive at the top, but proud, consenting, and happy in this knowledge which has liberated him from the snares of hope.

So there has been abundance of engagement: Marxist, Christian, even Nazi as in Heidegger's case (although it must be added that Heidegger, something like twenty years after the appearance of his *Time and Being,* one of the main sources of postwar existential-ism, has refused to let the term of existentialist be applied to his thought). But since this engagement remains always free, that is revocable, since every philosophical, political, religious *security* means a fall in the abyss of *inauthenticity* and a shying away from radical freedom and absolute responsibility, not only have the offers of collaboration been looked upon with certain misgivings from the authorities to which such temporary alliances were offered, but the engagement did not lead, and could not have led, to positive theories, models of ideal states, perfect societies, authentic churches. It could not lead but to the formal refusal of systematic thought, if under "systematic" is understood the attempt to bring into the form of consistent discourse the whole of reality, attitudes, ends, the whole of human experience and strivings. There have been excellent pieces of work in applied existentialism, if such an expression is permissible, and particular fields have certainly profited by it, be it only because subjectivity has been reinstated in its rights. The philosophy of religion, psychology, personal morals, psychiatry have taken from existentialism much that will probably prove of lasting value. If the results have been the same as far as philosophy proper is concerned remains a very open question.

It would be absolutely illegitimate to reduce existentialism to the historical conditions under which it was born. Not only were there forerunners (there always are, but then they become fore-runners only when the runners are on the track), but no idea is positively determined by such conditions, although it remains true that it would not have appeared on the scene if the whole setting had been different. But the success and the wane of an idea depend essentially on the worries, troubles, events of the times, on the whole of historical environment. So, it cannot be considered as fortuitous if existentialism made its appearance precisely between the two world wars in Germany, at the moment when the dream of German greatness had been shattered for the first time. The old system had broken down (there never was a revolution in Germany), and no new promise was visible, no cause for which to toil and fight and sacrifice oneself; the whole thing had become meaningless. It is not fortuitous either if existentialism spread over the whole of Europe after 1945. There was no meaning any more for young people in speaking of greatness (although the old traditions, to repeat it once more, had not disappeared); reconstruction was something for technicians and civil servants, empires were breaking down, and even the ideals of social justice and equality were losing much of their glamor once you saw that it was not so much a question of cutting the pudding into slices of about the same size, but of getting a bigger pudding in order that a relatively small piece might be absolutely bigger than a fair part of a smaller one, even if, in order to make it grow, you had to have more relative inequality. Good inspiring causes were becoming scarce. You could speak and write and organize in favor of Free Algeria, or of a better deal for the Mezzogiorno, or of disengagement in Indonesia and Africa if you were a "leftist." But as long as you did not break the rather liberal laws of your country, you took no edifying risks and, worse still, you found yourself in an unpleasant and disquieting alliance with people who for technical and economical reasons wanted, and even realized, the right thing for what you considered the wrong reasons. So, existentialism as a philosophy (or as substitute for philosophy) is on the wane, as are Marxism, liberalism, in fact every kind of -ism, at least as far as political and philosophical thought is concerned. It seems as if nothing has been left. Metaphysics has succumbed to existentialism, positivism has had no success, and existentialism has no power. What else is there? What else could there be?

There is of course a lot of tradition and of traditions. There is much, and much serious, teaching and research work. There are the institutions of learning which keep alive philosophy, be it only because they offer jobs and careers. On the other hand, philosophy is being talked about. There is even a widespread public interest for it, sometimes of a rather old-fashioned brand if you look less at the modern contents than at the way these contents are handled. The success of Fr. Teilhard de Chardin's speculations are a case in point, comparable to the impression made in Germany after World War I by Spengler's *magnum opus*. But all that is just tradition and traditional; will we have to declare that nothing remains but habit and intellectual manners?

There can be no clear-cut answer to such a question, and even the most circumspect answer will be presumptuous. The future lies on the knees of the gods. But certain trends are perhaps distinguishable, although any piece of really original thinking would of course belie all predictions if there would be ears to hear, which might not be the case if every sincerely felt need for philosophy were dying away.

The most significant fact is probably the new interest in the history of philosophy already mentioned, not only, and not predominantly, a scholarly and erudite pursuit, but an interest in the great systems of the past considered, if the formula is not too paradoxical, as contemporary thinking, as thinking for us. Evidently, people want to know what the masters have said and meant, and a remarkable amount of excellent editing, interpreting, commenting has been done and is constantly under way. The difference nevertheless is evident between, for instance, Zeller's classic and always indispensable *History of Greek Philosophy* or Ueberweg's textbook (of which, by the way, a new and extremely erudite edition is in view) and characteristically "modern" intentions. One of the signs of the change is certainly that no general history of philosophy has appeared, if one neglects the always necessary manuals (of which Fr. Coplestone's is one of the best). Instead, some authors seem to concentrate on them the philosophical fire, the most popular among them being Aristotle, Hegel, and Nietzsche.

This choice is in itself significant; but as significant is the absence of certain other names, precisely those of thinkers who were very much to the fore in the preoccupations of the preceding generations, Plato and Kant above all. (Descartes is a French national hero and is the subject of many studies, of purely historical or of predominantly systematic type; but the trend is specifically French, and it might be asked to what extent the French specialists don't read into Descartes what they want him to have been interested in.) Very tentatively, it might be submitted that the neglect of Plato and Kant could be explained by Nietzsche's presence. Nietzsche equals existentialism, for Nietzsche is being taken, to the exclusion of all the other ingredients of his thought—one ought probably to say, his thoughts—as the hero who has destroyed every "beyond," every *Hinterwelt*, every transcendence and who has liberated man by giving him the possibility, the duty, the right, and the unavoidable obligation of being just himself. Plato and Kant, both of them, are looked upon as the defenders of other worlds and of dogmatic faith. Notwithstanding some good scholarly work on both of them, they stay condemned, not as harshly as Nietzsche condemned them (together with Christianity), but nevertheless convicted, without the profit of due process of discussion, silently rejected rather than openly condemned.

This is not the place to ask if this judgment is well founded or could be well founded. What is interesting is its symptomatic value. It goes to show that Heidegger and the existentialists have carried the day, negatively. But that does not imply that existentialism is alone in the field after having beaten the enemy. Just the contrary. Aristotle and Hegel are certainly no existentialists in any possible meaning of this very ambiguous word. But in Hegel's *Phenomenology of the Spirit* certain traits do lend themselves to an existentialistic interpretation, and Aristotle's theory of the soul through its refusal of a soul-substance points in the direction existentialists as the late Merleau-Ponty (and nonexistentialist thinkers like Professor Gilbert Ryle) want to go. Then, there is the fact that Aristotle is Plato's main critic as Hegel is Kant's. And lastly, both of them, in opposition to Plato and Kant (at least as they have been seen by their interpreters of the nineteenth and early twentieth century) have not put their trust in mathematics and exact science and so can be considered as helpers in the holy war against scientism, the main form of antisubjectivism and unexistentialistic thinking, or, to quote Heidegger's expression, "the forgetfulness of Being"—a forgetfulness which stems from the addiction to things, matters of fact, techniques, science and sciences, from the interest in objects, a forgetfulness of which the best (or worst) expression is to be found in philosophical positivism.

All this would be quite natural if only Aristotle and particularly Hegel were not, and did not declare to be, systematic thinkers, thinkers who try to seize in a consistent discourse the whole of reality, natural, human, and, at least in Hegel's case, historical. The fact is that the older generation, Heidegger in Germany, Sartre and Merleau-Ponty in France (both of which largely ignored Aristotle) to mention only the best known names, have always had their misgivings, the first concerning Aristotle and Hegel, the other two concerning Hegel, and, despite their admiration for him, have often declared that they were unable to follow him precisely in his systematic philosophy of history. But the younger people don't write existentialistic books (even in literature there is at present a very conscious and programmed move away from subjectivity, if subjectivity is taken to mean that reality is interpreted from a psychologically consistent and historically developing subject's point of view). They try to understand Hegel. Of course, one of the mainsprings of this popularity is to be seen in the father-son relationship between Hegel and Marx, or, for a smaller number, between him and Kierkegaard. (Something similar is happening for Aristotle in Roman Catholic thinking. You cannot understand your own tradition unless you go back to its roots—from where people then often proceed toward Hegel.) But it seems remarkable that Marxists, not excluding very orthodox Communists, are engaging the discussion with a man who, ten or fifteen years ago, was just a dirty reactionary. People do read Hegel, not in order to refute him—anyhow younger people, as a rule, don't refute, they simply refuse—but because they want to learn from him.

What then do they want to learn, and why? The reason is probably to be looked for in the very victory of existentialism and of what Nietzsche called nihilism, a victory which has left the battlefield empty. Once it has been proclaimed that there is no transcendent security, that "values" depend on you, that it is you who give to history and action a meaning, you may go on proclaiming the same thing all over again. Being has been left out, man has delivered himself to "inauthenticity" and has objectified himself while objectifying, not so much the world, but whatever is present in a world whose character as the always hidden and always revealing presence of Being has been forgotten. You may then find your witnesses in poets and the darkest sayings of pre-Socratic thinkers; but in the not-so-long run that becomes boring, and you cannot live with purely negative statements. It is all right to insist upon the fact that human beings are always and unavoidably "in situation," that they are finite and neither omniscient nor omnipotent; you will always come to the point where your particular, real situation has to be apprehended, understood, put into a framework. And apprehending, understanding, establishing a system of references is precisely what Hegel pretended to do in all fields and what Aristotle offers in the field of natural philosophy, politics, and morals. It seems that the point has been reached where reality itself, not only its foundations in liberty and Being, has again become interesting.

It would be a grave misunderstanding if the preceding remarks were read as meaning that all young people had become Hegelians (or Aristotelians). If the success of Hegel is evident (there have been founded two Hegel Societies in the last years, both of which prosper and attract at their meetings an astonishingly large number of people), nobody is likely to buy the Hegelian system lock, stock, and barrel, just as nobody who looks to Aristotle for a way back to a Philosophy of Nature would accept his physics. What matters is not so much what they saw or said they saw as their way of looking at things, what is being called their *dialectics,* the will to see every fact, every thesis and its opposite without falling into skepticism, coordinating all of them, establishing, or discovering between them, understandable relations whose existence is the condition of the existence of an understandable world, even of a world which might become meaningful only through human action. No action would be thinkable in a disconnected and not connectable heap of unrelated data, and there would not even be the desire to act and to understand.

So it is a time of stock-taking, to use a formula. Marxism is very well, so is free enterprise, liberal planning, nationalism (for oneself or, more frequently in Europe, for other people). So is, on the other hand, existentialism and Nietzsche and phenomenology and the Philosophy of Being. But once you do not adher blindly, "naturally," naïvely to a credo, the question comes up: why rather this than that? There seems to be a feeling that a fundamental change is called for in outlook, fundamental in the sense that it has become urgent, not so much to revise the answers (there are only too many of them), but the very questions to which these answers correspond or, since they all go way back into the past, have corresponded. It could be that they have become irrelevant to our situation, that we have not really taken grip of our own problems but are going on as if the traditional ones were always with us. We go on as if, to give at random some examples, there were really a proletariat of the type Marx thought of, without anything to lose but their chains, while social insurance and state care eliminate progressively the threats of starvation and misery from loss of job, sickness, old age; while the worker is no more just a commodity in the market; while the technical changes are constantly reducing the proportion of those groups who conceive of themselves as proletarians, without possessions, without any share in cultural benefits, without even an interest in the prosperity of their country. It could be that nonrevolutionary change—Marx by the way foresaw that possibility—has transformed the real conditions to a point where the old theory does not apply any more, although no new one has replaced it as a global theory of State and Society, their relations and their interdependence. It is quite possible, to take one more case, that Freud was absolutely right in his time when he insisted on the importance of repressed sexual pulsions and desires and it would not be absurd to submit that he has brought into the open these tendencies, has abolished many of the traditional interdicts, and characterized another part of them as the very conditions of civilized life; and by doing that has just deprived the problem of its importance, at least for practically normal beings.

So it is conceivable that the problems of history, sociology, politics, psychology need not only correction, but radical reformulation. In other words, it looks as if Europe has come to a point where everything in the treasure-house of a very old culture has to be looked at anew, has to be weighed again and assayed. All questions would have to be asked again, but from the viewpoint of their consistency, of their basic unity, of their relevancy. The task would be not so much to solve the problems one by one—that would be the hopeless attempt to rely once more on unquestioned questions and "self-evident" practical axioms, an attempt which would lead back to nihilism. The relevance of the problems would have to be established, their importance, place, and function for a way of thinking leading toward a nonarbitrary unity of thought and life, a unity not given, but to be discovered—discovered in a very cool and very passionate quest.

Only a prophet could tell if that tremendously hard task will be undertaken and, if so, if it will be accomplished. The need, it seems, is acutely felt by thinking people all over the Old Continent; perhaps more felt than clearly understood. It might be that even intellectually courageous people will turn away from it. There is so much to be done; there are on the other hand such big potential audiences waiting for any new "final solution"; there are so many possibilities for comforts of every kind that, if you add to enough bread enough *circenses*, the sense for problems, as opposed to difficulties, may wither away. A pessimist would say that the resulting boredom, sometimes already visible as a social phenomenon, would lead to a new barbarism, the reign of violence, and the destruction of the perfect ant-heap, to borrow Nietzsche's expression. But that would be a pessimist's outlook. It is quite as possible that ants are content—or that human beings accept to think.

MICHEL CROZIER

The Cultural Revolution: Notes on the Changes in the Intellectual Climate of France

I The Problem

THE changes in the intellectual climate of France during the last twenty years and their relationship to changes in French society in general constitute a problem which cannot be dealt with adequately by a purely literary description.

There is, indeed, a surprising contrast between the France of the late 1940's and the new France of the 1960's. The economic, social and even moral climate of the Liberation was a climate of impotence and almost of despair. Everything seemed destined for failure in a country torn and disoriented, convinced that its future did not depend on itself. In this situation of prostration and pessimism—which affected most social groups equally and whose traces can be seen in public opinion polls—intellectual life was intense, enthusiastic and influential. Intellectual leaders enjoyed a very wide audience and their dramatic differences of opinion were treated as events of national importance. They were prepared to involve themselves in politics, or at least in social criticism; they felt that they were endowed with a mission and they sought by all available means to take part in action.

One could take each of these statements and say almost exactly the opposite about France in the 1960's. Optimism prevails in the economic and social spheres. While various social groups continue to complain of their lot and to demand aid, the French people in general seem to have regained confidence in a society and a world which, though imperfect, no longer seems impossible to improve. In this society, affluent and more confident about the future, intellectual life seems to have lost its fervor as well as its distinction. People smile at the emotional transports of the Liberation. Labor leaders and politicians talk of nothing but rates of economic growth and the necessity of planning, while bookish intellectuals turn their backs on these problems. The present intellectual fashion favors

602

formalism and detachment; the intellectuals stand aside deliberately and refuse to interest themselves in the profound changes that are revolutionizing social relations. At the same time, they seem to have lost both their power to fascinate and their wide audience. Intellectual life continues to be active and passionate, but it is no longer in the foreground in anything like the way it once was.

Such a situation cannot be satisfactorily explained by using only the criteria and methods of classical cultural analysis—whether neo-Marxist or existentialist*—because such analysis deals really with the products and not with the mechanisms of intellectual life. It considers products and methods as the reflection and expression of problems with which an era and a society are concerned. The analyst's intent is to clarify these factors, one in terms of the other, and to try to discover—through this game with mirrors—the significance of the dominant intellectual themes while arriving at a more accurate evaluation of the basic trends operating in society as a whole. The assumption is that culture can be understood exclusively as an instrument which develops, to be sure, but which remains fundamentally stable and can therefore register the anxieties and aspirations of a society in an impartial manner. This postulate was easy to accept up to the present, at least within the limits of western bourgeois society. Even while society experienced basic change, it was assumed that the function of the intellectual world that served it as a sounding-board and measuring instrument would not be altered thereby. This confidence in culture is now recognized to be impossible. At a moment when the crisis which had shaken the European states in the 1930's and 1940's were beginning to be forgotten, when a stabilized society accepted itself as it really was, and faith in its future was restored, people realized that the essential human measuring instrument (which they had never doubted before) had in fact been profoundly affected. The variations and the excesses of the intellectual climate in the latest postwar period no longer reflect simply the backwash of the outside world; they express primarily a crisis of the intellectual function itself. It would be a mistake to see in this the manifestation of a new and more fundamental crisis of the modern soul. Rather, it seems to me, it is the coming to light of a long delayed change in the role of the intellectual and of the mechanism of intellectual activity in Europe, whose scope is just beginning to be understood and whose consequences seem to me to be enormous.

I shall try to study this phenomenon, which for lack of a better

---

* Lukacs' style of criticism, which has such prestige in Europe and especially in France, seems to me completely inadequate from this point of view.

name, I shall call the *cultural revolution*, through an examination of the paradoxes of change in France. I believe, however, that the problem is quite general, and it is its general aspect that I believe the French example illustrates so clearly.*

II The Intellectual as an Agent of Change in Bourgeois Society

The great weakness of traditional Marxist or neo-Marxist analysis is that it always tends to consider the intellectual merely as a sort of "resounding echo" of the problems of his times, as if all culture constituted, in the long run, only a kind of superstructure. But if this aspect of culture, and of the role of the intellectual, is important and particularly interesting at a certain stage of social analysis, we should not forget that culture is also a means and a fundamental resource for a human being in his own development. Even if we leave aside the physical sciences and man's action on nature and limit ourselves only to institutions, morals and human relations, the intellectual quite as much as the man of action plays the role of an agent of change. The modes of reasoning and intellectual models he produces condition, directly or indirectly, all human activities. Changes in institutions and modes of organization —reappraisals of the "rules of the game," are possible only if man is capable of conceiving new types of human relations. In modern society it is the intellectual's role to explore, experiment with and make known his own feelings and conceptions, as well as those of others, for out of these conceptions new types emerge.

While change was rapid and profound in western society in the nineteenth and early twentieth centuries, human relations continued to be characterized by situations of subordination, distance and stratification, and any change of habit, any new conception of interpersonal relations, seemed to threaten the whole social equilibrium. As a result, change generally aroused opposition which often was overcome only at the time of great crisis. The classic European intellectual is one who foresees, prepares, dreads or flees the crisis, but he is always defined in relation to it.

French bourgeois society offers the most conspicuous example

* Here I am summarizing a model for the analysis of change which I have worked out on the basis of the bureaucratic system of organization prevailing in France. The first sketch of this model appeared in an article in *Esprit*, "France, terre de commandment" (December, 1957). It is set forth in detail in a book now in the process of publication by Editions du Seuil in Paris, *Le Phenomène Bureaucratique*. An English translation, *The French Bureaucratic System* (University of Chicago Press) is also about to be published.

of this phenomenon. To the problems posed by change, it responded by ever increasing centralization of institutions and of the system of social relations. As a consequence, a change in any part of the whole, even a minor one, really challenged the general equilibrium of society. In thus displacing the source of its rigidity from social relations to institutions, French society did not accelerate the rhythm of change, but made the mechanism more apparent.

In the other European nations, different types of rigidity prevailed and the individual was not paralyzed and stimulated in the same way by the institutions intended to protect him. Nevertheless, the same dichotomy was to be found between thought—irresponsible, categorical and ignorant of the means which it could not grasp —and action, which remained in the sphere of empiricism and compromise, and which necessarily involved practices unacceptable to anyone committed to the pursuit of an ideal. In such conditions, the myth and ideology of revolution naturally served as agents of change; they constituted at the same time, theoretically, the only acceptable way for action to become at last "the sister of the dream" and to be integrated into the sphere of intellectual activity.

This conception of change and the predominance of ideology do not depend only upon the logic of human relations. They depend also upon properly intellectual factors—the capacity to anticipate the future and to conceive the rational possibilities of action. These two categories of determinants are inextricably connected.

If change is to take place in a rational way, those who have to make decisions must understand both the real facts of the situation and the psychology of the actors who are affected by it and who will participate in it, but this is not possible, given the general mechanism of subordination and noncommunication; those who make decisions do not have sufficient knowledge of the problem to be resolved, while those who have a more direct experience have a very incomplete view themselves and no means of communicating it. Besides, subordinates at all levels need protection against an oppressive and authoritarian system of relations, and they use the very institutions which are the framework of the system as a protection. Any change affecting these institutions frightens them.

This attachment to paralyzing means, however, is first of all related to the impossibility of conceiving other, more direct, means. The conception of rationality, or rather of the possibilities of rational action, influences the system of human relations of which it is the expression as much as it is influenced or determined by that system. Indeed, in classical European bourgeois society, there is a rather narrow idea of rationality, which makes it extremely difficult to foresee and organize the future. The successive steps of action are clearly seen, but they are understood much more in a historical sense than in an experimental or prospective sense. More emphasis is placed on the study of material determinism than on the mechanisms of action or change.* People are incapable of integrating in their theory unforeseen results of action which are the counterpart of the means chosen to obtain the desired ends in an overall view. Theoretical as well as practical conceptions of action are founded upon a clear-cut distinction between the category of ends and the category of means. Ends are discussed in relation to moral, religious or philosophical principles, and means are analyzed in a mechanistic perspective. They deal only with the ideal functioning, the one best way, and refuse to take into account the role of independent human elements upon which they must rely.

Such a conception makes it impossible to discuss ends in terms other than value judgments, and it exaggerates the differences and conflicts of a metaphysical type through which real conflicts of interest can be expressed. Substantive issues have thus to be dealt with in such an intransigent way that they cannot be well understood, and one cannot therefore either resolve them or make them advance in a rational way.† Nor does such a conception provide understanding of the development of means that condition action more practically and are themselves changed through the crisis. As a result men make new monsters out of these forces they have no way to grasp such as technology, bureaucracy, the mass media.

Imprisoned in its system of human relations, society blinds itself both to its goals and to its acts. The intellectual has a very definite place in this situation, of which he is both the victim and the beneficiary. He is disarmed in his will to understand and to explain, and he constantly struggles with the ends-means contradiction. Society, in fact, forbids him to interfere in action and forces him to behave in a doctrinaire manner, but at the same time it considers him a being apart. He suffers from his false situation and from the demands hanging over him, but in exchange he enjoys a very great prestige. He is the "frontiersman" of the ideal, the one who presides over the establishment of norms and models. This separation, this distance from others, from which he suffers is also his glory, and it gives him certain advantages in a hierarchical so-

---

* It is true that the recognition of this determinism was a sign of great progress, and there were also many anticipations of future types of reasoning. The Marxists, for example, with the models of the "plus value" and of the reserve army of the unemployed, already applied an overall functional interpretation, but they did not preceive the methodological value of their discovery.

† Marxism does not really explain the actual conflicts of interests; it transcends them in a simplified model which makes them incomprehensible.

ciety. His real social status is often rather low, to be sure, but his ambitions remain unlimited and he shares in the sovereignty of the intellect. His word is law; he defines the true, the beautiful and the good. The intellectual who succeeds has something special, something personal, which places him above other men. The intellectual world is built around the notion of genius. The royalty, the liberty, the privileges accorded to a man of genius are the fundamental goods to which all intellectuals think they have a right and to which they profoundly aspire. Whether revolutionary or conservative, the intellectual is profoundly attached to this aristocratic situation which makes him the sovereign dispenser of new ways of feeling, of new norms.

The intellectual thus embodies a fundamental contradiction in society. On the one hand he is its principal agent of change, deriving his glory from this function, and on the other he is profoundly attached to the model of human relations which paralyzes all progress.

III *The Transformation of Western Society and its Repercussions on the Role of the Intellectual*

This whole system, in which social relations, relations of authority, the conception of rationality and the processes of change are interdependent parts, has been changing profoundly, at least since World War II. This explains the crisis in the intellectual world because these changes cannot help having repercussions on the role of the intellectual and the mechanisms of intellectual life which, as we have seen, are intimately connected with social change.

I shall not stress here the transformation of social relations and relations of authority. In a very general way we are witnessing in all the nations of western Europe a spectacular acceleration of change in this domain. The distance between social groups is narrowing, human relations are becoming easier; at work and in all social institutions the traditional subordination is tolerated with increasing impatience while those in authority, for their part, no longer dare give orders as they did only a short while ago. Even relations between parents and children, which are the foundation of all these types of relations, are being transformed and the conception of authority, that fundamental characteristic of the culture, is being weakened.

At the same time, the way in which rational action is conceived is undergoing a real revolution that completes, reinforces and makes possible the revolution in social relations and relations of authority from which it is inseparable. Society is becoming more conscious of itself and of its means. Men no longer depend on myths like that of the invisible hand which will harmoniously regulate conflicts of interests;* they refer less to principles which are supposed to dictate conduct and begin to see how the lessons of experience can be used to anticipate the future rather than to restrain action to the norms of the past.

This new consciousness of its own limits and means that society is discovering is the fruit of cumulative progress in the sciences and in technology, but it corresponds also to the development of a new form of rationality, of a new way of conceiving action. Discussion of ends no longer ignores consideration of means, and allowance can be made for unforeseen results of action. Of course, the politician and the man of action have always been conditioned by the resistance of their milieux, but they were scorned for their "deals" and their double game. What Weber called *Verantwortungsethik* could not be established as long as consideration of the ideal remained radically separated from consideration of the means of applying it.† Under the conditions of the time, it could only be a heroic dream, realizable only by supermen. The situation is entirely changed as soon as science can help in conceiving global systems including both ends and means. We are still only at the beginning, to be sure; our techniques are extremely limited, but already the resistance of human means is no longer unforeseen. It can be taken into account in advance and one can make predictions without having recourse to coercion to assure the accuracy of the predictions. This new way of action is basically connected with the transformation in human relations and with an easier access to information of which it in turn facilitates the discovery. Knowledge eliminates the necessity of force.

Such a change implies two essential novelties: first, there is the increasing gain in importance of the social sciences over the tradi-

* The liberal theory of an "invisible hand" which, it was believed, would regulate harmoniously all the conflicts between individuals provided the basic model of social thought in this conception of society.

† Weber himself foresaw the importance of the problem, but his discussion of the two forms of rationality, *Zweck* and *Wertrationalität*, implies a much more radical separation. Talcott Parsons has shown very clearly that Weber himself did not succeed in maintaining it (*Theories of Society* [New York: Free Press of Glencoe, 1962], p. 1063). The chief defect of his analysis, however, is that it does not recognize the importance of human means in the conditioning of action, so that rationality as regards ends (*Zweck*) can remain utilitarian and mechanical while rationality as regards values (*Wert*) becomes abstract and moralistic. Weber conceives of the two meeting only on the heroic or metaphysical plane.

tional normative disciplines—law, philosophy and the humanities— although the old disciplines are also being penetrated and renewed by the new ones. Second, and most important, the role of the intellectual is transformed. The intellectual is engaging much more directly in action. He does not thereby become a man of action, but his thought is much closer to action, much more pertinent and usable in a direct way. Action is no longer a world apart; compromises and deals are no longer shameful things, for they can be studied rationally. The intellectual no longer spends his time denouncing them in the name of an ideal but is trying to understand and to rationalize them.

This constantly increasing appropriation of action by the scientific intelligence constitutes a considerable step forward for the intellectual function, and the number of those who can be considered intellectuals is constantly growing. But at the same time the role of the intellectual and his prestige as an individual are losing in value. The man of genius is disappearing. The favorite image of nineteenth-century European romantic poets, of the sage on his mountaintop uttering prophetic words destined to renew the kingdom, appears strange and anachronistic today. As a class, the intellectuals have been profoundly affected by the narrowing of social distances and the greater flexibility of aristocratic relations. They are more numerous, nearer to others—and less revered.

The transformation of the role of the intellectual is often explained by the invasion of the mass media. This is, of course, a major aspect of the change, but its real significance can be little appreciated if it is studied outside the general context we have described. There is, in fact, a tendency to see in this transformation of the intellectual's role the degradation of the content of traditional culture, a transformation which would really lead one to believe that this barbarian invasion should be resisted and that the struggle to preserve true values should constitute the essential concern of the intellectual. But if it is legitimate to criticize pseudo-culture, a rear-guard action to arrest the improvement of the culture of the masses seems both reactionary and futile; above all, it would be to misunderstand totally the transformation of the role of the intellectuals. They have no less influence because they have lost their sacred character. Quite the contrary, their influence is only becoming more immediate and more responsible.

This general change is taking place in all industrial societies, but it is much more advanced in North America and especially in the United States. Europe, in this respect, up to this time has lagged behind, both because of its slower economic development and because of the power of vested interests in the traditional forms of organization. In western Europe, which had developed one of the most advanced, complex and efficient forms of classic culture, the transition—the conversion to a new form—is provoking a very profound crisis at the same time that the transition is called for, even demanded, by the developments of the old form itself. In my opinion, this explains the acuteness of French intellectual uneasiness much more than a general moral crisis of civilization itself.

In this context, all recent European intellectual movements can be analyzed from two complementary points of view. On the one hand, one can see in them a painful effort, often ill directed but consistent, to go beyond the old forms of rationality, to achieve more direct forms of communication among people in order to understand action more directly and more intimately. On the other hand, one can see a no less tenacious resistance to the loss of traditional privileges, an attachment to traditional habits of thought and forms of communication, to rationalizations and to flight-behavior, which in certain respects make the intellectual milieu one of the most conservative in contemporary society.

IV The Intellectual Climate of the Liberation

Let us now leave this preliminary and somewhat too theoretical general analysis and return to the concrete situations that we have used as a point of departure. It is well to begin with the paradoxical climate of the Liberation. I shall focus on the two basic tendencies which I have already distinguished in elaborating my model. Each of them suggests a complementary interpretation of the facts. On the one hand, change has certainly come about; traditions have been directly challenged; innovations are being made; new behavior patterns and new styles of life are found to be necessary. But on the other hand, the manner in which change has come confirms the classic model; it takes place through a crisis whose course mortgages the future and perpetuates the distinction between the sphere of morality and the sphere of real action, from which society already suffers.

At the same time, a third dimension, or rather the possibility of new light on the subject, will also emerge through an analysis of the mechanism of the illusions forged in the era of the Liberation itself. The role of these illusions was extremely important. In order to surmount the contradiction between these two tendencies, people needed indeed to be mistaken about the reality of change and the very existence of the goals they sought.

V *The Permanence of the Traditional Model*

We shall first take up the more conservative interpretation. All the phenomena of effervescence and romantic explosion which contrasted so profoundly with the practical impotence of society at the time of the Liberation can be clearly explained in the classic model of change through crisis. With hindsight, one discovers in the extraordinary climate of the Liberation the national resurgence of a fundamental characteristic of French bourgeois society, that is, opposition between static groups and institutions and dynamic individuals. This is another example of the brief moment of anarchy in an over-rigid society; the traditional barriers have cracked, the creative irresponsibility of individuals can at last have free rein. The golden age of the intellectuals, the "perfect moment"* of which they dream as individuals, has arrived.

In reality, in the confusion, the suffering and the conflicts of the troubled era of the Liberation there was an extraordinary individual freedom such as had not been seen for a long time. At least in intellectual circles people thought that everything was possible, that one could reconstruct from zero. Each intellectual was a sort of sovereign reformer, issuing a call to all other men. Sartre has elaborated the theory of this creative liberty and sovereignty of the writer.[1] Painters, moralists and novelists wanted to impose a new vision of the world.

But this sovereign, unbridled, creative liberty, this enthusiasm and effervescence, remained completely irresponsible. No one was concerned with the consequences. The intellectual, so progressive in his intentions and in his utterances, remained aristocratic in his style. He posed all the problems in moral terms and proposed to the world a model of intransigence which forbade all compromise. He thus perpetuated the chasm between thought and action which otherwise he claimed to bridge. He took advantage of the temporary weakness of the traditional institutions to make another voice heard, and people listened to him precisely because they had lost faith in the traditional distinctions and hierarchies; but his voice was exclusively negative. It overlooked the human factor to such an extent that it did not have the least practical effect.

The typical hero of the era was Albert Camus, young, charming, free, consumed with fraternal zeal, profoundly committed to the fray,† but miraculously successful in preserving his purity! Camus,

* The phrase is Sartre's; it describes an emotional state he discusses frequently.

† He was for months editor of a newspaper and served as the conscience of the left.

a lone man who appealed to other lone men in the name of the good, a good which was certainly far from the traditional morality but which was also, and above all, a morality. He was a revolutionary, but his revolution had nothing to do with the play of interests—it was a revolution of the intellect and of purity. His position was unassailable, his uprightness and his passion were touching, but his forays into the realm of action—due to a fortunate combination of circumstances—was a real gamble which could not last for long.

In contrast with this purity, the Communist party represented a permanent temptation because, at the price of a few relatively minor initial concessions, the party offered satisfaction of the need for liberty—the absolute thirst—and at the same time satisfaction of the desire for responsibility and for constructive commitment. The Communist intellectual of the 1940's was very close to the revolutionary hero in the style of Camus; it was with an equally complete liberty and equally great irresponsibility and, moreover, in the same terms that he criticized society and projected on the socialist future his dream of sovereignty and total individualism. But he did not have the same anxieties, because he was sure of being really committed in the world of action. Life in the party is certainly often mean and disagreeable, and for that very reason it is reassuring. This difficult service does not on the whole pose too many problems if one is willing to admit on the one hand that its adherents regard it only as a means, as a substitute for real life; and on the other hand that with its rigidity, its hierarchy and its system of obedience it is very similar to the traditional society it opposes. The passion for responsibility, for devotion, for efficiency attracted to Communism all those who were incapable of bearing the weight of liberty and solitude, which is the counterpart of the intellectual enthusiasm of the epoch. The Communist is part of the world in his zeal, in his concern for prosaic detail, in his militancy; and apart from the world in his utopian dream of a future society which would permit the illumination and resolution of all the problems of the world. Some later pushed the dichotomy to the point of absurdity, in entirely good faith. In any case, we observe that we find here, in a precise and exaggerated form, the divorce between thought and action which, in the classical model, constitutes at the same time both the consequence and the foundation of the social hierarchy.

Sartre, Merleau-Ponty* and their existentialist friends had foreseen the problem, and their philosophy can be interpreted as a

---

* Merleau-Ponty later returned to the ultra-heroic position of Weber.

desperate but always inadequate effort to find a solution for it. Sartre criticized bold spirits like Camus for their moralism and for their rejection of the world, and he equally criticized the Communists for having a too short-sighted view of action and for being cut off by too great a concern with immediate problems. But neither Sartre nor Merleau-Ponty succeeded in reintegrating action with the world of the intellect. They were incapable of going beyond discussion of principles, and when they tried to compromise on principle in order to escape the predicament, they became clerks who betrayed and not intellectuals who shed light on the world of action, as is seen in Sartre's bitter experience.

All these attempts naturally led rapidly to the failure for which they were destined: the years of disenchantment, disillusion and abandonment. Such a result was inevitable because no one was willing to understand the necessities of action, that is, to admit the existence of a real society, in crisis to be sure, but very much alive and which could be transformed only if it was understood.* The intellectuals wanted a new society, but one fallen from heaven, or at least one that would not be conditioned by the impure struggle that had to be waged against the old society. Misled by this profoundly conservative dream, they could not find a middle ground between the total liberty of the individual revolutionary and the total constraint of Stalinism, and they thus deprived themselves of all possibility of communication with others and therefore of constructive cooperation and rational action.

However unjust such a brief analysis may seem, these positions sum up the general trend of the intellectual movement as expressed in its articulate existentialist wing. In addition, there were, of course, numerous more subtle and more solid works in process, but they had absolutely no influence. Outside of revolutionary moralism, Communist alienation and the existentialist attempts at conciliation, no one proposed anything.† Between the rigid bourgeois society that they criticized and characteristically parodied without respite and the utopian society of which they dreamed, the intellectuals were incapable of conceiving or of shedding light on the society actually taking form, to which they themselves contributed without knowing it.

* Sartre tried, especially in his important essay, "Les Communistes et la Paix," but his analysis is nothing more than an academic exercise (*Les Temps Modernes,* April, 1954).

† Christian humanism, more responsible, more deeply rooted and profound than existentialism, would make its contribution later. In the enthusiasm of the Liberation period it can be considered as an attempt comparable to, and much influenced by, existentialism.

VI *The Contribution of the Intellectual Movement of the Liberation*

In spite of all these illusions and all this cultural conservatism disguised as social progressivism, something positive happened which should not be neglected, although its importance is quite other than what its agents thought. The intellectual movement of the Liberation, all things considered, had a decisive influence on philosophy and morality, on social customs and even on the conception of action. In spite of its naïveté, in spite of the deep conservatism of its intellectual vision of the world, it began to prepare the ground for change. In any case, it opened the way to the new disenchantment (*Entzauberung*) with the world, against which it fought in the names both of socialism and of culture.

Its main conscious effort consisted in demolishing the positivism and the narrow moralism of French bourgeois society. Jean-Paul Sartre and the existentialists were the impassioned leaders of this fight. Their intensity and eloquence were devastating. No one could withstand them; even their opponents never seriously entered the controvery on this level.* Whatever reservations they may have had, Marxists, Communists, Christians, individualists and liberals adopted the same highbrow disdain toward any trace of good conscience, toward all a priori claims of hierarchy and experience, and toward any analysis of human conduct in the black and white terms of traditional categories.† The basic vocabulary of the existentialist lingo, ambiguity and behavior in bad faith, enjoyed considerable popularity and became the key words of intellectual analysis.

If we reflect on the significance of this fashion, the two following points appear to be essential. First, the hierarchical order of the world, this closed, structured universe where everyone has his place, is radically challenged—and this not only in the abstract and theoretical way of the early Socialists, but concretely in everyday life and with respect to the most ordinary habits. There could be no more universal morality with its restraining but reassuring taboos. Second, the ambiguity of human motives and feelings is brought to light; black and white no longer exist. The traditional dichotomy

* At the time, there was something pathetic in the way the French intelligentsia rapidly trampled on the very foundations of its education, its morality and its vision of the world, led by thinkers who were themselves nourished in the academic atmosphere and who were so enraged precisely because they were at war with themselves.

† Which, of course, did not prevent them from having recourse to a still more rigorous moralism every time a positive judgment was called for. This moralism, so well exemplified in Camus, was an individual moralism lacking any philosophical foundation.

between the rigorous world of principle and the too tolerant world of application and human weakness maintained in the intellectual domain is denied in everyday morality. No one can get off cheap; everyone must assume his part of the responsibility for the conduct of the world.

This philosophical and moral change was directly reflected in daily life. Of course, people have too hastily connected existentialist philosophy (which, after all, is highly technical and sometimes austere) with the "existentialist bohemianism" of Saint-Germain-des-Prés, but this connection, all things considered, was legitimate, and the progress made through the excesses of life in the *caves* can be credited to the intellectual movement because existentialist thought contributed definitively to the liberation from a certain number of bourgeois taboos of the younger generation, and through them of all society. Hence its rapid and unexpected success, not only in Paris but throughout France and even Europe. It was not only a question of greater freedom in personal behavior—more apparent than real—but of the negation of distances and of constraints, of a new liberty in human relations, of a more spontaneous mode of communication between the sexes and among social groups. Saint-Germain-des-Prés, in the years after the Liberation, was a crucible where the traditional barriers were broken down and a new style forged which in a few years completely upset the equilibrium of French bourgeois life.[2]

But this progress, so clear on the level of social customs and the individual vision of the world, became much more uncertain on the level of action, for the entire intellectual movement is founded on the individual. Here again we find the opposition between the negative world of structures and the positive world of the individual who thinks he can liberate himself by ignoring the structures on which he depends. Sartre, who could unmask the deep bad faith behind the complicated network of individual motives with flawless licidity, became paradoxically naïve each time he dealt with institutions, political parties, techniques of organization or social structure in general. On the level of structures, Sartre made the black and white judgments that he—more than anyone—eliminated on the individual level. The subtle, complicated, supremely comprehensive man that he tried to become then reverted to an ideological bourgeois, peremptorily distinguishing between good and evil. Similarly, at their own level, the young existentialists lived a marginal life, rejecting the world *en bloc* or accepting only the Communist caricature of it.

The existentialists, Sartre first among them, were indeed conscious of the difficulty. For many years the intellectual world waited for Sartre's moral system. This is not the place to criticize the clumsy, contradictory and half-disenchanted work that he finally delivered to the public, a defense a posteriori, an effort to prolong artificially an era that was already past.[3] Sartre's moral system, implicit in all his works, is a heroic and individual morality which consists in making the individual assume the whole weight of the world at every moment. It makes no sense except in the context of rejection of the world. The total commitment it demands naturally leads to paralysis, and the young intellectuals who really practiced this philosophy lived in a sort of ghetto.

Even in this context, however, the existentialist school was not without purpose. True enough, a whole group of people for a long time abandoned themselves to the delights of this nirvana. But for the majority who gradually succeeded in overcoming it, the lesson they learned has played a fundamental role. It liberated them from a priori principles and categories and led them to understand, seriously and honestly, the alibis of good conscience and the detours and compromises necessary for any action. For them, and finally for society in general, the existentialist revolution really brought thought closer to action just as it contributed to diminishing the differences among people and to the lowering of social prestige.

VII *The Illusions of the Liberation Era and Their Mechanism*

Only through a discriminating interpretation can one contrast on the one side the method which seeks progress only through the old forms of action that paralyze it, and on the other the method which throws off the weight of the past by pushing to the furthest extreme the consequences of the intellectual tradition that is respected. The inherent contradiction is, in fact, found on all levels. In practice, however, during the Liberation era it was concealed by the illusions which both the intellectual and the practical worlds harbored about themselves. These illusions should not be summarily rejected, for their mechanism constitutes one of the essential foundations of the intellectual life. Perhaps no other era has been at the same time so perceptive and so blind about itself. It ignored both its liabilities and its assets. Cut off in the hopeless fight it was waging in the present, it refused to see the future it was bringing to birth; rather, it struggled violently against it and revolted against the type of society it was helping to create—all in the name of an ideal whose aristocratic aspects permitted it to keep its illusions and thus to continue to dream in complete security of the perfect revolutionary society.

This blindness about the future explains the pessimism of the movement. Sartre's intentions were surely honestly constructive. It is well known that the existentialists passionately proclaimed their commitment, but no one took them entirely seriously and they themselves did not feel very much at ease outside the familiar field of abstract speculation.* The negative moment of their vision of the world was really the great one, because it alone was spontaneous and authentic. It was natural that the public should retain only its nihilism and the taste for the absurd.

Behind all the different levels of illusion or make-believe one always comes back in the end to a fundamental trait that goes beyond the intellectual milieu and expresses one of the basic difficulties of the period: the fear of commitment. This may appear paradoxical at first sight, since the basic slogan of the existentialist movement was "commitment," but people wanted so much to discuss the theme and gave the intellectuals who played with it so much credit only because the necessary practical effort was psychologically difficult. In the atmosphere of psychological and social insecurity that prevailed, no one dared take the responsibility for his own acts. The spirit of initiative, the will to undertake things and to construct, had not disappeared—one would see its results later on—but they could not be avowed as such. Nothing constructive could be claimed openly. The most active artisans of the renewal professed or claimed to profess an ideal very different from that implied by their acts. At least in their relations with others, their undertakings were inadequate and contemptible pragmatic solutions to which they had to have recourse in order to save their skins and in order not to compromise the future too much. Many of them discovered only gradually the originality of what they had accomplished, and it is only when the climate changed that they at last decided to assume the responsibility for their actions.

Under such circumstances, the intellectual function took on a very special importance because it had the task of elaborating the illusions that paralyzed action but which at the same time, given the condition of crisis, were indispensable to it. Amid the fireworks of individualism, action—always collective, always besmirched by compromise—appeared impossible, futile and immoral. At the moment when the old constraints were being broken, people could not bear to create new ones. Yet they did it. They committed themselves for the future, but without wanting to acknowledge it, with-

---

* Some, like Francis Jeanson, have succeeded in finding a commitment that suits them in the struggle of the colonial peoples which is revolutionary, total and in the sphere of action all at the same time.

out wanting to apply their intellect to the problems raised. The bright flash of their understanding of the past and the present blinded them completely to the future. This mixture of clear perception and blindness was never more apparent or more laden with consequences than in relation to America.

VIII Attitudes toward America

The problem of relations with America assumed major importance for the entire intellectual movement after the Liberation. America, in fact, presented the only concrete image of a future; it was from America that the intellectual movement borrowed many of its ideas, and it was in following the American example that a new style and new habits were evolved. At the same time, European intellectuals were deeply shocked by this too realistic future they perceived through better acquaintance and as a result of their own first direct experience of change. Besides, official America—moderate and realistic, hampered by its innumerable responsibilities—really appeared to be a conservative power incapable of promoting change and even trying, consciously or unconsciously, to slow it down. This was a fine occasion for the Europeans to reverse the roles and to project on America their own fears of the future, their own conservatism, and to regain at slight cost the intellectual leadership of the world.

This combination of contradictory assumptions made America the ideal ground for the French—and European—intellectual confrontation. America provided the essential framework, and if many at the time chose the Soviet Union as their ideal, it was primarily about the United States that they talked. America was also the subject about which individuals and groups differed most radically. It was as if no one could either remain indifferent or resolve the contradictions that paralyzed debate on such a fundamental issue.

At the very beginning, in 1944–1945, enthusiasm predominated. Whatever reservations people might have had about the naïve or ill-informed policy of American leaders did not prevent the development of a cult about a generous and progressive America. With the passing of time people tend to forget the extent to which the intellectual generation of the Liberation—Communists included—was brought up on American jazz, novels and movies. The reading of Faulkner was for a long time its principal hallmark.* Avant-garde

---

* Faulkner was almost as important in the France of the 1940's as Bertold Brecht was to become ten years later. (Brecht incidentally was discovered in France later than in English-speaking countries.)

publishers were flooded with American translation, and magazines featured passionate studies on the American writers of the 1930's. The vision of the world, social customs and style of life in France were all profoundly influenced at this period by the American model; the intellectuals introduced the rest of the population to this influence.*

In a very short time, however, with the beginning of the cold war and the shattering of the illusion that progress could be easy and painless, the situation was completely reversed. The first step was to disassociate the "good America" of unions and intellectuals from the "bad America" of consumers and gadgets, anesthetized by materialism and more and more dominated by the trusts. Next, everything American was challenged, and the greater part of the intellectual left was submerged in anti-Americanism, rejecting as class enemies and enemies of peace all those who would not let themselves be blinded. The climax of this groundswell was reached at the time of the Rosenberg affair, which drew more attention in Paris, it is well known, than anywhere else in the world. America was for some time the scapegoat, the cause of all the difficulties encountered or feared by the intellectuals.

But already a reaction was setting in against such a loss of control. Opposition to the EDC, in which all prejudices, all resentment and all fears met, was the last great effort of the intellectual left. The ground was ideal—even too ideal. American imperialism was compromising itself openly with Prussian militarism—but the tone adopted could not be sustained for long; it was fatiguing and the futility of the whole undertaking came to light. This problem, which had aroused such passion, was settled quietly, and without anyone daring seriously to oppose it. With the accession of Pierre Mendès-France to power, other problems, more concrete and more specifically French, regained attention. The intellectual generation of the Liberation lost a great deal of its influence over the younger generation, and attitudes toward America again became more discriminating, more rational. Soon the anti-American left and the pro-American left would be reconciled in the drama of decolonization, while the right in its turn would pick up the torch of anti-Americanism.

What lies behind these actions whose violence may appear inexplicable and even paradoxical, given the extent to which the fashion for the American style of life and American values continued to grow? Those concerned claimed to explain it by an analysis of the political context. For them America appeared as the last remaining

---

* Scotch whisky was the preferred drink of the intellectuals before becoming the choice of the midddle class.

support of a capitalism which was morally indefensible at the same time that it was inefficient and vacillating. America was also the only western nation to have assumed its real responsibilities and it was therefore the only center of decision making on which the French intelligentsia could imagine itself exerting any effective influence. This analysis, in spite of the cynical turn which its advocates— Sartre, for example[4]—sometimes gave it was absolutely superficial in its rationalism, and it could in no way account for the passions that Franco-American relationships aroused.

In reality, an important two-fold reaction—nationalist and conservative—explains anti-Americanism and the resulting political choice. Anti-Americanism was all the more powerful since such reaction was unavoidable otherwise in the French context. The nationalism of the intellectuals of the French left is very different from the territorial and traditional nationalism of the right, but it is no less lively. The defeat of 1940 did not extinguish it directly, but France's loss of substance, the diminution of its universal mission, the general decline of the French style of reasoning, threatened it in the long run, and from this point of view, the anti-American reaction was natural because America, whose universalistic ideal is so close to the French, seemed in the process of taking over what used to be the glory of French culture. To learn from America had been possible and fruitful when America was still a bit far off and mythical and when the intellectuals had a monopoly of Franco-American intercultural relations. But as soon as the contacts became closer and involved other social groups, the risk became too great. Those who had launched the intellectual vogue of the New Deal bristled as soon as the Marshall Plan officially installed American influence in Europe.

Under these circumstances, Marxism and the Socialist Utopia offered the easiest means of re-establishing the equilibrium. France could admit its backwardness on the material plane, on the plane of technology and even in certain intellectual methods for which it did not have the necessary means of research, because it was regaining the advantage on the level that counted most, that of working out the future society. If everything is reduced to the Marxist common denominator, France returns to the avant-garde. Jacques Duclos has the right to castigate Earl Browder, and French intellectuals can patronize American intellectuals for being too naïve or too conformist. The argument ran that if only French intellectuals had at their disposal the extraordinary resources of American power, which was due to an accidental accumulation of material circumstances, the ideal rational society would already be well advanced. French intellectuals were indignant at the passivity of American intellectuals and union leaders; they showed impatience with their hesitations, they were angered at their betrayals. In contrast with an America crazed by fear and burdened by the moral weight of the atomic sin, the French intellectual could feel marvelously reasonable. He had a good conscience, he had extricated himself from a scrape, and he affirmed with the superiority of the intellect the scope and the supremacy of French values. The fever of the McCarthy period proved definitively for him the inferiority of "the American way of life."

The attitudes of French social scientists are particularly significant from this point of view. At the time of the Liberation, France was quite far behind in the most modern social sciences, those most accessible to technology and also those which were the harbingers of a new style of thinking. All the intellectuals of that time who were seriously interested in these new fields passionately applied themselves to learn from America. But at the same time, all or almost all of them were or soon became politically and culturally anti-American, for their politico-social commitment was not a secondary commitment for these French intellectuals; it was an important part of their professional life. Therefore they could respectfully admire their American colleagues for their professional qualities and at the same time reproach them violently for their naïveté, their lack of perspective and their misunderstanding of social phenomena. They saw themselves as rich in ideas but poor in methods and means. If only they had had at their disposal American resources, they would have at last constructed the all-embracing social science. In the meanwhile, they tried to learn from the Americans, or at least to take from them that famous "know-how" indispensable for progress. They certainly expected to use it against the Americans.

Of course this too convenient position was basically only a compensation for great weakness. Blocked by inhospitable university structures and an unreceptive intellectual milieu, the French social scientists opposed indiscriminately Marxist dialectic and American statistics to French intellectual tradition. They could not yet understand the long patience required for research. These ambivalent attitudes also reflected the hesitations and uncertainties which completely paralyzed them. Wishing to use techniques whose spirit they did not understand, they condemned themselves to misunderstanding even the methods of research. Lost on both planes, that of empiricism and that of overall synthesis, many gave up; some turned to methodology, and others returned to a literary style of dealing with social problems.

Nevertheless, at long last, after many detours, those who persevered finally attained their goal. The function they had assumed and the methods they had borrowed ended by transforming their vision of the world. The entire history of the development of the social sciences in France since the Liberation is the history of this unforeseen reversal. The social scientists began by using the weapons of America considered as an enemy—weapons which, moreover, they overestimated and idealized. Then they gradually realized that in trying to fight the Americans they were becoming like them. Finally they discovered that the antagonism they felt was due not so much to ideological differences but to the difficulties of a change in orientation that brought into question the very foundations of the intellectual function. As they ceased to idealize American techniques and methods and began to feel that they were capable of criticizing American studies directly and without an inferiority complex, anti-Americanism itself disappeared.*

IX The Present Situation

As sufficient perspective for a thorough analysis of the present situation is obviously lacking, I shall confine myself to a few hasty notes to indicate the main trend. I shall also try to explain the second part of the paradox noted at the beginning—the development of an intellectual climate of formalism and detachment at the very moment when economic and social confidence appears to be regained.

Different as the present intellectual climate is from that of the Liberation, it can be clearly explained in terms of the same two tendencies and the same two interpretive models that we used to undestand the earlier period. In fact we find again in the present both a confirmation of the traditional and aristocratic classic model of separation and the slow emergence of a new conception of rationality. Nevertheless, the balance between the two tendencies is not quite the same now as it was then. In particular, the illusions have largely disappeared and a more profound crisis seems to have taken their place.

At first sight the thread of continuity between the climate of the Liberation and the present may seem a bit arbitrary, so much do the interests and the very substance of intellectual life seem to have

---

* Often, moreover, those who have remained most anti-American are those who most idealize modern techniques. Thus we arrive at the paradox that, at present, the most distinguished American social scientists seem to be adventurous theorists while the young Europeans who attack them pose as rigorous empiricists. For a long time the great European tradition of Weber, Durkheim and Pareto aroused much more interest in the United States than in Europe. It is only to the extent that they have lost their feeling of inferiority to America that the young Europeans have begun, in turn, to respect it.

changed. It becomes clearer when one realizes that we have passed —following a traditional pattern—from the romantic period of crisis, when the irresponsible and creative individual partially succeeds in exploding the social structures, to a period of routine and retreat when the structures again become dominant.

If we are now in the dead part of the cycle, it is natural that the intellectual of the traditional type should no longer arouse echoes. The weight of social constraint has reappeared, but its effects have not been felt long enough for people to think seriously of revolt. They can no longer think that everything is possible, and they are not yet ready to think that everything should change. Such a period is naturally melancholy for the intellectual world because it tends to give the impression of retreat and decline. The illusions of the Liberation are being liquidated; men turn back on themselves and search their sinful souls rather than attack the world; self-criticisms and retrospective studies abound.

But in another sense, basically nothing has changed. A foreigner returning after a ten years' absence has an impression of remarkable continuity. It is still the same atmosphere, with its same types of human relations, its methods of judging and rejecting. There is still the same enthusiasm, the same liberty and conformity, zeal and perception—and capacity for illusion. The content and the tone may have changed but the form and the structure seem at first sight unaffected.

I am well aware that such an over-formal analysis accounts for only one part of the reality. Alongside this permanence of the old model or the natural return to it, we find some change. If the conservative tendency seems to have kept the higher road of the two, the important paths leading to change should not be neglected, for the search for a new form of rationality is also slowly becoming more important. It is also becoming more respectable, more easily acknowledged and more conscious.

The permanence of the old model is nevertheless more characteristic of the strictly literary and artistic world, which remains traditional. This world still exhibits the same intransigence, the same demand for perfection and totality, the same irresponsibility and the same arrogance. Skepticism and the passion for technical skill have replaced effervescence and commitment, but what the prophet has lost on the romantic side he has gained on the esoteric side. If the writer no longer has the halo of prestige appropriate to a genius capable of appealing to all men, he has at least kept his rank in society, thanks to the shield of his esoteric craft.

If the conservative tendency continues to dominate the central nucleus of the intellectual world, however, this nucleus itself is losing its influence, if not its prestige. The change is subtle. On the surface the difference is hardly perceptible; but below the surface a mutation has occurred. Literature has withdrawn and seems to be drowsing; more people are interested in it but they are less excited by it. No thinker seems in a position to assume leadership in the manner of Sartre, Camus or Picasso. On the other hand new forms of intellectual activity, more accessible to change, more concerned with the future and with the synthesis of thought and action, are growing in importance and tend to react on the literary milieu itself.

The first and most spectacular change concerns, if not politics as a profession, at least the type of interest the younger generation of intellectuals are taking in politics and the way they see the means of action and the possibilities of success. The necessity for revolution has disappeared or has at least changed direction. The fashion today is for reform by concrete commitment, for contacts through participation, for responsibility. The turning point came in the period of Pierre Mendès-France. His career, which suddenly gave new significance to a political game which had been made completely sterile by its remoteness from life, had a profound effect on the younger generation. The vicious circle of impotence and revolutionary verbiage as well as the lure of the Communist party—which up to that time had appeared to be the most extreme and most concrete of all commitments to change—seems to be broken. The vicissitudes of the Algerian war concealed and delayed this development, but even in that atmosphere of crisis the moral judgments, heroic attitudes and acts-on-principle which certainly abounded did not reproduce the irresponsibility and the liberty of the 1940's. The intellectual alienation and the practical sterilization of the intellectual left certainly persisted, but it was a defensive and declining position; leftist blackmail no longer pays off and the most extreme revolutionaries now borrow the voice of realism.

This change of climate is perceptible among students, among union members and peasants, in the Jeunes Patrons and in all the groups to which the new and more dynamic elements of society belong. It is the *raison d'être* of the democratic clubs and intellectual societies which have suddenly developed. What characterizes all these organizations is the need to make contact between category and category, between spiritual family and spiritual family, the horror of a priori formulas and systems, the passion for reform and the ideology of participation. Through these new and more concrete experiences a new elite is being formed which only partially coincides with the old intellectual milieu but which should be considered nevertheless as an intellectual milieu because its modes of action are essentially intellectual even though it is partly composed of practical men. This new elite also brings the whole sphere of political and social action and the strategy of reform into the intellectual field. Directly or indirectly, the new elite tends to transform both politics as a profession and at the same time its antithesis, revolutionary intellectualism.

The second sphere of change is that of the social sciences. The results gained here are so far not very evident, but the change whose paradoxical beginning I have analyzed is starting to yield some fruit. Transformed by the very methods they use, the social scientists have renounced their excessive ambitions. They have become aware of the means at their disposal, of their potential and of their real role. However slow their progress, they are now advancing under their own colors. Their research is becoming more positive and cumulative; they no longer claim to deal with everything at once; but at the same time they are understanding more and more how their work relates directly to action. On the organizational level they are still weak by comparison with the older disciplines which still dominate the universities, but they are beginning to influence the latter from within. Above all, they have a general influence far out of proportion to their small numbers. They are now attracting more attention, and increasing the demand for their services is greater than the supply they have to offer. Even within the intellectual world itself their influence is not negligible; they form a sort of link, in fact, between the intellectual tradition seeking to reform itself and the world of action which is trying to renew itself through a process of more scientific reasoning.

This third and final sphere, that of business or action in general, is not yet very open. But the progress made has been considerable and it is tending to increase. Intercultural exchanges and many missions to America have played a role in this reawakening of managerial thought. In any case, French business and administrative leaders could not escape the problems posed by the alternative between stagnation and irrevocable decline on the one hand and transformation of the modes of action on the other. To be sure, the business world claimed at first to act independently and undertook its own particular exchanges with its American opposite numbers, but it was forced to realize its impotence, and for the last ten years we have been witnessing a rapprochement of thought and action in France itself. The traditional boss, who prided himself on his culture but did not think for a second that this culture was of any use other than as a relaxation or as a stimulant, is tending to be replaced by business leaders who really believe in the virtue of education and are trying to encourage it. This evolution is intellectualizing the world of business and the top ranks of the civil service, who are leaving the role of judge and Maecenas for that of a participant in culture. The taste for exchange is also stimulated by the increase of knowledge which brings together businessmen, administrators and intellectuals and which thus tends to enlarge the limits of the intellectual world.

Behind these new developments, it would be easy to point out the permanence of the old forces which are reshaping the familiar traditions within the new context; but no progress, no social change, takes place in any other way, and in any event great progress had been made. Politics and business are always dominated by the immediate context and day-to-day decisions; the old dichotomy between principles and means consequently persists as a pragmatic problem that cannot be eliminated. A will for renewal is nevertheless apparent. Exchanges with other groups and looking to the future are gradually becoming the rule rather than the exception. Practice sometimes precedes, sometimes follows theory, but the idea is in the air and it is becoming irresistible.

This general social climate, more open, more fluid, more oriented toward the future, tends to influence the intellectual milieu whose traditional habits and conception of itself it challenges. I personally think that the general uneasiness of the intellectual world, the real crisis that we are seeing in avant-garde literature, can be explained only in this context.

This uneasiness and this crisis are particularly apparent in a phenomenon which has for some years held the attention of the intellectual world, namely, what has been called the new novel or *chosisme*. The new novel presents the reader with a sort of blank hero who never succeeds in existing. In a way he follows the existentialist pattern, the disintegration of the traditional rational personality, but he carries it so far that he offers a caricature or a criticism of it through absurdity. The existentialist found sense in commitment and in history. The *chosistes* go to the extreme, there is no sense at all, "things" decide for us.[5]

This "esthetic of absence," whatever may be its long-run literary merit, is primarily an ethic of regret and of denunciation. This abstract external universe of *chosisme* sends us constantly back to the absence of God and of meaning. The *chosiste* says, "I have searched, but in spite of my extraordinary thoroughness, I have nothing to bring back." The writer of the new novel, in fact, refuses to accept the monster (to him terrifying) that man's new power seems to make of him. Into the traditional world with its constraints and repressions, which was limited but clear ("fortunate limitations"), the existentialist introduced confusion and ambiguity and minimized the resulting difficulties by claiming that man could

626

assume everything at the same time. The *chosiste* novelist exaggerates the same difficulties in order to reject everything, and thus he finally arrives at the idea of objective action, with its own inherent logic outside of the sphere of man.

Such a simplistic if not absurd vision has an impact and esthetic value only because it reflects the anguish of modern man, too much on guard and too aware of the weight of decision. Classical rationalism was too narrow, but it was clear and reassuring. Without it man oscillates between the delirium of individual omnipotence and the schizophrenia of total determinism.

Although this conception may have long range repercussions, I am directly concerned only with its relation to the intellectual. It is the expression of the crisis that imposes on him a change of role. Hence the hyper-intellectualism, the esoteric character of the language—for initiates only—of the new novel. Hence also the importance given to the craft, to the act of creation itself. It is the sign of an embarrassment and of an obsession, caused by the difficulty of being an intellectual in this period of transition.

The traditional novelist created a world and he lightly assumed the role of God the Father. This corresponded to his right as a man of genius, separate from the world, to give the world new models of conduct. The author of the new novel understands all the futility of such make-believe, but he is not at all resigned to it, and in his will to go beyond it he presents a caricature of himself which is both a denunciation of the new times and an expression of regret for the past.

The emergence and the success of the new novel and, for that matter, of the new "cinema," should not, however, give the impression that the contemporary literary and artistic world is entirely dominated by conservative and negative tendencies. I grant that these are expressions of retreat in comparison to the more positive and more adventurous tendencies expressed in that part of the intellectual world which is now more directly and more seriously oriented t—award action; the dichotomy between thought and action is becoming a dichotomy within the intellectual world. Even in these reactions of retreat, however, there is a certain ambivalence; the intellectuals of the *nouvelle vague* also affect the sophisticated, craft-oriented, serious spirit of the times.* Besides, indirectly, they pose the problems of the new rationality. They are a crude expression of it, but an expression all the same.

* A glaring example of this ambivalence may be found in the extraordinary (if temporary) success of the "cinéma-vérité" (free interviewing of case stories) among the same circles that patronize the new novel.

This ambivalence is carried to extremes in a phenomenon which is developing parallel to the success of the new novel and which is, to some extent, connected with it—the fad for the work of Levi-Strauss.[6] In the last few years, Claude Levi-Strauss has become the intellectual hero and the new master thinker of the literary avant-garde. His influence is much narrower than that of Sartre, but it is equally profound. This influence has the effect of allowing the traditional intellectual world to penetrate the forbidden zone of the most modern social sciences.

Such a combination is somewhat surprising. It is made possible both by the originality and vigor of Levi-Strauss' thought and also by the fact that the intellectual elite, in retreat from the world, is fascinated by the new possibilities for comprehending the human adventure, and Levi-Strauss (through a misunderstanding such as often happens in history) provides a version which his rationalism and his pessimism make reassuring. He indeed brings off the tour de force of taming the new monster, even while allowing him to keep the forbidden and strong aspect which arouses interest. The ascetic initiation that he demands of those who follow him is painful, but at least at the first approach, it does not disturb the traditional intellectual universe. Levi-Strauss himself remains in some ways a *philosophe* of the old style, a rational and refined humanist.[7] At the same time, and more subtly, what the cultivated public passionately seeks in the work of this master, with whom they feel an affiliation, is the going beyond, the leap, which his thought accomplishes and allows others to accomplish by speculating on dead societies while still remaining safely under the protection of scientific standards. No one has done more than Levi-Strauss to condition the modern elite to the new type of reasoning demanded by the introduction of scientific method in the study of social phenomena. He proclaims and prepares the cultural revolution which implies taking its results into consideration in the actual conduct of human affairs. But at the same time he withdraws before this revolution. By pushing to the extreme the traditional dichotomy, he radically separates the sphere of thought and culture, for him all-powerful, from the sphere of nature and human arrangements, which he abandons to determinism and to scientific observation.

It is because of the many aspects of his thought that are similar to the traditional model that Levi-Strauss' system is so easily accessible to those who were educated in the rationalism of the nineteenth century, but in transposing the model into another logic, his thought tends to explode the model. To the notion of ambiguity contributed by Sartre, which remained exclusively psychological, Levi-

Strauss adds the notion of structure and the unassailable logic of the interdependence of signs and behaviors. In the same way that Sartre exploded the rationalist conception of the individual, Levi-Strauss explodes the rationalist conception of society; but this time there is no further recourse and we inevitably arrive at total pessimism. Sartre had projected on the social adventure the entire traditional metaphysics of personality. Levi-Strauss moves to the other extreme, from the deification of history to its total rejection. But the two philosophers are not far apart.* Both equally dodge the problems of change and action while opening indirectly, one after the other, new paths toward their comprehension. And from one to the other, despite appearances, progress is incontestable.

X The Possible Contribution of the New Europe

The analysis I have made, limited as it is to the case of France, may have seemed much more negative than positive. The European intellectual world is making progress, to be sure, but it is extremely painful and difficult for it to adopt new ways of conceiving its own role and of influencing action. The formation of a new style of thought is always very slow. But here we witness not only slowness but obstruction. If one admits that culture is a means, a resource, and not a treasure to be accumulated and kept under lock and key, contemporary Europe is paralyzed by its past successes. Its culture, too prematurely perfected and too advanced, has congealed in the past and finds itself inadequate to the tasks imposed by the modern world.

One might conclude that European inferiority is destined to continue, faced with an America which does not suffer from the same weight of social structure, but this would be to forget that the obstacles of a difficult accomplishment also have their advantages. Up to now, America has been able to progress more easily and it looks with a certain tenderness on the way Europeans continue to allow themselves to be separated by their local quarrels, by competition for leadership, by the impossibility of bridging the gap between rival ideologies and by their great compensatory dreams of revolution. But the integration of the various elements necessary for action that America has been able to accomplish is still quite limited. American rationalism, although broader than Cartesian rationalism, is still often quite narrow. From this point of view, certain European criticisms are not unjustified. In its facile universalism and in its

* We are of course dealing only with the philosophical aspects of Levi-Strauss' work.

really too naïve good will, America also dodges the problems posed by differences in culture and by the complexity and inevitability of the phenomena of power.

These are the very problems that are blocking the progress of the new Europe. Europe will overcome them only when Europeans understand that they cannot copy America in these matters, and that what they can find in America is a stimulus and not a solution. If Europe succeeds in this, it will in its turn contribute new and decisive progress to the formation of the style of thought and action required by the modern world. Such progress is not impossible; it is inherent in the logic of change itself. This is why the intellectual adventure of the new Europe may be just as stimulating to the mind as its economic and political progress, which, moreover, cannot really be brought to fruition until European intellectuals have finally accomplished the cultural revolution before which they are balking.

REFERENCES

1. In "Qu'est-ce que la Litterature?" a series of articles in *Les Temps Modernes*, Nos. 17–22 (February–July, 1947).

2. Jesse R. Pitts has analyzed this change very well. See *In Search of France* (Cambridge: Harvard University Press, 1963), pp. 299–300.

3. Jean-Paul Sartre, *Critique de la Raison Dialectique* (Paris: Gallimard, 1960).

4. In "Les Communistes et la Paix" (*Les Temps Modernes*, April, 1954).

5. For a sociological description of *chosisme* see Zwedei Barbu, " 'Chosisme' a Sociopsychological Interpretation," *The European Journal of Sociology*, Vol. IV (1963), No. 21, pp. 127–147.

6. For the connection between the new novel and the fad for Levi-Strauss, see Roland Barthes, "L'activité structuraliste," in *La France, Mère des Arts, Lettres Nouvelles* (Paris: Julliard, 1963).

7. This is especially noticeable in his last work, *La Pensée Sauvage* (Paris: Plon, 1960).

STEPHEN R. GRAUBARD

A New Europe?

EUROPEANS, looking back over the first four decades of the twentieth century, cannot fail to be saddened by that spectacle. The tragic happenings were neither anticipated nor prepared for; their consequences were unforeseen. Prescience was a commodity in very short supply throughout this period of fear interrupted by violence. Actually, given the character of the First World War and the unparalleled disorder that followed in its wake, it is not wholly surprising that men failed to perceive then what hindsight makes even now only partly intelligible. Opinions emphasizing "decline" and "decadence" were common in those years; they accorded well with a physical and moral chaos that impressed itself on all who claimed any sort of sensitivity. In these circumstances, theories of the kind proclaimed by Oswald Spengler flourished; they seemed to confirm and explain an anxiety which many had reason to feel.[1]

Toward the end of the Second World War when doubt assumed even more serious proportions, Alfred Weber, the distinguished German sociologist, completed a work which in its English translation carried the grim title, *Farewell to European History*.[2] Weber's principal thesis was less melancholy than his title, for his concern was largely with the future of European civilization. Finding in nineteenth- and twentieth-century nihilism the cause of many of Europe's misfortunes, Weber argued for an abandonment of immediately antecedent attitudes and a return to earlier traditions. Hope for Europe's physical and spiritual revival depended on such return being accomplished rapidly and completely. Weber recognized that Europe's political hegemony was lost,[3] but he questioned whether this need involve other losses as well. Although seeming to belong in its more pessimistic passages to the same tradition as Spengler's, the work reflected an important difference. Weber, despite his anxieties and fears, rebelled against the notion that Europe's death sentence had no appeal.

The book, while in many ways dated, is an excellent introduction to the postwar period. It expresses perfectly a sentiment that was increasingly felt after 1945. Europe's persistent refusal to admit the validity of any theory that questioned her capacity to survive with dignity in a world dominated by Soviet and American power, made the earlier alarms about inevitable European decline untenable. Such confidence could not have developed in the absence of tangible economic and social gains; these, in fact, came with remarkable frequency after 1950. In almost every aspect of life, Europe showed a vitality in these years greater than was once presumed possible. Rapid economic growth, which showed itself in increased trade as well as in new levels of production, and a quite extraordinary capacity for political and social invention, created a mood of well-being which communicated itself to almost all classes. While Europeans remained skeptical of the roseate views of those who prophesied a great new age, they were genuinely excited by the stirrings within their world and curious about what they might betoken. The immediate postwar pessimism was clearly outmoded; so, also, were the various forms of optimism that flourished immediately after the Liberation.[4] Both were replaced by an intense preoccupation with immediate problems. There was a genuine reluctance to attempt long-range prophecies; these had too often in the past proved wrong.

In the general optimism that prevailed it was easy to imagine that Europe was changing so rapidly that she would soon cease to resemble what she had been. This view had its advocates on both sides of the Atlantic, enjoying perhaps more support in the United States than in Europe. It coincided with a deap-seated prejudice, characteristic of the age, which assumed that large, radical and abrupt interruptions in human affairs were not only possible but likely. The vocabulary of the twentieth century—in politics certainly but in scholarship also—shows a partiality to the idea of "revolution," with all its promise of new beginnings. Men of this persuasion reacted in certain fixed ways to Europe's situation; they tended to exaggerate the gravity of individual events, attributing to essentially parochial circumstances a universal significance. After 1962, when, for example, de Gaulle's actions gave serious cause for offense, an importance was ascribed to them which must have surprised even the French president. In the more excited accounts, he appeared to stand between Europe and the possibility of effective political union. The loss suffered as a consequence of Great Britain's exclusion from the Common Market figured largely in such discussions; there was an attempt made to maintain the illusion that Europe stood at an important crossroads, confronted with major

options, on the resolution of which her future clearly, indeed irrevocably, depended. This was a time of talk about a so-called "inward-looking Europe," a particularly dangerous possibility at least
to those who invented the term.

There is no reason for surprise at such hyperbole. Happily, however, it is not the only interpretation of the contemporary European
scene. The magisterial studies of the great nineteenth-century
French historian, Alexis de Tocqueville, indicate a direction quite
different from that favored by men who insist on viewing every
day's decision as crucial, possibly vital. De Tocqueville argued that
change, while always difficult to effect, does in fact occur, but that
even in revolutionary situations it is rarely complete. Writing about
the French Revolution, he explained how the *ancien regime,* sup-
posedly destroyed by the events of 1789, in fact survived in many
of the so-called "new" institutions created by the Revolution.[5] De
Tocqueville's method reminds us to beware of thinking too exclusively in terms of "decline and fall." Both obviously occur, but less
frequently than is sometimes imagined. We should not forget the
significance of de Tocqueville's approach for our own thinking about
contemporary Europe.

The notion of a "new Europe," for example, needs to be interpreted with something other than literal exactness. Otherwise,
there is a tendency to write about Europe as if her history began at
the moment when Hitler lay dead in his Berlin bunker. To ignore
Europe's past and to dwell wholly on the present is to encourage
the view that change is easy, that Europe's capacity to adopt any
form, achieve any identity, pursue any goals, is in fact considerable.
By this interpretation, limits, whether imposed by tradition, habit
or experience, became secondary, and the only comparisons encouraged are those which contrast present-day societies without
reference to their historical antecedents. The method, inevitably,
concentrates on specific individuals and events, giving both an
importance which history is unlikely to confirm.

Europe is today the product of many influences, not the least
significant being those which derive from experiences having little
to do with the twentieth century. Unless this is frankly admitted—
and not simply accepted as a truism—the possibility for accurate
analysis of the contemporary situation is markedly reduced. While
it is of course theoretically possible that two great wars have so
transformed Europe that her earlier experience is largely irrelevant
to her present situation, the evidence for this view is not overwhelming. There are, indeed, numerous grounds for believing the opposite
to be true. To argue thus is not to underestimate the importance of
recent changes, or to raise doubts about their long-range signifi-

cance; it is only to suggest that tradition and habit assume many guises, and that a close search for both is always necessary. The dilemmas that confront Europe today may have less to do with a conflict between new ideas and old values than with a continuing concern to give modern expression to traditional drives which retain much of their former appeal. If this is true, then it becomes vital to know what Europe's past has been, what roles, ambitions and attitudes have seemed important to her people over many centuries.

At the risk of appearing overly schematic, I would suggest that these aspirations may be reduced to a very few categories; while several involve attitudes going back many centuries, others are of more recent origin and all remain vitally important. To begin with, Europe has generally been expansionist. By peaceful or aggressive means, she has sought to extend her influence beyond her own borders. Partly as a consequence, she came to know well peoples whose experience was vastly different from her own. The pride Europeans have traditionally felt about their society needs to be reflected on, since it was a major force in maintaining the illusion of European unity even when there seemed to be no basis for such a belief.

Contemporary hopes for European unity perpetuate a tradition whose earliest forms are to be found in classical and Christian example. While unity frequently existed more as an ideal than as a fact, its influence was felt even in those periods which were inhospitable to its aspirations. Foreign invasion, internal religious and social disorder, and exaggerated nationalist feeling successively threatened European unity, but never entirely succeeded in obliterating its values. The idea of a single European society commanded widespread support; England, needless to say, was always considered a member of this European community.

Europe, especially after the seventeenth century, became a principal model for even the most remote societies; her ideas, no less than her technology, developed as major items of export. Whether in the settlement of New Amsterdam or in trade with Indian princes, Europeans showed little hesitation in imposing their own particular values and institutions, which they assumed to be superior. This is not to suggest that Europe after the seventeenth century was entirely free of danger to herself, particularly from internal stresses. The characteristic response was a reaffirmed confidence in Europe's unique and distinctive qualities. This confidence was expressed in widely different intellectual and social circles, and is as important in its way as the constant exhortations to carry European influence abroad. The establishment of settlements in America and Africa created the possibility of novel experiment with European political and social systems. Europe was aware that many who left her shores regarded her civilization with suspicion, and, not infrequently, with disdain, but it was not until the twentieth century that she took seriously such hostile opinion.

The unity of Christendom and Empire disappeared as religious and national differences became paramount. Europeans turned to new utopian images to articulate their continuing fidelity to values more universal than sect or nation. Science and learning, technology and social reform—all the appurtenances of modern civilization—derived from European discovery and invention; their dissemination depended largely on European ingenuity. Nationalism, particularly widespread in the nineteenth century, seemed to give primary importance to such other values as *geist* and *macht*. When looked at closely, however, it becomes apparent that nationalism also attributed to particular nations the very qualities which at one time were thought to describe the whole of Europe. In this same century, when socialism emerged as an important political and ideological movement, with obvious universal aspirations, its advocates assumed as a matter of course that Europe would lead the world to the new and better social order.

In one form or another these ambitions and attitudes survive even today. A more detailed analysis both of Europe's past and of her present experience will make this even more apparent. Let us start with the simplest fact of all; Europe has never been inward-looking. Isolation has never seemed an attractive or hopeful option to her. Even in the Dark Ages, when there was every incentive to be self-regarding and to ignore the rest of the world, Europe sought constantly to maintain or establish contacts beyond her own frontiers. Europe's earliest memories are of association with others. When this was rendered difficult by outside invasion, as with the Saracens, there was no thought to retreat within Europe's narrow confines, better to defend the territory that remained. The object was always to regroup forces, "civilize" the would-be conquerors,[6] and expel those who refused submission to Europe's values. The thrust was invariably outwards; this is the leitmotif of centuries of European experience.

Europe is an "old world," but not simply because a new one came to be discovered in the fifteenth and sixteenth centuries. Her antiquity derives from the longevity of her past, and also, from certain patterns characteristic of her thought. Alfred North Whitehead, in describing ancient Egypt, said: "Probably the Egyptians did not know that they were governed despotically, or that the priests limited the royal power, because they had no alternative as a contrast either in fact or in imagination."[7] This could never have been

635

said of Europe, either in the sixth century or in the sixteenth. Monks, bankers, lawyers, kings and barons had a very precise notion of themselves and of their institutions; they conscientiously preserved records to remind themselves of what they had been, to measure their progress, but also, to record their losses. Extensive trade and travel, except in the most turbulent times, afforded that possibility of comparison which Whitehead claimed the Egyptians never knew. In the high Middle Ages, during the Crusades, for example, the failure to occupy and hold the Holy Land was only a partial verdict on an enterprise which restored to Europeans the vast riches of their ancient past. The ambition of Europe in that day may be gleaned from a twelfth-century English chronicler, William of Malmesbury, who wrote:[8]

The world is not evenly divided. Of its three parts, our enemies hold Asia as their hereditary home—a part of the world which our forefathers rightly considered equal to the other two put together. Yet here formerly our Faith put out its branches; here all the Apostles save two met their deaths. But now the Christians of those parts, if there are any left, squeeze a bare subsistence from the soil and pay tribute to their enemies, looking to us with silent longing for the liberty they have lost. Africa, too, the second part of the world, has been held by our enemies by force of arms for two hundred years and more, a danger to Christendom all the greater because it formerly sustained the brightest spirits—men whose works will keep the rust of age from Holy Writ as long as the Latin tongue survives. Thirdly, there is Europe, the remaining region of the world. Of this region we Christians inhabit only a part, for who will give the name of Christians to those barbarians who live in the remote islands and seek their living on the icy ocean as if they were whales? This little portion of the world which is ours is pressed upon by warlike Turks and Saracens: for three hundred years they have held Spain and the Balearic Islands, and they live in hope of devouring the rest.

At that time, when parochial concerns might have occupied the whole of Europe's energies, the ideal was not to defend what had been kept, but to press forward to regain what had been lost. Christian men pushed forward toward a larger unity that had ceased to exist, but of which tradition retained a very precise recollection. When Europe lost this religious impulse, and when secular concerns began to predominate, there was no diminution of the pride Europeans felt about their world and its peculiar institutions. Machiavelli, in writing about "the Turk and the King of France," was in fact contrasting Asia and Europe. The former, he believed, was despotic, characterized by a single individual ruling a body of men who were in effect his servants; the latter, by contrast, was free, with a king "surrounded by a large number of ancient nobles, recognized as such by their subjects, and loved by them; they have their prerogatives, of which the king cannot deprive them without danger to himself."[9] This sentiment, in many permutations, survived; Europeans never ceased to compare themselves with others, and only occasionally did they imagine that the comparison provided an unflattering portrait of themselves.

Machiavelli's life coincided with the development in Europe of the sort of nationalist feeling that was to become increasingly common. As Johan Huizinga, the distinguished twentieth-century Dutch historian, has pointed out, it is curious that it was during the Renaissance, when such deference was continually paid to ancient Greece and Rome, that Europe's more universal aspirations were abandoned in favor of local patriotisms. Erasmus, the greatest humanist of his day, argued against the new nationalism, but with little success; even his distinguished and learned friends felt the pull of this new power.[10] The idea of a common European civilization was not abandoned; it was simply added to, so that men now wished to identify themselves as well with a particular national state, whether it were France, Holland, England, or some other.

The Reformation, in fact, posed a more serious challenge to the idea of a single European society. When religious discord was added in the sixteenth century to other divisive influences, the possibility of a final breakup of the unity that had existed since the time of Rome became immediate. The conflict, on one level, revolved around questions of dogma, church organization and ritual. On another, it involved nothing less than how Europeans were to regard each other, what relations were to subsist between them, and what parts of a traditional pattern of behavior were to be retained. A modern comment on Thomas More's martyrdom emphasizes these larger issues, viewing them in a European, rather than in a purely English context; there is much to be gained from regarding the matter in such terms. Thus, More's behavior becomes something other than rebellion against a king who has turned against the true faith; it is seen as a commitment "not only to the cause of papal supremacy, but also to England's historic partnership in a Christian Europe."[11]

If the Reformation was a grave blow to the concept of a single European society, the growth of the national state, particularly after the seventeenth century, constituted an even more serious challenge to that possibility. Fortunately, at the moment when this was occurring, other influences were bringing Europeans to a new consciousness of their common identity. This no longer depended on their sharing a particular religious belief; now, it expressed itself in a whole set of scientific and technological pursuits based on common intellectual habits and procedures, which gave promise of creating new power for those who already regarded themselves as the most civilized peoples of the world. If Europe required proof of her superior qualities, it came in the readiness of others to learn from her example, and to copy her ways. Areas which had not been touched by Rome, ancient or Christian, began to fall under Europe's influence. Thus, for example, when Peter the Great set out to rationalize the Russian state, to improve its military capabilities and create a more extensive commerce, he chose Western Europe for his model. This policy, though modified many times by successive rulers, was generally persisted in; as Sir John Maynard has explained:[12]

> From Peter the Great's time Russia—or Russia's upper stratum—has always had some European country as its fashion and its idea. In Peter's time the admiration was for technique and the economic life: and Holland, Sweden and Germany were imitated. France attracted admiration under the Empresses Elizabeth and Catherine the Great. After 1815, England, the House of Commons, Bentham, Byron, the dandies and Adam Smith, had their turn. Under Nicholas I, Germany became the ideal: her absolutism and bureaucracy attracted the official mind, her philosophy opened a new world to the intellectuals.

That this consistent imitation of Europe created a counter-current in Russia, opposed to such innovation, and favoring instead models borrowed from a specifically Russian past, which took the form in the nineteenth century of Slavophilism, was important only for Russia itself. For Europe, the important thing was that the experience provided yet another confirmation of her power. As Athens had been the school of the ancient Greek world, so Europe increasingly assumed that role in the seventeenth century for the whole world. Europeans rarely questioned the superiority of their ideas or techniques. Fontenelle, in his *Entretiens sur la Pluralité des Mondes*, wrote, rather characteristically:[13]

> . . . there is a certain specific quality of mind or genius which you meet with nowhere but in Europe, or at any rate not far beyond it. It may be that it cannot, from its very nature, expand at once over an extended area, and that some decree of fate compels it to keep within a more or less restricted sphere. Be that as it may, let us make the most of it while it is ours. The great thing is, it is not confined to matters of science and arid philosophical speculation, it embraces art, and taste, and beauty, in which spheres I doubt if there is any race in the world to equal us.

Pride in Europe's unique qualities grew the more that Europeans became acquainted with the rest of the world. The philosophers of the Enlightenment were ardent propagandists for Europe; they did much to bring European achievement to the attention of a larger audience than the learned public. Could any greater praise have been accorded Europe than that which Voltaire chose to bestow in his biography of Louis XIV? He wrote:[14]

Already for a long time one could regard Christian Europe (except Russia) as a sort of great republic divided into several states, some monarchical, others of a mixed character; the former aristocratic, the latter popular, but all in harmony with each other, all having the same substratum of religion, although divided into various sects; all possessing the same principles of public and political law, unknown in other parts of the world. In obedience to these principles the European nations do not make their prisoners slaves, they respect their enemies' ambassadors, they agree as to the pre-eminence and rights of certain princes, such as the Emperor, kings and other lesser potentates, and, above all, they are at one on the wise policy of maintaining among themselves so far as possible an equal balance of power, ceaselessly carrying on negotiations, even in wartime, and sending each to the other ambassadors or less honourable spies, who can acquaint every court with the designs of any one of them, give in a moment the alarm to Europe, and defend the weakest from invasions which the strongest is always ready to attempt.

These words, written more than two centuries after the death of Erasmus, showed the influence of seventeenth-century theory on international relations; in the pride Voltaire felt concerning Europe's achievement, there is little to distinguish this statement from what might have been said in the time of Michelangelo. Voltaire was able to look away from national wars, religious strife, commercial rivalry, and see a single European civilization. His confidence in the vitality of that order was absolute. There was no disposition to question Europe's basic institutions or values. Voltaire, a citizen of France, was also a citizen of Europe. He thought about both, with equal solicitude, being quite incapable of separating one from the other.

When European civilization came to be threatened, as it was after 1789, it is noteworthy that the individual who made the most ardent plea for Europeans to join together to defeat the French revolutionaries was a British member of Parliament, Edmund Burke, who had made his name at Westminster in large part through his defense of the interests of individual nations and peoples—the American, the Irish, and the Indian. Burke had long insisted on the unique identities of specific communities; at the time of the American Revolution, he had said: "I was never wild enough to conceive that one method would serve for the whole; that the natives of Hindostan and those of Virginia could be ordered in the same manner."[15] After 1789, such differences seemed less important to Burke. European civilization stood in dire peril; Burke thought neither as a British M.P. nor as a man born in Ireland. Both for him were subsumed in a larger unity; the reality of Europe was never more obvious, and it was this tenet which made it possible for him to say:[16]

Nothing is more certain than that our manners, our civilization, and all the good things which are connected with manners, and with civilization, have, in this European world of ours, depended for ages upon two principles; and were, indeed, the result of both combined; I mean the spirit of a gentleman, and the spirit of religion.

The question of whether others would choose to define Europe as Burke had, while historically important, is not relevant to our discussion. What makes Burke's view significant is that he chose to regard Europe as an entity, to which, quite obviously, England and Ireland belonged. It never occurred to him that in such an emergency the interests of England could be substantially different from those, for example, of Spain. This attitude made possible the formation of those coalitions which, after many years and numerous failures, finally brought Napoleon down. The statesmen who gathered at Vienna to "restore" Europe came with plans which did not provide for very substantial changes in the way that Europe had been governed. They, however, were not the only men with schemes for the restoration of peace in Europe. A glance at a more utopian project tells something about the sentiment that prevailed in less conservative circles at the time. Henri St. Simon, the noted French socialist, proposed a "new Europe" which would be governed by a supra-national state. This international body would keep the peace, while maintaining intact the consciousness of Europe's identity. St. Simon's prescription for order is revealing; he wrote, more wisely than is sometimes admitted, the following:[17]

Without external activity there can be no internal tranquillity. The surest method of maintaining peace in the confederation will be ceaselessly to direct its efforts outside of itself and to occupy it without a let-up on great internal public works. To people the globe with the European race, which is superior to all other races, to open the whole world to travel and to render it as habitable as Europe, that is the enterprise through which the European parliament should continually engage the activity of Europe and always keep up the momentum.

This opinion, given its source, cannot be facilely interpreted. It is impossible to dismiss it as an expression of conventional European nationalism; much less can it be taken as the self-satisfied view of someone whose position in Europe made him idealize that world and disparage all others. St. Simon, in his concern to create safeguards against the recurrence of war, settled on a scheme which he believed fitted the European temperament. By these devices, he imagined, Europe could be led to channel energies into productive enterprises which would keep her fully occupied. St. Simon did not believe this to be a utopian venture; he constructed on the basis of a well-understood European disposition to expand. He was exploiting Europe's love of adventure, but also, the readiness of her people to emigrate.[18]

Until the early nineteenth century, the emigration had been continuous though quantatively small. After the Napoleonic Wars, however, and particularly toward the middle of the century, the numbers grew in almost geometric proportions. The United States, because it drew the greatest number of European immigrants, became the object of widespread European curiosity. The question of how the New World, peopled by citizens of Europe, compared with the Old, was of more than academic interest. Continued immigration depended in part on the impressions that were transmitted back; also, relations between the two continents, inevitably, would be influenced by opinions held by each about the other. The European traveler to America in the late eighteenth and early nineteenth centuries generally came away with the impression that the New World was not simply an extension of the Old. The settlers, while superficially following European ways, engaged in daily pursuits which had more to do with conquering a wilderness than with living in settled towns or in established agricultural communities. Even the most basic institutions in America showed the effects of contact with nature. European forms did not survive unchanged in the American environment.[19] Many who traveled to the New World returned with glowing reports of the freedom they found, and of the abundance which a largely unexplored continent gave promise of producing. Others, more skeptical of the virtues of the place, were disinclined to esteem it at the value set by the Americans themselves. All, however, accepted the Atlantic Ocean as a real barrier, recognizing that it separated two worlds obviously related but in no sense identical.

The most influential report on nineteenth-century America, at least for Europeans, was certainly that written by Alexis de Tocqueville. The interest of the work derived from the fact that it was not simply a report on America, but also a prophecy of what Europe must soon expect to become. De Tocqueville, traveling in America in the 1830's, came away with a novel interpretation of the differences between the Old World and the New. The originality of his account lay in the fact that he believed these differences would soon become less important, and that Europe would increasingly come to resemble America. The "passion for equality," which he believed was the most distinctive feature of American life, would also, he prophesied, soon overwhelm Europe. When it did, Europe's aristocratic forms would disappear, and with them would go the distinctive civilization that had been created over the centuries. Democratic ideas would prevail, and they would quickly destroy aristocratic ideals and practices. It was not to France, specifically, that de Tocqueville addressed his message, but to all who lived in the Old World and who remained faithful to traditional forms and beliefs. Europe could do nothing to prevent this evolution; she might, however, knowing a little more about the American scene, prepare for it.[20]

New societies are generally assumed to be moving in the direction of the old. De Tocqueville's argument implied a reversal of this order; he expected the old to become increasingly like the new. This was a prospect which many Europeans regarded with trepidation and misgiving. The European attitude to the United States was, as always, ambivalent. Uncertainty about the virtues of the American democratic experiment seemed amply justified, particularly in the middle decades of the century. The Civil War and Reconstruction period strained the confidence even of those who were prepared to think well of the United States. The American habit of caricaturing European society, making it appear servile and uncreative, did not encourage Europeans to admire their critics. How could they take seriously an opinion which so grossly distorted the European situation? The comments of a prominent Norwegian lawyer, O. M. Raeder, who traveled in the United States in the middle of the century and who had no reason to feel hostile towards the Americans, suggests how such opinion affected an intelligent European; Raeder wrote, quite candidly:[21]

> That which has annoyed me most in my associations with the Americans is their prejudice against Europe, which they regard as hopelessly lost in slavery and wretchedness. Three-fourths of the people in the East and ninety-nine hundredths of the people in the West are fully convinced that the other side of the Atlantic is nothing but a heap of medieval feudal states, which, indeed, show some slight indication of reform here and there, but have not made much political progress and have not enough vitality to rise from the abyss of misery and corruption into which they have fallen as the result of centuries of ignorance and despotism; their doom is inevitable. . . . It is rather a big job to defend all Europe; and I have on various occasions declined to do so, no matter how agreeable it might be once in a while to lay aside by little Norwegian, or even Scandinavian, patriotism and to pose as the champion of a whole continent. It does not help much to reject this constituency of 200,000,000 people, because people here do not recognize many differences among various nations; every European is responsible for the whole thing.

At a time when Europeans were becoming increasingly conscious of national difference, Americans insisted on seeing the Old World as a unity. This was a period in European history when leaders tended to concentrate on large industrial, commercial and imperial enterprises, calculated to bring credit to their several countries. Terms like "Holy Russia," "Imperial Germany," and "Republican France," were only partially descriptive; they were intended to evoke emotional responses, creating the illusion of large new national purposes suited to an age which placed great stock in such accomplishment. Nationalism, in its nineteenth-century form, was both romantic and disruptive; it served to make the more conventional attachments to Europe seem anachronistic. J. P. T. Bury, the British historian, has spoken of this period as one where "antagonisms fostered by nationalism . . . made not only for wars, insurrections, and local hatreds—they accentuated or created new spiritual divisions in a nominally Christian Europe."[22] Gordon Craig has shown how these developments coincided with an increasing reluctance on Great Britain's part to involve herself in Europe's affairs. As Craig explains: "Britain's growing isolation after 1865 further weakened the possibility of collaborative action in the interests of peace, because it became increasingly clear that she was unwilling to accept the kind of responsibility and assume the kind of commitments which would restrain the continental realists."[23] It was nineteenth-century nationalism, then, that made the Channel appear an important barrier, if only because it encouraged the illusion that it was possible to be in Europe while ignoring European affairs. This view enjoyed an exceedingly short life; two wars in the twentieth century proved its inadequacy.

Meanwhile, coinciding with the rise of nationalism, though repudiating many of its parochial values, another view developed which ignored traditional definitions of Europe, but which aspired to create a utopia with universal implications. This was the socialist view. The socialists, in their emphasis on class and alienation, described a world where neither would exist, where all men would enjoy equality, and where national states would be as irrelevant as private property. Karl Marx, more than those whom he dubbed "utopian Socialists," looked away from Europe, and thought only in international terms. He regarded Europe as he regarded the bourgeois class; history had given it a purpose, which was to contribute to a process that would eventually issue in a universal society. Unwittingly, Europe, even in her imperialist ventures, was creating the mechanisms which would press the world forward into the next stage. Marx's views on Great Britain's role in India are instructive; they are without sentimentality, either about one or about the other. Marx wrote in 1853:[24]

However melancholy we may find the spectacle of the ruin and desolation of these tens of thousands of industrious, peaceful, patriarchal, social groups . . . suddenly cut off from their ancient civilization and their traditional means of existence, we must not forget that these idyllic village communities . . . always provided a firm basis to oriental despotism, confining the human intelligence within the narrowest limits, making of it the obedient traditional instrument of superstition, stunting its growth, robbing it . . . of all capacity of historical activity; let us not forget the egoism of barbarians who, concentrated on an insignificant portion of earth's surface, watched unmoved while immense empires crumbled, unspeakable cruelties were committed, the populations of entire cities were butchered—observed this as if they were events in nature, and so themselves became the helpless victims of every invader who happened to turn his attention to them. . . . In causing social revolution in India, England was, it is true, guided by the lowest motives, and conducted it dully and woodenly. But that is not the point. The question is whether humanity can fulfill its purpose without a complete social revolution in Asia. If not, then England, in spite of all her crimes, was the unconscious instrument of history in bringing about this revolution.

Between the pretensions of nationalism and the ambitions of socialism, the concept of Europe lost much of its former appeal. The great war of 1914-1918 seemed almost a final judgment on a society which had been remarkably reckless in discarding whatever promised to create unity and order. The First World War, by its general excess, created a mood of violence which made itself felt as much in parliaments as on the battlefield. The propaganda of these years exceeded anything which Europe had ever known; each side accused the other of the most abominable intentions and crimes. Any suggestion that the interests of both might be served by a negotiated settlement was dismissed as defeatist or treasonable. Victory was made to appear all-important; in fact, all other benefits were believed to depend on military success. The "saving of Europe," insofar as it was thought of at all, was translated into military terms, each side arguing of course that its victory would also be Europe's. In these terrifying years, Europe seemed to show all those qualities which her detractors had always assumed to be characteristic of her so-called civilization. Belligerence could not have taken more unpalatable forms; arrogance could not have shown a more uncompromising character. Europe became involved in a whole series of enterprises from which she seemed incapable of extricating herself, enterprises which served only to raise doubts about the intelligence and humanity of those who formulated her policies.

The price of this war was paid in many installments; certain of the more onerous charges were computed only after the guns were silenced. The disillusion that set in after the Armistice reflected a failure not of a single individual but of a social and intellectual process. The postwar vocabulary, with its heavy emphasis on guilt and retribution, exploited attitudes which four years of Armageddon had made both familiar and acceptable. In these circumstances, utopian plans for Europe's reorganization came principally from men relatively untouched by such feelings, who in fact had little knowledge of Europe's character, and cared not at all for her traditional aspirations. This had many disadvantages, but in the situation that prevailed nothing else was possible. Woodrow Wilson and Jan Smuts, more than any European statesmen, conceived and promulgated the schemes for a better society which wartime propaganda had promised but had left ambiguous. The League of Nations—the major political innovation of the period—was constructed largely from materials and ideas provided by individuals and groups active in the United States, Great Britain, and in the latter's overseas Empire. It is not entirely an accident that a volume like Henry Winkler's *The League of Nations Movement in Great Britain, 1914-1919*, has never been written for France.[25] There simply did not exist there or elsewhere on the Continent an organized sentiment for this sort of solution to Europe's problems. Wilson and Smuts believed that if Europe were left to her own devices, there would be an early return to the aggressive policies of the past. As outsiders, theoretically uncommitted, able to view extreme nationalism dispassionately, they believed themselves to be particularly well-placed to recommend remedies for Europe's malady. That such ideas might not appeal to Europeans, or that they implied an adverse judgment on Europe's earlier history, never occurred to those who were persuaded that Europe was a "lawbreaker," and that only the introduction of competent restraints would prevent a repetition of the tragedy so recently terminated.[26]

The early reaction to the League of Nations, both on the Continent and in Great Britain, was, on the whole, favorable. At one time, in the mid-twenties, the League appeared to enjoy very considerable support. Only after the advent of Hitler did its insufficiencies begin to be commonly recognized. The League seemed incapable either of keeping the peace within Europe or of compelling others outside to do so. Even more serious was the fact that its power to compel member states to accept the responsibilities outlined in the Covenant, particularly in respect to restraining would-be aggressors, seemed severely limited. Europe was incapable of operating the instruments provided her by the Paris peacemakers, and she showed little ingenuity in inventing others more suited to her needs. The idea of creating new political and economic forms, transcending existing national institutions, scarcely entered the arena of political discourse. This was a time for timid and limited gestures; those with utopian visions imagined many things but rarely a united Europe.

The Second World War threw into grim relief the barren topography of these twenty years. From 1939 to 1945, first with only the major West European powers involved, together with Poland, and then, with all except Sweden, Switzerland, Spain and Portugal actually participating, Europe came to know a war as "total" as any the world had ever experienced. Invasion, by land, sea, or air, came to each in turn, with consequences always grave and sometimes tragic. The Second World War, almost from its beginning, assumed a character that made the idea of its being a European "civil war" quite inappropriate. The active participation of "outsiders" was too conspicuous this time; the major battles were fought on and over too many continents and in all the seas of the world. Europe's quarrel became the world's in a way that admitted of no misinterpretation. This was a coming together of many disputes, involving many parties, and not an ingenious gathering of support by Great Britain and France from friends, dependencies and allies beyond the seas. The military operations designed to destroy German power inside Europe, while appearing as primary to those actually suffering the terrors of Nazi occupation, were not, in fact, always as strategically important as those which occurred elsewhere. Reactions to V-E Day expressed perfectly the character of this second great war of the century; for Russia, Norway, Denmark, Belgium and the peoples of southern and eastern Europe, Germany's defeat constituted the end of hostilities in an effective sense; the French and Dutch, while equally relieved, accepted the fact that there was still an enemy to be overcome; the British probably felt this even more acutely, given the extent of their imperial holdings still under Japanese occupation, and the Americans understood it in the deepest sense. The difference in perspective reflected the extent to which the global nature of the conflict impressed itself on the various belligerents, and this, in turn, derived from the nature of their individual commitments to others.

While the war was proceeding, few predicted correctly its likely consequences. The material devastation, by its direct and overpowering assault on the physical senses, seemed at one time as important as anything else. The visible damage, in fact, proved to be a relatively simple matter to repair. While bombs and shells destroyed whole cities and laid waste great tracts of land, European ingenuity was more than equal to the task of rapid reconstruction. In this, American aid proved to be invaluable. It was quite another matter when it came to coping with the spiritual, moral and human losses. Military casualties, very heavy for certain of the belligerents,

constituted only a part of the appalling toll. Nazi bestiality sen-
tenced millions to death, and when Europe learned the full story of
this horror, there were no scales adequate to measure the offense.
Europe had no experience of such tragedy; it put into the shade
memories of trench warfare in 1914-1918, when hundreds of thousands fell in vain efforts to gain a few yards of shell-torn land.[27]

If Europe emerged from the war uncertain about the future,
the reasons were not hard to find. Certainty in this situation would
have been a form of hypocrisy. It was only gradually that indications began to appear, suggesting what the postwar European
world might in fact be required to contend with. The loss of power
—military and political—seemed obvious. This loss might be
remedied in time, but for the moment the United States and the
Soviet Union hovered over Europe as two colossi, influencing
everything—the establishment of new governments, the rate of
economic recovery, the stability of particular regimes.

Just as the war bore only a superficial resemblance to what had
happened in 1914-1918, so the post-war period quickly took a course
markedly different from what Europe had known in the 1920's
and 1930's. To begin with, there was almost no nostalgia for the
immediate past. No one thought to go back to "the good old days
before 1939"; no one deluded himself that they had been good.
More than that, a recognition grew that Europe's situation was in
certain respects fundamentally different from any she had known
in the past, a fact made immediately inescapable by the presence
of Soviet and American military forces. As Europeans reflected on
their prospects, they faced first a loss of power, which, in more
depressed moments, they chose to translate as a loss of independence.
They saw the continent riven by new and unnatural boundaries,
expressing the accidents of war more than the circumstances of
nationality, history, or geography. Formerly dependent peoples in
Asia and Africa rebelled against their European allegiances, or
made their intentions so unmistakable that Europeans, occasionally
recognizing the advantage of acting quickly, granted independence
almost as soon as it was demanded. A structure of relations, carefully built up through the eighteenth and nineteenth centuries,
seemed to disintegrate as if it had no substance whatever. In these
circumstances, more than sufficient reason existed for concern and
even alarm. The extraordinary thing about the postwar period
was that neither developed to the extent that might have been
predicted. It was as if the war itself had purged Europe of all fears.
So much had been experienced—the suffering and loss had been
so great—that these new blows fell almost without effect on peoples who had become habituated to adversity. It was as if a whole

society wished to skip a generation, forget the shame of two wars,[28] and even more, the disgrace of indecision, weakness and injustice of the first inter-war period, the true "locust years" of the century.

Europeans had every reason to despair, but accepted none of them. While their more remote past appeared almost irrelevant to their new situation, the spirit of enterprise characteristic of those days carried an appeal that caution, which had gone under the name of good sense in more recent times, wholly lacked. There were no Stanley Baldwins about, either in England or elsewhere, dispensing their mild prescriptions for guaranteed safety. This was a blessing. The concept of a single European society, which had gone out of fashion in the second half of the nineteenth century, having become largely the pejorative cliché of non-Europeans, returned to favor. There was no way of knowing how far the revival of European sentiment would go, or what its long-range consequences would be, but there was no denying its reality. Economic cooperation might stop with the Common Market and never proceed to political union, but this did not alter the fact that the second prospect had been raised in serious political debate throughout Europe, and that it had not been dismissed as visionary. The citizen of Milan, visiting London, came away with a renewed appreciation of the differences between English and Italian society, but the differences seemed less significant than they would have been three decades earlier. No Franco-German understanding could obliterate the distinctive character of each, or entirely cancel out recent history, but the fact that it occurred said something about those who conducted foreign policy in the second postwar era. The French citizen who argued, almost chauvinistically, the importance of language in creating a common civilization, was being no less sincere than the British politician who dwelled on the primary importance of Britain's Commonwealth ties; each, however, lived in a society which understood that these were only partial truths. Increasingly, the idea of Europe penetrated everyone's thinking; men might define the term differently, resist it, but they refused to deny it. A consciousness of Europe, once the property of educated men, became a common possession. As nationality had once won approval from both, so now, the idea of Europe seemed to be a democratic device with its own peculiar attractions.

Geographic proximity, which for so long had seemed the condition of national war and rivalry, emerged as a factor encouraging unity. European frontiers, in the West at least, became demilitarized; the Franco-German understanding was certainly as remarkable a development as any other in a century of diplomatic change. Soviet military power, which loomed ominously at times of crisis, seemed scarcely more threatening to Europeans after 1956 than it did to those more protected by distance. Technology had done much to eradicate the barriers of terrestrial space, and Europeans accepted with a certain stoicism the necessity of living in close proximity to Soviet power. If war came, Europe would almost certainly suffer acutely, but it was not a foregone conclusion that others would suffer less. This was no consolation, obviously, but Europeans had few illusions about what they might themselves do to prevent hostilities. They might try to restrain the Soviets, using argument to recommend caution, and they might employ the same weapon to reason with their American allies. These, however, were means of obviously limited efficacy. The Cuban affair in 1962 told Europeans what they had already guessed—on certain issues involving the security of the United States, Europe would be informed after rather than before the decision-making process was completed, and she would have little to say in what was finally done. It was difficult for any European to believe that a larger control, or even one so large, could ever be maintained over Soviet actions.

European statesmen hurried from conference to conference, flew the oceans of the world, and indicated by their every gesture a continuing interest in maintaining control over their own destinies and in influencing that of others. The incontrovertible reality remained. With severely limited resources, particularly in the military sphere, Europe was incapable of defending herself. This fact could never be lost sight of. Europe's reliance on American protection was total; this situation had no historic parallel. While the Soviet Union and the United States might be concerned with the state of their alliances, their national defense never depended entirely upon alliances being maintained in good repair. Europe was not in anything like the same situation. The connection with America, if impaired, opened at least the possibility of interference by the Soviet Union. The weapons available to Europeans were manifestly insufficient.

This loss of military self-sufficiency coincided with another development, less discussed, but which could prove to be equally important. Europe, for all practical purposes, was excluded from the scientific and technological pursuits associated with the exploration of space. For the first time in centuries major discoveries were taking place in another part of the world, to which Europeans contributed in only the most insignificant manner. All the early steps—including the important ones taken during the Second World War—were enormously indebted to European scientific and technological inventiveness. In the postwar phase, Europe was denied any important share in these activities.

This issue, rarely discussed, symbolized Europe's dilemma. In the pre-1945 world, Europe's centrality, while open to challenge, was never effectively denied. Her citizens succeeded in opening up the world; her ideas dominated in science as well as in the arts; her techniques were studied and copied by all who believed in the possibility of progress. This hegemony was achieved by a society of many states, with large national differences, given to extreme competitiveness, which might take the form of a trade war, but which frequently went beyond and became considerably more hazardous. Others were admitted to European benefits only on condition that they accepted her ways. While there is a danger in making too much of Europe's power before the middle of this century, the greater mistake is to esteem it too low.

Such a dominant position, perhaps, is beyond the capacity of any society today; if so, Europe is simply experiencing what the Americans and Soviets also feel, and what is in any case inevitable, given the facts of modern technology. Dominance once enjoyed, however, is not lightly abandoned, particularly when it seems to define the whole of a society's past experience. A feeling persists in Europe, rarely expressed, that Europe must not simply become the junior partner in a going enterprise, however magnificently managed.[29] Europe's continuing concern is with the possibility of becoming too much the political, intellectual and spiritual disciple of the United States. The opposition to Americanization—which is a sort of short-hand for the complex trends toward modernization—does not derive from underestimating the importance of steel production or the advantages of well-being. Rather, it expresses a sense of the necessity which Europeans feel, that they must continue to be something which Americans are not. This is a strange reversal of roles. Europe, in the twentieth century, is seeking the independence from the other which America so prided itself on securing in the eighteenth. The difficulty of achieving this identity in any meaningful way arises from the fact that there is so little in Europe's recent past that is immediately relevant to the present. The control of vast territories overseas, by economic or political means, is excluded. The destruction of class difference, even where it is more apparent than real, precludes the possibility of maintaining the values characteristic of a more aristocratic society. In the realm of ideas, it is difficult to conceive how Europe can achieve again the sort of primacy that she once enjoyed.

The difficulties of the situation do nothing to diminish or alter the ambition. Consciously or unconsciously, Europe has turned her back on extreme nationalism, imperial rivalry, and military build-up. It is as if the last seven or eight decades have been erased from memory. This, however, does not by itself provide a solution to the problem as it is presently defined. Europe's task is made all the more difficult by the necessity of being reasonable in her criticism of the United States. The freedom to invent clichés about the other —which Americans so much enjoyed in the nineteenth century precisely because no one was listening—is effectively denied Europeans today. It would be taken in bad grace, and, in any case, it would be no solution to Europe's problem. It would not create the distinction that is sought, since it would not be based on any real competence that could be pointed to. Yet, it is precisely this competence that is being sought.

Europe's experience is too deeply and permanently inscribed for illusions to exist about the possibility of starting over again.[30] There may be a "new Europe," but Europe is not a new world. The Flemish will not soon feel differently about the Walloons, though any number of rational arguments may be offered to demonstrate why they should. West Germans will not easily abandon talk of the "unification" of Germany, though many abroad would wish that they might. National pride may be purged of its xenophobic features, but this by itself does not destroy nationalism. Traditional myths and an obsolescent political vocabulary do not disappear simply because they no longer describe a present reality or a future potential. It is in this sense that Europe today, while vastly changed from what she was two and three decades ago, and while prepared to inter that past, is still its victim. Beyond that, there is a longer history with other myths and possibilities which again persist, and which require some sort of modern redefinition. Europe is not ashamed of that past; she instinctively seeks to recreate it.

For the moment, her energy appears to be expended particularly in planning. Cities are being built, industries developed, and agriculture rationalized. Each of these activities creates opportunities and problems. As in the past, politics concerns itself largely with the situations created by immediate developments. Tensions between groups, however defined, continue, and refer back to both long-standing and recent differences. In a relatively static society, education is rarely a problem. In one which is rapidly transforming itself, assuming new directions and developing aspirations which bear only slight resemblance to what was once thought adequate, it becomes a central issue. Funds are obviously required; more that that, there is a pressing need for new ideas. How to educate becomes as controversial as whom to educate. Both are aspects of a dilemma which would not have arisen in the first instance had the society been satisfied or able to remain where it was.

Prophecy is difficult in any century; in the twentieth it appears to be a lost art. No one foresaw in 1953 the Europe of today. There is no reason to believe that a prophecy, registered now about what Europe will be a decade hence, will have any greater validity. This situation is created, in part, by the fact that Europe is not entirely the mistress in her own house. What the United States and the Soviet Union elect to do in the next ten years will influence Europe, and there is only a limited sense in which Europe can determine these actions. More important, however, is the fact that Europe remains undecided about many things and uncertain about what parts of a long and distinguished past can be maintained or revived. As always, she looks at others for comparison and, increasingly, for guidance, but it is not yet clear that she is prepared to be the student of others in the way that Russia was in an earlier day. The abdication by Europe of her own distinctive forms is not easily accepted. If there are no twentieth-century "Slavophils" coming to the fore, reminding Europe of what she had once been, it is because the "Westernizers" remain cautious, and no one recommends complete "Americanization."

Europe's rebuilding and decolonizing tasks have so preoccupied her, have required such vast expenditures of physical and psychic energy, that there has been little incentive to recognize that these were essentially finite operations, which would not indefinitely make important demands on her. In the decade now opening, new preoccupations will undoubtedly assert themselves. More thought, almost certainly, will be given to relations between Western and Eastern Europe. While the Soviet's policy in this matter will be enormously influential, it may be less governing than in the past. Relations between Europe and the states of the Iberian peninsula may change rather dramatically; this "underdeveloped" region of Europe is not necessarily destined to remain so. European-Soviet and European-American relations will almost certainly be modified, in part because of the policies pursued by the great powers, in part because of Europe's own growing consciousness of her own capabilities. It would be hazardous to guess what these changes will be, but it would be wrong to assume that existing relations define what they are likely to be, even in the immediate future. The question of European political unity will certainly continue to be debated. It is not impossible that it will be as unsettled a matter a decade from now as it is today.

For those who are now old, and who have lived their lives in Europe, the century must appear as one of disappointment, with hopes many times raised, only to be finally denied. Neither the liberal nor the socialist utopias have fared well in this century. Nationalism, once thought to have some merit, is now in its extreme forms very properly questioned. If there is an unwillingness to construct new utopias, or to prophesy the certain realization of those now formulated, this reluctance need not be interpreted as evidence of fatigue or skepticism. Europe, by almost any standard that is relevant, shows remarkable vitality and hope. It should not surprise anyone if in the next half century she seeks again, with something approaching her former self-confidence, to be an "example" to the world. The task, while difficult, may be precisely the one to justify the use of that now overworked phrase, the "new Europe." The present efforts, seemingly chaotic, may in time be viewed as the uncertain strivings of an old society to renew itself, by taking what is best from its recollections of a not undistinguished past.

REFERENCES

1. Oswald Spengler, *The Decline of the West,* 2 vol. (New York: Knopf, 1926-28); see also H. Stuart Hughes, *Consciousness and Society* (New York: Knopf, 1958), p. 378. Mr. Hughes suggests that Spengler's work proved attractive to German readers because it seemed to explain the calamities that had befallen them. The same could be argued for Weber's work; it offered an explanation for the Second World War catastrophe.

2. Alfred Weber, *Farewell to European History* (London: Kegan Paul, Trench, Trubner, 1947).

3. *Ibid.,* p. 2. Weber wrote what was in effect Europe's epitaph in the following words: "The part Europe has played in world politics by reason of her will and spirit springs from her dynamism. Thanks to this unique dynamism she has been the mistress of the earth ever since A.D. 1500 and has made it dependent on her—something that Greece was never able to do in the small Mediterranean area."

4. The optimism of the immediate postwar years has been too little written about; see above, Michel Crozier, pp. 514–542; also Ernesto Rogers, pp. 358–372.

5. Alexis de Tocqueville, *L'Ancien Régime et la Révolution.* 2 vol. (Paris: Gallimard, 1953); it is interesting to note that such a thesis has been uncommon in twentieth-century studies of the Russian Revolution. I except the works of Nicolas Berdyaev which, however, cannot be compared with these of de Tocqueville. See Nicolas Berdyaev, *The Origin of Russian Communism,* 2nd ed. (London: Geoffrey Bles, 1948); *The Russian Idea* (London: Macmillan, 1948).

6. See, for example, Henri Pirenne, *Mohammed and Charlemagne* (New York: Norton, 1939), pp. 274-283.

7. Alfred North Whitehead, *Adventures of Ideas* (Harmondsworth: Penguin Books, 1948), p. 63.

8. Quoted in R. W. Southern, *The Making of the Middle Ages* (New Haven: Yale University Press, n.d.), p. 71.

9. Niccolò Machiavelli, *The Prince and the Discourses* (New York: The Modern Library, 1940), pp. 15-18.

10. Johan Huizinga, *Men and Ideas* (New York: Meridian Books, 1959), pp. 120-121.

11. Pieter Geyl, *Encounters in History* (New York: Meridian Books, 1961), p. 297.

12. John Maynard, *Russia in Flux* (New York: Macmillan, 1951), pp. 4-5.

13. Quoted in Paul Hazard, *The European Mind* (New Haven: Yale University Press, 1953), pp. 439-440.

14. Voltaire, *The Age of Louis XIV* (London: Everyman, 1926), pp. 5-6.

15. Edmund Burke, "A Letter to the Sheriffs of the City of Bristol," *Works* (London: Henry Bohn, 1846), vol. II, p. 119.

16. Edmund Burke, "Reflections on the Revolution in France," *ibid.*, Vol. III, p. 101.

17. Quoted in Frank E. Manuel, *The New World of Henri St. Simon* (Cambridge: Harvard University Press, 1956), p. 176.

18. *Ibid.*, pp. 171-179.

19. Oscar Handlin, *The Americans* (Boston: Little Brown, 1963), pp. 28-29.

20. Alexis de Tocqueville, *Democracy in America*, 2 vol. (New York: Knopf, 1960).

21. Oscar Handlin, *This Was America* (Cambridge: Harvard University Press, 1949), pp. 218-219.

22. *The New Cambridge Modern History* (Cambridge: Cambridge University Press, 1960), p. 245.

23. *Ibid.*, p. 272.

24. Quoted in Isaiah Berlin, *Karl Marx* (London: Oxford University Press, 1939), p. 187.

25. Henry R. Winkler, *The League of Nations Movement in Great Britain, 1914-1919* (New Brunswick: Rutgers University Press, 1952); see also, Laurence W. Martin, *Peace without Victory* (New Haven: Yale University Press, 1958).

26. Winston S. Churchill, *The Aftermath* (New York: Scribner, 1929). See particularly his comments on Woodrow Wilson.

27. There is no satisfactory study comparing the effects of World War I and World War II on Europe; this is a great lack.

28. In this matter, an exception must be made for Great Britain. Its recollections of the Second World War, for example, were substantially different from those of occupied and defeated states.

29. This is not adequately considered by even the better studies on the Atlantic Community.

30. This is explicitly recognized by the author of one of the best volumes on contemporary Europe, George Lichtheim, *The New Europe* (New York: Praeger, 1963).

Notes on Contributors

ACHILLE ALBONETTI, born in 1927, is Director of the Division of International Affairs and Economic Studies of the Italian Committee for Nuclear Energy. His extensive public service has included participation in the negotiations preparatory to the Euratom and the Common Market treaties. He also took part in the negotiations for the establishment of the European free exchange zone. His most recent publications are: *Préhistoire des Etats-Unis d'Europe* (1963) and *International Nuclear Coöperation* (1963).

RAYMOND ARON, born in 1905, is professor of sociology in the Faculty of Arts at the University of Paris. His publications include, among many others: *Introduction to the Philosophy of History; The Century of Total War; The Opium of the Intellectuals;* and *France, Steadfast and Changing: The Fourth Republic.* His essay, "Reflections on American Democracy," appeared in the Fall 1962 issue of *Dædalus.*

FRANK BOWLES, born in 1907, is the President of the College Entrance Examination Board. His annual presidential reports, together with his reports as director of admission at Columbia University (1934–1948), and other publications constitute an extensive review of problems and opportunities in higher education.

KARL DIETRICH BRACHER, born in 1922, has since 1959 been professor of political science and modern history at the University of Bonn, after spending the years 1950–1958 at the Free University of Berlin. His most recent publication is *Die nationalsozialistische Machtergreifung* (1960), with W. Sauer and G. Schulz. During the present year 1963–1964 he is a fellow at the Center for Advanced Study in the Behavioral Sciences, Stanford, California.

FABIO LUCA CAVAZZA, born in 1927, is a member of the board of editors of the journal *Il Mulino.* Research projects in which he has participated include, among others: a system of social security in Italy; the conditions of Italian universities (under a grant from the Ford Foundation); and patterns of political participation in Italy (in process for the Twentieth Century Fund).

WILLIAM CLARK, born in 1916, is Director of the Overseas Development Institute, a research center principally concerned with the study of developing countries.

MICHEL CROZIER, born in 1922, is a research fellow at the Centre Nationale de la Recherche Scientifique. A student of the sociology of organizations, his *The French Bureaucratic System* is to be published by the University of Chicago Press in December of this year. He was a fellow of the Center for Advanced Study in the Behavioral Sciences in Stanford, California during 1959–1960.

RALF DAHRENDORF, born in 1929, is professor of sociology, and director of the sociological seminar, at the University of Tübingen. His studies have embraced both political and industrial sociology. Early publications were: *Marx in Perspektive* (1953) and *Soziale Klassen und Klassenkonflikt* (1957). His most recent book is *Angewandte Aufklärung Gesellschaft und Soziologie in Amerika* (1963). He was a fellow at the Center for Advanced Study in the Behavioral Sciences in Stanford, California during 1957–1958.

CHARLES FRANKEL, born in 1917, is professor of philosophy at Columbia University. He is the author of *The Case for Modern Man* (1956); *The Democratic Prospect* (1962); and the principal author of the Rockefeller Panel Report on American Democracy, "The Power of the Democratic Idea" (1960).

LORD FRANKS, Privy Counsellor, G.C.M.G., K.C.B., C.B.E., born in 1905, is the Provost of Worcester College, Oxford. A member of the National Economic Development Council, he served as British Ambassador to the United States from 1948 to 1952. His subsequent publications have included: *The American Outlook in Foreign Affairs* (1954) and *Britain and the Tide of World Affairs* (1955).

STEPHEN R. GRAUBARD, born in 1924, is editor of *Dædalus* and of the American Academy of Arts and Sciences, and also research associate in the Center for International Affairs, Harvard University. His publications include *British Labour and the Russian Revolution* (1956) and *Burke, Disraeli and Churchill: Politics and Perseverance* (1961); and he is presently at work on the effects of World Wars I and II on Great Britain and France.

ALFRED GROSSER, born in 1925, is Director of Studies and Research of the Fondation Nationale des Sciences Politiques, and professor in the Institut d'Etudes Politiques in Paris. He has served as visiting professor at the Bologna Center, S.A.I.S., of The Johns Hopkins University, and at Stanford University. Among his principal publications are: *The Colossus Again: Western Germany from Defeat to Rearmament; Hitler: la presse et la naissance d'une dictature;* and *La Quatrième République et sa politique exterieure.* A new work, *La Politique en France* (with F. Goguel), is to be published early in 1964.

STEPHANE HESSEL, born in 1917, is the Director of International Coöperation in the French Ministry of National Education. His career has embraced service as Conseiller des Affaires Etrangères, as Councillor of the French Embassy in Viet Nam, and as adviser to the cabinet of Pierre Mendès-France. He is an Officier de la Légion d'Honneur, and a former inmate of Buchenwald Concentration Camp.

ALEXANDER KING, C.B.E., born in 1909, is now Director for Scientific Affairs of the Organization for Economic Cooperation and Development in Paris, following upon his earlier direction of various scientific and technical operations of that organization. His concern with the relation of scientific research to international policy led, among other appointments, to his becoming head of the United Kingdom Scientific Mission in Washington and Scientific Attaché of the British Embassy from 1943 to 1947. His publication has been extensive.

MAX KOHNSTAMM was born in Amsterdam in 1914. After the liberation of his country in May, 1945, he was appointed private secretary to Queen Wilhelmina. In 1948 he entered the Foreign Office as head of the German Bureau, later becoming director of European affairs. He was a member of the Dutch Schuman Plan delegation, and in 1952 became Executive Secretary to the High Authority. In 1956 he resigned to become Vice President of the Action Committee for the United States of Europe and President of the Institute of the European Community for University Studies, a post which he now holds. He is the author of *The European Coal and Steel Community*.

ERIC LARRABEE, born in 1920, was until recently managing editor of *Horizon* magazine. His volume, *The Self-Conscious Society*, appeared in 1960. He has also served as co-editor with Robert E. Spiller of *American Perspectives*, and with Rolf Meyersohn of *Mass Leisure*.

SEYMOUR MARTIN LIPSET, born in 1922, is professor of sociology and Director of the Institute of International Studies at the University of California at Berkeley. In 1962 he received the MacIver Award of the American Sociological Society for his book *Political Man: The Social Bases of Politics*. His most recent volume is *The First New Nation: The United States in Comparative and Historical Perspective*.

RICHARD MAYNE, born in 1926, was the first Englishman to work on the staff of the European Economic Community; he is now working in Paris with Jean Monnet. He is the author of *The Community of Europe* (1962), as well as of articles in such periodicals as the *Cambridge Historical Journal, The New Statesman, La Revue des Lettres Modernes* and *The Guardian*.

ALESSANDRO PIZZORNO, born in 1924, is professor at the Urbino University and Research Director at ILSES (Istituto Lombardo per gli Studi Economici e Sociali) in Milan. His most recent book is *Comunitá e Razionalizzazione* (1960); he has written articles in *Passato e Presente, Quaderni di Sociologia, Ragionamenti, Archives Européennes de Sociologie, Esprit* and *Arguments*.

ERNESTO N. ROGERS, born in 1909, combines occupancy of a professorship of architecture at Milan Polytechnic with the private practice of architecture. Throughout his career he has evidenced an interest in town planning complementary to his professional activities. His publications include: *Esperienze dell' Architettura; Auguste Perret;* and, in collaboration, *Piano Regolatore della Valle d'Aosta*.

MANLIO ROSSI-DORIA, born in 1905, is professor of agricultural economics at the University of Naples, and Director of the Center for Advanced Training and Research in Agricultural Economics in Portici. His long concern with the nature of social and structural change in agriculture in industrializing societies is reflected by his membership in the Italian Economic Planning Commission. Recent publications are: *Dieci Anni di Politica Agraria nel Mezzogiorno* and *Rapporto sulla Federconsorzi*.

ALAIN TOURAINE, born in 1925, is Director of Studies in the École Pratique des Hautes Etudes. Co-founder, in 1959, and co-editor of the quarterly journal *Sociologie du Travail*, he is the author of *Evolution du Travail Ouvrier aux Usines Renault* and *Ouvriers d'Origine Agricole*.

ERIC WEIL, born in 1904, is the holder of degrees from the University of Hamburg and from the Sorbonne. He is presently professor of philosophy at the University of Lille. In addition to articles in such periodicals as *Critique, Revue de Métaphysique et Morale*, and *Confluence*, he is the author of *Logique de la Philosophie, Hegel et l'Etat, Philosophie Politique, Philosophie Morale* and *Problèmes Kantiens*.

KLAUS EPSTEIN, born in Hamburg, Germany, in 1927, is professor of history at Brown University. His book *Erzberger and the Dilemma of German Democracy* was published in 1959 and his other publications deal with modern European history.

ERNST B. HAAS, born in Frankfurt, Germany, in 1924, is professor of political science at the University of California, Berkeley. He is recognized as an authority dealing with international relations and theories of national and international integration. His newest book, *Beyond the Nation: Functionalism and International Organization*, will be published this fall. His other works include *The Uniting of Europe* and *Consensus Formation in the Council of Europe*.

HANS KÜNG, born in Switzerland in 1928, has, since 1960, been a professor in the Catholic Theological Faculty of the University of Tubingen. He was a theological expert in attendance at the Vatican Council sessions, and his latest volume of papers has been published in America as *The Council in Action*. A spokesman for liberal reforms in Holy Office procedures, he has lectured widely in the United States, and in 1963 received an honorary doctorate of laws from the University of St. Louis.

KARL DIETRICH BRACHER, born in 1922, has since 1959 been professor of political science and modern history at the University of Bonn, after spending the years 1950–1958 at the Free University of Berlin. His most recent publication is *Die Auflösung der Weimar Republik* (1957; 3rd rev. ed. 1960) with Ring-Verlag, Stuttgart. Last year (1963–1964) he spent as a fellow at the Center for Advanced Study in the Behavioral Sciences, Stanford, California.

Index

Index

661